Our Inheritance of Faith:

Martin Davie is to be commended for writing a commentary on the Thirty-Nine Articles for the Twenty-First Century. Drawing on his strong command of the Scriptures, Church History, the English Reformers, later developments in Anglicanism and modern theologians as well.

Davie clearly tells the story of the Articles and their enduring witness to the 'faith once received'. As a result, Our Inheritance of Faith is not only thoroughly readable but also contemporarily relevant for Anglicans today.
The Revd Canon Dr Ashley Null, DFG-Cranmer-Projekt Humboldt-Universität zu Berlin

Our Inheritance of Faith provides an accessible, scholarly and thorough commentary on one of the key foundation documents of the Church of England. It will be valuable as an introduction and as a reference work.
The Rt Revd Dr Steven Croft, Bishop of Sheffield

All who are engaged with the Church of England's mission to proclaim the gospel afresh within a rapidly changing culture have reason to thank Martin Davie for this volume. The 39 Articles are part of the inheritance of faith to which Anglican clergy swear they will be loyal, and is provided as a source of inspiration for our mission to the nation. This book brings the Articles alive, roots them in scripture, and engages in contemporary apologetics. The result is a compendium of living biblical theology.
The Rt Revd Graham Cray, Archbishops Missioner

This book provides a thorough exposition of each of the 39 Articles in addition to tracing their origins, interpretation and application. It is an especially valuable addition to the literature on the Articles because it provides a lengthy detailed scholarly comment on the articles and a useful commentary on modern applications of the Articles after carefully weighing differing interpretations.

Martin Davie is a superb teacher, a precise scholar and a well read theologian. All of these qualities help to make this book a particularly valuable addition to the literature on the 39 Articles This book provides a thorough exposition of each of the 39 Articles in addition to tracing their origins, interpretation and application as well as discussing some of the more recent interpretations of the Articles.
Canon Dr Rudolph W. Heinze, Adjunct Professor Northern Seminary

We need this: a serious but accessible textbook to help theological students and clergy enter in to a vital part of their heritage.

Martin Davie opens the Articles up with great clarity and accessible scholarship.

This should be required reading for Anglican ordinands and candidates for Readership. It fills a particular gap, but is also a model of readable historical theology.
The Rt Revd Donald Allister, Bishop of Peterborough

Any attempt to understand Anglicanism needs to address its theology and any attempt to do that must engage with the 39 Articles. Sadly, fewer and fewer Anglicans—including clergy—are familiar with them. This excellent study should help rectify this lack as well as benefitting the wider church in its exposition of genuinely catholic and Reformed theology. It is packed with historical and theological insights into the Articles as it explores their origins, theology, interpretation and continued relevance and importance.

The Revd Dr Andrew Goddard, Associate Director of the Kirby Laing Institute for Christian Ethics (KLICE), Part-Time Tutor in Christian Ethics Trinity College Bristol

In this erudite study Martin Davie sets out to explode some myths about the 39 Articles, not least that they are of little importance to contemporary Anglicanism. He does so by providing not only a careful commentary on their origin, meaning and relevance but also, through them, a course in Christian doctrine that demonstrates their abiding value. This important study is essential reading for anyone who wants to understand the Christian Faith as the Church of England has received it.

The Rt Revd Christopher Cocksworth, Bishop of Coventry and Chair of the Faith and Order Commission of the Church of England

The 39 Articles have a renewed significance in the Anglican Communion. This theological commentary – in the tradition of Bicknell, Litton, Griffith Thomas and O'Donovan – introduces, explains and elucidates each Article. The historical formularies live again in this timely and important study. I warmly commend it to students of Anglicanism.

The Rt Revd Tim Dakin, Bishop of Winchester

Clear, illuminating and authoritative, just as the Articles themselves were intended to be. This should prove a welcome resource for ordinands and for anyone seeking a deeper understanding of Anglican identity.

The Revd Canon Andrew Norman, Principal, Ridley Hall Theological College Cambridge

This is an excellent study of the Thirty Nine Articles which manages to be comprehensive, relevant and useful. Martin Davie combines biblical, historical and doctrinal exposition in a fresh way to offer revealing insights into what the Articles meant in their original context, and what they might mean for Anglicans and others today. Its scholarship ranges widely and deeply but it is lucidly written. As such, it is set to become a valuable resource both for undergraduate and postgraduate study, and for general readers with an interest in the history and character of Anglicanism. I will certainly be commending it to my own students, and to anyone who wants to understand the enduring significance of the Articles.

The Revd Dr David Hilborn, BA, MA, PhD, Principal St John's College Nottingham

Our Inheritance of Faith:
A Commentary on the Thirty Nine Articles

Martin Davie

Gilead Books Publishing
www.GileadBooksPublishing.com

First published in Great Britain, April 2013
Reprinted March 2019, December 2019
4 6 8 10 9 7 5 3

British Library Cataloguing-in-Publication Data:
A catalogue record for this book is available from the British Library.

ISBN-13: 978-0-9568560-7-4

Cover design: Nathan Ward

Cover Images:
King Henry VIII 1542, Unknown Artist after Hans Holbein, Castle Howard
King Edward VI c.1546, Edward as Prince of Wales, Unknown Artist
Mary Tudor Queen of England 1554, Anthonis Mor, El Museo Nacional del Prado, Madrid
Queen Elizabeth I 1590, Unknown Artist, Jesus College Oxford
Archbishop Matthew Parker 16th Century, Unknown Artist
Book of Common Prayer 1662, John Baskerville edition 1762
William Reed Huntington: A Tribute of Love from William Wilkinson. New York: Trinity
Parish, 1909
Lambeth 2008 Bishops, ©Anglican Communion Office, www.anglicancommunio.org
Singing ©Anna Viljoen
Camp Worship ©Paul M. Walsh, Creative Commons License
Title page: Thomas Cranmer Theologe und Reformator Kupferstich 17 Jahrhundert
Signatur

Contents

Introduction

I	The Purpose and Nature of this Commentary	8
II	The Nature and Purpose of the Articles	10
III	The Development of the Articles	22
IV	The Subsequent History of the Articles	64
V	The Interpretation of the Articles	90
VI	The Shape of the Articles	95
VII	Bibliography	97

Commentary

The Doctrine of God: Articles I-V   **100**

Article I	Of Faith in the Holy Trinity	103
Article II	Of the Word, or Son of God, which was made very man	126
Article III	Of the going down of Christ into Hell	160
Article IV	Of the Resurrection of Christ	174
Article V	Of the Holy Ghost	214

Scripture and the Creeds: ArticlesVI-VIII   **237**

Article VI	Of the sufficiency of the Holy Scriptures for Salvation	240
Article VII	Of the Old Testament	269
Article VIII	Of the Three Creeds	286

Sin and Salvation: Articles IX-XVIII   **301**

Article IX	Of Original or Birth Sin	303
Article X	Of Free Will	311
Article XI	Of the Justification of Man	320
Article XII	Of Good Works	330
Article XIII	Of Works before Justification	342
Article XIV	Of Works of Supererogation	349
Article XV	Of Christ alone without Sin	357
Article XVI	Of Sin after Baptism	365
Article XVII	Of Predestination and Election	374
Article XVIII	Of obtaining eternal salvation only by the name of Christ	392

The Church and its Authority: Articles XIX-XXI   **400**

Article XIX   Of the Church   401
Article XX   Of the Authority of the Church   412
Article XXI   Of the Authority of General Councils   422

Errors to be avoided in the Church: Articles XXII-XXIV   **431**

Article XXII   Of Purgatory   432
Article XXIII   Of Ministering in the Congregation   447
Article XXIV   Of speaking in the Congregation in such a
    tongue as the people understandeth   457

The Sacraments: Articles XXV-XXXI   **466**

Article XXV   Of the Sacraments   467
Article XXVI   Of the Unworthiness of the Ministers, which
    hinders not the effect of the Sacraments   481
Article XXVII   Of Baptism   489
Article XXVIII   Of the Lord's Supper   503
Article XXIX   Of the wicked which do not eat the body of Christ,
    in the use of the Lord's Supper   516
Article XXX   Of Both Kinds   525
Article XXXI   Of the one oblation of Christ finished
    upon the Cross   532

The Discipline of the Church: Articles XXXII-XXXVI   **542**

Article XXXII   Of the Marriage of Priests   543
Article XXXIII   Of Excommunicated Persons, how they are
    to be avoided   550
Article XXXIV   Of the Traditions of the Church   561
Article XXXV   Of Homilies   572
Article XXXVI   Of Consecration of Bishops and Ministers   587

Christians and Civil Society: Articles XXXVII-XXXIX   **597**

Article XXXVII   Of the Civil Magistrates   598
Article XXXVIII   Of Christian men's goods which are not common   617
Article XXXIX   Of a Christian man's Oath   628

Subject Index   **635**

Index of Biblical Citations   **655**

Foreword

The Thirty-Nine Articles of Religion still represent a major strand in the Church of England's self-understanding; the inheritance of faith they transmit to us is affirmed in the Declaration of Assent made by the clergy of the Church of England as an authoritative standard – something offering 'inspiration and guidance', in the words of the preface to that Declaration. It may be true that the Articles no longer hold quite the place they did even fifty years ago in the minds of clergy and ordinands; but the fact remains that they are a central part of how the Church of England has located itself on the global map of Christian conviction.

Martin Davie gives us in this book a magisterial overview of the context and original significance of each of the Articles and of the text as a whole, and spells out the biblical and traditional elements that form the ground of what they teach. He rightly cautions against the glib conclusion that they are simply 'Calvinist', but leaves us in no doubt of their broadly Reformed intentions. As he notes, the current Declaration allows for some latitude as to how binding the precise formulation of this or that point may be. But this does not mean that they are of primarily historical interest, or that we are invited to affirm them in so vague and general a sense as to render them empty. In the language he helpfully borrows from Dr James Packer, the Articles call us into a twofold dialogue: a dialogue with the texts themselves as 'inspiration and guidance' – in which we allow ourselves to be questioned and challenged by them, and a dialogue between these and other doctrinal formulations and the words of Scripture – to test the authenticity of these human formulations against the primary words of revelation.

We have here a treasury of both historical and theological learning. This volume will take its place in a distinguished succession of commentaries on the Articles across the centuries, and will provide great stimulus and nourishment for all students of Anglican identity – and, I hope, for all exploring their calling to teach and minister in the Anglican tradition.

+Rowan Cantuar:
Lambeth Palace, London
Advent 2012

Acknowledgements

My thanks are due to my former students on the WEST course at Wycliffe Hall, Oxford and at Oak Hill College, London to whom I first taught the Articles and to those colleagues from the Church of England and other churches with whom I have worked since moving to Church House, Westminster thirteen years ago. All these people have challenged me to think through more deeply my understanding of the history and theology of the Articles and I am grateful to them.

I am grateful for Chris Hayes for all his hard work in preparing the text for publication and to Meg Davies for producing the indexes,

I am also grateful to Michael Green and the late John Wenham for first showing me that being an Anglican is a good way of being a Christian and above all to my wife Alyson and my son William for all their love and support while this book was being written.

Martin Davie
April 2013

To William

∞

Introduction

I. The Purpose and Nature of this Commentary

There are lots of myths floating around about the *Thirty Nine Articles* of the Church of England. They are said to be Calvinist. They are said to be written in such a way as to deliberately encompass a wide range of theological opinions. They are said to be outdated. They are said to be no longer authoritative.

As we shall see in the course of this commentary, all of these statements about the Articles are misleading. The Articles do not put forward a Calvinist view of predestination. They were not written with the intention of making space for diverse theological beliefs. What they have to say about God, the Church and the Christian life remains highly relevant for today and the Articles still form a key theological authority for the Church of England and for other parts of the Anglican Communion as well.

What the existence of these myths demonstrates, however, is that the Articles are not well understood. Although all Clergy and Readers in the Church of England have to affirm their loyalty to the Articles as part of the Church of England's inheritance of faith which they will use as their 'inspiration and guidance under God' in making the 'grace and truth of Christ' known to today's world,[1] all the evidence that we have suggests that many of them are not really certain what the Articles stand for or why they matter.

The purpose of this commentary is to help address this situation by providing a comprehensive, but accessible guide to the Articles that will help Clergy, Readers, theological students and anyone else who is interested in the theology of the Church of England to understand the history and theology of the Articles and their continuing relevance for today.

In order to be as helpful as possible for those who want to understand the Articles a commentary on them needs to have five characteristics.

- It should explain how the Articles as a whole came to be written and their overall purpose.

---

[1] The Canons of the Church of England, Canon C.15.

- It should explain the history of the Articles within the life of the Church of England and the Anglican Communion and the main traditions of interpreting them.

- It should explain the current status that the Articles have in the Church of England and the Anglican Communion.

- It should explain the history of each individual article, its intended purpose and what it says about the subject that it covers.

- It should address any points of difficulty that have arisen concerning the teaching contained in the Articles and how what they say relates to subsequent theological developments on the topics that they address.

In order to ensure that it contains all these characteristics, this commentary begins with an Introduction that explains the purpose of the *Thirty Nine Articles*, the history of their production, their subsequent history within the Church of England and Anglicanism in general and their status today. It then goes on to look at each of the articles individually, giving the text of the article in both English and Latin, explaining how each article reached its present form, what its purpose was and how it is to be understood. Where appropriate the commentary on an article will include one or more notes that will address particular points of difficulty raised by that article or consider how what is said in that article relates to later theological developments. In the Introduction to the commentary the main traditions of interpretation of the Articles are explained and in the body of the commentary constant reference is made to the work of previous commentators on the Articles, thus enabling the reader to understand how they have been interpreted down the centuries and to benefit from the theological riches contained in this interpretative tradition.

In this commentary Articles with a capital A is used to refer to the *Thirty Nine Articles* as a whole and article or articles with a small a is used to refer to the individual articles. A capital A is also used for the title of an individual article such as Article I.

II. The Nature and Purpose of the Articles

1. Statements of Faith and Order from the Bible to the Reformation

According to the Biblical narrative, from the very beginnings of the history of Israel the leaders of God's people have found it necessary to provide statements that define what the theology and practice of God's people should be, what we would now call questions of faith and order.

Two examples illustrate this point.

In Deuteronomy chapter six we find Moses giving instructions to the people of Israel prior to their final entry into the promised land. In verses 4 and 5 we find the *Shema,* the basic confession of faith of the people of Israel, what one commentator has called '...the touchstone for Israel's faith and life, the plumb line by which their relationship to the Lord of history was constantly being measured'[2]:

> Hear, O Israel: The Lord our God is one Lord; and you shall love the Lord your God with all your heart, and with all your soul, and with all your might.

What we also find in the chapter, however, are a series of specific instructions explaining how the people of Israel should live out this confession of faith. The people are given instruction on how to make sure that they take the words of the *Shema* to heart (vv.6-9), about the importance of not worshipping the gods of the peoples round about them (vv.10-15), about not putting God to the test as they had done during their journey through the wilderness but being obedient to Him (vv.16-19) and about telling subsequent generations about what God has done for His people and what He requires of them (vv.20-25).

In 1 Timothy chapter three we find a similar combination of instructions about faith and practice. In verses 3-12 there are practical instructions about the qualities that are to be looked for in bishops and deacons, but in the second half of the chapter we find St. Paul describing the truth which the Christian church is called on to uphold, what he calls the 'mystery of our religion':

> Great indeed, we confess, is the mystery of our religion:
> He was manifested in the flesh,

---

[2] P D Miller *Deuteronomy* Louisville: John Knox Press 1990 pp.97-98

vindicated in the Spirit,
seen by angels,
preached among the nations,
believed on in the world,
taken up in glory. (v16)

The word 'He' here refers to Christ and St. Paul seems to be quoting from an early Christian hymn in order to declare the basic Christian message about the incarnate, resurrected and glorified Christ as a contrast to the erroneous doctrines of the false teachers whom he goes on to censure in the next chapter. This, he is saying, is the true Christian faith from which they have departed.

Because of a concern that the Church should be faithful to God in its teaching and practice the early centuries of the Church's existence saw a continuation of the process of defining the faith and practice of the people of God. The classic examples of this are the definitions of faith and practice produced by the great ecumenical councils such as the Councils of Nicaea (325 AD) and Chalcedon (451 AD).

For example, as is well known, the Council of Nicaea defined the orthodox understanding of the Trinity in opposition to Arianism in the *Creed of Nicaea*, the forerunner of the *Nicene Creed* which is recited today. However, the Council not only produced this doctrinal definition but also twenty canons regulating various aspects of the Church's practice.

Canon IV, for instance, gives regulations concerning the appointment of bishops:

It is by all means proper that a bishop should be appointed by all the bishops in the province; but should this be difficult, either on account of urgent necessity or because of distance, three at least should meet together, and the suffrages of the absent [bishops] also being given and communicated in writing, then the ordination should take place. But in every province the ratification of what is done should be left to the Metropolitan.[3]

The process of defining the faith and practice of the Church in this way continued throughout the Middle Ages. The Fourth Lateran Council of

---

[3] Council of Nicaea Canon IV in *The Nicene and Post Nicene Fathers* 2nd series vol XIV Edinburgh & Grand Rapids: T&T Clark 1997 p.11

1215, for example, sets out the basic belief of the Church in Canon I and then covers a wide range of other issues in the life of the Church ranging from provincial councils to the relics of the saints.

In the 16th century all sides of the Reformation divides drew up their own statements setting out their understanding of what the faith and practice of the Church should be like. Thus the Lutheran *Augsburg Confession* of 1530 not only contains articles on issues of faith such as the doctrines of the Trinity, original sin and justification, but also matters of practice such as the marriage of priests, monastic vows and the power of bishops. Thus also the *Canons and Decrees of the Council of Trent*, finally published in 1563, covered a similar range of issues from a Roman Catholic perspective.

2. The Purpose of the Thirty nine Articles

The Church of England's Thirty Nine Articles emerged out of this Reformation context.

Following the breach with Rome in the early 1530's the Church of England was faced with the need to declare where it stood in relation to the religious controversies of the time. In the words of Stephen Neill: 'Amid the burning controversies that raged in the sixteenth century, it was necessary that a Church should know where it stood, and should make its position known both to friends and enemies.'[4]

In specific terms this meant that it had to define where it stood in relation to the teaching being propagated by those who remained loyal to Rome, by the mainstream Reformers in continental Europe such as Luther, Zwingli, Calvin and Bucer and by the theologians of the radical Reformation both on the continent and at home.[5]

Viewed in their historical context, the *Thirty Nine Articles* provide such a definition. As we shall see when we look at each of the Articles in turn, they set out where the Church of England stood in relation to the teaching of these various groups on a series of issues of faith and practice which were of pressing concern at the time when the Articles were produced.

---

[4] S C Neill *Anglicanism* 4th ed London: Mowbray 1977 p.81
[5] The groups associated with the radical Reformation have traditionally been described as 'Anabaptists'. However, this title is not now used as a general description of these groups since it is clear that not all of them practised believer's baptism.

If we enquire further we find that the motive that the Church of England had for defining where it stood in relation to the groups just mentioned was to try to achieve agreement on matters of religion. The title given to the Articles in their final form in 1571 was:

> Articles agreed upon by the Archbishops and Bishops of both provinces, and the whole clergy, in the Convocation holden at London in the year 1562, for avoiding of diversities of opinion, and for the establishment of consent touching true religion.[6]

The key point is contained in the final two clauses of this title. What the sixteenth century English Reformers who were responsible for the Articles wanted to avoid was diversity of opinion and what they wanted to achieve was agreement on true religion.

The reason they sought to avoid 'diversity of opinion' was that they believed that this was incompatible with maintenance of proper order in Church and state. Thus when Archbishop Matthew Parker and fourteen other bishops wrote to Queen Elizabeth I in 1566 asking her to give her official approval to a bill requiring subscription to the Articles from the clergy of the Church of England they declared that:

> ...the approbation of the Articles by your Majesty shall be a very good means to establish and confirm all your Highnesses' subjects in one consent and unity of true doctrine, to the great quiet and safety of your Majesty and this your realm; whereas now, for want of Articles of doctrine by law to be declared, great distraction and dissension of minds is at this present among your subjects.[7]

More fundamentally, it was also because they believed that to tolerate diversity on the topics which the Articles covered would mean tolerating error in important areas of the Church's faith and practice. The Articles were intended to prevent this happening by identifying and rejecting such error. As Parker and the other bishops explained in the same letter

---

[6] The fact that almost identical words had been used to describe the function of the *Ten Articles* of 1536 and the *Forty Two Articles* of 1553 highlights the fact that that this was a continuing concern of the Tudor Reformers.

[7] *The Correspondence of Archbishop Parker* Cambridge: CUP/ Parker Society 1853 p.294

to Queen Elizabeth, another reason for her giving her support to the Articles was that:

> ...divers and sundry errors, and namely such as have been in this realm wickedly and obstinately by the adversaries of the Gospel defended, are by the same Articles condemned.[8]

In contrast, what the Reformers of the Church of England wanted was 'consent touching true religion.' If we ask what they meant by the term 'true religion' the title of the earliest commentary on the Articles, the commentary by Thomas Rogers published in two parts in 1585 and 1587, provides us with the answer.

The title of this work is *The English Creede; consenting with the True, Ancient, Catholique and Apostolique Church in all the points and articles of Religion which everie Christian is to know and believe that would be saved* and what this title points us to is the fact that for the leaders of the 16th century Church of England true religion, that is to say religion the practice of which would enable you to be saved, was to be found in the teaching and practice of the 'true, ancient, catholic and apostolic Church'.

By this term they meant the teaching and practice of Jesus and His Apostles as recorded in the New Testament and expounded by the orthodox Fathers and Councils of the Church during the first few centuries of its history. As works such as Bishop John Jewel's *Apology for the Church of England* show, the Reformers of the Church of England believed that this teaching and practice had been corrupted by the Medieval Church and that what the Church of England and other Protestant churches had done was to re-discover it using the historical and linguistic tools newly available to sixteenth century scholars.

The *Thirty Nine Articles* were intended to help embody this re-discovered teaching and practice in the life of the Church of England as part of a wider series of projects that were designed to achieve this end. The Articles and the model sermons known as the *Homilies* were intended to set out in broad terms what the faith and practice of the Church of England should be as the basis for teaching, catechesis, and discipline. The *Book of Common Prayer* and its accompanying *Ordinal* were designed to express the faith of the Church of England through reformed liturgical practice. Finally, the proposed reform of Medieval

---

[8] Ibid p. 293

canon law, the *Reformatio Legum Ecclesiasticarum,* was designed to give the faith detailed legal application.

The explanation of the nature of the Articles offered by Bishop John Pearson in 1660 has often been quoted. In response to the argument of a Puritan writer called Cornelius Burges that the Articles were defective because there were important theological issues that they did not cover, Pearson stated that what he called the 'Book of Articles':

> ...is not, nor is pretended to be, a complete body of divinity, or a comprehension of all Christian doctrines necessary to be taught; but an enumeration of some truths, which upon and since the Reformation have been denied by some persons; who upon this denial are thought unfit to have any cure of souls in this Church or realm; because they might by their opinions either infect their flock with error, or else disturb the Church with schism, or the realm with sedition.[9]

What Pearson says in this quotation is true as far as it goes.

It is true that the Articles are not, and were never meant to be, a complete systematic theology, although they were meant to cover the key articles of the Christian faith. It is also true, as has already been indicated, that the Articles were intended to be, and were used from the outset as, a way of excluding from the ranks of the clergy those who were likely to teach error or spread dissension in Church and state.

However, to say that the Articles were intended simply to exclude those who were heretical, schismatic or seditious is to take too negative a view of their purpose. Like the other doctrinal statements referred to at the beginning of this introduction, the Articles were not intended primarily to combat error but rather to proclaim the truth. As has already been indicated, the Articles were intended to set out a basic framework of faith and practice for the Church of England, based on the Scriptures and the teaching of the Early Church, for '...the glory of God, the advancement of true religion, and the salvation of Christian souls.'[10]

---

[9] W Churton (ed) *John Pearson – Minor Theological Works* II, 1843, p.215.
[10] *Correspondence of Archbishop Parker* p.293

3. The Articles and comprehension

It is also often suggested that the Articles were intended to be an exercise in comprehension, in the sense that they were meant to give room for a variety of different theological opinions within the parameters of a broadly conceived Protestant orthodoxy, and that to achieve this purpose the Articles were written in a manner that was meant to leave room for more than one interpretation. In this connection reference is often made to the statement by Bishop Gilbert Burnet in his 1690 *Exposition of the XXXIX Articles* that the: '...the Articles are conceived in large and general words' and that: '...we ought to take that for a sure indication that the Church does not intend to tie men up too severely to particular opinions, but that she leaves all to such a liberty as is agreeable with the purity of the faith.'[11]

As in the case of Pearson's explanation of the purpose of the Articles, the suggestion that the Articles were intended to be comprehensive is true as far as it goes, but what is meant by 'comprehensive' in this context needs careful definition. In the words of J.I. Packer:

> It is often said that the Articles were deliberately framed to be as comprehensive as possible. This is true; but it is important to be clear on the precise sense in which it is true. The Articles are not vague, or ambiguous, or intentionally imprecise. They are not the product of doctrinal indifferentism, not the fruit of theological compromise. Their comprehensiveness does not consist in any of these things. It consists simply in this: that the Articles are deliberately and consciously minimal in their requirements. They define only those fundamental matters on which, in the compilers' view, agreement and assent are absolutely indispensable if the gospel as the Church of England understands it is to be preserved and the Church's order maintained. And those fundamental matters are defined no further than the compilers judged necessary as a means to this end. Beyond these necessary limits, the compilers were content for the clergy, in John Wesley's phrase, to 'think and let think.'[12]

---

[11] G Burnet *An Exposition of the XXIX Articles of the Church of England* Oxford: Clarendon Press 1819 pp.11-12

[12] J I Packer *The Thirty Nine Articles* London: Church Pastoral Aid Society 1961.

Burnet's suggestion that the Articles were intended to allow of more than one reading is understandable as a reaction to the bitter disputes about the precise meaning of the Articles that had marked the life of the Church of England for much of the 17th century. However, as an account of the intention of those who drew up the Articles his suggestion is ruled out by the evidence of Archbishop Thomas Cranmer, the principal author of most of the Articles, who wrote in a letter to the Polish Reformer John A Lasco in July 1548:

> We are desirous of setting forth in our churches the true doctrine of God, and have no wish to adapt it to all tastes and to trifle with ambiguities, but, laying aside all carnal and prudential motives, to transmit to posterity a true and explicit form of doctrine agreeable to the rule of the sacred writings.[13]

If Cranmer's motivation was shared by the others responsible for the Articles, and there is no reason to think that it was not, it follows that Burnet's idea of a deliberate ambiguity being built into the Articles from the beginning has to be rejected.

4. Are the Articles a creed?

Another issue in relation to the nature and purpose of the Articles is whether they were intended to be a creed. The idea that they are a creed is frequently denied. G W H Lampe, for example, states unequivocally:

> The Articles are not a creed. They look back to the Creeds, and are not a substitute for them. They do not, any more than the other [Reformation] Confessions, stand on the same level as those ancient professions of the Faith which have been received and tested by the universal Church since its early years.[14]

On the other hand Packer maintains that the Articles claim:

---

[13] T Cranmer *Original Letters* vol 1. p.17 quoted in E Tyrell Green *The XXXIX Articles and the Age of the Reformation* London: Wells, Darton Gardner & Co. 1896 p. 3

[14] G W H Lampe 'The Revision of the Articles' in J C de Satge et al *The Articles of the Church of England* London: A R Mowbray 1964 p.95

...to be what the ecumenical creeds are, explanatory echoes of the apostolic witness to Christ, and to exercise the same kind of authority as the creeds do. And any responsible assessment of the Articles must begin by taking this claim seriously.

The grounds on which it is sometimes maintained that the Articles have not the nature of a creedal statement are quite insubstantial. To the argument that they are not a creed because they are not a complete body of divinity, it is enough to reply that, complete or not, they contain a good deal more than the ecumenical creeds themselves do. To the argument that they are not a creed because they include statements on Anglican domestic order and discipline, one need only say that this means that they are more than a creed – not less! The argument that they are not a creed because they were sought out partly with a political motive, to settle strife and enable men to live together, is answered by the consideration that exactly the same was true of the Nicene Creed. The argument that they are not a creed because they have never given rise to an Anglican 'confessional' theology like the Lutherans is sufficiently met by pointing out that there has never been a confessionalism in the Reformed churches either, yet Reformed theology is as clear as Lutheran about the identical nature of patristic creeds and sixteenth-century confessions. The fact remains that the Thirty-nine Articles exhibit not only the same doctrines as other Reformation confessions do, but also the same concern to identify the faith they confess with the faith of the Fathers and the New Testament, and the same conviction that the road they fence is, in fact, the highroad of catholicity, from which Romans and Anabaptists alike had gone astray. Like the rest of the Reformation confessions, the Articles are a domestic creed, and their authority must be understood accordingly.[15]

Packer seems to have the better of the argument here. It is true that the Articles were never intended to be a substitute for the ecumenical creeds. They were, however, as Packer implies, intended to be a supplement to them. Like the other Reformation Confessions they were intended to be a supplementary echo of the apostolic witness to Christ in the context of

---

[15] Ibid pp.44-45

sixteenth century England. In that sense they were intended to be, as the title of Roger's commentary states, the 'English Creed.'

It is also true that the Articles do not possess the same degree of acceptance down the centuries and across the churches that the ecumenical creeds possess. However, as Article VIII makes clear, in the sixteenth century Church of England historical pedigree and ecumenical acceptance were not seen as the key issues when considering the authority of the creeds. What mattered was whether the contents of the creeds could be 'proved by most certain warrants of holy Scripture' and the Church of England believed this to be true of the *Articles* just as much as it was true for the Apostles, Nicene or Athanasian Creeds.

As W H Griffith Thomas argues it is best to see the relationship between the ecumenical Creeds and the confessional statements of the Reformation, such as the *Thirty Nine Articles,* not in terms of contrast but in terms of continuation and development:

> Creeds and Confessions are sometimes contrasted to the detriment of the latter, but a study of the historical order of emergence of these documents of the faith suggests a comparison rather than a contrast. As we follow in order the three Creeds themselves, the Apostles', the Nicene, and the Athanasian, we find that there is a tendency to elaboration, to a fuller theological statement, and to an exploration of what is involved in the original summary of belief. The confessions of faith in the sixteenth century are really only an extension, prolongation and development of the same process.[16]

5. Are the Articles Reformed in their theology?

A final issue that needs to be considered in this section of the Introduction is whether the Articles were intended to be specifically Reformed statement of faith and order. Packer claims that they were: 'They are demonstrably Protestant as opposed to Roman, and Reformed as opposed to Lutheran'.[17] The claim that the Articles are Protestant rather than Roman Catholic in their theology is not one that is open to serious question. As we shall see, the Articles repeatedly take a

---

[16] W H Griffith Thomas *The Principles of Theology* 4ed London: Church Book Room Press 1951 p. xxv. For a fuller statement of this idea see G Aulen *Reformation and Catholicity* London: Oliver & Boyd 1962
[17] Packer op.cit. p. 11

Protestant position in opposition to sixteenth century Roman Catholic faith and practice on a whole range of issues. However, the claim that the Articles are Reformed as opposed to Lutheran is more debatable.

There are two arguments that are normally put forward in support of this claim. The first is that the Articles were included in a harmony of Reformed statements on faith published in 1581[18] and the second is that Articles XVII and XXIX take a Reformed line on the issues of Predestination and the Eucharist. On the latter issue Eric Routley argues, for instance, that Articles XVII and XXIX exhibit a distinctively Calvinist theology.[19]

In response to the first argument, it is true that the Articles were included in the 1581 harmony. However, all that this tells us is that in the opinion of the person or persons who compiled the harmony the Articles were compatible with Reformed theology. Whether the Articles actually are distinctively Reformed in character is something that can only be determined from an examination of the Articles themselves.

In response to the second argument a number of points need to be made.

(a) The use of the term 'Calvinist' is problematic because although a theological tradition influenced by the work of John Calvin was in existence and influential within the Church of England by the end of the sixteenth century this tradition had not come into existence at the time when the Articles were drawn up. To say that any of the Articles were Calvinistic is thus, strictly speaking, anachronistic, even though one could argue that certain of the Articles had an affinity with later Calvinist thought.[20]

(b) As we shall see when we look at Article XVII in more detail, this Article does not have the characteristics that were to mark later Reformed or Calvinist thinking about predestination. Specifically, neither here nor elsewhere in the Articles, is there any reference to either double predestination or limited atonement. What we have in Article XVII is in fact a distinctive development of the thought of St. Paul as developed by

---

[18] *A Harmony of the Confessions of Faith of the Orthodox and Reformed Churches* Geneva 1581

[19] E Routley *Creeds and Confessions* London: Duckworth 1962 pp. 105-107

[20] For the development of Calvinism in England see R T Kendall *Calvin and English Calvinism to 1649* Carlisle: Paternoster Press 1649

St. Augustine, a development that cannot be identified with the approach taken by either the Lutheran or the Reformed traditions.

(c) In the case of Article XXIX and the general teaching of the Articles on the Eucharist we do find a Reformed rather than Lutheran approach to Eucharistic theology. It is also true that there are parallels between the Eucharistic theology of the Articles and the approach taken by John Calvin.

This means that one can say that there is an element of Reformed theology in the Articles and that aspects of the theology of the Articles do parallel the teaching of John Calvin. However, alongside this Reformed element we also find the influence of the Lutheran theology of the Augsburg and Württemberg Confessions, the theology of St. Augustine and the teaching of the ecumenical creeds. As Packer says, the Articles are:

> ...consciously eclectic. They set out the Trinitarian faith of the ecumenical creeds (1-5) as biblical and necessary to salvation (6-8), together with Augustine's doctrine of sin (9-10); Lutheran teaching on justification, grace, and the church (11-21, 23, 34, 37), as given in the Augsburg Confession of 1530 and Württemberg Confession of 1552 (used in the 1563 revision); and sacramental teaching of the Swiss sort, with at one point an anti-Lutheran edge (29).[21]

(d) To say that the Articles are a piece of Reformed theology (a 'Calvinistic creed' as the Earl of Chatham famously later called them) is to ignore the eclectic nature of their theological pedigree. Furthermore, it is also to overlook the fact that the reason for this eclecticism is that differences between 'Lutheran' and 'Reformed' approaches to theology seem simply to have not been that important to those Reformers of the English Church who were responsible for the production of the Articles. We do not find in the writings of these Reformers the idea that there were two opposed theological blocs, Lutheran and Reformed, between which one had to chose. What we find instead is a stress on the agreement between Protestant theologians about the basic tenets of the faith and a minimising of the significance of the differences between them.

---

[21] de Satge op.cit. p.31

III. The Development of the Articles

The Articles as we have them today are the product of thirty five years of theological development during which the Church of England marked its evolving theological position with a series of statements of faith and order.

1. The Ten Articles (1536)

The first of these statements was the *Ten Articles* of 1536. These set out the Church of England's theological position in the light of the negotiations that had taken place the previous year with Lutherans who accepted the Augsburg Confession. These seem to have been drawn up at the request of Henry VIII by a committee of moderate theologians and then subsequently approved by the Convocations of Canterbury and York.[22]

The teaching of the *Ten Articles* show that in 1536 the theology of the Church of England was in a transitional phase between Medieval Catholicism and Protestantism

As Gerald Bray explains in his introduction to these articles in his *Documents of the English Reformation*:

Lutheran influence is prominent in Article 5 on Justification, and following Luther's practice only three of the traditional seven sacraments are mentioned. On the other hand, traditional Catholic practices like the veneration of images, the cult of the saints and prayers for the dead are reaffirmed. Article 4 on the Lord's Supper allows for a breadth of interpretation which could permit either a Lutheran or a Catholic position on transubstantiation. The need to respond to Protestant attacks is particularly apparent in the defence of penance in Article 3. There is extensive appeal to Scripture in that Article, which suggests that there was a conscious attempt being made to persuade Protestants that penance had biblical warrant. Another concession to Protestant sensibilities is the rejection of purgatory and the devotional practices connected with it. With one exception, biblical quotations are in Latin, a reminder that there was as yet no official English translation of the Scriptures. On balance, the Ten

---

[22] See C Hardwick *A History of the Articles of Religion* London: George Bell & Sons 1895 pp 32-42

Articles represent an early stage in the process of reformation, when traditionalist views were still strong. However, the fact that a number of Protestant ideas were included, and given at least qualified approval, shows which way the wind was blowing.[23]

2. The Institution of a Christian Man/Bishops Book (1537)

In 1537 a synod of bishops and representative clergy from the Convocations of Canterbury and York was summoned by Henry VIII's Vicar General, Thomas Cromwell, and given the task of producing an improved statement of where the Church of England stood theologically.[24]

The book that was eventually produced, officially called *The Institution of a Christian Man*, became known as *The Bishops' Book* because it was published in the name of the two archbishops '....and all the other bishops, prelates and archdeacons of the realm' rather than with royal authority. Like the *Ten Articles* of the previous year, from which it drew much of its material, the new statement (which was designed to be read as sermons)[25] was a compromise between those who wanted the Church of England to retain as much as possible of the theology and practice of Medieval Catholicism and those led by Archbishop Cranmer who wanted it to move to a more definitely Protestant position.

In the words of Bishop Edgar Gibson in his commentary on the Articles:

This document contained 'the exposition or interpretation of the Common Creed, of the Seven Sacraments, of the Ten Commandments, and of the Pater Noster, and the Ave Maria, Justification and Purgatory.' The articles on Justification and Purgatory are copied verbatim from those in the Ten Articles, and in general the character of the teaching contained in the two documents is very similar. The 'Seven Sacraments' are retained, but abuses connected with extreme unction are carefully

---

[23] G Bray *Documents of the English Reformation* Cambridge: James Clark 1994 p.162

[24] For details see D MacCulloch *Thomas Cranmer* New Haven & London: Yale University Press 1996 pp.185-197.

[25] Ibid p. 206

restrained, and a marked distinction is drawn between Baptism, the Eucharist, and Penance, and all other sacraments.[26]

Because the new work never received the formal sanction of either the crown or the Convocations the *Ten Articles* officially remained in force as the Church of England's doctrinal standard.

3. The Act of the Six Articles

This Act was agreed by Parliament and the Convocations in 1539 in the face of opposition from Archbishop Cranmer and others with Protestant sympathies. Inspired by the religious conservatism of Henry VIII himself, the Act upheld six key points of traditional Catholic theology and practice and laid down severe penalties, up to and including the death penalty, against those who taught or acted against them.

The points in question were as follows:

> First, that in the most blessed sacrament of the altar, by the strength and efficacy of Christ's mighty word (it being spoken by the priest), is present really, under the form of bread and wine, the natural body and blood of our Saviour Jesus Christ, conceived by the Virgin Mary; and after the consecration there remaineth no substance of bread and wine, nor any other substance, but the substance of Christ, God and man.
>
> Secondly, that communion in both kinds is not necessary *ad salutem*, by the law of God, to all persons; and that it is to be believed, and not doubted of, but that in the flesh, under the form of the bread, is the very blood; and with the blood, under the form of the wine, is the very flesh; as well apart, as though they were both together.
>
> Thirdly, that priests after the order of priesthood received, as afore, may not marry, by the law of God.
>
> Fourthly, that vows of chastity or widowhood, by man or woman made to God advisedly, ought to be observed by the law of God; and that it exempts them from other liberties of Christian people, which without that they might enjoy.

---

[26] E C S Gibson *The Thirty Nine Articles* 6ed London: Methuen 1908 p. 5

Fifthly, that it is meet and necessary that private masses be continued and admitted in this the King's English Church and Congregation, as whereby good Christian people, ordering themselves accordingly, do receive both godly and goodly consolations and benefits; and it is agreeable also to God's law. Sixthly, that auricular confession is expedient and necessary to be retained and continued, used and frequented in the Church of God.[27]

The Act remained in force until King Henry's death in 1547 although the severity of some of its provisions were soon relaxed.

4. The Necessary Doctrine and Erudition for any Christian Man (1543)

This document, published in 1543, officially superseded the *Ten Articles* as the statement of the doctrinal position of the Church of England. It was the work of a committee of bishops, it was approved by Parliament and the Convocations and because it was published by Royal authority it became known as the *King's Book*.

Much of the material in this new document was drawn from the *Bishops' Book* of six years before, but it contained additional Articles on Free Will and Good Works, expanded material on the nature of the sacraments and a preface on Faith. These changes resulted in a more conservative statement than the previous work.

Specifically, the new statement emphasised traditional Catholic theology by teaching the legitimacy of receiving communion in one kind, the necessity of priestly absolution as part of the sacrament of penance, and the importance of the performance of good works for the 'increase of justification'. Like the *Six Acts* it reiterated the requirement of celibacy for the clergy and those who had taken monastic vows and over against the Protestant belief that everyone should be able to read the Bible it restricted the reading of the Scripture to the clergy and those of gentle birth.

The *Necessary Doctrine* remained in force as the Church of England's doctrinal statement until it was in turn superseded by the *Forty Two Articles* in 1553.

---

[27] Text in Bray op.cit p.224

5. The Thirteen Articles (1538)

In 1538 an embassy from the German Lutheran Princes was sent to England to see if it would be possible to achieve doctrinal agreement between the Lutherans of the *Augsburg Confession* and the Church of England. This embassy met with a committee of three bishops and four doctors (academics) from the Church of England appointed by the King, the most prominent of whom was Archbishop Cranmer, and although doctrinal agreement was not achieved a product of their discussions was a document known as the *Thirteen Articles* which was never published but was discovered among Cranmer's papers in the early 19th century.

The Articles, which were written in Latin, seem to have been drawn up by Cranmer and the topics they cover are: The Unity of God and the Trinity of Persons, Original Sin, The Two Natures of Christ, Justification, The Church, Baptism, The Eucharist, Penitence, The Use of the Sacraments, The Ministers of the Church, The Rites of the Church, Civil Affairs and The Resurrection of the Body and the Last Judgement.[28] As Gibson notes, of these Articles:

> ...the first three are taken almost word for word from the Confession of Augsburg, the influence of which may be traced in other parts of the Articles as well. But it is noteworthy that the sections on Baptism, the Eucharist and Penance are either entirely new or largely rewritten, while in that on the Use of Sacraments the language of the Lutheran Confession has been considerably strengthened, in order to emphasise the character of sacraments as channels of grace – apparently in order to satisfy the Anglican divines.[29]

Although the *Thirteen Articles* never had any official standing in the Church of England, and were never even published, nevertheless they are important for three reasons.

First, the context in which they were produced indicates that there was a desire both in England and on the Continent for there to be a doctrinal agreement leading to the establishment of communion between the Church of England and the Lutheran churches and also that, initially at least, it was believed that such an agreement might be possible.

---

[28] For the text of the *Thirteen Articles* see Ibid pp. 184-221
[29] Gibson op.cit. p.7

Secondly, they provided the channel by means of which the Lutheran theology of the *Augsburg Confession* became part of the official doctrine of the Church of England via the inclusion of large parts of them into the *Forty Two* and then the *Thirty Nine Articles*. To quote the Victorian writer Charles Hardwick in his *History of the Articles of Religion*, the Articles of 1538:

> ...not only indicate the disposition of our leading reformers to acquiesce in the dogmatic statements which had been put forward in the Augsburg Confession, but have also a prospective bearing of still more importance, as, in many ways, the ground-work of Articles now in use. No one can deny that the compilers of the Forty-two Articles in the reign of Edward VI drew largely from the Lutheran formulary of 1530; but the recent discovery of the Thirteen Articles has made it probable that such derivation, instead of being (as was hitherto supposed) direct, took place entirely through the medium of the Anglo-German channel. This conclusion is supported by the fact, 'that the expressions of Edward VI's Formulary, usually adduced to prove its connection with the Confession of Augsburg, are also found in the Book of Articles; while it contains others, which can be traced as far as the Book of Articles, but which will be sought for in vain in the Confession of Augsburg.' From what is known of their general character, the framers of the Edwardine Articles would be 'anxious, in the execution of their undertaking, to meet, if possible, the views of their brethren on the continent, as well as of their countrymen at home; and they could scarcely pursue a surer method of obtaining their object than by borrowing from a form of doctrine already approved by both.'[30]

Two examples will serve to illustrate the connection between the *Augsburg Confession, The Thirteen Articles,* and the *Thirty Nine Articles*.

The first example is the first article of the *Thirteen Articles* which contains the following words taken from the first article of the *Augsburg Confession*:

---

[30] Hardwick op.cit. pp.60-61

God, eternal, incorporeal, indivisible, of immense power, wisdom and goodness, creator and preserver of all things, visible and invisible, and yet there are three persons of the same essence and power, coeternal, Father, Son and Holy Spirit.[31]

Via the *Forty Two Articles* this eventually became Article I of the *Thirty Nine Articles*

There is but one living and true God, everlasting, without body, parts, or passions; of infinite power, wisdom, and goodness; the maker and preserver of all things both visible and invisible. And in unity of this Godhead there be three Persons, of one substance, power, and eternity; the Father, the Son, and the Holy Ghost.

The second example is the ninth article of the *Thirteen Articles,* which contains the following account of the sacraments taken from article thirteen of the *Augsburg Confession:*

We teach that the sacraments which have been instituted by the Word of God are not only signs of profession among Christians, but even more, sure witnesses and effective signs of grace and of God's good will towards us. Through them, God works in us invisibly, and pours his grace into us invisibly, if we receive them rightly, and faith is also awakened through them and confirmed in those who use them.

Via the *Forty Two Articles* this eventually became the basis for the first paragraph of Article XXV of the *Thirty Nine Articles*:

Sacraments ordained of Christ be not only badges or tokens of Christian men's profession, but rather they be certain sure witnesses and effectual signs of grace and God's good will towards us, by the which He doth work invisibly in us, and doth not only quicken, but also strengthen and confirm, our faith in Him.

---

[31] Bray op.cit p. 185

Thirdly, Cranmer's decision to produce his own set of articles which drew on the *Augsburg Confession*, but also contained new material of their own, and the inability of the Lutheran and Church of England sides to reach theological agreement, foreshadowed the fact that even when the Church of England became a definitely Protestant church in the reigns of Edward VI and Elizabeth I it did not become a Lutheran church with bishops like the Church of Sweden, but forged its own distinctive identity that combined elements from a number of different theological traditions.

6. *The Forty Two Articles*

(a) Their development

The death of Henry VIII and the accession of Edward VI in 1547 provided the opportunity for Cranmer and other like minded bishops such as Hugh Latimer and Nicholas Ridley to move away from the theological equivocation of Henry's reign and to take the Church of England in a definitely Protestant direction. Their willingness to grasp this opportunity is shown by their production of the *First Book of Homilies* of 1547 with its clear emphasis on the authority of Scripture and on the doctrine of justification by faith and by the introduction of the First and Second English Prayer Books in 1549 and 1552.

However, as I have already explained, until the very end of Edward's reign in 1553 the official doctrinal statement of the Church of England remained the conservative and traditionalist *Necessary Doctrine*. This delay has seemed surprising to most writers on the English Reformation, but the explanation seems to be that Cranmer wanted to wait and see if it might be possible to produce an agreed statement of faith that the other Protestant churches on the continent would also be able to adopt.

That this was the case is directly testified by John Rogers in the dedication to the 1607 edition of his commentary on the Articles. Addressing the then Archbishop of Canterbury, Richard Bancroft, he states:

> Most reverend Father in God, there is no one thing in this world, that of men truly zealous and Christian in these latter days of the world with greater earnestness hath been desired, than that by a joint and common consent of all the churches rightly, and according to the canons of the sacred scriptures, reformed, there

29

might be a draught made and divulged, containing and expressing the sum and substance of that religion, which they do all both concordably teach and uniformly maintain.

That holy man (of happy remembrance) D. Cranmer, who sometime enjoyed that room in our church which your grace now worthily possesseth, in the days of our godly young prince, Edward the Sixth, employed a great part of his time and study for the effecting of that work; and imparted his thoughts with the most principal persons, and of rarest note in those days for their wisdom, piety, and credit, among the people of God throughout Christendom. M. Calvin, understanding of his intent, addressed his letters unto the said archbishop, and offered his service, saying, 'That, might his labours stand the church instead, *Ne decem quidem maria*, it would not grieve him to sail over ten seas to such a purpose.'

But, this proving a purpose of much difficulty, if not altogether impossible in men's eyes, especially in those days to be brought about; the next course and resolution was, that every kingdom and free state, or principality, which had abandoned the superstitious, and antichristian religion of the church of Rome, and embraced the gospel of Christ, should divulge a brief of that religion, which among themselves was taught and believed, and whereby, through the mercy of God in Christ, they did hope to be saved.[32]

Cranmer still appears to have been working to achieve agreement for the production of this ecumenically agreed statement of faith as late as March 1552, but by the autumn of 1549 he also appears to have been working on a new document that would form the basis of the *Forty Two Articles*.[33] On December 27 1549 John Hooper, a Protestant theologian who was to become Bishop of Gloucester and then Worcester, wrote in a letter to the Swiss Reformer Heinrich Bullinger that:

---

[32] T. Rodgers *The Catholic Doctrine of the Church of England* Cambridge: CUP/Parker Society 1844 pp.3-4

[33] The surviving evidence does not tell us whether this was always intended to be a purely English document or whether Cranmer hoped that it might form the basis for a wider ecumenical statement.

The Archbishop of Canterbury entertains right views as to the nature of Christ's presence in the supper, and is now very friendly towards myself. He has some Articles of Religion to which all preachers and lecturers in divinity are required to subscribe, or else a license for teaching is not granted to them.[34]

These articles are also mentioned in a further letter from Hooper to Bullinger dated 5th February 1550:

The Archbishop of Canterbury, who is at the head of the King's Council gives to all lecturers and preachers their licence to read and preach; every one of them, however, must previously subscribe to certain Articles, which if possible I will send you; one of which respecting the Eucharist, is plainly the true one, and that which you maintain in Switzerland. [35]

The fact that Hooper, writing from a strongly Protestant perspective, refers so positively to the teaching on the Eucharist contained in these articles indicates that he is not referring to the *Necessary Doctrine*, but to a new and more definitely Protestant set of doctrinal articles.

Either these articles referred to by Hooper, or some developed form of them, appear to have been submitted by Cranmer to the English bishops for their comments in late 1551, and in May 1552 they were laid before the King's Council. They were returned to Cranmer in September 1552 and after he had re-ordered them and added titles to them they were sent to the King's secretary and tutor, Sir William Cecil and Sir John Cheke for their comments.

After further scrutiny by the six royal chaplains in October 1552, the Articles, which at this stage numbered forty five,[36] were returned to Cranmer for final revision. They were then sent by Cranmer to the Council and on 19 June 1553 were finally promulgated by royal authority, although the first edition of the Articles had already been published in May. The articles were published in both English and Latin.

---

[34] H Robinson (ed) *Original Letters relative to the English Reformation 1537-58* Cambridge: CUP/Parker Society 1846 p.71.

[35] Ibid p.76

[36] The long Article 29 on the Lord's Supper in the *Forty Two Articles* is four separate articles in the MS which went to the chaplains and which is still extant.

As Hardwick notes:

> With the sole exception of the form it had assumed when in the hands of the royal chaplains (Oct. 1552) we have no definite means of judging as to the degree of modification it [the Forty Two Articles] was made to undergo in the course of this protracted criticism; and yet the letter of the King to Ridley, bearing the date June 9, 1553, as well as that of the Archbishop to Cecil in the previous September, lead us to suppose that the amount of alteration had been considerable; for it describes the Articles, which were then publishing in their final form, as 'devised and gathered with great study, and by good advice of the greatest learned part of our bishops of this realm and sundry others of our clergy.' We are, therefore, justified in concluding that the work had been subject to a searching criticism, and gradually amended by a number of auxiliary hands, before subscription to it was enforced upon the clergy by royal mandate.[37]

An issue on which there has been continued debate is the issue of whether or not the *Forty Two Articles* were approved by the Southern Convocation at its meeting in London in March 1553.

The official title of the *Forty Two Articles* declared that they were 'Articles agreed on by the bishops and other learned men in the synod at London.' The Synod in question was the meeting of the southern Convocation and *prima facie* it would appear that the title must mean that the Articles were agreed by the Convocation and therefore had proper ecclesiastical as well as royal authority.

However, the truthfulness of this apparently straightforward declaration in the title of the Articles has been called into question for four reasons.

- There is no trace in the Convocation records of any such authorisation having been given.

- The royal letter requiring clergy and others to subscribe to the Articles made no mention of its having been agreed at Convocation.

---

[37] Hardwick op.cit p. 76

- The language used in the title is vague as to who precisely authorised the Articles, whereas in the subsequent promulgation of the *Thirty Nine Articles* in 1563 these are described in precise terms as having been: 'agreed upon by the archbishops and bishops of both provinces and the whole clergy'.

- In 1554, in the reign of Mary Tudor, Archdeacon John Philpot of Winchester and Archbishop Cranmer himself both specifically denied that the Articles had been authorised by Convocation. Philpot stated that they had been agreed by a committee authorised by Convocation and were in that sense authorised by it, while Cranmer stated that the title had been invented by the King's Council on the grounds that the Articles were produced: 'at the time of the Convocation.'[38]

On the other hand, those who accept the declaration in the title at face value put forward a number of counter arguments.

- It is true that the records of Convocation, which were destroyed in the Great Fire of London in 1666, were said by 17th century historians to have no record of any such authorisation. However, these historians also tell us that the records of the session in question were barren of almost any information apart from the names of those who were there. Assuming that the Convocation did undertake some business this must mean either that the records for the session in question were very badly kept or that they were deliberately mutilated in the following reign. In either case the argument from the silence of the Convocation records ceases to carry weight.

- The vagueness of the language in the title is not unique. Thus we know that the *Ten Articles* of 1536 were agreed by both the southern and the northern Convocations, but the royal declaration prefixed to them describes the Convocation as: 'the bishops and the other the most discreet and learned men of the clergy.' There does not appear to have been a fixed form of wording to describe the membership of Convocation.

---

[38] Hardwick op.cit. pp.105-108

- The statements by Archdeacon Philpot and Archbishop Cranmer refer specifically to 'the Catechism' and this is most naturally taken to be a reference not to the Articles themselves but to the catechism with which they were published.

- We have direct evidence from the summer of 1553 in the form of letters from the Vice Chancellor and Senate of Cambridge and from Sir John Cheke dated 1 and 7 June respectively that refer to the articles agreed by the synod of London.

- At the Convocation of 1563 and in the course of the dispute about the use of vestments in 1566 it was accepted without dispute that the *Forty Two Articles* had been agreed by the Convocation of 1553.[39]

The silence concerning the role of Convocation in the royal letter requiring subscription to the articles remains unexplained. However, this argument from silence has to be weighed against the strong contemporary evidence that the Articles were agreed by Convocation and on balance it seems clear that we may safely say that the Articles were thus agreed.

MacCulloch argues in his biography of Cranmer that:

> ...there were good reasons for not letting the whole Convocation loose on the articles, for there were conservatives present who would have given them a rough ride if they had been offered the chance, possibly even the remaining conservative bishops who were still clinging to their dioceses.[40]

This is a purely speculative argument and in the absence of any evidence to support it does not prove that Cranmer and his supporters did not decide to push the articles through the southern Convocation in spite of the possibility of the kind of conservative opposition to which MacCulloch refers. What seem good reasons to us may not have seemed good reasons to Cranmer.

---

[39] Hardwick op.cit pp.105-111
[40] MacCulloch op.cit. p.536

(b) Their contents

The list of articles that were promulgated in 1553 is as follows. Those that were eventually omitted from the *Thirty Nine Articles* are in italics. .

I	Of faith in the Holy Trinity
II	That the Word, or Son of God was made a very Man
III	Of the going down of Christ into hell
IV	Of the resurrection of Christ
V	The doctrine of Holy Scripture is sufficient to salvation
VI	The Old Testament is not to be refused
VII	The three Creeds
VIII	Of original or birth sin
IX	Of free will
X	*Of grace*
XI	Of the justification of Man
XII	Works before justification
XIII	Works of Supererogation
XIV	No Man is without sin, but Christ alone.
XV	Of sin against the Holy Ghost
XVI	*Blasphemy against the Holy Ghost*
XVII	Of Predestination and Election
XVIII	We must trust to obtain eternal salvation only by the name of Christ
XIX	All men are bound to keep the moral commandments of the law
XX	Of the Church
XXI	Of the authority of the Church
XXII	Of the authority of General Councils
XXIII	Of Purgatory
XXIV	No Man may minister in the Congregation, except he be called
XXV	Men must speak in the Congregation in such tongue, as the people understandeth
XXVI	Of the Sacraments
XXVII	The wickedness of the Ministers doth not take away the

effectual operation of God's ordinances

XXVIII Of Baptism

XXIX Of the Lord's Supper

XXX   Of the perfect oblation of Christ made upon the Cross

XXXI The state of single life is commanded to no Man by the word of God

XXXII Excommunicate persons are to be avoided

XXXIII Traditions of the Church

XXXIV Homilies

XXXV Of the books of Prayers and Ceremonies of the Church of England

XXXVI Of Civil Magistrates

XXXVII Christian Men's goods are not common

XXXVIII Christian Men may take an oath

XXXIX The resurrection of the dead is not yet brought to pass

XL   The souls of them that depart this life do neither die with their bodies nor sleep idly

XLI   Heretics called Millenarii

XLII   All Men shall not be saved at the length

(c) Their sources

These articles seem to have been largely drawn up from scratch by Cranmer and those who helped him to revise the material. There is no obvious continuity of content with the three official doctrinal statements of Henry VIII's reign, although Cranmer took material from the *Thirteen Articles* and incorporated it into Articles I, II, VIII, XXIV, XXVI, XXVII, and XXXIII.

(d) Their nature

A study of the content of these articles makes it clear that, as Gibson says, they were a 'two edged sword' designed to 'smite with equal impartiality' on the one hand the errors of Rome and on the other hand those of the radical Reformation.[41] A letter sent by John Hooper to Heinrich Bullinger from London in June 1549 illustrates the situation that they were intended to address, a situation in which the mainstream

---

[41] Gibson op.cit. p.21

Reformers felt that Church and state were threatened both by those radical groups whom Hooper calls the 'Anabaptists' and by those who remained committed to traditional Medieval Catholicism, what Hooper calls 'the popish faction':

> The Anabaptists flock to the place, and give me much trouble with their opinions respecting the incarnation of our Lord; for they deny altogether that Christ was born of the Virgin Mary, according to the flesh. They contend that a man who is reconciled to God is without sin, and free from all stain of concupiscence, and that nothing of the old Adam remains in his nature; and a man, they say, who is thus regenerate cannot sin. They add all hope of pardon is taken away from those who, after having received the Holy Ghost, fall into sin. They maintain a fatal necessity, and that beyond and beside that will of His, which He has revealed to us in the Scriptures, God hath another will, by which he altogether acts under some kind of necessity. Although I am unable to satisfy their obstinacy, yet the Lord by His word shuts their mouths, and their heresies are more and more detested by the people. How dangerously our England is afflicted by heresies of this kind, God only knows; I am unable indeed from sorrow of heart to express to your piety. There are some who deny that man is endued with a soul different from that of a beast and subject to decay. Alas, not only are these heresies reviving among us, which were formerly dead and buried, but new ones are springing up every day. There are such libertines and wretches, who are daring enough in their conventicles not only to deny that Christ is the Messiah and Saviour of the world, but also to call that blessed seed a mischievous fellow, and deceiver of the world. On the other hand a great portion of the kingdom so adheres to the popish faction, as to altogether set at nought God and the lawful authority of the magistrates; so that I am greatly afraid of a rebellion and civil discord. [42]

---

[42] Robinson (ed) op.cit p.65 For more details of the ideas of the 'Anabaptists' mentioned by Hooper see C J Clement *Religious Radicalism in England 1535-1565* Carlisle: Paternoster Press/Rutherford House 1997

The particular articles that respond to Rome and the radical Reformation respectively are as follows:

In response to Rome:

- Articles V and XXI reject the Roman claim that things that are not in Scripture may need to be believed by people in order for them to be saved

- Article XI insists that justification comes solely through faith in Jesus Christ over against the Roman teaching that justification is a result of both faith and good works.

- Article XII rejects the teaching of the Medieval scholastics that good works could make people worthy to receive grace (what was known as 'congruous merit).

- Article XIII rejects the idea that it is possible to earn extra merit with God by performing works that go beyond what He has specifically commanded.

- Article XX insists that the Church of Rome has erred both morally and theologically.

- Article XXII responds to the claims made by Rome for the Council of Trent (which had begun to meet in 1545) and for the Medieval Councils that preceded it.

- Article XXIII rejects the teaching of Rome concerning purgatory, pardons, images and the invocation of the saints.

- Article XXV defends liturgy in the vernacular against the Roman claim that the liturgy should be in Latin.

- Article XXVI rejects the idea the sacraments confer grace simply by virtue of the rite having been performed (*ex opere operato*)

- Article XXIX rejects the Medieval doctrine of transubstantiation upheld by Rome.

- Article XXX rejects the teaching of Rome about the sacrifice of the Mass.

- Article XXXI argues against the discipline of compulsory celibacy for the clergy upheld by Rome.

- Article XXXIII rejects the Roman claim that traditions and ceremonies need to be uniform throughout the Church.

- Article XXXVI rejects the jurisdiction of the Pope over the Church of England.

In response to the radical Reformation:

- Articles I-IV uphold the traditional doctrines of the Church concerning the Trinity and the person and work of Christ.

- Article V stresses the sufficiency Holy Scripture for salvation over against the stress by some of the radicals on the authority of the Spirit – an issue also touched in Article XIX

- Article VI rejects the radicals' belief that the Patriarchs in the Old Testament 'did look only for transitory promises.'

- Article VII upholds the authority of the Ecumenical Creeds.

- Article VIII rejects the teaching of Pelagius ('which also the Anabaptists do nowadays renew') that original sin consists in following Adam's bad example.

- Articles IX-X reject the radicals' stress on human free-will.

- Article XIV rejects the belief held by some radicals that it is possible for human beings to be free from sin.

- Article XV rejects the related idea that serious sin after baptism is the unpardonable sin against the Holy Spirit

- Article XVII upholds the Augustinian doctrine of predestination which many of the radicals rejected due to their stress on the freedom of the will and also insists that we must accept the will of God revealed to us in Scripture and not think that He has some secret additional will besides this.

- Article XVIII rejects the belief held by some radicals that people may be saved if they live according to the tenets of their own religious system and the light of nature.

- Article XIX rejects the belief of some radicals that the guidance of the Spirit was to be followed even when this was contrary to Scripture.

- Article XXIV rejects the radical belief that those who believed that they were called by God to exercise the office of preacher were bound to do so even though they were not authorised to preach by the Church.

- Article XXVII argues against the position held by some radicals that the personal unworthiness of the minister prevented the sacraments from being efficacious.

- Article XXVIII challenges the rejection of infant baptism by some radical groups.

- Articles XXXII and XXXIII challenge the radicals' rejection of ecclesiastical authority.

- Article XXXVI challenges the radical rejection of civil authority and, as a corollary, the radical rejection of capital punishment and espousal of pacifism.

- Article XXXVII teaches that the possessions of Christians should not be regarded as common property ('as certain Anabaptists do falsely boast').

- Article XXXVIII argues against the radical claim that the Bible forbids Christians to take oaths

- Articles XXXIX-XLII reject various errors put forward by the radicals in the area of eschatology.

In his commentary on the *Thirty Nine Articles* Gibson comments with regard to the *Forty Two Articles* that a:

> ...brief review of the objects and contents of the Forty-Two Articles will be sufficient to show that in the first instance the document must have been merely intended to be a provisional and temporary one. Every line of it bears witness to this. The idea that it would be maintained as a permanent test of orthodoxy cannot ever have occurred to its authors. For such a purpose it is singularly ill-suited. Many of the articles are purely negative, condemning in trenchant terms some existing error, but not attempting to define the positive truth opposed to it.[43]

What Gibson says in this quotation about the purely negative character of some of the articles is correct. For example, article XLI runs as follows:

Heretics called Millenarii
They that go about to renew the fable of heretics called Millenarii, be repugnant to Holy Scripture, and cast themselves headlong into a Jewish dotage.

This article does not say anything positive about eschatology. It simply condemns the beliefs of those who held that there would be a thousand year rule of Christ on earth.

However, it is arguable that Gibson fails to do justice to the positive nature of much of the material in the *Forty Two Articles* and it is also far from clear that Cranmer and his colleagues would have regarded

---

[43] Gibson op.cit p.26

the rejection of heresy as a purely temporary measure. They would have been aware that heresy was anathematised both by the authoritative Councils of the Early Church and by the New Testament itself (see Gal 1:9) and may well have seen this as indicating that the condemnation of heresy was of permanent significance.

Furthermore, when the Church of England sought to define its theological position once more in the reign of Elizabeth I, it did not simply reject the *Forty Two Articles* as a temporary statement without abiding value. As the full list of articles given above shows, thirty five of the *Forty Two Articles* of 1553 were carried over into the *Thirty Nine Articles* of 1571. Thirty four of these were kept as the basis for separate articles and article XIX was incorporated into article VII of the *Thirty Nine Articles*. Much of the material that was carried over into the 1571 Articles was either re-written or expanded, but a comparison of the two sets of Articles makes it clear that the *Thirty Nine Articles* was not a new work, but a revision, albeit a quite extensive revision, of the earlier one.

The positive teaching of the Forty Two Articles is as follows:

- They affirm the classical biblical and patristic account of the Trinity and the person and work of Christ (I-IV), a biblical and Augustinian approach to the doctrines of sin, grace and predestination (VIII-X) and the mainstream Reformation teaching about the unique authority of Scripture and about justification by faith (VI and XI-XIII). They also affirm that the death of Christ was the unique means of atonement for all the sins of the whole world (XXX).

- On the doctrine of the Church they affirm that the marks of the visible Church are the right preaching of the word and the due celebration of the sacraments and that the traditions and ceremonies of the Church do not have to be the same in all places (XX and XXXIII). Following Mt 18:17, they also argue that those who have been excommunicated by the Church should be treated as a 'heathen and publican' until such time as they are properly reconciled through penance and received back into the Church by a judge with proper authority (XXXII).

- On the sacraments they teach that Christ has 'knit together' his people by means of the two sacraments of baptism and the Lord's

Supper and that these are not simply external marks of Christian belonging, or of the love of Christians for each other, but are means by which God is invisibly at work in the lives of believers making them part of His people and confirming and strengthening their faith They also commend the practice of infant baptism and teach that the bread and wine at the Lord's Supper are a means of partaking in the body and blood of Christ to those who receive them with faith (XXVI, XXVIII, XXIX).

- On the formularies of the Church of England they teach that the 1547 *Homilies* are 'godly and wholesome' and should be read to the people, and that the English Prayer Book and Ordinal are 'godly' and agreeable to the 'wholesome doctrine of the gospel' and should therefore be received by the faithful members of the Church of England, and especially its ministers, and commended to the people of God (XXXV and XXXVI).

- On the relationship between Church and society they declare that the king of England is 'supreme head on earth, next under Christ' of the Church of England and Ireland, that authority of the civil magistrate is ordained by God, and that they therefore ought to be obeyed. They also declare that Christians may take part in lawful wars, that the goods of Christians are not a common possession (although they ought to use what they have to give alms as liberally as possible), and that it is proper for Christians to take oaths when the magistrate requires them to do so, providing it is done: 'in justice, judgement and truth' (Jer 4:2) (XXXVI-XXXVIII).

- Finally, they declare that our bodies will be raised up on the last day so that we may receive either reward or punishment depending on whether we have lived 'virtuously or wickedly' (XL).

7. The Elizabethan Articles

a. The Eleven Articles (1561)

The death of Edward VI on 6 July 1553 and the accession of his sister Mary Tudor led to a reversal of the religious policies followed by both Edward and his father and the reconciliation of the Church of England with Rome the following year. This meant that although the

Forty Two Articles were never officially abolished they were in practice replaced by a number of Articles and dogmatic definitions that were in line with Roman teaching.[44]

When Mary Tudor was in turn succeeded by her sister Elizabeth I in 1558 it was not immediately clear what Elizabeth's religious policy would be. However, the passing in 1559 of the *Act of Supremacy* which rejected Papal jurisdiction and declared Elizabeth to be 'supreme governor' of the Church of England and the *Act of Uniformity* which reintroduced the 1552 English Prayer Book, albeit in a slightly more traditionalist form, made it clear that Elizabeth intended to follow the approach of her father and her brother rather than that of her sister.[45]

Elizabeth's new Archbishop of Canterbury, Matthew Parker, was therefore faced with the task of continuing the reforming work begun by Archbishop Cranmer and his colleagues during the reigns of Henry VIII and Edward VI. Because the *Forty Two Articles* had never been abolished, but had merely fallen into disuse, it would have been possible, as Hardwick notes, for Parker to have maintained continuity with the Edwardine Reformation by offering them to the clergy: 'for adoption and subscription.'[46]

However, as he also notes, this was not what happened:

> The Articles in truth were kept almost entirely in the background, till submitted for discussion in the Convocation of 1563; nor, after they had been considerably remodelled in that Synod, was subscription to them regularly enforced until some further Acts of Parliament and Convocation in 1571.[47]

What happened instead was that from 1561-1571 the clergy were required to subscribe to the *Eleven Articles* which were drawn up in 1559 or early 1560 under the supervision of Archbishop Parker and agreed by the Archbishop of York and the other bishops of the Church of England. The Preface to these Articles explains their purpose and how they are to be used. It states that they are:

---

[44] Hardwick op.cit. p.113. For more detail on the doctrinal teaching of the Marian church see E Duffy *The Stripping of the Altars* New Haven & London: Yale University Press 1992 pp. 527-537

[45] For the Acts of Supremacy and Uniformity see Bray op.cit. pp. 318-334.

[46] Hardwick op cit p. 116

[47] Ibid p.117

A declaration of certain principal Articles of Religion set out by the order of both archbishops metropolitans and the rest of the bishops for the uniformity of doctrine, to be taught and holden of all parsons, vicars and curates, as well in testification [testimony] of their common consent in the said doctrine, to the stopping of the mouths of them that go about to slander the ministers of the church for diversity of judgement, as necessary for the instruction of their people; to be read by the said parsons, vicars and curates at their possession- taking, or first entry into their cures, and also after that, yearly at two several times, that is to say, the Sunday next following Easter day, and St. Michael the archangel, or on some other Sunday within one month after these feasts, immediately after the gospel.[48]

The Articles themselves begin with a statement that declares that they represent what the minister himself believes and what he requires his parishioners to assent to as well:

Forasmuch as it appertaineth to all Christian men, but especially to the ministers, and the pastors of the Church, being teachers and instructors of others, to be ready to give a reason of their faith, when they shall be thereunto required; I, for my part, now appointed your parson, vicar, or curate, having before my eyes the fear of God, and the testimony of my conscience, do acknowledge for myself, and require you to assent to the same ...[49]

The Articles then divide into six sections as follows:

- Articles I and II set out the basic theological beliefs of the Church of England, affirming faith in the Trinity, the Bible and the Catholic Creeds.

First, That there is but one living and true God, of infinite power, wisdom, and goodness, the Maker and Preserver of all things; and that

---

[48] Text in ibid p. 355
[49] Ibid p.357

in unity of this Godhead there be three Persons, of one substance, of equal power and eternity, the Father, the Son, and the Holy Ghost.

II. I believe also whatsoever is contained in the holy canonical Scriptures, in the which Scriptures are contained all things necessary to salvation, by the which also errors and heresies may sufficiently be reproved and convicted, and all doctrine and articles necessary to salvation established. I do also most firmly believe and confess all the articles contained in the three Creeds, the Nicene Creed, Athanasius' Creed, and our common Creed, called the Apostles' Creed; for these do briefly contain the principal articles of our faith, which are at large set forth in the Holy Scriptures.

• Article III defines the characteristics of true churches and the authority possessed by theses churches (such as the Church of England) to modify their own rites and ceremonies:

III I do acknowledge also that church to be the spouse of Christ, wherein the word of God is truly taught, the sacraments orderly ministered according to Christ's institution, and the authority of the keys duly used; and that every such particular church hath authority to institute, to change, clean to put away ceremonies, and other ecclesiastical rites, as they be superfluous, or be absurd, and to constitute other making more to seemliness, to order, or edification.

• Articles IV-VI discuss the issue of authority in the Church, rejecting the authority of private individuals or the Pope, and acknowledging instead the properly constituted ecclesiastical and secular authorities and the paramount authority of Queen Elizabeth I

IV. Moreover I confess, that it is not lawful for any man to take upon him any office or ministry, either ecclesiastical or secular, but such only as are lawfully thereunto called by their high authorities, according to the ordinances of this realm.

V. Furthermore, I do acknowledge the queen's majesty's prerogative and superiority of government of all estates, and in all causes, as well ecclesiastical as temporal, within this realm, and other her dominions and countries, to be agreeable to God's word, and of right to appertain to her highness, in such sort, as is in the late act of parliament expressed, and sithence [since] by her majesty's Injunctions declared and expounded.

VI. Moreover, touching the Bishop of Rome, I do acknowledge and confess, that by the Scriptures and word of God he hath no more authority than other bishops have in their provinces and dioceses; and therefore the power, which he now challengeth, that is, to be the supreme head of the universal church of Christ, and to be above all emperors, kings, and princes, is an usurped power, contrary to the Scriptures and word of God, and contrary to the example of the primitive church, and therefore is for most just causes taken away and abolished in this realm.

• Article VII defends the English Prayer Book, which had been restored to use in 1559

VII. Furthermore, I do grant and confess, that the book of Common Prayer and administration of the holy sacraments, set forth by the authority of parliament, is agreeable to the Scriptures, and that it is catholic, apostolic, and most for the advancing of God's glory, and the edifying of God's people, both for that it is in a tongue, that may be understood of the people, and also for the doctrine and form of ministration contained in the same.

• Articles VIII-X defend the way in which that Prayer Book omits traditional rites associated with baptism and private masses while restoring the cup to the laity at the Lord's Supper:

VIII. And although in the administration of baptism there is neither exorcism, oil, salt, spittle, or hallowing of the water now used, and for that they were of late years abused and esteemed necessary, where they pertain not to the substance and necessity of the sacrament, that they be reasonably abolished, and yet the sacrament full and perfectly ministered to all intents and purposes, agreeable to the institution of our Saviour Christ.

IX. Moreover, I do not only acknowledge, that private masses were never used amongst the fathers of the primitive church, I mean, public ministration and receiving of the sacrament by the priest alone, without a just number of communicants, according to Christ's saying, "Take ye and eat ye," etc., but also, that the doctrine, that maintaineth the mass to be a propitiatiory sacrifice for the quick and dead, and a mean to deliver souls out of purgatory, is neither agreeable to Christ's ordinance, nor grounded upon doctrine apostolic, but contrarywise most ungodly and most injurious to the precious redemption of our Saviour Christ, and his only sufficient sacrifice offered once for ever upon the altar of the cross.

X. I am of that mind also, that the holy communion or sacrament of the body and blood of Christ, for the due obedience to Christ's institution, and to express the virtue of the same, ought to be ministered unto the people under both kinds; and that it is avouched by certain fathers of the church to be a plain sacrilege, to rob them of the mystical cup, for whom Christ hath shed his most precious blood, seeing he himself hath said, "Drink ye all of this:" considering also, that in the time of the ancient doctors of the Church, as Cyprian, Hierom, Augustine, Gelasius, and others, six hundred years after Christ and more, both the parts of the sacrament were ministered to the people.

• Finally, Article XI rejects a number of superstitious devotional practices in favour of obedience to God's law and the performance of the works of faith:

Last of all, as I do utterly disallow the extolling of images, relics, and feigned miracles, and also all kind of expressing God invisible in the form of an old man, or the Holy Ghost in the form of a dove, and all other vain worshipping of God, devised by man's fantasies, besides or contrary to the Scriptures, as wandering on pilgrimages, setting up of candles, praying upon beads, and such like superstition; which kind of works have no promise of reward in Scripture, but contrarywise threatenings and maledictions; so I do exhort all men to the obedience of God's law, and to the works of faith, as charity, mercy, pity, alms, devout and frequent prayer with the affection of the heart, and not with the mouth only, godly abstinence and fasting, charity, obedience to the rulers, and superior powers, with such like works and godliness of life commanded by God in his word, which, as St. Paul saith, "hath promises both of this life and of the life to come," and are works only acceptable in God's sight.

The Articles conclude with a further exhortation from the minister in which he states that he accepts the preceding articles in good conscience and calls on his listeners to accept them too:

> These things above rehearsed, though they be appointed by common order, yet I do without all compulsion, with freedom of mind, and conscience, from the bottom of my heart, and upon most sure persuasion, acknowledge to be true and agreeable to God's word; and therefore I exhort you all, of whom I have cure, heartily and obediently to embrace and receive the same, that we all joining together in unity of spirit, faith, and charity, may also at length be joined together in the kingdom of God, and that through the merits and death of our Saviour Jesus Christ, to whom with the Father, and the Holy Ghost, be all glory and empire now and for ever. Amen.

What soon becomes clear from a study of the Eleven Articles is they are designed to do two things.

On the one hand they are designed to explain and to defend the new religious policy of Elizabeth I by explaining:

- Why the reformed Church of England is a true and orthodox church (Articles I-III)

- Why it is entitled to change traditional Church practices and ceremonies (Article III)

- The structure of authority under which the Church of England operates (Articles IV-V)

- Why the restored English Prayer Book should be accepted (Article VII)

- The nature of true Christian piety (Article XI)

On the other hand they are designed to counter those who remained loyal to the Pope and to those traditional rites and ceremonies that had been reintroduced under Mary by arguing that the Pope's authority was usurped (Article VI) and that the traditional rites and ceremonies were superfluous, superstitious or ungodly (Articles VIII-XI).

In so far as this is what the Articles are intended to do they are a successful piece of work. They are tightly focused on a particular set of issues, clearly argued and easy to follow.

However, their tight focus means that there are significant omissions in these Articles as compared with the *Forty Two Articles* of the previous reign. For example, they say nothing about the doctrine of the person of Christ, about justification or about how the sacraments function as means of grace.

Furthermore, the sole authority that the *Eleven Articles* possessed was the concurrence of the bishops who had agreed to it and the fact that it was produced by the royal press. Like the *Bishops' Book* of 1537 they lacked full legal authority because they were agreed neither by Convocation not by Parliament.

For these reasons, although church officials 'inquired of the semi-annual parochial readings of the Eleven Articles as later as 1582'[50] and although they were introduced into the Church of Ireland in 1566, Archbishop Parker and his fellow bishops decided that they were only a temporary solution to the Church of England's need for a doctrinal standard. What they opted for as a permanent solution was the production of a revised version of the Forty Two Articles agreed by Convocation and authorised by Parliament.[51]

b. The Thirty Eight Articles of 1563

The first meeting of the Convocation of Canterbury in the new reign took place in January 1563 and it appears that for some time before

---

[50] W P Haugaard, *Elizabeth and the English Reformation*, Cambridge: CUP, 1968, p.241.

[51] At some point at the end of 1560 or the beginning of 1561 the bishops also produced another set of doctrinal articles. There are twenty three of these articles and they overlap with both the *Forty Two* and the *Eleven Articles*. These articles exist in Latin in a collection of episcopal documents known as *The Interpretations of the Bishops*, but they never seem to have been made public. They can be found in W H Frere (ed) *Visitation Articles and Injunctions of the Period of the Reformation, Vol III 1559-1575*, London: Longmans Green and Co., 1910 pp.64-66.

this Parker, assisted by a number of his fellow bishops, especially Richard Cox, Bishop of Ely, and Edmund Guest, Bishop of Rochester, had been working on a revision of the Latin text of the *Forty Two Articles*.

The revision that was presented to the Convocation still consisted of Forty Two articles, but there had been major changes to the 1553 text with four articles added four articles taken away and amendments in the form of either additions or omissions to seventeen others. When Convocation met further discussions among the bishops and clergy led to the omission of a further three articles and a number of minor amendments to those that remained. Having previously been agreed by the bishops, these Thirty Nine Articles were finally agreed by the House of Clergy of the Southern Convocation in February 1563 and were then laid before the Queen in Council and published in Latin by the royal printer and under the direct authority of the Queen herself.[52]

The published version had two changes from the text that had been agreed by the bishops in January and that was preserved in manuscript form among the papers of Archbishop Parker:

- A new clause was added to the beginning of Articles XX stating: 'Habet Ecclesia ritus statuendi ius et in fidei controversiis auctoritatem' ('The Church hath authority to decree Rites or Ceremonies, and authority in Controversies of Faith').

- Article XXIX *'De manducatione corporis Christi, et impios illud non manducare'* ('Of the Wicked which eat not the Body of Christ in the use of the Lord's Supper') was omitted entirely, thus reducing the number of Articles to Thirty Eight.

These changes may have been introduced by the lower house of Convocation, but as Hardwick argues, it seems 'far more probable' that they were introduced: '...by the royal council in compliance with the wishes of the monarch or the scruples of her chief advisers'.[53] In the words of Gibson:

---

[52] As Hardwick notes: 'Though the northern Convocation, as a body, had no direct influence in the compiling of the Articles, its concurrence was to some extent implied in the signature of the archbishop of York and his two suffragans. In 1605 all doubts and scruples on this question were set at rest by the formal acceptance of the Articles in the Covocation of York.' Ibid p.140, footnote 1.

[53] Ibid p.141

The object of the affirmative clause to Article XX was to assert in strong terms the rights and powers of the Church with an eye to the position taken up by the Puritan party, who were denying to her [the Queen] the power to decree any rites and ceremonies, save such as could claim direct support from Holy Scripture. [54]

Gibson further argues that the omission of Article XXIX was due to a desire to conciliate those who remained loyal to traditional Catholic theology, and who held that the change in the bread and wine that took place as a result of the prayer of consecration at the Mass meant that everyone (including the 'wicked') ate the body of Christ, with the hope that this would enable them to accept the new regime in the Church of England.[55] W H Griffith Thomas, on the other hand, argues that the omission was due to a wish to conciliate Lutherans who held that the Presence of the body and blood of Christ 'in, with and under' the consecrated bread and wine meant that the wicked partook of Christ's body. He points out that there is no other sign in the Articles of a desire to conciliate those of traditional Catholic beliefs and that, on the contrary, the Articles are more critical of Roman Catholic theology than was the case with the *Forty Two Articles* of 1553.[56]

The differences that finally emerged between the *Forty Two Articles* of 1553 and the *Thirty Eight Articles* of 1563 were as follows:[57]

Changes introduced by Archbishop Parker in consultation with other bishops

(i) He deleted four existing articles
    Art. X. Of grace.
    Art. XVI. Blasphemy against the Holy Ghost.
    Art. XIX All men are bound to keep the commandments of the moral Law. (Though this was omitted as a separate article, part of it was embodied in Article VII of the revised series. See below)
    Art. XLI. Heretics called Millenarii.

---

[54] Gibson op.cit. p.49
[55] Ibid p. 49
[56] W H Griffith Thomas *The Principles of Theology* 4ed London: Church Book room Press 1951 p. xlv.
[57] This is an adapted form of the list of changes given in Gibson, op.cit. pp.32-37.

(ii) He added four new articles

Art. V. Of the Holy Ghost.

Art. XII. Of good works.

Art. XXIX. Of the wicked, which do not eat the body of Christ in the use of the Lord's Supper.

Art. XXX Of both kinds.

(iii) He re-wrote five articles

Art. XI. Of the justification of man.

Art. XXIV. Of speaking in the congregation in such a tongue as the people understandeth.

Art. XXXII. Of the marriage of priests.

Art. XXXV. Of homilies.

Art. XXXVI. Of consecration of bishops and ministers.

(iv) He deleted clauses from six articles

Art. VI 'Although it be sometimes received of the faithful as godly and profitable for an order and comeliness.'

Art. IX 'Which also the Anabaptists do nowadays renew.'

Art XVII 'Though the decrees of predestination are unknown to us.'

Art XXV 'Our Lord Jesus Christ hath knit together a company of new people with sacraments, most few in number, most easy to be kept, most excellent in signification, as is Baptism and the Lord's supper.'

'And yet that not of the work wrought [ex opere operato], as some men speak, which word, as it is strange and unknown to Holy Scripture, so it engendereth no godly but a very superstitious sense.'

Art. XXVIII. 'Forasmuch as the truth of man's nature requireth that the body of one and the self-same man cannot be at one time in diverse places, but must needs be in some one certain place: therefore the body of Christ cannot be present at one time in many and diverse places. And because (as Holy Scripture doth teach) Christ was taken up into heaven, and there shall continue unto the end of the world, a faithful man ought not either to believe or openly to confess the real and bodily presence (as they term it) of Christ's flesh and blood in the Sacrament of the Lord's Supper.'

Art. XXXVII 'The Civil Magistrate is ordained and allowed of God: wherefore we must obey him, not only for fear of punishment, but also for conscience' sake.'

(v) He added clauses to ten articles

Art. II. 'Begotten from everlasting of the Father, the very and eternal God, of one substance with the Father.'

Art. VI. The clauses on the Canon of Scripture with the list of the canonical books of the Old Testament, and specimens of the Apocrypha.

Art. VII. The clause on the Ceremonial and the Moral Law. ('Although the law given from God by Moses ... the commandments which are called moral.' This clause was drawn from the Nineteenth Article of 1553)

Art. VIII. 'And believed.'

Art. X. 'The condition of man after the fall of Adam is such, that he cannot turn and prepare himself by his own natural strength and good works to faith and calling upon God.'

Art. XVII. 'In Christ.'

Art. XXV. The two clauses on the number of the sacraments, and the five rites, commonly called Sacraments.

Art. XXVII. 'Overthroweth, the nature of a sacrament.'

'The body of Christ is given, taken, and eaten in the Supper only after an heavenly and spiritual manner: and the mean whereby the body of Christ is received and eaten in the supper is faith.'

Art. XXXIII. 'Every particular or National Church hath authority to ordain, change, and abolish ceremonies or rites of the Church, ordained only by man's authority, so that all things be done to edifying,'

Art. XXXVII. The explanation of the royal supremacy. ('Where we attribute to the Queen's majesty restrain with the civil sword the stubborn and evildoers.')

(vi) He introduced various changes to four other articles

54

Art. XXII. 'The Romish doctrine' (doctrina Romanensium) was substituted for ' the doctrine of school authors.'

Art. XXV. The order of the clauses was reversed.

Art. XXVII. The clause on Infant Baptism was rewritten.

Art. XXXVII. The-first paragraph was rewritten. ('The Queen's Majesty hath the chief power in this realm of England, and other her Dominions, and unto whom the chief government of all estates of this realm, whether they be ecclesiastical or civil, in all causes, doth appertain, and is not, nor ought to be, subject to any foreign jurisdiction," was substituted for "The King of England is supreme head in earth, next under Christ, of the Church of England and Ireland.').[58]

Changes introduced by Convocation

(i) Three additional articles were deleted

Art. XXXIX The resurrection of the dead is not yet brought to pass.

Art. XL The souls of them that depart this life do not die with the bodies nor sleep idly.

Art. XLII. All men shall not be saved at length.

(ii) A clause on Christ's descent to hell was deleted from Article III

'For the body lay in the sepulchre until the resurrection,
but his ghost departing from him was with the ghosts that were in prison, or in hell, and did preach to the same, as the place of St. Peter doth testify.'

Changes introduced by Queen Elizabeth I

(i) A new clause was added to Article XX

'The Church hath power to decree rites or ceremonies and authority in controversies of faith.'

(ii) Article XXIX 'Of the wicked, which do not eat the body of Christ in the use of the Lord's Supper.' was deleted

---

[58] Gibson op.cit pp. 32-37

As Gibson explains, a number of the changes made by Archbishop Parker reflect the influence of the *Confession of Wurtemburg,* a Lutheran confession of faith which was presented to the Council of Trent in 1552 by the ambassadors of the Lutheran state of Wurtemburg:

> From this is taken verbatim the clause in Article II concerning the Divine Nature of the Son; the Fifth Article ('Of the Holy Ghost'), and the additional statement concerning the canonical books of the Old and New Testament in Article VI; while the additional clause in Article X, the re-written Article XI, and the new Article XII ('On good works') as well as the affirmative clause in Article XX, are obviously suggested by it.[59]

It is important to note the influence of the *Confession of Wurtemburg* on the Articles because this reminds us that, although many of the leaders of the Elizabethan Church were those who had been exiled to the Continent during the reign of Queen Mary and had been influenced by Reformed theology, there were others who saw the future of the Church of England in terms of closer links with the churches of the Lutheran tradition. Indeed during the early years of Queen Elizabeth's reign there were negotiations for England to become part of the Lutheran Schmalkaldic league, although in the end these negotiations came to nothing. As was noted above, the omission of Article XXIX from the Articles of 1563 is probably to be attributed to a desire to meet Lutheran sensibilities in this context.

The overall character of the changes detailed introduced in 1563 is as follows:

- They fill some gaps in the previous Articles by providing an article on the person of the Holy Ghost (Art. V), an article on good works (Art. XII) and two additional articles on the Eucharist (Arts. XXIX-XXX).

- They omit material that had ceased to be relevant to the theological debates of the 1560s, such as the four articles at the end of the 1553 version (Arts. XXXIX-XLII) attacking the errors of the radical reformers with regard to eschatology, and material that was regarded as unnecessarily controversial, such as the two articles on grace and

---

[59] Ibid p. 38

blasphemy against the Holy Spirit (Arts X and XVI in the 1553 list) and the rejection of the real presence of Christ at the Eucharist in Article XXIX of the old list.

• They introduce clarificatory and explanatory material such as the material on Article II on the eternal generation of the Son, the lists of Old Testament and certain Apocryphal books in Article VI, and the definition of Royal headship in Article XXXVII.

• They tidy up the order of existing material by, for example, moving the discussion of the Old Testament commandments from the old Article XIX to form part of overall discussion of the Old Testament in the revised Article VII.

• They make more explicit the differences between the Church of England and the Church of Rome by for example rejecting the doctrinal authority of the Apocrypha in Article VI, attacking 'Romish doctrine' in Article XXII, and adding a denial of the jurisdiction of the Bishop of Rome to Article XXXVII.

However, in spite of all these changes, the basic character of these Articles was the same as the character of Cranmer's *Forty Two Articles* of 1553. The overall theological stance represented by the Articles remained unaltered.

(c) The final revision of the Articles in 1571.

Although the Articles of 1563 were thus approved by the Southern Convocation and printed by royal authority there was no requirement for the Clergy to subscribe to them and they had no parliamentary authority.

This situation was felt to be unsatisfactory and in December 1566, as part of a wider attempt by members of the Puritan party to take further the reform of the Church in a Protestant direction,[60] a bill was passed by the House of Commons requiring clerical subscription to the *Thirty Eight Articles*. The bill had the support of the bishops, but it was nonetheless stalled by royal command when it got to the House of Lords

---

[60] For details of this wider attempt at reform see P Collinson *The Elizabethan Puritan Movement* Oxford: OUP 1998 p. 116.

and it was lost completely when Parliament was dissolved by the Queen at the beginning of January.[61] The reason why the Queen refused to give her approval seems to have been twofold.

Firstly, as Griffith Thomas explains, Queen Elizabeth's policy at the time:

> ...was one of religious toleration, and this 'non-committal' attitude served her purpose, for as long as the clergy were not required to subscribe to the Articles, the Queen could appear free to deal with Rome, or to negotiate with the Lutherans, while subscription would mean a definite committal to one side.[62]

Secondly, it appears that the Queen objected in principle to religious matters being dealt with by Parliament. She felt that they should be dealt with by the Church under her supervision. Thus when the attempt to achieve subscription was revived in 1571 it was reported that:

> ...the Queen's Majesty having been made privy to the said articles, liketh very well of them and mindeth to publish them [i.e. in a fresh edition], and have them executed by the bishops, by direction of her majesty's regal authority of supremacy of the Church of England, and not to have the same dealt in by Parliament.[63]

By 1571 it was clear that the Queen's non-committal approach no longer made sense diplomatically. Negotiations with the Lutherans had come to an end and in 1570 the Queen had been excommunicated by Pope Pius V in the Bull *Regnans in Excelsis*. In this new situation the attempt to achieve subscription was revived and the Queen finally and reluctantly gave her assent to a Bill to this effect on 29 May 1571. Her reluctance to give her assent is shown by the fact she continued to oppose the Bill until its fourth reading in the House of Commons.

The Act thus enacted in May 1571 required subscription from all Church of England clergy to:

---

[61] Hardwick pp.145-146
[62] Griffith Thomas op,cit, p.xlvii
[63] D'Ewes *Journal of Parliament* 1682 p. 185 quoted in Hardwick op.cit. p.146-7

...all the articles of religion, which only concern the confession of the true Christian faith and the doctrine of the sacraments, comprised in a book imprinted, intituled : Articles, whereupon it was agreed by the archbishops and bishops of both provinces, and the whole clergy in the Convocation holden at London in the year of our Lord God one thousand five hundred sixty and two, according to the computation of the Church of England, for the avoiding of the diversities of opinions, and for the establishing of consent touching true religion put forth by the queen's authority.[64]

The Articles referred to here are the *Thirty Eight Articles* of 1563. They are dated to 1562 because until 1752 the New Year began on 25 March and so what we know as February 1563 was for the Elizabethans February 1562. The other striking thing about the Act is the way that it limits subscription to only those articles which are concerned with Christian doctrine or with the sacraments.

It has been suggested that what the Act means is that the Articles as a whole are concerned with Christian doctrine and with the sacraments, but this interpretation is difficult to argue grammatically and involves a very odd description of the contents of the Articles, which, as we have seen, are concerned with other issues as well. Furthermore we know that the leading supporters of the Act, such as the MPs William Strickland and Peter Wentworth, were Puritans who wanted to impose subscription to the Articles on the clergy (and ideally on the laity as well), but who also wanted to restrict subscription to those Articles which they considered to be sound, which were the ones concerned with doctrine and the sacraments.[65] In the words of Patrick Collinson:

> The puritans desired – in the interests of their own sensitive consciences – to restrict subscription to the more strictly doctrinal of the Articles and with that limitation to use them as a more searching test of lay as well as clerical orthodoxy.[66]

---

[64] 13 Elizabeth Cap.12 text in H Gee and W Hardy (eds) *Documents illustrative of English Church History* New York: Macmillan 1896 p.478.
[65] Hardwick op.cit. pp.224-225
[66] Collinson op.cit .p117

This Puritan programme was never implemented and the 1571 Act, though remaining on the statute book, became a dead letter. As we shall see below, when subscription to the Articles was imposed it was imposed only on the clergy and on students at Oxford and Cambridge rather than on the population as a whole, subscription was to all the Articles without exception and the Articles to which subscription was given were not the *Thirty Eight Articles* of 1563 but a revised version, the *Thirty Nine Articles* we have today.

As was then the custom, the Southern Convocation met at the same time as Parliament in the spring of 1571. As we have already noted, the records of Convocation were destroyed in the Great Fire of London and so we are unable to trace the course of its deliberations in any detail, but what we do know is that at the end of the Convocation the bishops sent to the Queen for her approval our current *Thirty Nine Articles* and that these were subsequently published in Latin and English with a royal ratification (which is still to be found in the *Book of Common Prayer* today) declaring that they were approved by Convocation:

> This Book of Articles before rehearsed, is again approved, and allowed to be holden and executed within the Realm, by the assent and consent of our Sovereign Lady Elizabeth, by the grace of God, of England, France and Ireland, Queen, Defender of the Faith, &c. Which Articles were deliberately read, and confirmed again by the subscription of the hands of the Archbishop and Bishops of the Upper-House, and by the subscription of the whole Clergy of the Nether-House in their Convocation, in the Year of our Lord 1571.

The revision of the *Thirty Eight Articles* that produced the Thirty Nine we know today seems to have been mainly the work of John Jewel, Bishop of Salisbury, though Archbishop Parker seems also to have played a part. The changes they introduced are as follows:

- The addition of the prefixes 'de' and 'of' to the Latin and English titles of the Articles and the revision of the Latin and English titles of Articles II, VI, VII, XV, XVI, XVIII, XXIII, XXIV, XXVI, XXXIII, XXXVIII, XXXIX

- The completion of the list of Apocryphal books in Article VI.

- The phrase 'Working in us' in Article IX of 1553 changed to 'working with us' in Article X

- The words 'or new birth' added to 'regeneration' in Article XXVII

- The ratification by Convocation of the first clause of Article XX

- The insertion of Article XXIX

As Hardwick notes, these changes left 'the character impressed upon the Articles of 1563 entirely unaffected.'[67] The only major change is the re-insertion of Article XXIX. As explained above this Article seems to have been part of the Articles that were agreed by Convocation in 1563 and was only subsequently deleted by the royal council for diplomatic reasons.

The fact that the 1571 revision made only minor changes to the Articles of 1563 meant that the *Thirty Nine Articles*, remained at heart the work of Archbishop Cranmer. As Oliver O'Donovan explains, both Elizabethan versions of the Articles were:

> ....a careful and thorough revision, undertaken by Matthew Parker with the assistance of other bishops, and then further amended in Convocation, of the forty two Articles which had been prepared by Thomas Cranmer (in both Latin and English) on the eve of the Marian crisis.[68]

and therefore:

> Cranmer is, in effect, the 'author' of our Thirty Nine Articles; for although Parker's revisions were extensive, especially in the second half of the document, Cranmer's conception and order were preserved, and his theological personality continued to give the Articles their distinctive character.[69]

---

[67] Hardwick op.cit. p.155
[68] O M T O'Donovan *On The Thirty Nine Articles* Exeter; Paternoster Press 1986 p. 10
[68] Ibid p.10
[69] Ibid pp.10-11

Because the *Thirty Nine Articles* were issued in both a Latin and an English version and because, in the words of O'Donovan, the English version is: 'not quite a straight translation of the Latin,'[70] the question that has occasionally been raised is which version should be given priority when deciding questions of interpretation. Are both forms equally authoritative or, where there is a variation between them,[71] is one more authoritative than the other? What is generally regarded as the correct answer to this question is that given by the eighteenth century theologian Daniel Waterland that both forms are equally authoritative:

> As to the Articles, English and Latin, I may just observe for the sake of such readers as are less acquainted with these things; *first*, that the Articles were passed, recorded, and ratified in the year 1562, and *in Latin only*. *Secondly*, that those Latin Articles were revised and corrected by the Convocation of 1571. *Thirdly*, that an authentic English translation was then made of the Latin Articles by the same Convocation, and the Latin and English adjusted as nearly as possible. *Fourthly*, that the Articles thus perfected *in both languages* were published the same year, and by the royal authority. *Fifthly*, subscription was required the same year to the English Articles, called the Articles of 1562, by the famous act of the 13 [year] of Elizabeth.
>
> These things considered, I might justly say with Bishop Burnet, that the Latin and English are both *equally authentical*. Thus much, however, I may certainly infer, that if in any places the English version be ambiguous, where the Latin original is clear and determinate; the Latin ought to fix the more doubtful sense of the other, (as also *vice versa*), it being evident that the

---

[70] Ibid p.10

[71] As Hardwick notes: A few such variations have been pointed out: e.g. in the ninth Article, the English, 'for them that believe and are *baptized* = the Latin 'renatis et credentibus;' and just before, the English, 'there be no condemnation' = the Latin 'nulla propter Christum est condemnatio.' Similarly, in the twelfth Article, the English, 'follow after justification' = Latin 'justificatos sequuntur' The English heading of Art. XVIII is, 'of obtaining eternal salvation only by the name of Christ' ; the Latin is 'Tantum in nominee Christi speranda est aeterna salus'. In Art XXV the Latin words. 'quomodo nec poenitentia,' have no English equivalent' (Hardwick op.cit. p.155 footnote 1)

Convocation, Queen, and Parliament intended the same sense in both.[72]

As well as revising the Articles, the Southern Convocation also discussed the issue of subscription to them. At the same time as Parliament was debating the bill requiring limited subscription to the Articles, the meeting of the Southern Convocation drew up regulations of its own on the same subject requiring a more comprehensive form of subscription. To quote Hardwick:

> ...while the House of Commons were thus exacting a subscription to the Articles (1) of all the clergy who had not been ordained according to the Edwardine form, and (2) of all future incumbents upon admission to their cures, the Convocation of the same year was actively engaged in devising a second and auxiliary provision. They enjoined that all persons approved as public preachers should have their licenses renewed only on the condition that they subscribe the Articles of Religion as agreed on at the Synod, and pledge themselves to preach in accordance with that standard. In like manner, every minister of a church before entering on his sacred functions is enjoined to give a satisfactory proof of the orthodoxy of his creed by subscribing (not some, but) *all* the Articles of Religion; where the prelates had obviously an eye to the notion that all the requirements of the Church were included in the recognition of what were deemed the *doctrinal* Articles; and consequently if subscription to the rest could not have been legally enforced, it is indisputable that the whole work was now binding on the clergy, at least *in foro conscientiæ*.[73]

As has already been indicated, and as we shall see in more detail below, it was the approach taken by Convocation rather than that taken by Parliament that was to prevail. What would be required of the clergy of the Church of England would be subscription to the *Thirty Nine Articles* in their entirety.

---

[72] D Waterland *Works* Vol II Oxford 1843. pp. 316-317
[73] Hardwick op.cit pp.226-227

IV. The Subsequent History of the Articles
(a) Attempts to supplement or revise the Articles

The Lambeth Articles of 1595

The question of whether the Church of England as a whole was 'Calvinist' in its theology at the end of the sixteenth century is one that is disputed. Nicholas Tyacke argues in his book *Anti-Calvinists* that: '...it is not an exaggeration to say that by the end of the sixteenth century the Church of England was largely Calvinist in doctrine'.[74] Others, however, have argued that Tyacke has overstated his case and has failed to distinguish adequately between those who held to an Augustinian belief in divine election and those who held to a specifically Calvinist belief in double predestination.[75]

Nevertheless, what is undeniable is that by the end of the sixteenth century there were many in the Church of England who did hold to specifically Calvinist beliefs and who wished it to be made clear that this was also the position of the Church of England as a corporate body. It was in this context that the Lambeth Articles were produced in 1595.

The immediate cause of their production was a sermon preached by William Barrett of Caius College Cambridge in which he attacked three key tenets of Calvinist theology: the idea that the elect were incapable of falling away from God (the 'indefectibility of grace'), that the elect could know that they were going to be saved ('assurance') and that God had predestined part of humankind to eternal damnation ('reprobation'). In addition he also criticised John Calvin, Peter Martyr, Theodore Beza, Girolamo Zanchius and other Reformed theologians.

Not surprisingly, his sermon caused outrage among those of the Calvinist persuasion and brought to a head the controversy in the University of Cambridge between those who were Calvinist and those who were not. The Regius Professor of Divinity at Cambridge, William Whitaker, a leading Calvinist, and a number of the Heads of the Cambridge colleges who were also Calvinists responded to the sermon by seeking not only a public recantation from Barrett but also the

---

[74] N Tyacke *Anti-Calvinists* Oxford: OUP 1987 p.3
[75] See for example P White *Predestination, policy and polemic* Cambridge: CUP 1992

authorisation of more explicitly Calvinist material to supplement Article XVII of the *Thirty Nine Articles*.

In order to achieve this latter objective a conference was called at Lambeth Palace in November 1595 to draft a response to Barrett and his supporters. When Whitaker and a colleague had produced a draft this was forwarded to the Archbishop of Canterbury, John Whitgift, for his comments and a series of Articles, known as the *Lambeth Articles* agreed by Whitaker, the Heads and Archbishop Whitgift were published on November 20, 1595.[76]

The Articles were originally published in Latin. Gerald Bray translates them as follows:

1. From eternity God has predestined some men to life and condemned others to death.

2. The moving or efficient cause of predestination to life is not the foresight of faith or of perseverance, or of good works, or of anything inherent in the persons predestined, but only the will of God's good pleasure.

3. There is a predetermined and fixed number of predestinate which cannot be increased or diminished.

4. Those not predestined to salvation will necessarily be condemned because of their sins.

5. A true, living and justifying faith, which the Holy Spirit sanctifies, cannot be extinguished, nor can it fall away or disappear in the elect, either finally or totally.

6. The true believer, i.e. one who possesses justifying faith, is certain, by the full assurance of faith, of the forgiveness of sins and of eternal salvation through Christ.

---

[76] For details of the history leading to the production of the Lambeth Articles see Hardwick op.cit Ch VII and V C Miller *The Lambeth Articles* Oxford: Latimer House 1994 Ch. 3.

7. Saving grace is not granted, communicated, or given to all men, so that they might be saved by it if they wished to be.

8. No-one can come to Christ unless it is given to him (to come), and unless the Father draws him. And not all men are drawn by the Father to come to the Son.

9. It is not placed in the will and power of any and every man to be saved.[77]

These nine articles are an emphatic re-statement of the Calvinist position and they specifically re-assert the three points disputed by Barrett. Articles 1-4 and 7-9 teach a fixed and unalterable division decreed by God between the saved and the lost, Article 5 teaches the indefectibility of grace and Article 6 teaches the doctrine of assurance.

These articles had the support of Archbishop Whitgift, but their circulation was vetoed by Queen Elizabeth in early December 1595. In the words of Victoria Miller:

> Elizabeth, having heard indirectly of the Articles, personally intervened to suspend them. She thought predestination 'a matter tender and dangerous to weak and ignorant minds.' She was also annoyed at Whitgift's participation in a synod of sorts without her authorization, and she characteristically wanted to avoid controversy over doctrinal matters, even at the universities.[78]

The Hampton Court Conference 1604

Following death of Queen Elizabeth I in 1603 and the accession of James I, the Puritan party pressed the King for further reform of the Church of England. They were given the opportunity to state their case at the Hampton Court Conference in 1604 and at this conference the Thirty Nine Articles were among the things they wanted reformed. Specifically, according to the account given by the historian Edward Cardwell in his *History of Conferences*[79] what they asked for was:

[77] Bray op.cit pp.399-400
[78] Miller op.cit p. 55 quoting from John Strype *The Life and Acts of John Whitgift DD* vol II Oxford: Clarendon Press 1822 p.286
[79] E Cardwell *History of Conferences* pp.179-181

- The addition of the *Lambeth Articles*

- The amendment of Article XVI to make clear the indefectibility of grace by stating that departure from grace was neither final nor total.

- The clarification of Article XXXIII to make it clear that lay people were not allowed to preach or celebrate the sacraments outside the context of congregational worship (the words 'ministering in the congregation' being thought to allow this loophole).

- The clarification of Article XXV to make it clear that Confirmation was not a result of the 'corrupt following of the Apostles', but was, as the Confirmation Service in the Prayer Book said, a proper following of the Apostles' example.

- The amendment of Article XXXVII by adding the clause 'nor ought to have' to the statement that 'the Bishop of Rome hath no jurisdiction in this land of England'.

- The introduction of a phrase into the Articles denying that the intention of the minister was of the essence of a sacrament.

These suggestions were dismissed by the Archbishop of Canterbury, Richard Bancroft, on the grounds that the doctrine of predestination was a topic that was best discussed at the Universities and that it was not necessary to: 'stuff the Book with all conclusions theological', that the suggested change to Article XVI would encourage people to neglect holiness of life and that the other changes were unnecessary once the Articles in question were rightly understood.

Bancroft's position prevailed and in the words of Hardwick 'the Formulary left exactly as it issued from the hands of Convocation in 1571.'[80]

The Royal Declaration of 1628

Disputes about predestination continued throughout the reigns of James I and his son Charles I as Calvinist theology came increasingly under attack from what came to be known as the 'Arminian' party (so

---

[80] Hardwick op.cit. p. 211

named after the anti-Calvinist Dutch theologian Jacobus Arminius). In response to these attacks those of the Calvinist party insisted that the *Thirty Nine Articles* should be glossed in a Calvinist direction and it was even suggested that no one who was unwilling to subscribe to the specifically anti-Arminian theology produced by the Dutch Synod of Dort in 1619 should be allowed to minister in the Church of England.

In an attempt to pacify this situation Charles I on the advice of Archbishop William Laud issued in 1628 the royal declaration which is still prefixed to the Articles in the *Book of Common Prayer*. This declaration declared that:

> ...in these both curious and unhappy differences, which have for so many hundred years, in different times and places, exercised the Church of Christ, We will, that all further curious search be set aside, and that these disputes shut up in God's promises, as they be generally set forth to us in the holy Scriptures, and the general meaning of the Articles of the Church of England according to them. And that no man hereafter shall either print or preach, to draw the Article aside any way, but shall submit to it in the plain and full meaning thereof: and shall not put his own meaning of the Article, but shall take it in the literal and grammatical sense.

On one level this is a helpful statement of interpretative principles, but in its original context it was, and was understood to be, a warning shot across the bows of the Calvinists telling them to stop insisting that the Articles had to be glossed in their particular fashion and not to insist on subscription to any doctrinal standard other than the Scriptures and the Articles. At the same time another royal proclamation was issued withdrawing from publication the leading statement on the Arminian side, Richard Montague's *Apello Caesarem*, in the hope that this action too would help take the heat out of the dispute.

The Westminster Assembly

The 1628 declaration did not succeed in taking the heat out of the controversies exercising the Church and when in 1643, during the Civil War, the Westminster Assembly was established by Parliament to further reform the Church of England, it was asked to consider the first nineteen of the Articles in order to: '...free and vindicate the doctrine of them from all aspersions and false interpretations.' By the time work on this project ceased fifteen of the Articles had been revised. The nature of the revisions is helpfully summarized by Hardwick as follows:

> The design of this revision, in the language of Neal, "was to render the sense of the Articles *more express and determinate in favour of Calvinism*". And a cursory examination of the phraseology adopted in the new series of definitions will leave no doubt as to the kind of influence which presided over that second reformation of the Church. The first, second, fourth, fifth, twelfth, fourteenth, and fifteenth, as we might expect from their character and purport, were left as they stood before or altered only in such a manner as to indicate but little of the ruling spirit. Of the rest, the *third* of the new series interprets the "descent into Hell" as equivalent to "continuing in the state of the dead, and under the power and dominion of death". The *sixth* omits all mention of the testimony of the Church in determining the canon of Scripture; it eliminates the Apocrypha altogether; it adds a list of the New Testament canon: and also substitutes for the canonicity of the sacred books the fact of their *inspiration* as the ground of our deference to their teaching. The *seventh* adds one clause implying that even the civil precepts of Moses should be urged upon Christians, provided they be not such as were peculiarly meant for the commonwealth of the Jews; and a second affirming that by the "moral law" we understand all the Ten Commandments taken in their full extent. The *eighth* on the Creeds was finally accepted with the proviso that they should be retranslated and explained in an Appendix to the contemplated edition of the Articles. The *ninth* on Original Sin bears the special impress of Geneva: (1) the divines insert that original sin consists of the "first sin imputed" as well as of inherent corruption; (2) that man is not only "very far gone from original righteousness" but "wholly deprived" of it; (3) that he is of his own nature inclined *only* to evil; (4) they substitute "regenerate" for "baptized"; and (5) affirm that concupiscence "is truly and properly sin". The *tenth* "Of Free-will" interpolates a clause which describes "the preventing grace" of God as "working so effectually in us as that it *determineth* our will to that which is good". The *eleventh* "Of the justification of man (before God)", in explaining the mode of our acquittal declare that the "whole obedience and satisfaction" of our Saviour "is by God

69

imputed unto us, and Christ with His righteousness apprehended and rested on by faith only": while the *thirteenth* changes the expression "works done before the grace of Christ and the inspiration of His Spirit" into "works done before justification by Christ and regeneration by His Spirit".[81]

The Articles Today

Although the revisions of the articles described by Hardwick were presented to Parliament and to Charles I during his imprisonment at Carisbrooke Castle matters went no further with the Assembly and Parliament choosing to replace the Articles in their entirety with the more detailed and explicitly Calvinist *Westminster Confession* of 1648.

When the monarchy was restored after the Commonwealth in 1660 the *Thirty Nine Articles* in their original 1571 form were restored as well. The Book of Common Prayer was slightly revised in 1662 but the Articles were left as they were.

Although in the centuries since then suggestions have been made from time to time that the Articles should be revised, no official revision has been undertaken and so the Articles today are exactly as they were agreed by Convocation in 1571. It is these un-revised Articles (which Canon A2 states are: 'agreeable to the Word of God and may be assented unto with a good conscience by all members of the Church of England') which are listed in Canon A5 as one of the sources of the Church of England's doctrine and which are subscribed to by Clergy, Readers and Licensed Lay Workers according to the form laid down in Canon C 15.

In 1926 a light revision of the Articles was produced by a committee of five bishops of the Church of England. Although this revision, which is believed to have largely the work of Bishop Henley Henson, was said to have been well received by the bench of bishops the matter did not go any further and the proposed revision was not made public. The question of the possible revision of the Articles was considered again in the 1960s by the Archbishops' Commission on Christian Doctrine (what became the Doctrine Commission) which between 1967 and 1968 looked at: '...the place of the Thirty Nine Articles in the Anglican Tradition and the question of Subscription and Assent to them.'[82] During the course of its deliberations two members of the

[81] Ibid. p.p. 213-215 quoting D Neal *History of the Puritans* vol III p.68
[82] *Subscription and Assent to the Thirty Nine Articles* London: SPCK 1968 p.7

Commission produced a draft light revision of the Articles. For example, in place of the statement in Article XIX:

> The visible Church of Christ is a congregation of faithful men, in the which the pure word of God is preached and the sacraments be duly ministered according to Christ's ordinance in all those things that of necessity are requisite to the same.

they suggested instead:

> The visible Church of Christ, instituted by him and dependent upon him for its continuing life, is a congregation of faithful men united with him and in him with one another to be both his witness to the world and the instrument [or means] whereby his will is to be accomplished in the world. Herein by the abiding presence of the Holy Spirit the pure Word of God is preached, the Sacraments are duly ministered according Christ's ordinance, and the Christian life is nourished under the protection of a godly discipline.[83]

However, in the end:

> The proposal of light revision did not on balance commend itself to the Commission. Such a revision might give relief to some troubled consciences; but it seemed clear that it would fail to satisfy either those who wish to retain the Articles as they stand or those who would prefer to dispense with them completely in favour of a contemporary statement of faith.[84]

The Commission also noted that:

> It might be possible to produce a Statement of Faith of a wholly different kind dealing with the contemporary situation in modern terms and divorced from articular form; but the Commission recognized that such a task could not be undertaken without long

---

[83] Ibid p. 57
[84] Ibid p. 42

and careful discussions, and would in any event be an entirely different construction from a set of Articles.[85]

The Commission felt that to: 'abolish subscription altogether might suggest that the Church no longer regarded doctrinal belief as important'[86] and so, in the light of all these factors, its recommendation was that:

> The most practicable method of avoiding giving distress to those who are happy to assent to the Articles as they stand while at the same time easing the consciences of those who cannot at the present make the required subscription without mental reservation is to modify the formula of assent.[87]

The Church Assembly accepted this recommendation and, as we shall see below, in due course a modified form of assent was introduced, thus creating the situation we have in the Church of England today.

The Commission also recommended that the Articles should still be bound up with *The Book of Common Prayer*. Its argument was that:

> The Prayer Book contains not only the services of the Church but also documents (such as the Catechism) of a different character. To discontinue the practice of appending the Articles to editions of the Prayer Book would make them difficult of access. The Bible is continually read and the Creeds frequently recited; if the Articles, which are another of the standards of doctrine of the Church of England were no longer to be bound up with the Prayer Book as a guarantee of their continued ready availability, they would, as a matter of psychological fact, lose much of their authority.[88]

This recommendation too was accepted, although the further recommendation by the Commission that the royal declaration of 1628 should be replaced by a new introductory paragraph was not.

---

[85] Ibid. p.43
[86] Ibid p.40
[87] Ibid p.43
[88] Ibid p.40

(b) Subscription to the Articles

As we have seen, the Southern Convocation stipulated in 1571 that the Clergy of the Church of England must subscribe to the 1571 Articles in their entirety and from then on the Court of High Commission (the supreme legal body dealing with Church matters) began to enforce subscription to them upon the clergy. However, no precise form of subscription had been lain down, and in 1583 Archbishop Whitgift acted to make good this omission as part of his wider programme to tighten the discipline of the Church following a period of relative laxity under his predecessor Archbishop Grindal. He produced what were known as 'Whitgift's Articles' which stated:

> That none be permitted to preach, read, catechise, minister the sacraments, or execute any ecclesiastical function, by whatsoever authority he be admitted thereunto, unless he first consent and subscribe to these Articles following, before the ordinary of the diocese...[89]

The first two of the following Articles concerned acceptance of the royal supremacy and the *Book of Common Prayer* and the *Ordinal* and the third stated:

> That he alloweth the Book of the Articles of Religion agreed upon by the archbishops and bishops of both provinces and the whole clergy in the Convocation holden at London in the year of our Lord 1562, and set forth by Her Majesty's authority, and that he believeth all the articles therein to be agreeable to the Word of God. [90]

The fact that the Articles of Religion that the clergy had to subscribe to are described as those agreed in 1562 seems odd given that the form of the Articles that was in use in 1583 was the *Thirty Nine Articles* of 1571. We do not know why Whitgift used this form of words but the obvious explanation is that the 1571 Articles were seen as simply a revised form of those of 1562 and, as such, covered by their authorisation.

---

[89] Strype, op.cit. Bk III Ch III
[90] Ibid

Whitgift's Three Articles were subsequently included almost verbatim in Canon XXXVI of the Canons of 1604. This declared that:

> No person shall hereafter be received into the ministry, nor either by institution or collation admitted to any ecclesiastical living, nor suffered to preach, to catechise, or to be a lecturer or reader of divinity, in either university, or in any cathedral or collegiate church, city, or market town, parish church, chapel, or in any other place in this realm, except he be licensed either by the archbishop, or by the bishop of the dioceses where he is to be placed, under their hands and seals, or by one of the two universities under their seal likewise; and except he shall first subscribe to the three articles following in such manner and sort as we have here appointed.[91]

As before, the first two of the following articles concerned acceptance of the royal supremacy, the *Book of Common Prayer* and the *Ordinal* and the third stated:

> That he alloweth the Book of Articles of Religion agreed upon by the archbishops and bishops of both provinces and the whole clergy in the Convocation holden at London in the year of our Lord God 1562; and that he acknowledgeth all and every of the Articles therein contained, being in number nine and thirty, besides the ratification, to be agreeable to the word of God.[92]

Canon XXXVI then went on to add that:

> To these Articles, whosoever will subscribe he shall, for the avoiding of all ambiguities, subscribe in this order and form of words, setting down both his Christian and surname, viz:- I, N.N., do willingly and ex animo subscribe to these three articles above mentioned, and to all things that are contained in them.[93]

---

[91] E Cardwell *Synodalia* vol 1 p.267
[92] Ibid p. 267
[93] Ibid p. 267

As Gibson notes: 'After the revolution of 1688 an attempt was made to get rid of the various forms of subscription and declaration required from the clergy'[94], and the 'Comprehension Bill' of 1689 attempted to bridge the difference between Anglicans and Non-Conformists in the aftermath of the Glorious Revolution of 1688 by relieving all ministers of the necessity of subscribing to the Articles. It substituted instead a Declaration which read: 'I do approve of the doctrine and worship of the Church of England by law established, as containing all things necessary to salvation, and I promise, in the exercise of my ministry, to preach and practise according thereunto.'[95]

The bill never became law and subscription to the Articles was still required of the clergy of the Church of England, the form normally used for this being a combination of the terms required under the 1571 Act of Parliament and the Canons of 1604:

> I, A.B. do willingly and from my heart subscribe to the Thirty-Nine Articles of Religion of the United Church of England and Ireland, and to the three Articles in the Thirty-Sixth Canon, and to all things therein contained. [96]

In addition the *Toleration Act* of 1689 laid down that Protestant Dissenting Ministers could legally minister providing that they declared their:

> ...approbation of and subscribe the Articles of religion mentioned in the statute made in the thirteenth year of the reign of the late Queen Elizabeth (1571), except the thirty-fourth, thirty-fifth and thirty-sixth, and these words of the twentieth Article, viz: 'the Church hath power to decree rites or ceremonies, and authorities in controversies of faith and yet'...[97]

The Act also provided that ministers that: 'scruple the baptizing of infants' did not have to subscribe to that part of Article XXVII relating to infant baptism.[98]

---

[94] Gibson op.cit. p.61
[95] Ibid p. 61
[96] Ibid p. 62
[97] Text in Bray op.cit. p.573
[98] Ibid p.574

The requirement that Dissenting Ministers should subscribe in part to the Articles was abolished in 1779. However, the requirement that Church of England clergy should subscribe to the Articles in their entirety remained in place.

In the eighteenth century a considerable number of the clergy of the Church of England came to question the traditional doctrines of the Trinity and the atonement and in order to respond to their wish to be free to believe as they felt fit a petition[99] to abolish subscription in favour of a simple declaration of belief in the Bible was introduced into the House of Commons on February 6 1772 by the member for Oxford, Sir Roger Newdigate. It was defeated by 217 votes to 71 and the matter lapsed.

The form of assent to the Articles remained unchanged until 1865. A few years previously another attempt to abolish the various forms of clerical subscription had been defeated in the House of Lords, but shortly afterwards a royal commission was appointed to consider the matter. As Gibson explains, the report of the commission: '...showed that the forms in use were unnecessarily numerous and complicated, and the commissioners were unanimous in recommending the substitution of a single declaration of assent in place of the cumbrous forms then in use.'[100] The Clerical Subscription Act was passed by Parliament to give effect to their recommendations and Canon XXXVI was duly amended by Convocation and the result was the following declaration of assent, which was required from all candidates for orders, as well as from all persons admitted to any benefice or licensed to preach:

> I A.B. do solemnly make the following declaration. I assent to the Thirty -Nine Articles of Religion, and to the Book of Common Prayer, and of ordering of Bishops Priests and Deacons; I believe the doctrine of the [United] Church of England [and Ireland] as therein set forth, to be agreeable to the word of God: and in public prayer and administration of the Sacraments, I will use the form in the said book prescribed, and none other, except so far as shall be ordered by lawful authority.[101]

---

[99] Normally known as the 'Feathers Tavern Petition'

[100] Gibson op.cit p.63

[101] Text in Ibid p. 64 The words in square brackets ceased to be used after the disestablishment of the Church of Ireland in 1869.

The Clerical Subscription Act also required that:

> ...every person instituted or collated to any benefice with cure of souls or licensed to a perpetual curacy, shall on the first Lord's Day on which he officiates in the church of such benefice or perpetual curacy, or on such other Lord's day as the Ordinary may appoint or allow, publicly and openly in the presence of the congregation there assembled, read the Thirty-Nine Articles of Religion, and after immediately after reading the same make the said declaration of assent.

It is often stated that the 1865 Act introduced a form of 'general assent' that excused the clergy from having to give total assent to each of the Articles individually. This view is mistaken. In the words of the 1968 report on *Subscription and Assent*:

> It is important to recognize that, contrary to what is sometimes supposed, the alteration in the form of subscription in 1865 did not in any way imply that henceforth a 'general' assent, in the sense of incomplete assent, to the Articles would be legally adequate. In law, assent must be taken to mean 'complete legal acceptance'...The Act of 1865 retained the word 'assent', and it is this, rather than any intentions expressed by individuals in the debates, which has legal force. Thus in law the situation remains essentially what it was.[102]

As was noted above, the present form of subscription to the Articles built on the recommendations of *Subscription and Assent*. This form of subscription, which was introduced in 1975[103], is contained in Canon C15, which contains a Preface followed by a Declaration of Assent.

The Preface first of all declares:

> The Church of England is part of the One, Holy, Catholic and Apostolic Church worshipping the one true God, Father, Son and

---

[102] *Subscription and Assent* p.12
[103] The history behind the wording of the Declaration of Assent is given in C Podmore *Aspects of Anglican Identity* London: CHP 2005 Ch 4.

Holy Spirit. It professes the faith uniquely revealed in the Holy Scriptures and set forth in the catholic creeds, which faith the Church is called upon to proclaim afresh in each generation. Led by the Holy Spirit, it has borne witness to Christian truth in its historic formularies, the Thirty-nine Articles of Religion, the Book of Common Prayer and the Ordering of Bishops, Priests and Deacons.

It then asks the person making the declaration of assent:

In the declaration you are about to make will you affirm your loyalty to this inheritance as your inspiration and guidance under God in bringing the grace and truth of Christ to this generation and making him known to those under your care?

The person making the declaration responds:

I A.B., do so affirm, and accordingly declare my belief in the faith which is revealed in the Holy Scriptures and set forth in the catholic creeds and to which the historic formularies of the church of England bear witness; and in public prayer and administration of the sacraments, I will use only the forms of service that are authorised by Canon.

The 1865 requirement that the Articles be read publicly no longer exists, but the Canon lays down that the above declaration has to be made by all who are ordained ministers in the Church of England prior to their ordination, when they are consecrated bishop and when they take up a new appointment. Canons E5 and E8 also lay down that an adapted form of the declaration has to be made by Readers and Licensed Lay Workers when they are licensed or admitted as lay workers.

The three things that need to be noted about the current form of subscription are that:

- In a tradition going back to Whitgift's Articles in 1583, assent is given not to the Articles in isolation but to all three Anglican formularies, the Articles, the Book of Common Prayer and the Ordinal.

- It stresses the importance of relating the Articles and other formularies to the contemporary situation. *Subscription and Assent* argued that in any new declaration of assent: 'The possibility of fresh understandings of Christian truth must be explicitly left open'[104] and that is why the Declaration of Assent in Canon C15 stresses that the Church as to proclaim the faith: 'afresh in every generation' and why it talks about using the inheritance of faith as: 'inspiration and guidance' to bring the grace and truth of Christ: 'to *this* generation.'

- As compared with the previous forms of subscription the focus of assent is now not on the Articles themselves but on the Christian faith to which the Articles and the other Church of England formularies bear witness. As the report of the Revision Committee that produced the final wording of the declaration puts it: 'Belief is expressed in the faith, not in particular documents, but this faith is expressed by reference to certain documents.'[105]

The fact that there is this new focus on the faith rather than on the Articles could be seen as giving room for dissent from at least some of the Articles in accordance with the principle expressed in *Subscription and Assent* that a new declaration should not: '...tie down the person using it to acceptance of every one of the Articles of 1571.'[106]

However, it also needs to be noted that:

(a) The faith in which belief is declared is defined as that to which the Articles and the other formularies bear witness. That is to say, if we ask the how the Church of England understands the faith that is 'revealed in the Holy Scriptures and set forth in the catholic creeds' the answer is that it understands it in line with the witness of the Articles and the other formularies. It is to the faith thus understood that the person making the Declaration gives his or her assent.

(b) In the Declaration of Assent the person making it is not given the option of saying that they will only take some of the Articles as the

---

[104] Ibid p.72
[105] GS 1116A 1973 p.6 paras 8-9 cited in Podmore op.cit p.53
[106] Ibid p.72

inspiration and guidance for their ministry. They affirm that they are loyal to the Articles as a whole, together with Scripture, the Catholic Creeds and the other Anglican formularies, as providing this inspiration and guidance.

Furthermore in two other Canons the Articles are affirmed in their entirety.

Canon A2 declares that: 'The Thirty Nine Articles are agreeable to the Word of God and may be assented to with a good conscience by all members of the Church of England.' If this is really what the Church of England believes it is difficult to see how it could think it right for an individual to dissent from the Articles.

Canon A5 states that:

> The doctrine of the Church of England is grounded in the Holy Scriptures, and in such teachings of the ancient Fathers and Councils of the Church as are agreeable to the said Scriptures.
>
> In particular such doctrine is to be found in the Thirty-nine Articles of Religion, the Book of Common Prayer and the Ordinal.

Here again there is no qualification. The Canon declares that the doctrine of the Church of England is to be found in the Articles as such and not just in some of them.

Although, as explained above, some of the Puritan leaders in the mid sixteenth century would have liked to make subscription to a modified form of the Articles compulsory for the laity as well as the clergy, the Church of England has not chosen to follow this path. The nearest it has come to it is in the Fifth Canon of the Canons of 1604 which declares that no one is allowed to affirm that the Articles are superstitious or erroneous :

> Whosoever shall hereafter affirm, That any of the Nine and Thirty Articles agreed upon by the archbishops and bishops of both provinces, and the whole clergy, in the Convocation holden at London, in the year of our Lord God one thousand five hundred and sixty-two, for avoiding diversities of opinions, and for the establishment of consent touching true religion, are in any part

superstitious or erroneous, or such as he may not with a good conscience subscribe to, let him be excommunicated *ipso facto*, and not restored, but only by the archbishop, after his repentance, and public revocation of such his wicked errors.

The key point to be noted is that this Canon (which seems to have been aimed at Puritan critics of the Articles) does not actually require assent to Articles. In the words of Gibson:

The Canon...strong as its language is, was apparently intended to prohibit the laity from impugning and attacking the Articles rather than to require a definite and formal assent to them. [107]

Historically, the Universities of Oxford and Cambridge required assent to the Articles from their students. The history of this is as follows:

At Oxford subscription to the Articles was required from all candidates for degrees from 1576 and from all those wishing to matriculate from 1581. From 1587 candidates for degrees had to make a declaration of assent to the Prayer Book as well and from 1617 candidates for all degrees except music had to subscribe to the Thirty Nine Articles, the 'Three Articles' of the Thirty Sixth Canon of 1604 and the Oath of Supremacy.

At Cambridge subscription to the 'Three Articles' was required from all candidates for degrees by an edict of James I in 1616 confirmed by the Heads of the Colleges in 1623.

From 1772 the University Senate allowed candidates at Cambridge for the degrees of BA and BCL, to substitute the declaration: 'I A.B. do declare that I am, *bona fide*, a member of the Church of England as by law established' and from 1779 the same rule was extended to cover candidates for the degrees of MB and MD. At Oxford the old form of subscription remained in place until 1854 when the *Oxford University Act* abolished the requirement for any person to make an oath or declaration with regard to religion in order either to matriculate or take the degrees of BA, BCL, BM or B Mus. However, such a degree would not constitute a qualification for holding any office hitherto reserved for members of the Church of England unless the person involved had made the necessary oaths and declarations. Finally the *Universities Test Act* of 1871 abolished

---

[107] Gibson, op cit pp.66-67

all declarations and oaths respecting religious beliefs at Universities with an exception for degrees in divinity and the restriction of certain posts such as divinity or Hebrew professorships to people in Anglican orders.

It should be remembered, however, that these requirements were made by the Universities themselves or by the Crown and were not imposed by the Church of England.

(c) The Articles in the Anglican Communion
The Church of Ireland

Although the Reformation never achieved the same degree of popular acceptance in Ireland as it did in England, the Church of Ireland was reformed at the same time as the Church of England. However, the *Thirty Nine Articles* were adopted by the Church of Ireland some time later than by the Church of England.

From 1566 until 1615 the official doctrinal standard of the Church of Ireland were Archbishop Parker's *Eleven Articles* of 1561. Then in 1615 the Convocation of the Irish Church, meeting in Dublin, agreed its own set of *Irish Articles*. Their nature is helpfully explained by Hardwick as follows:

> They are a long and discursive compilation, extending to one hundred and four paragraphs, arranged under nineteen general heads, and comprehend a variety of statements, or rather disquisitions, upon the following theological topics: The Holy Scripture and the three Creeds; faith in the Holy Trinity; God's eternal decree and predestination; the creation and government of all things; the fall of man, original sin, and the state of man before justification; Christ, the Mediator of the second Covenant; the communicating of the grace of Christ; justification and faith; sanctification and good works; the service of God; the civil magistrate; our duty towards our neighbours; the Church and outward ministry of the Gospel; the authority of the Church, General Councils, and bishop of Rome; the state of the Old and New Testament; the Sacraments of the New Testament; Baptism; the Lord's Supper; the state of souls of men after they be departed

out of this life, together with the general resurrection and the last judgement.[108]

As Hardwick further explains, the Irish Articles were based on both the *Thirty Nine Articles* and the *Lambeth Articles* of 1595:

> Many of the Articles contained in one or other of these divisions are borrowed from the authorized English series on corresponding points; some, again, are of a homiletic nature, relating wholly to Christian duties; others enter upon speculative questions, such as the fall of angels, and the primeval state of Adam; one absolutely pronounces that the pope is "the man of sin" and antichrist but the paragraphs which excited the strongest objection at the time of their first appearance, as well as in the later ages are those which include the Lambeth Articles, or bear upon the controversy out of which those Articles had issued. It is true that they are not incorporated altogether, being dispersed in various portions of the work, and that in the original copy there was not the slightest reference to the compilation of 1595; yet the resemblance, with one or two verbal exceptions, is so manifest and complete that we cannot possibly mistake the connexion between them.[109]

It is unclear whether any attempt was made to impose subscription to the 1615 Articles and in 1635 the Irish Convocation, under pressure to come into line with the Church of England, passed a Canon which declared:

> For the manifestation of our agreement with the Church of England in the confession of the same Christian faith and the doctrine of the sacraments, we do receive and approve the Book of Articles of Religion agreed upon by the archbishops and bishops and the whole clergy in the Convocation holden at London in the year of our Lord, 1562, &c. And, therefore, if any hereafter shall affirm that any of these Articles are in any part superstitious or erroneous, or such as he may not with a good

---

[108] Hardwick op.cit pp.180-181 the full text of the Irish Articles can be found in Bray op.cit. pp.437-52.
[109] Ibid p. 181

conscience subscribe unto, let him be excommunicated and not absolved before he make a public recantation of his error.[110]

Although the *Irish Articles* were not officially abolished by this Canon they effectively faded from view and the *Thirty Nine Articles* became the doctrinal standard of the Irish Church.

The Episcopal Church of the United States of America

A revised form of the Thirty Nine Articles was adopted by a convention of the Protestant Episcopal Church in the United States on September 12, 1801. The revisions that were made to the Articles reflect eighteenth century doubts about the acceptability of the Athanasian Creed and the changed political situation in the United States following the American War of Independence.

As *Subscription and Assent* explains, in the American version:

> The reference to the Athanasian Creed was omitted from Article 8 ('Of the Three Creeds,' retitled 'Of the Creeds'); in place of Article 21 ('Of the Authority of General Councils') there is a bracketed statement reading: 'The Twenty-first of the former Articles is omitted; because it is partly of a local and civil nature, and is provided for, as to the remaining parts of it, in other Articles'; Article 35 ('Of the Homilies') is followed by a bracketed gloss to the effect that the Homilies are useful in so far as they explain doctrine and instruct in piety and morals, but that references to the constitution and laws of England are inapplicable in America, so that the order for the reading of the Homilies is suspended pending their revision; and Article 37 ('Of the Civil Magistrates') is retitled 'Of the Power of the Civil Magistrates,' and replaced by a new Article reading; 'The power of the Civil magistrate extendeth to all men, as well Clergy as Laity, in all things temporal; but hath no authority in things purely spiritual. And we hold it to be the duty of all men who are professors of the Gospel, to pay respectful obedience to the Civil Authority, regularly and legitimately constituted.'[111]

---

[110] Text in Ibid p. 185
[111] *Subscription and Assent* p. 21

The Scottish Episcopal Church

After the Scottish Reformation the *Confession of Faith* drawn up by John Knox and others was adopted by the Scottish Parliament in 1560.[112] It remained the confessional standard of the Scottish Church until 1647 when it was officially superseded by the *Westminster Confession*. Scottish Episcopalians, however, continued to use the Confession of 1560 well into the eighteenth century.

In 1792 the *Scottish Episcopal Relief Act* which brought to an end a century of persecution of Episcopalians in Scotland required their acceptance of the *Thirty Nine Articles* and these were formally adopted by the Convocation held at Laurencekirk in 1804.

The Church of New Zealand

When the constitution of the Church of New Zealand was originally drawn up in 1857 it declared that:

> This branch of the Church doth hold and maintain the doctrine and sacraments of the Christ....as the United Church of England and Ireland hath explained the same in the Book of Common Prayer and the Thirty-nine Articles of Religion. And the general synod shall have no power to make any alteration in the authorized version of the Holy Scriptures, or in the above named formularies of the Church.[113]

However, in 1874the New Zealand General Synod, anxious to protect the right of self government of the New Zealand Church over against possible encroachment by the Colonial authorities, passed a statute that laid down that explanatory words should be appended to Articles XXI and XXXVII.

The words to be appended to Article XXI were: 'It is not to be inferred from this Article that the Church in the Colony is hindered from meeting in Council without the authority of the Civil Power.' The words to be appended to Article XXXVII were: 'It is not to be inferred from this Article that the Civil power has authority in this Colony, to determine purely Spiritual questions or to hinder the Church in the Colony from

---

[112] G H Henderson and J Bulloch, The Scots Confession of 1560, Edinburgh: St. Andrew Press, 1960.
[113] Text in Neill op.cit. p. 290

finally determining such questions by its own authority, or by Tribunals constituted under its authority.'[114]

These statements were included in the Third Schedule to the *Church of England Empowering Act,* which was passed by the New Zealand Parliament in 1928 and gave the Church in New Zealand the right to change its formularies and use translations of the Bible other than the Authorised Version, but the expanded form of these Articles has never been printed in any Prayer Book

The Lambeth Conferences

The development of new Anglican churches as a result of the great era of missionary activity in the second half of the nineteenth century led to the question being raised as to whether these new churches needed to adopt the *Thirty Nine Articles*. The answer to this question given by Resolution 19 of the Lambeth Conference of 1888 was 'No':

> ...as regards newly constituted Churches, especially in non-Christian lands, it should be a condition of the recognition of them as in complete intercommunion with us, and especially of their receiving from us episcopal succession, that we should receive from them satisfactory evidence that they hold substantially the same doctrine as our own, and that their clergy subscribe articles in accordance with the express statements of our own standards of doctrine and worship; but that they should not necessarily be bound to accept in their entirety the Thirty-nine Articles of Religion.[115]

At the Lambeth Conference in 1930 the report of a commission on the Anglican Communion further defined the identity of the Communion without reference to the Articles. The report stated that the Anglican Communion includes those:

> ...whose faith has been grounded in the doctrines and ideals for which the Church of England has always stood.

---

[114] Text in *Subscription and Assent* p.20
[115] R Coleman (ed) *Resolutions of the Lambeth Conferences 1867-1988* Toronto: Anglican Book Centre 1992 p.16

What are these doctrines? We hold the Catholic faith in its entirety: that is to say, the truth of Christ, contained in Holy Scripture; stated in the Apostles' and Nicene Creeds; expressed in the Sacraments of the Gospel and the rites of the Primitive Church as set forth in the Book of Common Prayer with its various local adaptations; and safeguarded by the historic threefold Order of the Ministry.[116]

The Lambeth Conference of 1968 went even further in demoting the importance of the Articles. Resolution 43 of that year runs as follows:

The Conference accepts the main conclusion of the Report of the Archbishop's Commission on Christian Doctrine entitled Subscription and Assent to the Thirty-nine Articles (1968) and in furtherance of its recommendation:

(a) suggests that each Church of our Communion consider whether the Articles need to be bound up with its Prayer Book.

(b) suggests to the Churches of the Anglican Communion that assent to the Thirty-nine Articles be no longer required of ordinands.

(c) suggests that, when subscription is required to the Articles or other elements in the Anglican tradition, it should be required, and given, only in the context of a statement which gives the full range of our inheritance of faith and sets the Articles in their historical context.[117]

Although (c) was in line with what the Commission had said (a) and (b) were directly contrary to it and the Chairman of the Commission, Bishop Ian Ramsey, voted against the resolution. As has already been indicated the Church of England as a whole also decided not to accept them, but to continue to bind the Articles in with the Book of Common Prayer and to require assent to the Articles from its ordinands.

---

[116] *The Lambeth Conferences 1867-1930* London: SPCK 1948 p.246.
[117] Coleman (ed) op.cit. p.165

The situation today

The most recent survey of the place of the Articles in the Anglican Communion is by Peter Toon. He writes that:

> The Churches of Ireland, Scotland, Wales, Australia, Canada and New Zealand, along with those of Uganda, Ruanda-Burundi-Zaire, Nigeria and West Africa have retained them. The Churches of Kenya and Tanzania make them an option an individual diocese may adopt. At least in their Constitutions the rest of the Churches do not specifically refer to the Articles. However, in some cases it is possible that there is an implicit reference to them when the claim is made that the same faith is shared with the mother Church of England. [118]

In 1999 the General Synod of the Church of Ireland re-affirmed the importance of the Articles along with its other formularies as part of the Church's inheritance of faith:

> The Church of Ireland is part of the one, holy, catholic, and apostolic Church, worshipping the one true God, Father, Son, and Holy Spirit. It professes the faith uniquely revealed in the Holy Scriptures and set forth in the catholic creeds: which faith the Church is called upon to proclaim afresh in each generation. Led by the Holy Spirit, it has borne witness to Christian truth in its historic formularies, the Thirty–nine Articles of religion, the Book of Common Prayer and the Declaration prefixed to the Statutes of the Church of Ireland (1870).
>
> These historic formularies are a definition of the faith as proclaimed by the Church of Ireland, and thus form an important part of the inheritance through which this Church has been formed in its faith and witness to this day. The formularies that have been passed on are part of a living tradition that today must face new challenges and grasp fresh opportunities.[119]

---

[118] P Toon 'The Articles and Homilies' in S Sykes and J Booty (eds) The Study of Anglicanism London: SPCK 1988 p.141

[119] The text of the General Synod declaration can be found at http://ireland.anglican. org/worship/13

However, speaking in an Irish context where differences between the various Christian traditions have been deeply felt and have frequently contributed to communal conflict, the General Synod also sought to make clear that the words of these formularies did not necessarily represent the Church of Ireland's attitude towards other Christians today:

> Historic documents often stem from periods of deep separation between Christian Churches. Whilst, in spite of a real degree of convergence, distinct differences remain, negative statements towards other Christians should not be seen as representing the spirit of this Church today.
>
> The Church of Ireland affirms all in its tradition that witnesses to the truth of the Gospel. It regrets that words written in another age and in a different context should be used in a manner hurtful to or antagonistic towards other Christians.
>
> The Church of Ireland seeks the visible unity of the Church. In working towards that goal this Church is committed to reaching out towards other Churches in a spirit of humility and love, that together all Christians may grow towards unity in life and mission to the glory of God.[120]

The Jerusalem Declaration and the Anglican Covenant

Two recent international statements of Anglican belief have also referred to the continuing importance of the *Thirty Nine Articles*.

Article 4 of *The Jerusalem Declaration*, a statement of Anglican belief produced in 2008 by the Global Anglican Futures Conference (GAFCON), a gathering of conservative Anglicans from around the world, states:

> We uphold the Thirty-nine Articles as containing the true doctrine of the Church agreeing with God's Word and as authoritative for Anglicans today.[121]

In paragraph 1.1.2 of the Anglican Covenant, which was produced on behalf of the Anglican Communion as a whole in 2009, the *Thirty Nine Articles*, together with the *Book of Common Prayer* and the *Ordinal* are

---

[120] Ibid
[121] http://fca.net/resources/the_jerusalem_declaration/

seen as bearing 'authentic witness' to the Catholic and apostolic faith. In this paragraph each church adopting the Covenant declares its commitment to:

> The catholic and apostolic faith uniquely revealed in the Holy Scriptures and set forth in the catholic creeds, which faith the Church is called upon to proclaim afresh in each generation The historic formularies of the Church of England, forged in the context of the European Reformation and acknowledged and appropriated in various ways in the Anglican Communion, bear authentic witness to this faith.[122]

V. The Interpretation of the Articles
Traditions of Interpretation

As we saw when considering the history of the Articles in the seventeenth century, at that time there was a division of opinion as to whether the Articles should be interpreted in a Calvinist or an Arminian direction, and different traditions of interpretation have persisted ever since.

As Toon explains:

> Generally speaking, expositions of the Articles from the seventeenth to the twentieth century have fallen into four types – (1) Evangelical and Reformed (2) Broad Church and Latitudinarian (3) High Church and generally Arminian, and (4) Anglo-Catholic.[123]

Examples of the first category would include the commentaries by Rogers and Griffith Thomas. The second is classically represented by the commentary by Burnet. The third category includes the commentaries by Bishop William Beveridge[124], and by Gibson. The final category includes the commentaries by Bishop A P Forbes[125] and by E J Bicknell.[126]

---

[122] http://www.anglicancommunion.org/commission/covenant/final/text.cfm
[123] Toon art cit p. 137
[124] W Beveridge *Ecclesia Anglicana Ecclesia Catholica* Oxford: OUP 1846
[125] A P Forbes *An Explanation of the Thirty Nine Articles* Oxford: Parker 1878
[126] E J Bicknell *A Theological Introduction to the Thirty Nine Articles of the Church of England* 2ed London: Longmans, Green & co 1947

The distinction between these different types of interpretation are that:

- The first stresses the Protestant and Reformed character of the Articles and the distinction between this and Roman Catholic teaching.

- The second seeks to distance the Articles from both Calvinism and Roman Catholicism and to show how the Articles can make rational sense to reasonable people.

- The third emphasises the continuity between the Articles and the teaching of the early and undivided Church. It seeks to distance the Articles from the Reformation tradition while also being wary about Roman Catholic theology.

- The fourth follows the third except in that it seeks to emphasise what it sees as agreement between the teaching of the Articles and Roman Catholic theology.

It should be noted, however, that these categories are not absolute and that, in Toon's words: 'some expositors have had feet in two traditions of interpretation.'[127] Bicknell, for instance, takes a 'liberal Catholic' approach that at times comes close to the latitudianarian approach of Burnet.[128]

The significance of these different traditions of interpretation is twofold:

Firstly, it needs to be understood that they have both reflected and reinforced wider differences of theological approach within the Church of England and the wider Anglican Communion. When theological colleges were established in the nineteenth century, commentaries on the Articles were used as text books for training ordinands and this resulted in a situation where clergy trained at one college would understand the Articles in a way that was very different from those trained at another college of a different tradition.

This situation helps to explains why the use of the Articles for educating clergy came under a cloud in the latter part of last century. In the words of O'Donovan, writing from an Evangelical perspective in the 1980s:

---

[127] Toon Art cit. p.137
[128] This point is made by Packer in de Stage (ed) op.cit. p. 33

When I began teaching theology at an English college some years ago, I would have reacted to the idea that I should use this document as a text for instruction with frank distaste. We still lived under the shadow of the old party controversies which had raged about the Articles for a hundred years or more because of the requirement of subscription by candidates for ordination. We were trying, if anything, to wean our students away from the old handbooks on the Articles which had provided the staple doctrinal teaching for a previous generation of clergymen. They were conceived as manuals for induction into a party tradition, comfortably reassuring about what it was permissible for an Anglican parson of the right persuasion to believe, uncomfortably challenging to the doubtful convictions of the other party. They inculcated minute scholarship on details, disagreeable prejudices on generalities. The picture that they gave of the Articles was lopsided, preoccupied by the polemical concerns of the late Victorian age.[129]

Secondly, the existence of this polemical (mis)use of the Articles raises the question of how to interpret the Articles in a theologically responsible fashion. What are the rules for rightly understanding them?

Principles of interpretation

In his history of the Articles Hardwick provides a set of rules for the interpretation of the Articles which have been widely accepted. He writes:

It is desirable:

First, to weigh the history of the Reformation movement in the midst of which the Articles had been produced.

Secondly, to read them in this light, approximating as far as possible to the point of view that had been occupied by the leading compilers.

---

[129] O 'Donovan op.cit. p.9

Thirdly, to interpret the language of the formulary in its plain and grammatical sense (*i.e.* the sense which it bore in the Edwardine and Elizabethan periods of the Church), bestowing on it "the just and favourable construction which ought to be allowed to all human writings, especially such as are set forth by authority."

Fourthly, where the language of the Articles is vague, or (as might be expected from their history) we meet with a comparative *silence* in respect of some theological topic, to ascertain the doctrine of the Church of England on that point, by reference to her other symbolical writings— the Prayer Book, the Ordinal, the Homilies, and Canons.

Fifthly, where all these sources have been tried without arriving at *explicit* knowledge as to the intention of any Article, to acquiesce in the deductions which "the catholic doctors and ancient bishops" have expressly gathered on that point from Holy Scripture; in accordance with the recommendation of the Canon of 1571, in which subscription to the Articles of Religion had been enjoined upon the clergy.[130]

The strength of these rules is that they take seriously the need to read the Articles according to their grammatical sense, in the light of their historical context, and with reference both to the other Anglican formularies and to the teaching of the Fathers, which the Church of England regards as a significant doctrinal norm (see Canon A5).

However, these rules also have two important weaknesses.
Firstly, they say nothing about the need to read the Articles with reference to the contemporary context. If the Articles are to be more than simply a theological museum piece and are indeed to be used as a means of 'bringing the grace and truth of Christ to this generation', then we have to ask not only what the Articles meant at the time when they were written, but also what their teaching means for us today.

Secondly, they say nothing about fundamental importance of reading the Articles in constant dialogue with Scripture. According to the Articles themselves the primary norm for Christian theology is the Bible,

---

[130] Hardwick op.cit p.221

and so the most important task of any theologian when approaching the Articles is to ask how they relate to the Biblical witness.

This latter point is well made by Packer, who argues that an Anglican theologian is called to be in constant dialogue with the Creeds and the Articles, allowing them to challenge him or her about his or her fidelity to the biblical witness and also challenging them about whether what they say is truly in accord with that same witness:

> It belongs to the Anglican theological vocation to live in continuous dialogue of this sort with the Creeds and the Articles. It is part of our proper theological discipline to expose ourselves to the questions which they ask us and to allow them constantly to challenge our lopsidedness, to correct our aberrations, to rebuke our 'negligences and ignorances,' to point us insistently back to the Scriptures, and to press upon us their classic clarifications of basic biblical and evangelical issues. Not that the dialogue should be one-sided: as the Articles cross-examine us in the name of Scripture, so we must cross-examine them with questions like: Why do you say this? What do you mean? What biblical warrant have you for it? [131]

As he goes on to say:

> No Anglican has any business to try to evade this instructive and corrective dialogue, and anyone who has in any measure experienced the benefit of it will regard the man who does try to evade it as, not merely an inadequate Anglican, but foolish into the bargain. One test of the quality of a creed is the fruitfulness of this kind of dialogue with it. By this test, the Articles must be rated a very good creed indeed. In this way, then, they may still play a vital part in the theological life of twentieth [or twenty first!] –century Anglicanism, by ensuring that, while we address ourselves to new problems and preoccupations, we do not lose touch with the old gospel from which the answers to modern perplexities must be drawn. There is no greater service that they could do us.[132]

---

[131] Packer in de Satge (ed) op.cit p.52
[132] Ibid pp.52-53

VI. The Shape of the Articles

Over the centuries there has been a debate about the shape of the Articles and commentators have offered a variety of different analyses.[133] The following analysis is offered as a contribution to this debate.

1. The Doctrine of God I-V

I.	Of Faith in the Holy Trinity
II	Of Christ the Son of God
III.	Of his going down into Hell
IV	Of his Resurrection
V	Of the Holy Ghost

2. Scripture and the Creeds VI-VIII

VI	Of the Sufficiency of the Scripture
VII	Of the Old Testament
VIII	Of the Three Creeds

3. Sin and Salvation IX- XVIII

IX	Of Original or Birth-sin
X	Of Free-Will
XI	Of Justification
XII	Of Good Works
XIII	Of Works before Justification
XIV	Of Works of Supererogation
XV	Of Christ alone without Sin
XVI	Of Sin after Baptism
XVII	Predestination and Election
XVIII	Of obtaining Salvation by Christ

4. The Church and its Authority XIX-XXI

XIX	Of the Church
XX	Of the Authority of the Church

---

[133] See, for example, Gibson op.cit. p.69, Griffith Thomas op.cit. pp. lix-lxi and Tyrell Green p. 18

XXI   Of the Authority of General Councils

5. Errors to be avoided in the Church XXII-XXIV

XXII   Of Purgatory
XXIII   Of Ministering in the Congregation
XXIV   Of speaking in the Congregation

6. The Sacraments XXV-XXXI

XXV   Of the Sacraments
XXVI   Of the Unworthiness of Ministers
XXVII   Of Baptism
XXVIII Of the Lord's Supper
XXIX   Of the Wicked which eat not the Body of Christ
XXX   Of both kinds
XXXI   Of Christ's one Oblation

7. The Discipline of the Church XXXII-XXXVI

XXXII   Of the Marriage of Priests
XXXIII Of Excommunicate Persons
XXXIV   Of the Traditions of the Church
XXXV   Of the Homilies
XXXVI   Of Consecrating of Ministers

8. Christians and Civil Society XXXVII-XXXIX

XXXVII Of Civil Magistrates
XXXVIII Of Christian men's Goods
XXXIX   Of a Christian man's Oath.

The commentary that follows will be structured according to this analysis.

VII. Bibliography

1. Commentaries on the Articles

W Beveridge, *Ecclesia Anglicana Ecclesia Catholica,* Oxford: OUP 1846

E J Bicknell, *A Theological Introduction to the Thirty Nine Articles of the Church of England*, 2ed, London: Longmans, Green & co 1947

G Bray, *The Faith We Confess,* London: Latimer Trust, 2009

E H Browne, An *Exposition of the Thirty Nine Articles*, London: John W Parker, 1847.

G Burnet, *An Exposition of the XXIX Articles of the Church of England*, Oxford: Clarendon Press, 1819

A P Forbes, *An Explanation of the Thirty Nine Articles,* Oxford: Parker 1878

E C S Gibson, *The Thirty Nine Articles*, 6ed, London: Methuen 1908

W H Griffith Thomas, *The Principles of Theology*, 4ed, London: Church Book Room Press 1951

R W Jelf, *The Thirty Nine Articles of the Church of England*, London, Oxford and Cambridge: Rivingtons 1873

O M T O'Donovan, *On The Thirty Nine Articles*, Exeter; Paternoster Press 1986

T. Rodgers, *The Catholic Doctrine of the Church of England*, Cambridge: CUP/Parker Society, 1844

E Tyrell Green, *The XXXIX Articles and the Age of the Reformation*, London: Wells, Darton Gardner & Co. 1896

W G Wilson and J H Templeton, *Anglican Teaching*, Dublin: Association for Promoting Christian Knowledge 1962.

2. Primary background material

G Bray, *Documents of the English Reformation*, Cambridge: James Clark 1994

G Bray, *Tudor Church Reform*, Woodbridge, Boydell Press/ Church of England Record Society, 2000

G E Corrie (ed), *Nowell's Catechism*, Cambridge: Parker Society/CUP, 1853

W H Frere (ed) *Visitation Articles and Injunctions of the Period of the Reformation,* Vol III, 1559-1575, London: Longmans Green and Co., 1910

The Homilies, Bishopstone: Brynmill/Preservation Press, 2006

3. Secondary studies

C J Clement, *Religious Radicalism in England 1535-1565,* Carlisle: Paternoster Press/Rutherford House, 1997

P Collinson, *The Elizabethan Puritan Movement,* Oxford: OUP, 1998

M Davie, 'The Augsburg Confession and the Thirty Nine Articles' in D Wendebourg (ed) *Sister Reformations,* Tubingen: Mohr Siebeck, 2010, pp. 191-211

A G Dickens, *The English Reformation,* 2ed, London: B T Batsford, 1993

E Duffy, *The Stripping of the Altars,* New Haven & London: Yale University Press, 1992

C Hardwick, *A History of the Articles of Religion,* London: George Bell & Sons 1895

W P Haugaard, *Elizabeth and the English Reformation,* Cambridge: CUP, 1968

R T Kendall, *Calvin and English Calvinism to 1649,* Carlisle: Paternoster Press 1997

J Leith (ed) *Creeds of the Churches,* rev ed, Oxford: Blackwell, 1973

D MacCulloch, *Thomas Cranmer,* New Haven & London: Yale University Press, 1996

V C Miller, *The Lambeth Articles,* Oxford: Latimer House, 1994

J R H Moorman, *A History of the Church of England,* 3ed, Harrisburg PA: Morehouse Publishing, 1980

S C Neill, *Anglicanism,* 4th ed, London: Mowbray, 1977

J H Newman, *Tracts for the Times, Remarks on Certain Passages in the Thirty-Nine Articles,* (Number 90), http://anglicanhistory.org/tracts/tract90

J I Packer, *The Thirty Nine Articles,* London: Church Pastoral Aid Society 1961

C Podmore, *Aspects of Anglican Identity,* London: CHP 2005, Ch 4.

E Routley, *Creeds and Confessions.* London: Duckworth, 1962

J C de Satge et al. *The Articles of the Church of England.* London: A R Mowbray, 1964. *Subscription and Assent to the Thirty Nine Articles,* London: SPCK, 1968

P Toon 'The Articles and Homilies' in S Sykes and J Booty (eds) *The Study of Anglicanism* London: SPCK 1988 pp.113-143

The Doctrine of God: Articles I –V

As noted in the Introduction, the *Thirty Nine Articles* begin with five articles that are concerned with the doctrine of God. Article I is concerned with God the Holy Trinity, articles II-IV are concerned with the person and work of God the Son and article V is concerned with God the Holy Spirit.

Articles I-IV are the same in order and largely the same in content as the corresponding articles in the *Forty Two Articles*. Article V, however, is a new article added by Parker in 1563. These facts raise two questions. (1) Why did Cranmer and following him Parker begin their Articles with four articles concerned with God the Holy Trinity and God the Son? (2) Why did Parker add a new article on the Holy Spirit?

The question as to why the Articles begin as they do arises when we consider the fact that other doctrinal statements from the sixteenth and seventeenth centuries start differently. Thus the *First and Second Swiss Confessions* of 1536 and 1566 start with issues of theological method by looking at Scripture as the source of our knowledge of God before going on to talk about God Himself, and the same approach is taken by the *Irish Articles* of 1615 and the *Westminster Confession* of 1647. Cranmer and Parker could have taken this alternative approach, but they chose not to. Why?

The honest answer is that we have no hard information as to why they made their decision, but what seems likely is that they were concerned to demonstrate at the outset the orthodox nature of the Church of England's teaching and to make it clear that, unlike some of the radical Protestant groupings, the Church of England was not reviving any of the Trinitarian or Christological heresies that had plagued the early Church.

Whatever the historical reason for their choice, their decision to begin the Articles in this way can be defended as the right choice theologically. This is a point made by O'Donovan in his study of the Articles. He argues that the Articles are right to begin with God rather than to follow the Swiss model and start with questions of theological method:

...it is hard not to feel that the Tudor theologians had a true Christian instinct in putting God before method. 'There is but one living and true God.' Is that not the right way for a Christian to begin stating his faith – however much he may wish, as a theologian, to comment on methodological questions at a later stage? The whole theological undertaking arises from the simple affirmation of the believer: 'I believe in God.' [134]

As O'Donovan goes on to argue, Cranmer and Parker were also right to start with God rather than with Christ:

Perhaps Article 1 might have begun, as did Zwingli's Articles of 1523, 'The sum of the gospel is, that Christ, the Son of the living God, made known to us the will of his heavenly Father, and that his innocence redeemed us from eternal death and reconciled us to God.' In the order of knowledge that sequence is correct. The Christian claims to know what he knows about God, because God has made himself known in Jesus. 'No one knows the Father except the Son and any one to whom the Son chooses to reveal him' (Matt 11:27). But in the order of reality things are the other way round. Jesus does not exist in or for himself. 'The Son can do nothing of his own accord, but only what he sees the Father doing; for whatever he does, that the Son does likewise' (Jn 5:19). There is a priority of the Father to the Son. The Son exists for the Father, and is orientated towards him. For the Anglican Reformers, who were deeply concerned with epistemological questions, reality, nevertheless, was, in the last resort, more important even than knowledge itself.[135]

If we move on to the question of why Parker added an article on the Holy Spirit, the answer again has to be that we do not know for certain why he decided to do this. However, there are two probable explanations. The first is that he wanted to counteract heretical teaching about the Holy Spirit by some of the Protestant radicals. However, since this teaching seems to have been most prevalent in Cranmer's time rather than Parker's, a second and more likely explanation is that Parker simply felt

---

[134] O'Donovan op.cit. p.18
[135] Ibid p.18

that an Article on the Spirit was required for the sake of theological completeness. Given the presence of Article II on the Son of God Parker may well have felt it necessary to provide an article on the Holy Spirit in order to give a proper balance and symmetry to the opening section of the Articles, even if such an article was not specifically required to combat heresy.

Parker may also have wished to make the order of the first five Articles correspond with the Trinitarian structure of the Apostles and Nicene Creeds, by starting with an article on God the Creator (Article I) followed by Articles on God the Son (Articles II-IV) and an Article on the Holy Spirit (Article V).

Article I

∞

Of Faith in the Holy Trinity

There is but one living and true God, everlasting, without body, parts, or passions; of infinite power, wisdom, and goodness; the maker and preserver of all things both visible and invisible. And in unity of this Godhead there be three Persons, of one substance, power, and eternity; the Father, the Son, and the Holy Ghost.

De fide in Sacrosanctam Trinitatem

Unus est vivus et verus Deus, aeternus, incorporeus, impartibilis, impassibilis, immensae potentiae, sapientiae, ac bonitatis, creator et conservator omnium, tum visibilium tum invisibilium. Et in unitate huius divinae naturae tres sunt Personae eiusdem essentiae, potentiae, ac aeternitatis, Pater, Filius, et Spiritus Sanctus.

This article was taken over practically unchanged from the first of the *Forty Two Articles*, the only alteration being the omission of the words 'and he is' before 'everlasting.'. It is based on the first of the *Thirteen Articles* of 1538 which began as follows:

Concerning the unity of the divine essence and the three persons we hold the decree of the council of Nicaea to be true and without any doubt to be believed, viz. that there is one divine essence which is both called and is God, eternal, incorporeal, indivisible, of immense power, wisdom and goodness, creator and preserver of all things visible and invisible, and yet there are three persons of the same essence and power, coeternal, Father, Son and Holy Spirit.[136]

---

[136] Text in Bray op.cit. p.185

The Article also parallels the statement on the Trinity in the *Reformatio Legum Ecclesiasticarum* which states:

> All children of God who are born again by Jesus Christ, shall believe with a pure heart, a good conscience and an unfeigned faith, and they shall confess that there is one living and true God, eternal and incorporeal, impassible, of unlimited power, wisdom and goodness, the creator and preserver of all things, both visible and invisible, and that in the unity of that divine nature there are three persons, of the same essence and eternity, the Father, the Son and the Holy Spirit, and that the Father is of himself, neither begotten of anyone else nor proceeding, and that the Son is begotten of the Father and that the Holy Spirit proceeds from the Father and the Son, and that no diversity or inequality is to be understood in this distinction of persons, but that according to the divine substance, or (as they say) essence, they share everything alike and equally. [137]

Two reasons can be suggested for the inclusion of this article.

Firstly, Cranmer and Parker may have included this article simply because they thought what it said was true and constituted the foundation of Christian faith and theology.

Secondly, they may also have wanted to dissociate the Church of England from the contemporary revival of Trinitarian heresies. In the words of Gibson:

> The need of such an Article as this is shown by the formidable spread of Anabaptism in this country as well as on the continent. Contemporary documents show how very many of the Anabaptists had lost all faith in the doctrine of the Holy Trinity. Some were reviving the Sabellian heresy and denying that there was more than one person in the Godhead; others were teaching a

---

[137] *Reformatio Legum Ecclesiasticarum* I.2 text in G Bray (ed) *Tudor Church Reform*, Church of England Record Society – 8, Woodbridge: The Boydell Press 2000 pp.171-3

form of Arianism, denying the Divinity of the Second person, while others again maintained that Christ was 'a mere man.'[138]

This statement can be illustrated by a letter written by Bishop Nicholas Ridley to John Bradford shortly before his death in 1555 in which he refers to:

> ...the outrageous rule that Satan, our ghostly enemy, beareth abroad in the world, whereby he stirreth, and raiseth so pestilent and heinous heresies, as some to deny the blessed Trinity, some the Divinity of our Saviour Christ, some the Divinity of the Holy Ghost.[139]

The article is in two parts, which correspond with its two sentences. The first part concerns the unity and the attributes of God and the second concerns the threefold nature of God.

There is but one living and true God

This statement is based on the clear teaching of a number of biblical texts.

- That God is *one* is taught in texts such as Deut 6:4, Mk 12:32, 1 Tim 2:5

- That God is the *living* God is taught in texts such as Ps 42:2, Jer 10:10, 2 Cor 3:3

- The God is the *true* God is taught in texts such as 2 Chron 15:3, Jn 17:3, 1 Thess 1:9

The key to the statement, however, is the word 'but', which this context means 'only'. What the statement is saying is not simply that God is one instead of many, that He is living rather than dead, that is He is true rather than false, but that He is the only God, the only God who really

---

[138] Gibson op.cit. p.91
[139] H Christmas (ed) *The Works of Nicholas Ridley* Cambridge: CUP/Parker Society 1843 p.367

lives, the only God who is the genuine article and in that sense the true God.

Here again the article is following the biblical witness which uses the terms 'one', 'living' and 'true' to contrast the God of Israel with other claimants to deity.

Deut 4:35 'To you it was shown, that you might know that the Lord is God; there is none other besides him'

Jer 10:10 'But the Lord is the true God; he is the living God and the everlasting King.'

Jn 17:3 'that they may know thee the only true God'

1 Cor 8:4 '...there is no God but one.'

1 Thess 1:9 '...how you turned from idols to serve a living and true God.'[140]

As Patrick Miller notes in his commentary on Deut 6:4-5 (what is known as the *'Shema'* - 'Hear, O Israel: The Lord our God is one Lord; and you shall love the Lord your God with all your heart, and with all your soul, and with all your might'), the biblical teaching, echoed by this article, that there is only one God has both a theological and an anthropological significance.

The theological significance has to do:

> ...with the freedom and power of God. That is, the monotheism that arises out of this Deuteronomic center claims that there is only one ultimate or absolute – the power that undergirds all reality is one and not multiple, faithful and not capricious, a whole

---

[140] It is sometimes suggested that the Old Testament is not consistently monotheistic and that in some passages it allows the existence of other gods alongside the God of Israel, while forbidding them from being the subjects of Israel's worship or obedience. For a helpful treatment of this issue which exposes the weakness of this argument see R Bauckham 'Biblical Theology and the Problem of Monotheism' in C Bartholomew et al (eds) *Out of Egypt: Biblical Theology and Biblical Interpretation* Carlisle & Grand Rapids Paternoster: Zondervan 2004 pp. 187-232.

and not divided, and therefore capable of purpose and power because this one is not controlled and limited by other forces. The only limitation on the freedom and power of God is the self-limiting step that is taken by God in the act of creation. Without this freedom and power in God uncontrolled by outside forces, one would have to raise serious questions about the possibility of the accomplishment of the divine purpose or even the clarity of speaking of a divine purpose. For it is difficult to assume an order and a purpose to the universe if there is not a center or ground of being, value and meaning that is one, comprehensive and consistent. [141]

The anthropological significance is:

...the impossibility of human sharing of a loyalty that is meant to be ultimate. Penultimate loyalties to those beings and things that do not ground human existence, do not call human life into being or shape its destiny, are quite possible and indeed necessary and desirable; but the loyalty to the Creator, the Lord and giver of life, Savior and Judge, cannot be satisfactorily divided. This claim is not merely abstract and theoretical. It is indeed personal and ultimately pastoral. For the oneness of the reality that grounds existence, God, is what keeps life from being chaotic and divided beyond the limits of human management. In the face of the multiple pulls and dimensions of human life and experience, human existence is kept together and in order by that one and absolute object of our allegiance and loyalty. We do not find conflicting claims on our ultimate loyalty, only on our secondary interests and loyalties. It is possible to deal with these secondary claims if we have a sense that our ultimate and full allegiance is directed towards one alone. The demand of the Shema is, therefore, finally not just a demand. It is also what makes human life possible. All claims on human life are relativized and subsumed within the one total claim of God so that the demand is ultimately the gift of grace.[142]

---

[141] P D Miller *Deuteronomy* Louisville: John Knox Press 1990 p.103
[142] Ibid pp.103-104

...everlasting, without body, parts, or passions

This clause begins to identify the characteristics of the one living and true God and it does this by making it clear that God is not be regarded as if He were a human being like ourselves, only slightly bigger and more powerful. As W G Wilson and J H Templeton explain in their commentary on the Articles, the clause is intended to guard against this error by reminding us that God is not subject to our human limitations:

> Our lives are subject to all the limitations imposed upon us by time and space, but God is 'everlasting'[Ps 90:2, Rom 1:20, 16:26, Rev 1:8].There was no moment of time when He first came into being. Time does not hamper His knowledge or His power. He does not grow old or weary [Isa 40:28]. Because He is Spirit [Jn 4:24], He is *without body* unlimited by any considerations of space, and can be present in all places at the same time [Ps 139, Prov 15:3, Acts 17:27] He is also *without parts* (Latin, *impartibilis),* incapable of being divided in any sense. We may suffer from inner conflicts, but He is at one within Himself. What from our standpoint are separate attributes such as His love and His wrath are really 'aspects of one consistent and unchanging being'. Likewise He is *without passions* (Latin, *impassibilis); He* is not fickle and does not change [Mal 3:6, Jas 1:17] or do anything inconsistent such as contradicting Himself [2 Tim 2:13], or telling a lie [Heb 6:18, Num 23:19, 1 Sam 15:29]. [143]

The fact that God is free from limitations in this way is an important aspect of Christian teaching because it means that He is a God in whom we can put our trust. Thus:

• The fact that God is not limited by space and time means that His love revealed to us in the particular historical life of Jesus Christ is available for us at all times and everywhere (Mt 28:20).

• The fact that God is undivided and does not suffer from inner conflict and the fact that he is not fickle and does not change means

[143] W G Wilson and J H Templeton *Anglican Teaching* Dublin: Association For Promoting Christian Knowledge, 1962, p.p. 15-16. Biblical references in the original.

that we can always rely upon God to be one he has declared Himself to be in Jesus Christ.

In spite of the positive aspects of this teaching, and in spite of the biblical texts which can be appealed to in its support, it has been questioned for three reasons.

First, the question has been raised as to how this teaching is compatible with the biblical texts that refer to God in terms that imply that God has a human body. Examples of such texts would be Ps 102:25 which refers to God's hands, Job 40:9 which refers to God's arm, and Ps 34:15 which refers to God's eyes and ears. Do not these texts, it is asked, suggest that God does have a body like ours?

The classic Christian answer to this question is that these sorts of references are figures of speech that are used to describe God's activity in the world in ways that we can easily understand. In his commentary on the Articles, Bishop Burnet writes, for example, that:

> ...though God is spoke of as having a face, eyes, ears, a smelling, hands and feet, and as coming down to view things on earth, all this is expressed after the manner of men, and is to be understood in a way suitable to a pure spirit. For the great care that was used, even under the most imperfect state of Revelation, to keep men from framing any image or similitude of the Deity, shewed that it was far from the meaning of those expressions, that God had an organized body. These do therefore signify only the several varieties of Providence. When God was pleased with a nation, his face was said to *shine* upon it; for so a man looks towards those whom he loves. The particular care he takes of them, and the answering their prayers, is expressed by figures borrowed from *eyes* and *ears*: the peculiar dispensations of rewards and punishments are expressed by his *hands*; and the exactness of his justice and *wisdom* is expressed by *coming down* to view the state of human affairs.[144]

Secondly, the question has been raised as to how the belief that God is unchanging is compatible with the fact that God is said to possess emotions such as love (Hos 11:1), anger (Jn 3:36), grief (Ps 78:40) and

---

[144] Burnet op.cit pp.33-34. Italics in the original

jealousy (Deut 32:16) and with fact that God is said to repent (Jer 18:8). Do not the existence of these varying emotions and the fact that God repents mean that there is in fact real change in God?

One possible response to this would be to say that these too are figures of speech that refer to the way in which God's unchanging attitude towards mankind is experienced by human beings at any given time. However, there are two problems with this approach.

(a) Unlike in the case of references to God's hands, eyes, etc., there is no indication in Scripture itself that God's emotions and God's repentance are not to be taken literally.

(b) We end up not being able to say anything at all about how God really feels about us. If all we can talk about is our experience of God and not how God really is then the Bible does not reveal God to us in the way that the Bible itself and the subsequent Christian tradition claim that it does.

A better approach is to follow the argument of Karl Barth in *Church Dogmatics* II.1 and talk about God changelessness in terms of God remaining 'constant' in the sense of true to Himself while at the same time being free to change in terms of His emotions and His actions:

> ...it would not be a glorifying, but a blaspheming and finally a denial of God, to conceive of the being and essence of this self-consistent God as one which is, so to speak, self-limited to an inflexible immobility, thus depriving God of the capacity to alter his attitudes and actions, as they are manifested in His revelation in concurrence or sequence. And he himself does not alter in the alteration of his attitudes and actions (Ps 102.26f). In all of them He intends and maintains Himself, His love and His freedom. He neither loses Himself nor becomes untrue to Himself. Yet he is not prevented by this continuity from advancing and retreating, rejoicing and mourning, laughing and complaining, being well pleased and causing His wrath to kindle, hiding or revealing Himself. And in all these things He can be always Himself, and therefore He can be them seriously, yet still according to the

order of His essence, and therefore in a definite sequence and gradation. [145]

Thirdly, the question has been raised about whether the idea of God's changelessness means that He cannot suffer. The classic argument that it does mean this has been that because suffering is a change imposed on someone by some outside force it is not something that can be predicated of God. God, it is said, is both sovereign and changeless and to say that He suffers would be a denial of both.

On the other hand it is argued:

- That in Scripture God is described as suffering. This can be seen most clearly in the suffering of Christ on the Cross but it can also be seen, for example, in the repeated statement that God has 'compassion' for His people (Deut 30:3, Isa 49:14-16, Hos 11:8-9) since having compassion means experiencing pain because of someone else's affliction or distress.

- That if God was incapable of suffering He would be morally deficient. The argument here is that it is a moral good to experience pain over the suffering of others and if God does not, or cannot experience this, then He is more morally limited than the human beings He has made.

How should we respond to these contrasting arguments? Building on what Barth says about God's ability to remain constant in the midst of change, the best approach in the light of the biblical evidence would seem to be to say that God does indeed suffer but that He does not do so out of compulsion, but as a result of his free choice. Packer puts it like this:

> God is impassible. This means, not that God is impassive and unfeeling (a frequent misunderstanding), but that no created being can inflict pain, suffering and distress on him at their own will. In so far as God enters into suffering and grief (which

---

[145] K Barth *Church Dogmatics* II.1 Edinburgh: T&T Clark 2004 pp.498-9

Scriptures many anthropapathisms,[146] plus the fact of the cross shows that he does), he is never his creatures' hapless victim.[147]

Having said what God is not, the article next moves on to say what God is.

...of infinite power, wisdom, and goodness

As Bishop Beveridge notes:

> Having seen what God is not, we are now to consider what he is: when we speak of imperfections, he is utterly destitute of them, but as for perfections they are all infinite in him; he is without body, without parts and without passions; but of infinite power, infinite, wisdom, and of infinite goodness. He is of infinite power, so as to be able to do whatever is possible to be done: of infinite wisdom, so as to know whatever is possible to be known: and of infinite goodness, so as to be more goodness in himself, than can possibly be conceived by us.[148]

These perfections of God are further explained by Bicknell.
Concerning God's infinite power he writes:

> 'With God all things are possible' (Mt 19:26). God's omnipotence is the perfection of His will. He is almighty, i.e. all-sovereign: unfettered by any limitations in His actions, unbounded in His resources. All the power that exists in the universe, of body, mind or will, is in origin His. He is pleased to lend it to beings whose wills are free. As such, they may pervert or misuse it. But its source is all the time in Him and its exercise is never withdrawn from His control. 'Precisely in this way above all others, that He is omnipotent over a free world, does God reveal the greatness of His power most clearly.' Thus God is not hindered in His activity by any foreign or independent power in the world. Nor yet is God limited by creation in the sense that He has exhausted His resources in it. He has inexhaustible power and wisdom in

---

[146] Descriptions of God as suffering human emotions.
[147] J I Packer 'God' in S B Ferguson & D F Wright (eds) *New Dictionary of Theology* Leicester: IVP 1988 p.277
[148] Beveridge op.cit p. 35

reserve. On all such points God's infinite power is contrasted with man's finite power.

But God's infinite power does not mean that God can do anything whatever. He cannot lie or contradict Himself (2 Tim 2:13). He cannot do wrong or undo the past or make men holy apart from their own efforts. For all these things are contrary to His own laws. These laws are not imposed upon Him by any external necessity, but are the free expressions of His own character and purpose. As Hooker writes: 'The Being of God is a kind of law to his working.' 'God is a law both to Himself and to all other things besides.' 'Nor is the freedom of the will of God any whit abated, let or hindered by means of this, because the imposition of this law upon Himself is his own free and voluntary act'.[149]

Concerning God's infinite wisdom he declares:

'Omniscience is the perfection of God's mind as omnipotence is the perfection of God's will.' He is 'the only wise God' (Rom 16:27). Not only has God an immediate and perfect knowledge of the smallest detail of every event that happens upon this earth (Mt 10:29-30, etc), but He knows all the manifold intricacies of His universe. Every piece of truth gained, of whatever kind, is so far an entering into the mind of God. Science has been defined as 'thinking God's thoughts after Him.' Further, God knows all the possibilities that lie before the world. Nothing that happens can every take him unawares (Heb 4:13). In what way God views the future we cannot say. All that we can affirm is that no contingency is unforeseen by Him or outside His control.[150]

Finally, concerning God's infinite goodness he states:

The Latin *bonitatis* shows that goodness here means 'kindness' rather than 'holiness' It refers to God's infinite blessings to

---

[149] Bicknell op.cit pp.38-39
[150] Ibid p.39

mankind 'the riches of his goodness (Rom 2:4, cp Tit 3:4) as shown in creation, preservation and redemption.[151]

The importance of the fact that God is infinitely powerful, wise and good in the way just described is that is His power, wisdom and goodness are the foundations for his action in the world.

- Because God's kindness is infinite we can be sure that His purposes are good.

- Because God's wisdom is infinite we can be sure that He knows the best way to carry out these purposes.

- Because God's power is infinite He has the ability to put these purposes into effect, and because His use of His power is limited by His character and purpose we can be sure that He will never misuse it.

It is these three principles that are the basis of Christian confidence that God will keep His promises set out in Scripture and fulfil His good plan for us and for all creation.

...the maker and preserver of all things both visible and invisible.

The fact that God is the maker and preserver of all things is taught in a whole series of biblical texts (see, for example, Gen 1, Ps 104, Isa 42:5, Mt 6:25-30, Acts 17:26-28, and Col 1:16-17). For this reason it has been affirmed consistently by Christian theologians from the earliest days of the Church.

Thus at the end of the second century St. Irenaeus of Lyons declares in opposition to the various Gnostic groups that denied that the world was God's creation that Christians believe that God:

> ...is the creator of heaven and earth and all the world, and maker of angels and men, and Lord of all, through whom things exist and by whom all things are sustained.[152]

---

[151] Ibid p. 39

[152] Irenaeus *Demonstration of the Apostolic Preaching* 6 in I M Mackenzie (ed) Irenaeus's *Demonstration of the Apostolic Preaching* Aldershot: Ashgate 2002 p.3

This belief was subsequently affirmed in the *Apostles* and *Nicene* Creeds and it was accepted without question by the reformed Church of England. How it was understood by the Tudor Church is clearly expressed in the *Catechism* produced by the Elizabethan Dean of St. Paul's, Alexander Nowell:

Master. How dost thou say that God created all things?

Scholar. That God, the most good and mighty Father, at the beginning and of nothing, by the power of his Word, that is, of Jesus Christ his Son, framed and made this whole visible world, and all things, whatsoever they be that are contained therein, and also the uncorporal spirits whom we call angels.

M. But dost thou think it godly to affirm that God created all spirits, even those wicked spirits, whom we call devils?

S. God did not create them such: but they, by their own evilness, fell from their first creation, without hope of recovery, and so are they become evil, not by creation and nature, but by corruption of nature.

M. Did God think it enough to have once created all things, and then to cast away all further care of things from thenceforth?

S. I have already briefly touched this point. Whereas it is much more excellent to maintain and preserve things created, than to have once created them; we must certainly believe, that when he had so framed the world and all creatures, he from thenceforth hath preserved and yet preserveth them. For all things would run to ruin, and fall to nothing, unless by his virtue, and, as it were by his hand they were upholden. We also assuredly believe, that the whole order of nature and changes of things, which are falsely reputed the alterations of fortune, do hang all upon God: that God guideth the course of the heaven, upholdeth the earth, tempereth the seas, and ruleth this whole world, and that all things obey his divine power, and by his divine power all things are governed: that he is the author of fair weather and of tempest, of rain and of drought, of fruitfulness and of barrenness, of health and of sickness: that of all things that belong to the sustentation and preserving of our life, and which are desired either for necessary use or honest pleasure; finally, of all things that nature needeth, he hath ever given, and yet most largely giveth abundance and plenty with most liberal hand; to this end, verily, that we should so use them as becometh mindful and kind children.[153]

It is this understanding of God's creative and sustaining activity that is reflected in the teaching in Article I that God is: 'the maker and preserver of all things both visible and invisible'. In the minds of many people today this teaching raises three questions.

Firstly, is it still possible to believe in the existence of angels and devils in the way that Nowell clearly does?

Ever since the Enlightenment a belief in angels and devils has increasingly come to be seen as a relic of pre-scientific superstition and this feeling has also come to be shared by many people within the Church. This situation is reflected, for example, in the 1938 report *Doctrine in the Church of England* in which the members of the Archbishops' Commission on Christian Doctrine that produced the report write that:

> To believe positively, whether on the ground of Scripture, or on the ground of tradition as interpreting Scripture and as lending weight to an inherent probability, in the existence of spiritual beings other than human is in no way irrational.
>
> Nevertheless the Commission desires to record its conviction that it is legitimate for a Christian either to suspend judgement on the point, or alternatively to interpret the language, whether of Scripture or of the Church's liturgy with regard to angels and demons in a purely symbolical sense.[154]

What the Commission does not tells us is why they regard it as legitimate either to be agnostic about the existence of angels and demons or to interpret the references to them in a symbolic way.

As the Commission itself concedes, belief in angels and demons cannot be seen as irrational. Not only is there no reason why God could not have chosen to create angelic beings, but if there are purely spiritual

---

[153] G E Corrie (ed) *Nowell's Catechism* Cambridge: CUP/Parker Society 1853 p????
[154] *Doctrine in the Church of England* London: SPCK 1938 p.47

beings then science (in the sense of the natural sciences) has nothing to say either for or against their existence since it is concerned with the study of the material universe ('things visible').

This leaves the question of whether angels and demons exist as a matter of biblical interpretation, and as the Commission itself accepts:

> The belief in such beings is an unquestioned element in the intellectual world-view of the New Testament writers, by whom it was held that there exists, in the supernatural world, a variety of spiritual agencies, both evil and good; that the Son of Man came upon earth as the Conqueror of Demons and as the Deliverer of all them that were 'under the tyranny of the devil'; and that there are angels who as 'ministering spirits' are 'sent forth to do service for the sake of them that shall inherit salvation.' The Gospels present our Lord Himself as practising exorcism, and as sharing (in this and other respects) the current beliefs of His time.[155]

This being the case, there seems no good reason to depart from the consistent practice of the Christian tradition and to re-interpret the references to angels and demons in a symbolic rather than a literal fashion (except in the case of the Book of Revelation where the whole narrative section of the book - and not just its references to angels and demons - seems to require a symbolic interpretation).

Secondly, is Nowell's view of God's providential action in the world consistent with what we now know about the way in which the world is governed by the operation of the laws of nature? To put it simply, do these laws allow any room for the action of God?

This issue is helpfully tackled by David Broughton Knox in his study of the *Thirty Nine Articles*. He comments that:

> ...God is the author of the laws of nature and He is not thwarted in His purposes by them, nor limited in His power. He works His purposes through nature which He created. Because He is an 'unchanging God' He works uniformly and not capriciously and so we designate the observed uniformity of nature as 'laws of nature'. However, God is not limited in His freedom of action by this regularity, known to us as 'laws of nature'. Yet many modern

---

[155] Ibid p.46

Christians have fallen into this mistake. For example, they are diffident in praying for seasonable weather, on the view that the weather is controlled by meteorological laws and that as a consequence God has limited Himself in this area. But if limited here, He is limited everywhere, so that all prayer becomes impossible. For there are, in fact, no 'gaps' in nature, though there may still be gaps in our knowledge. But God works through the laws of nature. His sovereignty is not in the slightest degree affected by them. It is God who sends the rain, so Jesus taught. Droughts are his judgement; the drought and the breaking of the drought of Elijah's time were the result of prayer, according to James. If we prefer to think of the weather as caused by meteorological laws, we must remember that these are secondary causes. God's 'infinite power' is primary and we may have access to Him by prayer.[156]

Thirdly, if we say that the world is ruled by God's providential care this raises the question of why there is so much suffering in the world. The classic biblical and Christian answer to this question is that suffering comes from living in a world that has been disrupted by sin and that what God has done and is doing is to work to heal and renew it. This a point brought out by Bishop N T Wright in his recent commentary on Romans. He writes as follows on St. Paul's account of the groaning of creation in Rom 8:18-25:

> When we look at the world of creation as it is in the present, we see a world in the same condition as the children of Israel were in when they were enslaved in Egypt. Just as God allowed the Israelites to go down into Egypt, so that in bringing them out he could define them for ever as the freedom-from-slavery people, so God has allowed creation to be subjected to its present round of summer and winter, growth and decay, birth and death. It's beautiful, yes, but it always ends in tears or at least a shrug of the shoulders. If you happen to live at the sharp end of the corruption of creation – on an earthquake fault line, for instance, or by an active volcano – you may sense the awe of that futile power.

---

[156] D B Knox *Thirty Nine Articles – The Historic Basis of Anglican Faith* London: Hodder & Stoughton 1967 p.15

Creation can sometimes appear like a caged buffalo; all that energy, and it's not achieving anything. And, thinking of wild animals, what about that promise of the wolf and the lamb lying down together? Is it just a dream?

No, says Paul, it isn't a dream. It's a promise. All these things are signs that the world as it is, though still God's good creation and pregnant with his power and glory (Rom 1.20), is not at present the way it should be. God's 'covenant faithfulness' was always about his commitment that, through the promises to Abraham, he would one day put the whole world to rights. Now at last we see what this meant. The human race was put in charge of creation (as so often, Paul has Genesis 1-3 not far from his mind). When human beings rebelled and worshipped parts of creation instead of God himself (Rom 1.21-23), creation fell into disrepair. God allowed this state of slavery to continue, not because the creation wanted to be like that but because he was determined eventually to put the world back to rights according to the original plan (just as, when Israel let him down, he didn't change the plan, but sent at last a faithful Israelite). The plan had called for human beings to take their place under God and over the world, worshipping the creator and exercising glorious stewardship over the world. The creation isn't waiting to *share* the freedom of God's children, as some translations imply. It is waiting to benefit wonderfully when God's children are glorified. It is waiting – on tiptoe with expectation, in fact – for the particular freedom it will enjoy when God gives to his children that glory, that wise rule and stewardship, which was always intended for those who bear God's glorious image.[157]

The obvious objection to this explanation is that the natural sciences tell us that suffering, death and decay do not appear to be an intrusion into the created order. They are built into it in the sense that they are simply a result of the normal operation of the laws of nature. However, this objection overlooks the fact that all the natural sciences are able to describe is the world as it is, not the world as it would have been without the effects of sin, nor the world as it is going to be when God's purposes

[157] N T Wright *Paul for Everyone - Romans Part I* London: SPCK 2004 pp. 151-152

are fulfilled. The operation of natural laws in a fallen world cannot tell us how that world is meant to be.

And in unity of this Godhead there be three Persons, of one substance, power, and eternity; the Father, the Son, and the Holy Ghost.

Not only has the Christian Church held from the earliest times that God is the maker and preserver of all things, but it has also consistently held that this God is Father, Son and Holy Spirit. For example, St. Irenaeus writes:

> This then is the order of the rule of our faith, and the foundation of the building, and the stability of our conversation: God the Father, not made, nor material, invisible; one God, the creator of all things: this is the first point of our faith. The second point is: The Word of God, Son of God, Christ Jesus our Lord, who was manifested to the prophets according to the form of their prophesyings and according to the method of the dispensation of the Father, through whom all things were made; who also at the end of the times, to complete and gather up all things, was made man among men, visible and tangible, in order to abolish death and show forth life and produce a community of union between God and man. And the third point is: The Holy Spirit, through whom the prophets prophesied and the fathers learned the things of God, and the righteous were led forth into the way of righteousness; and who in the end of times was poured out in a new way upon mankind in all the earth, renewing man unto God.[158]

It is this belief in God as Father, Son and Holy Spirit that is the subject of the second part of Article I.

The biblical basis for this belief is helpfully summarised by Griffith Thomas, who argues that in the New Testament we find two lines of teaching:

---

[158] Mackenzie (ed) op.cit. p.3

(a) One line of teaching insists on the unit of the Godhead (1 Cor 8:4; Jas 2:19); and (b) the other reveals distinctions within the Godhead (Matt 3:16, 17; 28:19, 2 Cor 13:14). We see clearly that (1) the Father is God (Matt 11:25; Rom 15:6; Eph 4:6); (2) the Son is God Jn 1:1, 18; 20:28; Acts 20:28; Rom 9:5; Heb 1:8; Col 2:9; Phil 2:6; 2 Pet 1:1); (3) the Holy Spirit is God (Acts 5:3, 4; 1 Cor 2:10, 11; Eph 2:22); (4) the Father, Son and Holy Spirit are distinct from one another, sending and being sent, honouring and being honoured. The Father honours the Son, the Son honours the Father, and the Holy Spirit honours the Son (Jn 15:26; 16:13,14; 17:1, 8, 18, 23). (5) Nevertheless, whatever relations of subordination there may be between the Persons in the working out of redemption, the Three are alike regarded as God. The doctrine of the Trinity is the correlation, embodiment and synthesis of the teaching of these passages.[159]

In the words of St. Augustine:

O Lord our God, we believe in Thee, the Father and the Son and the Holy Spirit. For the Truth would not say, Go, baptise all nations in the name of the Father and of the Son and of the Holy Spirit, unless thou wast a Trinity. Nor wouldest thou, O Lord God, bid us to be baptized in the name of Him who is not the Lord God. Nor would the divine voice have said, Hear, O Israel, the Lord thy God is one God, unless thou wert so a Trinity as to be one Lord God. And if thou, O God, wert thyself the Father, and wert thyself the Son, Thy Word Jesus Christ, and the Holy Spirit your gift, we should not read in the book of truth, 'God sent his Son;' nor wouldst Thou, O Only-begotten, say of the Holy Spirit, 'Whom the Father will send in my name;' and 'Whom I will send to you from the Father.' [160]

Although the Trinitarian nature of God is only explicitly taught in the New Testament it is also important to note that, as B S Childs puts it, the

[159] Griffith Thomas op,cit p. 24. For a detailed exploration of these passages see A W Wainwright *The Trinity in the New Testament* London: SPCK 1962 and E J Fortman *The Triune God* London: Hutchinson 1972.

[160] St. Augustine *On the Trinity* XV:28 in *The Nicene & Post Nicene Fathers* Vol III Edinburgh and Grand Rapids: T&T Clark/ Eerdmans 1998 p.227

doctrine of the Trinity is: '...not a battle *against* the Old Testament, but rather a battle *for* the Old Testament.'[161] That is to say, when the Church has confessed God as Father, Son and Holy Spirit it has always insisted that these are not new gods, over against the God of Israel. Rather, it has insisted that they are identical with the one God of Israel confessed in the *Shema*. The one God of Israel *is* the God who is Father, Son and Holy Spirit.

And in unity of this Godhead there be three Persons...

In expressing its belief in God as Father, Son and Holy Spirit Article I uses the technical term 'Person' inherited from the debates about the Trinity in the Early Church.

What it means by this term is explained by the corresponding article in the *Thirteen Articles*. This states: '...we use the name Person in the same sense as it was used by the Church Fathers, i.e. as signifying not a part or a quality in another being, but what subsists in itself.'[162]

That is to say, the term Person does not mean that a part of God is the Father, and a part of God is the Son and a part of God is the Spirit. This would mean that there was a division in God, an idea that the Article has already ruled out as compromising God's essential oneness.

Furthermore, the term Person does not mean the one God has the qualities of Fatherhood, Sonship and Spirithood. This would compromise the reality of the distinctions between the Persons referred to by St. Augustine. It would, for instance, make nonsense of the statement that God the Father sent His Son for our salvation.

What the term Person does mean is that the Father, Son and Holy Spirit each truly exists in their own right with the personal, eternal, existence that is proper to the being of God.

This might be understood to mean that the Father, the Son and the Holy Spirit were three eternally existing separate individuals. This would however, be Tri-theism (a belief in three Gods) and contrary to the biblical insistence on the oneness of God. That is why the Article states that the Persons exist 'in unity of this Godhead.' What this means, in the words of St. Augustine, is that the Persons are 'so a Trinity as to be one

---

[161] B S Childs *Biblical Theology of the Old and New Testaments* Minneapolis: Fortress Press 1992 p.376.
[162] Bray *Documents of the English Reformation* p.185

Lord God'. In other words, the one God exists eternally and simultaneously as Father, Son and Holy Spirit.

...of one substance, power, and eternity

The unity of the Persons is underlined when the articles goes on to say that the persons are 'of one substance, power and eternity'. The point that is being made here is explained more fully in a passage from the *Reformatio Legum Ecclesiasticarum* quoted above which declares:

> ...that no diversity or inequality is to be understood in this distinction of persons, but that according to the divine substance, or (as they say) essence, they share everything alike and equally.

The word substance is another technical term from the Trinitarian debates of the Early Church and, as the quotation says, it is used to refer to the essence of God, the one divine nature the possession of which makes God God. This means that when it is said that the Persons are of one substance it means that as God each of the Persons possesses this one divine nature in all its fullness.

As a result each of the Persons possesses all the divine attributes 'alike and equally.' The article illustrates this point by stating that they possess one 'power and eternity'.

As we have seen, the one God is omnipotent and eternal, and this means that God the Father is omnipotent and eternal, God the Son is omnipotent and eternal, and God the Holy Spirit is omnipotent and eternal. However, there are not three gods who are omnipotent and eternal, but one omnipotent and eternal God who exists in these three ways.

Although this kind of technical theology is necessary in order to safeguard the truth of the biblical witness to who God is, it can very often seem irrelevant to the concerns of most Christians. 'Why', it is asked,' does the doctrine of the Trinity matter?' The answer to this question, and the reason St. Athanasius and others fought so hard to safeguard the doctrine, is that the Trinitarian nature of God is what makes our salvation possible.

This is a point that is implicit in the quotation from St. Irenaeus at the beginning of this section, and is stressed by the Doctrine Commission in its 1995 report *The Mystery of Salvation*.

The report explains that the doctrine of the Trinity:

> ...insisted that all three Trinitarian persons are truly and equally God, because it is as these three that God gives himself to us in salvation. If the incarnate Jesus were less than truly God or if the indwelling Spirit were less than truly God, salvation would be jeopardised. It would not be God's gift of himself. The gift of the Son would be a gift of something less than God himself, and the gift of the Spirit would be a gift of something less than God himself. The divine activity in salvation – the gift of the Son and the gift of the Spirit – would not be the activity of divine self-giving that the New Testament witness sees in it.[163]

And it also goes on to say that the doctrine affirms:

> ...that God is his own divine self really is such that God can share himself with his creation. God is not only the utterly other who infinitely transcends creation; God can also be deeply and intimately present within creation, as the Spirit, and God can also be one of us, a genuinely human person, as Jesus Christ the Son. Therefore God can and does open up his own life for us to share. Moreover, because God is Trinity God can share his life even with those created beings, ourselves, who are alienated from God and opposed to God. As incarnate Son and indwelling Spirit, God enters our situation of evil, suffering and mortality, shares with us the pain of our alienation, bears for us the pain of overcoming our enmity and healing our estrangement, sustains us in the struggle to be truly human, redirects our lives towards the Father as the source and goal of our being. The New Testament summary narratives of Trinitarian self–giving imply all this. It is as Father, Son and Holy Spirit that God can and does save us.[164]

The fact that is as Father, Son and Holy Spirit that God can and does save us is something that is implicit in the *Thirty Nine Articles* as well. It is because God is in himself the God of Article I, the God who is the Father, Son and Holy Spirit, that he is the incarnate Son of Article II-IV and the

---

[163] *The Mystery of Salvation* London: CHP 1995 p.41
[164] Ibid p.43

Holy Spirit of Article V. This in turn means that he is the God who died and rose for us and who chooses, calls, justifies, adopts and sanctifies us, and who acts in our lives through the sacraments (Articles II-IV, IX-XVIII, XXV-XXXI.)

Article II

∞

Of the Word, or Son of God, which was made very man

The Son, which is the Word of the Father, begotten from everlasting of the Father, the very and eternal God, and of one substance with the Father, took man's nature in the womb of the blessed Virgin, of her substance: so that two whole and perfect natures, that is to say, the Godhead and manhood, were joined together in one person, never to be divided, whereof is one Christ, very God and very man, who truly suffered, was crucified, dead, and buried, to reconcile His Father to us, and to be a sacrifice, not only for original guilt, but also for all actual sins of men.

De Verbo, sive Filio Dei, qui verus homo factus est

Filius, qui est Verbum Patris, ab aeterno a Patre genitus, verus et aeternus Deus, ac Patri consubstantialis in utero beate Virginis ex illius substantia naturam humanam assumpsit: ita ut duae naturae, divina et humana, integre atque perfecte in unitate personae, fuerint inseparabiliter coniunctae: ex quibus est unus Christus, verus Deus et verus homo: qui vere passus est, crucifixus, mortuus, et sepultus, ut Patrem nobis reconciliaret, essetque hostia non tantum pro culpa originis verum etiam pro omnibus actualibus hominum peccatis.

Like Article I, this article is an edited version of the corresponding article in the *Forty Two Articles*. In this case the editing took the form of the addition in 1563 of the clause: 'begotten from everlasting of the Father, the very and eternal God, and of one substance with the Father' which was taken from Article II of the *Wurtemburg Confession*.

The original 1553 article was taken almost word for word from the third of the *Thirteen Articles* which read:

We also teach that the Word, that is, the Son of God, took unto him human nature in the womb of the blessed virgin Mary, so that there are two natures, the divine and the human, inseparably joined together in unity of person; true God and true man, born of the Virgin Mary; (who) truly suffered, was crucified, dead and buried, that he might reconcile the Father unto us, and might be a sacrifice, not only for original guilt, but also for all actual sins of men.[165]

As in the case of Article I, Article II can be seen to have had a dual function. Its primary function was to set out the orthodox understanding of the person and work of Christ, but in so doing it was probably also intended to counteract two different heresies being promulgated by radical Protestant groups.

The first of these was the Arian heresy referred to above, which denied the divinity of Christ. The second was a heresy that denied that Christ took human nature from the Virgin Mary.

Both these errors are noted, for example, in the section of the *Reformatio Legum Ecclesiasticarum* dealing with heretical beliefs. The fifth heresy identified in this section is concerned with the two natures of Christ and it is described in the following terms:

Concerning the double nature of Christ there is a pernicious error which takes different forms. Some are of the sect of the Arians, holding that Christ is man in such a way as to deny that he is God. Others consider that he is God in such a way that they do not recognize him as a man, and concerning his body, they pretend that he fell in [an] assumed one of a divine nature from heaven, and fell into a virgin's womb, rather as if he were in transit through Mary and flowed through her as through a canal or tube...Some say that the body itself was often reincarnated here of earth... All of which errors are to be corrected by the authority of Holy Scripture in such a way that Christ is to be accepted as the eternal God in his higher nature, and therefore as the equal of God the Father, but that in his human nature he has a body, made and manifested in time, not more than once, nor of any matter other than the true and sole substance of the virgin Mary, which body

---

[165] Text in Bray *Documents of the English Reformation* p.186

indeed, just as it was made only once, so also it was lifted up on the cross for our salvation only one single time, and there offered to God the Father, and was circumscribed by the limits of finitude just as other human bodies are. [166]

The significance of this quotation is, first, that it makes clear why the Article maintains both the true divinity and the true humanity of Christ. Both were being questioned and both therefore needed to be upheld. When he came to revise Cranmer's article Parker clearly felt that although it adequately upheld Christ's true humanity it needed to uphold his true divinity as well. That is why he added the new clause from the *Wurtemburg Confession*.

Secondly, it explains why the article goes on to talk not just about the incarnation, but also the death of Christ. In order to tackle the idea that that there might have been numerous re-incarnations of the heavenly body of Christ it was necessary to make the point that the incarnation was a once for all event that began with the birth from the Virgin Mary and led to the Cross. That is to say, the incarnation was linked to a series of specific historical events that ensured our salvation and, as such, was unrepeatable and therefore unrepeated. It is this point that is implicit in the Article III of the Thirteen Articles and subsequently in Article II of the *Forty Two* and *Thirty Nine Articles*.

The Son, which is the Word of the Father, begotten from everlasting of the Father, the very and eternal God, and of one substance with the Father...

This part of the Article is intended to combat the revived Arianism of the sixteenth century. It draws on the orthodox understanding of the divinity of Christ which was developed in opposition to the original Arian heresy in the fourth century.

Arius, who was a presbyter of the Church of Alexandria taught that the Son of God was not truly God, but was an angel, a spiritual being created by God out of nothing like the rest of the created order.[167] This teaching was rejected by the Church as a whole for two reasons:

---

[166] Text in Bray *Tudor Church Reform* pp.189-91.
[167] For Arius' teaching see R Williams *Arius* London: SCM 2001

- It was contrary to the teaching of Scripture which explicitly and implicitly taught that the Son of God was God and not just an angel.

- For the reasons outlined in the comments on Article I, a denial of the divinity of Christ was held to involve a denial of Christ's ability to save.

The formula that was eventually drawn up in to enshrine the orthodox belief in the divinity of Christ over against Arianism was the Nicene Creed, the second part of which states a belief in:

> ...one Lord Jesus Christ, the only begotten Son of God, Begotten of his Father before all worlds, God of God, Light of Light, Very God of very God, Begotten, not made, Being of one substance with the Father...

The first section of Article II embodies the theology of this section of the Nicene Creed and echoes some of its language. However, it is not simply based on the Creed. More fundamentally it is based on the prologue to St. John's Gospel (Jn 1:1-18) as is shown by the reference to the 'Word', a key term in the prologue, but one that is not found in the Creed. What we have in the opening section of Article II is a summary of the teaching of Jn 1:1-18 expressed largely in language drawn from the Creed.

Even though He is not mentioned directly within it,[168] it is clear from the rest of St. John's Gospel that the subject of the prologue is the Son of God. The rest of chapter 1, for example, goes on seamlessly to discuss how first John the Baptist and then Nathanael confessed that Jesus was the Son of God and the prologue is clearly intended to tell us who it was that they were confessing.

The prologue describes the Son of God as being God's 'Word' (1:1, 1:14). As numerous commentators have pointed out, this word seems to have been intended by St. John to carry two meanings, based on the teaching of the Old Testament and of Greek philosophy respectively. To quote Archbishop William Temple:

---

[168] The evidence seems to indicate that Jn 1:18 should read 'only God' not 'only Son'

It is the word of the Lord by which the heavens were made, and which came by the Prophets. It is also the Rational Principle which gives unity and significance to all created things.[169]

As Temple goes on to say, by using this term with these two meanings:

St. John has thus established common ground with all his readers. If they are Jews they will recognise and assent to the familiar doctrine of the Old Testament concerning the Word of God. If they are Greeks they will recognise and assent to the declaration that the ultimate reality is Mind expressing itself. To both alike he has announced in language easily received that the subject for which he is claiming their attention is the ultimate and supreme principle of the universe.[170]

According to St. John this Word both exists *alongside* God (He is the Son who exists alongside the Father) and *is* God – 'the Word was with God and the Word was God' (Jn 1:1).[171]

Article I had already discussed the distinction in unity of the Persons of the Trinity and Article II does not repeat the point here. Instead, in order to emphasise the deity of the Son in opposition to the revival of Arianism it focuses on St. John's teaching that 'the Word was God'. It does this by echoing the teaching of the Creed and saying that the Word is 'begotten from everlasting from the Father, the very and eternal God, and of one substance with the Father.'

The meaning of the word 'very' in this description is explained by the use of the word 'verus' in the Latin version of Article II. Verus means 'true' so what the phrase literally says is that the Word is 'the true and eternal God'. However, in order to convey better the point that the article is making here it is better to put the phrase into contemporary English by saying that the Word is 'truly and eternally God'. Over against the Arian teaching that the Word was an angel with the honorific title of God the article says 'No, the Word is truly God'. Over against the Arian teaching that the Word came into being in time (as the Arian tag had it 'there was when he was not') the article says 'No, the Word is eternally God'.

---

[169] W Temple *Readings in St. John's Gospel* London: Macmillan 1947 p.3
[170] Ibid p.5
[171] A similar point is made in the body of the gospel when Christ says in 10:30 'I and the Father are one.'

This latter point is also derived from the prologue to St. John's Gospel. Deliberately echoing Gen 1:1, Jn 1:1 declares 'In the beginning was the Word.' In the eternity before all things began the Word was there with the Father.

The eternal nature of the Word is further underlined by the opening clause of this section of the article, 'begotten from everlasting from the Father.' The point that is being made here is well summarized by Tyrell Green:

> ...**begotten** expresses here not an event, but a relationship which has subsisted from **everlasting**. He is 'begotten' or else he would not be 'Son,' but 'from everlasting' or else he would not be God (Col. 1:15; Heb. I.5-12).[172]

What is meant when it is said that the Son is begotten is explained by Harold Browne in his commentary on the Articles. He writes:

> ...our Lord speaks of Himself, as deriving His own eternal Being from God the Father. 'As the living Father hath sent Me, and I live by the Father' (John vi.57), and again, 'As the Father hath life in Himself, so hath He given to the Son to have life in Himself' (John v.26). From which we learn, that the mode of existence, which the Father possessed from all eternity, He communicated to the Son. All created beings have their existence from, and their life in God. But the son, who is uncreated, derives indeed His being from the Father; but it is a Being of the same kind as the Father's, and therefore not dependent, like a creature's, but independent, self-existent, having life in itself.
>
> Accordingly the Son is farther called 'the Brightness of His Father's glory, the express Image of His Person,' Heb 1.3; words, which in the Greek indicate a relation of the Son to His Father, like that of brightness to light, like that of the impression of a seal on wax to the seal, which it answers to. [173]

---

[172] Tyrell Green op.cit p.31. Bold in the original.
[173] E H Browne *An Exposition of the Thirty-Nine Articles* London: John W Parker 1854 pp.65-66

In human beings begetting takes place in time. However, this cannot be true with regard to the Son because, as we have already seen, as God His existence is eternal. Therefore the orthodox Christian tradition has insisted that His begetting is eternal or, as Article II puts it 'from everlasting'. As Tyrell Green notes, if the Son were not begotten from everlasting He would not be God.

The final clause in this section tells us that the Son or Word is 'of one substance with the Father'. This phrase is taken from the Nicene Creed and theologically as well as grammatically it follows on from the preceding two clauses. If the Son is eternally begotten of the Father, and if as a result it is true that he is truly and eternally God, it follows that He must possess the same divine 'substance', or, in other words, the same divine nature, as the Father.

The phrase 'of one substance' was criticised when it was used in the context of the Arian debates of the fourth century, and has been criticised subsequently, on the grounds that it is not a biblical phrase. However, as its defenders have pointed out, what matters is not the word itself, but the truth it is used to defend, namely the belief that the Son is truly God and as such is able to be our saviour. In the words of Alasdair Heron: '...what really matters is to grasp what it means – that in Christ God has come among us, identified himself in solidarity with us, and claimed us as his own.'[174]

> *...took man's nature in the womb of the blessed Virgin, of her substance: so that two whole and perfect natures, that is to say, the Godhead and manhood, were joined together in one person, never to be divided, whereof is one Christ, very God and very man*

For it to be true that in Christ God has come among us and identified himself in solidarity with us, it is not only necessary that Christ should have possessed the divine nature, but it is also necessary that He should have possessed human nature as well. That the latter is the case is what is affirmed in this section of the article in opposition to the idea that He possessed a heavenly body that passed through the virgin Mary like water through a pipe.

---

[174] A I C Heron 'Homoousios with the Father' in T F Torrance (ed) *The Incarnation* Edinburgh: The Handsel Press 1981 p.76.

If we break the section down into its component parts what we find is that the first part down to the colon describe what happened at the incarnation and the second part explains how we are to understand who Christ is as a result.

...took man's nature in the womb of the blessed Virgin, of her substance

In his commentary on the Apostles' Creed Wolfhart Pannenberg explains that:

> ...in the church of the first centuries the virgin birth counted as being the special token of Jesus' true humanity, in opposition to the Gnostics, who did not want to allow the Redeemer a truly human birth and either made the Son of God live among men with an apparent body, or thought that he was only seemingly united with Jesus the man. In either case the idea was that the unchangeable God could not be truly one with a changeable suffering and dying man, born in time. Contrary to this view, the creed stresses with the 'anti-Gnostic' fathers of the second century that the Son of God himself was born through Mary.[175]

Faced with a similar denial of Christ's true humanity, Cranmer responded in the same way as the second century Fathers before him by stressing that the Son of God was born of the Virgin Mary. This meant that He was truly human since He took human nature from the human nature ('substance') of His mother.

Ironically, although in the second and sixteenth centuries the virgin birth was understood to be the guarantee of Christ's humanity, more recently it has been seen to call it into question. Thus *Doctrine in the Church of England* records that:

> There are...some among us who hold that a full belief in the historical Incarnation is more consistent that our Lord's birth took place under the normal conditions of human birth. In their minds the notion of a Virgin Birth tends to mar the completeness

---

[175] W Pannenberg *The Apostles Creed* London: SCM 1972 p.71

of the belief that in the Incarnation God revealed Himself at every point in and through human nature.[176]

There are two responses that need to be made to this line of argument.

First, the teaching about God the creator contained in Article I reminds us that, whatever the natural processes that brought them into being, all created things are as they are because God wills them to be so. We can see this if we consider the gospel stories of the conversion of water into wine (Jn 2:1-11) and the multiplication of loaves and fishes (Jn 6:1-14). In both cases what came into being came into being miraculously rather then naturally. Nevertheless, we are told that what resulted was wine, bread and fish. What God creates is truly created. This means that if God chooses to create human nature from the Virgin Mary then what He takes *is* truly human nature even though it came into existence through the miraculous activity of the Holy Spirit rather than as a result of sexual intercourse.

Secondly, we need to note the point made by C S Lewis in his book *Miracles* that what we see in the case of the virgin birth is simply a telescoped version of what takes place in all human births.

> In a normal act of generation the father has no creative function. A microscopic particle of matter from his body, and a microscopic particle from the woman's body meet. And with that there passes the colour of his hair and the hanging lower lip of her grandfather and the form of humanity in all its complexity of bones, sinews, nerves, liver and heart, and the form of those pre-human organisms which the embryo will recapitulate in the womb. Behind every spermatozoon lies the whole history of the universe: locked within it lies no inconsiderable part of the world's future. The weight or drive behind it is the momentum of the whole interlocked event which we call Nature up-to-date. And we know now that the 'laws of Nature' cannot supply that momentum. If we believe that God created Nature that momentum comes from Him. The human father is simply an instrument, a carrier, often an unwilling carrier, always simply the last in a long line of carriers – a line that stretches far beyond his ancestors into pre-human and pre-organic deserts of time,

---

[176] Doctrine in the Church of England p.82

back to the creation of matter itself. That line is in God's hand. It is the instrument by which He normally creates a man. For He is the reality behind both Genius and Venus; no woman ever conceived a child, no mare a foal, without Him. But once, and for a special purpose, He dispensed with that long line which is His instrument: once His life-giving finger touched a woman without passing through the ages of interlocked events. Once the great glove of Nature was taken off His hand. His naked hand touched her.[177]

The importance of all this, writes Lewis, is that like the other nature miracles recorded in the gospels:

> ...the miraculous conception is one more witness that here is Nature's Lord. He is doing now, small and close, what He does in a different fashion for every woman who conceives. He does it this time without a line of human ancestors: but even when He uses human ancestors it is not the less He who gives life. The bed is barren where that great party, Genius, is not present.[178]

Because, as Lewis argues, what we see in the birth of Christ is what is fundamentally true of all births, namely, that they are the result of the creative activity of God bringing new life into being in the body of a woman, it follows that what happened in the case of the birth of Christ cannot call His true humanity into question. If the action of God means that Christ was not truly human then the truth that Lewis highlights means that no other baby is truly human either (a position which no one has yet sought to defend).

Even if we set aside this theological objection to the virgin birth there is another objection that needs to be considered, which is that there are problems with the historicity of the accounts of the birth of Christ in Mt 1:18-25 and Lk 1:26-2:20

The specific problems that are normally raised are:

- The lack of references to the virgin birth elsewhere in the New Testament.

---

[177] C S Lewis *Miracles* London: Harper Collins 2002 pp.224-225
[178] Ibid p. 226

- The fact that there are two different accounts of the birth in the gospels of Matthew and Luke.

- The fact that the genealogies in these gospels trace Jesus' descent through Joseph thereby implying that he was Jesus' father.

- What are identified as 'legendary' elements in the stories such as the revelation through dreams and the ministry of angels which suggest that the stories are not historical in character.

It is suggested that the accounts were either based on pagan stories of miraculous births or were created in order to show that the birth of Christ had fulfilled Old Testament prophecy. [179]

On the other hand, in support of the historicity of the accounts, we need to note that:

- References to the miraculous birth of Christ can be found in texts such as Mk 6:3, Jn 1:13, 6:41-42, Rom 1:3, Gal 4:4, and Phil 2:7 and belief in the virgin birth was an unquestioned part of Christian belief from the early second century onwards.

- The gospels present us with two independent but complementary witnesses to a miraculous birth having taken place.

- The genealogies are careful to make it clear that Joseph was not the father of Jesus (Mt 1:16, Lk 3:23) so that what is being traced is legal not biological descent.

- The 'legendary' elements are only legendary if one rejects in advance the biblical teaching that God uses dreams and angels to communicate with human beings.

- There are no parallels between the gospel accounts and pagan stories about the begetting of children by the gods.

---

[179] For these points see, for example, A and R Hanson *Reasonable Belief* Oxford: OUP 1981 p.77

- The belief that the Messiah would be born of a virgin does not seem to have been a part of contemporary Jewish expectation and what we know about both how St. Matthew and St. Luke worked and contemporary Jewish practice make the idea that they created the stories from scratch to fulfil Old Testament prophecy implausible.

Above all, as Ben Witherington argues:

> ...both narratives collapse without the assumption of a virginal conception. Furthermore, the arguments of both Evangelists about the theological significance of Jesus' origins are predicated on the assumption by both writers of the virginal conception. Otherwise there would be no need for the sort of apologetics and adjustment of genealogies that we find in these narratives.[180]

and:

> It is difficult if not impossible to explain why Christians would create so many problems for themselves and invite the charge of Jesus' illegitimate birth by promulgating such an idea if it had no historical basis.[181]

If we accept that Christ's birth did take place in the way described in the gospels and which the Church has believed down the centuries, we are still left with the issue of the theological significance of His being born in this way. A way into this issue is provided by the relevant section of *Nowell's Catechism* which gives us a Tudor perspective on the matter.

> *M.* But why was he conceived of the Holy Ghost, and born of the Virgin Mary, rather than begotten after the usual and natural manner?

> *S.* It behoved that he that should and could satisfy for sins, and entirely restore wicked and damned persons, should not himself

---

[180] B Witherington III 'Birth of Jesus' in J B Green, S McKnight & I H Marshall *Dictionary of Jesus and the Gospels* Downers Grove and Leicester: IVP 1992
[181] Ibid p.70. The most thorough and comprehensive defence of the historicity of the virgin birth remains J G Machen *The Virgin Birth of Christ* Cambridge: James Clarke 1958.

be defiled or blemished with any stain or spot of sin, but be
endued with singular and perfect uprightness and innocency.
Therefore when the seed of man was wholly corrupt and defiled,
it behoved that in conception of the Son of God, there should be
the marvelous and secret working of the Holy Ghost, whereby he
might be fashioned in the womb of the most chaste and pure
Virgin, and of her substance that he should not be defiled with the
common stain and infection of mankind. Christ, therefore, that
most pure Lamb, was begotten and born by the Holy Ghost and
the conception of the Virgin without sin, that he might cleanse,
wash, and put away our spots, who, as we were first conceived
and born in sin and uncleanness, so do still from thenceforth
continue in unclean life.[182]

That Christ needed to be holy in order to save is indisputable (see 2 Cor
5:21, Heb 7:26-28, 1 Pet 1:19, 2:22). What is also indisputable is that His
holiness flowed from the activity of the Holy Spirit in the womb of the
Virgin Mary. Luke 1:35 is specific about this point:

> And the angel said to her, 'The Holy Spirit will come upon you,
> and the power of the Most High will overshadow you; therefore
> the child to be born will be called holy, the Son of God.

In St. Matthew's account, similarly, we are told in Mt 1:18 and 1:20 that it
is through the Holy Spirit that Mary bears a son who will 'save His people
from their sins' and whose name will be 'God with us'.

As Karl Barth argues, the teaching that it is work of the Holy Spirit
that leads to the birth of the Son of God has a twofold significance.

First, it makes it clear that what we are dealing with is the direct
activity of God, and not some bizarre natural phenomenon:

> ...when we regard the Holy Spirit by whom Jesus Christ is
> conceived as in the strict sense God Himself, God the Lord, we
> forestall and eliminate any attempt to come to the assistance of
> the saying about the Virgin birth of Christ with any speculation
> from physics or with any more or less genuine scientific
> information of a biological sort. In other words, if we are clear

---

[182] Corrie (ed) op.cit p.??

that with the Holy Spirit God himself is declared to be the author of the sign of the Virgin birth, then we know that in acknowledging the reality of this sign we have a priori renounced all understanding of it as a natural possibility, even when we are tempted to do so by a consideration so inviting as that of natural parthenogenesis.[183]

Secondly, it makes it clear that what takes place in the case of the birth of Christ is a prototype of what happens to Christians subsequently. In the birth of Christ human nature is made open to God, and therefore participates in God's holiness, through the work of the Holy Spirit, and this is what happens to Christians as well. In their case too, it is the work of the Spirit that makes them sons and daughters of God sharing in God's holiness.

As Barth puts it:

> Through the Holy Spirit and only through the Holy Spirit can man be there for God, be free for God's work on him, believe, be a recipient of His revelation, the object of the divine reconciliation. In the Holy Spirit and only in the Holy Spirit has man the evidence and guarantee that he really participates in God's revealing and reconciling action. Through the Holy Spirit and only through the Holy Spirit does God make His claim on us effective, to be our one Lord, our one Teacher, our one Leader...

> It is this freedom of the Holy Spirit and in the Holy Spirit that is already involved in the incarnation of the Word of God, in the assumption of human nature by the Son of God, in which we have to recognise the real ground of the freedom of the children of God, the real ground of all conception of revelation, all lordship of grace over man, the real ground of the Church. The very possibility of human nature's being adopted into unity with the Son of God is the Holy Ghost. Here, then, at this fontal point in revelation, the Word of God is not without the Spirit of God. And here already there is the togetherness of Spirit and Word. Through the Spirit it becomes really possible for the creature, for

---

[183] K Barth *Church Dogmatics* I/2 Edinburgh: T&T Clark 2004 pp.197-198

man, to be there and to be free for God. Through the Spirit flesh, human nature, is assumed into unity with the Son of God. Through the Spirit this Man can be God's Son and at the same time the Second Adam and as such 'the firstborn among many brethren' (Rom 8:29), the prototype of all who are set free for His sake and through faith in Him. As in Him human nature is made the bearer of revelation, so in us it is made the recipient of it, not by its own power, but by the power conferred on it by the Spirit, who according to 2 Cor 3:17 is Himself the Lord. [184]

The truth of what Barth says here is confirmed by the clear parallel between what is said about the birth of Christ in the gospels of Matthew and Luke and what we are told in Jn 1:13 about how Christians become children of God: 'not of blood, nor of the will of the flesh nor of the will of man, but of God' – God here meaning specifically the Holy Spirit as Jn 3:1-15 makes clear.

What also needs to be noted is that if it is true that it is the work of the Holy Spirit, and only the work of the Holy Spirit, that makes human nature open to God, then we have to question Nowell's statement that Christ was born: '....in the womb of the most chaste and pure Virgin, and of her substance *that he* should not be defiled with the common stain and infection of mankind' (italics added)

What the words in italics seem to imply are that it was not simply because of the work of the Holy Spirit, but because He took His human nature from 'the most pure and chaste Virgin' that Christ was free from sin. This suggestion is problematic not only because it adds an idea that is not found in Lk 1:35, Mt 1:18 and 20, or anywhere else in Scripture, but also because it means that the human race, in the person of the Virgin Mary, was able to contribute to its own salvation, a notion that is contrary to the biblical teaching that salvation is the work of God from beginning to end.

If we look at the biblical account of the birth of Christ and consider the place of Mary's virginity within it what we find, by contrast, is that her virginity has no positive significance of its own. It is, purely and simply, the human not working that as such highlights the working of God. Like the biblical accounts of births from barren mothers such as those of Isaac (Gen 18:9-15, 21:1-7), Samson (Judg 13:1-20) and Samuel

---

[184] Ibid p.198-199

(1 Sam 1:1-2:11) there is a contrast between human inability and divine ability that mirrors the bigger biblical picture of the way in which God relates to human kind.

Once again this point is picked up by Barth who notes that from the biblical perspective the absence of human sexual activity in connection with the birth of Christ is not because heterosexual sexual activity is considered sinful per se, but because it is a sign of the fact that human striving and achieving comes under the judgement of God and is set aside in favour of the work of God.

He writes that human virginity too comes under God's judgement, in the sense that it is not Mary's virginity but the work of the Spirit that brings about the birth of Christ, but that by grace it also becomes a sign of the divine activity:

> Human virginity, far from being able to construct for itself a point of connexion for divine grace, lies under its judgement. Yet it becomes, not by its nature, not of itself, but by divine grace, the sign of the judgement passed upon man, and to that extent the sign of divine grace. For if it is only the *virgo* who can be the mother of the Lord, if God's grace considers her alone and is prepared to use her for His work upon man, that means that as such willing, achieving, creative sovereign man is not considered, and is not to be used for this work. Of course, man is involved, but not as God's fellow-worker, not in his independence, not with control over what is to happen, but only –and even that because God has presented him with Himself – in his readiness for God. So thoroughly does God judge sin in the flesh by being gracious to man. So much does God insist that He alone is Lord by espousing the cause of man. This is the mystery of grace to which the *natus ex virgine* points. The sinful life of sex is excluded as the source of the human existence of Jesus Christ, not because of the nature of sexual life nor because of its sinfulness, but because every natural generation is the work of willing, achieving, creative, sovereign man. No event of natural generation will be a sign of the mystery indicated here.[185]

---

[185] Ibid p.192

...so that two whole and perfect natures, that is to say, the Godhead and manhood, were joined together in one person, never to be divided, whereof is one Christ, very God and very man

The two opening words of this section of the article 'so that' make it clear that what is affirmed in it follows on from what has gone before. Because at the incarnation the eternal Son of God, the second person of the Trinity, took human nature upon himself what resulted was the fact that in Christ there was one person with two natures, one human and one divine.

This idea that Christ is one person with two natures was taken from the teaching of the Council of Chalcedon in 451. The *Chalcedonian Definition* produced by that council stated that:

> Following the holy Fathers we teach with one voice that the Son [of God] and our Lord Jesus Christ is to be confessed as one and the same [Person], that he is perfect in Godhead and perfect in manhood, very God and very man, of a reasonable soul and [human] body consisting, consubstantial with the Father, as touching his Godhead, and consubstantial with us as touching his manhood; made in all things like unto us, sin only excepted; consubstantial with the Father as touching his Godhead, and consubstantial with us as touching his manhood; made in all things like unto us, sin only excepted; begotten of his Father before the worlds according to his godhead; but in these last days for us men and for our salvation born [into the world] of the Virgin Mary, the mother of God according to his manhood. This one and the same Jesus Christ, the only-begotten Son [of God] must be confessed to be in two natures, unconfusedly, immutably, indivisibly, inseparably [united], and that without the distinction of natures being taken away by such union, but rather the peculiar property of each nature being preserved and being united in one Person and one subsistence, not separated or divided into two persons, but one and the same Son and only-begotten, God the Word, our Lord Jesus Christ, as the Prophets of old time have spoken concerning him, and as the Lord Jesus

Christ hath taught us, and as the Creed of the Fathers hath delivered two us.[186]

The language used by this definition is complex and daunting for many readers today, but if it is studied carefully it can be seen that it makes three basic affirmations which ruled out a number of heresies which had troubled the Early Church.

• Over against the Arian heresy that claimed Christ was a superior angel it affirms that Christ is truly God and therefore possesses a divine nature.

• Over against the Docetic heresy which claimed that Christ only appeared to be human, the Apollinarian heresy which denied that he had a rational human soul, and the Eutychian heresy which claimed that his humanity was swallowed up by His deity, it affirms that Christ is truly human and therefore possesses a human nature.

• Over against the Nestorian heresy which claimed that Christ was a union of two persons, one human and one divine, it affirms that that there is one person, one self, who possesses the two natures and operates through both of them.

These are also the three basic points that are made in this section of Article II. It tells us that Christ is one person with two whole and perfect natures, one human and one divine, and that therefore he is truly God and truly human ('verus Deus et verus homo').

If we turn to the New Testament we find clear evidence to support each of these points.

First, it is clear that Christ is truly God. As has already been noted in connection both with this article and with Article I, the Son, as the second Person of the Trinity, eternally begotten of the Father, possesses the same divine substance or nature as the Father and the Holy Spirit.

Secondly, it is equally clear that Christ is truly human. In the words of Beveridge:

---

[186] Text in *Nicene and Post Nicene Fathers* vol XIV Edinburgh & Grand Rapids: T&T Clark/Eerdmans 1997 pp.264-265.

...this Son of God became very man, so that he was not more like to God, yea, very God in his Divine, than he was like to man, yea very man in his human nature; and as he was begotten of the same substance with God the Father from eternity, so was he conceived of the same substance with us men in time; and therefore is there nothing that belongs to us as men, but what he took upon himself. Have we a body? So had he, Heb x.5.10. Have we flesh and blood? so had he, Heb ii.14. Have we hands and feet? so had he, Luke xxiv.39. Have we a soul? so had he, Matt xxvi.38. Are we hungered? so was he, Matt iv.2: and weary? so was he, John iv.6: and heavy and sorrowful? so was he, Mark xiv.33. Do we grow in stature and knowledge? so did he, Luke ii.52. Do we die? so did he, he gave up the ghost too, John xix.30. Thus was he in all things tempted like us, but only in sin, Heb ii.7, iv.15 so well may he be called the man Christ Jesus, 1 Tim ii.5. 1 Cor xv.21 and Christ Jesus the son of man, Matt xxvi.2.[187]

Thirdly, it is clear that Christ was one person, in the sense of one self. Throughout the New Testament there is one person described or referred to, never two, and if we ask who that person was, the answer is, as we have already indicated, that it was the eternal Word or Son of God who took human nature upon Himself at the incarnation (Jn 1:14). It was the one who was rich with the glory of heaven who became poor for our sake (2 Cor 8:9). It was the one who 'descended' from heaven to earth at the incarnation who ascended 'far above all the heavens' (Eph 4:9-10). It was the one who was eternally 'in the form of God' who 'emptied himself', took upon himself 'the form of a servant' and was 'born in the likeness of men' (Phil 2:7). It was the one who 'reflects the glory of God and bears the very stamp of his nature, upholding the universe by his word of power' who partook of our nature for the sake of our salvation (Heb 1:3 and 2:14-18). In short, according to the witness of the New Testament, it was the eternal Son, the second Person of the Trinity who was the self who possessed the two natures of Christ.

---

[187] Beveridge op.cit. p. 84. Many modern New Testament scholars have argued that the term Son of Man refers either to the representative of the Saints of the Most High in Dan 7:14 or is a form of self reference equivalent to 'I'. However, in both senses the term refers to one who is a human being and so Beveridge's basic point stands.

To use the technical theological terminology this means that the human nature was *anhypostatic* - that is to say, the human nature is not possessed by a human person. Instead the human nature was *enhypostatic* – that is to say, it was the human nature that was possessed by God the Son. [188] This is the teaching that underlies the reference to the 'one person' of Christ in Article II.

Furthermore, as Richard Hooker explains, because Christ was one person or subject possessed of both a divine and a human nature it follows that we can talk about Him in terms that refer to Him as both God and Man:

> A kind of mutual commutation there is whereby those concrete names, God and Man, when we speak of Christ, do take interchangeably one another's room, so that for truth of speech it skilleth not whether we say that the Son of God hath created the world, and the Son of Man by his death hath saved it, or else the Son of Man did create, and the Son of God die to save the world. Howbeit, as oft as we attribute to God what the manhood of Christ claimeth, or to man what his Deity hath right unto, we understand by the name of God and the name of man neither the one nor the other nature, but the whole person of Christ in whom both natures are.[189]

It is because it is right to use language in this way that the Church has felt able to affirm down the centuries that it was God who suffered and died for our salvation. Thus the Second Council of Constantinople in 553 declared: 'our Lord Jesus Christ who was crucified in the flesh is true God and the Lord of Glory and one of the Holy Trinity'[190] and the Orthodox Liturgy of St. John Chrysostom proclaims:

> O only-begotten Son and Word of God, immortal being, you who deigned for our salvation to become incarnate of the holy Mother of God and ever-virgin Mary, you who without change became

---

[188] See for example Capitula V of the Second Council of Constantinople of 553 and St. John of Damascus *The Orthodox Faith* Bk III: 7-9.
[189] R Hooker *The Laws of Ecclesiastical Polity* Bk V:LIII.4 in J Keble (ed) *The Works of Richard Hooker* Vol I Oxford: Clarendon Press 1841 p.607
[190] Second Council of Constantinople Capitula IX in *Nicene and Post Nicene Fathers* vol XIV p. 314.

man and were crucified, O Christ our God, you who by your death have crushed death, you who are one of the Holy Trinity, glorified with the Father and the Holy Spirit, save us.[191]

Strictly speaking it was the human nature of Christ that was crucified, but because that nature was the human nature of God the Son, and because in and through that nature He experienced suffering and death, we can rightly say that on the cross it was God who suffered and died.

In recent centuries there have, however, been three objections put forward to this traditional Christian understanding of Christ.

The first objection is that this traditional account is based on an artificial division between Christ's humanity and divinity whereby some things, such as Christ's weariness, suffering and tears, are ascribed to his humanity, while other things, such as His working miracles and his supernatural knowledge, are to be ascribed to His divine nature. As Hanson and Hanson comment:

> This strikes many modern theologians as unsatisfactory: surely, if Jesus was both God and man, both the divinity and the humanity ought to be expressed in everything he did. Otherwise we seem to have a purely artificial arrangement, quite inconsistent with a real, historical figure.

The response to this is that it is necessary to distinguish between the two natures because there are certain things that can be said of Christ's humanity that cannot be said of his divinity and vice versa. Thus to be hungry is not something that can be predicated of the divine nature because God is in His divine nature incorporeal spirit and therefore Christ's hunger must be attributed to his humanity. Conversely, human nature does not have the power to control the weather so the calming of the storm must be attributed to Christ's divinity. If we fail to make this kind of distinction we end up with absurdities like saying that the divine nature came into existence as a baby or that the human nature was everywhere present throughout time and space.

---

[191] *Liturgy of St. John Chrysostom* Troparion O monogenes Text in *Catechism of the Catholic Church* London: Geoffrey Chapman 1994 p.105

Furthermore, even while making this kind of necessary distinction we can still maintain that the divinity and humanity were expressed in everything Christ did. Thus we can say that the hunger that Christ felt was the hunger felt in His human nature by God and that when Christ touched people and healed them it was God acting through His human nature that healed them. What we seen in the Gospels is what John Webster calls a 'concurrence', a coming together, of the distinct two natures in the one historical person of Christ.[192]

The second objection is that if the human nature possessed by Christ was not attached to a human person then Christ was not truly human. To quote Hanson and Hanson:

> What we encounter in Jesus Christ, according to the orthodox view, is not *a* man, but a non personal humanity, a humanity that is expressed, not in a human person, but in the divine mode of being, God the Word. It is moreover true that orthodox doctrine has nearly always taught that what God the Word assumed at the incarnation was not personal humanity, but impersonal humanity. Strictly speaking, orthodox doctrine is not that God became *a* man, but that God became man. The critics would object that impersonal humanity is a contradiction in terms. The essence of humanity is to be personal. If God in Jesus Christ assumed impersonal humanity, the incarnation was not a manifestation of God in real humanity.[193]

The answer to this objection is, quite simply, that the critics have not understood orthodox teaching properly. It has never been taught that in Christ there was an impersonal humanity. Rather it has been held that from the moment of conception the humanity of Christ was personal in that it was the humanity of the second Person of the Trinity.

Moreover, As H M Relton argues, the fact that the person involved was God the Son does not make Christ's humanity any less human. God is not less personal than we are, but more so, and as those made in God's image our personhood is a reflection of the divine archetype. It follows, says Relton, that the incarnation of the Son:

---

[192] J Webster *Word and Church* Edinburgh: T&T Clark 2001 p.148
[193] Hanson & Hanson op.cit p.90. Italics in the original

... brought to the human nature he assumed, not an alien element such as would render a truly human life for the God-man an impossibility, but just that which alone could make the life of Christ in every stage of its growth and development a truly and perfectly human life. The Divine Logos was capable of being the Ego, not only of His Divine but also of His Human Nature; because His Personality in virtue of its Divinity already embraced all that is most distinctive of a truly human personality. The human and the Divine are not two contradictory, but two complementary terms, and the less is contained in the greater. His Divine self-consciousness was, in virtue of its Divinity, a truly human self-consciousness. His ego was Divine – it was also human; therefore it could be the subject of both natures.[194]

The third objection is that to believe that the person involved in the incarnation was God the Son makes it impossible to account for elements of the gospel accounts such as Christ's growth in wisdom and knowledge (Lk 3:52) or his ignorance of the date of the last day (Mk 13:32) or his inability to do miracles (Mk 6:5-6). Surely as God He would be subject to no such limitations?

The classic answer to this objection has been to think in terms of voluntary self limitation. P T Forsyth declares, for example that:

The omniscience of God does not mean that it is incapable of limitation, but rather that, with more power than finitude has, it is also more capable of limitation. Only it is self-limitation: He limits Himself in the freedom of holiness for the purposes of His own end of infinite love. [195]

The issue here is analogous to that of God's ability to suffer that we considered in connection with Article I. Just as God cannot be made to suffer, but may choose to undergo suffering, so likewise God cannot lack either knowledge or power, but may choose not to exercise them. Thus we can say that God the Son chose only to know those things and to be able to do those things that were compatible with His living a truly

---

[194] H M Relton *A Study in Christology* London: SPCK 1934 p.227
[195] P T Forsyth *The Person and Place of Jesus Christ* cited in Wilson and Templeton op.cit p.31. See also the discussion of Christ's knowledge in *Catechism of the Catholic Church* p.104.

human life and fulfilling the mission given to Him by the Father. As Gibson argues, in the Gospels we find passages indicating that Christ was able to know things and do things beyond the capacity of ordinary human beings:

> But there is another side as well to the portrait drawn in the Gospels, and from many passages we can see that, although for all purposes of His divine mission and work our Lord's manhood was supernaturally enlightened and endowed with divine powers, yet in ordinary matters, outside the sphere of the special work He had come to do, He accepted the limitations common to men in general, and natural to His position as born in a particular spot, at a particular time in the world's history. Though he miraculously fed the five thousand in the wilderness, yet when He was Himself an hungered, He was content to wait which his disciples went into the city to buy food to supply His needs (S. John iv.8). In reference to His human intellect, it is said that He 'increased in wisdom' (S. Luke iii.52). Of the day and hour of the last judgement He Himself tells us that He did not know. 'Of that day and hour knoweth no one, not even the angels in heaven, *neither the Son*, but the Father' (S. Mark xiii.32). He raised the dead to life, but when His hour was come, Himself submitted to the power of death. Both classes of passages to which attention has been drawn refer to one and the same Person and that Person the Eternal Son of God. That which explains them is the fact that in taking upon Him our nature He voluntarily limited Himself. In S. Paul's phrase...He 'emptied Himself' – not of His Godhead, for that were impossible, but of the exercise of His divine prerogatives.[196]

...who truly suffered, was crucified, dead, and buried, to reconcile His Father to us, and to be a sacrifice, not only for original guilt, but also for all actual sins of men.

Having explained who Christ is, the article concludes by describing how He suffered and died for our salvation. As we have noted, this conclusion to the article had the specific function in the sixteenth century context of

---

[196] Gibson op.cit p.143

helping to emphasise the once for all nature of the incarnation, but, as Beveridge explains, it also completes the sequence of thought in the article by describing the purpose and outcome of the incarnation:

> That the Second Person in the sacred Trinity was begotten from the First in eternity, and conceived by the Third in time, and that in the womb of a virgin; and so became both perfectly God and perfectly man, perfectly united together in the same Person, we have seen in the foregoing part of this article. And in this we are to dive into the reason of this so great a mystery, why did the Son of God thus become the Son of man? Why did he thus take the human nature into his Divine Person? When he came from heaven to earth, what did he before he went again from earth to heaven? How did he deport himself towards his fellow-creatures, and how did they carry themselves towards him? Did they not highly honour and extol him, who had so honoured and extolled them as to assume their humanity into his Divinity? No: he was so far from being honoured amongst them, that he truly *suffered, was crucified, dead and buried*. But it is strange so great a Deity should be loaded with so much ignominy. Was it for his own sake he suffered all this? No: it was to reconcile God to our souls, and to be a propitiation for our sins.[197]

The fact that the article follows the Apostles and Nicene creeds by moving straight from Christ's birth to His death raises the question as to why all the other parts of His life on earth as recorded in the Gospels are overlooked. We have no direct evidence as to why Cranmer and Parker followed the creeds in this regard, but what seems to plausible explanation is provided by Nowell in his *Catechism*:

> *M.* But why doth the Creed omit the story of his life, and passeth straight from his birth to his death?

---

[197] Beveridge op cit p.98 Italics in the original.

S. Because in the Creed are rehearsed only the chief points of our redemption, and such things as so properly belong to it that they contain as it were the substance thereof. [198]

In other words, it is Christ's incarnation and death that are decisive for our salvation and it is therefore on these that the creeds and the article focus. Whereas much modern theology in the Liberal Protestant tradition has seen the importance of Christ in terms of His being a teacher or a moral example, and whereas much recent Anglican thought has seen His importance in terms of the union between God and humanity achieved by the incarnation, for the older Christian tradition represented by the article what was really important about Christ was that He took our nature upon Him in order to die for our salvation.

The article begins its account of the death of Christ by emphasising the reality of Christ's sufferings, insisting that Christ 'truly suffered, was crucified, died and was buried.' As the quotation from the *Reformatio Legum Ecclesiasticarum* at the beginning of the commentary on this article makes clear, this emphasis, like the earlier emphasis on the reality of the two natures of the incarnate Christ, is intended to refute those who taught that Christ did not assume a truly human body, but had a heavenly body that was incapable of suffering and death.

Having emphasised the reality of the death of Christ in this way, the article goes on to explain the purpose of His dying. The important point to notice at the outset about what it says in this regard is that the two final clauses of the article are parallel rather than incremental. That is to say, they are not saying that Christ died to reconcile the Father to us and in addition was a sacrifice for sin. Rather, what it is saying is that Christ's sacrifice for sin was the means by which our reconciliation to the Father took place.

This point is important because it defines the terms within which the article uses the term sacrifice. The term sacrifice is a word that can carry a number of different meanings. For example, sacrifice can mean the offering of the self to God (Rom 12:1) or it can be a means of giving thanks to God (Ps 66:13-15), but in the context of the article what sacrifice means is the achievement of reconciliation with God in the face of the alienation caused by sin.

---

[198] Corrie (ed) op.cit p??

The statement in the article that Christ died 'to reconcile His Father to us' has often been criticised on the grounds that it misrepresents the way that the language of reconciliation is used in the New Testament. In the words of Gibson: '...the Bible speaks of the need for men to be reconciled to God, but says nothing of God being reconciled to man.'[199]

This can be seen if we look at the four New Testament passages in which the word 'reconcile' occurs in connection with the death of Christ.

> Rom 5:10-11 For if while we were enemies we were reconciled to God by the death of his Son, much more, now that we are reconciled, shall we be saved by his life. Not only so, but we also rejoice in God through our Lord Jesus Christ, through whom we have now received our reconciliation.

> 2 Cor 5:18-20: All this is from God, who through Christ reconciled us to himself and gave us the ministry of reconciliation; that is, in Christ God was reconciling the world to himself, not counting their trespasses against them, and entrusting to us the message of reconciliation. So we are ambassadors for Christ, God making his appeal through us. We beseech you on behalf of Christ, be reconciled to God.

> Eph 2:16 ...and might reconcile us both to God in one body through the cross, thereby bringing hostility to an end.

> Col 1:19-20 For in him all the fullness of God was pleased to dwell, and through him to reconcile to himself all things, whether on earth or in heaven, making peace by the blood of his cross.

At first sight the evidence of these four passages seem to tell decisively against the language used by Article II. However, if we think further about the matter the picture changes. The key issue to consider is what the reconciliation achieved by Christ involved. Was it the removal simply of our enmity towards God or also of His enmity towards us?

The 1571 *Homily of Repentance* makes it clear how the Tudor Church of England regarded the matter.

---

[199] Gibson op.cit p.145

> We have a need of a Mediator for to bring and reconcile us unto Him, who for our sins is angry with us. The same is Jesus Christ; who; being true and natural God, equal and of one substance with the Father; did at the time appointed take upon Him our frail nature, in the blessed Virgin's womb, and that of her undefiled substance; so that he might be a Mediator betwixt God and us, and pacify His wrath.[200]

The point that is being made in this quotation is that human beings were, as Romans 5 says, God's enemies in the sense that we were the objects of God's wrath and Christ's death was needed to pacify that wrath. In saying this what the homily is doing is simply following through the logic of St. Paul's teaching in Rom 1:18-3:26. According to this teaching (which is a summary of the teaching of the Old Testament and is itself summarised in Eph 2:1-3), all human beings without exception are sinners and as a result are subject to the wrath of God both now and at the final judgement. As we shall see, the way that they are saved from this situation is by the death of Christ. The wrath of God against us is removed by the death of Christ and it is for this reason that, as St. Paul goes on to say: 'we have peace with God through our Lord Jesus Christ.' (Rom 5:1).

It is this big picture that St. Paul has in mind when he says that in Christ God has reconciled us to Himself and this is also what the Tudor theologians had in mind when they said that Christ died to reconcile His Father to us. Understood in this way the language of Article II can be said to be justified even if it does not correspond directly with the way in which the New Testament uses the word 'reconcile.'

When thinking about this biblical picture it is important to note a point of which the Tudor theologians were well aware, which is that the death of Christ was not the cause of God's love for us. Rather Christ died to deal with the wrath of God against our sin because God loved us in spite of our sinfulness. The point is well made by St. Augustine:

> Our being reconciled by the death of Christ must not be understood as if the Son reconciled us, in order that the Father, then hating, might begin to love us, but that we were reconciled to him already, loving, though at enmity with us because of sin. To

---

[200] Text in Tyrell Green op.cit p.33

the truth of both propositions we have the attestation of the Apostle, 'God commendeth his love towards us, in that while we were yet sinners Christ died for us' (Rom 5:8). Therefore he had this love for us even when, exercising enmity towards him, we were the workers of iniquity. Accordingly, in a manner wondrous and divine, loved us even when he hated us. For he hated us when we were such as he had not made us, and yet because our iniquity had not destroyed his work in every respect, he knew in regard to each one of us, to hate what we had made, and to love what he had made.[201]

The language that the article uses about 'original guilt' and 'all the actual sins of men' also fits into this big biblical picture. 'Original guilt' here means the same as 'original sin' in Article IX. What is being described is the situation described in Rom 1-3 in which human rebellion against God (which in Romans 5:12-21 St. Paul traces back to the sin of Adam) leads to a fallen human nature which is in turn manifested in the particular personal sins ('the actual sins') that we all commit.

As Gibson notes, the fact that both here and in the parallel language of Article XXXI the death of Christ is said to be a sacrifice for both original and actual sin:

> ...is accounted for by the fact that teachers were found within the Roman communion who, following the guidance of some among the schoolmen, actually taught that, though Christ suffered on the cross for original sin, the sacrifice of the altar was daily offered for original sin.[202]

The *Augsburg Confession* specifically mentions this teaching, referring to the: '...abominable error...according to which it was taught that our Lord Christ had by his death made satisfaction only for original sin, and had instituted the Mass as a sacrifice for other sins.'[203]

In opposition to this error the article insists that Christ's death was a sacrifice that was sufficient to deal with *all* sin. It is also important to note with Gibson that this stress on the fact that Christ's death dealt with all

---

[201] Augustine of Hippo *Tract in John* 110

[202] Gibson op.cit p.149

[203] *Augsburg Confession* XXIV text in J H Leith Creeds of the Churches rev ed Oxford: Blackwell 1973 p.84

sin implies that the atonement was universal in extent, a point that was appreciated by those of a Calvinist persuasion who omitted the word 'all' from copies of the Articles and sought to officially delete in the revision instituted by Parliament in 1643.[204]

In using the language of sacrifice to describe the death of Christ the article faithfully reflects the witness of a number of biblical passages such as Jn 1:29, Rom 3:25, 1 Cor 5:7, Eph 5:2, Heb 9:26 and 1 Pet 1:19 which use sacrificial language to express the meaning of the cross. I Cor 5:7, for example, declares: 'Christ our paschal lamb has been sacrificed and Heb 9:26 tells us that Christ: '...has appeared once for all at the end of the age to put away sin by the sacrifice of himself.' This fidelity to the biblical witness means that this section of the article provides a good model for subsequent theologians writing about the cross to follow. As *The Mystery of Salvation* insists: '...if we are to think in line with the Scriptures about the death of Christ, sacrifice must remain a normative model.'[205]

What the article does not do, however, is explain how the language of sacrifice enables us to make sense of the cross. As we have said, the article states that the sacrificial death of Christ enables us to be reconciled to God, but it does not tell us how it made this reconciliation possible.

The same is also true of other doctrinal and liturgical material from the Church of England in the sixteenth century. For example, Archbishop Cranmer's homily *Of the Salvation of Mankind* tells us that Christ died: '...to make a sacrifice and satisfaction, or (as it may be called) amends to his Father for our sins, to assuage his wrath and indignation conceived against us for the same.'[206] What it does not tell us is either how Christ's death assuaged God's wrath and indignation by making amends for our sins or how the use of sacrificial language enables us to make sense of how it did so.

We are therefore left with the question of how are to understand the biblical language about sacrifice and its application to the death of Christ in the New Testament. Here Barth is once again helpful.

---

[204] Gibson op.cit pp.149-150
[205] *The Mystery of Salvation* p.115
[206] T Cranmer *Of the Salvation of Mankind* in ibid p.240

In his study of the biblical material about sacrifice in *Church Dogmatics* IV.1 Barth notes that at the heart of the Old Testament sacrificial system lay the idea of dealing with the discord between God and His people:

> The member of the covenant people still belongs to Yahweh even though he has a part in the rebellion and transgression in which this people is caught up. He cannot forget Him. He cannot escape his guilt and responsibility in relation to Him, his commitment to Him. He can and must make an offering (this is where the mediatorial ministry of the priest is so important). Offerings are substituted for what he really ought to render to God, but never does and never will. They are gifts from the sphere of his most cherished possessions which represent or express his will to obey, which symbolise the life which has not in fact been offered to God. He can bring these gifts. He ought to do so. He acknowledges Yahweh and the fact that he belongs to Him by bringing them. He recognises his guilt and obligation.[207]

In this way, says Barth, the Old Testament sacrifices are: 'a provisional and relative fulfilment of the will and commandment of God.'[208] The problem with the Old Testament sacrificial system, however, was not only that people could misuse it in the way criticised by the prophets and the psalmists (see Isa 1:10-11, Jer 7:21-23, Amos 5:21-24, Ps 40:6), but that even at its best it could not deal with sin:

> The real problem of sacrifice is not the imminent misuse to which like any cult it can be put, but the fact that in the face of the sin of man, while it can mean an impressive summons to repent and convert, a cheerful encouragement to do the best we can, and even a serious encouragement, and while its fulfilment does call us to remember the presence and will and commandment of the holy and merciful God, it does not in any way alter either sin itself or the situation of conflict and contradiction brought about by sin.[209]

---

[207] K Barth *Church Dogmatics IV.1* Edinburgh: T&T Clark 2004 p.278
[208] Ibid p.278
[209] Ibid p. 278

In the coming of Christ, however, that which is provisional is done away with:

> He now wills and demands the fulfilment of the covenant, the new man who not only knows and recognises and actively gives it to be understood, but lives wholly and utterly by the fact that he belongs to God, that He is His man. He wills and demands not merely the bridging and lessening of the conflict between Himself and us, but its removal, not only light in darkness, but as on the first day of creation the dispersal of darkness by light. He wills and demands the sacrifice of the old man (who can never be this man, who can only die). He wills and demands the setting aside of this man, his giving up to death, which is not fulfilled merely by giving up this or that, even the best he has. God wills and demands the man himself, to make an end of him, so that the new man may have air and space for a new life. He wills and demands that he should go through death to life. He wills and demands that as the man of sin he should abandon his life, that his blood as this man should finally be shed and fall to the ground and be lost, that as this man he should go up in flames and smoke. This is the meaning and end of sacrifice. And that is the judgement that is not fulfilled in any other sacrifices. It is fulfilled in the sacrifice of Jesus Christ, in the shedding of His 'precious blood' (1 Peter 1:19). It has the power of a real offering and taking away of the sinful man, the power to bring about his end and death as such, and therefore to create a new situation in which God no longer has to do with this man, in which His own faithfulness will meet a faithful people and a faithful man. In the sacrifice of Jesus Christ the will of God is fulfilled in this turning, in this radical conversion of man to himself which posits an end and therefore a new beginning.[210]

According to Barth, the reason that this sacrifice fulfilled the will of God in the way that previous sacrifices did not is because in the death of Christ:

---

[210] Ibid p.280

...it is God Himself who not only demands but makes the offering. He makes it in that He the Lord willed to become a servant, in that His Son willed to go into the far country, to become one with us and to take our place as sinners, to die for us the death of the old man which was necessary for the doing of the will of God, to shed our wicked blood in His own precious blood, to kill our sin in His own death. In Israel's sacrifices in obedience to the command of God this could only be intended and willed and attested and represented – because they were made within and under the presupposition of a constant rebellion against God, and in the sign of the constant provocation of His wrath. But now it has actually taken place – taken place because and to the extent that in Jesus Christ God himself has acted in place of the human race, Himself making the real sacrifice which radically alters the situation between himself and man. In Him God not only demands but He gives what He demands. In him He does that which has to take place to set aside sin and to remove the conflict. He shows himself to be pure and holy and sinless by not refusing in Him to become the greatest of all sinners, achieving the penitence and conversion which is demanded of sinners, undertaking the bitter reality of being the accused and condemned and judged and executed man of sin, in order that when He Himself has been this man no other man can or need be, in order that in place of this man another man who is pleasing to God, the man of obedience, may have space and air and be able to live.[211]

There are four great strengths to Barth's approach.

Firstly, what he says helps us to make sense of those New Testament texts that describe Christ's death as a sacrifice, particularly Heb 9:1-10:18 with its stress on the replacement of the Old Testament sacrifices by the one perfect sacrifice of Christ, in the light of the overall biblical account of the relationship between God and humanity.

Secondly, it makes clear why it was necessary for Christ to be both truly God and truly human. In Christ God offers on behalf of the human race, as its representative and substitute, the one perfect sacrifice that human

---

[211] Ibid pp.280-281

beings should offer to God, but which in and of themselves they cannot offer.

Thirdly, it makes clear why, as Article II says, the death of Christ reconciled the Father to us, why His wrath was assuaged. As St. Augustine argues, God's wrath is His hatred of that in us which we have made, that which distorts and destroys the true humanity intended by God at creation. Through Christ's sacrificial death, that which we have made is done away with once and for all. The death of Christ was the death of our old sinful humanity and so that which caused God's wrath no longer exists. 'If any one is in Christ, he is a new creation, the old has passed away, behold the new has come' (2 Cor 5:17). 'For our sake he made him to be sin who knew no sin, so that in him we might become the righteousness of God' (2 Cor 5:21).

Fourthly, it stresses that what Christ did He did for everyone. As St. Paul insists in Rom 5:12-21 and 1 Cor 15:45-50, Christ is the second Adam, the one who undoes the work of the first Adam by bringing renewal to the whole human race. The sacrifice of Christ was universal in extent. Christ died not just for a limited number of the elect, but for everyone. We shall return to this point when looking at Articles XV, XVII and XXXI.

Article III

∞

Of the going down of Christ into Hell

As Christ died for us, and was buried, so also is it to be believed that He went down into Hell.

De descensu Christi ad inferos

Quemadmodum Christus pro nobis mortuus est, et sepultus, ita est etiam credendus ad inferos descendisse.

This Article is ultimately derived from the statement in the Apostles Creed: 'He descended into hell.' The fact that there is no corresponding clause in the Nicene Creed points us to the fact that the descent into hell does not appear to have been part of the earliest creedal tradition of the Church and never became part of the creedal tradition of the Eastern Church. It is found in Western creeds from the fourth century onwards and only seems to have become a generally accepted part of the Apostles Creed from the seventh century.

However, as Gibson notes:

> Although the clause 'He descended into hell' has never formed part of the creed of the Eastern Church, and only made its way into that of the West in comparatively late times, it is remarkable how prominent a position the fact of the descent occupied in the belief of the early Christians, and how very general was the belief that it was instrumental in changing for the better the condition of the faithful who had died before the coming of Christ.[212]

---

[212] Gibson op.cit p.175

Three examples will serve to illustrate the general Patristic testimony on this matter:

First, St. Ignatius of Antioch, writing to the church in Magnesia in about 115 asks how it is possible to give Christ:

> ...no place in our lives when even the prophets of old were themselves pupils of His in spirit, and looked forward to Him as their Teacher? Indeed, that was the very reason why He, whom they were rightly awaiting, came to visit them, and raised them from the dead.[213]

Secondly, St. Athanasius, writing in the fourth century to Epictetus, Bishop of Corinth, argues that the descent of Christ to the dead shows that a distinction has to be made between the body of Christ and the Word which inhabited it:

> And this above all shows the foolishness of those who say that the Word was changed into bones and flesh. For if this had been so, there would have been no need of a tomb. For the Body itself would have gone by itself to preach to the spirits in Hades. But as it was, He Himself went to preach, while the Body Joseph wrapped in a linen cloth, and laid it away at Golgotha. And so it is shown to all that the Body was not the Word, but Body of the Word.[214]

Thirdly, St. John of Damascus declares in his *Exposition of the Orthodox Faith* in the eighth century that Christ's soul:

> ...descended in Hades, in order that, just as the Sun of Righteousness rose for those upon the earth, so likewise He might bring light to those who sit under the earth in darkness and shadow of death: in order that just as He brought the message of peace to those upon the earth, and of release to the prisoners, and of sight to the blind, and became to those who believed the

---

[213] Ignatius *Letter to the Magnesians* 9 text in M Staniforth (ed) *Early Christian Writings* Harmondsworth: Penguin 1978 p.89

[214] Athanasius *Letter LIX Ad Epictetum* in The Nicene and Post Nicene Fathers 2nd series vol IV Edinburgh and Grand Rapids: T&T Clark/Eerdmans 1998 p. 572

Author of everlasting salvation and to those who did not believe a reproach of their unbelief, so he might become the same to those in Hades: *That every knee should bow to Him, of things in heaven, and things in earth and things under the earth.* And thus after He had freed those who had been bound for ages, straightway He rose again from the dead, showing us the way of resurrection. [215]

In the *Thirteen Articles* Archbishop Cranmer followed exactly the wording of the Apostles Creed, with Article 3 simply declaring that Christ 'descended into hell'.[216] In the *Forty Two Articles* of 1553, however, this statement was considerably expanded to read:

As Christ died and was buried for us: so also it is to be believed that He went down into hell. For the body lay in the sepulchre until the resurrection: but His ghost departing from Him was with the ghosts that were in prison or in hell, and did preach to the same as the place of St. Peter doth testify.

The reference to the 'place of St. Peter' is a reference to 1 Peter 3:18-20, and 'ghost' means a disembodied soul. This expanded article follows the Patristic teaching about Christ's preaching to the dead that we have noted above.

In 1563 the expanded article was radically pruned by the bishops in Convocation to produce the Article we have today. The reason for this pruning seems to have been a desire to avoid unnecessary theological controversy.

On 20 May 1550 the Flemish reformer Martin Micronius wrote from London to Heinrich Bullinger and reported that: '...they are disputing about the descent of Christ into Hell.'[217] In 1563 Bishop William Alley of Exeter again mentioned this controversy in a paper drawn up in preparation for the meeting of Convocation:

First, for matters of Scripture, namely for this place which is written in the Epistle of S. Peter, that *Christ in Spirit went down to*

---

[215] John of Damascus *Exposition of the Orthodox Faith* Bk III:29 in *The Nicene and Post Nicene Fathers* 2nd series vol IX Edinburgh and Grand Rapids: T&T Clark/Eerdmans 1997 pp.72-73
[216] Text in Bray *Documents of the English Reformation*
[217] Robinson (ed) op.cit. vol II p.561

Hell, and preached to the souls that were in Prison. There have been in my diocese great invectives between the preachers, one against the other, and also partakers with them; some holding that the going down of Christ, His soul to Hell, was nothing else but the virtue and strength of Christ, His death, to be made manifest and known to them that were dead before. Others say that Descendit ad inferna is nothing else but that Christ did sustain upon the cross the infernal pains of hell, when He called *Pater, quare me dereliquisti*, i.e. *Father, why hast Thou forsaken me?* Finally, others preach that this article is not contained in other symbols, neither in the symbol of *Cyprian*, or rather *Rufine.* And all these sayings they ground upon Erasmus and the Germans, and especially upon the authority of Mr.*Calvin* and Mr. *Bullinger*. The contrary side bring for them the universal consent, and all the Fathers of both churches, both of the *Greeks* and the *Latins*.[218]

What is clear from Bishop Alley's paper is that the interpretation of 1 Pet 3:18-20 and the statement in the Apostles Creed based upon it had become a fault line dividing those who looked for theological guidance primarily to the Fathers and those who looked for theological guidance to the Continental Reformation. The former held that the descent into hell was a distinct event, subsequent to the cross, in which Christ proclaimed to the dead the triumph of the cross. The latter held that the descent into hell was not a distinct event, but simply a way of talking about the way in which Christ suffered the pains of hell on the cross, as manifested in the cry of dereliction.

An example of the latter approach, although dating from before the time of Bishop Alley's paper, is provided by Bishop John Hooper's 1550 *Brief and Clear confession of the Christian Faith*. In this Hooper declares:

> I believe also that while he was on the cross dying and giving up His Spirit unto God His Father, He descended into hell; that is to say, He did verily taste and feel the great distress and heaviness of death, and likewise the pains and torments of hell, that is to say, the great wrath and severe judgement of God upon Him, even as if

---

[218] J Strype *Annals* vol.1 p.348 cited in Gibson op.cit p.161

God had utterly forsaken Him, yea, as though God had been His extreme enemy; so that He was constrained with loud voice to cry, 'My God, my God why hast thou forsaken me?' This is simply my understanding of Christ, his descending into hell.[219]

At the conclusion of his paper Bishop Alley wrote to his fellow bishops:

Thus, my Right Honourable good Lords, your wisdoms may perceive what tragedies and dissensions may arise for consenting to, or dissenting from this article. Wherefore, your grave, wise, and godly learning might do well and charitably, to set some certainty concerning this doctrine; and chiefly because all dissensions, contentions, and strifes may be removed from the godly affected preachers.[220]

Although we have no direct evidence, it seems likely that it was the concern expressed about this issue by Bishop Alley that led to pruning of the article, which had been left untouched by Archbishop Parker in his preliminary revision of the *Forty Two Articles* prior to Convocation.

If we look at the article as amended by the bishops, it is clear that it is a compromise. On the one hand, the explicit link between the descent into hell and 1 Pet 3:18-20 is removed, presumably to avoid dissension about the meaning of this particular text. On the other hand, the structure of the revised article implies that the descent in hell is not simply a way of describing what took place on the cross. It describes how Christ died, and was buried and then states 'so also is it to be believed that He went down into Hell.' The implication seems to be that this was a separate event following on from Christ's death and burial and preceding His resurrection and ascension which are described in Article IV.

In order to understand more precisely the teaching of Article III as it now stands, what needs to be noted is that hell/*inferos* does not mean here the place of eternal punishment to which the damned are sent after the last judgement.

---

[219] C Nevinson (ed) *Later Writings of Bishop Hooper* Cambridge: CUP/Parker Society 1852 p.30
[220] Gibson op.cit. p.561

It is a translation of the Hebrew word *sheol* and the Greek word *haides* which are used to refer to the place of all of the dead in texts such as Ps 16:10, Ps 86:13, Isa 14:9-10, Mt 11:23 and Rev 1:18. As Bishop Wright explains, in the Old Testament itself *sheol* is, for the most part envisaged as the final destination of the dead. It is:

> ...a place of gloom and despair, a place where one can no longer enjoy life, and where the presence of YHWH himself is withdrawn. It is a wilderness, a place of dust to which creatures made of dust have returned. Those who have gone there are 'the dead'; they are 'shades', *rephaim*, and they are 'asleep'. As in Homer there is no suggestion that they are enjoying themselves; it is a dark and gloomy world. Nothing much happens there. It is not another form of real life, an alternative world where things continue as normal. [221]

Although this is the main Old Testament picture what we also find are the beginnings of a hope that God will not abandon His people to *sheol* but grant them life with him beyond death (Ps 16:9-11, 49:15, 73:24, Jb 19:25-26.) and, specifically, the belief that God will raise to a re-embodied life those who have died (Isa 25:8, 26:19, Dan 12:2).

In New Testament times there was a diversity of beliefs within Judaism about the fate of the dead, as shown by New Testament texts such as Mk 11:18-27 and Acts 23:6-10. However, a belief in the eventual resurrection of the dead by God on the last day had become increasingly prevalent and it is this belief that is presupposed by the writers of the New Testament.

This belief in resurrection mean that *sheol/haides* was no longer seen as the final resting place of the dead but as an intermediate state, a place of waiting. As Bishop Wright further explains, if we ask who or what the dead are according to this world view the answer is that:

> They are, at present, souls, spirits or angel-like beings, held in that state of being not because they were naturally immortal but by the creative power of YHWH. Where are they? They are in the hands of the creator God; or in paradise; or in some kind of Sheol, understood now not as a final but as a temporary resting place.

---

[221] N T Wright *The Resurrection of the Son of God* London: SPCK 2003 pp. 88-89

What's wrong? They are not yet re-embodied, not least because their God has not yet completed his purposes for the world and for Israel. What's the solution? Ultimate re-embodiment, which will be caused by YHWH's power and spirit. [222]

Two New Testament texts help to illustrate this quotation. The first is Acts 12:15 where the maid Rhoda claims to have seen St. Peter's 'angel'. What this means is that she believes that St. Peter has been executed by King Herod and that what she has encountered is the apostle's disembodied spirit.

The second is 2 Cor 5:2-4 in which St. Paul declares:

> Here indeed we groan, and long to put on our heavenly dwelling, so that by putting it on we may not be found naked. For while we are still in this tent, we sigh with anxiety; not that we would be unclothed, but that we would be further clothed, so that what is mortal may be swallowed up in immortality.

We know from 2 Cor 5:8, and Phil 1:23 that St. Paul believed that those Christians who died before the final resurrection would go and be with Christ. However, this situation, although one of happiness and contentment would be one of disembodiment and: '...his preference is for the final state, in which one will be given a new body to be put over the top of the present one, clothing the Messiah's people in a new kind of physicality whose main characteristic is incorruption.'[223]

From the evidence of the apocryphal book of Enoch and from Rabbinic sources we also know that the existence of the dead in *sheol/haides* was not regarded as a single undifferentiated state. Rather it was a state in which the disembodied dead received a foretaste of their ultimate fate after the final judgement. The unjust were thus in misery while the righteous were in place of blissful enjoyment described variously as 'paradise', the 'Garden of Eden', 'beneath the throne of glory' and 'in Abraham's bosom.' [224]

---

[222] Ibid p.203. The lower case g originally used by Wright in this quotation to refer to YHWH has been replaced by a capital G to avoid confusion.
[223] Ibid p.367
[224] Browne op.cit. pp.80-81, Gibson op.cit pp.164-16

What Article III states is that when Christ died He entered into this disembodied state and that He remained there until His resurrection on the third day. There are two New Testament texts that explicitly support this statement.

The first is Lk 23:43 in which Christ says to the penitent thief: 'Truly, I say to you, today you will be with me in Paradise.' As Gibson comments, these words:

> ...assume and sanction the current belief that Paradise, or the Garden of Eden, was the part of that unseen region to which the name of Sheol was given, in which the souls of the faithful departed were preserved. And thus the passage appeals to us with the weight of a direct statement from our Lord Himself that after His death He would pass into the region of departed souls, i.e. would 'descend into hell.'[225]

The second is Acts 2:24-31 in which St. Peter talks to the crowd on the day of Pentecost about the fulfilment of the prophetic words of King David in Ps 16:10: '...thou wilt not abandon my soul to Hades, nor let thy Holy One see corruption.' The apostle declares that these words were not true of David himself, but were true of Christ: '...he foresaw and spoke of the resurrection of the Christ, that he was not abandoned to Hades, nor did his flesh see corruption.' Like the verse from St. Luke's gospel previously cited, these words indicate that when Christ died He went to *sheol/haides,* although He did not remain there because God raised Him up from the dead.

A third text which is sometimes quoted in support of the belief that Christ descended to the place of the dead is Eph 4:9 which states that Christ 'descended into the lower parts of the earth'. It is possible to read the 'lower parts of the earth' as a reference to *sheol/haides,* but commentators generally take it as meaning 'the lower parts, namely the earth' in contrast to heaven from which Christ descended at the incarnation and to which He ascended at the resurrection. FF Bruce writes, for example:

> In the Fourth Gospel the ascent is from earth to heaven and the preceding descent from heaven to earth; and so it is here. That is

---

[225] Gibson op. cit. p.166

to say, 'the lower parts of the earth' should be understood as meaning 'the earth below.' [226]

What is clear from Lk 24 and Acts 2 is that when He died Christ did indeed descend, as a disembodied soul possessed by God the Son, into the place of the dead referred to in the Apostles Creed and in Article III by the use of the word 'hell'.

Note: The use of 1 Peter 3:17-22 in the *Book of Common Prayer*

That Christ descended to the place of the dead as a disembodied soul is the sole belief to which members of the Church of England are committed by Article III itself. However, as Canon A5 states, the doctrine of the Church of England is found in the *Book of Common Prayer* as well as in the *Articles*. In the *Book of Common Prayer* 1 Peter 3:17-22 is set as the Epistle for Holy Communion on Easter Eve and this gives implicit endorsement to the patristic tradition noted above that Christ not only descended to the place of the dead but also preached to those who were there.

There are two biblical texts that are cited as giving support to this tradition. The first, as has been said, is 1 Pet 3:18-20:

> For Christ also died for sins once for all, the righteous for the unrighteous, that he might bring us to God, being put to death in the flesh but made alive in the spirit; in which he went and preached to the spirits in prison, who formerly did not obey, when God's patience waited in the days of Noah, during the building of the ark in which a few, that is, eight persons, were saved through water.

The second is 1 Pet 4:6:

---

[226] FF Bruce *The Epistles to the Colossians, to Philemon and to the Ephesians* Grand Rapids: Eerdmans 1984 p.343. Bruce cites John Calvin's comment: 'A comparison is drawn, not between one part of the earth and another, but between the whole earth and heaven; as if he had said, "From that lofty habitation He descended into our deep gulf."'

> For this is why the gospel was preached even to the dead, that though judged in the flesh like men, they might live in the spirit like God.

In the case of 1 Pet 3:18-20 there are three schools of interpretation about what 'preaching to the spirits in prison' means.

- The first sees Christ as preaching the gospel, during his sojourn in the place of the dead, to the souls of those sinners who disobeyed God at the time of the flood.

- The second sees Christ as proclaiming to the fallen angels referred to in Jude 6 and 2 Peter 2:4 his victory on the cross and their consequent doom.

- The third sees the preaching as referring to an activity of the pre-incarnate Christ which took place during the time of Noah.

The problem with the second approach is that it is not clear why the fallen angels referred to in Jude 6 and 2 Pet 2:4 should be identified with the 'spirits' referred to in 1 Pet 3:20, who in context seem to be human sinners who were disobedient to God at the time of the flood (Gen 6:12). Seeing them as human sinners also seems to make more sense if those referred to in 1 Pet 3:20 are the same as 'the dead' referred to in 1 Pet 4:6 as the flow of thought in this section of the Epistle seems to require. Furthermore, the connection with 4:6 makes it more likely that the Greek verb *kerusso* used in 3:20 carries its normal New Testament sense of the proclamation of the gospel rather than referring to a declaration to the fallen angels that their doom was sealed.

The problem with the third approach is that it seems to make little sense in the context of the discussion of Christ's death and resurrection that immediately precedes it in 3:18 and to which the argument of the Epistle returns in 3:22-4:1. It is also difficult to connect with 4:6.

The first approach seems the most persuasive given that it fits best into the immediate context in the Epistle and connects most easily to what is said subsequently in 4:6. Therefore, as Charles Cranfield puts it, we may take it that:

...the meaning of vv19-20a is that in the interval between his death and resurrection Christ preached to the souls of the dead (the men who died in the flood being specially mentioned as outstanding sinners.)[227]

In the case of 1 Peter 4:6 there are again three schools of thought.

- The first sees 'the dead' as being the 'spirits in prison' previously referred to in 3:19.

- The second sees them as those who were spiritually dead.

- The third sees them as being Christians who had the gospel preached to them while they were alive, but have subsequently died.

As before, the second and third interpretations are problematic. In the previous verse the dead are the physically dead and as it is the mention of these that seems to lead into v 6 it seems most likely that the dead referred to in v 6 are the physically dead also. It is possible that the dead are Christians who have now died, but this does not seem an obvious meaning, is difficult to connect to 3:19-20, and makes it difficult to make sense of the use of the Greek word *kai,* meaning 'even or 'also'. Why is it a matter for comment that the gospel was preached 'even' or 'also' to the dead if the dead in question had the gospel preached to them while they were alive? Something additional to the normal preaching of the gospel seems to be in mind.

To quote Cranfield once more:

> ...the most natural interpretation is surely to connect it with 3:19 and to understand a reference to 'the spirits in prison'. Though 'that they might be judged' and 'live' are co-ordinate grammatically it is best to take the former as subordinate to the latter in thought, so that the meaning will be: 'in order that, though they have died, as all men must (death being regarded as God's judgement), they might nevertheless live by God's power in the spirit'. In the opinion of men the dead have had their

---

[227] C E B Cranfield *I & II Peter and Jude* London: SCM 1960 p.103.

judgement; but the good news has been preached even among them, in order that those who responded to it might live eternally.[228]

If 1 Pet 3:18-20 and 4:6 are to be understood along the lines just suggested, this means that the patristic tradition that the Christ's descent into hell involved preaching to the dead has some biblical support. It also means that Archbishop Cranmer was correct in what he wrote in the *Forty Two Articles* and the Church of England has been right to retain 1 Pet 3:17-22 as the Epistle for Easter Eve.

In his commentary on the *Thirty Nine Articles* O'Donovan declares that the difficulty with Cranmer's approach:

> ...was that it evoked a fundamentally mythical world of disembodied beings who are supposed to share our time but not our space...But just as the dead have no place within our space other than their tombs, so they have no existence at this point in our time except as memory or remains.[229]

It is clear that 'mythical' is being used here to mean 'legendary' or 'non-existent' and what is being denied is that we can say of the dead that they have a time that is related to our own. However, the biblical evidence would seem to indicate that that is precisely what we must say. As we have seen, the Jewish belief presupposed by the New Testament is that the dead do still exist in a temporal existence that, like ours, is leading towards the final judgement and the resurrection. The New Testament also teaches that during the period between His death and resurrection Christ entered into their realm of existence and while there proclaimed the gospel to some at least of the dead.

If we ask what the doctrinal significance of this biblical evidence is, the answer is that is has a fivefold significance.

First, it underlines the reality of Christ's human nature. As we have seen, according to the Jewish understanding of the fate of the dead accepted by the New Testament, when people die their bodies lie in their graves while their disembodied souls or spirits go to *sheol/haides*. This is precisely

---

[228] Ibid p. 110
[229] O Donovan op.cit p.39

what happened also to Christ. Because He had a full human nature He had, as the Chalcedonian definition puts it, 'a reasonable soul and body' and when He died on the cross His body lay in Joseph of Arimathea's tomb while His soul went to the place of the disembodied dead. If this did not happen it would have meant that Christ was not truly human.

Secondly, by underlining the reality of Christ's human nature it also underlines God's full identification with us in both life and death. In the words of B F Westcott, belief in the descent into hell:

> ...completes our conception of the Lord's death. To our minds death is the separation of body and soul. According to this conception Christ in dying shared to the full our lot. His body was laid in the tomb. His soul passed into that state on which we conceive that our souls shall enter. He has won for God and hallowed every condition of human existence. We cannot be where he has not been. He bore our nature as living: He bore our nature as dead.[230]

Thirdly, 1 Pet 3:19-20 provide further evidence of that ministry to sinners which is so strong a feature of the Gospel accounts of Jesus' ministry on earth. As Cranfield argues, those humans who perished in the flood were: '...generally regarded as the most notorious and abandoned of sinners: if there was hope for them, then none could be beyond the reach of Christ's saving power.'[231]

Fourthly, it sheds some degree of light on the question of the fate of those who have died in ignorance of the promises of God in Christ. To quote Cranfield again, 1 Pet 3 indicates that the interval between Christ's death and resurrection was:

> ...not without significance, and that in it, as at other times, Jesus Christ was active as the Saviour of the world. The best thing is to realize that we encounter here a mystery, which is still a secret from us, and reverently to accept the hint that is given to us. It is a hint within the canon of scripture that the atoning efficacy of

---

[230] B F Westcott *The Historic Faith* London: Macmillan 1893 p.? 76
[231] Cranfield op.cit p.102

Christ's death was available to those who died in paganism in the ages before Christ, and also, surely, a hint that those who in subsequent ages have died without ever having had a real chance to believe in him are not beyond the reach of his saving power.[232]

Fifthly and finally, it gives at least some support to the patristic belief noted above that Christ proclaimed the victory of the cross to the dead patriarchs and prophets of Old Testament times. As Gibson notes, the question with which we are faced when comparing the teaching of 1 Pet 3 with the patristic tradition is whether those specified by St. Peter were the only ones to whom Christ preached:

> One generation, and one generation alone is specified by the apostle; and that just the generation of which it might be said that it received exceptional treatment on earth. It may, therefore, have been the subject of a special extension of mercy to the unseen world of Hades. But...there is an extraordinarily strong tradition among the fathers that Christ descended to the patriarchs and prophets of the Old Dispensation and preached to them, and bettered their condition. There is no other passage of Holy Scripture from which such a tradition can have originated; and it would therefore seem that the Fathers took it that those mentioned by S. Peter were but specimens, so to speak, of a class – of those, that is, who had lived and died under the Old Covenant. It *may* be so. But this is all that can be said. When Scripture is silent, such an inference must be more or less precarious, and though the opinion may appear a probable one, it can only be held (if at all) as a 'pious opinion' which cannot be pressed upon any as part of the faith. In any case, it would be rash in the extreme to infer from this passage the possibility of an extension of the day of grace, or an opportunity of repentance beyond the grave, for Christians whose case is wholly different. It cannot be said that the apostle's words afford the slightest grounds for expecting a second offer of salvation to any of those who have slighted or misused God's revelation made 'in His Son.'[233]

---

[232] Ibid p.104
[233] Gibson op.cit pp.174-175 Italics in the original

Article IV

∞

Of the Resurrection of Christ

Christ did truly rise again from death, and took again His body, with flesh, bones, and all things appertaining to the perfection of man's nature, wherewith He ascended into heaven, and there sitteth until He return to judge all men at the last day.

De Resurrectione Christi

Christus vere a mortuis resurrexit, suumque corpus cum carne, ossibus, omnibusque ad integritatem humanae naturae pertinentibus, recepit, cum quibus in coelum ascendit, ibique residet, quoad extremo die ad iudicandos homines reversurus sit.

This article remained practically unchanged between 1553 and 1571 except for two minor changes. The Latin title of 1553 and 1563 'Resurrectio Christi' was changed to the current Latin title in 1571 in order to harmonize with the titles of all the other articles, and the word 'all' in the last clause was added to the English editions of the article in 1563 and 1571 although with no equivalent change in the Latin text.

The equivalent section of the third of the *Thirteen Articles* declares that Christ:

> ...truly rose again on the third day. Afterward he ascended into heaven to sit at the right hand of the Father, and reign for ever, and have dominion over all creatures; and to sanctify those who believe in him by sending the Holy Spirit into their hearts to rule, comfort and quicken them, and defend them against the Devil and the power of sin. The same Christ shall openly return to judge the living and the dead etc. as the Apostles' Creed states.[234]

---

[234] Text in Bray *Documents of the English Reformation* pp. 186-187

A comparison between this statement and Article IV indicates that the focus of Archbishop Cranmer's concern in 1553 was to uphold the belief that when Christ rose from the dead and ascended into heaven he retained the human nature that He assumed at the incarnation.

The reason that he had this focus is explained by the reference in the list of heresies contained in the *Reformatio Legum Ecclesiasticarum* to the fact that:

> Some resuscitate the delusion of Eutyches concerning the body of Christ [and] assert that the Word was changed into the nature of flesh, which they claim was immediately once more turned back and absorbed into the divine nature as soon as it was taken up into heaven from the dead.[235]

Over against this teaching by some of the Protestant radicals, Article IV insists that precisely the same human nature that was assumed at the incarnation, that died and that descended into hell was raised from the dead on the third day and taken into heaven. Having made this point, the article finally completes its teaching about Christ by following the Creed in declaring that the ascended Christ will return to judge all humankind at the last day.

Christ did truly rise again from death, and took again His body, with flesh, bones, and all things appertaining to the perfection of man's nature

The reason for this section of the article has been indicated above. How we are to understand it is explained with great clarity by Bishop Beveridge in his commentary of this article. He writes as follows:

> ...Christ did truly rise from death. As he did truly suffer, was truly crucified, truly dead, truly buried, and did truly descend into hell; so did he also truly rise again from death. The soul of Christ; being breathed from his body, went down to hell; the body of Christ, being deprived of its soul, was carried to the grave. And here they both continued, the one in the grave, and the other in hell, until the third day after the divorce was made: at which time the soul

---

[235] Text in Bray *Tudor Church Reform* p. 191

that went from the body down to hell, comes up again from hell unto the body. And, as it left the body upon the cross, it now finds it in the grave; even the selfsame body that, three days before, was nailed to the cross; not any way broken, bemangled or corrupted, but in the same condition the soul had left it in. This selfsame body, which the soul before was forced from, is it now again united to. After which union of the soul to the body, immediately follows the return, or resurrection both of soul and body from the state of death. The separation of the soul from the body had brought (though not the soul, yet) the human nature into a state of death; the union of the soul to the body brings it back again to the state of life. So that Christ after his resurrection, as well as before his passion, had all things appertaining to the human nature; having the same soul and the same body, the same flesh and the sane bones that he had before, and the same of every thing that belongeth to the perfection of man's nature. So that whatever is essential to the constitution of the human nature, without which he could not be man as well as God, that was the Lord Christ invested with after his resurrection, as well as before his passion.[236]

If we ask what the evidence is that Christ rose in soul and body from the tomb in the way summarised in the article and expounded by Beveridge the answer is twofold.

First, as we have already noted in connection with *Article III* belief in the resurrection in the first century Jewish context meant precisely the re-embodiment of a disembodied soul in a resurrected body in the way described by Beveridge. To quote Wright again:

'Resurrection', with the various words that were used for it and various stories that were told about it, was never simply a way of speaking about 'life after death.' It was one particular story that was told about the dead: a story in which the *present* state of those who had died would be replaced by a *future* state in which they would be alive once more...'resurrection' was a life after 'life after death', the second of two stages in the post-mortem

---

[236] Beveridge op.cit p.139

programme. Resurrection was, more specifically, not the *redefinition* or *redescription* of death, a way of giving a positive interpretation to the fact that the breath and body of a human body had ceased to function, leading quickly to corruption and decay, but the *reversal* or *undoing* or *defeat* of death, restoring to some kind of bodily life those who had already passed through that first stage. It belonged with a strong doctrine of Israel's God as the good creator of the physical world. [237]

What this means is that when the New Testament talks about the 'resurrection' of Christ the use of the term necessarily implies not that His soul continued to exist in some post-mortem state, or that His influence lived on in some vague fashion, but that in His case the resurrection of the dead expected at the end of time had already occurred with His soul being re-united with His resurrected body.

Secondly, the descriptions in the New Testament of what happened on the third day and subsequently all support the picture just given.

As we have seen, St. Peter's exposition of Ps 16 on the day of Pentecost (Acts 2:22-34) makes clear that what had not happened to King David had happened to Christ. King David remained dead with his soul in Hades and his body in a well known Jerusalem tomb, but Christ was alive with His soul liberated from Hades and His body freed from the corruption of death.

In the Gospels we find this picture supported by the accounts both of the empty tomb (Mt 28:1-8, Mk 16:1-8, Lk 24:1-11, Jn 20:1-18) – empty because the body of Christ has been raised, and by the accounts of the encounters of the disciples with the risen Christ, who is specifically said not to be a 'ghost' (i.e. a disembodied soul) but someone who is capable of being seen, talking, eating food and being touched (Lk 24:36-43, see also Lk 24:30, Mt 28:9, and Jn 20:26-28, 21: 9-14). It is clear that His body could do things that normal bodies cannot, such as appear and disappear and go through locked doors (Lk 24:31, Jn 20:19 & 26). In context, however, it is clear that this does not mean that the body is any way unreal. It is simply that it is a body that through God's power is able to do things that are not normally possible.

---

[237] Wright op.cit. p. 201. Italics in the original, but with God being given a capital G as before.

In 1 Cor 15:3-5 St. Paul repeats what Gordon Fee describes as: '...a very early creedal formulation that was common to the entire church.'[238] This formulation declares that:

> Christ died for our sins in accordance with the scriptures, that he was buried, that he was raised on the third day in accordance with the scriptures, and that he appeared to Cephas, then to the twelve.

As Fee further argues, the clause 'that he was buried':

> ...functions to verify the reality of the death. In the present context it emphasizes the fact that a dead corpse was laid in the grave, so that the resurrection that follows will be recognized as an objective reality, not merely a 'spiritual' phenomenon. Therefore, even though the point is incidental to Paul's own concern, this very early expression of Christian faith also verifies the reality of the empty tomb stories. It is common in some quarters of NT scholarship to deny this latter, but that seems to be a case of special pleading. The combined emphasis on death, burial and third day resurrection would have had an empty tomb as its natural concomitant, even if not expressed in that way. Given this language, embedded in the heart of the earliest tradition, the early Christians and Paul would find it unthinkable that some would deny that they believed that the tomb was also empty, or that those stories were the creation of a later generation that needed 'objective verification' of the resurrection. One may not believe that Jesus rose and that the tomb was therefore empty; but one may scarcely on good historical grounds deny that they so believed.[239]

The statement that Christ was raised 'on the third day' also points us in the same direction. To quote Wright again:

> The phrase 'after three days', looking back mainly to Hosea 6:2 is frequently referred to in rabbinic mentions of the resurrection.

---

[238] G D Fee *The First Epistle to the Corinthians* Grand Rapids: Eerdmans 1993 p.718
[239] Ibid pp.725-726.

This does not mean that Paul or anyone else in early Christianity supposed that it was a purely metaphorical statement, a vivid way of saying 'the biblical hope has been fulfilled'. In fact, the mention of any time-lag at all between Jesus' death and his resurrection is a further strong indication of what is meant by the latter: not only was Jesus' resurrection in principle a dateable event for the early Christians, but it was always something that took place, not immediately upon his death, but a short period thereafter. If by Jesus 'resurrection' the early church had meant that they believed he had attained a new state of glory with God, a special kind of non-bodily post-mortem existence, it is difficult to see why there should have been any interval at all; why should he have had to wait? If, however, the early church knew from the first that something dramatic had happened on the third day (counting inclusively) after the Friday when Jesus died, then not only the appeal to Hos 6.2 and the wider tradition thereby represented, but also the shift represented by the Christian use of Sunday as 'the lord's day', is fully explained. [240]

What all this means is that when St. Paul goes on to mention the list of the earliest witnesses to the resurrection in 1 Cor 15:5, and then goes on to add some more witnesses of his own in verses 6-8, he is telling us about is people who did not simply have subjective visionary experiences, but people who had an actual historical encounter with the Christ who was able to appear to them because He was no longer dead but had been raised from the grave in body and in soul.

Acceptance of the reality of the bodily resurrection of Christ still leaves us with the question of the significance of this event. Within the Bible Christ is not the only person who is described as returning from the dead. This is also true, for example, of the son of the widow of Zarephath (1Ki 17:17-24), of Lazarus (Jn 11:1-44) and of the dead saints in Jerusalem mentioned by St. Matthew (Mt 27: 51-53). What, then, is it about the resurrection of Christ that makes it uniquely important?

Article IV itself does not answer this question, but the answer given to it by the Elizabethan Church of England and presupposed by the Article is contained in the homily 'Of the Resurrection of Our Saviour Jesus Christ' in the *Second Book of Homilies*.

---

[240] Wright op.cit p. 322

This homily tells us that Christ's resurrection was uniquely significant because by it, as the completion of what he achieved on the cross, Christ defeated sin, death and the devil and purchased life and righteousness for all believers. The homily declares:

> If death could not keep Christ under his dominion and power, but that he arose again, it is manifest that his power was overcome. If death be conquered, then must it follow that sin, wherefore *death was appointed as the wages* (Romans 6:23), must be also destroyed. If death and sin be vanished away, then is the devil's tyranny vanished, *which had the power of death*, and was the author and brewer of sin, and the ruler of hell. If Christ had the victory of them all by the power of his death, and openly proved it by his most victorious and valiant resurrection (as it was not possible for his great might to be subdued of them) and it is true, that Christ died for our sins, and rose again for our justification; why may not we, that be his members by true faith, rejoice and boldly say with the Prophet Osee, and the Apostle Paul, *Where is thy dart, O death? Where is thy victory, O hell? Thanks be unto God*, say they, *which hath given us the victory by our Lord Christ Jesus* (Hosea 13:14, 1 Corinthians 15:55, 57). [241]

It then goes on to say:

> This is the mighty power of the Lord, whom we believe on. By his death, hath he wrought for us this victory, and by his resurrection, hath he purchased everlasting life and righteousness for us. It had not been enough to be delivered by his death from sin, except by his resurrection we had been endowed with righteousness. And it should not avail us, to be delivered from death, except he had risen again, to open for us the gates of heaven, to enter into life everlasting. And therefore St. Peter thanketh *God, the Father of our Lord Jesus Christ for his abundant mercy, because he hath begotten us* saith he *unto a lively hope by the resurrection of Jesus Christ from death, to enjoy an inheritance immortal, that never shall perish, which is laid up in heaven for them that bee kept by the power of God through faith* (1

---

[241] *The Homilies*, Bishopstone: The Brynmill Press/Preservation Press: 2006, p.314.

Peter 1:3-5). Thus hath his resurrection wrought for us life and righteousness. He passed through death and hell, to the intent to put us in good hope, that by his strength we shall do the same. He paid the ransom of sin that it should not be laid to our charge. He destroyed the devil and all his tyranny, and openly triumphed over him, and took away from him all his captives, and hath raised and set them with himself, among the heavenly citizens above (Ephesians 2.6). He died, to destroy the rule of the devil in us: and he rose again, to send down his holy Spirit to rule in our hearts, to endow us with perfect righteousness.[242]

The homily also follows St. Paul in declaring that the resurrection has consequences for Christian behaviour. It is not only something to believe in intellectually as a historical fact, but also a summons to a new way of life:

If we then we be risen with Christ by our faith to the hope of everlasting life: let us rise also with Christ, after his example, to a new life, & leave our old. We shall then be truly risen, if we *seek for things that be heavenly*, if we *have our affection on things that be above, and not on things that bee on the earth*. If ye desire to know what these earthly things be which ye should put off, and what be the heavenly things above, that ye should seek and ensue, St. Paul in the Epistle to the Colossians declareth, when he exhorteth us thus. *Mortify your earthly members* and old affections of sin, *as fornication, uncleanness, unnatural lust, evil concupiscence, and covetousness, which is worshipping of idols, for the which things, the wrath of God is wont to fall on the children of unbelief, in which things once ye walked, when ye lived in them But now put ye also away from you, wrath, fierceness, maliciousness, cursed speaking, filthy speaking, out of your mouths. Lie not one to another, that the old man with his works be put off, and the new be put on* (Colossians 3.1-2, 5-9). These be the earthly things which Saint Paul moved you to cast from you, and to pluck your hearts from them. For in following these, ye declare yourselves earthly and worldly. These be the fruits of the earthly Adam. These should ye daily kill, by good diligence, in withstanding the desires

[242] Ibid, pp.314-315.

of them, that ye might rise to righteousness. Let your affection from henceforth *be set on heavenly things*, sue and search for *mercy, kindness, meekness, patience, forbearing one another, and forgiving one another. If any man have a quarrel to another, as Christ forgave you, even so do ye* (Colossians 3:12-13) If these and such other heavenly virtues ye ensue in the residue of your life, ye shall show plainly that ye be risen with Christ, and that ye be the heavenly *children of your Father in heaven* (Matthew 5:45) , from whom, as from the giver, cometh these graces and gifts (James 1.17). Ye shall prove by this manner, that your conversation is in heaven, where your hope is: and not on earth, following the beastly appetites of the flesh (Philippians 3.20).[243]

...wherewith He ascended into heaven

The point of the word 'wherewith' here is to stress over against the heretical ideas mentioned in the *Reformatio Legum Ecclesiasticarum* that when Christ ascended into heaven He did not slough off His resurrected body but took it with Him into the presence of God. In the words of O'Donovan, it makes clear that the ascension is:

> ....a material event which involves the material body of Jesus; it leaves this spatio-temporal order to enter the immediate presence of the Creator.[244]

This is clearly what is described by St. Luke in Acts 1:6-11. It is the same Jesus with the same physical body who has met with the disciples over the forty days since the resurrection that is taken up into a cloud out of their sight.

Today, however, many people question whether the ascension is to be regarded as an historical event. There are two reasons for this.

- First, it is argued that St. Luke alone describes the ascension as a distinct event. All the other New Testament writers, it is said, seem to conflate together the resurrection and ascension as two aspects of the same event.

---

[243] Ibid, pp.317-318.
[244] O'Donovan op.cit p. 37

- Second, it is argued that what St. Luke appears to describe involves a view of the world that we now know to be impossible, one in which heaven is physically located 'beyond the bright blue sky'.

In response it needs to be noted:

Firstly, the ascension is mentioned as a distinct event not only in Acts 1:6-11, 2:33-34 and 3:21, but it is also referred to in a number of non-Lukan texts, Jn 6:62, 20:17, Eph 4:8-10, 1 Thess 1:10, 1 Tim 3:16, Heb 4:14, 9:24, 1 Pet 3:22, Rev 5:6. It is also found in the longer ending of St. Mark's Gospel at Mk 16:19.

Secondly, there is nothing in Acts to suggest that St. Luke believed that this event was any less historical than any of the other events that he describes. It is noteworthy that four times in Acts 1:9-11 St. Luke mentions the disciples seeing the events described. It is clear that he thinks he is describing an event for which there were eyewitnesses.

Thirdly, what has to be explained is why the early Christians (a) believed that post-resurrection appearances of Christ on earth had come to an end and (b) that Christ was now at the right hand of God in heaven from which He would return in glory at the end of time. The Lukan account of the ascension provides a plausible explanation for these facts that are otherwise unaccounted for. The suggestion that the session at God's right hand is based on Ps 110:1 depends on the belief that the early Christians made up events on the basis of biblical texts. The evidence that we have, however, is that they followed the Jewish practice of seeking to interpret events with reference to biblical texts.

Fourthly, it is true that in the Christian tradition the ascension has been interpreted in terms of a cosmology which sees heaven as a place above the earth to which Christ travelled. Thus Bishop John Pearson writing in the seventeenth century in his exposition of the Apostles' Creed interprets belief in the ascension as meaning that:

> I am fully persuaded that the only-begotten and eternal Son of God, after he rose from the dead, did, with the same soul and body with which he rose, by a true and local translation convey himself from the earth on which he lived, through all the regions of the

air, through all the celestial orbs, until he came unto the heaven of heavens, the most glorious presence of the majesty of God.[245]

If belief in the ascension did depend upon this belief in a 'local translation' of Christ's body then there would be a serious problem. However, it is important to note that nothing in the Lukan account supports Pearson's account of what the ascension involved. All that St. Luke himself tells us is that: 'he was lifted up and a cloud took him out of their sight' (Acts 1:9). As in the story of the transfiguration (Lk 9:34-35) the cloud is a symbol of the divine presence, so what St. Luke is telling us is simply that Christ was taken up into the presence of God. How the presence of God -'God's place' – is related to our place in cosmological terms is something upon which neither St. Luke nor any other New Testament writer speculates.

If we are still worried even by the degree of movement implied by the statement that Christ was 'lifted up' we need to remember that, as C S Lewis remarks:

> Movement (in any direction but one) away from the position momentarily occupied by our moving Earth will certainly be to us movement 'upwards'. To say that Christ's passage to a new 'Nature' could involve no such movement, or no movement at all, within the 'Nature' he was leaving, is very arbitrary. Where there is passage there is departure; and departure is an event in the region from which the traveller is departing.[246]

A moment's consideration will show that if after the resurrection Christ genuinely possessed a human body it follows that it either had to remain permanently located in our space and time or it had to go somewhere else. If it went somewhere else this will necessarily have involved movement and to say this movement could not, initially at least, have involved a movement upwards is, as Lewis says, simply arbitrary.

A further issue which arises in relation to the belief that Christ ascended to heaven is how this belief relates to Christ's promise in Mt 28:20: 'I am with you always, to the close of the age.' If Christ has ascended to heaven how is He still with His people?

---

[245] J Pearson *Exposition of the Apostles Creed* p.376
[246] Lewis op.cit p.255

He is clearly not present in the physical body He assumed at the incarnation. As we have said, the ascension involved a movement of Christ's body from our place to God's place and like any other physical body it cannot be in two places at once.

However, the ascension does not cancel out the incarnation. The second person of the Trinity, God the Son, still has a human as well as a divine nature and when He acts through either of His two natures He acts as the one who possesses both. What this means is that through His divine nature God the Son is everywhere present, but He is everywhere present as Jesus Christ, the one who was born as human being, lived among us, suffered, died and rose again. In this way we can say that although Christ's physical body is in heaven He is nevertheless with us always according to His promise.

Furthermore, as Hooker points out, we also need to remember that the human nature of the ascended Christ is not just an historical memory. It is not simply that the ascended Christ acts as the one who once lived a human life here on earth. Rather the human nature of Christ is at work co-operating with the divine nature in everything that He does. As we shall see shortly, the ascended Christ is active in His three roles as prophet, priest and king, and in all of them the human nature of Christ is involved through the operation of His human will and understanding.

As Hooker puts it, the government over the universe that Christ exercises as ascended Lord seated at God's right hand:

> ...he exerciseth both as God and as man, as God by essential presence with all things, as Man by co-operation with that which essentially is present. Touching the manner how he worketh as man in all things; the principal powers of the soul of man are the will and understanding, the one of which two in Christ assenteth unto all things, and from the other nothing which Deity doth work is hid; so that by knowledge and assent the soul of Christ is present with all things which the Deity of Christ worketh.[247]

We have already mentioned that the ascended Christ is active as prophet, priest and king and in order to understand the significance of the ascension more fully we shall now look at each of these three roles in more detail.

---

[247] Hooker *The Laws of Ecclesiastical Polity* Bk V: lv:8 in Keble (ed) vol I p.621

Christ as prophet

The role of the prophet is to proclaim God's word to Israel and to the world, and this is also the role of the ascended Christ. In Acts 3:22-23 St. Peter declares that the ascended Christ is the eschatological prophet foretold in Dt 18:15, the second and greater Moses who will finally and definitively reveal the will of God:

> Moses said, 'the Lord God will raise up for a prophet from among your brethren as he raised me up. You shall listen to him in whatever he tells you. And it shall be that every soul that does not listen to that prophet shall be destroyed from the people.'

When considering Christ's prophetic role highlighted in this passage there are three things that need to be noted.

First, because Christ is God's Word and God's Son (Jn 1:1, Heb 1:2) and as such Himself God it follows that, unlike in the case of all the other prophets, in His case the message and the messenger are identical. He is not only the proclaimer, but the content of the proclamation. What He has to declare is what God has done in and through Him for the salvation of the world.

Secondly, since the ascension means that Christ is no longer present in the world in bodily form, the way that Christ's prophetic message is proclaimed is through the witnesses Christ has appointed inspired by the Spirit that He sends at Pentecost (Acts 1:8, Jn 15:26-27). In the words of Torrance:

> The Church is the bodily and historical form of Christ's existence on earth through which He lets his Word be heard, so that the Church bears witness to him and proclaims the Gospel of salvation in his Name, he himself through the Spirit is immediately present validating that Word as his own and communicating himself to men through it.[248]

---

[248] Torrance op,cit. p120

It is because the Church is the form of Christ's existence on earth through which He performs His prophetic role that St. Luke tells Theophilus that his Gospel was about what Jesus '*began* to do and teach' (Acts 1:1), the point being that his second volume will be about what the ascended Christ continued to do and teach through the activity of His Church. A case could indeed be made out for saying that the most appropriate title for Acts is not the Acts of the apostles, but the Acts of the ascended Christ by His Spirit through His Apostles.

Thirdly, the warning that every soul that will not listen to the prophet will be cut off from the people is understood in the New Testament as meaning that everyone who refuses to listen and to be obedient to Christ will be excluded from the kingdom of God, a point to which we shall return when looking at the coming of Christ in judgement.

Christ as priest

The priestly role of the ascended Christ has again got three aspects to it.

First, as the Epistle to the Hebrews declares, the ascended Christ is our great High Priest who, having made the perfect sacrifice for sin, enters into the presence of God on our behalf:

> For Christ has entered, not into a sanctuary made with hands, a copy of the true one, but into heaven itself, now to appear in the presence of God on our behalf. Nor was it to offer himself repeatedly, as the high priest enters the Holy Place yearly with blood not his own; for then he would have to suffer repeatedly since the foundation of the world. But as it is, he has appeared once for all at the end of the age to put away sin by the sacrifice of himself. (Heb 9:24-26)

It is important to note that there is no thought in Hebrews of Christ as our High Priest perpetually re-offering to the Father the sacrifice of the cross. In words of Westcott, the:

> ...conception of Christ pleading in heaven His passion, 'offering His blood' on behalf of men has no foundation in the Epistle. His glorified humanity is the eternal pledge of the absolute efficacy of

his accomplished work. He pleads, as older writers truly expressed the thought, by His presence on the Father's throne.[249]

What is important to the author of Hebrews is that Christ is present in heaven on our behalf as the one who understands and can therefore truly represent us, and that, as a result, we can have confidence in coming to God though Him:

> Since therefore we have a great high priest who has passed through the heavens, Jesus, the Son of God, let us hold fast our confession. For we have not a high priest who is unable to sympathize with our weakness, but one who in every respect has been tempted as we are, but without sin. Let us then with confidence draw near to the throne of grace, that we may receive mercy and find grace to help in time of need.

Secondly, the ascended Christ is the one through whom we offer our worship. To quote Hebrews once more: 'Through Him then let us continually offer up a sacrifice of praise to God, that is, the fruit of lips that acknowledge his name.' (Heb 13:15). The key phrase here is 'through him'. As Torrance writes, what this means is that:

> We worship the Father not in our name, nor in the significance of our own prayer and worship, but solely in Christ's name who has so identified himself with us as to make his prayer and worship ours, so really ours that we appear before God with Christ himself as our one true prayer and our only worship. That identification is so profound that through the Spirit Christ's prayers and intercessions are made to echo in our own, and there is no disentangling them from our own weak and stammering and altogether unworthy acts of devotion. [250]

Thirdly, the ascended Christ is the one who blesses his people (Lk 24:50-51). To quote Torrance again:

---

[249] B F Wetscott *The Epistle to the Hebrews* London and New York: Macmillan 1889 p. 230
[250] Torrance op.cit p.117

In his ascension Jesus Christ blessed his people, and fulfilled that blessing in sending down upon us the presence of the Holy Spirit. The language which the New Testament uses to speak of these aspects of Christ's heavenly priesthood is taken from the Old Testament accounts of Melchizedek's blessing of Abraham, and from the Aaronic blessing of God's people after the completion of the sacrificial liturgy on the Day of atonement. We recall the account given of Christ's ascension, and of the lifting up of his hands in blessing upon the disciples with the promise of the power of the Spirit (Acts 1:1-11). Pentecost is the content and actualisation of that high priestly blessing. He ascended in order to fill all things with his presence and to bestow gifts of the Spirit upon men.[251]

Christ as king

The kingly role of the ascended Christ is expounded by St. Peter in Acts 2:34-35 and by St. Paul in 1 Cor 15:24-25 on the basis of Ps 110:1: 'The Lord says to my lord; sit at my right hand till I make your enemies your footstool'.

In Acts 2 and 1 Cor 15 this verse from the Psalm is understood as an address of God the Father to Christ, and it is used to convey three ideas.

- The reference to sitting at the right hand is an image of the delegation of authority and so what it means is what Christ Himself declares in Mt 28:18: 'All authority in heaven and on earth has been given unto me.'

- The second is that Christ exercises this authority until God the Father causes His enemies to submit to Him.

- The third is that Christ exercises this authority only *until* all His enemies submit to Him.

As a way into understanding the first two of these ideas it is useful, first of all, to consider the picture given to us in Rev 5:1-10:

---

[251] Ibid pp.117-118

And I saw in the right hand of him who was seated on the throne a scroll written within and on the back, sealed with seven seals; and I saw a strong angel proclaiming with a loud voice, 'Who is worthy to open the scroll and break its seals?' And no one in heaven or on earth or under the earth was able to open the scroll or to look into it, and I wept much that no one was able to open the scroll or to look into it. Then one of the elders said to me, 'Weep not, the Lion of the tribe of Judah, the Root of David, has conquered, so that he can open the scroll and its seven seal.

And between the throne and the four living creatures and among the elders, I saw a Lamb standing, as though it had been slain, with seven horns and with seven eyes, which are the seven spirits of God sent out over all the earth; and he went and took the scroll from the right hand of him who was seated on the throne. And when he had taken the scroll, the four living creatures and the twenty-four elders fell down before the Lamb, each holding a harp and with golden bowls full of incense which are the prayers of the saints and they sang a new song, saying, 'Worthy art thou to take the scroll and to open its seals, for thou wast slain and by thy blood didst ransom men for God from every tribe and tongue and people and nation, and hast made then a kingdom and priests to our God, and they shall reign on earth.'

In this picture the one seated on the throne is God the Father and the living creatures and the elders symbolise the created order and the people of God respectively. As George Caird explains, the scroll is 'God's redemptive plan, foreshadowed in the Old Testament, by which he means to assert his sovereignty over a sinful world and so to achieve the purpose of creation'[252] Opening the scroll means putting this plan into effect and no one is able to do it.

St John is informed that the scroll can be opened by the promised Messiah of the House of David, the sort of conquering king originally envisaged in Ps 110:1. However, we are then told that this Davidic Messiah is in fact a slain Lamb with seven horns and seven eyes. What is being said here is that true fulfilment of the hope of Israel lies not in a warlike Messiah but in the crucified Christ (the slain lamb) for it is he

---

[252] G B Caird *The Revelation of St. John the Divine* London: A&C Black 1971 p.72

who possesses God's power and wisdom (the seven horns and the seven eyes) and it is he who from whom God's Spirit goes out into all the world (the seven spirits of God).

The significance of all this is that, to quote Richard Bauckham, by juxtaposing the images of the Davidic Messiah and the slain lamb St. John has:

> ...forged a new symbol of conquest by sacrificial death. The messianic hopes evoked in 5:5 are not repudiated: Jesus really is the expected Messiah of David (22:16). But insofar as the latter was associated with military violence and narrow nationalism, it is reinterpreted by the image of the Lamb. The Messiah has certainly won a victory, but he has done so by sacrifice and for the benefit of people from all nations (5:9). Thus the means by which the Davidic Messiah has won his victory is explained by the image of the Lamb, while the significance of the image of the Lamb is now seen to lie in the fact that his sacrificial death was a victory over evil.[253]

What this means in terms of understanding the kingly authority of the ascended Christ and the submission of His enemies to Him is that His authority is the authority to carry out God's good purposes by manifesting in history the victory over sin and death achieved by His cross and resurrection. The defeat of His enemies means the overcoming of all the forces of evil that stand in way of this being achieved. Christ's kingly rule and defeat of His enemies are thus simply the means for achieving that renewal of humankind and of the whole created order that we have seen to be the purpose underlying the cross and resurrection.

It also needs to be noted that just as Christ's prophetic role is exercised through the Church so also is His kingly role. We can see this if we look at Rev 12:10-11 where we read:

> And I heard a loud voice heaven, saying, 'Now the salvation and the power and the kingdom of our God and the authority of his Christ have come, for the accuser of our brethren has been thrown down, who accuses them day and night before our God.

---

[253] R Bauckham *The Theology of the Book of Revelation* Cambridge: CUP 1993 p. 74

And they have conquered him by the blood of the lamb and the word of their testimony, for they loved not their lives even unto death.'

What is being celebrated here is the defeat of Satan and his fallen angels and what St. John tells us is that their conquest has been achieved by Christ in and through His people. As Bauckham notes, discussing the final part of the quotation above:

> ...the reference to the 'blood of the Lamb' is not purely to Christ's death but to the deaths of the Christian martyrs who, following Christ's example, bear witness even at the cost of their lives. But this witness even as far as death does not have an independent value of its own. Its value depends on its being a continuation of its witness. So it is by the Lamb's blood they conquer. Their deaths defeat Satan only by participating in the victory of the Lamb won over Satan by his death.[254]

What is true in these two verses is true in the book of Revelation as a whole. If we read Revelation carefully what we find is that behind the often violent military imagery is a paradoxically non-violent message. Christ's victory is made effective in the world not by the exercise of naked supernatural power, but in the lives of His followers who bear faithful witness to Him even to the point of death. It is this, teaches St. John, that is God's chosen method of bringing about the conversion of the nations.[255]

The third idea, that Christ will reign only until His foes submit, is explicitly taught by St. Paul who writes in 1 Cor 15:24 and 28 that:

> Then comes the end, when he delivers the kingdom to God the Father after destroying every rule and authority and power...When all things are subjected to him, then the Son himself will also be subjected to him who put all things under him, that God may be everything to everyone.

---

[254] Ibid p.77

[255] For the development of these points see the works by Caird and Bauckham mentioned above.

In order to make sense of this teaching it is necessary to note the distinction that has been made in Trinitarian theology between the equality of being and differentiation of order within the Trinity. As we have seen, the witness of Scripture points us to an equality of being between the Father and the Son in the sense that they are both equally God. However, the witness of Scripture in verses such as those just cited indicate that there is a differentiation of order between them which means that in terms of the relation between the persons of the Father and the Son the Son is eternally and joyfully obedient to the Father. We can see this most clearly in St. John's Gospel where the Word who is with God and is God acts always and only in accordance with the Father's will and commandment (see for example John 4:34, 5:19, 6:38, 7:16-18, 8:28, 10:25, 12:49, 17:4). See in this perspective, the handing over the kingdom to the Father by the Son makes perfect sense. The final establishment of the kingdom means the final establishment of the right order of things and this necessarily includes the subjection of the Son to the Father.

...and there sitteth until He return to judge all men at the last day

The idea of Christ sitting at the right hand of the Father can easily be seen as a purely passive image conveying the idea that Christ having ascended into heaven waits around until it is time for Him to return in judgement. However, to see things in this way would be to misunderstand the imagery that is being used here. As we have already noted, Christ's sitting at the right hand of the Father means the exercise of the authority over the created order given to Him by the Father to finally defeat the powers of evil and so usher in God's eternal kingdom.

The time between the ascension and the return in judgement is thus not a hiatus in Christ's activity, but a time when He is at work in His roles as prophet, priest and king in the ways previously described.

The fact that Christ is present and at work in the world raises, of course, the question of what it means to say that He will 'return.' How can Christ return to somewhere from which He has never been absent? The answer is that what is meant by the return of Christ is the return of His manifest presence in the world. Since the ascension Christ has not been visibly present in the world. His presence has been seen indirectly through His presence in the Church. At His return this indirectness will cease and: 'every eye will see him' (Rev 1:7).

As Barth puts it:

...He will issue out of the hiddenness in which He still remains for us to-day, where He is proclaimed and believed by the Church, where He is present to us only in His Word. The New Testament says of this future coming that 'He shall come on the clouds of heaven with great power and glory' and 'as the lightning goeth out from the East to the West, so shall be the coming of the Son of man.' These are metaphors, but metaphors of ultimate realties, which at least indicate that it takes place no longer in secrecy but is completely revealed. No one will any more be able to deceive themselves about this being reality. So He will come. He will rend the heavens and stand before us as the person He is, sitting at the right hand of the Father. He comes in possession and in the exercise of divine omnipotence. He comes as the One in whose hands our entire existence is enclosed. Him we are expecting, He is coming and will be manifest as the One whom we know already. It has all taken place; the only thing that is wanting is that the covering be removed and that all may see it. He has already accomplished it and has the power to make things manifest.[256]

The final thing we are told in this article that Christ's return will usher in the universal judgement. How this was understood by the Tudor Church of England is well illustrated by Nowell.

He first outlines what He thinks will happen at the end of time:

Christ shall come on the clouds of the heaven with most high glory, and with most honourable and reverend majesty, waited on and beset with the company and multitude of holy angels. And at the horrible sound and dreadful blast of trumpet all the dead that have lived from the creation of the world to that day, shall rise again with their souls and bodies whole and perfect, and shall appear before his throne to be judged, every one for himself, to give account of their life, which shall be examined by the uncorrupted and severe Judge according to the truth.

---

[256] K Barth *Dogmatics in Outline* London: SCM 1949 p.133

He then goes on to explain the proper Christian attitude to what is going to happen.

> *M.* Ought the godly at thinking upon this judgement be stricken and abashed with fear, and to dread it and shrink from it?
>
> *S.* No. For He shall give the sentence, which was once by the Judge's sentence condemned for us, to the end that we, coming under the grievous judgement of God, should not be condemned but acquitted in judgement. He, I say, shall pronounce the judgement in whose faith and protection we are, and which hath taken upon him the defence of our cause. Yea, our consciences are cheerfully stayed with a most singular comfort, and in the midst of the miseries and woes of this life, do leap for joy that Christ shall one day be the Judge of the world; for upon this hope we chiefly rest ourselves, that then at last we shall, with unchangeable eternity, possess that same kingdom of immortality and everlasting life, in all parts fully and abundantly perfect, which hitherto hath been but begun, and which was ordained and appointed for the children of God before the foundations of the world were laid. But the ungodly, which either have not feared the justice and wrath of God, or have not trusted in his clemency and mercy by Christ, and which have persecuted the godly by land and sea, and done them all kinds of wrong, and slain them with all sorts of torments and most cruel deaths, shall, with Satan and all the devils, be cast into the prison of hell appointed for them, the revenger of their wickedness and offences, and into everlasting darkness, where, being tormented with conscience of their own sins, with eternal fire, and with all and most extreme execution, they shall pay and suffer eternal pains.

What Nowell says in these two extracts is based on the teaching of the New Testament in passages such as Mt 25:31-46, Jn 5:25-9, 1 Cor 15:51-52, 2 Cor 5:9-10, 2 Thess 1:7-10, and Rev 20:11-15 and represents the traditional position of the Christian Church from the earliest times.

If we unpack what he is saying it is clear that there are four elements to it:

- The dead will be raised for judgement.

- In this judgement everyone will judged on the life they have led.

- This judgement will have a dual outcome.

- As Christians we can nevertheless look forward to the judgement with confidence and hope.

If we look at the first of these four elements the first question that it raises is why there will be a judgement. The answer to this question lies in the moral perfection of God, which would be called into question if He did not make a final judgement between good and evil. As Packer puts it:

> The truth is that part of God's moral perfection is His perfection in judgement. Would a God who did not care about the difference between right and wrong be a good and admirable Being? Would a God who put no distinction between the beasts of history, the Hitlers and Stalins (if we dare use names), and His own saints, be morally praiseworthy and perfect? Moral indifference would be an imperfection in God, not a perfection. But not to judge the world would be to show moral indifference. The final proof that God is a moral Being, not indifferent to questions of right and wrong, is the fact that He has committed Himself to judge the world.[257]

Furthermore, we need to note that the justice of God that is revealed in His judgement of the world is not something that is opposed to His mercy. In the words of Tom Smail:

> The God who speaks in the Scriptures is both just and merciful in everything that he does; the two are entirely consistent because the God who exercises both of them is entirely consistent with himself and faithful to himself and his purposes in all his works and ways.
>
> That comes out clearly in the way the Old Testament prophets, and in particular Isaiah, speak of God's justice. He speaks for example of Jerusalem as the place 'once full of fair judgement, where saving justice used to dwell' (1:21). When he is looking forward to God's people returning from exile he says to

---

[257] J I Packer *Knowing God* London: Hodder & Stoughton 1990 p.159

the anxious, 'Be strong, fear not, your God is coming with judgement, coming with judgement to save you' (35:4), and in the second part of the book God identifies himself to the prophet, 'There is no God apart from me, a righteous God and a Saviour' (45:21) where the meaning clearly is not 'a righteous God and in spite of that a Saviour,' but rather 'a righteous God and therefore a Saviour.'

Verses like that could be multiplied from the Psalms and other Old Testament writings. We should not forget either that in the Old Testament we have a book of Judges which tells the story not of legal officials holding courts and imposing sentences but of men and women God raised up precisely to save and deliver his people from the oppressing Philistines. All this serves to make the point that in God righteousness and salvation, justice and mercy, are not in conflict but are complementary descriptions of how consistently and faithfully he pursues his single purpose for his people and his world. In the God who revealed himself in word to the prophets and even more in the person and passion of Jesus Christ, mercy is at the heart of justice, and his justice is his faithful commitment to mercy.[258]

To put it another way, God's mercy is shown by the fact that He has not abandoned His universe to the destructive forces of sin and death, but has come in person to defeat these forces and to create a new heaven and a new earth where His creatures can find their perfect fulfilment. However, in order for this to happen there needs to be a divine act of judgement in which all the forces of evil and all human beings who have chosen to identify with them are finally and decisively prevented from ever again being able corrupt God's good creation. This is what we see described in Rev 20:7-14 as the prelude to the coming of the new heaven and the new earth and that is why, paradoxical though it may seem, God's judgement is ultimately an expression of God's mercy.

The fact that God's justice and mercy go together in the way just described also explains why it is Christ who executes judgement before handing over the kingdom to the Father. As we have seen, Christ's kingly role involves the defeat of the forces of evil and His execution of final

---

[258] T Smail *Windows on the Cross* London: Darton, Longman and Todd 1995 pp.42-3

judgement is simply the last expression of this role, the completion of the task given to Him by the Father.

If that is why there will be a judgement, a further question that needs to be answered is why it is that the final judgement will be preceded by the general resurrection. Why does there need to be resurrection in order for there to be judgement? The answer would seem to be the same as the answer to the question of why there needs to be a resurrection at all. As human beings we were created by God to be a combination of soul and body. That is who we truly are and it is therefore as this that we are judged. The self that deserves and will receive either eternal life or eternal damnation is the self that consists of both body and soul and therefore both body and soul together need to be raised for judgement. In the words of Athenagoras:

> ...if it is not proper that either the soul alone should receive the wages of the deeds wrought in union with the body (for this of itself has no inclination to the faults which are committed in connection with the pleasure or food and culture of the body), or that the body alone should (for this of itself is incapable of distinguishing law and justice), but man, composed of both of these, is subjected to trial for each of the deeds wrought by him; and if reason does not find this happening either in this life (for the award according to merit finds no place in the present existence, since many atheists and persons who practise every iniquity and wickedness live on to the last, unvisited by calamity, while, on the contrary, those who have manifestly lived an exemplary life in respect of every virtue, live in pain, in insult, in calumny and outrage, and suffering of all kinds) or after death (for both together no longer exist, the soul being separated from the body, and the body itself being resolved into the materials out of which it was composed, and no longer retaining anything of its former structure or form, much less the remembrance of its action): the result of all this very plain to everyone – namely, that, in the language of the apostle, 'this corruptible (and dissoluble) must put on incorruption,' in order that those who were dead, having been made alive by the resurrection, and the parts that were separated and entirely dissolved have been again united,

each one may, in accordance with justice, receive what has been done by the body, whether it be good or bad.[259]

Moving on to the second of these four elements, it is clear that according to the teaching of the New Testament we will indeed be judged on the basis of the life we have lived. In 2 Cor 5:10, for example, St. Paul declares:

> ...we must all appear before the judgement seat of Christ, so that each one may receive good or evil, according to what he has done in the body.

Similarly, in Rev 20:11 the picture of the last judgement is a picture of God's record books being opened: 'And the dead were judged by what was written in the books, by what they had done.'

If we ask why it is that we will be judged by our deeds, the answer is that our deeds reveal who we truly are. To quote Packer again:

> Final judgement, as we saw, will be according to our *works* – that is, our *doings*, our whole course of life. The relevance of our 'doings' is not that they ever merit an award from the court – they are too far short of perfection for that – but that they provide an index of what is in the heart – what, in other words, is the real nature of each agent. Jesus once said, 'on the day of judgement men will render account for every careless word they utter; for by your words you will be justified, and by your words you will be condemned' (Mt 12:36f RSV). What is the significance of the words we utter (which utterance is, of course, a 'work' in the relevant sense)? Just this: the words show what you are inside. Jesus had just made this very point. 'The tree is known by its fruit...how can you speak good, when you are evil? For out of the abundance of the heart the mouth speaks (verse 33ff.). Similarly, in the sheep- and-goats passage appeal is made to whether men had or had not relieved Christians' needs. What is the significance of that? It is not that one way of acting was meritorious while the other was not, but that from these actions one can tell whether

---

[259] Athenagoras *On the Resurrection of the Dead* XVIII in The Ante-Nicene Fathers vol II p. 159

there was love for Christ, the love that springs from faith, in the heart. (see Matthew 25:34ff).[260]

The third of these four elements, the fact that the New Testament teaches that there will be a dual outcome at the last judgement with some going to heaven and other going to hell, is one that causes problems for many people today for two reasons.

The first reason is an unwillingness to believe in the possibility that anyone could be lost. Surely, it is argued, a God who is love will ensure that everyone will be saved in the end.

In response to this argument the first point that needs to be made is that priority has to be given to the biblical witness over our own ideas about God and the biblical witness is clear about the possibility of individuals being damned as well as saved (see for example Mt 7:13-14, Jn 5:28-29, 2 Thess 1:8-9, and Rev 21:11-15). We cannot responsibly use the biblical teaching about the loving nature of God as a reason for ignoring other, more uncomfortable, parts of the biblical picture.

The second point that needs to be made is that it is in fact precisely the fact that God is love and that heaven is a communion of love that prevents us from saying that no one will be lost. In the words of *The Mystery of Salvation*:

No one can be compulsorily installed in heaven, whose characteristic is the communion of love. God whose being is love preserves our human freedom, for freedom is the condition of love. Although God's love goes, and has gone, to the uttermost, plumbing the depths of hell, the possibility remains for each human being of a final rejection of God, and so of eternal life.[261]

As C S Lewis declares in his chapter on hell in his book *The Problem of Pain*:

In the long run the answer to all those who object to the doctrine of hell, is itself a question: 'What are you asking God to do?' To

---

[260] Packer *Knowing God* p.161 As we shall when we look at Article XVIII it can be argued that those whose needs are either met or not met in the parable of the sheep and goats are not specifically Christians but anyone in need, but even if this point is accepted it does not undermine the main point that Packer makes here.
[261] *The Mystery of Salvation* p.198

wipe out their past sins, and, at all costs, to give them a fresh start, smoothing every difficulty and offering every miraculous help? But He has done so, on Calvary? To forgive them? They will not be forgiven. To leave them alone? Alas, I am afraid that is what He does?[262]

The second reason people have difficulty with the idea of a dual outcome at the final judgement is an inability to believe in the traditional pictures of damnation (as found , for instance, in the art of the Middle Ages) in which the lost burn for ever in flames of real fire and are perpetually tormented by demons with pitchforks.

In response to this, the point that needs to be made is that the images of hell that are found in the Christian tradition only carry weight if they are based on the teaching of Scripture and that the images of hell that are found in Scripture itself are not intended to be taken literally. As Bauckham writes:

> The NT pictures of hell are markedly restrained by comparison with Jewish apocalyptic and with later Christian writings. The imagery used derives especially from Isa 66:24 (cf Mk 9:48) and Gen 19:24, Is.34: 9 f (cf Rev 14.10f; also Jude 7 Rev 19:3). It is clearly not intended literally but indicates the terror and finality of condemnation to hell, which is less metaphorically described as exclusion from the presence of Christ (Mt 7:23, 25:41, 2 Thess 1:9).[263]

If the images of damnation that are found in Scripture are not to be taken literally the question that inevitably arises is: 'What is the reality to which these images are meant to point us?'

One answer to this question that has been increasingly favoured in recent years is that hell should be understood in terms of the lost ceasing to exist after the final judgement. *The Mystery of Salvation*, for instance, argues that:

---

[262] C S Lewis *The Problem of Pain* London: Harper Collins 2002 p. 130.
[263] R J Bauckham 'Eschatology' in J D Douglas et al (eds) *The Illustrated Bible Dictionary* Vol 1 Leicester: IVP 1980 p.475

Hell is not eternal torment, but it is the final and irrevocable choosing of that which is opposed to God so completely and so absolutely that the only end is total non-being. Dante placed at the bottom of hell three figures frozen in ice – Judas, Brutus and Cassius. They were the betrayers of their friends, and through that they ceased to have the capacity for love and so for heaven. Annihilation might be a truer picture of damnation than any of the traditional images of the hell of eternal torment. If God has created us with the freedom to choose, then those who make such a final choice choose against the only source of life, and they have their reward.[264]

The belief that the damned simply cease to exist has seemed attractive to many people because it avoids having to believe that the lost will remain in torment for ever, but whatever the attractions of this belief the key issue is whether or not it is a convincing interpretation of the biblical teaching about the fate of the lost.

In his book *I Believe in the Second Coming of Jesus*, Stephen Travis notes that there are two arguments that are put forward to support the belief that the biblical accounts of damnation are compatible with the idea of the damned finally ceasing to exist.

Positively, it is argued that: '...biblical images such as 'fire' and 'destruction', suggest annihilation rather than continued conscious existence.'[265] Negatively, it is maintained that:

...New Testament references to 'eternal punishment' (Mt 25:46; cf 2 Thessalonians 1:9; Hebrews 6:2) do not automatically mean what they have traditionally been assumed to mean. 'Eternal' may signify the permanence of the result of judgement rather than the continuation of the act of punishment itself. So 'eternal punishment' means an act of judgement where results cannot be reversed, rather than an experience of being punished forever.[266]

---

[264] *The Mystery of Salvation* p. 199
[265] S H Travis *I Believe in the Second Coming of Jesus* London: Hodder & Stoughton 1982 p.198
[266] Ibid p. 199 for a more detailed exposition of these ideas see J W Wenham 'The Case for Conditional Immortality' in N M de S Cameron (ed) *Universalism and the Doctrine of Hell* Carlisle: Paternoster Press 1992 pp.161-191 and B F C Atkinson *Life and Immortality* Taunton: Phoenx Press N.D.)

Both these arguments have been challenged by those who hold that the Bible teaches the continued existence of the damned rather than their annihilation.

On the subject of 'fire' it is noted that Christ Himself talked not just about fire but about 'eternal' and 'ever burning' fire. J A Motyer writes, for example:

> The passages in question are Matthew 18:8 and Mark 9:48. The former speaks of 'eternal fire', and the latter, recapitulating the same teaching of the Lord, quotes him as saying that 'the fire is not quenched'. In both passages...the topic is the destiny of the unsaved and we are therefore bound to hold that the intention of the divine Teacher is the same and His wording consistent.
>
> But did He also teach that the unsaved would experience eternally this 'eternal fire'? Presumably an 'eternal fire' could burn on but yet annihilate once and for all those who are thrown into it. The rest of the New Testament is against this conclusion. Whenever it uses the Lord's imagery of the 'eternal fire', it either teaches or implies a conscious and continuing experience. The same teaching was conveyed by our Lord when He said that 'their worm dieth not.' At least, it can be put this way. As far as we can tell, these words would only have been understood in one way by our Lord's hearers, and He, had he not intended this meaning, must either have avoided or else otherwise explained them. The origin of this expression is Isaiah 66:24, where the undying worm and the unquenched fire is the lot of 'the men that have transgressed against me.' The pathway whereby this reached the New Testament and the meaning it had for New Testament times may be discerned in the references contained in the Apocrypha. Judith 16:17, with the same topic in hand, reads: 'The Lord Almighty will take vengeance of them in the day of judgement, to put fire and worm in their flesh, and they shall weep and feel their pain for ever.' [267]

---

[267] J A Motyer *After Death – A Sure and Certain Hope?* London: Hodder & Stoughton 1965 pp.45-46

On the subject of 'destruction' it is noted that the Greek terms translated as 'destruction' do not necessarily imply the cessation of existence[268] and that in 2 Thess 1:9, which is the one passage in which the fate of the lost is specifically described as eternal destruction, the context makes it clear that annihilation is not what St. Paul has in mind. In this verse St. Paul tells us that on the last day the ungodly: '...shall suffer the punishment of eternal destruction and exclusion from the presence of the Lord and from the glory of his might'. In this verse the second half also explains the meaning of the first half. As David Williams puts it in his commentary on 1 and 2 Thessalonians:

> As eternal life lies in knowing God and of necessity Jesus Christ through whom alone he can be known (Matt 11:27), so eternal destruction lies in being 'separate from Christ...and (therefore in being) without God' (Eph 2:12 cf Rom 6;23). It would seem that separation, not annihilation, is intended by this destruction...It is destruction in the sense of deprivation 'away from' (*apo*) the face of the Lord, depicted in NIV as being shut out from his presence.[269]

On the subject of 'eternal punishment' it is noted that in Matt 25:46 the term 'eternal punishment' used of the damned is paralleled by the term 'eternal life' used of the blessed, and that it is therefore reasonable to assume that the word 'eternal' means the same in both cases. In the case of the blessed it is agreed that 'eternal life' involves the enjoyment of life without end and therefore in the case of the damned 'eternal punishment' must involve the suffering of punishment without end. In the words of Motyer:

> The notion of 'eternity', in so far as it is revealed to us in the New Testament use of the word, excludes the idea of termination; and the noun 'punishment' wherever it is used signifies painful experience.[270]

---

[268] Ibid pp.41-44
[269] D J Williams *1 and 2 Thessalonians* Carlisle: Paternoster Press 1995 p.116. It is worth noting that the only other place where the phrase 'eternal destruction' is used is in 4 Macc 9:9 in the Greek Old Testament where it is used in parallel with 'eternal torment by fire' and therefore clearly does not mean annihilation.
[270] Motyer op.cit. p.45

Understanding 'eternal punishment' in this way would also make it consistent with the use in Mt 25:41 of the corresponding term 'eternal fire' which we have looked at above, and with what we know to have been the prevailing Jewish understanding of the fate of the wicked.

Looking at the arguments on both sides it appears that those on the traditionalist side are more convincing both because they make better sense of the relevant texts in context and because they correspond better to what we know of first century Jewish eschatology, which was the matrix out of which Christian eschatology emerged.

If the fate of the lost is unending punishment and if the images that are used to describe that punishment are not necessarily to be taken literally the question that still has to be answered is what the nature of their punishment will be. A helpful approach to this issue is that taken by Packer in *Knowing God*. His approach is helpful because it highlights the fact that the essence of hell will be that the damned are given the fate that they have chosen for themselves. God does not inflict upon them an arbitrary punishment but ratifies the terrifying choice that they themselves have made:

> ...what does it mean to lose our souls? To answer this question, Jesus uses His own solemn imagery – 'Gehenna' (hell in Mark 9:47 and then other gospel texts), the valley outside Jerusalem where rubbish was burned; the 'worm' that 'dieth not' (mark 9:47), an image, it seems for the endless dissolution of the personality by a condemning conscience; 'fire' for the agonising awareness of God's displeasure; 'outer darkness' for knowledge of the loss, not merely of God, but of all good, and everything that made life seem worth living; 'gnashing of teeth' for self-condemnation and self-loathing. These things are, no doubt, unimaginably dreadful, though those who have been convicted of sin know a little of their nature. But they are not arbitrary inflictions; they represent, rather, a conscious growing into the state in which one has chosen to be. The unbeliever has preferred to be by himself, without God, defying God, having God against him, and he shall have his choice.[271]

---

[271] Packer *Knowing God* pp.169-170

The idea that the damned receive the fate that they have chosen also helps us to begin to make sense of the issue of why the damned remain in hell forever. In the same way that it has traditionally been held that those who are saved move beyond the possibility of sin into a state in which it is no longer possible for them to turn away from God, it is possible to conceive that those who are damned enter through their own choice into a state in which they are no longer capable of responding to the love of God with anything other than hatred and rejection. In the words of Lewis:

> They enjoy forever the horrible freedom they have demanded, and are therefore self-enslaved: just as the blessed, forever submitting to obedience, become through all eternity more and more free.[272]

Lewis explores this idea in more detail in his novel *The Great Divorce* in which he envisages the possibility of the damned enjoying what he calls a 'refrigerium', that is to say, a holiday or excursion to heaven, and looks at how those who come up from hell either accept or reject the life of heaven. In this book he writes that:

> ...a damned soul is nearly nothing: it is shrunk, shut up in itself. Good beats upon the damned incessantly as sound waves beat on the ears of the deaf, but they cannot receive it. Their fists are clenched, their teeth are clenched, their eyes fast shut. First they will not, in the end they cannot, open their hands for gifts, or their mouths for food, or their eyes to see.[273]

In the same book he also considers to the question of how the saved can be joyful in heaven while the damned remain outside, challenging the idea that: '...the loss of one soul gives the lie to all the joy of those who are saved.'[274] The response that Lewis puts into the mouth of the Teacher whose role it is to explain to the hero of the story what is happening is that:

---

[272] Lewis *The Problem of Pain* p.130
[273] C S Lewis *The Great Divorce* Glasgow: Fontana 1974 pp.113-114
[274] Ibid p.110

Either the day must come when joy prevails and all the makers of misery are no longer able to infect it: or else for ever and ever the makers of misery can destroy in others the happiness they reject for themselves. I know it has a grand sound to say ye'll accept no salvation which leaves even one creature in the dark outside. But watch that sophistry or ye'll make a Dog in a Manger the tyrant of the universe.[275]

The final element of Alexander Nowell's approach to the topic of the final judgement is an insistence that we can look forward to it with confidence and hope. How can this be when there is the possibility of damnation as well as salvation and when we are aware that our continuing sinfulness means that damnation is the fate that we deserve?

The answer to this question is that we can have confidence because, as we have seen, Christ died to put to death our old sinful nature and rose again to give us a new nature freed from sin. In the words of St. Paul, this means that if we are Christians, those who are 'in Christ', then we are a 'new creation' (2 Cor 5:17), 'dead to sin and alive to God' (Rom 6:11), and as such free from the threat of condemnation at the last judgement. There are sins that still beset us, but they are no longer a threat to our eternal destiny and we shall be delivered from them once and for all when we die.

In the words of Bishop Wright:

...the glorious news is that, although during the present life we struggle with sin, and may or may not make small and slight progress towards genuine holiness, our remaining propensity to sin is finished, cut off, done with all at once, in physical death. 'The body is dead because of sin' declares Paul, 'but the spirit is life because of righteousness' (Rom 8:10).[276]

We can therefore approach the last judgement in confidence and hope knowing that:

---

[275] Ibid p. 111
[276] Wright *For all the Saints?* p.32

'There is therefore no condemnation for those who are in Christ Jesus. For the law of the Spirit of life in Christ Jesus has set me free from the law of sin and death.' (Rom 8:1-2)

What should not be overlooked here is the reference to the Spirit. It is the Holy Spirit, the 'Spirit of life in Christ Jesus' who makes what Christ has done for us real in us and thereby delivers us from condemnation. We shall look in more detail at who the Spirit is and His role in our lives as Christians as we go on next to explore the teaching of Article V.

Note 1: Responding to scholarly scepticism about the resurrection

It is popular in some scholarly circles today to dismiss the possibility of the bodily resurrection of Christ out of hand. The New Testament scholar Robert Funk records, for example, how he once presented the proposition that the resurrection was an event in the life of Jesus to the members of the American academic group the Jesus Seminar:

> My proposition was received with hilarity by several Fellows. One suggested that it was an oxymoron....Others alleged that the formulation was meaningless, since we all assume, they said, that Jesus' life ended with his crucifixion and death. I was surprised by this response. I shouldn't have been. After all, John Dominic Crossan has confessed 'I do not think that anyone, anywhere, at any time brings dead people back to life.' That's fairly blunt. But it squares with what we really know, as distinguished from what many want to believe. Sheehan is even blunter: 'Jesus, regardless of where his corpse ended up, is dead and remains dead.'[277]

In response to this scepticism three points need to be made.

First, such scepticism is nothing new. St. Luke records that when St. Paul preached the resurrection of the dead to the Athenian intellectuals on the Areopagus he was met with mockery as well as with faith (Acts 17:32). Pagans in the first century Mediterranean world were just as sceptical about belief in the resurrection of the dead as Western intellectuals are today and for precisely the same reason, an *a priori* conviction that once

---

[277] R W Funk *Honest to Jesus* New York: Harper Collins 1996 p.258

you are dead you are dead and that is all there is to be said. There are no new reasons for denying the resurrection, simply the age old assumption that such a thing could not happen.

Secondly, as Christian apologists have consistently pointed out down the centuries, such an assumption leaves out of account the power and purposes of God. As the second century Christian writer Athenagoras puts it in his treatise *On the Resurrection of the Dead*:

> ...that [God's] power is sufficient for the raising of dead bodies is shown by the creation of these same bodies. For if, when they did not exist, He made at their first formation the bodies of men and their original elements, He will, when they are dissolved, in whatever manner that may take place, raise them with equal ease: for this too, is equally possible to him.[278]

Furthermore, says Athenagoras, if God does not raise the dead, then the way He has made human beings as a combination of body and soul is pointless, an idea which it is impossible to accept given that God is the all-wise and all-good creator:

> ...if no resurrection were to take place, the nature of men as men would not continue. And if the nature of men does not continue, in vain has the soul been fitted to the need of the body and to its experiences; in vain has the body been fettered so that it cannot obtain what it longs for, obedient to the reins of the soul, and guided by it as with a bridle; in vain is the understanding, in vain is wisdom, and the observance of rectitude, or even the practice of every virtue, and the enactment and enforcement of laws, - and to say all in a word, whatever is noble in men or for men's sake, or rather the very creation and nature of men. But if vanity is utterly excluded from all the works of God, and from all the gifts bestowed by Him, the conclusion is unavoidable, that, along with the interminable duration of the soul, there will be a perpetual continuance of the body according to its proper nature.[279]

---

[278] Athenagoras *On the Resurrection of the Dead* III in *The Ante-Nicene Fathers* Vol II Edinburgh and Grand Rapids: T&T Clark/Eerdmans 2001 p.150
[279] Athenagoras *On the Resurrection of the Dead* XV in Ibid p.157

Thirdly, the historical evidence points to the resurrection having taken place. As Bishop Wright states, the combination of the existence of the empty tomb and the meetings that people had with Christ is the sole plausible historical explanation for the emergence of early Christianity:

> The empty tomb and the 'meetings' with Jesus, when combined, present us with not only a sufficient condition for the rise of early Christian belief, but also, it seems, a necessary one. Nothing else historians have been able to come up with has the power to explain the phenomena before us....The early Christians did not invent the empty tomb and the 'meetings' or 'sightings' of the risen Jesus in order to explain a faith they already had. They developed the faith because of the occurrence, and convergence of these two phenomena. Nobody was expecting this kind of thing; no kind of conversion-experience would have generated such ideas; nobody would have invented it, no matter how guilty (or how forgiven) they felt, no matter how many hours they pored over the scriptures. To suggest otherwise is to stop doing history and to enter into a fantasy world or our own, a new cognitive dissonance in which the relentless modernist, desperately worried that the post-Enlightenment worldview seems in imminent danger of collapse, devises strategies for shoring it up nevertheless. In terms of the kind of proof which historians normally accept, the case we have presented, that the tomb-plus-appearances combination is what generated early Christian belief is as watertight as one is likely to find.[280]

If we then go on to ask why the tomb was empty and why it was that people in their hundreds (1 Cor 15:6) were able to meet with Christ, converse with Him and even touch Him, the only plausible explanation is that the tomb was empty because Christ was no longer dead but alive and therefore able to meet with them.

---

[280] Wright op.cit pp.706-707 For further detail on this argument see Wright Ibid Part V, W L Craig *Assessing the New Testament Evidence for the Historicity of the Resurrection of Jesus Christ* Lewiston, Queenstown and Lampeter: The Edwin Mellen Press, 1989 and M Licona, *The Resurrection of Jesus*, Downers Grove and Leicester: IVP Academic/Apollos, 2010,

Note 2: The corporate and cosmic significance of the resurrection.

As noted above, the Tudor Church of England stressed the importance of the resurrection for individual believers. What also needs to be emphasised is its corporate and cosmic significance.

As Archbishop Michael Ramsey in his study *The Gospel and the Catholic Church* in which he declares that a central part of our dying and rising with Christ is the fact that we die to self and rise to a new corporate life in the Church:

> 'Individualism' therefore has no part in Christianity, and Christianity verily means its extinction. Yet through the death of 'individualism' the individual finds himself; and through membership in the Body the single Christian is discovered in new ways and becomes aware that God loves him, in all his singleness, as if God had no one else to love. He can speak of a conscious union between his single self and Christ: 'He loved me, and gave Himself for me,' Hence two kinds of language have always been legitimate for Christians, the one which dwells upon the Body of Christ wherein the individual is merged, the other which dwells upon the individual Christian in his conscious union with Christ. But both kinds of language describe what is really one fact. For the individual Christian exists only because the Body exists already. The self is known in its reality as a self when it ceases to be solitary and learns its utter dependence, and the 'individuality' of Christians, with all its rich variety, springs from their death and resurrection in the Body which is one. In the Body the self is found, and within the 'individual experience' the Body is present.[281]

It also needs to be noted that the resurrection of Christ is the start of the renewal not just of the lives of human beings, but of the creation as a whole. We have already touched on this point when looking at the issue of the presence of evil in creation in connection with *Article I*, noting that according to the teaching of St. Paul in Rom 8:18-22 the final outcome of God's saving work through the cross and resurrection will be the re-birth of the whole created order as human beings finally taken on the role of

---

[281] M Ramsey *The Gospel and the Catholic Church* 2ed London: SPCK 1990 p.38

stewardship and oversight that was given to them at creation, but which the effects of sin have made it impossible for them to fulfil. To quote *The Mystery of Salvation*:

> The resurrection of Jesus is the beginning within history of a process whose fulfilment lies beyond history, in which the destiny of humanity and the destiny of the universe are together to find their fulfilment in a liberation from decay and futility.[282]

As this quotation makes clear, although Christians participate already in the resurrection (Jn 11:25, Rom 6:1-11, Eph 2:6, Col 2:12) the resurrection also has future dimension.

For human beings this means, as St. Paul declares, that:

> ...the trumpet will sound, and the dead will be raised imperishable, and we shall be changed. For this perishable mature must put on the imperishable, and this mortal nature must put on immortality. (1 Cor 15:52-53)

Earlier in 1 Cor 15 St. Paul talks about this change in terms of our acquiring a 'spiritual body' (v44). It is important to recognise that spiritual here does not mean 'non-physical'. The apostle does not mean that our present physical bodies will be replaced by non-physical ones. As Wright explains, what St. Paul is doing here is making a comparison with the story of the creation of the first Adam in Gen 2:7.

In the Genesis account Adam, the first human being, becomes a living being because he is animated by the breath/spirit of God breathed into his nostrils. In a similar fashion, argues St. Paul, we shall be given a new existence through the Holy Spirit that comes from Christ the second Adam (1 Cor 15:45). What we shall then possess is: 'a body animated by, enlivened by, the Spirit of the true God.'[283] It is in this way that we shall acquire immortality and an imperishable nature.

St Paul's statement in 1 Cor 15:50 that: 'flesh and blood cannot in inherit the kingdom of God' might seem to tell against the idea that St. Paul believes that our physical bodies will be the ones in which we dwell

---

[282] *The Mystery of Salvation* p.192
[283] Wright Ibid p.354

with God for ever, but it is important to note that in this verse 'flesh and blood' is used as a parallel for that which is 'perishable'. What will not inherit the kingdom of God is not our physical bodies as such, but our physical bodies in their present perishable state, and this is something that God will change.

Although the Bible does not explicitly say so, if the rest of the created order is to share in God's kingdom it too will presumably need to undergo the same sort of transformation. To quote *The Mystery of Salvation* again:

> The new creation will be a world freely reconciled to God in Christ (Col 1.20), a transfigured universe completely suffused with the divine presence. The 'matter' of such a world can coherently be supposed to possess new properties not seen in our present experience, so that the new creation is not a second attempt at a creation out of nothing, but is the eschatological transformation of the old creation. It will be a *cosmos pneumatikos* – a universe animated by God's Spirit, in the most intimate connection to its creator.[284]

---

[284] *The Mystery of Salvation* pp.194-195

Article V

∞

Of the Holy Ghost

The Holy Ghost, proceeding from the Father and the Son, is of one substance, majesty, and glory with the Father and the Son, very and eternal God.

De Spiritu Sancto

Spiritus sanctus, a Patre et Filio procedens, eiusdem est cum Patre et Filio essentiae, maiestatis, et gloriae, verus ac aeternus Deus.

As we noted in the introduction, this article, which was taken verbatim from the *Wurtemburg Confession*, was added by Archbishop Parker in 1563. As we have already noted in the introduction to Articles I-V, two reasons can be suggested as to why it was added.

The first reason is the need to combat the denial of the distinct identity and the deity of the Holy Spirit. This emerged in the 16th century as part of a wider rejection of traditional Trinitarian theology. Evidence that some were denying the distinct identity of the Spirit can be found at the end of the first of the *Thirteen Articles* of 1538, which combats this denial by saying:

> We also condemn the Adoptionists, ancient and modern, who argue that there is only one person, and daringly and impiously prate that the Word and the Holy Spirit are not distinct persons, but that the Word is just a verbal utterance and the Spirit just a movement created in things.[285]

---

[285] Bray *Documents of the English Reformation* p.185

Evidence for the denial of the deity of the Spirit can be found in the list of heresies in the *Refomatio Legum Ecclesiasticarum,* which includes a section entitled 'Of the Holy Spirit' that states:

> And just as these gangrenous members, who have such perverse notions of Christ its head, are to be cut out of the body of the church, so also is the execrable impudence of those who, with Macedonius, have conspired against Holy Spirit, not recognizing him as God.[286]

Given that both these documents date from the time of Archbishop Cranmer the question that naturally arises is why he, or those who worked with him, did not feel it necessary to include an article on the Holy Spirit in the *Forty Two Articles.* The best suggestion is that they felt that orthodox belief about the Spirit had been sufficiently maintained in the general teaching about the Trinity in Article I. If this was the case, this still leaves us with the issue of why Archbishop Parker felt that a separate article on the Spirit was required.

The second reason why Parker may have felt it necessary to add an article on the Holy Spirit may have been a desire to give a proper balance and symmetry to the Articles. In the words of Gibson:

> If there was an Article on the Son of God, it may well have been felt that the lack of a corresponding Article on the Third Person of the Holy Trinity was a deficiency which it would be wise to supply, for the sake of symmetry and proper balance, even though there was no positive necessity for it arising from heresy, without which it would not be excluded.[287]

The article that Parker added divides into two parts. The first part concerns the procession of the Holy Spirit and the second concerns the deity of the Holy Spirit.

We shall now look at each of these in turn.

---

[286] Bray *Tudor Church Reform* p.193
[287] Gibson op.cit p.199

The Holy Ghost, proceeding from the Father and the Son...

The first thing that needs explanation in connection with these words is that the word 'Ghost' is simply an old English word meaning 'spirit'. Like the corresponding word 'Spiritus' in the Latin form of the article it could mean the disembodied spirit of a dead person and hence a ghost in the modern sense of the term, but the context makes it obvious that that is not what is intended here.

The second thing that needs explanation is what is meant by the term 'proceeding'.

This is a technical theological term that is used to describe the relationship of the Holy Spirit to the Father and the Son within the life of the Holy Trinity. The biblical evidence that lies behind it can be summarised as follows.

On the one hand it is clear in Scripture that the Holy Spirit is the Spirit of the Father who comes from the Father.

- In the narrative of Christ's baptism the Spirit is described as 'the Spirit of God', with God here meaning God the Father. (Matthew 3:16). The Spirit is also described as the Spirit of God with the same meaning in other passages such as Rom 8:9 and 1 Cor 3:16.

- In Matthew 10:20 Christ tells His disciples that when they bear witness in the face of persecution 'the Spirit of your Father' will speak through them.

- In Romans 8:11 the Spirit is described as the 'Spirit of him who raised Jesus from the dead.'

- In Luke 11:13 and John 14:16 the Spirit is said to be given by the Father.

- In Jn 14:26 the Spirit is sent by the Father.

- In John 15:26 the Spirit proceeds from the Father.

- In Acts 2:33 the risen Christ receives the Spirit from the Father.

On the other hand it is also clear that the Holy Spirit is the Spirit of the Son who comes from the Son.

- In Romans 8:9, Phil 1:19 and 1 Pet 1:11 the Spirit is called the 'Spirit of Christ'

- In Galatians 4:6 we read that 'God has sent the Spirit of his Son into our hearts'.

- In Acts 16:17 the Spirit is called the 'Spirit of Jesus'.

- In John 15:26 and 16:7 the Spirit is said to be sent by the Son.

- In John 20:22 and Acts 2:33 the Spirit is bestowed by the Son.

It is sometimes objected that it has been an illegitimate move by the Christian tradition to take this biblical material as the basis for thinking about the eternal relationships within God. The reason for this objection is that it argued that the passages cited above tell us about how the Holy Spirit comes to us in the course of God's interaction with our history. They are not intending to describe what God is eternally like in Himself.

However, as Tom Smail points out in his book *The Giving Gift* it is not wrong to take the statements in the New Testament about the relationships between the Persons of the Trinity as showing us what God is like in Himself because:

> The gospel offers us not just a knowledge of our own situation and of God's gracious and abundant provision for us, but a knowledge of God himself. It is not a matter of our storming the heavens to invade his secrets. Rather he himself has come into our human world and shown himself to us and invited us to known him as he eternally is. For if the gospel does not show us God as he really and eternally is, then it is a deception and not the truth, a concealment and not a revelation.[288]

In the words of Barth:

---

[288] T A Smail *The Giving Gift*: London: Hodder and Stoughton 1988 p.145

The reality of God in His revelation cannot be bracketed by an 'only' as though somewhere behind His revelation there stood another reality of God; the reality of God which encounters us in His revelation is His reality in all the depths of eternity.[289]

If we ask why it is that the tradition has used the term procession to describe the derivation of the Holy Spirit from the Father the answer is that (a) procession is a biblical term and (b) although the precise meaning of the term 'procession' is a mystery, the fact that the term 'procession' is used of the Holy Spirit but not of the Son points us to the fact that the Son and the Holy Spirit have distinct identities.

Because of His mode of derivation from the Father the Holy Spirit is the Holy Spirit rather than being a second Son. The Son is the Son because He is generated or begotten by the Father, whereas the Spirit is the Spirit because He proceeds from the Father.

As we have noted, it has been accepted that the precise meaning of the 'procession' of the Holy Spirit is ultimately a mystery.

In the subsequent theological tradition in both Eastern and Western Christianity it has been agreed that just as the Son eternally derives His being from the Father in a manner that is described as 'generation'[290] so likewise the Spirit eternally derives His being from the Father in a manner that is described as 'procession'. It has been accepted that what the term 'procession' denotes in relation to God is a mystery in just the same way the meaning of the term 'generation' is a mystery, but the term has been used to point to the fact that the Spirit comes from the Father in some way that makes Him different from the Son.

In the words of St. John of Damascus:

...the Father is without cause and begotten: for He is derived from nothing, but derives from Himself His being, nor does He derive a single quality from another. Rather He is Himself the beginning and cause of the existence of all things in a definite and natural manner. But the Son is derived from the Father after the manner of generation and the Holy Spirit is likewise derived from the Father, yet not after the manner of generation, but after that of procession. And we have learned that there is a difference

---

[289] K Barth *Church Dogmatics* I/1 T&T Clark 1980 p.479
[290] See the discussion of this on pp 22-23. above

between generation and procession, but the nature of that difference we in no way understand. [291]

However theologians have nevertheless sought to try to make some sense of this distinction. One of the ways that they have done so is to build on the biblical idea of the Spirit as the breath of God (Gen 2:7, Ps 33:6, Ezek 37:1-14, Jn 20:22) by talking about the procession of the Spirit as meaning the Spirit's being breathed out by the Father in distinction to the Son being begotten by Him.

As Tom Smail explains in his book *The Giving Gift*, this way of understanding what is meant by the procession of the Holy Spirit is a helpful way to begin to make sense of what is distinctive about the Spirit over against the Son.

> What perhaps they were getting at, in using these two different verbs to describe how Son and Spirit derive from the Father, is that the coming forth of the Son is like a human begetting, in that it results in the production of another centre of personal life who is of the same 'stuff' as his Father, but who stands over against him as a second person distinct from him. They are one in their deity; yet, like any parent a child they are sufficiently distinct for the one to love and be loved by the other.
>
> On the other hand the coming forth of the Spirit from the Father is more like the production of a divine breath that carries within it God's being, life, truth and power. In the Son the Father finds a partner for his love and in the Spirit he finds a way of communicating that love first to the Son and then to us. The Son is the primary object of the Father's love: it makes good New Testament sense to say 'The Father loves the Son' (John 5:20). However, there is no equivalent statement that 'The Father loves the Spirit,' for that would be an inappropriate thing to say. The Spirit is not the personal *object* of the Father's love, but rather its personal *communication*. The special relationship of the Spirit to the Father's love is expressed in Romans 5:3: 'God has poured out his love into our hearts by the Holy spirit whom he has given us.' The difference between the begetting of the Son and the breathing

---

[291] St. John of Damascus *Exposition of the Orthodox Faith* Ch VIII in *The Nicene and Post Nicene Fathers* 2nd series vol IX Grand Rapids: Eerdmans 1997 p.9

out of the Spirit has something to do with the difference between originating someone to love and originating someone else by whom that love can be conveyed.[292]

Although both Eastern and Western Christianity are agreed about the Spirit's procession from the Father, where they have historically disagreed is about whether or not it is also right to say that there is a procession of the Spirit from the Son.

This brings us to the third thing that needs explanation, which is that the words 'proceeding from the Father and the Son' are based on what is known as the 'filioque clause.'

The Latin word *filioque* means 'and the Son' and the 'filioque clause' is the name that is given to the addition of the words 'and the Son' to the original statement in the Nicene Creed that the Spirit 'proceeds from the Father.' The historic and continuing disagreement between the Eastern and Western churches is whether it was and is legitimate to add these words to the original text of the Creed.

The Creed of Nicaea in 325 merely stated 'And [we believe] in the Holy Spirit'. The Nicene–Constantinoplian (or Nicene Creed as it is generally known) associated with the Council of Constantinople in 381 and endorsed by the Council of Chalcedon in 451 expanded this to read 'And [we believe] in the Holy Spirit, the Lord and life-giver, who proceeds from the Father, Who with the Father and the Son is together worshipped and glorified, Who spoke through the prophets'.

The original text of the Nicene Creed reflects the traditional belief of the Eastern Church that the Holy Spirit proceeds from the Father alone, what is known as the 'single procession' of the Spirit.

In the Western Church, however, the idea that the Spirit proceeds from the Father as well as the Son, what is known as the 'double procession', had been taught as far back as the time of St. Hilary of Poitiers in the fourth century, who writes of the Spirit: 'proceeding...from Father and Son' and that 'The Spirit of Truth proceeds from the Father, He is sent by the Son and receives from the Son.'[293] It was given classic expression by St. Augustine in Book XV of his work *Of the Trinity*, 'The

---

[292] Smail op.cit. p. 122
[293] Hilary of Poitiers On the Trinity II:29 and VIII:26 in The Nicene and Post Nicene Fathers 2nd series vol ix Edinburgh & Grand Rapids: T&T Clark/ Eerdmans 1997 pp. 60 and 145.

Spirit of Truth proceeds from the Father, He is sent by the Son and receives from the Son' in which he writes that:

> ...as the Father has in Himself that the Holy Spirit should proceed from Him, so has He given to the Son that the same Holy Spirit should proceed from Him, and be both apart from time: and that the Holy Spirit is so said to proceed from the Father as that it be understood that His proceeding also from the Son, is a property derived by the Son from the Father.[294]

and again:

> ...the Son is born of the Father; and the Holy Spirit proceeds from the Father principally, the Father giving the procession without any interval of time, yet in common from both [Father and Son].[295]

From the time of St. Augustine onwards belief in the double procession of the Holy Spirit became accepted as Catholic orthodoxy in the Western Church and when, at the end of the sixth century, the Visigoths in Spain converted from Arianism to Catholic orthodoxy they therefore embraced the double procession as part of orthodox Catholic teaching.

In 589 the Visigothic king Reccared summoned a council at Toledo to officially mark the fact that the Visigothic Church was now Catholic in its theology. At this council he gave an exposition of the Catholic faith in which he declared that:

> In equal degree must the Holy Spirit be confessed by us, and we must preach that He proceeds from the Father and the Son and is of one substance with the Father and the Son: moreover that the Person of the Holy Spirit is the third in the Trinity, but that He nevertheless shares fully in the divine essence with the Father and the Son.[296]

As John Kelly comments:

---

[294] Augustine *On The Trinity* XV:47 in *The Nicene and Post Nicene Fathers* vol III p.225
[295] Ibid p.225
[296] Text in J N D Kelly *Early Christian Creeds* 3ed Harlow: Longman 1991 p.361

Evidently the doctrine was regarded as clinching the case against Arianism. It implied that the Son, as the source equally of the Spirit, was in no sense inferior to the Father, and that all three persons were completely coordinate and participated equally in the divine essence.[297]

Following the king's lead the council went on to declare:

> Whoever does not believe in the Holy Spirit, or does not believe that He proceeds from the Father and the Son, and denies that He is coeternal and coequal with the Father and the Son, let him be anathema. [298]

It has traditionally been held that the Council of Toledo was the point at which the filioque clause was inserted into the Nicene Creed as recited by the Church in Spain, either as a deliberate addition, or because the Visigoths were so convinced that the double procession was integral to Catholic orthodoxy that the scribe who translated the Creed from Greek into Latin for their benefit assumed that the absence of the clause must be due to a scribal error and therefore put it in to repair the omission.[299]

As Kelly notes, however, this tradition may be mistaken:

> The evidence of the MSS, however, is not free from ambiguity on the point. Many years ago A E Burn drew attention to the fact that several important MSS containing the acts of the council either lack the crucial word or exhibit it inserted by a later hand. The matter still requires investigation but the conclusion seems inescapable that, as originally recited at the council of Toledo, the text of C [the Nicene Creed] was the pure one without the filioque.[300]

Whatever the truth of the matter, what is indisputable is that at some point either at or after the Council of Toledo the Nicene Creed began to be

---

[297] Ibid p. 361
[298] Ibid pp. 361-362. To say that someone was anathema was to say that they were cursed by God (see Gal 1:9).
[299] See Gibson op.cit pp. 215-220
[300] Kelly op.cit p. 362

used in Spain with the addition of the filioque clause. From Spain this practice spread north to Gaul and by the beginning of the ninth century had become the standard practice in Spain, Gaul, Germany and Northern Italy.

Initially at least, the churches in the West that accepted the doctrine of the double procession seem not to have realised that this represented a development of earlier teaching. For example, as we have said, the Visigoths at the Council of Toledo seem to have sincerely believed that the doctrine of the double procession of the Holy Spirit was Catholic orthodoxy and at the Synod of Hatfield in 680 (presided over by Bishop Theodore of Tarsus who was himself from the East) the English church produced a profession of faith which explicitly stated that the doctrine of the double procession was what had been taught by the earlier orthodox councils:

> We acknowledge and glorify our Lord Jesus Christ as they glorified Him, neither adding nor subtracting anything, and we anathematise with heart and voice those whom they anathematised, and we acknowledge those whom they acknowledged, glorifying God the Father without beginning, and His only-begotten Son, begotten of the Father before all ages, and the Holy Spirit proceeding in an inexpressible manner from the Father and the Son, as those holy apostles and prophets taught whom we have mentioned.[301]

Eventually, however, representatives of these churches met with representatives of churches that held to the original form of the Creed and taught that the Holy Spirit proceeded only from the Father. This first seems to have happened at the Council of Gentilly in 767, and thereafter the issues of the procession of the Spirit and the addition of the filioque clause to the Creed became a source of conflict between East and West, a conflict exacerbated by the fact that the Western Emperor Charlemagne used the dispute as a way of seeking to exert his own authority over against that of the Eastern Byzantine Empire.

At first the Papacy backed the Eastern point of view. In a letter to Charlemagne in 794 Pope Hadrian I defended the teaching of the Patriarch of Constantinople, Tarasius, who had taught that the Holy Spirit

---

[301] Bede *The History of the English Church and People* 4:17 text in Kelly ibid p.363

proceeded from the Father through the Son, and in 808 Pope Leo III refused to support Charlemagne in a dispute caused by Western monks in Jerusalem chanting the Nicene Creed with the addition of the filioque clause. The chronicler Anastasius tells us that after this episode Pope Leo had two silver shields erected in St. Peter's in Rome with the original text of the Creed without the filoque clause written upon them in Greek and Latin.[302]

The opposition of the Papacy to the introduction of the filioque clause does not seem to have been based on opposition to the doctrine of the double procession as such. Pope Leo agreed with Charlemagne that this doctrine was an essential part of Christian orthodoxy. Rather, as Kelly argues, the Roman position seems to have been due to a range of other motives:

> No doubt sturdy traditionalism was one motive: reluctance to follow in the footsteps of provincial churches may be another, although the period of Roman borrowing from the Gallican liturgy was beginning. There must also have been a very understandable determination on the part of the papacy not to put itself irretrievably in the wrong in the eyes of Constantinople. It was one thing for churches on the fringe to naturalize the controversial clause in their creeds: for the Holy See it involved far more to take the inevitable step.[303]

The Papacy maintained its opposition to the introduction of the filioque clause until the eleventh century. Why it changed its position and accepted the addition of the clause at this date is not clear. However, a plausible suggestion is that it was due to pressure being placed on Pope Benedict VIII in 1014 by the Holy Roman Emperor Henry II for Rome to adopt the practice of chanting the Nicene Creed (with the addition of the filioque clause) during the celebration of the Mass.

After this point the addition of the filioque clause became standard throughout the Western Church and this was one of the contributory factors behind the official split between the Eastern and Western Churches from 1054 onwards. At the Reformation the Church of England continued to follow the traditional Western approach on the

---

[302] Kelly ibid pp.363-366
[303] Kelly ibid p.366

matter and it is this approach which is reflected in the wording of Article V.

The Eastern Church has continued to this day to see addition of the filioque clause to the Creed as illegitimate, and in recent years some Western theologians, seeking ecumenical rapprochement with the churches of the East, have agreed that its use should be discontinued.

For example, the *Moscow Agreed Statement* produced by the Anglican-Orthodox Joint Doctrinal Commission in 1976 states:

The Anglican members therefore agree that:

(a) because the original form of the Creed referred to the origin of the Holy Spirit from the Father,

(b) because the *Filioque* clause was introduced into this Creed without the authority of an Ecumenical Council and without due regard for Catholic consent, and

(c) because this Creed constitutes the public confession of faith by the People of God in the Eucharist, the *Filioque* clause should not be included in this Creed.[304]

The *Moscow Agreed Statement* was influential in that it was one of the contributory factors that led to the 1978 and 1988 Lambeth Conferences recommending that Anglican churches should consider omitting the filioque clause from the Nicene Creed.[305] However, the argument that it puts forward for omitting the filioque clause presents a number of difficulties.

Firstly, it is true that the original form of the Nicene Creed did not contain the clause. However, the original Creed of Nicaea of 325 did not contain most of the material about the Holy Spirit that is contained in the Nicene Creed itself and yet this material is accepted and recited by churches in both East and West along with the other additions to the Creed of Nicaea contained in the Nicene Creed. It follows that it is difficult

---

[304] *Anglican Orthodox Dialogue – The Moscow Agreed Statement* London: SPCK 1977 p.88
[305] See Coleman (ed) Resolutions of the Lambeth Conferences pp.192 and 201.

to consistently maintain that additions to existing creedal material are wrong in principle.

Secondly, although it is true that the filioque clause was introduced into the Creed: 'without the authority of an Ecumenical Council and without due regard for Catholic consent,' this is also true of the additions made to the Creed of Nicaea by the Nicene Creed. As we shall see in more detail in connection with Article VIII, research on the origins of the Nicene Creed indicates that it was a local adaptation of the Creed of Nicaea that was adopted by the First Council of Constantinople in 381 and then formally endorsed by the Council of Chalcedon in 451. It follows that if the local adaptations of the Creed of Nicaea contained in the Nicene Creed could be granted retrospective endorsement there is no reason in principle why the same should not be true of the filioque clause.

Thirdly, while it is undoubtedly important that the Creed that is recited at the Eucharist should unite and not divide the people of God omission of the filioque clause by the West is only one way that this unity might be upheld. It could also be upheld by the East adopting the filioque clause or by an agreement by both East and West that it was and is legitimate to recite the Creed with or without the addition.

Fourthly, the objections to the use of the clause in the *Moscow Agreed Statement* all skirt around the most fundamental issue which is whether the theology of the double procession contained in the clause is correct. As we shall see when we come to look at Article VIII, from a traditional Church of England perspective the important thing about the Creeds is that they are summaries of the teaching of Scripture and this means that if an addition to the Creed makes it a better summary of Scripture then there is a good case for adopting it whatever its provenance might be.

The fundamental issue, then, is whether we should accept the theology of the double procession and it is to this issue that we now turn.

As Smail argues, the Eastern idea of the procession of the Spirit from the Father alone has the great strength that it duly recognises the priority of the Father within the Holy Trinity:

> ...in the New Testament the Father is the prime source and the ultimate end of everything that the Son does and is. Within the divine being that they both share, the Father is first and the Son is second. It is true both of his time on earth and from eternity to

eternity in heaven that 'the Father and I are one' (John 10:30) and that 'the Father is greater than I' (John 14:28).

The same is true of the Spirit. If we turn again to what John says about the giving of the Spirit, we shall see that even when the immediate focus is on the Son's part in sending the Spirit, there is nearly always a reference to the Father as the ultimate source from whom the Spirit comes. For example in John 15:26, although the Spirit is sent by the Son, nevertheless the point of origin is 'from the Father'. In the other passages we reviewed earlier in this chapter the Spirit is given in response to the prayer or to the completed work of the Son; nevertheless it is the Father rather than the Son who gives him. If it is the Son who baptises with the Spirit, it is because he himself at his own baptism received the Spirit from the Father.

To sum up, if the relationships between Father, Son and Spirit that come to light in the life of the incarnate Son reflect and reveal the eternal relationships between Father, Son and Spirit within the life of God, we have every reason to join our eastern Orthodox brethren in holding that the primary and most basic thing to say about the Spirit is that he 'proceeds from the Father'. The New Testament basis for that statement is clear and sure.[306]

On the other hand, there is also a strong basis for the Western position in those New Testament passages that talk about the Holy Spirit being sent by the Son as the counsellor or 'paraclete' and that talk about the Spirit as being breathed out by the risen Jesus. To quote Smail again:

> The strength of the western creedal claim that the Son has a central part to play in the giving of the Spirit is that it accurately reflects what the relevant scriptural passages say. If the Paraclete passages in John make it clear that the Father is the primary source of the Son – the eastern emphasis – they make it equally clear that the Spirit is sent by the Son – the western emphasis.
>
> We need only recall such passages as John 15:26 which speaks of 'the Counsellor whom I will send to you from the Father' and John 16:7, 'If I go I will send him to you', and also the risen Jesus breathing upon his disciples and saying 'Receive the

---

[306] Smail *The Giving Gift* p.124

Holy Spirit' (John 20:22). To such passages the West appeals for biblical backing and such an appeal is fully justified. The western emphasis on the strong relation between the Spirit and the Son is part of the gospel as given and is needed as bulwark against the Christless mysticism, religious pluralism and charismatic excess which can easily intrude when we try to enter into life in the Spirit as something apart from life in the Son.[307]

The standard Eastern response to the passages cited by Smail is to say that they only refer to the sending of the Spirit in this world and do not tell us anything about the eternal relationship between the Son and the Spirit within the life of the Trinity. However, as we have already noted, it is theologically illegitimate to try to distinguish between God as we encounter Him in His revelation and God as He is in Himself. Either God is as He is in His revelation or we cannot know God at all.

Given the strengths of both the Eastern and the Western positions is there any way that we can bring them together? One suggestion that has been gaining ground in recent years is to say that the Holy Spirit proceeds from the Father *through* the Son.

The idea that the Spirit proceeds from the Father through the Son is not a recent innovation, but one that has ancient roots. It can be found, for example, in the teaching of St. Gregory of Nyssa in the Fourth century. In his work *On the Holy Spirit* he compares the procession of the Spirit to the lighting of three torches:

> It is as if a man were to see a separate flame burning on three torches (and we will suppose that the third flame is caused by the first being transmitted to the middle, and then kindling the end torch)...[308]

As Smail notes, what St. Gregory is saying in this quotation is that: 'The Spirit has his being from the Father, although he receives that being not directly and immediately but through the Son.'[309] If we compare this understanding of the procession of the Spirit with the one put forward by

---

[307] Ibid p. 132
[308] Gregory of Nyssa *On the Holy Spirit* in *Nicene and Post Nicene Fathers* 2nd series vol V Edinburgh & Grand Rapids: T&T Clark / Eerdmans 1994 p.317
[309] Smail *The Giving Gift* p.128

St. Augustine to which we referred earlier what we find is a fundamental agreement between the two.

Both St. Augustine and St. Gregory hold that the principal source of the Holy Spirit is the Father, but that He also has His being from the Son to whom the deity possessed by the Father has also been given. Given that, as has been said, the teaching of St. Augustine lies at the root of the Western doctrine of the double procession, the agreement between his teaching and that of St. Gregory is highly significant. What it means is that in Fathers from both East (Gregory) and West (Augustine) we can find an agreement that takes us beyond the apparent impasse between the doctrines of the single and double processions of the Spirit.

What it means is that we can say with both Scripture and the Eastern tradition that the Father is the fount of deity, the one from whom the Son and the Spirit eternally have their being. Therefore we have to say that the Spirit is the Spirit of the Father who proceeds from the Father.

It also means that we can say with both Scripture and the Western tradition that the Spirit does not have His being apart from the Son, but eternally has His being from the Father through the Son. Therefore we have to say that the Spirit is the Spirit of the Son who proceeds from the Son as well as from the Father.

In terms of the Nicene Creed what this means is that the West needs to recognise that it is legitimate to say that the Holy Spirit 'proceeds from the Father' providing this is understood to mean that the Father is the ultimate source of the Spirit and does not preclude the idea that the Spirit proceeds from the Father but through the Son. It also means that the East needs to recognise that it is legitimate to say that the Holy Spirit 'proceeds from the Father and the Son' as long as it is recognised that 'from' has to be understood in the sense of 'from the Father through the Son' and not as meaning that the Son is a separate and distinct source of the Spirit's being alongside the Father.

In his commentary on Article V Bishop Gibson draws attention to the fact that at the Council of Alexandria in the Fourth Century it was accepted that the different terminologies used by Eastern and Western Christians to describe the Trinity were both legitimate. He suggests that given the kind of basic theological agreement described above this provides a model for handling the differences over the inclusion or exclusion of the filioque clause from the Creed.

There was a difference of phraseology between different portions of the Church as regards an important matter of faith. But so soon as it was discovered that, in spite of varying language, the meaning of both parties was identical, it was felt that a difference of phraseology was, after all, but a minor inconvenience, which might well be endured without causing any schism in the Church, and it was agreed that both parties might keep to their own traditional mode of expressing the doctrine which they held in common. So also, if Greeks and Latins are really at one in the doctrine, it is possible to look forward to the day when similar wise counsels may prevail, and the acceptance of the [Nicene] Constantinoplian Creed, either with or without the *Filioque*, may be admitted as a basis for intercommunion between the long estranged branches of the Church in the East and West.[310]

...is of one substance, majesty, and glory with the Father and the Son, very and eternal God.

In its original context the picture by St. Gregory of Nyssa of three torches with the second and third being lit from the first was part of an argument for the full deity of the Holy Spirit. The point he is making is that because the Holy Spirit has His being from the Father through the Son He is fully God in just the same way as one fire lit from another fire is none the less fully fire.

In a similar fashion the logic of Article V is that because the Holy Spirit proceeds from the Father and the Son that He is 'of one substance, majesty, and glory with the Father and the Son, very and eternal God.' As Bishop Beveridge puts it in his commentary on the Articles:

> ...as the Son doth so receive his Divine essence from the Father, as to be the selfsame individual God with the Father; so doth the Spirit receive his essence from the Father and Son to be of one substance and glory with the Father and the Son. The Father did not communicate another, but his own numerical or individual nature to the Son, and so both Father and Son being of one nature betwixt themselves communicate that their nature to the Spirit; by which means though he proceed from both, and so is a distinct

---

[310] Gibson op.cit pp228-229

Person from both, yet he hath the same nature and substance with both, and so is as truly that one God which we worship and adore, as either or both of them. Insomuch that as though the Father be the root, origin and fountain of Deity to the Son, and yet the Son hath as much of the Divine nature in him as the Father; so here though it be from the Father and the Son that the Spirit doth proceed, yet he hath the Divine nature in him as perfectly as either of them, and so is truly and eternally God, that one God blessed for evermore, which angels and men are continually bound to worship and adore.[311]

Because the Holy Spirit is 'very and eternal God' it therefore follows that He possesses the one divine essence or 'substance' possessed also by the Father and the Son, that He possesses the same divine 'majesty' as the Father and the Son and that He possesses the same 'glory' as they do.

The fact that the Holy Spirit is 'very and eternal God' is shown by three converging pieces of biblical evidence.

First, the Holy Spirit is implicitly called God:

- In Acts 5:3-4 the lie told by Ananias to the Holy Spirit is said to be a lie told to God.

- In 2 Cor 3:18 the Spirit is given the divine name 'the Lord'.

- A comparison of Lk 11:20 and Mt 12:28 shows that the 'finger of God' in St. Luke is identical with the 'Spirit of God' in St. Matthew.

- In Acts 28:25-28 the words of God in Isa 6:9-10 are ascribed to the Holy Spirit.

- In 1 Cor 3:16 and 6:19 the presence of God in the bodies of believers, which are now the Temple of God, is specifically identified as the presence of the Holy Spirit.

Secondly, divine characteristics and actions are ascribed to Him:

---

[311] Beveridge op.cit p.179

- In Mk 3:29 blasphemy against the Holy Spirit is described as the unforgivable sin and such a sin would only be possible if the Holy Spirit is God.

- In Heb 9:14 He is said to possess eternity, being described as 'the eternal Spirit'.

- In 1 Cor 2:10-11 He is said to possess omniscience in that it is said that 'Spirit searches everything, even the depths of God.'

- In Ps 139:7-12 He is said to possess omnipresence in that the Psalmist parallels the Omnipresence of God with the omnipresence of God's Spirit: 'Whither shall I go from thy Spirit? Or whither shall I flee from thy presence?

- The actions of the Spirit in creation (Gen 1:2, Ps 33:6), in inspiring the prophets (Isa 61:1 2 Pet 1:21), in bringing about the incarnation (Lk 1:35) and in giving new birth to Christians (Jn 3:5-7, Tit 3:5) so that they are 'born of God' (1 Jn 3:9) are actions which only make sense if the Holy Spirit is God rather than a creature.

Thirdly, he is ranked alongside the other members of the Trinity:

- We see this most clearly in the threefold baptismal formula in Mt 28:19, but also in other three membered passages such as 1 Cor 12:4-6, 2 Cor 3:14, Eph 4:4-6, 1 Pet 1:2 and Jude 20-21, all of which again only make sense on the basis that the Holy Spirit is a member of the Godhead alongside the Father and the Son rather than a creature.

The cumulative weight of this witness is well summarised by St. Basil in his work *Against Eunomius*:

> Seeing what is common to the Father and the Son is common also to the Spirit; seeing by the same things that God the Father and the Son are characterised and described in scripture, by the same things is the Holy Ghost characterised and described; it is hence gathered that the Spirit is of the same Deity as the Father. Seeing that whatsoever is in the Father as God only and not as a father, and whatever is in the Son as God only and not as a son, the same

also is in the Holy Ghost, but not in any creatures, as names and things incommunicable to the creatures, common only to the Trinity, it is hence gathered that the Trinity is of one substance and glory.[312]

It might theoretically be possible to maintain that, while the Holy Spirit is God, He is an impersonal attribute of God and that that is why He has the impersonal name 'Spirit' rather than a personal name like 'Father' or 'Son'. However, this idea is ruled out by the biblical evidence which clearly teaches the personal identity of the Spirit.

We see this first of all in the 'farewell discourse' in Jn 14-17. In these discourses the Spirit is given the personal title of the 'paraclete' or 'counsellor' (14:16, 26, 15:26, 16:7), He is referred to by the masculine singular pronoun *ekeinos* ('he') and as Bishop Gibson writes: '....such personal activities are ascribed to Him as teaching, reminding, bearing witness, convicting of sin, guiding into truth, declaring things to come, glorifying Christ, taking of the things of Christ, and declaring them to the disciples (14:26, 15:26, 16:8-14).'[313] As Henry Swete comments, throughout this whole discourse:

> ...the role of a personal advocate is ascribed to the Spirit. He takes the place of the absent Christ. He is sent by the Christ from the Father, and when He has come He will guide believers as Christ had guided them hitherto, will teach as Christ taught, will take of that which is Christ's and declare it to them, will convict the world which the ministry of Christ failed to convict. That this advocate will be invisible and purely spiritual does not make against his personality; it is in that which is most spiritual in ourselves that we find evidence of our own personal life. That He fulfils the whole of our Lord's personal functions towards the Church, that He belongs to the category of Paraclete – Teacher, Director, Protector Counsellor – this invests Him with all the essential attributes of that which we understand by personality.[314]

---

[312] St. Basil *Against Eunomius* 1.5 quoted in Beveridge op.cit p.185
[313] Gibson op.cit. p.202
[314] H B Swete *The Holy Spirit in the New Testament* London: Macmillan 1910 p. 292

We also see it in the rest of the New Testament where we are told that the Holy Spirit 'intercedes' for the saints (Rom 8:26-27), apportions spiritual gifts 'as He wills' (1 Cor 12:4-11), 'leads' Christians into living holy lives (Gal 5:18), and can be 'grieved' (Eph 4:30). As we have seen, it is also possible to lie to the Spirit (Acts 5:4) and to blaspheme against Him (Mk 3:29). In the words of Bishop Gibson: 'Language such as this is surely conclusive. It would be inexplicable if the Holy Spirit were only an attribute, influence, gift, or operation.'[315]

The final issue that we need to consider in looking at Article V is how we are to understand the role of the Holy Spirit within the life of God. If He is indeed the Third Person of the Trinity who proceeds from the Father and (through) the Son how does He relate to them and enable them to relate to each other?

Smail is helpful on this issue. Building on the teaching of St. Augustine that the Holy Spirit is the bond of love between the Father and the Son and drawing on the work of the Roman Catholic theologian Heribert Muhlen on the Holy Spirit as the product and expression of the relationship between them, he writes:

> Because the Father and the Son share one divine being and nature, their love for each other can become person in one Holy Spirit, who in his origin is the Spirit of the Father whom he gives to his Son, the eternal partner of his divine life, and within that life becomes the Spirit of the Son in whom he gives himself to the Father. He is not just the relationship of love between the two, but the personal product and expression of that relationship in which the Father initiates and the Son responds to his initiative. He proceeds from the Father to the Son and he returns from the Son to the Father.
>
> This, in a way that affirms both the priority of the Father, for which eastern Orthodoxy rightly contends, and the essential involvement of the Son, on which western Christians rightly insist, he is the Spirit of the Father and of the Son. He is the Father's Gift of himself in person to the Son; he is the Son's answering Gift of himself in person to the Father. He is the third Person who originates in the self giving of the first Person to the

---

[315] Gibson op.cit p.204

second, and expresses the responsive self-surrender of the second Person to the first.[316]

According to Smail, it is this pattern of relationship within God that we see expressed in the saving activity of God in the incarnation:

> It is this Spirit who comes to us. Because he is in himself the personal product of the self-giving of the Father and Son within the eternal life of God, he can express that self-giving savingly in human history and experience. The Father who in the Son has given himself before all words to his eternal Son now gives himself in the same way to his incarnate Son in the context of his human life. He gives himself in his Spirit to his Son first to bring him to human birth at Christmas. He gives himself in another way to the same Son in the Spirit to anoint him with divine authority in his baptism. He gives himself in a third way to the same Son in the same Spirit to transform him into the *eschatos Adam*, the ultimate Man in his resurrection. In these historical events the Father is doing what he has always done, giving himself in his Spirit to his Son.
>
> In the same way the Son who before all worlds gives himself to the Father as to his source and origin, now in his incarnation gives Himself to his Father in the context of his human life. In the Spirit from whom he has his birth he grows into his Father's favour and pledges himself to be about his Father's business (Luke 2:52,49). In the Spirit who comes upon him in his baptism he gives himself in life and death to fulfil his Father's purpose. That purpose is our salvation and it is accomplished in a way that is entirely consonant with the eternal being of God, namely in the giving of the Father to the Son in the Spirit and in the giving of the Son to the Father in the same spirit. God is self-giving and it is when that self-giving becomes human history that fallen humanity is redeemed and renewed.[317]

---

[316] Smail *The Giving Gift* p.160
[317] Ibid pp.160-161

Finally, Smail notes that it is through the Holy Spirit that God the Father and the Son dwell in us and we are enabled to receive and to respond to what God has done for us:

> Christians are temples indwelt by the Father and the Son. This indwelling is effected by the Holy Spirit in such a way that the personal relationship between them and us is preserved in its integrity. They do not become us and we do not become them. Yet in the Spirit they give themselves across the relationship to us, just as in their own life they give themselves across the Father-Son relationship to each other. The indwelling of the Father and the Son in us is the Holy Spirit, who is their personalised self-giving to us. The Spirit is the originating love of the Father and the responding love of the Son given to us in personal form. The Spirit of the Father and the Son comes to us to enable our reception of and our response to what God has done for us in Christ.[318]

To put the same thing in more explicitly biblical terms, what this means is that the love of God the Father: 'has been poured into out hearts through the Holy Spirit which has been given to us' (Rom 5:5) and as a result we are able through the same Spirit to respond with God the Son by crying: 'Abba! Father!' in return (Rom 8:15, Gal 4:6).

---

[318] Ibid p.162

Scripture and the Creeds: Articles VI-VIII

Having considered the doctrine of God in Articles I-V, the *Thirty Nine Articles* move on to look at Scripture and the Creeds in Articles VI-VIII.

These articles are an expansion by Archbishop Parker of articles V-VII of the *Forty Two Articles* and like their predecessors they are designed to establish the Church of England's position over against the Roman Catholics on the one hand and the radical Protestants on the other.

A careful study of the relationship between Articles VI-VIII reveals that the key to the sequence of thought which they contain is the statement of the sufficiency of Scripture for salvation in the first paragraph of Article VI. The statement in this paragraph that Holy Scripture contains everything necessary for salvation leads into a series of statements about a number of other issues relating to Scripture that are tackled in the remaining paragraphs of Article VI and then in Articles VII and VIII.

These issues are:

(1) The practical consequence of the fact that Scripture contains everything necessary for salvation.

According to Article VI the consequence is that no one can be required to accept anything that is not in Scripture or that cannot be proved on the basis of what is in Scripture as either a necessary part of the Christian faith or as essential for their salvation.

(2) Which books constitute Scripture?

One of the dividing lines between Roman Catholic and Protestant theologians at the Reformation was the issue of which books constituted Scripture. The Roman Catholic position, eventually defined at the Council of Trent, was that some of the books of the Apocrypha were part of Scripture. The Protestant position was that they were not.

Article VI takes the Protestant side of this issue, defining Scripture in terms of the thirty nine Old Testament and twenty seven New Testament books accepted by the later Patristic and Medieval Western Church.

(3) The value of the Apocrypha.

If the books of the Apocrypha were not part of Scripture what value did they have? The answer Article VI gives to this question is that although they do not provide a basis for Christian doctrine they nevertheless continue to be read by the Church because they provide examples of holy living and moral instruction

(4) The unity of the Old and New Testaments.

Over against the idea that in the Old Testament people are promised blessings only in this world whereas in the New Testament they are offered everlasting life that begins in this world and continues in the world that is to come, the first part of Article VII declares that there is a unity between the two Testaments in that in both of them everlasting life is offered through Christ.

(5) The continuing authority of the Old Testament law.

The second part of Article VII rejects two opposing errors concerning the laws in contained in the Old Testament. The first is the idea that these laws have no authority for Christians and the second is the idea that Christians should continue to obey all of them. Rejecting these two errors, Article VII argues instead that while Christians are not called upon to observe either the ceremonial and ritual laws of the Old Testament or those laws relating to the civil government of Israel, they are called upon to observe the basic moral commandments that the Old Testament contains.

(6) The authority of the Creeds.

The Protestant emphasis on the unique authority of Scripture reflected in Article VI necessarily raised the issue of the authority of the Creeds. Given that they were not part of Scripture did they still have to be accepted? Article VIII declares that the three Creeds used in the Western Church, the Apostles', Nicene and Athanasian Creeds, do have to be accepted because their contents reflect the teaching of Scripture itself.

Within the wider structure of the *Thirty Nine Articles* the opening sentence of Article VI also leads into the discussion of issues concerning salvation in Articles IX-XVIII. What Article VI does is to lay down the principle that such matters need to be based on the teaching of Scripture, and what Articles IX-XVIII do is to expound what Scripture teaches about salvation with reference to particular sixteenth century controversies.

Article VI

∞

Of the sufficiency of the Holy Scriptures for Salvation

Holy Scriptures containeth all things necessary to salvation: so that whatsoever is not read therein, nor may be proved thereby, is not to be required of any man, that it should be believed as an article of the faith, or be thought requisite or necessary to salvation. In the name of Holy Scripture, we do understand those Canonical books of the Old and New Testament, of whose authority was never any doubt in the Church.

Of the names and number of the Canonical Books:

Genesis	First Book of Chronicles
Exodus	Second Book of Chronicles
Leviticus	First Book of Esdras
Numbers	Second Book of Esdras
Deuteronomy	Book of Esther
Joshua	Book of Job
Judges	Psalms
Ruth	Proverbs
First Book of Samuel	Ecclesiastes, or the Preacher
Second Book of Samuel	Cantica, or Songs of Solomon
First Book of Kings	Four Prophets the Greater
Second Book of Kings	Twelve Prophets the Less

And the other books (as Hierome saith) the Church doth read for example of life and instruction of manners; but yet doth it not apply them to establish any doctrine; such are these following:

Third Book of Esdras	Baruch the Prophet
Fourth Book of Esdras	The Song of the Three Children
Book of Tobias	The Story of Susanna
Book of Judith	Of Bel and the Dragon
The rest of the Book of Esther	The Prayer of Manasses
Book of Wisdom	First Book of Maccabees
Jesus the Son of Sirach	Second Book of Maccabees

All the books of the New Testament, as they are commonly received, we do receive, and account them canonical.

De divinis Scripturis, quod sufficiant ad salutem

Scriptura sacra continet omnia, quae ad salutem sunt necessaria, ita, ut quicquid in ea nec legitur, neque inde probari potest, non sit a quoquam exigendum, ut tanquam articulus fidei credatur, aut ad salutis necessitatem requiri putetur.

Sacrae Scripturae nomine, eos Canonicos libros Veteris et Novi Testamenti intelligimus, de quorum authoritate in Ecclesia nunquam dubitatum est.

De nominibus et numero librorum sacrae Canonicae Scripturae veteris Testamenti.

Genesis, Exodus, Leviticus, Numeri, Deuteronomium, Iosuae, Iudicum, Ruth, Prior liber Samuelis, Secundus liber Samuelis, Prior liber Regum, Secundus liber Regum, Prior liber Paralipomenon, Secundus liber Paralipomenon, Primus liber Esdrae, Secundus liber Esdrae, Liber Hester, Liber Iob, Psalmi, Proverbia, Ecclesiastes vol Concionator, Cantica Solomonis, quatuor Prophetae maiores, duodecim Prophetae minores.

Alios autem libros (ut ait Hieronymus) legit quidem Ecclesia ad exempla vitae et formandos mores; illos tamen ad dogmata confirmanda non adhibet: ut sunt:

Tertius liber Esdrae, Quartus liber Esdrae, Liber Tobiae, Liber Iudith, Reliquum libri Hester, Liber Sapientiae, Liber Iesu filii Sirach, Baruch Propheta. Canticum trium puerorum, Historia

Susannae, De Bel et Dracone, Oratio Manassis, Prior liber Machabaeorum, Secundus liber Machabaeorum.

Novi Testamenti omnes libros (ut vulgo recepti sunt) recipimus, et habemus pro Canonicis.

Article VI is a development of Article V of the *Forty Two Articles*. That was entitled 'The doctrine of the Holy Scripture is sufficient to salvation' and contained only the first sentence of the current article and in the following, slightly different, form:

> Holy Scripture containeth all things necessary to salvation: so that whatsoever is neither read therein, nor may be proved thereby, *although it be some time received of the faithful as godly, and profitable for order and comeliness*: yet no man ought to be constrained to believe it as an article of faith or repute it requisite to the necessity of salvation.

When the Articles were revised in 1563 the title was retained, but the words we have put in italics were omitted and the final clause of the sentence was slightly reworded.

As Griffith Thomas notes, the reason that the italicised words were omitted was: '...because the Article deals with questions of faith not order, the latter being dealt with in Article XX and XXXIV.'[319]

The remaining part of the current article was also added, but with a shorter list of apocryphal books consisting of 3 and 4 Esdras, Wisdom, Jesus the Son of Sirach, Tobit, Judith and 1 and 2 Maccabees.

In 1571 the present title was adopted, the rest of the Book of Esther, Baruch the Prophet, the Song of the Three Children, the Story of Susanna, Bel and the Dragon and the Prayer of Manasses were added to the list of apocryphal books and one or two other minor verbal changes were made.

The language of the beginning of Article VI is similar to that of the *Reformatio Legum Ecclesiasticarum*, which follows a list of the books contained in Scripture with the words:

---

[319] Griffith Thomas *The Principles of Theology* p. 104

This is the sum of the Holy Scripture, in which we believe that all things which must be believed for salvation are fully and perfectly contained, so that if something is not read or contained in it, neither does it follow nor is it deduced from it, cannot be demanded of anyone that it should be believed as an article of faith.[320]

The second sentence of the article: 'In the name of Holy Scripture, we do understand those Canonical books of the Old and New Testament, of whose authority was never any doubt in the Church' was taken by Parker from the Article 'De Sacra Scriptura' in the *Wurtemburg Confession*.

The statement by St. Jerome on the Church's use of the Apocrypha that the Article paraphrases comes from his preface to the books of Solomon (Proverbs, Ecclesiastes and the Song of Solomon). In this he refers to the Wisdom of Solomon and Ecclesiasticus and comments with reference to these:

> As, then, the Church reads Judith, Tobit and the Books of Maccabees, but does not admit them to the canonical Scriptures, so let it read these two volumes for the edification of the people, not to give authority to the doctrines of the Church. [321]

As I have already indicated, Article VI, like Articles VI-VIII as a whole, is intended to establish the Church of England's position with regard to Scripture over against the radical Reformation on the one hand and the Roman Catholics on the other.

In the sixteenth century a number of the radical Protestant groupings played down the importance of the Bible and emphasised the importance of direct revelation through the Holy Spirit instead. Their beliefs in this respect are criticised both in the *Forty Two Articles* and in the *Reformatio Legum Ecclesiasticarum*

Article XIX of the *Forty Two Articles* declares:

---

[320] *Reformatio Legum Ecclesiasticarum* 1:9 in Bray *Tudor Church Reform* p.171
[321] St. Jerome, 'Prefaces' in *The Nicene and Post Nicene Fathers: Second Series*, Vol. VI, Edinburgh and Grand Rapids, T &T Clark/Eerdmans, 1996, p.492.

>...they are not to be hearkened unto, who affirm that Holy Scripture is given only to the weak, and do boast themselves continually of the Spirit, of whom they say they have learned such things as they teach, although the same be most evidently repugnant to the Holy Scriptures. [322]

In similar fashion, the account of current heresies in chapter two of the *Reformatio Legum Ecclesiasticarum* states that the 'most frightening' form of heresy is that taught by those:

>...who misread and distort the Holy Scriptures to the hurt of weak men only, thus all the while confirming that they have no respect for their authority, and they arrogate to themselves some special spirit by which they claim that they are supplied with the knowledge of things, demonstrating that they do not think themselves bound by their authority, but boast of some special spirit by which they say that everything they teach and do is revealed to them.[323]

The argument in this quotation is not easy to follow, but it is clear that its overall thrust is same at that of Article XIX, namely that there are heretics abroad who teach that the Scriptures are only for the spiritually weak, while the spiritually mature rely on the direct teaching of the Holy Spirit.

The fact that Archbishop Parker left out the section of Article XIX quoted above when he revised the *Forty Two Articles* seems to indicate that the threat of this heresy was not regarded as being as serious in the 1560s as it had been in the 1540s. Nevertheless the existence of this heresy forms part of the background to Article VI. What Article VI is implicitly saying is that Scripture is not just for the spiritually immature, but for all Christians. It contains all that you need to know in order to be saved and therefore it is a mistake either to base your religion on what are alleged to be the direct teachings of the Spirit or to insist that it is necessary to obey such teachings even when they contradict the testimony of Scripture itself.

The other part of the background to the article is the Roman Catholic response to the emphasis on the authority of the Holy Scripture

---

[322] Text in Bray *Documents of the English Reformation* p.296
[323] *Reformatio Legum Ecclesiasticarum* 2:3 in Bray *Tudor Church Reform* p.189

by the Protestant Reformers. In response to Lutheran teaching that contrasted the authority of Scripture with that of the traditions of the Church, the fourth session of the Council of Trent in April 1546 declared that:

> This [Gospel], of old promised through the Prophets in the Holy Scriptures, our Lord Jesus Christ, the Son of God, promulgated first with His own mouth, and then commanded it to be preached by His Apostles to every creature as the source at once of all saving truth and rules of conduct. It also clearly perceives that these truth and rules are contained in the written books and in the unwritten traditions, which, received by the Apostles from the mouth of Christ Himself, or from the Apostles themselves, the Holy Ghost dictating, have come down to us, transmitted as it were from hand to hand. Following, then, the example of the orthodox Fathers, it receives and venerates with a feeling of piety and reverence all the books both of the Old and New Testaments, since one God is the author of both; also the traditions, whether they relate to faith or to morals, as having been dictated orally by Christ or by the Holy Ghost, and preserved in the Catholic Church in unbroken succession.[324]

These words have been interpreted in two ways. Some have understood them to mean that the Council of Trent teaches a 'coincidence' view of the relationship between Scripture and tradition. Others have held that it teaches a 'supplementary' view of this relationship.

According to the 'coincidence' view the contents of Scripture and tradition coincide. They are two different channels by which one and the same divine revelation is passed on to us. According to the 'supplementary' view the contents of Scripture supplement the contents of Scripture. Things are revealed to us in tradition that are not also revealed to us in Scripture.[325]

---

[324] Council of Trent 'Decree Concerning the Canonical Scriptures'. Text in Leith *Creeds of the Churches* p.402

[325] For more detail on these two views of the relationship between Scripture and tradition see R Bauckham *God and the Crisis of Freedom* Louisville: Westminster John Knox Press 2002 pp. 92-94.

The debate about precisely which view the Council of Trent intended to endorse still continues.[326] However, the majority of the theologians at Trent took the supplementary view[327] and, as Richard Bauckham notes:

> After Trent, its decree was almost universally interpreted by Roman Catholic theologians from the sixteenth to the nineteenth century as teaching the supplementary view.[328]

The sixteenth and early seventeenth century Roman Catholic apologist Cardinal Robert Bellarmine writes, for instance:

> The controversy between us and the heretics [i.e. the Protestants] consists in two things. The first is, that *we* assert, that in Scripture is not expressly contained all necessary doctrine, whether concerning faith or morals, and therefore that, besides the written word of God, there is moreover needed the unwritten word, i.e. Divine and Apostolical Tradition. But *they* teach, that all things necessary for faith and morals are contained in the Scriptures, and that therefore there is no need of the unwritten word.[329]

It seems probable that Archbishop Cranmer and Archbishop Parker understood the Roman Catholic position in the terms in which it is expounded by Cardinal Bellarmine and that it is this position that Article VI is in part designed to oppose.

As I have already explained above, as well as emphasising the importance of tradition alongside Scripture, the fourth session of the Council of Trent also declared that some of the books of the Apocrypha were part of Scripture. The books in question were Tobit, Judith, Wisdom, Ecclesiasticus, Baruch and 1 and 2 Maccabees and Trent listed these as part of the Old Testament.[330]There can be no doubt that when Archbishop

---

[326] For details of the debate see, for example, Y M J Congar, *Tradition and Traditions,* London: Burns and Oates 1966 pp.164-169, and G Moran *Scripture and Tradition: A Survey of the Controversy*, New York: Herder and Herder 1963 pp. 34-38, 48-54, 63-68.

[327] See H Jedin *A History of the Council of Trent*, vol. 2, Edinburgh: Nelson 1961 p75

[328] Bauckham op.cit. p.94

[329] R Bellarmine *De Verbo Dei non Scripto* Bk IV. Ch 3 cited in Browne *An Exposition of the Thirty Nine Articles* p. 124

[330] See Leith op.cit pp.402-3

Parker drew up the list of canonical books in the second part of Article VI he was fully aware of the decision of the Council of Trent about the matter and that he intended to distance the Church of England from it as well as from the views of those Protestants who thought that no use should be made of the Apocrypha at all.

Holy Scriptures containeth all things necessary to salvation

The English Reformers of the sixteenth century accepted the belief that had always been held in the Christian Church that every one of the words of Scripture was inspired by God. We can see this, for example, in the following extract from a sermon preached by John Jewel, Bishop of Salisbury in 1570. Referring to the words of St. Paul in 2 Tim 3:16, Bishop Jewel comments:

> Many think that the apostle's speech is hardly true of the whole scripture, that all and every part of scripture is profitable. Much is spoken of genealogies, and pedigrees, of lepers, of sacrificing goats and oxen, &c: these seem to have little profit in them, but to be vain and idle. If they show vain in thine eyes, yet hath the Lord not set them down in vain. 'The words of the Lord are pure words, as the silver tried in a furnace of fire fined seven times.' There is no sentence, no clause, no word, no syllable, no letter, but it is written for thy instruction: there is not one jot but it is sealed and signed with the blood of the Lamb. Those oxen and goats were sacrificed teach thee to kill and sacrifice the uncleanness and filthiness of thy heart: they teach thee that thou art guilty of death, when thy life must be redeemed by the death of some beast: they lead thee to believe the forgiveness of sins by a more perfect sacrifice; because it was not possible that the blood of bulls and goats should take away sins. That leprosy teacheth thee to know the uncleanness and leprosy of thy soul. These genealogies lead us to be the birth of our Saviour Christ. So that the whole word of God is pure and holy: no word, no letter, no syllable, no point or prick thereof, but is written and preserved for thy sake.[331]

---

[331] J Ayre (ed) *The Works of John Jewel Bishop of Salisbury - The Fourth Portion* Cambridge: Parker Society/CUP 1850 pp.1174-5.

What is noteworthy in this extract, apart from Bishop Jewel's emphasis on the divine inspiration of every word in the Bible, is his emphasis on the practical result of this inspiration. For Bishop Jewel, following St. Paul, the inspiration of the Bible and its 'profitable' nature are inseparable. What the inspiration of Scripture means is that its words are called into being by God in order to enable us to become rightly related to Him by showing us our sinfulness, how God has made provision for our salvation through Christ and how we are meant to live in response.

This same practical emphasis is found in the opening words of Article VI. This article is not concerned with the sort of matters that pre-occupy many modern debates about Scripture, such as the historical accuracy of the Bible or its relationship to scientific discoveries.[332] What it is concerned about is the fact that the Bible contains all you need to know in order to be saved.

This point is made by Archbishop Cranmer in more detail in his 1547 homily *A Fruitful Exhortation to the Reading and Knowledge of Holy Scripture*. As its title suggests, this homily is meant to encourage people to read the Bible for themselves. The reason it gives that people should read the Bible is that only if they read it will they gain the knowledge necessary in order to find their way to God.

As the opening words of the homily put it:

> Unto a Christian man there can be nothing either more necessary or profitable, then the knowledge of holy Scripture, forasmuch as in it is contained God's true word, setting forth his glory, and also mans duty. And there is no truth nor doctrine necessary for our justification and everlasting salvation, but that is (or may be) drawn out of that fountain and well of truth. Therefore as many as be desirous to enter into the right and perfect way unto God, must apply their minds to know holy scripture; without the which, they can neither sufficiently know God and his will, neither their office and duty.[333]

---

[332] This is not to say that these natters are unimportant, simply to observe that they are not matters with which Article VI is concerned.

[333] T Cranmer *A Fruitful Exhortation to the Reading and Knowledge of Holy Scripture* in Leith op.cit. p. 231

In two subsequent sections of the homily Archbishop Cranmer explains in more detail what he means by these opening words.

In the first he declares:

> ...in holy scripture is fully contained what we ought to do, and what to eschew; what to believe, what to love, and what to look for at God's hands at length. In these Books we shall find the Father from whom, the Son by whom, and the Holy Ghost, in whom all things have their being and keeping up, and these three persons to be but one God, and one substance. In these books we may learn to know ourselves, how vile and miserable we be, and also to know God, how good he is of himself, and how he maketh us and all creatures partakers of his goodness. We may learn also in these books to know God's will and pleasure, as much as (for this present time) is convenient for us to know. And (as the great clerk and godly preacher Saint John Chrysostom saith) whatsoever is required to salvation of man, is fully contained in the Scripture of God. He that is ignorant, may there learn and have knowledge. He that is hard hearted, and an obstinate sinner, shall there find everlasting torments (prepared of God's justice) to make him afraid, and to mollify or soften him. He that is oppressed with misery in this world, shall there find release in the promises of everlasting life, to his great consolation and comfort. He that is wounded by the Devil unto death, shall find there medicine whereby he may be restored again unto health. If it shall require to teach any truth, or reprove false doctrine, to rebuke any vice, to commend any virtue, to give good counsel, to comfort or to exhort, or to do any other thing requisite for our salvation, all those things (saith Saint Chrysostom) we may learn plentifully of the Scripture.[334]

In the second he states:

> The words of holy Scripture be called words of everlasting life [Jn 6:68]: for they be God's instrument, ordained for the same purpose. They have power to turn through God's promise, and they be effectual through God's assistance, and (being received in

---

[334] Ibid pp.232-3

a faithful heart) they have ever an heavenly spiritual working in them: they are lively, quick, and mighty in operation, and sharper then any two edged sword, and entereth through, even unto the dividing asunder of the soul and the spirit, of the joints and the marrow [Heb 4:12]. Christ calleth him a wise builder, that buildeth upon his word, upon his sure and substantial foundation [Mt 7:24]. By this word of God we shall be judged: for the word that I speak (saith Christ) is it, that shall judge in the last day [Jn 12:48]. He that keepeth the word of Christ, is promised the love and favour of God, and that he shall be the dwelling place or temple of the blessed Trinity [Jn 14:23]. This word, whosoever is diligent to read, and in his heart to print that he readeth, the great affection to the transitory things of this world, shall be minished in him, and the great desire of heavenly things (that be therein promised of God) shall increase in him. And there is nothing that so much strengtheneth our faith and trust in God, that so much keepeth up innocency and pureness of the heart, and also of outward godly life and conversation, as continual reading and recording of God's word. For that thing, which (by continual use of reading of holy Scripture, and diligent searching of the same) is deeply printed and graven in the heart, at length turneth almost into nature. And moreover, the effect and virtue of God's word is, to illuminate the ignorant, and to give more light unto them, that faithfully and diligently read it, to comfort their hearts, and to encourage them to perform that, which of God is commanded. It teacheth patience in all adversity, in prosperity, humbleness: what honour is due unto God, what, mercy and charity to our neighbour. It giveth good counsel in all doubtful things. It sheweth of whom we shall look for aid and help in all perils, and that God is the only giver of victory, in all battle and temptations of our enemies, bodily and ghostly [1 Sam 14:4-23, 2 Chron 20:7, 17, 29, 1 Cor 15:57, 1Jn 5:4].[335]

The two key points made by Archbishop Cranmer in this pair of quotations are that:

---

[335] Ibid p.233 – biblical references added.

- Scripture gives us all the knowledge we need in order to be rightly related to God

- Scripture is the instrument ordained and employed by God that makes this knowledge fruitful in us by making us the people that God wants us to be.

It is these two characteristics of Scripture that mean it contains everything necessary for salvation. If Scripture gives us all the knowledge and power we need to be rightly related to God then what more can possibly be needed?

In his recent book *Holy Scripture* John Webster notes that:

> ...revelation is the self-presentation of the triune God, the free work of sovereign mercy in which God wills, establishes and perfects saving fellowship with himself in which humankind comes to know, love and fear him above all things.[336]

What Archbishop Cranmer is claiming is that the primary location of this revelation is Holy Scripture and it is this fact that means that Scripture gives us all that we need in order to be saved.[337]

In his homily Archbishop Cranmer refers to the words of St. John Chrysostom to support the points He is making. The significance of this is that it reminds us that when the English Reformers argued that Scripture

---

[336] J Webster *Holy Scripture – A Dogmatic Sketch* Cambridge: CUP 2003 p.13

[337] It is a welcome sign of ecumenical convergence that the Second Vatican Council's Dogmatic Constitution on Divine Revelation, *Dei Verbum,* stresses from a Roman Catholic perspective how Scripture is central to God's saving activity:

> ...in the sacred books, the Father who is in heaven meets His children with great love and speaks with them; and the force and power in the word of God is so great that it stands as the support and energy of the Church, the strength and faith for her sons, the food of the soul, the pure and everlasting source of spiritual life. Consequently these words are perfectly applicable to Sacred Scripture 'For the word of God is living and active'(Heb 4:12) and 'it has power to build you up and give you your heritage amongst all those who are sanctified (Acts 20:32; see 1 Thess 2:13). (*Dei Verbum* 21 in W M Abbott SJ (ed) *The Documents of Vatican II* London: Geoffrey Chapman 1965 p.125)

contains all we need to know for salvation they were consciously following in the footsteps of the Fathers. As they saw it they were not innovators but were returning to the Patristic position.

This is a point that has also been made subsequently by many commentators on this Article. In his commentary on this article Bishop Browne, for example, cites a long list of Fathers who argue for the sufficiency of Scripture. Thus he quotes, amongst others:

St Hippolytus:

> There is one God, whom we do not otherwise acknowledge, brethren, but out of the Sacred Scriptures. For as he, who would profess the wisdom of this world cannot otherwise attain to it, unless he read the doctrines of the philosophers; so whosoever will exercise piety towards God, can learn it nowhere but from the Holy Scriptures.

St Athanasius:

> These are the fountains of salvation, that he who thirsts may be satisfied with the oracles contained in them. In these alone the doctrine of salvation is contained. Let no man add to, or take from them.

St Augustine:

> In those things which are plainly laid down in Scripture all things are found, which embrace faith and morals.

and St. John of Damascus:

> All things, that are delivered to us by the Law, the Prophets, the apostles and the Evangelists, we receive, acknowledge and reverence, seeking for nothing beyond these.[338]

The argument that Archbishop Cranmer gives us in his homily for the sufficiency of Scripture for salvation is a coherent and persuasive one, but

---

[338]E H Browne *An exposition of the Thirty Nine Articles* pp 141-142 .

a number of contemporary writers would want to supplement it by arguing that in order to understanding how Scripture functions as God's saving word to us we need to pay attention to the character of the Bible as story.

The reason for this is that even a cursory glance at the Bible reveals that it is a complex rather than a simple entity. As biblical criticism has emphasised over the past two centuries, the Bible is not simply one book, but a collection of a large number of different books, which are written in a variety of different literary genres and each of which addresses a particular historical context or, indeed, a series of different contexts. This means that there is great diversity within Scripture and this in turn raises the question of what, if anything, gives coherence in the midst of this diversity.

How can we talk about Scripture rather than simply about the writings that make up the Bible? How can we talk about the Scripture as a whole as God's word to us when it contains so many different words that seem to say such a bewildering variety of different things?

The answer that a number of recent writers have given to these questions is that what gives coherence to the Bible is that the biblical writings all bear witness in their distinctive ways to a single overarching story concerning the relationship between God and the world that He has created. In the words of Richard Bauckham:

> The one comprehensive category within which we can locate all the biblical materials is that of story, meaning the total biblical story of the world and God's purposes for it, stretching from creation to new creation. A key place within this overarching story is occupied by the Gospel story of Jesus, but the Gospel story is incomplete and lacks its fully biblical meaning apart from the more comprehensive story in which the Bible places it. The category of story includes not only biblical narratives – the many smaller narratives, many of them relatively self-contained but also prophecy and apostolic teaching insofar as these illuminate the meaning of the story and point its direction towards its still future completion. This total biblical story is also the context within which the other biblical genres – law, wisdom, psalms, ethical instruction, parables and so on – are canonically placed.

> Story is the overarching category in which others are
> contextualised. [339]

If the overarching category that enables us to make coherent sense of the biblical material is that of story, the issue that then arises is how the biblical story can be God's authoritative word to us, showing us how to live rightly in relationship to Him. Once again Bauckham provides us with a helpful answer:

> To accept the authority of this story is to enter into it and to inhabit it. It is to live in the world as the world is portrayed in this story. It is to let this story define our identity and our relationship to God and to others. It is to read the narratives of our own lives and of the societies in which we live as narratives that take their meanings from this metanarrative that overarches them all. To accept this metanarrative as the one within which we live is to see the world differently and to live within it differently from the way we would if we inhabited another metanarrative or framework of universal meaning. [340]

To put this another way, accepting the authority of the Bible means accepting that the Bible gives us the overarching story of the relationship between God and His world. This in turn enables us to make sense of what it means to live rightly before God as those whose lives are part of this continuing story.

As I have said, Bauckham makes a helpful contribution to understanding the importance of understanding Scripture in terms of story. However, there are three ways in which what he says needs further development.

First, the proposal to see the Bible in terms of story has raised concerns in the minds of people who have thought that this means that the Bible is 'only a story' in the sense of being a fictional rather than a factual account of the world in which we live and its relationship with God. In order to meet these concerns the point that needs to be made is that the Scriptural story is a true story. It describes the relationship

---

[339] Bauckham op.cit. p.64
[340] Ibid pp.64-65

between God and His world as it truly is and it is because it does so that it possesses authority.

As G K Chesterton observes in his book *The Everlasting Man*, it was precisely because the Christian faith offered the world the true story about God and the world that it was able to bridge the age long division between the story tellers and the philosophers, between the human desire for romance and the human quest for truth.

> ...the sanity of the world was restored and the soul of man offered salvation by something which did indeed satisfy the two warring tendencies of the past. It met the mythological search for romance by being a story and the philosophical search for truth by being a true story.[341]

Secondly, Bauckham's account focuses exclusively on human activity. It is an account of *our* reading of the Bible. However, what must not be overlooked is the point made by Cranmer and Webster, that Scripture can only rightly be understood in the context of the *self*-revelation of God. Scripture is not simply a passive text that we have to make sense of. It is rather the instrument of God's self-presentation. It is the means by which we are actively addressed by God and summoned and enabled to live rightly before Him in the way described by Archbishop Cranmer.

Thirdly, we need a more precise account of the content of the biblical story. Bauckham talks about the: '...total biblical story of the world and God's purposes for it, stretching from creation to new creation', but he does not give any further details. The problem with this is that it means that he does not give us any clues about what it means properly to understand the biblical story.

It is on this point that N T Wright makes a helpful contribution. In his recent work *Scripture and the Authority of God*, he proposes that we should see Scripture in terms of a five act drama:

> The acts are: creation, 'fall', Israel, Jesus and the church; they constitute the differentiated stages in the divine drama which scripture itself offers.[342]

---

[341] G K Chesterton *The Everlasting Man* San Francisco: Ignatius Press 1994 p. 248
[342] N T Wright *Scripture and the Authority of God* London: SPCK 2005 p.89

Having outlined this five act model, Wright then argues that we live in the fifth act:

> This act began with Easter and Pentecost; its opening scenes were the apostolic period itself; its charter text is the New Testament; its goal, its intended final scene, is sketched clearly in such passages as Romans 8, 1 Corinthians 15 and Revelation 21-22. The key point of the whole model, which forms the heart of the multi-layered view of how 'the authority of scripture' actually works, runs as follows. Those who live in this fifth act have an ambiguous relationship with the four previous acts, not because they are being disloyal to them but precisely because they are being loyal to them as part of the story. If someone in the fifth act of All's Well that Ends Well were to start repeating speeches from earlier acts, instead of those which belonged to the fifth act itself, the whole play would begin to unravel. We must act in the appropriate manner for this moment in the story; this will be in direct continuity with the previous acts (we are not free to jump suddenly to another narrative, a different play altogether), but such continuity also implies discontinuity, a moment where genuinely new things can and do happen. We must be ferociously loyal to what has gone before and cheerfully open about what must come next. [343]

Wright gives a number of examples to illustrate what he means by 'discontinuity'. For instance he argues that:

> We are not members of Israel BC; so – as one example out of many – we ought not to rebuild the Jerusalem Temple and offer animal sacrifices in it.

and also that:

> We are not living during the time of Jesus' public career, and must not assume that e.g. the temporary prohibitions on preaching the gospel to non-Jews (Matthew 10:5-6) apply to us.[344]

---

[343] Ibid p.90
[344] Ibid p 91

He also stresses that we also need to recognise: '...that our relationship to the New Testament is not the same as our relationship to the Old.'[345] This is because:

> The New Testament is the foundation charter of the fifth act. No change of act in God's drama with the world (despite manifold changes in human culture) has occurred between the time of the apostles and evangelists and our own; there is nothing that would correspond to the great double change of act (from Act 3 to Act 4, and from Act 4 to Act 5) which occurred between their time and that of Torah, Prophets and Writings...
>
> We who call ourselves Christians must be totally committed to telling the story of Jesus both as the climax of Israel's story and as the foundation of our own. We recognize ourselves as the direct successors of the churches of Corinth, Ephesus and the rest, and we need to pay attention to what was said to them as though it was said to us. We cannot relativize the epistles by pointing out the length of time that has passed between them and us, or by suggesting any intervening seismic shifts that would render them irrelevant or even misleading. It is an essential part of authentic Christian discipleship both to see the New Testament as the foundation for the ongoing, and still-open ended, fifth act and to recognize that it cannot be supplanted or supplemented. The fifth act goes on, but its first scene is non-negotiable, and remains the standard by which various improvisations of subsequent scenes are to be judged. That is what it means to live under the authority of scripture, or rather, as I have stressed all along, under God's authority mediated through scripture.[346]

The term 'improvisations' used by Wright in this last quotation is his short hand for what he has referred to earlier as being: '...ferociously loyal to what has gone before and cheerfully open about what must come next'. He further explains this idea as follows:

---

[345] Ibid p. 92
[346] Ibid p. 92

Our task is to discover, through the Spirit and prayer, the appropriate ways of improvising the script between the foundation events and charter on the one hand and the complete coming of the kingdom on the other. Once we grasp this framework, other things begin to fall into place.

The notion of 'improvising' is important, but sometimes misunderstood. As all musicians know, improvisation does not at all means a free-for-all where 'anything goes,' but precisely a disciplined and careful listening to all the other voices around us, and a constant attention to the themes, rhythms and harmonies of the complete performance so far, the performance of which we are now called to continue. At the same time, of course, it invites us, while being fully obedient to the music so far, and fully attentive to the voices around us, to explore fresh expressions, provided that they will eventually lead to that ultimate resolution which appears in the New Testament as the goal, the full and complete new creation which was gloriously anticipated in Jesus' resurrection. The music so-far, the voices around us, and the ultimate multi-part harmony of God's new world: these, taken together, form the parameters for appropriate improvisation in the reading of scripture and the announcement and living out of the gospel it contains. All Christians, all churches, are free to improvise their own variations to take the music forwards. No Christian, no church, is free to play out of tune. To change the metaphor back to the theatre: all the actors, and all travelling companies of which they are a part (i.e. different churches) are free to improvise their own fresh scenes. No, actor, no company is free to improvise scenes from another play, or one with a different ending.[347]

Drawing together all the points noted so far in relation to Article VI, we can say that:

• The concern of Article VI is with the issue of how people can be saved.

---

[347] Ibid p.93

• From a Christian perspective being saved means responding rightly to what God has done for us in His acts of creation and redemption.

• The Bible is central to our salvation because it is the key instrument that God uses to enable us to make this response.

• What gives unity to the Bible is that it contains the one overarching story of God's creative and saving activity, and it is as we learn to inhabit this story and listen to God speaking to us through it that God makes known to us who He is, what He has done for us, and How we wants us to live before Him (the points highlighted by Archbishop Cranmer in his homily).

• In order to hear the biblical story rightly and respond to it appropriately we have to understand that it is a developing drama that has a number of distinct acts within it.

• As those who live in the final, unfinished, act of the drama, we are called to a life of responsible improvisation, an improvisation which involves both continuity and discontinuity with previous acts of the drama and draws particularly on the New Testament, in which the opening scenes of the final act are recorded for us and in which the final end of the drama is made known to us in general terms.

...so that whatsoever is not read therein, nor may be proved thereby, is not to be required of any man, that it should be believed as an article of the faith, or be thought requisite or necessary to salvation.

The opening words here – 'so that' – make it clear that what is said is dependent on what has gone before. These words are the negative corollary of the previous positive declaration that the Scriptures contain everything necessary for our salvation.

In order to understand properly what is being said here it is important to note precisely what is being ruled out.

We are not being told that we should not believe anything that is not in Scripture. The English Reformers did not push their belief in the sufficiency of Scripture to the absurd extent of holding that it tells us everything that we need to know about everything. Even a very brief glance at the writings of the English Reformers shows us that they were happy to believe many things, about the history of the Church for example, that they did not derive from a study of Scripture.

We are not being told that only that which is explicitly stated in Scripture can be a necessary article of faith. As Article VIII makes clear, the Tudor theologians believed that theological formulations such as the three Catholic creeds could be regarded as binding on the faithful even though they are not to be found in the biblical text itself because they are based in what is in the biblical text. In the terms of Article VI, even though such formulations are not 'read therein' they may nevertheless be 'proved thereby.'

We are not being told that that nothing can be done in the Church except if it has an explicit or implicit biblical basis. As we shall see when we go on to look at Article XX, the Elizabethan Church of England believed that the Church did have authority under God to decree 'rites and ceremonies' not found in Scripture providing that these were not contrary to anything that was in Scripture.

What we are being told is that no one should be asked to believe as an article of faith anything that is not in Scripture[348] and that nothing that is not in Scripture should be thought necessary for salvation. This necessarily follows from the claim that the Scriptures contain everything that we need to know and believe in order to be rightly related to God. If this is true then nothing further can be required.

To return to an analogy that we looked at earlier, if Scripture contains the script of the divine drama in which we are called to play our part, then if would be wrong to insist that something from outside the script is necessary in order for us to play our part correctly.

As the references to this same idea in Articles XX and XXI make clear, the point of this clause in the Article in its original context is to set limits to the authority of churches and of General Councils. Neither churches nor Councils can impose anything that is not in Scripture as an

---

[348] This point is also made in the Reformatio Legum Ecclesiasticarum 1:9:

> This is the sum of Holy Scripture, in which we believe that all things which must be believed for salvation are fully contained, so that if something is not read or contained in it, neither does it follow nor is it deduced from it, cannot be demanded of anyone that it should be believed as an article of faith. (Bray (ed) *Tudor Church Reform* p.179)

article of faith or as necessary for salvation. In the words of Bishop Burnet:

> If this is our rule, our entire and only rule, then such doctrines as are not in it ought to be rejected; and any Church that adds to the Christian religion, is erroneous for making such additions, and becomes tyrannical if she imposes them upon all her members, and requires positive declarations, subscriptions and oaths concerning them. In so doing she forces such as cannot have communion with her, but by affirming what they believe to be false, to withdraw from that which cannot be had without departing from the truth.[349]

Burnet goes on to criticise the Church of Rome for behaving in precisely this manner and there can be no doubt that the original intention of this part of Article VI was to make an implicit protest at what were seen as the oppressive claims of that particular church. However, in principle what is said applies with equal force to any and every church or council of churches that proposes as necessary for salvation anything that is not in Scripture.

It is also interesting to note that in the *Ordinal* attached to the *Book of Common Prayer* the promise about the conduct of their ministry required from all clergy before their ordination to the priesthood embodies exactly the same principles that are set out in Article VI:

> *The bishop*: Are you persuaded that the Holy Scriptures contain sufficiently all doctrine required of necessity for eternal salvation, through faith in Jesus Christ? And are you determined, out of the said Scriptures, to instruct the people committed to your charge, and to teach nothing, as required of necessity to eternal salvation, but that which you shall be persuaded may be concluded and proved by Scripture?
>
> *Answer*: I am so persuaded, and have so determined by God's grace.

---

[349] G Burnet *An Exposition of the XXXIX Articles* pp.103-104

A number of older commentators on this article support its insistence that nothing that goes beyond Scripture can be required by referring to a number of biblical texts which forbid making additions to the biblical material. Thus Thomas Rogers[350] cites:

> Deut 4:2 'You shall not add to the word which I command you, nor take from it; that you may keep the commandments of the Lord your God which I command you.'

> Deut 12:32 'Everything that I command you, you shall be careful to do; you shall not add to it or take from it.'

> Prov 30:5-6 'Every word of God proves true; he is a shield to those who take refuge in him. Do not add to his words, lest he rebuke you and you be found a liar.

> Rev 22:18-19 I warn every one who hears the words of the prophecy of this book: if any one adds to them, God will add to him the plagues described in this book, and if any one takes way from the words of the book of this prophecy, God will take away his share in the tree of life and in the holy city, which are described in this book.

There is an obvious problem about taking these as direct 'proof texts' that support the second clause of Article VI, which is that in their original contexts the verses from Deuteronomy and from Revelation apply to the Mosaic law and to the prophecies in the Book of Revelation and not to Scripture as such. On the other hand the verses from Proverbs set out a general truth, that human beings should not add to the words of God, which can be seen to underlie what is said in Deuteronomy and Revelation and which is capable of being applied to Scripture as a whole.

The fundamental point here is that if Scripture as a whole is God's word, then we should neither take away from what it says nor rank traditions of our own alongside it as if they too were also God's word. The fundamental objection of Archbishop Cranmer and the other English Reformers to requiring adherence to anything outside Scripture as an article of faith or as necessary for salvation was that it amounted to doing

---

[350] T Rogers *Catholic Doctrine of the Church of England* p.76

precisely this, ranking human traditions alongside God's word as if they possessed equal value.

In the name of Holy Scripture, we do understand those Canonical books of the Old and New Testament, of whose authority was never any doubt in the Church.

Of the names and number of the Canonical Books:

Genesis	First Book of
Exodus	Chronicles
Leviticus	Second Book of Chronicles
Numbers	First Book of Esdras
Deuteronomy	Second Book of Esdras
Joshua	Book of Esther
Judges	Book of Job
Ruth	Psalms
First Book of Samuel	Proverbs
Second Book of Samuel	Ecclesiastes, or the
First Book of Kings	Preacher
Second Book of Kings	Cantica, or Songs of
	Solomon
	Four Prophets the Greater
	Twelve Prophets the Less

And the other books (as Hierome saith) the Church doth read for example of life and instruction of manners; but yet doth it not apply them to establish any doctrine; such are these following:

Third Book of Esdras	Baruch the Prophet
Fourth Book of Esdras	The Song of the Three
Book of Tobias	Children
Book of Judith	The Story of Susanna
The rest of the Book of Esther	Of Bel and the Dragon
Book of Wisdom	The Prayer of Manasses
Jesus the Son of Sirach	First Book of Maccabees
	Second Book of Maccabees

All the books of the New Testament, as they are commonly received, we do receive, and account them canonical.

If the claims about Scripture made in the opening clauses of Article VI are to have any practical value in the life of the Church it follows that what is meant by Scripture has to be defined. There is no point in saying to someone that Scripture contains all things necessary to salvation and then not telling them what 'Scripture' is.

The final section of Article VI declares what the Church of England thinks that Scripture is. As Griffith Thomas notes, the opening sentence of the section, 'In the name of Holy Scripture, we do understand those Canonical books of the Old and New Testament, of whose authority was never any doubt in the Church,' is usually:

> '...regarded as a difficulty, since it cannot apply to all the books and all the Churches, for the Reformers knew well the doubts about some of the books.'[351]

The perceived difficulty here is, however, based on a misunderstanding. The section of the article which it introduces is concerned with the distinction between the books of the Old and New Testaments and the books of the Apocrypha. This is also what the sentence is concerned with. It is not addressing the issue of which books should be regarded as canonical. On that issue the Elizabethan Church was happy to go with the accepted list of canonical books, those that 'are commonly received' as the article goes on to say. What it is addressing is the issue of whether all the books received as canonical should be accorded the same authority.

That is to say, the English Reformers inherited an accepted list of canonical books from the Medieval Church. This list included not only the books of the Old and New Testaments, but also the books of the Apocrypha. However, they were aware that Fathers such as St. Jerome (the 'Hierome' referred to in the article), St. Rufinus and St. Hilary of Poiters in the West, and St. Athanasius and St. Gregory Nazianzen in the East had made a distinction between the canonical books of the Old and New Testaments and the books of the Apocrypha and it is this distinction that is referred to in the sentence with which we are concerned. The books of the Old and the New Testaments are the canonical books 'of whose authority there was never any doubt in the Church,' whereas there was doubt about the authority of the books of the Apocrypha, as reflected in the quotation from St. Jerome cited by the article which gives a lesser

---

[351] Griffith Thomas, *The Principles of Theology*, p.107.

authority to the Apocrypha than that given to the Old and New Testaments. The English Reformers, like the Protestant Reformers on the Continent, held that this distinction between the books of the Old and New Testaments on the one hand and the books of the Apocrypha on the other meant that only the former could properly be referred to as Scripture.

It should be noted, however, that the English Reformers were not consistent in their usage in this regard. In the First and Second Books of Homilies the books of the Apocrypha are referred to as the 'word of God' and as 'Scripture.' For example the homily 'Against Swearing and Perjury' introduces a quotation from Ecclesiasticus 23:11 with the words 'And Almighty God by the Wise Man saith' and the homily on 'Almsdeeds and Mercifulness toward the Poor and Needy' introduces a quotation from Tobit 4:10-11 with the formula 'The same lesson doth the Holy Ghost teach in sundry places of the Scripture.' As Gibson suggests, the best explanation for this is that 'habit and custom' were too strong for the Reformers on these occasions leading them to refer to the Apocryphal books in ways inconsistent with what is said in Article VI.

Having made this distinction between those books which are Scripture and those which are not, the article then goes on to say which books are in which category. It begins by listing the thirty nine canonical books of the Old Testament. In this list the First and Second Books of Esdras are what we now call Ezra and Nehemiah. These Old Testament books were all accepted as canonical by the Patristic and Medieval Church and the English Reformers were content to follow this precedent.

The article then refers to 'the other books' which, following St. Jerome, it says are to be read 'for example of life and instruction of manners' rather than 'to establish any doctrine.' It provides a list of fourteen books than come into this category. Although this is not explicitly stated, as we have already noted the purpose of the reference to St. Jerome is to indicate that the Apocryphal books have a lesser authority than the Old Testament books previously listed and therefore should not be viewed as Scripture properly so called.

Finally, the article declares that the Church of England receives and accounts as canonical 'the books of the New Testament as they are commonly received.' It does not say what these books are (presumably because it was thought that everyone knew what they were), but from the list contained in the Reformatio Legum Ecclesiasticarum[352] and also from the books contained in the 16th century English translations of the New Testament and the lectionary in the Book of Common Prayer we know that the books concerned are the twenty seven books that came to be accepted as canonical during the Patristic period and were accepted as canonical during the Middle Ages, namely the four Gospels, Acts, Romans, I and II Corinthians, Galatians, Ephesians, Philippians, Colossians, I and II Thessalonians, I and II Timothy, Titus, Philemon, Hebrews, James, I and II Peter, I, II and III John, Jude and Revelation.

Although the article outlines which books are Scripture and which are not it does not give any reason for this decision. It states that the books contained in Scripture are those who authority was not doubted in the Church, but it does not say that Church's decision is the reason that they are to be counted as authoritative.

All that the article commits Anglicans to, therefore, is a distinction between those books which constitute Scripture and a number of other books which are edifying but not doctrinally authoritative. The question remains, however, as to why we should accept this distinction.

First of all, why should we accept the thirty nine books of the Old Testament and the twenty seven books of the New Testament as canonical Scripture and therefore as authoritative?

In the case of the Old Testament the answer is that it can be shown that the books of our Old Testament Canon were those books which were accepted as Scripture by Christ himself and by the Apostolic Church. For Our Lord and for the Apostolic Church these were the books inspired by God himself through his Spirit (2 Timothy 3:16, 2 Peter 1:21).[353]

In the case of the New Testament it can be shown that the writings which it contains were written by the Apostles or those associated with them and that they were intended to carry God's own authority in the sense that they were intended to be the vehicles by which God's transformative work in the world could take place. As Wright puts it:

> ...the New Testament authors believed themselves called to exercise their calling as 'authorized' teachers, by the guidance and

---

[352] Bray, *Tudor Church Reform*, p.177
[353] For this see R T Beckwith, *The Old Testament Canon of the New Testament Church*, London: SPCK, 1985.

power of the Spirit, writing books and letters to sustain, energize, shape, judge and renew the church. The apostolic writings, like the 'word' which they now wrote down were not simply about the coming of God's kingdom into all the world; they were, and were designed to be, part of the means whereby that happened, and whereby those through whom it happened could themselves be transformed into Christ's likeness.[354]

As Wright goes on to say:

> Those who read these writings discovered, from very early on, that the books themselves carried the same power, the same authority in action, that had characterised the initial preaching of the word. [355]

The recognition of the New Testament writings as constituting canonical Scripture alongside the writings of the Old Testament, a process which seems to have begun in the first century[356] and which eventually produced the New Testament canon accepted by the Church of England, thus had a two fold basis. It was recognition that these were the writings that came from the Apostles or their associates and thus carried the authority given by Christ to the Apostles and that these were the writings in which the authoritative preaching of the word by the Apostles continued in the Church.[357]

Secondly, why should we accept the books of the Apocrypha as lacking doctrinal authority, but nonetheless being edifying reading?

The answer to the first part of this question is that although the books of the Apocrypha were valued by Greek speaking Jews at the time of Christ and formed part of the Greek version of the Old Testament, the Septuagint, the evidence that we have tells us that they were not regarded as Scripture either by Christ or by the Apostolic Church.[358]

---

[354] Wright, op.cit,. p.38.
[355] Ibid p.38
[356] 2 Peter 3:16 appears to indicate a recognition of St. Paul's letters as Scripture alongside the existing Old Testament Scripture.
[357] For the development of the New Testament canon see B M Metzger, *The Canon of the New Testament*, Oxford: OUP, 1987.
[358] See Beckwith, op,cit,.

If we are to be faithful to their example this means that we cannot regard them as Scripture either. If they are not Scripture they are not part of the divinely inspired witness to God's self-revelation in the history of Israel and in Jesus Christ on which Christian doctrine in based. It therefore follows that they cannot be regarded as doctrinally authoritative.

On the other hand the books of the Apocrypha do have a two fold value. First, they help to fill in a gap in our knowledge by giving us information about the history of Israel in the inter-testamental period. Secondly, they provide us with valuable instruction in what it means to live a godly life, by means of examples such as the stories of the heroism and faithfulness of the Jewish martyrs in the Books of Maccabees and direct teaching such as the instructions in practical godliness contained in the book of Ecclesiasticus.

Particularly for the latter reason, it is appropriate that the Church continues to do what it has done since the time of the Early Fathers, namely to read these books 'for example of life and instruction of manners' It is for this reason that the English Reformers set the Benedicite from the Song of the Three Children as a Canticle for use at Morning Prayer, appointed lessons from the Apocrypha to be read at Morning and Evening Prayer, took two of the offertory sentences in the service of Holy Communion from the Book of Tobit and included material from the Apocrypha in the Homilies.

Article VII

∞

Of the Old Testament

The Old Testament is not contrary to the New; for both in the Old and New Testament everlasting life is offered to mankind by Christ, who is the only Mediator between God and man, being both God and man. Wherefore there are not to be heard which feign that the old fathers did look only for transitory promises. Although the law given from God by Moses, as touching ceremonies and rites, do not bind Christian men, nor the civil precepts thereof ought of necessity to be received in any commonwealth; yet, notwithstanding, no Christian man whatsoever is free from the obedience of the commandments which are called moral.

De Veteri Testamento

Testamentum Vetus Novo contrarium non est, quandoquidem tam in Veteri quam in Novo per Christum, qui unicus est Mediator Dei et hominum, Deus et Homo, aeterna vita humano generi est proposita. Quare male sentiunt, qui veteres tantum in promissiones temporarias sperasse confingunt. Quanquam lex a Deo data per Mosen, quoad ceremonias et ritus, Christianos non astringat, neque civilia eius praecepta in aliqua republica necessario recipi debeant: nihilominus tamen ab obendientia mandatorum quae moralia vocantur nullus quantumvis Christianus est solutus.

Article VII was created in 1563 by bringing together material from two separate articles in the *Forty Two Articles*.

The first of these was Article VI, 'The Old Testament is not to be refused':

The Old Testament is not to be put away as though it were contrary to the New, but to be kept still, for both in the Old and New Testaments everlasting life is offered to mankind by Christ, who is the only Mediator between God and man, being both God and man. Wherefore they are not to be heard which feign that the old fathers did look only for transitory promises.

Testamentum Vetus, quasi Novo contrarium sit, non est repudiandum, quando-quidem tam in veteri quam in novo per Christum unicus est Mediator Dei et hominum, Deus et homo, aeterna vita humano generi est proposita. Quare non sunt audiendi, qui veteres tantum in promissiones temporarius sperasse confingunt.

The second was Article XIX, 'All men are bound to keep the moral commandments of the Law:'

The Law, which was given of God to Moses, although it bind not Christian men, as concerning the ceremonies, and rites of the same; neither is it required, that the civil precepts and orders of it should of necessity be received in any commonwealth: yet no man (be he never so perfect a Christian) is exempt and loose from the obedience of those commandments which are called moral. Wherefore they are not to be hearkened unto, who affirm that Holy Scripture is given only to the weak, and do boast themselves continually of the Spirit, of whom (they say) they have heard such things as they teach, although the same be most evidently repugnant to the Holy Scripture.

Lex a Deo data per Mosen, licet quoad ceremonias et ritus Christianos non astringat, neque civilia eius praecepta in aliqua Repub. necessario recipi debeant, nihilominus ab obedientia mendatorum quae Moralia vocantur, nullus quantumvis Christianus est solutus. Quare illi non audiendi, qui sacras literas tantum infirmis datas esse perhibent, et spiritum perpetuo iactant, a quo sibi quae praedicant suggeri asserunt, quanquam cum sacris literis apertissime pungent.

When the articles were revised in 1563 it was clearly felt that as the two articles of the 1553 version were both concerned with combating erroneous views of the Old Testament it made sense to bring them together in one composite article on the general topic of the Old Testament and to include this as part of the sequence of articles on Scripture and the Creeds.

Article VI of the *Forty Two Articles* was incorporated in its entirety as the first half of Article VII while the second half of Article VII consists of an edited version of the first sentence of the old Article XIX. The second half of Article XIX was dropped, either because the error it addressed was no longer seen as pressing, or because the error it addressed was seen as not relating specifically to the issue of how the Old Testament should be understood.

Article VII addresses three different errors regarding the Old Testament, put forward by certain radical Protestant groups.

The first error is the belief that the promises that were made to those lived in Old Testament times involved only material blessings in this world and that they were excluded from the gift of eternal life brought by Christ. The existence of this error is noted, for example, by William Alley, Bishop of Exeter at the beginning of Elizabeth I's reign, who writes in a work called *Poor Man's Library* about:

> ...the temerity, ignorance and blasphemy of certain phantastical heads, which hold that the prophets do write only to the people of the Old Testament, and that their doctrine did pertain only to their own time; and would seclude all the Fathers that lived under the law from the hope of eternal salvation.[359]

The second error is the belief that the entire Old Testament law still applies to Christians today. The list of heresies in the *Reformatio Legum Ecclesiasticarum* notes, for example, the error 'of those who cling so firmly to the Old Testament that they call us back to a need for circumcision and other ceremonies instituted by Moses.'[360]

The third error is the belief that Christians are totally free of all the commands given under the Old Testament, including the moral

---

[359] Text in Hardwick, op.cit., p.395.
[360] Bray, *Tudor Church Reform*, p.189.

precepts which it contains. The *Reformatio Legum Ecclesiasticarum* goes on to talk about the error:

> ...of those who think that by the death of Christ such great licence has been given to us and liberty to do anything and everything has been so permitted, that we are not even bound by those solemn moral precepts of the Ten Commandments nor by any of the other holy ordinances of life, with which the Holy Scriptures are saturated.[361]

The Old Testament is not contrary to the New; for both in the Old and New Testament everlasting life is offered to mankind by Christ, who is the only Mediator between God and man, being both God and man. Wherefore they are not to be heard which feign that the old fathers did look only for transitory promises.

The first two sentences of Article VII address the first of the three errors noted above. They argue that there is continuity rather than discontinuity between the Old and New Testaments in that in both of them 'everlasting life is offered to mankind by Christ.'

The theological thinking underlying this argument is set out in a passage in the homily 'A short declaration of the true, lively and Christian faith' in the *First Book of Homilies*. Referring to the list in Hebrews 11 of people from Old Testament times who demonstrated faith, the passage that their faith was in fact Christian faith:

> All these Fathers, Martyrs, and other holy men, whom St. Paul[362] spake of, had their faith surely fixed in God, when all the world was against them. They did not only know God to be the Lord, Maker, and Governor of all men in the world: but also they had a special confidence and trust, that he was and would be their God, their comforter, aider, helper, maintainer, and defender. This is the Christian faith which these holy men had, and we also ought to have. And although they were not named Christian men, yet was it a Christian faith that they had; for they looked for all

---

[361] Ibid, p.189.

[362] This reference to St. Paul reflects the traditional belief in the Western Church that St. Paul was the author of Hebrews.

benefits of God the Father, through the merits of his Son Jesu Christ, as we now do. This difference is between them and us; for they looked when Christ should come, and we be in the time when he is come. Therefore saith St. Augustine, 'The time is altered and changed, but not the faith. For we have both one faith in one Christ.' (Augustine, *In Ioannis Evangelium* Tract. 45.9) The same Holy Ghost also that we have, had they, saith St. Paul (2 Corinthians 4:13). For as the Holy Ghost doth teach us, to trust in God, and to call upon him as our Father: so did he teach them to say, as it is written, *Thou Lord art our Father and Redeemer, and thy Name is without beginning and everlasting* (Isaiah 63:16).. God gave them the grace to be his children, as he doth us now. But now, by the coming of our Saviour Christ, we have received more abundantly the Spirit of God in our hearts, whereby we may conceive a greater faith, and a surer trust, than many of them had. But in effect they and we be all one: we have the same faith, that they had in God, and they the same that we have.[363]

The quotation in this passage from St. Augustine indicates that this way of understanding the Old Testament reflects the teaching of St. Augustine in his *Homilies on the Gospel of John*. In the forty fifth homily Augustine comments on Jesus' claim in John 10:7 to be the 'door of the sheep,' the means by which human beings can enter God's sheepfold, and declares that this was as true in the Old Testament as it is in the New. In both testaments faith in Christ is the doorway through which people come to God:

Before the advent of our Lord Jesus Christ, when He came in humility in the flesh, righteous men preceded, believing in the same way in Him who was to come, as we believe in Him who has come. Times vary, but not faith. For verbs themselves also vary with the tense, when they are variously declined. He is to come, has one sound; He has come, has another: there is a change in the sound between He is to come, and He has come: yet the same faith unites both,- both those who believed that He would come, and those who have believed that He is come. At different times, indeed, but by the one doorway of faith, that is, by Christ, do we

[363] *The Homilies*, p.30.

see that both have entered. We believe that the Lord Jesus Christ was born of the Virgin, that He came in the flesh, suffered, rose again, ascended into heaven: all this, just as you hear verbs of the past tense, we believe to be already fulfilled. In that faith a partnership is also held with us by those fathers who believed that He would be born of the Virgin, would suffer, would rise again, would ascend into heaven; for to such the apostle pointed when he said, 'But we having the same spirit of faith, according as it is written, I believed, and therefore have I spoken; we also believe, and therefore speak.' (2 Corinthians 4:13) The prophet said, "I believed, therefore have I spoken:"(Psalm 116:10) the apostle says, 'We also believe, and therefore speak.' But to let you know that their faith is one, listen to him saying, 'Having the same spirit of faith, we also believe.'[364]

Augustine summarises his argument slightly later in the homily when he states:

As many, then, at that time as believed, whether Abraham, or Isaac, or Jacob, or Moses, or the other patriarchs or prophets who foretold of Christ, were sheep, and heard Christ. His voice, and not another's, did they hear.[365]

Seen in the light of these passages from the *First Book of Homilies* and the work of St. Augustine the claim that is made in the first two sentences of Article VII makes sense. In the view of the English Reformers, following Augustine, Christ was made known to the faithful of the Old Testament era and they believed in him and in the eternal salvation which was promised to them in him. Therefore it is not right to say that 'the old fathers did look only for transitory promises.'

This way of reading the Old Testament is one that does not come easily to us today. We tend to think of Christian faith as something that developed in response to the life, death and resurrection of Christ and therefore by definition not something that was possible who lived before Christ's coming. However, the position taken by the English Reformers

---

[364] St. Augustine, 'Homilies on the Gospel of John,' Tractate XLV:9, in *Nicene and Post Nicene Fathers*, First Series, Vol VII, Edinburgh and Grand Rapids: T &T Clark/Eerdmans, 1991, p.252.
[365] Ibid, p.252.

and before them by St. Augustine can be seen to reflect several converging strands of the New Testament witness.

First, there is the teaching of Christ in Luke 24:25-27 and 44-47 and John 5:39 that the Old Testament Scriptures bear witness to him, teaching which was subsequently reflected in the proclamation of the early Church (see, for example, Acts 2:22-36, 3:18, 8:30-35,13:27). This teaching implies that those in Old Testament times knew of Christ, because only if they knew of him could they bear witness to him.

Secondly, there is the explicit teaching in John 8:56 and 12:41 that Abraham and Isaiah saw the day of Christ and the glory of Christ: 'Your father Abraham rejoiced that he was to see my day; he saw it and was glad'; 'Isaiah said this because he saw his glory and spoke of him.'

Thirdly, there is the way in which the faith of those in Old Testament times and the faith of Christian believers are seen as one and the same thing. We can see this in St. Paul's account of the faith of Abraham in Romans 4 and Galatians 3:6-9, and in the way in which the faith of Old Testament believers is seen in Hebrews 11 as providing examples of faith for Christian believers. It is noteworthy that in Hebrews 11:26 Moses is said to have been willing to undergo 'abuse suffered for the Christ.' As FF Bruce puts it in his commentary on Hebrews, what the author of Hebrew's is saying is that 'by his obedience to the heavenly vision Moses, like Abraham at an earlier date, looked forward to the day of Christ.'[366]

Fourthly, there is the teaching of St. Paul in 1 Corinthians 10:1-4 about how the Israelites were fed by Christ in the wilderness in the same way that Christians are fed by Christ at the Eucharist:

> I want you to know, brethren, that our fathers were all under the cloud, and all passed through the sea, and all were baptized into Moses in the cloud and in the sea, and all ate the same supernatural food and all drank the same supernatural drink. For they drank from the supernatural Rock which followed them, and the Rock was Christ.

Commentators on these verses have noted that the final words of these verses 'and the Rock was Christ,' point to the belief that Christ was

---

[366] FF Bruce, *Commentary on the Epistle to the Hebrews*, London and Edinburgh: Marshall, Morgan and Scott, 1967, p.320.

present with the people of Israel in Old Testament times. A T Hanson, for example, writes that 'In 1 Cor 10 we have an instance of the real presence of Christ in Israel's history of old'[367] and Andrew Bandstra comments 'Christ himself, the pre-existent Christ, was present with the Israelites in their wilderness journey' and Christ 'was as much the source of the spiritual food and drink of the Israelites as he is the one present in the Lord's Supper at Corinth.'[368]

Fifthly, there is the teaching of 1 Peter 1:10-12 that the salvation made available through Christ was revealed in advance to the Old Testament prophets:

> The prophets who prophesied of the grace that was to be yours searched and inquired about this salvation; they inquired what person or time was indicated by the Spirit of Christ within them when predicting the sufferings of Christ and the subsequent glory. It was revealed to them that they were serving not themselves but you, in the things which have now been announced to you by those who preached the good news to you through the Holy Spirit sent from heaven, things into which angels long to look.

Sixthly, there is the teaching of Hebrews 11:10 and 11:13-16 that the Old Testament Patriarchs were looking for the fulfilment of God's promises to them not in terms of an earthly country, but in terms of the heavenly city prepared for them by God:

> For he [Abraham] looked forward to the city which has foundations, whose builder and maker is God...These all died in faith, not having received what was promised, but having seen it and greeted it from afar, and having acknowledged that they were strangers and exiles on the earth. For people who speak thus make it clear that they are seeking a homeland. If they had been thinking of that land from which they had gone out, they would have had opportunity to return. But as it is, they desire a better country, that is, a heavenly one. Therefore God is not ashamed to

---

[367] A T Hanson, *Studies in Paul's Technique and Theology*, London: SPCK, 1974, p.100.
[368] A Bandstra, 'Interpretation in 1 Cor 10:1-11,' *Calvin Theological Journal* 6 (1971), p.14.

be called their God, for he has prepared for them a city.

This city for which the Patriarchs were looking is the same as the city described in Hebrews 12:22 as 'Mount Zion...the city of the living God, the heavenly Jerusalem' and participation in the life of this city means the same as eternal life in the gospel of John.

The fact that the promises of God to Israel in the Old Testament have their fulfilment in the heavenly city is also made by St. John in the Book of Revelation. His description of the 'holy city, new Jerusalem' in Revelation 21-22 draws on the promises of a new Jerusalem in Isaiah 60 and Ezekiel 47-48 and makes it clear that these promises are to be seen as referring not to a renewed Jerusalem created as a result of human effort or political activity, but to a city 'coming down out of heaven from God' (21:10) that will exist following the resurrection of the dead, the last judgement and the creation of a new heaven and a new earth.

What all these strands of the New Testament witness tell us is that the people of God in Old Testament times did indeed have the same basic faith as those in New Testament times. They too knew Christ, believed in him and were fed spiritually by him. They looked forward to the salvation that Christ would bring about through his life death and resurrection and to the fulfilment of God's promises in the eternal life of the heavenly city of God.

The claim that is made in the opening two sentences of Article VII is thus justified. If we follow the New Testament witness this is how the Old Testament needs to be understood. The challenge to us is to learn once again to understand the Old Testament in this way.

A further point that is worth noting is that the reference to the 'Spirit of Christ' in 1 Peter 1: 11 indicates that the homily on the 'True, lively and Christian faith' is correct in saying the Holy Spirit was given to the people of God in the Old Testament as well as in the new. In the Old Testament as in the New God's people know the God who is the Father and the Son through the witness of the God who is the Spirit.

Although the law given from God by Moses, as touching ceremonies and rites, do not bind Christian men, nor the civil precepts thereof ought of necessity to be received in any commonwealth; yet, notwithstanding, no Christian man whatsoever is free from the obedience of the commandments which are called moral.

If the first two sentences of Article VII emphasise the continuity between the Old Testament and the New, the final sentence of the article emphasises that there is both continuity and difference.

This sentence addressed the second and third errors noted above, the belief that the entire Old Testament law still applies to Christians today and the belief that Christians are totally free of all the commands given under the Old Testament, including the moral precepts which it contains.

The first part of the sentence addresses the first of these errors. It declares that there is a difference between the Old and New Testaments in that under the New Testament dispensation Christians are no longer bound by the 'ceremonies', 'rites' or 'civil precepts' set down in the Old Testament law. By ceremonies and rites the article has in mind the laws concerning circumcision, ritual purity, sacrifice and the observation of holy days contained in the Old Testament and by civil precepts it means the laws referring to matters such as crime and punishment, the holding of land, and the conduct of warfare.

No explanation is given for the claim that Christians are no longer bound by the ceremonies and rites contained in the Old Testament law, but this claim draws on a range of New Testament passages such as Mark 7:14-23, Acts 10:9-16, Acts 15:1-29, Romans 14:14, Galatians 2:1-21, 5:1-12, Colossians 2:16-23 and Hebrew 7:11-10:18 These passages teach that the Old Testament laws concerning circumcision, ritual purity, sacrifice and the observation of holy days are no longer binding upon Christian believers.

No explanation is given either for the claim that Christians are no longer bound by the 'civil precepts' of the Old Testament, but this claim too is based on the New Testament. As Rogers puts it in his commentary on Article VII:

> The truth thereof appeareth by the apostles' decree; which showeth whereunto only the primitive church necessarily was tied (Acts 15:20, 28-29)
>
> By the apostles' doctrine, which enjoineth Christians to yield obedience unto the ordinances of their lawful governors and commanders whatsoever (Romans 13:1, 1 Peter 2:13-14).

By the apostles' example, and namely of the blessed St. Paul, who took benefit and made good use of the Roman and imperial laws (Acts 16:37, 22:25, 25:11-12).[369]

Rogers makes two points here. First, when the Council of Jerusalem in Acts 15 decided what laws the Gentile churches needed to observe the civil precepts of the Old Testament were not among them. Secondly, the fact that the apostles taught Christians to be obedient to the laws of whatever country they found themselves in and were prepared to make use of Roman law shows that Christians do not need to live under the laws appertaining to Israelite society in Old Testament times in order to be obedient to God.

The overall point here is that there is nothing in the New Testament by way of either precept or example to suggest that Christians are called to try re-create the civic life of Old Testament Israel either amongst themselves or in the life of society as whole. That this is the case was understood by the Christians of the early Church who were content to live as normal members of the various societies in which they lived and according to the laws of those societies. As the second century *Epistle to Diognetus* puts it:

Christians do not live apart in separate cities of their own, speak any special dialect, nor practise any eccentric way of life...They pass their lives in whatever township – Greek or foreign- each man's lot has determined; and conform to ordinary local usage in their clothing, diet, and other habit...They obey the prescribed laws.[370]

Even when Christian states came into existence from the end of the third century onwards no attempt was made to make those states conform to the civic laws of the Old Testament in their entirety. Certain aspects of Old Testament Israel were taken as models by these states. For example, the kings of these states were seen as the successors of the kings of Old Testament Israel and their clergy were seen as the successors of the Priests, Levites and Prophets. Thus Christian kings were anointed by the

---

[369] Rogers, op.cit., p.90.
[370] *The Epistle to Diognetus* 5 in M Staniforth, *Early Christian Writings*, Harmondsworth: Penguin 1978, pp. 176-177.

clergy in a direct echo of the practice of Ancient Israel (see 1 Samuel 10:1, 1 Samuel 16:13, 1 Kings 1:38-40) However, no attempt was made to perpetuate the practice of Levirate marriage or the laws of Jubilee in Leviticus 25 or to replicate the way the land of Israel was divided between the various tribes.

The position taken by Article VII thus conforms to the New Testament evidence and the subsequent practice of the Church.

The second part of the last sentence of the article emphasises continuity rather than difference. It addresses the belief the Christians are free not only from the ritual and ceremonial laws of the Old Testament and its civil precepts, but from all the commandments it contains. It rejects this belief, declaring that 'no Christian man whatsoever is free from the obedience of the commandments which are called moral'

As R W Jelf notes in his commentary on this passage 'the expression 'called' moral, may at first sound singular, as if they could be called moral without being moral.' However, as he goes on to say:

> ...it means simply those which are technically called moral by theologians – moral as contradistinguished, not from religious commandments, with which they coincide; but from ceremonial or civil regulations.[371]

Article VII itself does not tell us where in the Old Testament we find these moral commandments, but this is made clear in the homily 'Of Good Works annexed unto Faith.' in the *First Book of Homilies*. This homily addresses the question 'what are the good works that Christians need to perform?' and argues that this question was best answered

> ...by our Saviour Christ himself who was asked of a certain great man the same question. *What works shall I do*, said a prince, *to come to everlasting life?* To whom Jesus answered, *If thou wilt come to everlasting life, keep the commandments* (Matthew 19.16-17). But the prince, not satisfied herewith, asked further; *Which commandments?* The scribes and Pharisees had made so many of their own laws, and traditions to bring men to heaven, besides

---

[371] R W Jelf , *The Thirty Nine Articles of the Church of England*, London, Oxford and Cambridge: Rivingtons, 1873, pp. 125-126.

God's commandments, that this man was in doubt, whether he should come to heaven by those laws and traditions or by the laws of God; and therefore he asked Christ, which commandments he meant. Whereunto Christ made him a plain answer, rehearsing the commandments of God, saying: *Thou shalt not kill; Thou shalt not commit adultery; Thou shalt not steal; Thou shalt not bear false witnesses; Honour thy father and thy mother; and Love thy neighbour as thyself* (Matthew 19.18-19). By which words Christ declared, that the laws of God be the very way, that doth lead to everlasting life, and not the traditions and laws of men. So that this is to be taken for a most true lesson, taught by Christ's own mouth, that the works of the moral commandments of God be the very true works of faith which lead to the blessed life to come.[372]

From this quotation we learn that the 'moral commandments of God' are to be found in the Ten Commandments (Exodus 20:2-17 , Deuteronomy 5:6-21) and in the twofold summary of the law in terms of the commands to 'love the Lord your God with all your heart, and with all your soul and with all your mind, and with all your strength' and 'love your neighbour as yourself' (Deuteronomy 6:4, Leviticus 19:18, Matthew 22:34-40, Mark 12:28-34).

If the quotation from the homily was considered on its own it might appear that the moral commandments mean simply the ethical commands in the last five of the Ten Commandments plus the command to love one's neighbour because these are the only commandments that are actually quoted. However, there are two reasons why this is unlikely.

First, in the section of the homily that follows on from the passage just quoted the idolatry of the people of Israel is cited as an example of breach of the commandments and since this is clearly a breach of the first and second of the Ten Commandments this indicates that 'the commandments' means all ten and not just the last five.

Secondly, we know that the Tudor Church of England viewed all Ten Commandments and both parts of the summary of the law as forming an integrated and comprehensive set of commandments which Christians needed to obey.

We can see this in the Catechism in the *Book of Common Prayer*. This specifies that there are ten commandments which Christians need to

---

[372] Ibid, pp.37-38.

keep, the Ten Commandments in Exodus 20 and Deuteronomy 5, and then goes on to expound these commandments in terms of the twofold summary of the law as follows:

Question. What dost thou chiefly learn by these Commandments?

Answer. I learn two things: my duty towards God, and my duty towards my Neighbour.

Question. What is thy duty towards God?

Answer. My duty towards God is to believe in him, to fear him, and to love him, with all my heart, with all my mind, with all my soul, and with all my strength; to worship him, to give him thanks, to put my whole trust in him, to call upon him, to honour his holy Name and his Word, and to serve him truly all the days of my life.

Question. What is thy duty towards thy Neighbour?

Answer. My duty towards my Neighbour is to love him as myself, and to do to all men as I would they should do unto me: To love, honour, and succour my father and mother: To honour and obey the Queen, and all that are put in authority under her: To submit myself to all my governors, teachers, spiritual pastors and masters: To order myself lowly and reverently to all my betters: To hurt nobody by word nor deed: To be true and just in all my dealing: To bear no malice nor hatred in my heart: To keep my hands from picking and stealing, and my tongue from evil-speaking, lying, and slandering: To keep my body in temperance, soberness, and chastity: Not to covet nor desire other men's goods; but to learn and labour truly to get mine own living, and to do my duty in that state of life, unto which it shall please God to call me

For the Tudor Church of England, therefore, the commandments of God binding upon Christians, the 'commandments which are called moral' in Article VII, are the Ten Commandments and the commands to love God and neighbour and it is these as a whole that Christ is seen as referring to in the story of the rich young ruler, even though it is only the last six commandments and love of neighbour that are specifically mentioned.

In seeing the Ten Commandments and the two fold summary of the law as binding upon Christians Article VII is following the teaching of the New Testament.

This can be seen in the stories of the rich young ruler and Jesus' summary of the commandments (Matthew 19:16-30, Mark 10:17-31, Luke 18:18-30, Matthew 22:34-40, Mark 12:28-34). In these stories the continuing authority of the Ten Commandments and the two fold summary of the law are affirmed.

This can also be seen in the Epistles. Romans 3:21-23, 7:7-12, 13:8-10, Galatians 5:14 and James 2:8-13 all imply that the Ten Commandments and the twofold summary of the law are still binding on Christians. As in the gospel story of the rich young ruler, what is explicitly mentioned in the last three passages is the second half of the Ten Commandments and the command to love your neighbour, but this is explained by the fact that in all three passages it is the behaviour of Christians to their neighbours that is in view. There is no implication that the first Christians saw the first five commandments and the command to love God as not having continuing validity. This idea is ruled out, for example, by the fact that in Acts 15:20, Romans 1:22, 1 Corinthians 10:14-22 and 1 John 5:21 the second commandment is seen as still binding and by the way in which 1 John as a whole construes obedience to God's commandments in terms of love for God and neighbour.

Note: The continuing authority of the Old Testament as a whole.

It would be a mistake to conclude on the basis of Article VII that the fact that it is the moral commandments of the Old Testament rather than its ceremonies and rites or its civil precepts that are binding on Christian believers means that everything in the Old Testament except the Ten Commandments and the two fold summary of the law can be disregarded by Christians. Such an approach is ruled out by the clear teaching of Christ in Matthew 5:17-21 that he has come to fulfil rather than to abolish 'the law and the prophets' and that 'not an iota, not a dot will pass from the law until all is accomplished' and the words of St. Paul in 2 Timothy 3:16 that 'All scripture is inspired by God and profitable for teaching, for reproof, and for training in righteousness, that the man of God may be complete, equipped for every good work.'

Both these passages clearly imply that the Old Testament as a whole still has continuing authority for Christians.

The question that therefore arises is how to affirm the continuing authority of the Old Testament as a whole while at the same time acknowledging that large parts of it are not binding on Christians today. A helpful approach to this issue is provided by Oliver O'Donovan in his commentary on the Articles. He notes that:

> It had been said consistently since the early fathers of the Church that the religious law of ancient Israel was determined by its structure in salvation-history, as an order of sacraments which communicated the benefits of Christ yet to appear. In the middle ages an additional point was made: that the law of ancient Israel was determined by its contingent character as a society; by its social, educational, moral structure within history. These two elements of contingency in Old Testament law are recognised in the remark that 'the law as touching ceremonies and rites, do (sic) not bind Christian men, nor the civil precepts thereof ought of necessity to be received in any commonwealth.' Thus a division is set between the Old Testament era and the society to which the Old Testament (as law) bears witness. The dialectic of historical development is acknowledged. The order by which the social good was mediated in ancient Israel cannot claim us immediately, but is part of the historical dialectic through which the gospel of Christ was revealed.[373]

He also notes, however, that:

> ...this contingent social order was also a mediation of the universal good: to understand it is not enough to understand its contingency, but we must understand its relation to the universal good as well. Hence we detect also within this law a revelation of created order and the good to which all men are called, a 'moral law' by which every human being is claimed and which belongs fundamentally to men's welfare. The theologian's task in expounding the Old Testament is to allow the contingent and the universal to emerge distinctly. If the universal does not shine

---

[373] O' Donovan, op.cit., pp. 63-64.

through the contingent, then what is done is not theology, but only history: if the universal does not shine through the contingent, then what is done is bad theology, not founded in the narration of God's might deeds in saving history, and so inadequately Christian.[374]

The task of the Christian reader of the Old Testament is thus to discern how in any given part of the Old Testament the good that is willed by God for all people at all times and everywhere is revealed in and through what is contingent and to think how this universal good applies to us as Christians today in our own particular contingent historical situation.

---

[374] Ibid, p.64.

Article VIII

∞

Of the Three Creeds

The three Creeds, Nicene Creed, Athanasius' Creed, and that which is commonly called the Apostles' Creed, ought thoroughly to be received and believed; for they may be proved by most certain warrants of Holy Scripture.

De Tribus Symbolis

Symbola tria, Nicaenum, Athanasii, et quod vulgo Apostolorum appellatur omnino recipienda sunt et credenda; turarum testimoniis probari possunt.

This article originated as Article VII of the *Forty Two Articles*. In 1563 the words 'and believed' ('et credenda') were added to the article and in 1571 the word 'Apostolorum' was substituted for the original 'Apostolicum' in the Latin text. The present titles of the article were also substituted for the original titles 'The three Creeds' ('Symbola tria').

During the Patristic and early Medieval periods three creeds came in to general use in the Western Church, the Nicene Creed, the Apostles Creed and the Athanasian Creed.

• The Nicene Creed is a creed of unknown origin, written in Greek, that embodies the Trinitarian theology upheld by the Council of Nicaea. It seems to have been used at the Council of Constantinople in 381 which re-affirmed the Nicene faith and it was officially recognised as summarising the theology of that Council by the Council of Chalcedon in 451. Thereafter it came to be viewed as a touchstone of Christian orthodoxy in both East and West and from the sixth century onwards it became the Creed recited at the Mass. [375]

---

[375] See J N D Kelly, *Early Christian Creeds*, 3ed, London: Longman, 1972

- The Apostles Creed is a Western creed, written in Latin, which has it roots in the Old Roman Creed that can be traced as far back as the second century, but which in its present form seems to have originated in what is now South West France some time in the seventh century. Under the influence of the Emperor Charlemagne it came to be used in the Western Church as the standard statement of basic Christian belief from the ninth century onwards.[376]

- The Athanasian Creed, also known as the *Quicunque vult* from the opening words of the original Latin text, is another Western creed written in Latin. It was produced in the area of Lerins what is now Southern France some time in the sixth century and seems to have been associated in some way with the work of St. Caesarius, who was Bishop of Arles, also in Southern France from 502-542. It reflects the Trinitarian theology of St. Augustine, and its association with St. Athanasius seems to have come about because he was known to have been a champion of Trinitarian orthodoxy and so the term 'Athanasian' was used as a shorthand way of referring to a Trinitarian creed at a time when:

> 'orthodox' had not yet come into common use and the word 'catholic' would have been reserved for a creed that had received the official stamp of approval from an ecumenical council like that of Nicaea.[377]

In the Western Church it came to be viewed alongside the Nicene Creed as a key benchmark of theological orthodoxy.[378]

In line with the practice of the Western Church as a whole, in the Medieval Church of England the Nicene Creed was recited at the Mass, the Athanasian Creed was recited at the monastic service of Prime and the Apostles Creed was regarded as the basic statement of Christian belief and was used as the basis for catechetical instruction.

After the Church of England broke away from Rome in the 1530s it continued to emphasise the importance of these three Creeds. Thus

---

[376] Kelly, ibid
[377] G Bray, *The Faith We Confess*, London: Latimer Trust, 2009, p.67.
[378] For details on the Athanasian Creed see J N D Kelly, *The Athanasian Creed*, London: A & C Black., 1964.

Article 3 of the *Ten Articles* of 1536 declares that all bishops and preachers:

> ...ought and must most constantly believe and defend all those things to be true, which be comprehended in the whole body and canon of the Bible, and also in the three creeds, or symbols, whereof one was made by the apostles, and is the common creed which every man useth; the second was made by the holy council of Nicaea, and is said daily in the mass; and the third was made by Athanasius, and is comprehended in the Psalm *Quicunque vult*; and they ought and must take and interpret all the same things according to the selfsame sentence and interpretation, which the words of the selfsame creeds or symbols do purport, and the holy approved doctors of the church do entreat and defend the same.[379]

A comparison of this statement with what is said in Article VIII makes clear the intention of the latter.

Like the statement in the *Ten Articles*, Article VIII makes clear that the three Creeds continued to be accepted by the Church of England. There is no specific evidence that explains why it was felt necessary to say this, but it seems probable that like the defence of traditional Trinitarian and Christological orthodoxy in Articles I-V what is said in Article VIII was intended to be both an assertion of the theological orthodoxy of the Church of England and a response to the rejection of the Creeds by a number of the radical Protestant groups. In the words of Gibson, the leaders of these groups 'utterly ignored and set aside these summaries of the faith, together with the faith itself contained in them.'[380]

Where Article VIII is unlike the Ten Articles, however, is that whereas the *Ten Articles* could be seen to suggest that there are two equal theological authorities on which the Church of England's teaching should be based, the Bible and the Creeds, Article VIII firmly subordinates the Creeds to the Bible.

The final clause of the article thus does double duty. Against the Protestant radicals on the one hand and anyone who wanted to put the Creeds on the same theological level as Scripture on the other, the clause

---

[379] Bray, *Documents of the English Reformation*, p.165.
[380] Gibson, op.cit., p.297.

asserts that the Creeds ought to be believed and received because (and only because) 'they may be proved by most certain warrants of Holy Scripture.'

The same point is also made in the *Reformatio Legum Ecclesiasticarum* which states that: '...we receive and embrace these three creeds as summaries of our faith, for they can easily be proved by the most certain testimonies of the divine and canonical Scriptures.'[381]

The three Creeds, Nicene Creed, Athanasius' Creed, and that which is commonly called the Apostles' Creed, ought thoroughly to be believed and received

The names given to the three Creeds in the article are those by which they were commonly known at the time. By the fifteenth century doubts had already begun to be expressed about the legend that said that the Apostles Creed was literally the work of the Apostles (this may be reflected in the words 'which is commonly called') and subsequent critical study of the Creeds has made it clear that the Nicene Creed was not the creed produced by the Council of Nicaea and that the Athanasian Creed was not actually the work of St. Athanasius.

As early as the end of the seventeenth century Burnet thus had to admit that none of the creeds 'are named with any exactness.'[382] The question that then arises is whether the historically inaccurate names given to the Creeds by the article make any theological difference for us today. The answer is that they make no difference at all. First, the traditional names for the Creeds used in the article are those which are still in common use today so it is clear which creeds are being referred to. Secondly, the reason the article gives for believing and receiving these Creeds is not the traditional view of their provenance. It is the fact that the contents of the Creeds can be proved from Scripture that is theologically important for the article and thus the historical issue of whether or not these creeds were produced by the Apostles, the Council of Nicaea or St. Athanasius is of no importance.

It is not clear whether there is any particular significance in the order in which the three creeds are named. Griffith-Thomas suggests that:

---

[381] Bray, *Tudor Church Reform*, p.175.
[382] Burnet, op.cit. p.126.

The Nicene Creed probably comes first because it was used at Holy Communion; the Athanasian comes next because it was used daily at Prime; while the Apostles' is mentioned last because connected with ordinary use. [383]

This suggestion may be correct, but Griffith Thomas does not put forward any evidence to support it and no evidence about the historical reasons for the order of the Creeds has been put forward by other commentators on the article. The truth seems to be that we simply do not know why this order was chosen. As we have seen, the order in the *Ten Articles* and the *Reformatio Legum Ecclesiasticarum* is Apostles, Nicene and Athanasian.

Having specified the Creeds that are under discussion the article next goes on to say what attitude people ought to adopt to them. As Griffith Thomas notes:

> The wording of the Article is important. These confessions of our faith 'ought thoroughly to be received and believed' The Latin equivalent of 'thoroughly' is *omnino*, 'altogether,' emphasising very much more than intellectual credence, While the form of the Creeds is not strictly Scriptural and Apostolic, the contents are considered to be so, and on this account they call for thoroughness of acceptance. It is important to see from this where the Church of England stands in regard to the fundamental truths expressed in these formularies. Nothing could be clearer than this statement in committing the Church of England to a thorough belief in the verities set forth in the Creeds.[384]

...for they may be proved by most certain warrants of Holy Scripture.

As has already been noted this statement is intended to respond both to the radical Protestant claim that the Creeds should be disregarded because they are unbiblical and any argument from a more traditionalist Catholic perspective that that the Creeds have an intrinsic authority of their own. The former position is wrong, the article says, because the Creeds are not unbiblical. The latter position is wrong because the authority of the Creeds is not intrinsic, but extrinsic. That is to say, the

---

[383] Griffith-Thomas, op.cit. p.147.
[384] Ibid p.147.

Creeds are only authoritative because their contents faithfully reflect the teaching of Holy Scripture and therefore share in its authority.

When the article says that Creeds 'may be proved by most certain warrants of Holy Scripture' this does not mean that there are specific statements in the Bible that give authority to the three Creeds as such. No one, including the English Reformers, has ever suggested this idea. As we have just indicated, what it does mean is that what the Creeds teach can be shown to be a faithful reflection of the teaching of Scripture itself.

The article itself does not provide any evidence to support this argument and the English Reformers do not provide evidence for it anywhere else. Nevertheless the fact that this argument is correct can be seen from a consideration of the contents of the Creeds.

The Apostles' Creed is in three sections. The first section affirms belief in God as the almighty Father who is the creator of heaven and earth. The second section affirms belief in the incarnation, passion, resurrection and ascension of Christ and his return in judgement. The third section affirms belief in the Holy Spirit, the Church, the communion of Saints, the forgiveness of sins, the resurrection of the body and everlasting life.

Each of these three sections can be seen to reflect the teaching of Scripture We have already seen the biblical evidence concerning God as Father, Son and Holy Spirit in relation to Articles I-V. The affirmation in the Creed about the Church, the communion of Saints, the forgiveness of sins, the resurrection of the body and everlasting life can be seen to correspond to the teaching of the Bible in passages such as Matthew 16:18, Ephesians 1:3-3:21, 1 Peter 2:4-10 and Revelation 7:4-17 (the Church and the communion of saints), Luke 15:11-32, Romans 3:21-4:8, Colossians 2:13-15 1 John 1:8-9 (the forgiveness of sins) and John 3:16, 1 Corinthians 15:1-58, 1 Thessalonians 4:13-18, Revelation 21:1-22:5 (the resurrection of the body and eternal life)

The Nicene Creed is also in three sections. It has similar content to the Apostles' Creed except that:

- It expands the affirmation of belief in God as creator by saying that God the Father is the creator 'of all things visible and invisible'

- It declares explicitly the deity of Christ by affirming the belief that He is

...the only begotten Son of God, begotten of his Father before all worlds, God of God, light of light , very God of very God, begotten not made, being of one substance with Father by whom all things were made.

- It declares implicitly the deity of the Holy Spirit by affirming belief in the Holy Spirit:

...the Lord and giver of life, who proceedeth from the Father and the Son, who with the Father and the Son together is worshipped and glorified, who spake by the prophets.

- In the third section it links forgiveness and baptism, acknowledging 'one baptism for the remission of sins'

These additions also have a clear biblical basis. We have considered the biblical evidence for God as the creator of all things visible and invisible in connection with Article I, the evidence for the deity of Christ and the Spirit in relation to Articles II and V and the linkage between baptism and forgiveness can be seen in passages such as Acts 2:38, Romans 6:1-11 and Colossians 2:8-15

The Athanasian Creed affirms the Trinitarian nature of God, the divinity and humanity of Christ, and Christ's passion, resurrection, ascension and coming in judgement.

The language of the Athanasian Creed is more detailed and more technical than the language used in the Apostles and Nicene Creeds.

For example, in explaining the Trinitarian nature of God the Athanasian Creed declares:

So the Father is God, the Son is God: and the Holy Ghost is God.
And yet they are not three Gods: but one God.
So likewise the Father is Lord, the Son Lord: and the Holy Ghost Lord.
And yet not three Lords: but one Lord.
For like as we are compelled by the Christian verity: to acknowledge every Person by himself to be God and Lord;
So are we forbidden by the Catholick Religion: to say there be three Gods, or three Lords.
The Father is made of none: neither created, nor begotten.

The Son is of the Father alone: not made, nor created, but begotten.

The Holy Ghost is of the Father and of the Son: neither made, nor created, nor begotten, but proceeding.

Likewise, in expounding the Christian belief in Christ as God incarnate it states:

...our Lord Jesus Christ, the Son of God, is God and Man;

God, of the Substance of the Father, begotten before the worlds: and Man, of the Substance of his Mother, born in the world;

Perfect God, and Perfect Man: of a reasonable soul and human flesh subsisting;

Equal to the Father, as touching his Godhead: and inferior to the Father, as touching his Manhood.

Who although he be God and Man: yet he is not two, but one Christ;

One, not by conversion of the Godhead into flesh: but by taking of the Manhood into God;

One altogether, not by confusion of Substance: but by unity of Person.

For as the reasonable soul and flesh is one man: so God and Man is one Christ.

Both of these statements are dense and complex pieces of theology that take considerable amounts of thought to understand properly. However, when they are understood properly it can be seen that they express the biblical teaching about the Trinitarian nature of God and about the person of Christ that we looked at in connection with Articles I, II and V. The basic point being made by the first quotation is that the Father, the Son and the Holy Spirit are all truly God, but that there is nonetheless only one God and that what distinguishes the Persons from one another is that the Father begets the Son and sends forth the Spirit, the Son is begotten from the Father and the Spirit proceeds from the Father and the Son. The point being made in the second quotation is that Jesus Christ is one person who has two natures since he is both truly divine and truly human.

The way in which these points are made can be off putting to those not use to this way of expressing theological truth and may be a good reason for not using the Athanasian Creed regularly in regular public worship. However, the very precise way in which the Athanasian Creed expresses what it wants to say was necessary in the sixth century to rule out various forms of theological error and, when properly understood, still helps to rule out such error today.

As well as finding the style of the Athanasian Creed off putting many people also take offence at the so called 'damnatory clauses' which it contains. The first of these, which is at the start of the creed, declares:

> Whosoever will be saved: before all things it is necessary that he hold the Catholick Faith.
> Which Faith except every one do keep whole and undefiled: without doubt he shall perish everlastingly.

The second, which is towards the end of the creed, declares: 'This is the Catholick Faith: which except a man believe faithfully, he cannot be saved.'

There are two questions which are raised by these clauses.

The first question is what do they mean? What they do not mean is that those who have never heard of the Christian faith or have never been instructed as to its meaning are condemned because of their ignorance. The use of the words 'keep' and 'hold' in the first quotation indicate that what the creed has in mind are people who possess the Catholic faith. You cannot keep or hold what you do not possess.

The creed is thus issuing a warning to those who hold the Catholic faith about the dangers of letting it go. In the words of Burnet:

> ...these condemnatory expressions are only to be understood to relate to those who, having the means of instruction offered to them, have rejected them, and have stifled their own convictions, holding the truth in unrighteousness, and choosing darkness rather than light: upon such as do thus reject this great article of Christian doctrine, concerning one God and Three Persons, Father, Son and Holy Ghost, and that other concerning the Incarnation of Christ, by which God and man was so united as to make one person, together with the other doctrines that follow these, are these anathemas denounced; not so as if it were hereby meant, that every man who does not believe this in every tittle

must perish, unless he hath been furnished with certain means of conviction, and that he has rejected and hardened himself against them.[385]

If this is what the clauses mean, the second question is can they be justified theologically? The answer is that they can be, because they reflect the severe warnings contained in the New Testament about the consequences of rejecting the Christian faith (see Mark 16:16, John 3:18, 36, Galatians 1:8, 2 Corinthians 11:4 and 13-15, 1 John 2:22-23, 2 John 7-9). In the words of Browne:

> It is, in the main, unquestionably true, that he who having the means of learning the truth of Christ, shall yet reject and disbelieve it, shall on that account be condemned. It is probable that the damnatory clauses in the Creed of Athanasius mean no more than the words of our Lord 'He that believeth not shall be damned' (Mark 16:16). What allowance is to be made for involuntary ignorance, prejudice or other infirmities, is one of the secret things which belong on to the Lord our God; concerning which we may hope, but cannot pronounce. The Gospel declares, that unbelief in the truth shall be the cause of condemnation; and the Church is thereby justified in saying the same.[386]

As Browne goes on to say:

> The extreme earnestness and, as to some it seems, harshness, with which the Creed expresses it, resulted from that imminent danger, at the time it was composed of the most noxious heresy, and the need there was to hedge round the field of the Church, as it were, with thorns and briars. If we think such language unnecessarily severe; still we must remember that nothing human is free from the mark of human infirmity, and should be slow to doubt the value of a Catholic exposition of the Faith, because one or two expressions seem a little unsuited to modern phraseology.[387]

---

[385] Burnet, op.cit. p.143.
[386] Browne, op.cit., p.225.
[387] Ibid, p.225.

Note 1: The text of the three Creeds as given in the *Book of Common Prayer*

The Nicene Creed

I BELIEVE in one God the Father Almighty, Maker of heaven and earth, And of all things visible and invisible:

And in one Lord Jesus Christ, the only-begotten Son of God, Begotten of his Father before all worlds, God of God, Light of Light, Very God of very God, Begotten, not made, Being of one substance with the Father, By whom all things were made: Who for us men and for our salvation came down from heaven, And was incarnate by the Holy Ghost of the Virgin Mary, And was made man, And was crucified also for us under Pontius Pilate. He suffered and was buried, And the third day he rose again according to the Scriptures, And ascended into heaven, And sitteth on the right hand of the Father. And he shall come again with glory to judge both the quick and the dead: Whose kingdom shall have no end.

And I believe in the Holy Ghost, The Lord and giver of life, Who proceedeth from the Father and the Son, Who with the Father and the Son together is worshipped and glorified, Who spake by the Prophets. And I believe one Catholick and Apostolick Church. I acknowledge one Baptism for the remission of sins. And I look for the Resurrection of the dead, And the life of the world to come.

The Athanasian Creed

Quicunque Vult

Whosoever will be saved: before all things it is necessary that he hold the Catholick Faith.
Which Faith except every one do keep whole and undefiled: without doubt he shall perish everlastingly.
And the Catholick Faith is this: That we worship one God in Trinity, and Trinity in Unity;
Neither confounding the Persons: nor dividing the Substance.

For there is one Person of the Father, another of the Son: and another of the Holy Ghost.

But the Godhead of the Father, of the Son, and of the Holy Ghost, is all one: the Glory equal, the Majesty co-eternal.

Such as the Father is, such is the Son: and such is the Holy Ghost.

The Father uncreate, the Son uncreate: and the Holy Ghost uncreate.

The Father incomprehensible, the Son incomprehensible: and the Holy Ghost incomprehensible.

The Father eternal, the Son eternal: and the Holy Ghost eternal.

And yet they are not three eternals: but one eternal.

As also there are not three incomprehensibles, nor three uncreated: but one uncreated, and one incomprehensible.

So likewise the Father is Almighty, the Son Almighty: and the Holy Ghost Almighty.

And yet they are not three Almighties: but one Almighty.

So the Father is God, the Son is God: and the Holy Ghost is God.

And yet they are not three Gods: but one God.

So likewise the Father is Lord, the Son Lord: and the Holy Ghost Lord.

And yet not three Lords: but one Lord.

For like as we are compelled by the Christian verity: to acknowledge every Person by himself to be God and Lord;

So are we forbidden by the Catholick Religion: to say there be three Gods, or three Lords.

The Father is made of none: neither created, nor begotten.

The Son is of the Father alone: not made, nor created, but begotten.

The Holy Ghost is of the Father and of the Son: neither made, nor created, nor begotten, but proceeding.

So there is one Father, not three Fathers; one Son, not three Sons: one Holy Ghost, not three Holy Ghosts.

And in this Trinity none is afore, or after other: none is greater, or less than another;

But the whole three Persons are co-eternal together: and co-equal.

So that in all things, as is aforesaid: the Unity in Trinity, and the Trinity in Unity is to be worshipped.

He therefore that will be saved: must thus think of the Trinity.

Furthermore it is necessary to everlasting salvation: that he also believe rightly the Incarnation of our Lord Jesus Christ.

For the right Faith is that we believe and confess: that our Lord Jesus Christ, the Son of God, is God and Man;

God, of the Substance of the Father, begotten before the worlds: and Man, of the Substance of his Mother, born in the world;

Perfect God, and Perfect Man: of a reasonable soul and human flesh subsisting;

Equal to the Father, as touching his Godhead: and inferior to the Father, as touching his Manhood.

Who although he be God and Man: yet he is not two, but one Christ;

One, not by conversion of the Godhead into flesh: but by taking of the Manhood into God;

One altogether, not by confusion of Substance: but by unity of Person.

For as the reasonable soul and flesh is one man: so God and Man is one Christ.

Who suffered for our salvation: descended into hell, rose again the third day from the dead.

He ascended into heaven, he sitteth on the right hand of the Father, God Almighty: from whence he shall come to judge the quick and the dead.

At whose coming all men shall rise again with their bodies: and shall give account for their own works.

And they that have done good shall go into life everlasting: and they that have done evil into everlasting fire.

This is the Catholick Faith: which except a man believe faithfully, he cannot be saved.

Glory be to the Father, and to the Son: and to the Holy Ghost;

As it was in the beginning, is now, and ever shall be: world without end. Amen

The Apostles' Creed

I believe in God the Father Almighty, Maker of heaven and earth:

And in Jesus Christ his only Son our Lord, Who was conceived by the Holy Ghost, Born of the Virgin Mary, Suffered under Pontius

Pilate, Was crucified, dead, and buried: He descended into hell; The third day he rose again from the dead; He ascended into heaven, And sitteth on the right hand of God the Father Almighty; From thence he shall come to judge the quick and the dead.

I believe in the Holy Ghost; The holy Catholick Church; The Communion of Saints; The Forgiveness of sins; The Resurrection of the body, And the Life everlasting.

Note 2 The use of the three Creeds by the English Reformers

The English Reformers followed the practice of the Medieval Church by retaining the Nicene Creed as the Creed to be recited at Holy Communion.

They set the Apostles' Creed as the Creed to be recited daily at Morning and Evening Prayer and in line with the Medieval practice of using it as the basic statement of Christian belief they also made provision for it to be used for the visitation of the sick and at services of Baptism. For the same reason it is also the statement of Christian belief used in the Prayer Book Catechism.

Finally, they made provision for the Athanasian Creed to be said or sung at Morning Prayer in the place of the Apostles Creed on Trinity Sunday and thirteen other feast days including Christmas Day, Easter Day and Pentecost.

In the *Reformatio Legum Ecclesiasticarum* the Creeds are also given a key role in the interpretation of Scripture:

> Moreover, in expounding Holy Writ, the main points of the faith (which we call articles) derived from the clearest passages of Holy Scripture and briefly summarised in the creeds, are to be kept continually in view, so that we shall not interpret or define anything which is contrary to them.[388]

Note 3 The use of the three Creeds in the Church of England today

The use of the Creeds in the *Book of Common Prayer* remains unchanged.

In the contemporary services in the *Common Worship* collection modern translations of the Nicene and Apostles' Creeds are provided for

---

[388] Bray, op.cit,. p.181.

use at Holy Communion and Morning and Evening Prayer respectively. The Apostles' Creed is also set for use at Baptism services.

There is no provision in *Common Worship* for the recitation of the Athanasian Creed, but an abbreviated version without the damnatory clauses is provided as one of a number of alternative affirmations of faith which may be used when this is judged appropriate.

In the Declaration of Assent in Canon C15 ministers of the Church of England declare their belief in 'the faith which is revealed in the Holy Scriptures and set forth in the catholic creeds.' The Nicene, Apostles and Athanasian Creeds are the creeds that are meant.

Sin and Salvation: Articles IX – XVIII

Articles IX-XVIII form the longest sequence of articles within the *Thirty Nine Articles*

Articles IX and X begin the sequence by declaring that everyone needs salvations because the effects of original sin mean that all human beings are deserving of 'God's wrath and condemnation' and are unable in their own strength to turn back to God and behave in the way that he requires.

Articles XI-XII then go on to consider justification and good works. They explain that this salvation which human beings require has been achieved for them by Christ and is given to them as a gift to be received through faith (justification by faith), and that although good works cannot of themselves bring about salvation those who have been saved will necessarily perform them.

Articles XIII –XVI then consider errors relating to salvation propagated by Medieval Catholicism on the on hand and radical Protestantism on the other. Articles XIII-XIV reject the teaching of the scholastic theologians of the Middle Ages that good works performed prior to justification can make someone worthy to receive it and that good works performed by someone who is justified that go beyond what God has commanded (works of supererogation) can make them deserving of a spiritual reward than can them be passed on to someone else. Articles XV-XVI reject the ideas put forward by some radical Protestants that it is possible for believers to be free from sin in this life and that sins committed after baptism are unforgiveable.

Article XVII tackles the topic of predestination to salvation. It contends that there is predestination to life and that the knowledge that this is the case is beneficial to the godly. However, to avoid the spiritual dangers caused by the mishandling of the notion of predestination we should not seek to uncover the secret mind of God, but instead focus on God's self-revelation in Scripture and what this tells us about what God promises to us and requires from us in response.

Article XVIII completes the sequence by rejecting the idea put forward by some radical Protestants that if people are sincere in following their own beliefs they will be saved by so doing even if they reject Christ. In response to this idea it declares that it is only through Christ that people can be saved (although this does not involve as a consequence the damnation of those who have not come to faith in Christ).

Article IX

∞

Of Original or Birth Sin

Original sin standeth not in the following of Adam (as the Pelagians do vainly talk), but it is the fault and corruption of the nature of every man that naturally is engendered of the offspring of Adam, whereby man is very far gone from original righteousness, and is of his own nature inclined to evil, so that the flesh lusteth always contrary to the spirit; and therefore in every person born into this world, it deserveth God's wrath and damnation. And this infection of nature doth remain, yea, in them that are regenerated, whereby the lust of the flesh, called in Greek φρόνημα σαρκὸς (which some do expound the wisdom, some sensuality, some the affection, some the desire of the flesh), is not subject to the law of God. And although there is no condemnation for them that believe and are baptized, yet the Apostle doth confess that concupiscence and lust hath itself the nature of sin.

De Peccatum Origiali

Peccatum originis non est (ut fabulantur Pelagiani) in imitatione Adami situm, sed est vitium et depravatio naturae eiuslibet hominis ex Adamo naturaliter propagati, qua fit ut ab originali iustitia quam longissime distet, ad malum sua natura propendeat, et caro semper adversus spiritum concupiscat; unde in unoquoque nascentium iram Dei atque damnationem meretur. Manet etiam in renatis haec naturae depravatio, qua fit ut affectus carnis, Graece phronema sarcos (quod alii sapientiam, alii sensum, alii affectum, alii studium carnis interpretantur), legi Dei non subiiciatur. Et quanquam renatis et credentibus, nulla propter Christum est condemnatio, peccati tamen in sese rationem habere concupiscentiam fatetur Apostolus.

This article is based on Article VIII of the *Forty Two Articles*. Four changes were introduced when the article was revised in 1563.

1. The words 'which also the Anabaptists do nowadays renew,' which followed from the words 'as the Pelagians do vainly talk' in the 1553 version, were left out, possibly because the danger from the Anabaptists was seen to be less pressing.

2. In the definition of original sin in the first sentence the words 'his former righteousness which he had at his creation' were replaced by 'original righteousness.'

3. In the same sentence 'given to evil' was replaced by 'inclined to evil.'

4. In the second sentence 'baptised' was replaced by 'regenerated.'

In the last three cases the aim of the changes seems to have been to bring the English text into closer conformity with the Latin.

The article is in two parts. The first part explains the nature of original sin in opposition to the Pelagian heresy. The second part explains that the effects of original sin remain even in those who have been baptised.

Original sin standeth not in the following of Adam (as the Pelagians do vainly talk), but it is the fault and corruption of the nature of every man that naturally is engendered of the offspring of Adam, whereby man is very far gone from original righteousness, and is of his own nature inclined to evil, so that the flesh lusteth always contrary to the spirit; and therefore in every person born into this world, it deserveth God's wrath and damnation.

This part of the article is a response to the revival by some of the radical Protestant groups at the Reformation of the teaching of Pelagius and his followers ('the Pelagians'). Pelagius was a British theologian who taught in Rome in the late fourth and early fifth centuries and he and his followers maintained that the fall of Adam only affected his descendants in so far as he set an example of sinning which almost all subsequent human beings have followed.

The precise error which the article is tended to address is set out in section seven of the list of heresies contained in the *Reformatio Legum Ecclesiasticarum*. This section declares:

> In the inheritance of sin which is contracted at our birth, which we call original sin, we must first of all avoid the error of the Pelagians and also of the Anabaptists, whose agreement on this point goes against the truth of the Holy Scriptures, because they say that original sin belonged only to Adam and did not extend to his descendants, nor did it contribute any perversity to our nature, except in so far as Adam's sin set forth a bad example of sinning which invites people to imitate and take over the same depravity.[389]

In the light of this statement it is clear that the words 'standeth not in the following of Adam' in the first clause of Article IX mean 'does not consist in the imitation of Adam's example.'

That is what is rejected by the article. What it teaches instead is that original sin consists in 'the fault and corruption of the nature of every man that naturally is engendered of the offspring of Adam.' That is to say, it teaches that original sin means that there is something wrong with the nature of every descendant of Adam or, in other words, every human being (Christ being the sole exception as Article XV later points out).

The biblical basis for this position is the witness to universal human sinfulness borne by a range of biblical texts such as Genesis 8:21, Psalm 14:1-3, Ecclesiastes 7:20, Isaiah 53:6, Romans 3:23 and Ephesians 2:3 understood in the light of the teaching of St. Paul in Romans 5:12-21 and 1 Corinthians 15:21-22, passages which declare that Adam's transgression led to sin and therefore death spreading to all his descendants.

It is sometimes suggested that what we now know from evolutionary biology about the origins of the human race rules out belief in original sin and therefore we need to abandon this idea. This suggestion is problematic for three reasons.

---

[389] *Reformatio Legum Ecclesiasticarum*, *De haeresibus* 7. Text in G Bray (ed), *Tudor Church Reform*, Woodbridge: The Boydell Press/Church of England Record Society, 2000, p.193.

a) The God given nature of Scripture means that we cannot set aside what it teaches even if this seems to conflict with what we think we know from other sources.

b) Although evolutionary biology can tell us about how human beings have developed physically it is incapable of telling us anything about human beings have developed morally and in terms of their relationship with God.

c) If we do not believe in the Christian doctrine of the Fall 'the only alternative is to believe that God, when he created man, intended him to be as he now is – a far more pessimistic conclusion, and one far more inimical to any idea of progress.'[390]

Having said that original sin consists in the fact that there is something wrong with the nature of every human being, the article next goes on to explain what precisely is wrong.

The first point it makes in this regard is that 'man is very far gone from original righteousness.' 'Original righteousness' means that right relationship with God for which human beings were created and in which the first human beings existed prior to the Fall. As a result of the Fall human beings have now departed 'very far' from this relationship. As Griffith Thomas notes, the Latin version of the article expresses this by saying that Man has departed 'quam longissime' "as far as possible,' meaning thereby as far as he can, consistent with essential human nature.'[391]

Secondly, Man 'is of his own nature inclined to evil, so that the flesh lusteth always contrary to the spirit.' The article itself does not go into detail about what this inclination towards evil involves. However, light is shed on what the article has in mind by the Homily 'Of the Misery of All Mankind' in the *First Book of Homilies* and by the general confession in the services of Morning and Evening Prayer in the *Book of Common Prayer*. The former states:

---

[390] T M Parker , *The Re-creation of Man*, London: The Dacre Press, 1940 , p.64.
[391] W H Griffith Thomas, *The Principles of Theology*, London: Church Book Room Press, 1951,p.164.

For truly there be imperfections in our best works: we do not love God so much, as we ought to do, with all our heart, mind, and power; we do not fear God so much, as we ought to do; we do not pray to God, but with great and many imperfections; we give, forgive, believe, love, and hope unperfectly; we speak, think, and do unperfectly; we fight against the devil, the world, and the flesh unperfectly.[392]

The latter declares:

We have erred, and strayed from thy ways like lost sheep, we have followed too much the devices and desires of our own hearts, we have offended against thy holy laws, we have left undone those things which we ought to have done, and we have done those things which we ought not to have done, and there is no health in us.

In order to explain why it is that we behave in these ways the article points us to the teaching of St. Paul about the internal division which exists in fallen human beings. When the article says 'the flesh lusteth always contrary to the spirit' it is referring to the teaching of St. Paul in Galatians 5:17 about how 'the desires of the flesh are against the Spirit, and the desires of the Spirit are against the flesh; for these are opposed to each other, to prevent you from doing what you would' and also to his more extended account in Romans 7:7-25 about how the power of sin in his fallen nature prevents him from living in obedience to God.

The point that the article is making by means of these Pauline references is that even on our fallen state we can know what God requires of us, and we may even desire to do it, but the power of sin within us is such that we are unable to perform it.

The final part of this section of the article declares that 'in every person born into this world, it deserveth God's wrath and damnation.' It is important to note that the object here is original sin. It is the sin dwelling in human beings rather than human beings as such that is said to be subject to God's wrath and condemnation.

As Griffith Thomas notes:

---

[392] *The Homilies*, Bishopstone: Brynmill Press/ Preservation Press, 2006, p.14.

This is sometimes charged with being philosophically incorrect, but it is certainly true spiritually, for while everyone is born into this world with the evil principle within derived and inherited, it is only as the individual asserts himself and does what is wrong that he is personally subject to the Divine condemnation.[393]

As he further observes:

> The word 'deserveth' is also important, expressing the Divine justice and emphasising what sin in entitled to receive. It does not for a moment say that every case of divine sinfulness actually receive the Divine judgement, but only refers to its essential nature in the sight of God.[394]

'God's wrath and damnation' are his righteous anger and the judgement that flows from it. If we ask why they are exercised against the sin that exists in human beings the answer is that it is because God is a good and loving God who actively rejects all that is against his loving purposes. According to the biblical witness God's purpose is to unite to himself the human race and the all creation with it (Ephesians 1:10) and he rejects and condemns original sin because it stands in the way of the achievement of this purpose.

And this infection of nature doth remain, yea, in them that are regenerated, whereby the lust of the flesh, called in Greek φρόνημα σαρκὸς (which some do expound the wisdom, some sensuality, some the affection, some the desire of the flesh), is not subject to the law of God. And although there is no condemnation for them that believe and are baptized, yet the Apostle doth confess that concupiscence and lust hath itself the nature of sin.

The second half of the article draws on the teaching of St. Paul in Romans 8:6-7 about the 'mind set on the flesh' (the φρόνημα τῆς σαρκὸς) that is 'hostile to God, it does not submit to God's law, indeed it cannot.' It sees the existence of the 'mind set on the flesh' as the result of the infection of human lives by original sin and it declares that 'this infection doth

---

[393] Griffith Thomas, op.cit. p.166
[394] Ibid p.167

remain, yea, in them that are regenerated.' As the final sentence of the section makes clear, 'regenerated' is short hand for those who are born again to a new life through faith and baptism and so what the article is saying is that belief and baptism do not free a person from the effects of original sin.

Once again drawing on Romans 8, specifically Romans 8:1 'there is therefore now no condemnation for those who are in Christ Jesus,' the article concludes by affirming that 'there is no condemnation for them that believe and are baptized,' and yet that 'the Apostle doth confess that concupiscence and lust hath itself the nature of sin.' 'The Apostle' means St. Paul and the passages that the article appears to have in mind are passages such as Romans 6:12, and 7:7, Galatians 5:17 and Colossians 3:5 in which St. Paul seems to identify ἐπιθυμία (desire/lust/concupiscence) and sin.

The article makes this final point in response to the teaching of the Council of Trent. The 'Decree concerning original sin' produced by the fifth session of the Council of Trent in June 1546 taught that concupiscence remains in those who are baptised, but that;

> ...this concupiscence, which the Apostle sometimes calls sin, the holy council declares the Catholic Church has never truly understood to be called sin in the sense that it is truly and properly sin in those born again, but in the sense that is of sin and inclines to sin.[395]

The English Reformers saw this reading of St. Paul as mistaken. As they saw it, what arises from sin and leads to sin is truly and properly sin. The concluding statement in the article is therefore designed to correct Trent's error.

Charles Gibson[396] and E Tyrell Green[397] in their commentaries on the Articles suggest that the wording in Article IX that concupiscence 'hath...the nature of sin' takes a cautious middle line between the statement of Trent and the clear teaching of Protestant statements such

[395] Text in J H Leith (ed), *Creeds of the Churches*, rev ed. Oxford: Blackwell, 1973, p.408.
[396] C Gibson, *The Thirty Nine Articles*, 6ed, London, Methuen, 1908, p.376.
[397] E Tyrell Green, The XXXIX Articles and the Age of the Reformation, London: Wells, Gardner, Darton & Co. 1896, p.76.

as the *Gallican Confession* that concupiscence is truly sin. However, as Griffith Thomas comments:

> ...there seems to be some confusion here, because the paragraph in the Article is concerned with what is 'true and proper sin in the regenerate' since 'concupiscence and lust' must, of necessity, mean the same as 'this infection of nature.' Either, therefore, it is sin or it is not, and it is noteworthy that the first Commentary on the Articles, by Rogers, dated 1587-1607 clearly teaches that concupiscence is sin and opposes those who teach otherwise.[398]

---

[398] Griffith Thomas op.cit. pp.172-3.

Article X

∞

Of Free Will

The condition of man after the fall of Adam is such that he cannot turn and prepare himself, by his own natural strength and good works, to faith and calling upon God. Wherefore we have no power to do good works pleasant and acceptable to God, without the grace of God by Christ preventing us that we may have a good will, and working with us when we have that good will.

De Libero Arbitrio

Ea est hominis post lapsum Adae conditio, ut sese, naturalibus suis viribus et bonis operibus, ad fidem et invocationem Dei convertere ac praeparare non possit. Quare absque gratia Dei, quae per Christum est, nos praeveniente ut velimus, et cooperante dum volumus, ad pietatis opera facienda, quae Deo grata sint et accepta, nihil valemus.

This article was created in three stages

Article IX of the *Forty Two Articles* read:

> We have no power to do good works pleasant and acceptable to God, without the grace of God by Christ preventing us that we may have a good will, and working in us when we have that good will.

The language of this article was suggested by the statement of St. Augustine in his anti-Pelagian work *On Grace and Free Will*: 'We can, however, ourselves do nothing to effect good works of piety without Him either working that we may will, or co-working when we will.'[399]

The purpose of this original article seems to have been to reject the view put forward by certain of the radical Protestant sects that it was possible to live rightly before God without the need of God's grace in Christ. As section 7 of the list of heresies in the *Reformatio Legum Ecclesiasticarum* puts it:

> ...we must take steps against those who put such confidence in the freewill of our strength and nerves, that they contend that people can live rightly and perfectly by that alone without any other special grace of Christ.[400]

In 1563 Archbishop Parker added the opening section of the present article, using words from the article De Peccato in the *Confession of Wurtemburg*. The purpose of this opening clause is to provide an explanation as to why we are not able to do good works without the help of God's grace. The linking word 'wherefore' ('for which reason') makes this point clear.

Finally in 1571 the words 'with us' were substituted for 'in us' in the final clause of the English version of the article in order to make it clear that God's grace works with our co-operation as the word 'cooperante' in the Latin version already indicated.

Of Free Will

The title of this article is not quite accurate in that what the article is concerned with is not human free will in the abstract, but the specific issue of the need of grace. As Gibson comments:

> What is denied in the Article is the power and ability to turn to God and do good works without the assistance of God Himself: what is asserted is the absolute need of grace preventing and co-operating: but of 'Freewill' in itself nothing whatever is directly said. [401]

---

[399] St. Augustine, *On Grace and Free Will*, Ch 33 in *The Nicene and Post Nicene Fathers*, 1st Series, Vol V, Edinburgh & Grand Rapids: T&T Clark/ Eerdmans, 1997, p. 458.
[400] *Reformatio Legum Ecclesiasticarum, De haeresibus* 7, in Bray (ed), op.cit. p.193.
[401] Gibson, op.cit. p.379

The condition of Man after the fall of Adam is such that he cannot turn and prepare himself, by his own natural strength and good works, to faith and calling upon God.

This statement in the first part of the article follows on from what was said about original sin in the previous article. What we are told here is that a consequence of original sin is that human beings are unable in their own strength to turn to God. The article itself offers no explanation or justification of this claim, but the thinking that it reflects is set out for us in the Homily 'Of the Misery of All Mankind' in the *First Book of Homilies*.

This tells us that:

> ...in ourselves, as of ourselves, we find nothing (2 Corinthians 3.5), whereby we may be delivered from this miserable captivity, into the which we were cast, through the envy of the devil, by breaking of God's commandment in our first parent Adam. We are all become unclean: but we all are not able to cleanse ourselves, nor to make one another of us clean (Psalms 51.1-10). We are *by nature the children of God's wrath* (Ephesians 2.3), but we are not able to make ourselves the children and inheritors of God's glory. We are *sheep that run astray* (1 Peter 2.25): but we can not of our own power come again to the sheepfold: so great is our imperfection and weakness. In ourselves therefore may we not glory, which of ourselves, are nothing but sinful. Neither may we rejoice in any works that we do, which all be so unperfect and unpure, that they are not able to stand before the righteous judgement seat of God, as the holy Prophet David saith: *Enter not into judgement with thy servant, O Lord; for no man that liveth, shall be found righteous in thy sight* (Psalms 143.2).[402]

Wherefore we have no power to do good works pleasant and acceptable to God, without the grace of God by Christ preventing us that we may have a good will, and working with us when we have that good will.

---

[402] *The Homilies*, p.15.

Like the extract from the homily quoted above the second half of the article moves from the inability of fallen humanity to turn back to God to the inability of fallen human beings to perform good works.

The implicit logic of the article is that good works are the fruit of a right relationship with God and that since we are unable to achieve such a relationship in our own strength it follows that we are unable to do good works either. This argument is made explicit in the homily 'Of good works annexed unto faith' in the *First Book of Homilies*, which makes reference to the teachings of St. Ambrose, St. Augustine and St. John Chrysostom. We shall look at this argument in detail when we consider the teaching of Article XIIII about the status of good works performed 'before justification.'

The solution that Article X goes on to offer to the problem of the inability of fallen human beings to do good works is God's preventing and co-operating grace: 'the grace of God by Christ preventing us that we may have a good will, and working with us when we have that good will"

The term preventing grace (*gratia praeveniens*) seems to have originated with St. Augustine and is based on the Latin version of Psalm 59:10 'Deus meus misericordia eius praeveniet me' (the God of my mercy will precede me). It refers to the grace of God that precedes our human response, inclining our wills to choose the good.

The term co-operating grace (*gratia co-operans)* also goes back to St. Augustine. It refers to the grace of God that assists us to act once our wills have already been inclined to choose the good.

The combination of these two forms of grace can be seen in the collect for Easter Day in the *Book of Common Prayer*:

> Almighty God, who through thine only-begotten Son Jesus Christ hast overcome death, and opened unto us the gate of everlasting life; We humbly beseech thee, that, as by thy special grace preventing us thou dost put into our minds good desires, so by thy continual help we may bring the same to good effect; through Jesus Christ our Lord, who liveth and reigneth with thee and the Holy Ghost, ever one God, world without end. Amen.

The biblical basis for a belief in prevenient grace is found in passages such as:

John 6:44 'No one can come to me, unless the Father who sent me draws him.'

Acts 16:14 'The Lord opened her heart to give heed to what was said by Paul.'

Romans 10:20 'I have been found by those who did not seek me; I have shown myself to those who did not ask for me.'

Ephesians 2:10 'For we are his workmanship created in Christ Jesus for good works, which God prepared beforehand that we might walk in them.'

As Harold Browne notes in his commentary on the Articles:

Such passages, and all others, which speak of new birth and new creation, shew plainly, that God's grace prevents us, waits not, that is, for us to make advances to Him, but graciously comes forward to help us, whilst we are yet without strength.[403]

The biblical basis for a belief in co-operating grace is found in passages such as:

John 15:4-5 Abide in me, and I in you. As the branch cannot bear fruit by itself, unless it abides in the vine, neither can you, unless you abide in me. I am the vine, you are the branches. He who abides in me, and I in him, he it is that bears much fruit, for apart from me you can do nothing.

I Corinthians 15:10 But by the grace of God I am what I am, and his grace toward me was not in vain. On the contrary, I worked harder than any of them, though it was not I, but the grace of God which is with me.

Galatians 2:20 I have been crucified with Christ; it is no longer I who live, but Christ who lives in me; and the life I now live in the

---

[403] H Browne, *An Exposition of the Thirty Nine Articles*, London: John W Parker & Son, 1844, p.270.

flesh I live by faith in the Son of God, who loved me and gave himself for me.

Philippians 2:12-13 Therefore, my beloved, as you have always obeyed, so now, not only as in my presence but much more in my absence, work out your own salvation with fear and trembling; for God is at work in you, both to will and to work for his good pleasure.

What we see in these verses is both the grace of God and genuinely free human willing and acting, with neither excluding the other. As Oliver O'Donovan puts it, the grace of God in Christ 'acts on us first, producing in us a good will; and then it goes on working with us, because there is never a time when we can become independent of God for our response to him.'[404]

Article X of the *Forty Two Articles*, which was omitted by Archbishop Parker in 1563 also dealt with the subject of grace. It ran as follows:

Of Grace

The grace of Christ, or the Holy Ghost by Him given doth take away the stony heart and giveth an heart of flesh. And though, those that have no will to good things, He maketh them to will, and those that would evil things, He maketh them not to will the same: yet nevertheless He enforceth not the will. And therefore no man when he sinneth can excuse himself, as not worthy to be blamed or condemned, by alleging that he sinned unwillingly or under compulsion

De Gratia

Gratia Christi, seu Spiritus Sanctus qui per eundem datur, cor lapideum aufert, et dat cor carneum. Atque licet ex nolentibus quae recta sunt volentes faciat, et ex volentibus prava, nolentes reddat, voluntati nihilominus violentiam nullam infert. Et nemo hacde causa cum peccaverit, seiipsum excusare potest, quasi nolens aut

---

[404] O O'Donovan, *On the Thirty Nine Articles*, Exeter: Paternoster, 1986, p. 75.

coactus, pecacaverit, ut eam ob causam accusari non mereatur aut damnatur.

According to Charles Hardwick in his history of the Articles, this article by Cranmer was intended to refute the teachings of those radical Protestants who were:

> ...pushing their belief in absolute predestination to such frightful lengths that human actions were esteemed involuntary, and the evil choices of Man ascribed to a necessitating fiat of his Maker.[405]

Parker omitted the article either because he felt that the danger of this teaching was no longer pressing or because he did not wish to offend exiles returning from exile on the continent after the reign of Queen Mary who were disposed towards Continental Reformed theology and who may have felt this article gave to much weight to human freewill. However, in retrospect his decision to exclude it was unfortunate because this article makes four important points:

- Grace is not an impersonal force but the personal action of the Holy Spirit in a person's life;

- The work of the Holy Spirit in this way is the fulfilment of the promise given to Ezekiel 'A new heart I will give you, and a new spirit I will give you; and I will take out of your flesh the heart of stone and give you a heart of flesh. And I will put my spirit within you, and cause you to walk in my statutes and be careful to obey my ordinances' (Ezekiel 36:26-27);

- God's grace does not operate by enforcing the will. The human will remains free. Human beings do not become robots or puppets;

- The freedom that human beings have means that they cannot blame God for their sinful desires and actions.

---

[405] C Hardwick, *A History of the Articles of Religion*, London: George Bell and Sons, 1895, p.99

Because it makes these points this article provides an important supplement to what is said in Article X of the *Thirty Nine Articles*. As Browne notes:

> God must give the will, must set the will free from its natural slavery, before it can turn to good; but then it moves in the freedom which He has bestowed upon it, and never so truly uses that freedom, as when it follows the motions of the Spirit. Yet clearly there remains some power to resist and do evil. For 'those that hath no will to good things God maketh them to will;... Yet, nevertheless, He enforceth not the will.' And so, although He must work in us, yet we, under His influences, must strive and press forward, not resisting Him, not neglecting, but stirring up His gifts in our hearts.[406]

Although it is not mentioned in Article X, the work of the Holy Spirit in enabling to walk in God's way was taught by the Elizabethan Church of England in the Whitsunday homily 'The Coming Down of the Holy Ghost and His Manifold Gifts' in the *Second Book of Homilies*. This homily notes that:

> ...as there are three several and sundry Persons in the Deity, so have they three several and sundry offices proper unto each of them: the Father to create, the Son to redeem, the Holy Ghost to sanctify and regenerate.[407]

Building on this definition of the office of the Holy Spirit, the homily then explains that it is

> ...the Holy Ghost, and no other thing, that doth quicken the minds of men, stirring up good and godly motions in their hearts, which are agreeable to the will and commandment of God, such as otherwise of their own crooked and peruerse nature they should never have. *That which is born of the flesh*, saith Christ, *is flesh, and that which is born of the Spirit, is Spirit* (John 3.6). As who should say: Man of his own nature is fleshly and carnal, corrupt and

---

[406] Browne, op.cit. pp.272-273.
[407] *The Homilies*, p.332

naught, sinful and disobedient to God, without any spark of goodness in him, without any virtuous or godly motion, only given to evil thoughts and wicked deeds. As for the works of the Spirit, the fruits of Faith, charitable and godly motions, if he have any at all in him, they proceed only of the Holy Ghost, who is the only worker of our Sanctification, and maketh us new men in Christ Jesus.[408]

The same understanding of the work of the Holy Spirit is also expressed in summary form in the Catechism in the *Book of Common Prayer*. In this the candidate for confirmation expresses his or her belief 'in God the Holy Ghost, who sanctifieth me and all the elect people of God.'

In the light of what is said in the homily and the Catechism and what was taught in Article X of the *Forty Two Articles* it is legitimate to gloss the second sentence of the present Article X to read

Wherefore we have no power to do good works pleasant and acceptable to God, without the grace of God by Christ *given to us through the Holy Spirit* preventing us that we may have a good will, and working with us when we have that good will.

---

[408] Ibid, p.332.

Article XI

∞

Of the Justification of Man

We are accounted righteous before God, only for the merit of our Lord and Saviour Jesus Christ by faith, and not for our own works or deservings: Wherefore, that we are justified by faith only is a most wholesome doctrine, and very full of comfort; as more largely is expressed in the Homily of Justification.

De Hominis Iustificatione

Tantum propter meritum Domini ac Servatoris nostri Jesu Christi, per fidem, non propter opera et merita nostra, iusti coram Deo reputamur. Quare sola fide nos iustificari, doctrina est saluberrima, ac consolationis plenissima; ut in Homilia de Iustificatione hominis Fusius explicatur.

This article dates from the first Elizabethan revision of the Articles in 1563. Article XI of the *Forty Two Articles* read: 'Justification by only faith in Jesus Christ in that sense, as it is declared in the Homily of Justification, is a most certain and wholesome doctrine for Christian men' ('Justificatio ex solo fide Jesu Christi, eo sensu quo in Homilia de justificatione explicatur, est certissima et saluberimma Christianorum doctrina').

This was replaced by the present article.

The present article makes the same basic point as the article it replaces and retains its reference to the 'Homily on Justification'. However, it adds an opening main clause that explains the reasons that we are justified and the reasons that we are not. This clause provides the explanation for the claim in the second main clause that the statement that we are justified by faith only is 'wholesome' and 'full of comfort.' The word 'wherefore' ('for this reason') acts as the connection between the two main clauses.

The language used by Archbishop Parker in the first clause seems to have been influenced by the *Würtemburg* and *Augsburg* Confessions. Article V of the former declares 'For man is accepted by God and is accounted righteous before Him for the sake of the only Son of God, Our Lord Jesus Christ, by faith' and Article IV of the latter states that 'men cannot be justified by God by their own strength, deserts or works, but are freely justified for Christ's sake, by faith.'

Article XI is designed to make clear the position of the Church of England in relation to the debates about justification that took place during the Reformation. Specifically, it is designed to rule out the theories of human merit that were prevalent in Western Church of the Middle Ages and it may also have been aimed at the tenets of certain of the Protestant radicals who, in the words of the *Consultation* by the reforming Archbishop of Cologne, Hermann Wied:

> ...boste themselves to be ryghtuous and to please God, not purely and absolutely for Christes sake, but for theyr owne mortification of themselves, for theyr owne good workes and persecution, if they suffer any. [409]

Both the original 1553 article and its 1563 replacement make clear that the meaning of what these articles say about justification is explained in more detail in the 'Homily of Justification.' What they are referring to is the homily 'Of the Salvation of Mankind' by Archbishop Cranmer in the *First Book of Homilies*. It is therefore to this homily that we need to turn in order to understand Article XI properly.

We are accounted righteous before God

The homily nowhere offers a precise definition of what the terms 'justification' or 'righteousness' mean. However, the opening paragraph of the homily does contain two passages which enable us to infer what the two terms mean in the homily and therefore also in the article.

The first passage is the opening words of the homily which declare that:

---

[409] Cited in Tyrell Green, op.cit. p.84.

> Because all men be sinners and offenders against God, and breakers of his law and commandments, therefore can no man by his own acts, works, and deeds, seem they ever so good, be justified and made righteous before God; but every man of necessity is constrained to seek for another righteousness or justification, to be received at God's own hands, that is to say, the remission, pardon and forgiveness of his sins and trespasses in such things as he hath offended. And this justification or righteousness which we so receive of God's mercy and Christ's merits, embraced by faith, is taken, accepted, and allowed of God for our perfect and full justification.[410]

The second passage, which comes slightly later in the opening section, states that:

> ...they which in act or deed, do sin after their baptism, when they convert, and turn again to God unfeignedly, they are likewise washed by this sacrifice from their sins in such sort that there remaineth not any spot of sin, that shall be imputed to their damnation. This is that justification or righteousness which St. Paul speaketh of when he saith, *No man is justified by the works of the law, but freely by faith in Jesus Christ.* And again he saith, *We believe in Jesus Christ that we be justified freely by the faith of Christ and not by the works of the law, because that no man shall be justified by the works of the Law* (Galatians 2.16).[411]

From these two passages it appears that 'righteousness' as used by St. Paul in Galatians 2 means being in the right in the sight of God and that, in the face of human sinfulness, 'justification' or 'being accounted righteous' means coming to be in the right in the sight of God through the forgiveness of our sins.

This understanding of what justification means in the homily, and therefore also in Article XI, is supported by the fact that this understanding of what justification means is in line with the definition of justification contained in the *Ten Articles* of 1536 and the *Thirteen Articles* of 1538.

---

[410] *The Homilies*, p.17
[411] Ibid pp. 17-18.

Article V of the *Ten Articles* declares that

> This word justification signifieth remission of our sins and our acceptance or reconciliation into the grace and favour of God, that is to say, our perfect renovation in Christ.[412]

In similar fashion, Article IV of the *Thirteen Articles* states

> ...concerning justification we teach that properly speaking, it signifies the forgiveness of sins and our acceptance, i.e. reconciliation into the grace and favour of God, that is, true renewal in Christ. [413]

These two definitions and what is said in the homily indicate an agreed understanding that justification is about how God deals with our sins so that we are once again acceptable in his sight. It is this understanding that must be seen as the meaning of justification in Article XI. Why are we 'accounted righteous before God?' We are accounted righteous before God because our sins have been forgiven.

not for our own works or deservings

As the first passage from the homily also explains, none of us can be in the right before God by reason of what we do or are in ourselves because we are all 'sinners and offenders against God, and breakers of his laws and commandments.' This statement reflects the view of the sinfulness of fallen humanity that we have already looked at in connection with Articles IX and X.

only for the merit of our Lord and Saviour Jesus Christ

Just as the homily nowhere defines the meaning of the terms 'righteousness' or 'justification' so also it nowhere defines the term 'merit'. However, as before, the meaning of the term can be inferred from what the homily does say.

---

[412] Text in G Bray, *Documents of the English Reformation*, Cambridge: James Clarke,1984, pp. 170.
[413] Ibid p.187.

What the homily tells us is that God is both just and merciful. Because this is the case it follows that God would neither:

> ...by his justice condemn us, unto the everlasting captivity of the devil, and his prison of hell, remediless forever without mercy, nor by his mercy deliver us clearly, without justice or payment of a just ransom.[414]

Because we are sinners we cannot pay this just ransom. According to the homily, this is where the work of Christ comes into the picture. As the homily explains, God has shown his great mercy to us by:

> ....delivering us from our former captivity, without requiring of any ransom to be paid or amends to be made upon our parts; which thing by us had been impossible to be done. And whereas it lay not in us that to do, he provided a ransom for us, that was, the most precious body, and blood, of his own most dear and best beloved Son Jesus Christ; who besides his ransom fulfilled the law for us perfectly. And so the justice of God, and his mercy, did embrace together, and fulfilled the mystery of our redemption.[415]

It is this coming together of God's justice and mercy, says the homily, which St. Paul is referring to when he talks in the letter to the Romans about God justifying us:

> *And of this justice and mercy of God, knit together, speaketh St. Paul in the third chapter to the Romans:* All have offended and have need of the glory of God, but are justified freely by his grace, by redemption which is in Jesus Christ, whom God hath set forth to us for a reconciler and peacemaker, through faith in his blood, to show his righteousness. *(Romans 3.23-25). And in the tenth chapter,* Christ is the end of the law unto righteousness to every man that believeth *(Romans 10.4). And in the eighth chapter:* That which was impossible by the Law, inasmuch as it was weak by the flesh, God sending his own Son, in the similitude of sinful flesh, by sin damned sin in the flesh, that the righteousness of the Law

---

[414] *The Homilies* p.18.
[415] Ibid, p.18.

might be fulfilled in us, which walk not after the flesh, but after the Spirit *(Romans 8.3-5).*[416]

It is clear from these passages that the 'merit' of Christ means what Christ has done for us to satisfy the requirements of God's justice and mercy by dying for us on the cross to pay the price of rescuing us from our sins and by obeying God's law perfectly on our behalf. As the homily summarises the matter:

> He for them paid their ransom by his death. He for them fulfilled the law in his life. So that now in him, and by him, every true Christian man may be called a fulfiller of the law; forasmuch as that which their infirmity lacked, Christ's justice hath supplied.[417]

The punishment due to us for our sins and our need to obey God's law are thus both met in what Jesus Christ has done for us. This is his 'merit' and this is the reason why we are now in the right before God.

by faith

The teaching that we are justified by faith, based on the statements of St. Paul in Romans 3:21-5:9, 9:30-10:13, Galatians 2:20-3:29, Ephesians 2:8-9 and Philippians 3:2-11, could be taken, and in the history of the Church has been taken, to mean that it is our act of believing in what Christ has done for us that puts us in the right before God, as if all that God requires of us has been reduced to the single requirement that we believe.

However, the homily stresses that this is not what is meant when it is said that we are justified by faith:

> ...the true understanding of this doctrine, We be justified freely, by faith without works, or that we be justified by faith in Christ only, is not that this our own act, to believe in Christ, or this our faith in Christ, which is within us, doth justify us, and merit our justification unto us; for that were to count ourselves to be justified by some act, or virtue that is within ourselves.[418]

---

[416] Ibid, p.18.
[417] Ibid, p.19.
[418] Ibid, pp.21-22.

What, then, does 'by faith' mean? What it means is that we must look away from ourselves and our virtues and good works, and even our own faith, as the cause of our justification and instead trust wholly in Christ and what he has done for us. As the homily goes on to say:

> ...the true understanding and meaning thereof is, that although we hear God's word, and believe it, although we have faith, hope, charity, repentance, dread, and fear of God within us, and do never so many good works thereunto, yet we must renounce the merit of all our said virtues of faith, hope, charity, and all our other virtues and good deeds, which we either have done, shall do, or can do, as things that be far too weak, and insufficient and unperfect, to deserve remission of our sins and our justification; and therefore we must trust only in God's mercy, and in that sacrifice, which our High Priest and Saviour, Christ Jesus, the Son of God, once offered for us upon the cross, to obtain thereby God's grace, and remission, as well of our original sin, in baptism, as of all actual sin committed by us after our baptism, if we truly repent and turn unfeignedly to him again. So that as St. John Baptist, although he were never so virtuous and godly a man, yet in this matter of forgiving of sin, he did put the people from him and appointed them unto Christ, saying thus unto them, *Behold, yonder is the Lamb of God which taketh away the sins of the world* (John 1.29); even so, as great and as godly a virtue as the lively faith is, yet it putteth us from itself and remitteth or appointeth us unto Christ, for to have only by him remission of our sins or justification. So that our faith in Christ, as it were, saith unto us thus: It is not I that take away your sins, but it is Christ only; and to him only I send you for that purpose, forsaking therein all your good virtues, words, thoughts, and works, and only putting your trust in Christ.[419]

The article not only tells us that we are justified 'by faith,' but that we are justified 'by faith *only*.' The use of the word 'only' goes beyond what St. Paul actually says in passages such as Romans 3:25 and Galatians 2:16. The English Reformers were aware of this fact and the homily explains why it is nonetheless right to use the word 'only.' It declares that:

---

[419] Ibid, p.22.

...forasmuch as it is all one sentence in effect to say, Faith without works, and Only faith, doth justify us, therefore the old ancient fathers of the Church, from time to time have uttered our justification with this speech: *'Only faith justifieth us,'* meaning no other thing than St. Paul meant when he said, "Faith without works justifieth us" (Galatians 2.16).[420]

Only is thus a gloss meaning 'without works.' As the homily also explains, the 'ancient fathers of the church' referred to here are Patristic writers such as St. Basil, St. Hilary and St. Ambrose all of whom use the expression 'by faith only' in their writings.[421]

is a most wholesome doctrine, and very full of comfort

In the light of what is said in the homily, the reason why the doctrine of justification by faith is 'wholesome', that is, spiritually health giving, is because it teaches us to stop trusting in ourselves and our works for our salvation and to trust instead in Christ and his works. By doing this it enables us to be in the right in the sight of God.

Furthermore, because it teaches us that because of what Christ has done for us we can be in the right in the sight of God and therefore delivered from God's condemnation at the last judgement, the doctrine is also 'very full of comfort.'

The doctrine of justification by faith has been understood in a variety of different ways in the history of the Christian Church.[422] However, for the purposes of understanding Article XI what matters is how the English Reformers understood the doctrine. How they understood is set out in the 'Homily of Justification' in the way described above. This is what they and the article mean by justification by faith.

There are four further points that need to be noted in relation to Article XI.

---

[420] Ibid, p.23.
[421] In addition to the Fathers already mentioned, the Homily also adds Origen, St. John Chrysostom, St. Cyprian, St. Augustine, Prosper, Oecumenicus, Photius, St. Bernard, St. Anselm and 'many other authors, Greek and Latin.' (p.20).
[422] See A E McGrath, *Iustitia Dei*, 3ed, Cambridge: CUP, 2005.

1. What is said in this Article is integrally related to what will be said about the sinlessness of Christ in Article XV. It is because Christ was sinless that he was able to justify us by dying for us on the cross and perfectly fulfilling God's law on our behalf.

2. Although the point is not made in either the article or the homily, what they both teach about justification by faith on the basis of the merits of Christ requires that the believer is united with Christ so that God views him or her in the light of what Christ has achieved through his perfect obedience to God's law and his death on the cross. This point is emphasised by Richard Hooker in a sermon on justification by faith. Hooker states:

> In him God findeth us, if we be faithful, for by faith we are incorporated into him. Then, although in ourselves we be altogether sinful and unrighteous, yet even the man who in himself is impious, full of iniquity, full of sin, him being found in Christ through faith, and having his sin in hatred through repentance, him God beholdeth with a gracious eye, putteth away his sin by not imputing it, taketh quite away the punishment due thereunto, by pardoning it, and accepteth him in Jesus Christ as perfectly righteous, as if he had fulfilled all that is commanded him in the law: shall I say more perfectly righteous than if himself had fulfilled the whole law? I must take heed what I say; but the Apostle saith, "God made him who knew no sin to be sin for us, that we might be made the righteousness of God in him (2 Cor 5:21). Such we are in the sight of God the Father as is the very Son of God himself.[423]

3. As Oliver O'Donovan notes, the statement in Article XI that it is because of the merit of Christ that we are accounted righteous before God establishes that justification has an ethical basis.

> There is no suggestion that goodness and moral integrity do not matter. God has never ceased to be pleased by the righteousness

[423] R Hooker, 'A learned discourse of justification' in J Keble (ed), *The works of that learned and judicious divine Mr.Richard Hooker*, Vol II, Oxford: OUP, 1851, p.606.

of mankind. He is pleased with the one man who is truly righteous, Jesus.[424]

Furthermore God is still pleased when the righteousness of Christ begins to be reflected in believers which is why Article XII will go on to talk about the importance of the good works that flow from faith.

4. As O'Donovan further notes, the fact that Article XI understands justification in terms of our being 'accounted' righteous rather than, as in much Medieval discussion, our being made righteous by a process of sanctification defends the finality of what Christ achieved on behalf of his people by his resurrection from the dead.

> God having raised up the righteous representative and set him at the right hand, what remains for him to do? Shall we say that he has many further tasks ahead of him, the making of numerous believers righteous? Shall we say that with only one man yet exalted to the throne of God, the redeeming work is hardly begun? Shall we say that with the Second Person home and dry, the Third person has still to run his race? No, we may say none of these things. We must say that all is finished and complete. The sanctification of the many can do no more than realize the implications of what has already been accomplished. The coming of the Spirit to struggle with the flesh is simply a communication of the triumph that is won for all time. The doctrine of representation permits us to say no less and no more.[425]

---

[424] O O'Donovan, *On the Thirty Nine Articles*, p.78
[425] Ibid, p.79.

Article XII

∞

Of Good Works

Albeit that good works, which are the fruits of faith and follow after justification, cannot put away our sins and endure the severity of God's judgement, yet are they pleasing and acceptable to God in Christ, and do spring out necessarily of a true and lively faith, insomuch that by them a lively faith may be as evidently known as a tree discerned by the fruit.

De Bonis Operibus

Bona opera, quae sunt fructus fidei et iustificatos sequuntur, quanquam peccata nostra expiare et divini iudicii severitatem ferre non possunt, Deo tamen grata sunt et accepta in Christo, atque ex vera et viva fide necessario profluunt, ut plane ex illis aeque fides viva cognosci possit atque arbor ex fructu iudicari.

Article XII was one of four new articles added in the revision of the Articles in 1563. *The Forty Two Articles* moved straight from Article XI on justification to Articles XII on works before justification, but it was decided by Archbishop Parker that an article on good works needed to be inserted at this point.

We do not have any direct evidence as to why Parker thought that the addition was necessary, but we may presume that, like the articles on good works in the *Augsburg* and *Würtemburg* Confessions, the article was intended to refute the argument of those loyal to Rome that that doctrine of justification by faith implied that good works were unimportant and to correct any misguided people on the Protestant side who were tempted to think the same thing.

The article seems to have been newly composed for the 1563 revision, but the word 'follow after justification' in the second clause seem to have been taken from Ch XIV of the treatise *On Faith and Works* by St. Augustine and the third clause seems to have drawn on the statement in Article VII of the *Würtemburg Confession* that 'all good works that we do are imperfect and cannot endure the severity of God's judgement.'[426]

Albeit that good works, which are the fruits of faith and follow after justification, cannot put away our sins and endure the severity of God's judgement...

This clause makes two points.

First, what we are talking about in this article are the good works that are produced by Christian believer as a result of their faith in Christ.

Secondly, because, as Articles IX and XV teach, believers are still sinners it follows that their good works will always be imperfect and therefore unable to withstand the scrutiny of God's judgement. Furthermore, as the previous article and the homily to which it refers make clear, because they are imperfect they cannot do away with our sins. Only the death of Christ and his prefect fulfilment of God's law can do that.

...yet are they pleasing and acceptable to God in Christ,...

The key words here are 'in Christ.' Because, as we noted when looking at Article XI, believers are united with Christ their works are therefore acceptable to God. In the words of Browne in his commentary on this article:

> The words 'In Christ' are introduced to remind us, that whatever is good in us must spring from the grace of Christ, and whatever in us is acceptable to God is acceptable for Christ's sake. In all the servants of Christ, God sees the image of His Son. In all the members of Christ, God sees the Sprit of His Son, descending from the Head to the members, like the holy oil on Aaron's head, which flowed down to the skirts of his clothing. In all the branches of the heavenly Vine, God sees the fruits thereof, as put forward by

---

[426] Text in Tyrell Green, op.cit, p.380.

virtue of the life and nourishment derived from the Vine itself; and that Vine is Christ.[427]

Browne goes on to say that for this reason 'the Scriptures constantly, when they speak of Christians and the work of Christians as pleasing to God, teach us that it is 'in Christ.'[428] As evidence for this he points to passages such as:

Colossians 3:17 'And whatever you do, in word or deed, do everything in the name of the Lord Jesus, giving thanks to God the Father through him;'

Hebrews 13:15 'Through him then let us continually offer to up a sacrifice of praise to God, that is, the fruit of lips that acknowledge his name;'

1 Peter 2:4-5 'Come to him, to that living stone, rejected by men, but in God's sight chosen and precious; and like living stones be yourselves built into a spiritual house, to be a holy priesthood, to offer spiritual sacrifices acceptable to God through Christ Jesus.'

...and do spring out necessarily of a true and lively faith, insomuch that by them a lively faith may be as evidently known as a tree discerned by the fruit.

The statement here that a tree is discerned by the fruit is a reference to Matthew 12:33 where Jesus declares 'either make the tree good, and its fruit good; or make the tree bad, and its fruit bad; for the tree is known by its fruit.'

This verse is referred to in the same connection in the homily 'A short declaration of the true, lively, and Christian faith' in the *First Book of Homilies.* This homily amplifies what is said in the article about good works necessarily springing forth from a lively faith and, as in the case of Article XI, the article needs to be read in the light of what is said in the homily.

---

[427] Browne, op.cit. p.319
[428] Ibid, p.319.

The homily distinguishes between two kinds of faith that are described in Scripture. There is the 'dead faith' referred to by St. James (James 2:17-19) 'which bringeth forth no good works, but is idle, barren and unfruitful.' By contrast there is also another kind of faith, referred to by St. Paul:

> ...which is not as the foresaid faith, idle, unfruitful, and dead, but *worketh by charity*, as St. Paul declareth Gal.5[:6]: which, as the other faith is called a dead faith, so may this be called a quick and lively faith.[429]

The homily exhorts Christians to look at their lives and to consider whether they are producing the fruit of good works that indicates that they have a lively rather than a dead faith.

> Let us therefore, good Christian people, try and examine our faith what it is: let us not flatter ourselves, but look upon our works, and so judge of our faith, what it is. Christ himself speaketh of this matter and saith, *The tree is known by the fruit* (Matthew 12.33). Therefore let us do good works and thereby declare our faith to be the lively Christian faith. Let us, by such virtues as ought to spring up out of faith, show our election to be sure and stable; as St. Peter teacheth, *Endeavour yourselves to make your calling and election certain by good works* (2 Peter 1.10). And also he saith, *Minister* or declare *in your faith virtue, in virtue knowledge, in knowledge temperance, in temperance patience, in patience godliness, in godliness brotherly charity, in brotherly charity love* (vv. 5-7). So shall we show indeed, that we have the very lively Christian faith; and may so both certify our conscience the better, that we be in the right faith, and also by these means, confirm other men. If these fruits do not follow, we do but mock with God, deceive ourselves, and also other men. Well may we bear the name of Christian men, but we do lack the true faith that doth belong thereunto. For true faith doth ever bring forth good works; as St. James saith, *Show me thy faith by thy deeds* (James 2.18). Thy deeds and works must be an open testimonial of thy faith; otherwise thy faith, being without good works, is but the devil's

---

[429] *The Homilies*, p.27.

faith, the faith of the wicked, a phantasy of faith, and not a true Christian faith.[430]

What the article does not tell us is what constitutes good works. This was a major issue at the Reformation because the question arose as to whether traditional forms of Medieval piety such as going on pilgrimage and adoring the relics of the saints counted as good works.

This issue is addressed in another homily from the *First Book of Homilies*, 'Of Good Works annexed unto Faith.' This homily follows on from the homily on 'The true, lively and Christian faith' previously cited and in its second and third sections it specifically tackles the question 'what manner of works they be, which spring out of true faith, and lead faithful men, unto everlasting life.'[431]

In a section which we have already noted in connection with Article VII, the homily declares that the best answer to this question was given by Christ himself:

...who was asked of a certain great man the same question. *What works shall I do*, said a prince, *to come to everlasting life?* To whom Jesus answered, *If thou wilt come to everlasting life, keep the commandments* (Matthew 19.16-17). But the prince, not satisfied herewith, asked further; *Which commandments?* The scribes and Pharisees had made so many of their own laws, and traditions to bring men to heaven, besides God's commandments, that this man was in doubt, whether he should come to heaven by those laws and traditions or by the laws of God; and therefore he asked Christ, which commandments he meant. Whereunto Christ made him a plain answer, rehearsing the commandments of God, saying: *Thou shalt not kill; Thou shalt not commit adultery; Thou shalt not steal; Thou shalt not bear false witnesses; Honour thy father and thy mother; and Love thy neighbour as thyself* (Matthew 19.18-19). By which words Christ declared, that the laws of God be the very way, that doth lead to everlasting life, and not the traditions and laws of men. So that this is to be taken for a most true lesson, taught by Christ's own mouth, that the works of the

---

[430] Ibid pp.33-34.
[431] Ibid, p.37

moral commandments of God be the very true works of faith which lead to the blessed life to come.[432]

The homily then goes on to explore the difference between the commands of God and the 'traditions and laws of men,' arguing that ever since the Fall human beings have preferred to make up their own laws and traditions rather than follow the commandments of God and that this is the explanation for pagan religion, the frequent lapses into idolatry of the people of Israel, the Jewish traditions criticised by Jesus in the gospels and the 'papistical superstitions and abuses' that were prevalent in the English church until the Reformation.

Rather than going down that route, says the homily, producing the fruit of good works means living a live of obedience to the way of life that God has commanded. In the closing words of the homily this way of life is described as follows:

> Wherefore, as ye have any zeal to the right and pure honouring of God, as ye have any regard to your own souls and to the life that is to come, which is both without pain and without end, apply yourselves chiefly above all things, to read and hear God's word: mark diligently therein what his will is you shall do, and with all your endeavour apply yourselves to follow the same.
>
> First ye must have an assured faith in God and give yourselves wholly unto him, love him in prosperities and adversity, and dread to offend him evermore.
>
> Then for his sake love all men, friends and foes, because they be his creation and image and redeemed by Christ, as ye are. Cast in your minds how ye may do good unto all men, unto your powers and hurt no man. Obey all your superiors and governors, serve your masters faithfully and diligently, as well in their absence as in their presence, not for dread of punishment only, but for conscience's sake, knowing that ye are bound so to do by God's commandments. Disobey not your fathers and mothers, but honour them, help them, and please them to your power. Oppress not, kill not, beat not, neither slander, nor hate any man; but love all men, speak well of all men, help and succour every man as ye may, yea even your enemies that hate you, that

---

[432] Ibid, pp.37-38.

speak evil of you and that do hurt you. Take no man's goods nor covet your neighbour's goods wrongfully, but content yourselves with that which ye get truly, and also bestow your own goods charitably, as need and case requireth.

Flee all idolatry, witchcraft, and perjury. Commit no manner of adultery, fornication, or other unchasteness, in will nor in deed, with any other man's wife, widow, maid, or otherwise. And travailing continually during this life, thus in keeping the commandments of God, wherein standeth the pure, principal, and right honour of God, and which wrought in faith, God hath ordained to be the right trade and pathway unto heaven, ye shall not fail, as Christ hath promised, to come to that blessed and everlasting life where ye shall live in glory and joy with God forever; to whom be praise, honour, and empery [empire] forever and ever.[433]

Looked at carefully, this quotation can be seen to be based on a variety of different biblical passages, including the Ten Commandments, the Sermon on the Mount and the ethical teaching contained in the New Testament letters. The vision that it offers of a practical, Bible based piety also corresponds closely to the vision of the Christian life contained in the Prayer Book catechism in which the Ten Commandments are recited and then expounded in terms of 'duty towards God' and 'duty towards my neighbour.'

Taken together, Articles XI and XII put forward a balanced approach to the issue of the importance of good works. On the one hand, they emphasise that our good works will not, of themselves, put us into a right relationship with God. On the other hand, they emphasise that a living faith in Christ will necessarily produce good works and so we must ensure that we perform them. As the seventeenth century commentator on the articles, Bishop Gilbert Burnet, puts it in his closing remarks on Article XII, what the articles teach us is that:

...we must keep a just temper in this matter, neither to ascribe so much to our own works as to be lifted up by reason of them, or to forget our daily need of a Saviour both for pardon and intercession; nor on the other hand so far to neglect them, as to

---

[433] Ibid, pp.44-45.

take no care about them. The due temper is to *make our calling and election sure, and to work out our own salvation with fear and trembling* (Philippians 2:12); but to do *all in the name of the Lord Jesus*, ever trusting to him, and *giving thanks to God by him* (Colossians 3:7).[434]

Note 1: Justification in ecumenical agreements

Agreement about the doctrine of justification by faith in line with teaching of Articles XI and XII has been a feature of ecumenical agreements between the Church of England and other churches,

Paragraph 20 of the 1983 report of the Anglican-Lutheran European Regional Commission, *Anglican Lutheran Dialogue* declares:

> We therefore share a common understanding of God's justifying grace, i.e. that we are accounted righteous and are made righteous before God only by grace through faith because of the merits of our Lord and Saviour Jesus Christ, and not on account of our works or merits...Both our traditions affirm that justification leads and must lead to 'good works'; authentic faith issues in love.[435]

This declaration has since been echoed in the ecumenical agreements that the Church of England has entered into with the Evangelical Church in Germany,[436] with the other British and Irish Anglican churches and the Nordic and Baltic Lutheran churches,[437] with the Moravian Church in Great Britain and Ireland,[438] and with the other British and Irish Anglican churches and the French Lutheran and Reformed churches.[439]

The covenant between the Church of England and the Methodist Church of Great Britain also affirms that both churches teach 'the

---

[434] G Burnet, *An Exposition of the XXXIX Articles*, Oxford: Clarendon Press, 1819, p. 180.

[435] *Anglican Lutheran Dialogue,* London: SPCK, 1983.

[436] *The Meissen Agreement,* Texts, London: CCU, 1992, para 15(vi), p.18.

[437] *The Porvoo Common Statement,* London: CCU, 1993, para 32 c, p.18.

[438] *Anglican-Moravian Conversations*, London: CCU, 1996, para 32 f, pp.18-19.

[439] *Called to witness and service,* London: CHP, 1999, para 31 c, p. 26.

justification of the penitent believer by unmerited grace through faith in Christ.'[440]

Agreement on the doctrine of justification was also reached by the Anglican and Roman Catholic theologians of the second Anglican-Roman Catholic International Commission (ARCIC II) in their report *Salvation and the Church*. In this report they noted how the Protestant and Catholic theologians of the Reformation era used the term justification in different ways and how this difference led the two sides to be suspicious of each other's theology:

> The theologians of the Reformation tended to follow the predominant usage of the New Testament, in which the verb dikaioun usually means "to pronounce righteous". The Catholic theologians, and notably the Council of Trent, tended to follow the usage of patristic and medieval Latin writers, for whom justificare (the traditional translation of dikaioun) signified "to make righteous" Thus the Catholic understanding of the process of justification, following Latin usage, tended to include elements of salvation which the Reformers would describe as belonging to sanctification rather than justification. As a consequence, Protestants took Catholics to be emphasising sanctification in such a way that absolute gratuitousness of salvation was threatened. On the other side, Catholics feared that Protestants were so stressing the justifying action of God that sanctification and human responsibility were gravely depreciated.[441]

In the face of this traditional theological difference the theologians of ARCIC II reached an agreed understanding of justification. They agreed that justification means that 'instead of our own strivings to make ourselves acceptable to God, Christ's perfect righteousness is reckoned to our account.'[442] They further agreed that 'justification and sanctification are two aspects of the same divine act' (1 Cor 6:11) and that when we are justified God imparts to us 'a righteousness which is his and becomes

---

[440] *An Anglican Methodist Covenant*, Peterborough and London: MPH/CHP, 2001, para 110, p.37.
[441] *Salvation and the Church with commentary and study guide*, London: CTS/CHP, 1989, para 14, pp.24-25.
[442] Ibid, para 18, pp.25-26

ours.'[443] Finally, they agreed that 'good works necessarily spring from a living faith'[444] and that these good works are the result of the righteousness of Christ at work in our lives by means of which:

> We are freed and enabled to keep the commandments of God by the power of the Holy Spirit, to live faithfully as God's people and to grow in love within the discipline of the community bringing forth the fruit of the Spirit.[445]

This agreed understanding of justification corresponds to the traditional Protestant understanding of justification reflected in Articles XI and XII in which justification consists of God's impartation of the righteousness of Christ to us as a gift and in which a living faith necessarily brings forth the fruit of good works. It also helpfully combines this with the traditional Catholic emphasis that justification involves sanctification[446] and from this perspective makes clear that the good works that are the fruit of faith are also the fruit of divine grace in that they are the result of the righteousness of God at work in us.

The ARCIC report does not actually use the term 'justification through faith,' but this is clearly implied by the report in that it says that 'salvation is the gift of grace; it is by faith that it is appropriated'[447] and this statement forms the background to its subsequent discussion of justification.

Note 2: Justification and the 'new perspective' on Paul

During the twentieth century, and continuing today, a number of New Testament scholars have put forward what has been called a 'new perspective' on St. Paul.[448] These scholars have not necessarily agreed

---

[443] Ibid, para, 15 p.24.
[444] Ibid para 19, p.28.
[445] Ibid, para 19, p.29.
[446] As the ARCIC report notes, the view that righteousness also means sanctification was acknowledged in the sixteenth century by Richard Hooker who said that the perfect righteousness of Christ was imputed to us, but also 'imparted; to us 'as when grace is inwardly bestowed while we are on earth, and afterwards more fully our souls and bodies be made like unto his glory' (Laws of Ecclesiastical Polity V.lvii.11)
[447] Ibid, para 9, p.18.
[448] See, for example, J D G Dunn, *The Theology of Paul the Apostle*, Grand Rapids: Eerdmans, 1998, E P Sanders, *Paul and Palestinian Judaism*, London: SCM 1977, K

with each other, but what their approaches to St. Paul have had in common is that they have all been attempts to get behind the Reformation debates about his theology and to see in its original first century context.

The most prominent representative of this way of looking at St. Paul at the moment is the former Bishop of Durham, N.T. Wright, and in his writings on this topic he has argued that we need to take a fresh look at St. Paul's teaching on justification. His argument is that justification involves 'God's declaration that certain people are within the covenant.'[449] In his view, when St. Paul talks about justification by faith, what this means is that someone's faith shows that by God's grace they are a Christian. That is to say, they are part of the new covenant people that God has created through the life, death and resurrection of Christ and as such are in the right before God. As he puts it:

> Justification is not how God makes someone a Christian: it is his righteous declaration that someone is already a Christian. Faith is not an achievement which earns salvation, but the evidence of saving grace already at work. Only a renewed heart can believe in the resurrection: only the penitent heart can submit to Jesus as saviour and Lord.[450]

There are three points to note about Wright's interpretation of the Pauline teaching on justification:

First, Wright's view of justification is a topic of continuing scholarly debate,[451] and at the moment it only has the status of a scholarly proposal. It has not yet achieved general acceptance amongst New Testament scholars and there are plenty of scholars who still defend the tradition Reformation interpretation of Paul's teaching on justification. This being the case it would be premature for the Church of England to

Stendahl, *Paul among Jews and Gentiles*, Philadelphia: Fortress Press, 1976, N T Wright, *Paul: Fresh Perspectives*: London: SPCK, 2005.
[449] N T Wright, 'Justification: the biblical basis' in T Baker, G Carey, J Tiller & T Wright, *The Great Acquittal*, London: Fount, 1980, p.15.
[450] Ibid, pp.16-17.
[451] See N T Wright, *Justification*, London: SPCK, 2009, B McCormack, *Justification in Perspective: Historical Developments and Contemporary Challenges*, Edinburgh: Rutherford House, 2006, J Piper, *The Future of Justification: A Response to NT Wright*, Wheaton Il, Crossway Books, 2007 and S Westerholm, *Perspectives Old and New on Paul*, Grand Rapids: Eerdmans, 2004.

conclude that taking biblical scholarship seriously means having to re-consider its traditional understanding of justification.

Secondly, if Wright's proposal did come to be generally accepted Article XII would be unaffected. Wright is clear that those who are justified will live holy lives in obedience to God. However Article XI would need to be re-worded to make it clear that the teaching of the Homily that justification is the means by which we come to be in the right before God is incorrect and that according to St. Paul justification is instead God's declaration that we are already in the right before him and are part of his new covenant people.

Thirdly, if Wright's proposal did come to be accepted this would not affect the heart of the English Reformer's teaching about how we cone to be rightly related to God. Wright still maintains, just like the Reformers, that according to St. Paul we come to be rightly related to God not through our efforts or good works, but through what God has done for us in Christ and that those who are in the right with God are those who have faith in Christ. To quote Wright again:

> The message of justification by faith for us as individuals, as evangelicals, as churchmen, is this. Because God is the covenant God, he has kept his covenant with Abraham, and is even now restoring his kingly rule over the world by creating us in Christ as a renewed people for his own possession. Because God is love, he has sent his own Son to die for us, and his own Spirit to live in us. Because God is righteous, he declares in the present time that all who believe in the risen Lord Jesus are in the right, that their sins are forgiven.[452]

---

[452] 'Justification: the biblical basis,' p. 37.

Article XIII

∞

Of Works before Justification

Works done before the grace of Christ and the inspiration of the Holy Spirit, are not pleasant to God, forasmuch as they, neither do they make men meet to receive grace, or (as the School authors say) deserve grace of congruity: yea, rather for that they are not done as God hath willed and commanded them to be done, we doubt not but they have the nature of sin.

De Operibus ante Iustificationem

Opera quae fiunt ante gratiam Christi et Spiritus eius afflatum, eum ex fide Iesu Christi non prodeant, minime Deo grata sunt, neque gratiam (ut multi vocant) de congruo merentur: imo cum non sint facta ut Deus illa fieri voluit et praecepit, peccati rationem habere non dubitamus.

This article has remained unchanged since the *Forty Two Articles*. It seems to have been freshly composed for those Articles. There is no corresponding article in the *Augsburg Confession* and the language of the article has not been traced back to any other earlier source.

In the English version of the article the phrase 'as the School authors say' is used to explain more precisely what is meant by phrase 'ut multi vocant' ('as many say') used in the Latin version.

It has been suggested by Gibson in his commentary on this article that there is a discrepancy between the title of the article and its contents. The title of the article talks about 'works before justification' whereas the article itself talks about 'works done before the grace of Christ.' The issue Gibson raises is whether 'works before justification' and 'works before grace' are the same thing. He argues that they are not the same thing because the examples of the multitude who were 'cut to the heart' after hearing St. Peter on the day of Pentecost (Acts 2:37) and of St.

Paul who was praying prior to his baptism by Ananias (Acts 9:11) show that it is possible for people to be granted divine grace prior to their justification.[453]

In his view there is therefore a discrepancy between the title and the contents of the article and he traces this discrepancy back to the original drafting of the article between 1552 and 1553. He notes that a draft copy of the article exists in which the opening words are 'opera quae fiunt ante justificationem' ('works done before justication') and he declares that:

> It is evident that Cranmer and those working with him afterwards felt that this was inaccurate, and therefore modified the wording of the Article before publication, introducing the phrase which we now read in it, 'Works before the grace of Christ,' etc, although the old title was still allowed to remain, inexact though it was.[454]

In response to Gibson's argument, the key point that needs to be noted is that the article itself explains what it means by works done before grace. It says that such works 'spring not of faith in Jesus Christ.' In order to be consistent with the three preceding articles 'faith' here must mean 'justifying faith' and therefore what 'grace' must mean is the grace that people receive when they are justified and that results in their works being performed by 'the inspiration of the Holy Spirit.' There is thus no discrepancy between the title of the article and its contents although it remains unclear why the Cranmer and his colleagues substituted 'before the grace of Christ' for 'before justification' in the final version of the *Forty Two Articles*.

...or (as the School authors say) deserve grace of congruity

The purpose of the article is to relate the principle previously stated in Article X that fallen human beings are unable to prepare themselves by their 'own natural strength and good works, to faith, and calling upon God' to the teaching about 'congruent grace' which had existed among the

---

[453] Gibson, op.cit, p.416-417.
[454] Ibid, p.418. The draft text can be found in Hardwick, op.cit. p.281.

scholastic theologians of the Western Church (the 'school men') during the Middle Ages.[455]

As Gibson explains, some among the scholastic theologians had argued that people might be entitled to receive grace as a reward for actions performed in their own strength without the aid of the Holy Spirit. Starting from the view that the Fall left man's natural faculties intact:

> ...they taught that the exercise of these faculties was the natural transition to grace, and that a good use of them was the medium of grace, or in their phraseology, merited it *of congruity* (de congruo). God, they said, was not bound to reward such actions, but it was congruous or fitting that He should. [456]

As Gibson further notes:

> The stock instance to which they made their appeal was the case of Cornelius (Acts X), whose 'prayers and alms came up for a memorial before God,' and drew down God's grace upon him.[457]

Works done before the grace of Christ and the inspiration of the Holy Spirit, are not pleasant to God ...neither do they make men meet to receive grace, ...yea, rather for that they are not done as God hath willed and commanded them to be done, we doubt not but they have the nature of sin.

The article rejects the scholastic argument just described. It holds that the works performed by those who have not been justified by faith do not merit grace. This is because they 'are not pleasant to God' but rather have the 'nature of sin' since 'they are not done as God hath willed and commanded them to be done.'

---

[455] The 'school men' or 'scholastics', who included figures such as St. Thomas Aquinas, Peter Lombard and Gabriel Biel, taught philosophy and theology in the universities of Europe during the Middle Ages. They are generally seen as having sought to synthesise the teaching of the Bible and the Fathers into a consistent theological system.

[456] Gibson. op.cit, p.419.

[457] Ibid, p. 419.

As was noted above in connection with Article X, the thinking underlying this position is set out in the homily 'Of good works annexed unto faith' in the *First Book of Homilies* which argues in its opening section that no works can be good in the sight of God unless they are the result of faith.

The opening paragraph of the homily states that without faith:

> ...can no good work be done accepted and pleasant unto God. For, *as a branch cannot bear fruit of itself*, saith our Saviour Christ *except it abide in the vine, so cannot ye, except ye abide in me. I am the vine, and ye be the branches; he that abideth in me and I in him, he bringeth forth much fruit. For without me, ye can do nothing* (John 15.4-5). And St. Paul proveth that Enoch had faith, *because he pleased God; For without faith,"* saith he *"it is not possible to please God* (Hebrews 11.6). And again to the Romans he saith, *Whatsoever work is done without faith, it is sin* (Romans 14.23).[458]

The homily then goes on to declare that without faith:

> ...all that is done of us is but dead before God, although the work seem ever so gay and glorious, before man. Even as the picture graven or painted, is but a dead representation of the thing itself and is without life, or any manner of moving, so be the works of all unfaithful persons before God. They do appear to be lively works, and indeed they be but dead, not availing to the everlasting life. They be but shadows and shows, of lively and good things and not good and lively things indeed. For true faith doth give life to the works; and out of such faith come good works that be very good works indeed; and without faith no work is good before God.[459]

In support of the argument that good works performed by someone without faith are not in fact good the homily explains that this is because 'good deeds be not measured by the facts themselves' but 'by the ends and intents for which they are done.' Because this is the case, it follows, says the homily, that:

---

[458] *The Homilies*, p.35
[459] Ibid.p.35.

If a heathen man clothe the naked, feed the hungry, and do other such like works; yet, because he doeth them not in faith, for the honour and love of God, they be but dead, vain and fruitless works to him.[460]

In support of its argument the homily cites St. Augustine and pseudonymous works attributed to St. Ambrose and St. John Chrysostom.

It quotes Augustine, *Enarratio in Psalm. 31.2*, as saying:

> We must set no good works before faith, nor think that before faith, a man may do any good work. For such works, although they seem unto men, to be praiseworthy, yet indeed they be but vain.[461]

It also quotes *De Vocatione Gentium* 1:7, attributed to Ambrose, as saying:

> He that by nature would withstand vice, either by natural will or reason, he doth in vain garnish the time of this life, and attaineth not the very true virtues: for without the worship of the true God, that which seemeth to be virtue is vice.[462]

Finally, it quotes a work attributed to Chrsysostom, *De Fide et Lege Naturae* 1, as saying:

> You shall find many, which have not the true faith, and be not of the flock of Christ, and yet as it appeareth, they flourish in good works of mercy; you shall find them full of pity, compassion, and given to justice; and yet for all, they have no fruit of their works, because the chief work lacketh. For when the Jews asked of Christ what they should do to work good works, he answered, *This is the work of God, to believe in him whom he sent,* so that he called faith *the work of God* (John 6.29). And as soon as a man hath faith, anon

---

[460] Ibid, p.36.
[461] Ibid p. 35
[462] Ibid, p.36.

he shall flourish in good works: for faith of itself is full of good works, and nothing is good, without faith.[463]

What the homily makes clear is that what the English Reformers thought they were doing when they rejected the idea that works performed prior to faith merit saving grace was to re-assert the teaching of the Bible and the Fathers over against the misleading ideas introduced by the 'school men.'

The conclusion that they came to on this basis often puzzles people today. How is it, they ask, that we can say that good works performed by non-Christians are not good, but sinful? The answer is that for the English Reformers no human works, whether performed Christians or non-Christians, can be good in themselves. As we have already seen when looking at Articles X-XII, the Reformers held that, because all human beings are sinners, all their works, whether done before or after justification, lack true goodness, both because of the imperfect nature of what is done and the imperfect motives that cause it to be done. In the words of the *Authorised Version's* translation of Isaiah 64:6 'all our righteousnesses are as filthy rags.' It is for this reason that the article says that works performed before justification 'have the nature of sin.'

As we have also seen, for the Reformers there is one exception to the tale of human sinfulness. In his life and his death Jesus Christ offered God that perfect obedience that all other humans ought to offer him but are unable to.

It is because they are united to Christ and their actions are therefore viewed by God in the light of his perfection that the deeds of Christians are good in God's sight. Justifying faith unites Christians with Christ and it is for this reason that the Reformers declare that it is faith that makes our works good.

The fact that the article declares that works done before justification do not deserve grace also causes people to worry about what this means for the members of other religions. Does it mean that they have no chance of salvation?

The problem with this argument is that it presumes that the only reason people can be saved is because their deeds merit salvation. However, the overall argument of the English Reformers as expressed in

---

[463] Ibid, pp.36-37.

the Articles is that no one, whether Christians or non-Christians, is saved on the basis of their own merit. Salvation is through the life, death and resurrection of Jesus Christ.

It follows that the belief that the good works of those belonging to other religions do not merit salvation does not mean that it is impossible for them to be saved. It merely means that if they are saved it will be through Christ and what he has done for them rather than because of anything that they have done (which is true for Christians as well).

In conclusion, the purpose of this article is to tackle a particular error that was common among the scholastic theologians of the Middle Ages. The article does not teach that good works do not matter, but it does teach us humility in that it reminds us that the grace that we have received through Christ was not something that we deserved because of the good deeds that we performed. If follows that, to quote Bishop Burnet again:

> ...this Article is not to be made use of to discourage men's endeavours, but only to increase their humility; to teach them not to think of themselves above measure, but soberly; to depend always on the mercy of God, and ever to fly to it.[464]

---

[464] Burnet, op.cit. p.183.

Article XIV

∞

Of Works of Supererogation

Voluntary works besides, over and above, God's commandments which they call Works of Supererogation, cannot be taught without arrogancy and impiety. For by them men do declare that they do not only render unto God as much as they are bound to do, but that they do more for His sake than of bounden duty is required: Whereas Christ saith plainly, When ye have done all that are commanded to do, say, We be unprofitable servants.

De Operibus Supererogationis

Opera quae Supererogationis appellant non possunt sine arrogantia et praedicari. Nam illis declarant homines non tantum se Deo reddere quae tenentur, sed plus in eius gratiam facere quam deberent: eum aperte Christus dicat: Cum feceritis omnia quaecunque praecepta sunt vobis, dicte, Servi inutiles sumus.

Like the previous article this article dates from 1553. There were two small changes made in the reign of Elizabeth I. In 1563 the word 'impiety' was substituted for 'iniquity' in the first sentence as a more accurate rendering of the Latin term impietate. In 1571 the title was changed from 'Works of Supererogation' (Opera Supererogationis) to the present title.

The article seems to have been newly composed for the 1553 Articles and its purpose is to reject the teaching about supererogation developed by the Western Church during the Middle Ages and maintained by Rome at the Reformation.

The concern about this teaching which underlies the article is expressed in the section on heresies in the *Reformatio Legum Ecclesiasticarum*. Part 8 of this section declares that:

....the arrogance of those who have introduced certain works of supererogation, by which they think that not only have they fully and completely satisfied the laws of God, but that they have also done something more than what the commands of God require, on which basis they can obtain merit for themselves and apply their merits to others, must be restrained and bridled by the authority of the laws.[465]

Voluntary works besides, over and above, God's commandments which they call Works of Supererogation...

The term supererogation comes from the Latin verb 'supererogare' which means to pay over and above what is required. Its earliest occurrence is in the Latin versions of the New Testament in which the words of the good Samaritan to the innkeeper in Luke 15:35 'whatever more you spend' are translated 'quodcunque supererogaveris.' This translation is found in a homily on Luke's gospel by St. Ambrose and in the Old Latin version of the Bible and it became universal in the Western Church as the translation found in the Vulgate.

In the course of time the substantive supererogatio was formed from the verb and in the later Middle Ages the term 'opera supererogationis' was coined to describe the idea that it was possible to do good works that went beyond what God commanded and in that sense could be said to pay God more than was required.

As Griffith Thomas explains in his commentary on this article, from the Patristic period onwards:

...there sprang up in the Church a profound regard for virginity, based, as it was supposed on the teaching of St. Paul in 1 Cor. 7:25; 'Concerning virgins I have no commandment of the Lord, but I give my advice.' From this arose a distinction between 'commandments' and 'judgements,' between that which is necessary and that which is advisable. Together with this the story of the rich young ruler was employed (Mark 10:22) for the purpose of obtaining a similar distinction between precepts of obedience and counsels of perfection, between the ordinary and

---

[465] Bray (ed), *Tudor Church Reform*, p.195.

the extraordinary, between the necessary and the voluntary (though desirable).[466]

Once this distinction had been made the further step was then taken of arguing that by following the counsels of perfection:

> ...a Christian could do more than was really demanded by God, and from this arose the thought of a special value or 'merit' attaching to particular aspects of life. Eventually the idea of works of supererogation developed, being applied to works done in compliance with counsels.[467]

The view that developed amongst the scholastic theologians of the thirteenth century, such as Alexander of Hales, Albertus Magnus and St. Thomas Aquinas, was that outlined in the *Reformatio Legum Ecclesiasticarum*, that by following the counsels of perfection people 'can obtain merit for themselves and apply their merits to others.' The argument that was put forward was that it would be unjust of God not to reward those saints who have not only obeyed his commandments, but gone beyond them. The saints therefore have a spiritual reward or 'merit' from God and as they do not need this reward or 'merit' for themselves they can give it to others in the Church who have not managed to obey God's laws.

As the sixteenth century Roman Catholic English version of the New Testament, the *Douai-Reims New Testament*, puts it:

> Holy saints, may, in measure of other men's necessities and deservings, as well allot unto them the supererogation of their spiritual works, as those that abound in worldly goods may give alms of their superfluities to them that are in necessity. [468]

It came to be held that the merits of the saints, together with the infinite merits of Christ formed a 'treasury of merit' which the Pope, as the one holding the keys of the kingdom of heaven, could use on behalf of the Church to release people from the temporal penalties due to sin, whether

---

[466] Griffith Thomas, op.cit. pp 216-217.
[467] Ibid p.217.
[468] Cited in Ibid p.217.

they be the performance of penance in this life or suffering the pains of purgatory in the life to come. The name that came to be given to this release from the temporal penalties of sin was an 'indulgence.'

...cannot be taught without arrogancy and impiety. For by them men do declare that they do not only render unto God as much as they are bound to do, but that they do more for His sake than of bounden duty is required:

In 1517 Pope Leo X declared that those who contributed to the re-building of St. Peter's Basilica in Rome would receive an indulgence consisting in release from the pains of purgatory either for themselves or for those who had already died. Martin Luther began the German Reformation by opposing this declaration, and at the heart of his arguments was a rejection of the idea of supererogation:

> The saints have no extra credits. Every saint is bound to love God to the utmost. There is no such thing as supererogation. If there were any superfluous credits, they could not be stored up for subsequent use. The Holy Spirit would have used them fully long ago. Christ indeed had merits, but until I am better informed I deny that they are indulgences. His merits are freely available without the keys of the pope.[469]

The Roman Catholic side continued to maintain a belief in the legitimacy of issuing indulgences and in the theology of supererogation underlying them. As a result, attitudes to the idea of supererogation became one of the major fault lines between Protestants and Roman Catholics at the Reformation.

Article XIV makes clear that the reformed Church of England was on the Protestant side of this fault line and if we ask why this was the case the clue lies in the opening words of the article which describe works of supererogation as 'voluntary works besides, over and above, God's commandments.' This description uses three prepositions to describe the character of these voluntary works ('besides', 'over' and 'above') for the sake of emphasis and what is being emphasised is that these works are deeply wrong.

---

[469] Quotation in R Bainton, *Here I Stand,* Tring: Lion, 1978, p.83.

As we saw in our discussion of Article XII, the English Reformers held that good works were only good if they were performed in obedience to God's laws. For them the problem with the human race since the time of Adam was that human beings had substituted works of their own devising in place of what God had commanded. If follows that for them the fact that works of supererogation were works done 'besides, over and above' God's law mean that they were not acts of piety but, rather, prime examples of 'arrogancy and impiety.'

This understanding of Article XIV is supported by the first commentator on the Articles, Thomas Rogers, whose comments on this article were first published in 1579.

He writes that:

Works of supererogation (which are voluntary works besides, over and above the commandments of God) are often condemned in the holy scripture, where we are commanded to walk, not after the laws of men, but according to the statutes of God, and to hear, not what man speaketh, but what Christ doth say: and he, teaching the duty of Christians, setteth before them, as their rule and direction, the law and word of God ; and more than that he doth neither urge nor require.(Joshua 1:7, Ezekiel 20:1, Mark 9:7, Matthew 5:19).

And against man's injunctions: 'They worship me in vain (saith he) who for doctrine teach the commandments of men' (Mark 7:7). 'Teach them to observe all things whatsoever I have commanded you' (Matthew 28:20). 'My sheep hear my voice, and know not the voice of strangers' (John 10:27 & 5).

Which doctrine, ordinances and works whatever (besides, over and above that which God hath revealed or imposed), is called of the apostle, sometimes ordinances of the world, voluntary religion, sometimes the doctrine of devils, and cursed (Colossians 2:20 & 23, 1 Timothy 4:1, Galatians 1:8).[470]

Continuing the same theme, Rogers goes on to add that:

---

[470] T Rogers, *The Catholic Doctrine of the Church of England*, Cambridge: CUP/Parker Society, 1854, p.129.

> Where the works of supererogation are taught, and in regard, the law of God there is broken, against the will of Christ, and men's traditions may be observed (Matthew 5:19, Mark 7:7). The holy scripture must be contemned, as not sufficient enough to bring men unto the knowledge of salvation, which St. Paul saith is able to instruct in righteousness, that the man of God may be absolute, made perfect unto all good works (2 Timothy 3:16-17). God who is only wise, is made unwise, in not prescribing so necessary works (1 Timothy 1:17).[471]

Rogers also argues that in addition to undermining the importance of God's commandments the teaching of supererogation also undermines justification by faith:

> Faith and other spiritual and most special virtues are brought unto oblivion. Perfection is imputed not unto faith in Jesus Christ, but unto works: and, what is most detestable, unto the works too not commanded, but forbidden of God, ordained by men. The law of God is thought to be thoroughly satisfied, and more duties performed than man needed to have done.[472]

Whereas Christ saith plainly, When ye have done all that are commanded to do, say, We be unprofitable servants.

In this last clause the article contrasts the 'arrogancy and impiety' underlying the idea of works of supererogation with the attitude that Christians ought to have to the obedience of God's commandments as expressed in Luke 17:10.

The article itself does not explain how it understands this verse, or the parable which it concludes, but the context indicates that what the writer of the article had in mind was an understanding of the parable in Luke 17:7-10 along the lines of the one put forward by George Caird in his commentary on Luke's gospel:

> The parable of the master and slave is a warning against the book-keeping mentality, which thinks that it can run up a credit

---

[471] Ibid, p.131.
[472] Ibid, p.131.

balance with God. The slave's labour belongs to his master, and a full day's work is no more than his duty. There are no works of supererogation. Nothing he can do constitutes a claim on his master's gratitude or puts his master in his debt. The demands of God are equally exacting; his servants can neither earn his approval nor put him under an obligation. 'Unworthy servants' does not mean useless servants; even the best service is no more than God is entitled to expect, since it gives him nothing more than belongs to him by right. The whole idea of merit is be abandoned in our approach to God.[473]

Note: The ecumenical significance of the treasury of merit.

The Roman Catholic Church continues to teach the existence of a treasury of merit. *The Catechism of the Catholic Church* teaches that in this treasury there are the infinite merits of Christ, the prayers and good works of the Blessed Virgin Mary and:

> ...the prayers and good works of all the saints, all those who have followed in the footsteps of Christ the Lord and by his grace have made their lives holy and carried out the mission the Father entrusted to them. In this way they have attained their own salvation and at the same time co-operated in saving their brothers in the unity of the Mystical Body.[474]

The *Catechism* also teaches that indulgences can be obtained on the basis of the treasury of merit:

> An indulgence is obtained through the Church who, by virtue of the power of binding and loosing granted her by Christ Jesus, intervenes in favour of faithful Christians and opens up for them the treasury of the merits of Christ and the saints to obtain from the Father of mercies the remission of the temporal punishments due for their sins.[475]

---

[473] G B Caird, *Saint Luke*, Harmondsworth: Penguin, 1963, p.194.
[474] *The Catechism of the Catholic Church,* para 1477, London: Geoffrey Chapman, 1994, p.332.
[475] Ibis, para 1478, p.333.

This continuing teaching by the Roman Catholic Church constitutes an important difference from the teaching of churches like the Church of England that have been shaped by the Reformation. It is therefore a topic that needs to be the subject of ecumenical dialogue as part of the continuing attempt to overcome the divisions stemming from the Reformation.

Article XV

∞

Of Christ alone without Sin

Christ in the truth of our nature was made like unto us in all things, sin only except, from which He was clearly void, both in His flesh and in His spirit. He came to be the lamb without spot, who by sacrifice of Himself once made, should take away the sins of the world: and sin, as S. John saith, was not in Him. But all we the rest, although baptized and born again in Christ, yet offend in many things: and if we say we have no sin, we deceive ourselves, and the truth is not in us.

Nemo praeter Christum est sine peccato

Christus in nostrae naturae veritate per omnia similis factus est nobis, excepto peccato, a quo prorsus est immunis, tum in carne tum in spiritu. Venit ut agnus absque macula esset, qui mundi peccata per immolationem sui semel factam tolleret: et peccatum, ut inquit Iohannes, in eo non erat. Sed nos reliqui, etiam baptizati et in Christo regenerati, in multis tamen offendimus omnes: et, si dixerimus quia peccatum non habemus, nos ipsos seducimus, et veritas in nobis non est.

Like Article XIV, this article dates from 1553 and it has undergone no alteration since that time. Its language cannot be traced back to any earlier sources.

Three suggestions have been made about the purpose of this article.

One suggestion is that the article was designed to counter belief in the immaculate conception of the Blessed Virgin Mary.

Thus Hardwick, referring to the article as the fourteenth article of the articles of 1553, declares:

The fourteenth article, affirming that our blessed Lord alone was born without sin, impugns the Romish doctrine with regard to the immaculate conception of the blessed Virgin.[476]

As we shall see, it is likely that Article XV does include Mary within its scope. However, there are two reasons why it is unlikely that the article is intended to address belief in the Immaculate Conception.

1. There is no mention of Mary in the article which would be unlikely if the article was concerned with belief in her preservation from sin. In the words of Gibson:

> As a rule the Articles are perfectly direct and plain spoken in their condemnation of erroneous views, and if their compilers had had this doctrine in view it is unlikely that they would have contented themselves with so *indirect* a condemnation of it. [477]

2. Most of the article is unnecessary if the end in view was simply to reject belief in the Immaculate Conception. To quote Gibson again:

> Why was it needful to say so much about Christ's perfect humanity and atonement in order to condemn the doctrine of the Immaculate Conception?[478]

A second suggestion is that Article XV continues the attack on the doctrine of supererogation begun in Article XIV. This is the view taken, for example, by Burnet who states:

> This Article relates to the former, and is put here as another foundation against all the works of supererogation: for that doctrine, with the consequences of it, having given the first occasion to the Reformation, it was thought necessary to overthrow it entirely: and because the perfection of the saints

---

[476] Hardwick, op.cit, p.100.
[477] Gibson, op.cit, p.440.
[478] Ibid, p.440.

must be supposed, before their supererogating can be thought on, that was therefore here opposed. [479]

There can be no doubt that Article XV does act as a counter to a belief in works of supererogation in that its emphasis on the sinfulness of all Christians rules out the idea that the saints are in a position to produce a surplus of merit which the Church can then draw on for the benefit of other believers. However, it is unlikely that Burnet is correct in his claim that Article XV was intended as a supplement to what is said in Article XIV.

1. On Burnet's own logic, if Article XV was intended to deny the possibility of the perfection of the saints in order to overthrow the presupposition of the idea of supererogation then what is said in this article ought to have preceded rather than followed what is said in Article XIV.

2. As with the suggestion that the article is aimed at belief in the Immaculate Conception, the suggestion that it is aimed at belief in works of supererogation is rendered unlikely by the fact that the article nowhere mentions this belief.

3. As we have seen, the objection to belief in supererogation set out in Article XIV focuses on the idea that people can earn merit by performing voluntary works 'besides over and above, God's commandments.' Article XV, by contrast, focuses on a new topic, the continuing presence of sin in the life of believers. This means that rather than being linked to the article that precedes it, Article XV forms a pair with the article that follows it, which also deals with this topic although from a different angle.

If we see Article XV as forming a pair with Article XVI this points us to the third and most likely explanation of the purpose of Article XV, namely that it was designed to counter the errors of some of the radical Protestant groups.

In a letter to Heinrich Bullinger written shortly before the preparation of the Forty Two Articles, the Bishop of Gloucester, John Hooper notes the trouble he is being given by the Anabaptists who, amongst other errors:

---

[479] Burnet, op.cit, p.191.

...contend that a man who is reconciled with God is without sin and free from all stain of concupiscence, and that nothing of the old Adam remains in his nature; and a man, they say, who is thus regenerate cannot sin. They add all hope of pardon is taken away from those who, after receiving the Holy Ghost, fall into sin.[480]

Section 9 of the list of heresies in the *Reformatio Legum Ecclesiasticarum,* which was produced a couple of years later than Bishop Hooper's letter was written, links together the same two errors:

Those who believe that the justified can no longer fall into sin even though they are still living in this world, or that if they happen to do something which is forbidden by the laws of God, God will not count that as sin, also have a perverse concept of justification. Opposed to this opinion, but equally ungodly, are those who believe that any sin which may be committed by our will after we have received baptism is mortal, and who say that all such sin has been done against the Holy Spirit and cannot be forgiven.[481]

In this quotation the words 'also have a perverse concept of justification' refers back to the previous section dealing with those who argue for works of supererogation. The use of the word 'also' is a further indication that this is a different error from a belief in works of supererogation and propagated by a different group of people.

What the evidence from Bishop Hooper's letter and the *Reformatio Legum Ecclesiasticarum* points us to is the existence of two errors held by those on the radical wing of the Reformation. On the one hand there was the belief that the regenerate can no longer sin and on the other hand there was the belief that there is no forgiveness for sin committed after baptism. Articles XV and XVI are designed to address each of these errors in turn, with Article XV addressing the first error and Article XVI addressing the second.

---

[480] John Hooper to Heinrich Bullinger, June 25 1549, in H Robinson (ed), *Original Letters relative to the English Reformation,* vol 1, Cambridge: CUP/Parker Society, 1846, p.65.
[481] Bray, *Tudor Church Reform,* p.195.

Christ in the truth of our nature was made like unto us in all things, sin only except, from which He was clearly void, both in His flesh and in His spirit.

Article XV begins by affirming the likeness between Christ and all other human beings. In line with the affirmation in Article II that Christ took 'Man's nature in the womb of the blessed virgin, of her substance: so that two whole and perfect Natures, that is to say the Godhead and Manhood, were joined together in one person,' Article XV affirms that Christ 'was made like us in all things'. At this point the wording of the article echoes the statement in Hebrews 2:17 that Christ was 'made like his brethren in every respect'. The words 'in the truth of our nature' mean 'in respect of everything that makes us truly human.'

Having said that Christ was made like us in every respect, the article then notes the one exception, 'sin only except'. Here there seems to be another reference to Hebrews, this time to Hebrews 4:15 which talks about Jesus as someone 'who in every respect has been tempted as we are, yet without sin.' Other New Testament passages such as John 8:46, Acts 3:14, 2 Corinthians 5:21 and 1 Peter 2:22 which also affirm that Christ was without sin may be in the background here as well. The statement that Christ was void of sin in both 'His flesh and His spirit' means that he was without sin in every part of his human nature, free from sin arising from both the physical and the psychological aspects of his humanity. The accounts of the temptation in the wilderness in Matthew 4:1-11 and Luke 4:1-13 illustrate this point in that they tell us that Christ was not tempted to sin either by his physical hunger or by the devil's attack on his mind.

He came to be the lamb without spot, Who by sacrifice of Himself once made, should take away the sins of the world: and sin, as S. John saith, was not in Him.

This next section of the article is made up of references to a number of New Testament passages. 'He came to be the lamb without spot' is a reference to Hebrews 9:14 which talks about 'Christ who through the eternal Spirit offered himself without spot to God' and 1 Peter 1:19 which declares that Christians are redeemed 'with the precious blood of Christ, like that of a lamb without blemish or spot.' 'Who, by sacrifice of Himself once made, should take away the sins of the world' refers to John 1:29

'behold the lamb of God who takes away the sins of the world' and Hebrews 7:27, 9:12 and 10:10 which talk about the sacrifice of Christ made 'once for all.' 'And sin,' as S. John saith, 'was not in him' gives a direct quotation from 1 John 3:5.

The purpose of this section of the article is reinforce the idea that Christ was without sin by making the point that this is directly taught in 1 John and that the purpose of his coming into the world was to be a perfect sacrifice for sin, something that would only be possible if he was free from any taint of sinfulness. As has already been noted, this connects up with the Reformers understanding of justification. It is because Christ was sinless and therefore righteous before God that we are able to be righteous before God in him

But all we the rest, although baptized and born again in Christ, yet offend in many things: and if we say we have no sin, we deceive ourselves, and the truth is not in us.

Having affirmed the sinlessness of Christ the article goes on in its final section to note that sinlessness is true only of Christ. It refers to two further New Testament passages, James 3:2 'we all offend in many things' and 1 John 1:8 'if we say we have no sin, we deceive ourselves, and the truth is not in us' to support this claim and declares that the teaching of these two passages applies to all Christians even though they have been baptised and therefore born again in Christ.

The reference to the existence of post-baptismal sin picks up what has already been said in Article IX and points forward to what will be said in Article XVI and the claim that through baptism we have been born again once again points back to the link between regeneration and baptism in Article IX and forward to the declaration in article XXVII that baptism is 'a sign of regeneration and new birth.'

As Gerald Bray explains in his commentary on this article, its overall teaching is that it was:

> ...because Jesus had no sin in him that he could and did take away our sin (1 John 3:5). But what exactly does 'taking away our sin' mean? Can we say that we have been cleansed from sin in such a way as to become perfect? Here the answer must be no, and the article quotes 1 John 1:8 to reinforce this point. Our sins are taken away, not in the sense that we become sinless as Jesus was, but in

the sense that they no longer stand as a barrier blocking our access to God. We go on being sinners and therefore we go on sinning. Even if we can learn not to commit particular sins deliberately, every action of ours has something sinful about it because of our inherent sinfulness.[482]

Note – Article XV and the Virgin Mary

As we have noted, Article XV was not intended to counter the doctrine of the Immaculate Conception. Does this means, however, that it has nothing to say on the issue of whether Mary was preserved from sin?

The ARCIC II report *Mary: Grace and Hope in Christ* states that:

> Articles IX and XV affirmed the universality of human sinfulness. They neither affirmed nor denied the possibility of Mary having been preserved by grace from participation in this general human condition.[483]

It is true that neither Article IX nor article XV specifically mention that Mary was a sinner. However, in view of the fact that the articles affirm the sinfulness of all human beings without exception apart from Christ it would seem likely that if those who wrote them had wished to say that Mary was exempted from sin by a special act of divine grace they would have made this clear.

Furthermore, Thomas Rogers, in the earliest commentary on Article XV, is clear that among the 'enemies and adversaries' to the truth upheld in the article is the teaching that 'the blessed virgin was pure from all sin original and actual.'[484]

It is true that English Reformers talk about Mary and her status as a virgin with veneration and respect. Thus the homily 'Of Repentance' in the *Second Book of Homilies* talks about Jesus being born of Mary's 'undefiled substance, '[485] the homily 'Against Disobedience and Wilful Rebellion' in the same book refers to her as a 'most noble and virtuous

---

[482] G Bray, *The Faith We Confess*, London: Latimer Trust, 2009, 85.

[483] *Mary: Grace and Hope in Christ*, London and Harrisburg: Morehouse Publishing, 2005, p.42.

[484] Rogers, op.cit, p.134. Other early commentators such as Burnet and Beveridge also take the article to mean that Mary was a sinner.

[485] *The Homilies*, p.384.

lady'[486] and the collect for Christmas Day in the *Book of Common Prayer* talks about her as a 'pure Virgin.' However, none of this amounts to the specific claim that she was preserved from all sin original and actual. That is a claim that the English Reformers never make.

---

[486] Ibid, p. p.413.

Article XVI

∞

Of Sin after Baptism

Not every deadly sin willingly committed after Baptism is sin against the Holy Ghost, and unpardonable. Wherefore the grant of repentance is not to be denied to such as fall into sin after Baptism. After we have received the Holy Ghost, we may depart from grace given and fall into sin, and by the grace of God we may arise again and amend our lives. And therefore they are to be condemned, which say they can no more sin as long as they live here, or deny the place of forgiveness to such as truly repent.

De Peccato post Baptismum

Non omne peccatum mortale post Baptismum voluntarie perpetratum, est peccatum in Spiritum Sanctum, et irremissibile. Proinde lapsis a Baptismo in peccata locus penitentiae non est negandus. Post acceptum Spiritum Sanctum possumus a gratia data recedere atque peccare, denuoque per gratiam Dei resurgere ac resipiscere. Ideoque illi damnandi sunt qui se quamdiu hic vivant, amplius non posse peccare affirmant, aut vere resipiscentibus veniae locum denegant.

Like its two predecessors, this article also dates back to the *Forty Two Articles* of 1553. Its original title was 'Of Sin against the Holy Ghost' (De Peccato in Spiritum Sanctum). In order to reflect the contents of the article more accurately this was altered in 1563 to 'Of sin after Baptism.' The Latin title in 1563 was De Lapsis post Baptismum and this was altered to the current Latiin title De Peccato post Baptismum in 1571 in order to make it correspond more closely to the English title.

In the second sentence of the article locus penitentiae was translated as 'place for penitents' in 1553, 'place for penitence' in 1563 and finally in 1571 by the present words 'grant of repentance.' In the final sentence the words 'place for pentitents'/locus penitentiae were replaced by the present words place of forgiveness/ veniae locum in 1571.

As we saw when looking at Article XV, this article was intended to be the second of two articles concerning with two types of erroneous teaching about post baptismal sin that were being put forward by radical Protestant groups. The first type of teaching, which is tackled in Article XV, held that those who were baptised were free from the possibility of sinning. The second type of teaching, which is tackled in this article, held that all voluntary sin committed after baptism was unforgiveable.

The early theologian Origen held that when those who had received the Holy Spirit in baptism turned again to sin this was the sin against the Holy Spirit referred to by Jesus in Matthew 12:31-37, Mark 3:28-30 and Luke 12:10 and as such unpardonable. A similar view was taken from the third century onwards by a rigorist group in the Western Church known as the Novatians. The view that eventually came to be accepted in both the Eastern and Western churches, however, was that forgiveness was available for even serious sins committed after baptism.

At the Reformation the more rigorous approach taken by Origen and the Novatians was revived, but the English Reformers stuck to the accepted position and it is this position that is defended in Article XVI.

Not every deadly sin willingly committed after Baptism is sin against the Holy Ghost, and unpardonable. Wherefore the grant of repentance is not to be denied to such as fall into sin after Baptism.

The first sentence of the article sets out the position which the article is intended to counter. As the sentence makes clear what was being proposed by the radical Protestants was that deadly sin, voluntarily committed after baptism, constituted the sin against the Holy Spirit.

The article does not define what is meant by 'deadly sin' but when the phrase is used here and in the Litany – 'from fornication, and all other deadly sin; and from all the deceits of the world, the flesh, and the devil, Good Lord, deliver us' – it appears to mean serious and deliberate sin as opposed to sin committed through ignorance and weakness. As Burnet puts it in his commentary on this article:

> ...we are far from the conceit of the Stoics, who made all sins alike. We acknowledge that some sins of ignorance and infirmity may consist with a state of grace; which is either quite destroyed, or at

least much eclipsed and clouded by other sins, that are more heinous in their nature, and more deliberately gone about. It is in this sense that the word *deadly sin* is to be understood in the Article: for though in the strictness of justice every sin is *deadly*, yet in the dispensation of the Gospel, those sins are only *deadly*, that do deeply wound the conscience and that drive away grace.[487]

The reason that those who drew up the Articles did not see every deadly sin committed after baptism as unforgiveable is not explained in Article XVI itself. However, it is explained in the homily on 'Repentance and true reconciliation unto God' in the *Second Book of Homilies*.

This homily declares that:

> ....we do not without a just cause, detest and abhor the damnable opinion of them, which do most wickedly go about, to persuade the simple and ignorant people, that if we chance, after we be once come to God and grafted in his Son Jesus Christ, to fall into some horrible sin, repentance shall be unprofitable unto us - there is no more hope of reconciliation, or to be received again into the favour and mercy of God.[488]

It goes on to explain that those who advocate this opinion appeal to Hebrews 6:4-8 and 2 Peter 2:20-22 in support of their position, but that they fail to consider:

> ....that in those places the holy apostles do not speak of the daily falls that we, as long as we carry about this body of sin, are subject unto, but of the final falling away from Christ and his Gospel which is a sin against the Holy Ghost that shall never be forgiven; because that they that do utterly forsake the known truth, do hate Christ and his word, they do crucify and mock him (but to their utter destruction), and therefore fall into desperation, and cannot repent (Matthew 12.31, Mark 3.29).And that this is the true meaning of the Holy Spirit of God it appeareth

---

[487] Burnet, op cit, pp.194-5.
[488] *The Homilies*, p.386.

by many other places of the Scriptures, which promiseth unto all true repentant sinners, and to them that with their whole heart do turn unto the Lord their God, free pardon and remission of their sins.[489]

As examples of these many other places of the scriptures it cites:

> Jeremiah 4:1 'If thou return, return unto me, saith the Lord; and, if thou put away thine abominations out of my sight, thou shalt not be moved;'

> Isaiah 55:7 'Let the wicked forsake his own ways, and unrighteous his own imaginations, and turn again unto the Lord, and he will have mercy upon him, and to our God, for he is ready to forgive;'

> and Hosea 6:1 'Come and let us turn again, unto the Lord: for he hath smitten us, and he will heal us; he hath wounded us, and he will bind us up again.'[490]

The conclusion which the homily draws from these passages is that

> ...unto all them that will return unfeignedly unto the Lord their God, the favour and mercy of God, unto forgiveness of sins, is liberally offered. Whereby it followeth necessarily, that although we do - after we be once come to God and grafted in his Son Jesus Christ - fall into great sins (*for there is no righteous man upon the earth that sinneth not, and if we say we have no sin, we deceive ourselves, and the truth is not in us* (Ecclesiastes 7:20, 1John 1:8)), yet if we rise again by repentance, and with a full purpose of amendment of life, do flee unto the mercy of God, taking sure hold thereupon, through faith in his Son Jesu Christ, there is an assured and infallible hope of pardon and remission of the same, and that we shall be received again into the favour of our heavenly Father.
> [491]

---

[489] Ibid, p.386. In the *Forty Two Articles* there was a separate article, article XVI,
[490] Ibid, p.387.
[491] Ibid, p.387.

Because there is this assured hope for the forgiveness of even great sins committed after baptism, Article XVI goes on to say that 'the grant of repentance is not to be denied to such as fall into sin after Baptism.' As Gibson points out, those who produced the final version of the article in 1571 introduced a distinction between the 'grant of repentance' referred to here and the 'place of forgiveness' referred to at the end of the article. It is unlikely that that this revision was either accidental or purely stylistic. The most probable explanation is that offered by Gibson who argues that the whereas the 'place of forgiveness' at the end of the article refers to the forgiveness offered directly by God, the 'grant of repentance' refers to the reconciliation of sinners to the Church on the basis of repentance, thus allowing them to receive Holy Communion.[492]

This would mean that the Church of England rejected the argument put forward by some in the patristic period that while God might be willing to forgive those who had committed deadly sin on the last day the Church had no power to offer them pardon and reconciliation in this life.[493] It instead took the position that had come to be accepted by the Church as whole in the patristic period, namely, that since God himself granted forgiveness for deadly sins committed after baptism the Church should reflect this by granting repentant sinners pardon and reconciliation. In the *Thirty Nine Articles* this position is also reflected in what is said in Article XXXIII about how those who have been excommunicated should be avoided by the faithful until they are 'openly reconciled by penance.'

After we have received the Holy Ghost, we may depart from grace given and fall into sin, and by the grace of God we may arise again and amend our lives.

This section of Article XVI is intended to underline the point made in the opening sentence of the article by making the point that although we may fall into sin after we have received the Holy Spirit at our baptism we should not despair if this happens because God's grace is available to help us to start again and change our lives for the better.

---

[492] Gibson op.cit. pp.452-445.
[493] Gibson, p.454, refers to Tertullian, *On Modesty*, Ch XIX, as an example of this position.

This teaching reflects what is said in more detail in the homily 'How Dangerous a Thing it is to Fall from God' in the *First Book of Homilies.* This homily describes the various ways in which people can fall away from God and how long suffering God is to those who do fall way. However, it also warns that if people persist in a state of sin without repentance it is possible for them to reach a stage at which God turns his face from them with the result that:

> ...they shall be no longer governed by his Holy Spirit, they shall be put from the grace and benefits that they had and ever might have enjoyed through Christ, they shall be deprived of the heavenly light, and life which they had in Christ, whiles they abode in him. They shall be (as they were once) as men without God in this world, or rather in worse taking.

Such people, says the homily 'shall be given into the power of the devil' who 'beareth the rule in all them that be cast away from God' and the evidence that people are in this state is that they believe either that God cannot or will not 'take them again to his favour and mercy' or that even if they continue in their 'sinful and detestable living' God will be merciful to them in the end.

The homily declares that there is hope even for people who are in this state if they turn again to God, but it also argues that there is no guarantee that this will happen and issues a general warning against presuming on God's mercy:

> Let us beware therefore, of such naughty boldness to sin. For God, which hath promised his mercy, to them that be truly repentant, although it be at the latter end, hath not promised to the presumptuous sinner, either that he shall have long life, or that h shall have true repentance, at his last end. But for that purpose he hath made every man's death uncertain, that he should not put his hope in the end, and in the mean season, to God's high displeasure, live ungodly.

The homily's conclusion is that Christians should follow the teaching of Ecclesiasticus and make no delay in turning back to God:

Let us *not put off from day to day, for suddenly shall his wrath come and in time of vengeance he will destroy the wicked* (Ecclesiasticus 5:7). Let us therefore turn betimes and when we turn let us pray to God as Osee teacheth, saying *Forgive all our sins, receive us graciously* (Hosea 14.2). And if we turn to him, with an humble and a very penitent heart, he will receive us to his favour and grace for his holy name's sake, for his promise's sake, for his truth's and mercy's sake, promised to all faithful believers in Jesus Christ his only natural Son.

The teaching in the homily and the article is addressed to all baptised Christians. All alike may fall from grace and all alike may be restored if they make no delay, but turn again to God in repentance while there is still time. This teaching, as expressed in Article XVI became a source of difficulty to those in the Church of England who held to a Calvinist theology. This is because it was seen as contrary to the Calvinist belief in 'indefectible grace,' the belief that those elected by God can never fall away completely and finally from grace, but are assured of their final salvation

Repeated attempts were made by those of a Calvinist persuasion to correct the Article on this point. In 1572, the authors of a Puritan manifesto called the second *Admonition to Parliament* declared that 'the book of the articles of Christian religion speaketh very dangerously of falling from grace, which is to be reformed because it savoureth too much of error.'[494] As was explained in the Introduction, in 1595, a set of additional doctrinal articles known as the *Lambeth Articles* was produced, although never authorised, and the fifth of these articles states that 'a true, lively and justifying faith, and the sanctifying Spirit of God, is not lost nor does it pass away either finally or totally in the elect.'[495] In 1604, at the conference held at Hampton Court to consider the Puritan arguments for the further reformation of the English Church, the suggestion was made by the Puritans the statement that those who have received the Spirit 'may depart from grace given' should be qualified by the addition of the words 'yet neither totally nor finally.'[496]

---

[494] Gibson, op.cit, p.458.
[495] Text in V C Miller, *The Lambeth Articles*, Oxford: Latimer House, 1994, p.49.
[496] Gibson, op.cit. p.458.

None of these attempts to amend or supplement Article XVI was successful. The teaching of the Church of England remained (and remains) the teaching expressed in the article and the homily that it is possible for baptised believers to fall away from grace with no automatic guarantee that they will be restored. This teaching is also reflected, for instance, in the *Book of Common Prayer* in the words of the Collect for the second Sunday in Advent 'that by patience and comfort of thy Holy Word, we may embrace and ever hold fast the blessed hope of everlasting life' and in the words of the Burial Service 'O holy and merciful Saviour, thou most worthy Judge eternal, suffer us not, at our last hour, for any pains of death, to fall from thee.' Both of these prayers reflect the possibility of falling from God and so not attaining everlasting life and ask for God's help to avoid this happening. .

The Church of England thus offers believers no absolute guarantee against permanently falling away from God. On the other hand, as we shall see when we look at Article XVII, it does not teach a doctrine of double predestination either. This means that, unlike Calvinist theology, the doctrine of the Church of England does not teach that anyone is predestined to fall away from God after a period of temporary faith. It also means that according to the Church of England there is always the possibility of anyone who has fallen away being restored by the grace of God providing they are willing to repent and seek God's mercy and forgiveness.

And therefore they are to be condemned, which say they can no more sin as long as they live here, or deny the place of forgiveness to such as truly repent.

This final section of the article sums up the teaching of both Articles XV and XVI by condemning on the one hand those who teach that believers can be free from sin and on the other those who teach that that those who do sin cannot be forgiven. According to these articles there is no hope of complete freedom from sin in this life, but the mercy of God means that there is always hope of forgiveness for those who truly repent.

Note: the nature of the sin against the Holy Spirit

In 1553 *The Forty Two Articles* contained an article, Article XVI, which was entitled 'Blasphemy against the Holy Ghost.' This article declared that:

> Blasphemy against the Holy Ghost is, when a man of malice and stubbornness of mind, doth rail upon the truth of God's word manifestly perceived, and being enemy thereunto persecuteth the same. And because such be guilty of God's curse, they entangle themselves with a most grievous and heinous crime, whereupon this kind of sin is called and affirmed of the Lord unpardonable. [497]

In the revision of the articles in 1563 this article was omitted. Gibson suggests that this was probably due to 'an unwillingness to define the nature of this sin, and a desire not to bind the conscience of the clergy to a particular interpretation of a difficult set of passages.'[498] Given that the homily 'On Repentance and true reconciliation unto God,' which we have looked at in connection with Article XVI of the *Thirty Nine Articles* and which contained an alternative definition of blasphemy against the Holy Spirit, had been authorised for reading in every parish church the previous year, the argument that Archbishop Parker and his fellow bishops were unwilling to put forward an authorised definition of the nature of this sin is untenable.

A more convincing explanation is that they believed that the definition of blasphemy against the Holy Spirit offered in the homily 'On repentance' was preferable to the definition offered in Article XVI of the *Forty Two Articles*. They therefore omitted the article concerned in the belief that what was said about 'sin against the Holy Ghost' in Article XVI of the *Thirty Nine Articles* would be understood in the light of the improved teaching about this subject contained in the homily.

---

[497] Bray, Documents of the English Reformation, pp.293-294.
[498] Gibson, op.cit, p.348.

Article XVII

∞

Of Predestination and Election

Predestination to life is the everlasting purpose of God, whereby, before the foundations of the world were laid, He hath constantly decreed by His counsel secret to us, to deliver from curse and damnation those whom He hath chosen in Christ out of mankind, and to bring them by Christ to everlasting salvation as vessels made to honour. Wherefore they which be endued with so excellent a benefit of God be called according to God's purpose by His Spirit working in due season; they through grace obey the calling; they be justified freely; they be made sons of God by adoption; they be made like the image of His only-begotten Son Jesus Christ; they walk religiously in good works; and at length by God's mercy they attain to everlasting felicity.

As the godly consideration of Predestination and our Election in Christ is full of sweet, pleasant, and unspeakable comfort to godly persons and such as feeling in themselves the working of the Spirit of Christ, mortifying the works of the flesh and their earthly members and drawing up their mind to high and heavenly things, as well because it doth greatly establish and confirm their faith of eternal salvation to be enjoyed through Christ, as because it doth fervently kindle their love towards God: so for curious and carnal persons, lacking the Spirit of Christ, to have continually before their eyes the sentence of God's Predestination is a most dangerous downfall, whereby the devil doth thrust them either into desperation or into wretchlessness of most unclean living no less perilous than desperation.

Furthermore, we must receive God's promises in such wise as they be generally set forth in Holy Scripture; and in our doings that will of God is to be followed which we have expressly declared unto us in the word of God.

De Praedestinatione

Praedestinatio ad vitam est aeternum Dei propositum, quo, ante iacta mundi fundamenta, suo consilio, nobis quidem occulto, constanter decrevit eos, quos in Christo elegit ex hominum genere, a maledicto et exitio liberare, atque ut vasa in honorem efficta per Christum ad aeternam salutem adducere. Unde qui tam praeclaro Dei beneficio sunt donati, illi Spiritu eius opportuno tempore operante, secundum propositum eius vocantur; iustificatur gratis; adoptantur in filios Dei; unigeniti eius Iesu Christi imagini efficiuntur conformes; in bonis operibus sancti ambulant; et demum ex Dei misericordia pertingunt ad sempiternam felicitatem.

Quemadmodum Praedestinationis et Electionis nostrae in Christo pia consideratio dulcis, suavis, et ineffabilis consolationis plena est vere piis et his qui sentiunt in se vim Spiritus Christi, facta carnis et membra quae adhuc sunt super terram mortificantem, animumque ad coelestia et superna rapientem, tum quia fidem nostram de aeterna salute consequenda per Christum plurimum stabilit atque confirmat, tum quia amorem nostrum in Deum vehementer accendit: ita hominibus, curiosis carnalibus et Spiritu Christi destitutis, oboculos perpetuo versari Praedestinationis Dei sententiam perniciosissimum est praecipitium, unde illos diabolus protrudit vel in desperationem vel in aeque pernitiosam impurissimae vitae securitatem.

Deinde promissiones divinas sic amplecti oportet, ut nobis in sacris literis generaliter propositae sunt; et Dei voluntas in nostris actionibus ea sequenda est quam in verbo Dei habemus deserte revelatam.

This Article, which is the longest of the Articles, was one of the original *Forty Two Articles* of 1553. It was revised in two ways in 1563. First, the words 'in Christ' were added to the definition of predestination in the opening clause. Secondly, the original opening to the final paragraph:

'Furthermore, although the decrees of predestination are unknown unto us, yet we must receive...' was shortened to the one we have today.

Although the original Article appears to have been Cranmer's own composition rather than being based on existing material, it has parallels with the work of Peter Martyr, Martin Luther and Philip Melancthon.

The Article has three purposes. The first is to explain what predestination is, the second is to warn of the potential dangers of the doctrine of predestination and the third is to insist that God's will needs to be sought by looking at what is said openly in the biblical revelation rather than by trying to determine God's hidden purposes.

Predestination to life is the everlasting purpose of God, whereby, before the foundations of the world were laid, He hath constantly decreed by His counsel secret to us, to deliver from curse and damnation those whom He hath chosen in Christ out of mankind, and to bring them by Christ to everlasting salvation as vessels made to honour. Wherefore they which be endued with so excellent a benefit of God be called according to God's purpose by His Spirit working in due season; they through grace obey the calling; they be justified freely; they be made sons of God by adoption; they be made like the image of His only-begotten Son Jesus Christ; they walk religiously in good works; and at length by God's mercy they attain to everlasting felicity.

This opening paragraph of the Article is intended to define what predestination is. It is similar to the definition of predestination given by the Italian Reformer Peter Martyr Vermigli in his commentary on the Epistle to the Romans, which seems to have been written about the same time as Cranmer's original Article while Vermigli was Regius Professor of Divinity at Oxford. Vermigli states:

> Predestination is the most wise purpose of God, whereby from all eternity, He has constantly decreed to call those he hath loved in Christ to the adoption of sons, to justification by faith, and at length to glory through good works, that they may be conformed

to the image of the Son of God, and that there may be declared in them the glory and mercy of the Creator.[499]

In the absence of any common source on which they are both drawing, the similarity between the two definitions of predestination suggest that Cranmer's approach may have been influenced by that of Vermigli. Diarmaid MacCulloch also suggests that Cranmer's thinking about this issue was influenced by the anti-Pelagian treatises of St. Augustine of Hippo and by the work of Augustine's follower, the fifth century theologian St. Prosper of Aquitaine.[500]

The most important influences on this paragraph, however, seem to have been four passages from St. Paul's letters to the Romans and Ephesians.

In canonical order the first passage is Rom 8:28-30 in which the Apostle declares:

> We know that in everything God works for good with those who love him, who are called according to his purpose. For those whom he foreknew he also predestined to be conformed to the image of his Son, in order that he might be the first-born among many brethren. And those he predestined he also called; and those whom he called he also justified; and those whom he justified he also glorified.

The second passage is Rom 9:23-24 in which the Apostles describes God's desire:

> ...to make known the riches of his glory for the vessels of mercy, which he has prepared beforehand for glory, even us whom he has called, not only from the Jews but also from the Gentiles...

The third passage is Eph 1:4-5 in which the Apostle writes that:

> [God the Father] chose us in him [Christ] before the foundation of the world, that we should be holy and blameless before him. He

---

[499] P Martyr *Epistle to the Romans* p.411 cited in E Tyrell Green *The XXXIX Articles and the Age of the Reformation* London: Wells, Darton, Gardner & Co. 1896 p.385
[500] D MacCulloch *Thomas Cranmer* London & New Haven: Yale UP 1996 pp.211-212

destined us in love that we should be holy and blameless before him. He destined us in love to be his sons through Jesus Christ, according to the purpose of his will...

The fourth passage is Eph 1:11-12 in which the Apostles states that:

In him [Christ] according to the purpose of him who accomplishes al things according to the counsel of his will, we who first hoped in Christ have been destined and appointed to live for the praise of his glory.

If we compare these four passages with opening paragraph of Article XVII we find that the coincidence of both language and thought between them indicates that both Cranmer and the revisers of 1563 had these passages in mind when they drew up the Article. Whatever influence Vermigli, St. Augustine of Hippo and St. Prosper of Aquitaine may have had, the primary influence on the definition of predestination put forward by Article XVII is these four passages of Scripture and the primary intention of the definition is to reflect their teaching.

In the Article a reference to the work of the Holy Spirit is inserted into St. Paul's teaching in Rom 8:30 about the way in which justification follows on from calling. This insertion was probably felt to be justified because of what the New Testament teaches in passages such as Jn 3:1-13, Rom 8:1-17 and Eph 1:13-14 about the role of the Spirit in making God's eternal purpose effective in the lives of believers.

Predestination to life is the everlasting purpose of God

It is important to note the contrast between these opening words of the definition of predestination in Article XVII and the definitions of predestination offered in three subsequent sets of Articles from the within the Anglican tradition which offer a more explicitly Calvinist approach to this topic.

The *Lambeth Articles* of 1595, which were intended to be a supplement to the Thirty Nine Articles, were drawn up by William Whitaker, the Regius Professor of Divinity at Cambridge, and were approved by the Archbishops of Canterbury and York and a number of other bishops at a meeting held at Lambeth Palace on 20th November 1595. They never received official authority because Elizabeth I withheld her approval of them, but they indicate the prevailing view in the English church at the end of the sixteenth century. The first of the *Lambeth Articles* states that: 'From eternity God has predestined some men to life and condemned others to death.'[501]

The *Irish Articles* were drawn up at a Synod held in Dublin in 1615 and, as their name suggests, they were intended as Articles for the Protestant Church of Ireland. They were influenced by the *Lambeth Articles* and the opening paragraph of their Third Article, 'Of God's Eternal Decree, and Predestination,' declares that:

> God hath predestinated some unto life and reprobated some unto death; of both of which there is a certain number known only to God, which can neither be increased nor diminished.[502]

The *Westminster Confession* of 1647, which was drawn up by an Assembly consisting for the most part of Puritan clergy in Church of England orders, was an attempt to provide a replacement for the *Thirty Nine Articles* that could act as the statement of faith of a united church in England, Scotland and Ireland. Article 3 is entitled 'Of God's Eternal Decrees.' It states that:

> By the decree of God, for the manifestation of his glory, some men and angels are predestinated unto everlasting life and others foreordained to everlasting death.
>
> These angels and men, thus predestinated and foreordained, are particularly and unchangeably designed, and their number so certain and definite that it cannot be either increased or diminished. [503]

If we compare these later Articles to what is said in Article XVII the difference is that they follow the teaching of John Calvin in *Institutes* III.XXI.5 in teaching that there is a double predestination to both eternal life and eternal damnation whereas Article XVII teaches only predestination to life.

---

[501] *The Lambeth Articles* Article I text in G Bray (ed) *Documents of the English Reformation* Cambridge: James Clarke 1994 p.399
[502] *The Irish Articles* Article 3 text in Ibid p.439
[503] *The Westminster Confession* Article 3 in Ibid p.490

In the words of W H Griffith Thomas: 'The Article strictly and significantly limits the reference to the predestination of the believer to life, and there is no reference to anything else.'[504] As he goes on to say, this limitation of predestination to predestination to life:

> ...seems to be in strict agreement with the important distinction found in Scripture between the origination of good and evil. Thus, in speaking of 'vessels of wrath' and 'vessels of mercy' (Rom 9:22-23), St. Paul makes a marked difference. Of the former simply uses the passive participle, 'fitted to destruction,' while of the latter he uses the active voice of the verb, and the preparation is distinctly attributed to God as the originator, 'which He had afore prepared unto glory.' To the same effect is the distinction made between the sentences to be passed on those on His right hand and those on His left. To the former the words are: 'Come, ye blessed of My Father; ' to the latter, it is simply 'Depart from Me, ye cursed,' the omission to the latter being a mere indication that the curse was solely of themselves. Nor is it possible to overlook the departure from strict parallelism in other words of that passage. 'The kingdom prepared for you' is contrasted with 'everlasting fire, prepared for the devil and his angels.' Thus the Article in limiting attention to predestination to life seems clearly to follow Scripture in ascribing to God the work of grace for the believer, and associating evil and the doom of evil with men themselves. The election of believers is invariably referred to 'the good pleasure of God's will,' but nothing else is mentioned in this connection (Eph 1:5-9, Phil 2:13, 2 Thess 1:11). So that whatever may be argued on purely logical grounds it is in every way trust, safest, and best to keep divine predestination where Scripture places it. [505]

In response to the teaching of double predestination by John Calvin and those who adopted his position, the followers of the Dutch Reformed theologian Jacobus Arminius (known subsequently as the Arminians) argued for a doctrine of conditional election in which what God has

---

[504] W H Griffith Thomas *The Principles of Theology* 4ed London: Church Book Room Press 1951 p.238
[505] Ibid pp.238-239

eternally determined is to save those who believe in Christ and persevere in faith and obedience to the end of their lives. Thus the first article of the Arminian *Remonstrance* of 1610 states:

> That God, by an eternal and unchangeable purpose in Jesus Christ his Son, before the foundation of the world, hath determined, out of the fallen, sinful race of men, to save in Christ, for Christ's sake and through Christ, those who, through the grace of the Holy Ghost shall believe on this his son Jesus, and shall persevere in this faith and obedience, through this grace, even to the end; and, on the other hand, to leave the incorrigible and unbelieving in sin and under wrath, and to condemn them as alienate from Christ, according to the word of the Gospel in John 3:36; 'He that believeth on the Son hath everlasting life: and he that believeth not the Son shall not see life; but the wrath of God abideth on him,' and according to other passages of Scripture also.

This statement agrees with Article XVII in that it holds that salvation is rooted in a decision made by God before the foundation of the world. It disagrees with Article XVVI over the question of what precisely it is that God has decided.

The Arminian position is that God has chosen to save all those who satisfy the twin conditions of faith and perseverance. The position of Article XVII, and of those biblical passages on which it is based, is that God has eternally determined to save in Christ specific individuals and that their faith and perseverance is the result of this divine choice. For the Arminian the issue of whether we are saved is ultimately left up to us. We either respond to the grace of the Holy Spirit by choosing to believe and persevere or we do not. For Article XVII, on the other hand, it is God and God alone, who decides whether we are saved. We are saved because God has eternally determined to save us.

A further position that is incompatible with teaching of the Article is what is known as 'ecclesiastical election', that is to say the idea that that to which we are elected is the privilege of being members of the Church through baptism.

As Harold Browne puts it in his comments on this Article:

> Some have held that as the Jews of old were God's chosen people, so now is the Christian Church; that every baptized member of

the Church is one of God's elect, and that this election is from God's irrespective and unsearchable decree. Here, therefore, election is to baptismal privileges, not to final glory; the elect are identical with the baptized, and the election constitutes the Church.[506]

It is true that in both the Old and New Testaments the community of God's people is described as being 'chosen' or 'called' by God. We can see this in the Old Testament in passages such as Deut 7:6-7, Ps 105:6 and Ps 135:4. We can see it in the New Testament in passages such as Rom 1:6-7, 1 Cor 1:2 and 1 Pet 1:1.

It is also true that the view of the Church as God's elect is also found in the formularies of the Church of England. Thus the Homily for Whitsunday describes the Church as: 'an universal congregation or fellowship, of God's faithful and elect people'[507] and in the Collect for All Saints Day in the *Book of Common Prayer* God is said to have: 'knit together His elect in one communion and fellowship in the mystical body' of His Son.

Nevertheless, to say that election is simply to be seen in terms of being called into the Church through baptism does not do justice to the whole of what is said about election either in Article XVII or in the Bible. This is because both in the Article and in the biblical passages on which it draws, the end result of election is not simply that we become baptized members of the Church, but that we: 'attain to everlasting felicity.'

Election, that is to say, is not just about membership of the Church. It *is* about attaining eternal salvation.

by His counsel secret to us...

The point of these words in the context of Article XVII is to highlight the truth set out in Deut 29:29: 'The secret things belong to the Lord our God; but the things that are revealed belong to us and our children for ever, that we may do all the words of this law.'

In the case of the doctrine of election this means that we need to accept the fact that the specific identities of the elect are among the secret things that belong to the Lord our God. They are something that God has

---

[506] H Browne *On the Articles* London: John Parker & Sons 1854 p.393
[507] *The Homilies* Bishopstone: The Brynmill Press 2006 p. 336

not revealed to us. There is no list of the elect to be found either in the pages of Scripture or anywhere else. It follows that it is a waste of time engaging in abstract speculation about whether we (or anyone else) has been chosen by God.

As the final paragraph of the Article will make clear, what we need to do instead is focus on what has been made known to us, the promises and warnings that the Bible contains, and shape our lives according to these. This is because although we cannot know in the abstract whether we are among the elect we can know concretely that we have been chosen by God if the fruits of election are manifest in our lives through our faith in God's promises and our obedience to His warnings and commands.

in Christ...

The inclusion of the words 'in Christ' to the 1563 version of the Article on the basis of Eph 1:4 was an important addition because the inclusion of these words gives the Article's account of predestination a proper Christological focus. As Oliver O'Donovan notes, the truth that these words emphasise is the fact that we participate in the eternal relationship of love between the Father and the Son:

> Predestination, like justification, is salvation in Christ; but where justification associates us with the righteousness of Christ manifest in his human life, predestination associates us with the eternal relation between the Son and the Father before all time. Who was the object of God's glad goodwill before the foundations of the world were laid? The one who could say, 'I will tell of the decree of the Lord. He said to me, 'You are my son, today I have begotten you. Ask of me and I will make the nations your heritage' (Ps 2:7). When we speak of man's salvation as 'predestined' we are saying that the whole history of creation and salvation springs out of the eternal love which the Father bears to the Son, the love whereby he is resolved to give him a heritage, to make him 'the first-born of many brethren' (Rom 8:29). The phrase 'chosen in Christ' is not to be understood as though *we* were chosen and *he* was merely the instrument by which our choosing was given effect. We are chosen in him, because *he* is the chosen one, the eternal object of the Father's good pleasure. Just as our

justification means our participation in his righteousness, so our 'predestination,' our 'election' means our participation in his position as the object of the Father's favour from eternity.[508]

out of mankind

The words 'out of mankind' in this first paragraph of the Article highlight the fact that predestination necessarily means selection. This is a point that is clearly made in a number of the biblical passages that talk about election. Thus in Deut 7:6 we read: 'For you are a people holy to the Lord your God; the Lord your God has chosen you to be a people for his own possession out of all the peoples that are on the face of the earth.' In similar fashion St. Paul in Rom 9:13 illustrates the principle of election with reference to the words of Mal 1:2-3, 'Jacob I loved, but Esau I hated.'

However, the fact that the idea of selection is a necessary part of the doctrine of predestination does not stop it being a stumbling block to many people. As they see it, the idea that God selects some people rather than others makes it seem as if God acts in a purely arbitrary manner. 'Why', they ask, 'does God behave like this?' 'If God is a God of love, why does He choose some and not others?'

At the root of this objection to the doctrine of predestination lies the point noted by O'Donovan that:

> The classic doctrine of predestination posits a self-justifying division of mankind into two camps; this division serves no purpose in redemption, but it is simply given.[509]

What O'Donovan says about the classic doctrine of predestination in general also applies to what is said about predestation in Article XVII. The Article is silent about *why* God chooses to select some people, it merely assets *that* He does so. The reason that the Article is silent on this point is because of a wider failure in the Articles to see the calling of Christians in the light of the *missio dei*, the mission of God to bring salvation to humankind and all creation.

---

[508] O O'Donovan *On the Thirty Nine Articles* Exeter: Paternoster Press 1986 p.83
[509] Ibid p.87

When we see the doctrine of predestination in this context we are able to see that God's choice of some people is not an arbitrary decision that they should enjoy a salvation that is denied to others. Rather, God chooses people precisely so that those who are chosen may be the vehicles through which His salvation can be shared with those around them. To quote O'Donovan again:

> How, then, shall we understand the phrase 'out of' mankind? First we must say, as the Article does, that we are chosen to enjoy that salvation which God has wrought *for* mankind in Christ. But then we must add that our election out of mankind, like that of Christ himself, is intended to serve mankind. We are to be carriers of the blessing which is for the rest of mankind as well as for us. He, the Chosen One, was chosen that we might be chosen 'in him.' We are chosen in him that others may be chosen in him through us. Election is like the effect of a magnet passing over iron filings; the magnet picks up some filings immediately, and then, through hem, picks up others, which pick up others, and so on. Election is not election unless it works *through* us, as well as being enjoyed *by* us.[510]

A similar point is made by the Baptist theologian Stanley Grenz in his *Theology for the Community of God*. He writes that:

> ...the biblical concept of election includes being chosen as a people in history for participation in the ongoing sweep of God's activity in the world. In the Old Testament, the primary electing event was the Exodus, and its goal was that Israel belonged to God (Deut 7:6-8) as a people through whom God could bless all the nations of the earth (Gen 12:3). God elected Israel in order that they might fulfil a mission to the Gentiles (Isa 2:3; 42:1), thereby serving God's historical purposes. This forms the context for the inauguration of the New Testament church as the expression of the elected people of God. The great electing event was the coming of Jesus Christ and the pouring out of the Spirit. By virtue of our incorporation into Christ's body, God has elected us and mandated us to proclaim the gospel in all the world (Matt

---

[510] Ibid p. 87

28:16-20. Consequently, we invite people everywhere to join us in serving the grand purpose of God in history which will culminate in the coming of the eschatological community. [511]

Understood in this way, predestination is not a contradiction of the truth that 'God desires all men to be saved and come to a knowledge of the truth' (I Tim 2:4). It is, rather, the means by which this truth is put into effect as God works out His purposes in human history.

As Karl Barth insists: 'we cannot follow the classical doctrine and make the open number of those who are elect in Jesus Christ into a closed number to which all other men are opposed as if they were rejected.' [512] We have instead to think in terms of God's eternal will to bless humankind in Christ being put into effect in history through his constant calling of individual men and women both to enjoy this blessing for themselves and to be the means which God uses to call others so that they can enjoy it too.

Wherefore they which be endued with so excellent a benefit of God be called according to God's purpose by His Spirit working in due season; they through grace obey the calling; they be justified freely; they be made sons of God by adoption; they be made like the image of His only-begotten Son Jesus Christ; they walk religiously in good works; and at length by God's mercy they attain to everlasting felicity.

This final sentence of the first paragraph of the Article describes the outworking of predestination to life in the lives of particular individuals. It describes this outworking in terms of seven steps:

(1)   Vocation
(2)   obedience to vocation through grace
(3)   free justification
(4)   sonship by adoption
(5)   conformity to the image of our Lord
(6)   a religious life, and

---

[511] S Grenz *Theology for the Community of God* Carlisle: Paternoster Press 1994 p.591
[512] K Barth *Church Dogmatics* II.2 Edinburgh: T&T Clark 1957 p. 422

(7)   eternal felicity.[513]

As Gibson explains in his commentary on the Articles, the reason that these steps are set out in the Article is that 'they form a most important safeguard against Antinomian perversions of the doctrine, showing how much is really involved in predestination to life.'[514] That is to say, by setting out these steps the Article is saying that confidence in election cannot be detached from justification by grace through faith and the holiness of life that flows from it. If we want to know whether we are elect the question we need to ask is whether we have a living faith in Christ and, specifically, whether the existence of this living faith is shown by a growth in holiness as we are gradually transformed into the likeness of Jesus Christ.

To illustrate this point Gibson quotes the speech made by Richard Bancroft, then Bishop of London, at the Hampton Court conference between the English bishops and the leaders of the Puritan party in the Church of England that was convened by James I in 1604:

> The Bishop of London took occasion to signifie to His Majesty, how very many in these daies, neglecting holiness of life, presumed too much of persisting of grace, laying all their religion upon predestination, If I shall be saved, I shall be saved; which he termed a desperate doctrine, showing it to be contrary to good divinity and the true doctrine of predestination, wherein we should reason rather *ascendo* than *descendo*, thus 'I live in obedience to God, in love with my neighbour, I follow my vocation etc.; therefore O trust that God hath elected me, and predestinated me to salvation;' not thus, which is the usual course of argument, 'God hath predestinated and chosen me to life, therefore though I sin never so grievously, yet I shall not be damned; for whom He once loveth, He loveth to the end.[515]

It is also important to note that the Article does not give separate treatment to the issue of final perseverance, the issue of whether those who have been chosen and called by God can then subsequently fall away

---

[513] E Gibson *The Thirty-Nine Articles* London: Methuen 1908 p.481
[514] Ibid p.481
[515] Ibid p. 482

and be lost. Both the *Lambeth Articles* and the *Westminster Confession* have separate sections on this issue, but Article XVII does not. This is not an oversight, but is because Cranmer and those who revised the Article in 1563 took the view that the issue of final perseverance was not one that could be treated separately since it was necessarily linked to the existence of faith and holiness of life.

That is to say, they took the view that the question 'Will I finally be saved?' could only be answered is relation to two other questions 'Am I trusting in Christ?' and 'Am I showing the fruits of faith in a holy life?' Only a person who could answer 'Yes' to these latter questions could have confidence in their election and hence in their final state before God.

As the godly consideration of Predestination and our Election in Christ is full of sweet, pleasant, and unspeakable comfort to godly persons and such as feeling in themselves the working of the Spirit of Christ, mortifying the works of the flesh and their earthly members and drawing up their mind to high and heavenly things, as well because it doth greatly establish and confirm their faith of eternal salvation to be enjoyed through Christ, as because it doth fervently kindle their love towards God: so for curious and carnal persons, lacking the Spirit of Christ, to have continually before their eyes the sentence of God's Predestination is a most dangerous downfall, whereby the devil doth thrust them either into desperation or into wretchlessness of most unclean living no less perilous than desperation.

Having defined what predestination is in its first paragraph, the Article goes on in its second paragraph to set out the practical consequences of the doctrine of predestination. It sees these consequences as both positive and negative.

The first part of the paragraph sets out the positive consequences of the doctrine in the lives of the godly. The point that is being made is explained more fully in the section on Predestination in the *Refomatio Legum Ecclesiasticarum,* the code of Canon Law drawn up by Archbishop Cranmer during the reign of Edward VI.

This declares that the 'diligent and serious understanding' of predestination will 'reward the minds of godly people' who feel:

...the subjection of their flesh and members, and who look upwards to heavenly things with the sweetest and most joyful consolation, since it confirms our faith in the eternal salvation which will come to us through Christ, lights the strongest flame of love towards God, stirs us most remarkably to give thanks, and takes us far away from sin since we have been chosen by God and declared to be his children, which singular and exalted condition demands the highest propriety in behaviour and the most excellent perfection of virtue from us. Furthermore, it reduces our arrogance, lest we believe that we are ruled by our own strength, which is blessed by the free beneficence and infinite goodness of God. [516]

To put it simply, what belief in predestination does in the lives of godly people is to strengthen their faith (since they know that their salvation is dependent of God's grace and not on their own efforts), stir up their love and lead them away from sin.

The second part of the paragraph then sets out the negative consequences of the doctrine in the lives of the ungodly, whom it describes as 'curious and carnal persons,' that is to say, those whose approach to the doctrine of predestination is based on abstract intellectual curiosity or who are unwilling to forsake sin and embrace a life of holiness. In the case of such people, it says, the Devil uses the doctrine to either lead people to despair (since they cannot find out whether they are elect or not) and/or to the recklessness ('wretchlessness') of an ever more sinful way of life (since how they behave will, they think, have no effect on whether or not they will enjoy salvation).

Once again, the *Reformatio Legum Ecclesiasticarum* illustrates the point that is being made here. It notes that:

On the fringe of the Church there are many who live in a wild and dissolute way, who when they get interested in the subject, being dissipated by excess and completely cut off from the Spirit of Christ, always toss predestination and rejection, or (as they call it), reprobation into their speech arguing that since God by his

---

[516] *Reformatio Legum Ecclesiasticarum* 22 in G Bray (ed) *Tudor Church Reform* London: Boydell Press 2000 p. 211

eternal counsel has already determined something, both concerning salvation and concerning destruction, they have some excuse for their wrongdoings and crimes and all manner of evil. And when pastors upbraid their dissipated and disgraceful life, they blame God's will for their crimes and by that defence consider that the reprimands of admonitions are wasted, and so also, under the devil's leadership, they are tossed headlong into despair or drawn into some dissolute and soft security of life, without either repentance or any consciousness of wrongdoing.[517]

Furthermore, we must receive God's promises in such wise as they be generally set forth in Holy Scripture; and in our doings that will of God is to be followed which we have expressly declared unto us in the word of God.

As Archbishop Laurence suggests in his 1804 Bampton Lectures, this last paragraph of the Article seems to draw on the work of Melancthon. It is sometimes suggested, by Gibson for example,[518] that the purpose of this paragraph is to rule out the Calvinist belief in 'particular redemption,' the belief that Christ did not die for all, but only for the elect. There are two reasons why this suggestion is unlikely. First, the issue of particular redemption seems only to have become an issue of theological dispute within the Church of England after the Articles were written. Secondly, there is nothing in the wording of the paragraph that explicitly addresses this issue even though the first clause could be argued to address it indirectly.

The key to understanding this paragraph correctly is to note that (as the opening word 'furthermore' indicates) it follows on from the paragraph that precedes it. It is still concerned with the pastoral problem of how to avoid people lapsing into despair or antinomianism because they are either uncertain of whether they are among the elect or too confident that this is the case. It offers two solutions to this problem

The first solution is to insist on the principle that the promises of God concerning salvation contained in the Bible are to be understood generically, or, in other words, as applying not just to some few of the elect but to everyone who belongs to the genus 'human being' (that is

---

[517] Ibid p.211
[518] Gibson op.cit.pp. 485-6

what is meant by the Latin 'generaliter propositae sunt'). The importance of this principle is that it rules out despair by saying that no one need think that God's promises do not apply to him or her.

The second solution is to insist is that what we should take as the guide for our behaviour ('our doings') is the will of God revealed to us in the Bible rather than some supposed hidden will of God that might be different from this.

It should be noted that when the clause talks about 'that will of God' it is pointing us to where the will of God is to be found rather than suggesting that there might be some other will of God, but that we are not to follow it. Article I has already insisted that God is without 'parts,' that is to say, there is no division within God and He cannot have two contrasting wills, one hidden and one revealed. There is one will of God, the will revealed to us in Scripture and so we cannot excuse immoral behaviour by saying that we are not sure that this will applies to us. [519]

In summary, the article teaches that there is predestination to life and that the knowledge that this is the case is beneficial to the godly. However, to avoid problems caused by the mishandling of the notion of predestination it also teaches us that we should not seek to uncover the secret mind of God, but instead focus on God's self-revelation in Scripture and what this tells us about what God promises to us and requires from us in response. In the words of Martin Luther:

> Men should not turn their eyes on the secret sentence of election, foreknowledge and predestination, as they are called; for such speeches lead to doubt, security or despair, - are you elected? no fall can hurt you, and you cannot perish, - are you not elected? there is no remedy for it. These are shocking speeches, and men ought not to fix their heads on such thoughts; but the gospel refers us to the proclaimed word of God, wherein He has revealed His will, and through which He will be known and will work.[520]

---

[519] The fact that this is the right way to understand the paragraph is made clear by the parallel section of the *Reformatio Legum Ecclesiasticarum* in which Cranmer states:
> ...everyone must be warned by us that in undertaking actions they should not rely on the decrees of predestination, but adapt their entire way of life to the laws of God, and contemplate that both promises as well to the good and threats to the bad are generally set forth to him in the Holy Scriptures. (pp.212-13)

[520] M Luther Letter No.1753 in Gibson op. cit p. 485

Article XVIII

∞

Of obtaining eternal salvation only by the name of Christ

They also are to be had accursed that presume to say that every man shall be saved by the law or sect which he professeth, so that he be diligent to frame his life according to that law and the light of nature. For Holy Scripture doth set out to us only the name of Jesus Christ, whereby men must be saved.

De speranda aeterna salute tantum in nomine Christi

Sunt et illi anathematizandi qui dicere audent unumquemque in lege aut secta quam profitetur esse servandum, modo iuxta illam et lumen naturae accurate vixerit: eum sacrae literae tantum Iesu Christi nomen praedicent in quo salvos fieri homines oporteat.

This article was originally published in1553 as Article XVIII of the *Forty Two Articles*. The language of the article cannot be traced back to any earlier source.

The original titles of the article were 'We must trust to obtain to eternal life only by the name of Christ' (Tantum in nomine Christi speranda est aeterna salus). These were changed to the current titles in 1571 in order to bring the forms of the title into line with that of the other articles. There is a slight difference, the reason for which is not known, between the English title which talks about 'obtaining' eternal salvation only through Christ and the Latin which talks about 'hoping' *(speranda)* for eternal salvation only though Christ.

In 1553 the words 'and abhorred' were included in first line of the article after 'accursed' but these were omitted in 1563 thus bringing the English text into line with the Latin. The word 'et' in the Latin text was omitted in1563 but restored in 1571, thus keeping the Latin text in line with the English.

Article XVIII is the last of the set of articles starting with Article IX that are concerned with issues of sin and salvation. Article XVIII does not follow on from the discussion of predestination in the precious article and it seems most likely that the place it occupies was simply a matter of convenience. As an article concerning salvation it obviously needed to be part of the set of articles on issues of sin and salvation. However it did not fit in as part of a sequence of articles within that set and so it was included as a stand alone article at the end.

The word 'also (et) in the first line has been taken as reference back to either Article XVI or Article XVII.[521] If the reference is to Article XVII then the connection of thought would be that Article XVII shows that salvation only comes through Christ. However, the use of the words 'they also are to be accursed' at the start of Article XVIII seems an odd way to make that connection. If the reference is to Article XVI then it would follow on from the statement 'they are to be condemned' in the last sentence of that article and this seems to be the most probable explanation. If this is correct then 'accursed' in Article XVIII would be equivalent to 'condemned' in Article XVI.

Like Articles XV and XVI, Article XVIII is concerned with an error emanating from one of the radical Protestant groups of the reformation period. In the words of Hardwick:

> The eighteenth article is levelled at a philosophical theory of the rationalistic school of Anabaptists, who contended that if men were sincere only in following out their own systems, their deliberate rejection of the Saviour of the world would prove no obstacle to their salvation.[522]

This teaching is described in section eleven of the list of heresies in the *Reformatio Legum Ecclesiasticarum*. This states:

> Horrible and insane is the daring of those who maintain that salvation may be hoped for in every religion or sect which men have professed, as long as they strive as hard as they can for innocence and integrity of life according to the light that has been put into them by nature, for plagues of this kind are condemned

---

[521] Gibson, op.cit., p488, Griffith Thomas, op.cit. p.259,
[522] Hardwick,op.cit.p.101.

by the authority of Holy writ. For there the one and only name of Jesus Christ is commended to us, that all salvation may come to us from him.[523]

They also are to be had accursed that presume to say that every man shall be saved by the law or sect which he professeth, so that he be diligent to frame his life according to that law and the light of nature. For Holy Scripture doth set out to us only the name of Jesus Christ, whereby men must be saved.

A comparison between the quotation just given from the *Reformatio Legum Ecclesiasticarum* and the first sentence of Article XVIII makes it clear that this sentence is intended to summarise the heresy to which the *Reformatio* also refers. It sets out the error that is to be rejected.

The second sentence of the article then explains with reference to the teaching of St. Peter in Acts 4:12 why this error is to be rejected. In the words of Griffith Thomas in his commentary on this article:

In opposition to the error condemned by the Article, the teaching of Holy Scripture is inculcated, that 'only the Name of Jesus Christ' is set out to us 'whereby man must be saved.' This truth is clearly the fundamental reality of the New Testament, and the Article evidently refers to the well-known statement of St. Peter: 'Neither is there salvation in any other; for there is none other name under heaven given among men, whereby we must be saved' (Acts 4:12). Even Cornelius, with all his moral advantages, needed Jesus Christ and His salvation (Acts 10:2-5), and in various other connections the same truth is taught. Indeed it is only another way of saying that 'Christianity is Christ,' for it is only by means of the redemption provided by God in the Person of His Son that human salvation becomes possible (Mark 16:16; John 3:26; 1 Corinthians 3:11; 1 Corinthians 15:1-2; Galatians 1:8-9).[524]

The belief that salvation is solely to be obtained through Christ is also something that follows on from what has been said both negatively and positively in the articles from Article IX onwards. If all human beings

[523] Bray, *Tudor Church Reform*, p.197,
[524] Griffith Thomas, op. cit. p.259

without exception are sinners and are incapable of making themselves acceptable to God on the basis of their own efforts as Articles IX, X and XIII make clear then the idea that human beings can save themselves by their own religious activities and their adherence to the law of nature is ruled out. If we are 'accounted righteous only for the merit of our Lord and Saviour Jesus Christ' (Article XI), if he alone is the 'Lamb without spot, who by sacrifice of himself once made, should take away the sins of the world' (Article XV) and if God has eternally chosen us in Christ that we might be brought by him to everlasting salvation (Article XVII), then it follows that there is neither need nor room for any other source of salvation.

However, this having been said, there is also a general consensus amongst the commentators on the Articles that Article XVIII does not address the issue of whether it is possible for someone to be saved by Christ if he or she has not come to conscious faith in Christ and has not been baptised.[525] The article certainly rules out non-Christian philosophical or religious systems ('the law or sect which he professeth') as alternative sources of salvation. What it does not do is say that those who adhere to them cannot be saved.

In this connection Burnet makes a helpful distinction in his comments on this article between being saved *by* a law or sect and being saved *in* a law or sect:

> ...a great difference is to be observed between the words *saved by the law* and *saved in the law*; the one is condemned, but not the other. To be *saved by a law* or *sect*, signifies, that by the virtue of that *law* or *sect* such men who follow it may be saved: whereas to be *saved in a law* or *sect* imports only, that God may extend his compassions to men that are engaged in false religions. The former is only condemned by this Article, which affirms nothing concerning the other.[526]

To quote Browne, we can therefore say that Article XVIII:

---

[525] See, for instance, Browne, op. cit. 435-443, Burnet , op. cit. p.p.239-244, Gibson, op. cit. p.p.490-491, Griffith Thomas, op. cit. p.259.
[526] Burnet, ibid, p.240.

...condemns that latitudinarianism, which makes all creeds and all communions alike, saying that all men may be saved by their own sect, so they shape their lives according to it, and according to the law of nature. The ground, on which it protests against this view of matters, is that the Scriptures set forth no other name but Christ's whereby we may be saved. The opinion here condemned therefore, is not a charitable hope, that persons, who have never heard of Christ, or who have been bred in ignorance or error, may not be inevitably excluded from the benefit of His atonement; but that cold indifference to faith and truth, which would rest satisfied and leave them in their errors, instead of striving to bring them to faith in Christ and to His Body the Church, to which alone the promises of the Gospel are made, and to which, by actual revelation God's mercies are annexed.[527]

Note: two recent Church of England statements on the status of those of other faiths.

The issue raised by Article XVIII of the status in regard to salvation of those belong to religions other than Christianity has been addressed from a Church of England perspective in the 1984 report from the Board for Mission and Unity *Towards a Theology for Inter-Faith Dialogue* and in the 1995 Doctrine Commission report *The Mystery of Salvation..*

Towards a Theology for Inter-Faith Dialogue suggests that the basis for interfaith dialogue is provided by the biblical pointers that:

> The Triune God is a God who moved in creation into a relationship with all that is created; who as the Word, is incarnate in Jesus and yet encountered in other places; and who as Holy Spirit, present in the Church and in the lives of baptised Christians, is also active among those of other faiths and cultures. It is the same God whose saving grace is at work outside the Church as well at within it.

These 'powerful biblical pointers,' it says:

---

[527] Browne, op. cit. p.440.

...must inform a Christian understanding of our relationships with those of other faiths. What would be contrary to the biblical witness would be the abandonment of a defining loyalty to Jesus Christ as the one in whom God was reconciling the whole world himself and any proposal that this message of reconciliation through Christ need no longer be offered to those of other faiths. The inclusive invitation of God goes now, as always with the demand for exclusive loyalty to his Anointed.[528]

In its chapter on 'Christ and World Faiths' *The Mystery of Salvation* explores what we can learn from the Bible that is relevant to this issue and 'the witness of those who have lived closely with other faiths over a long period.' It declares that:

> It is incompatible with the essential Christian affirmation that God is love to say that God brings millions into the world to damn them. The God of Love also longs for all to come into relationship with him, and this is his purpose in creation. When he chooses certain peoples, such as Israel, or certain persons such as the prophets or Apostles, he chooses them not for exclusive privilege or salvation, but for a purpose in the expression of God's self revelation and showing of his saving love for all.[529]

However, it also goes on to affirm that the way that God will achieve his loving purpose in creation is through Jesus Christ:

> Ultimately, we believe, and that is why we are Christians, that it is through Jesus Christ that God will reconcile all things to himself. How that will come about, we can only be agnostic about, whether it is through some real but unconscious response to the Christ within them now, or whether it is in response to some eschatological revelation, or by some other means.[530]

If we think of salvation in the broadest sense as encompassing all that heals and enhances human life then clearly aspects of

---

[528] *Towards a Theology for Inter-Faith Dialogue*, London: CIO, 1984, p.27.
[529] *The Mystery of Salvation*, London: CHP, 1995, p. 173.
[530] Ibid p. 181

salvation are available in many ways, not only explicitly through Jesus Christ. In the ultimate sense, salvation is defined by having Jesus Christ as its source and goal. To use the terms we deliberately put aside earlier, this pluralism and this exclusivism are reconciled, not in some form of inclusivism is in the usual sense but eschatologically, in the final purposes of God. To recognise the life, death and resurrection of Jesus as constitutive of salvation as well as revelatory, as Christians do, is to anticipate that he will prove to be the definitive focus of salvation in its fully comprehensive meaning. It may be too that our understanding of Christ will itself be enhanced when people of other faiths are gathered in.[531]

Because this is the case, because 'ultimate salvation is found in Christ,' it follows that:

...mission remains the central task of the Christian Church. The task is to proclaim by word and to display in action that God has created a world that is good, and that we are responsible for that creation; that the kingdom of God, the kingdom of justice and peace, has already begun in Christ, and that we can be assured of its future consummation through him; that the gift and assurance of salvation and eternal life is available now, and the mark of this life is love. We deny the fullness of that love if we deny the truth and goodness which Christ, as Logos, and God by the Spirit, can also inspire in those of other faiths and of none. We believe that God has chosen to provide the fullest revelation of himself in Christ, and the fullest revelation of his love for all humanity in the cross and resurrection. Hence we naturally pray that God will bring all people, including those of other faiths, to explicit faith in Christ and membership of his Church. This is not because we believe that the God revealed in Christ is unable to save them without this, but because Christ is the truest and fullest expression of his love, and we long for them to share it. In the Lord's words in St. John's Gospel, 'I came that they may have life, and have it abundantly' (John 10.10).[532]

---

[531] Ibid.p.184
[532] Ibid p. 184

Both of these statements go beyond what is said in Article XVIII in the sense that they make a positive affirmation about God's saving activity outside the bounds of the Christian Church. However, what they say is compatible with the teaching of Article XVIII in that neither of them suggests that those of other faiths can be saved by adherence to the tenets or practices of those faiths or by living according to the light of nature. Both of them also insist that the Church must continue its mission of making Christ known to those of other faiths in the hope that they will come to faith in him and into membership of his Church.

The Church and its Authority: Articles XIX-XXI

Articles XIX –XXI are the first of four sets of articles concerning the Church. This set of articles are concerned with what the visible church is and the nature and limits of its authority.

Article XIX set out the Church of England's understanding of the nature of the visible Church in order to respond to the arguments of those who held that a visible Church had to be under the authority of the Church of Rome.

Article XX then goes on to consider the Church's authority in matters of faith and order. It argues that the Church does have a proper authority in these matters, but that this is subject to what is taught in Scripture.

Article XXI looks at the authority that belongs to General Councils of the Church as a particular example of the Church's authority. It argues that such councils cannot be called without the authority of the civil rulers appointed by God and the fact that they are liable to error means that their decisions should only be accepted if they are in accord with Scripture.

Article XIX

∞

Of the Church

The visible Church of Christ is a congregation of faithful men, in the which the pure word of God is preached and the sacraments be duly ministered according to Christ's ordinance in all those things that of necessity are requisite to the same. As the Church of Jerusalem, Alexandria, and Antioch have erred: so also the Church of Rome hath erred, not only in their living and manner of ceremonies, but also in matters of faith.

De Ecclesia

Ecclesia Christi visibilis est coetus fidelium, in quo verbum Dei purum praedicatur et sacramenta, quoad ea quae necessario exiguntur, iuxta Christi institutum recte administrantur. Sicut erravit Ecclesia Hierosolymitana, Alexandrina, et Antiochena: ita et erravit Ecclesia Romana, non solum quoad agenda et caeremoniarum ritus, verum in his etiam quae credenda sunt.

This article is the first of two seriess of articles about the Church running from Article XIX to Article XXIV. It originated as Article XX of the *Forty Two Articles*. Its definition of the marks of the Church may have been influenced by Article 7 of the *Augsburg Confession* which states that the Church is 'the assembly of all believers among whom the Gospel is preached in its purity and the holy sacraments are administered according to the Gospel.'[533] However, there is no evidence that Article XIX is verbally dependent on either the Augsburg article or any other existing source. It appears to have been freshly written for the *Forty Two Articles.*

---

[533] Text in Leith, *Creeds of the Churches*, p.70.

Slight verbal changes were introduced into the English text of the article during the reign of Elizabeth I in order to bring this into more exact agreement with the Latin text, which remained unchanged. 'And manner of ceremonies' was added in 1563 and 'their' was omitted before 'faith' in 1571.

As in the case of other articles, the purpose of Article XX is made clear by the list of heresies in the *Reformatio Legum Ecclesiasticarum*. Article 21 of this list is entitled 'Of the Roman Church and of the power of the Roman pontiff.' It states:

> Also the insanity of those who think that the Roman church was founded on a rock of such a kind that it has neither erred nor can err, must be restrained by limits imposed by law, since many of its errors can be repeated by the longer memory of our elders, and may even be recalled by our memory, partly in those things by which our life ought to be guided and partly also in those things by which our faith ought to be determined. For this reason the error of those who want the universal church of the whole Christian world to be governed by the bishop of Rome alone is intolerable. For we define the visible church like this; it is an assembly of faithful people in which Holy Scripture is sincerely taught and the sacraments (at least in those parts of them that are essential) are administered according to the command of Christ.[534]

The very close similarity between what is said in this quotation and the contents of Article XIX make it clear that the purpose of the article was to provide a definition of the Church that would refute the arguments of those who maintained that the visible Church had to be under the authority of the Church of Rome.

The fact that this was the purpose of the article explains why it is says nothing about the invisible Church. At the time that the article was written the theologians of the Church of England undoubtedly believed in the existence of the invisible Church. Thus in the article on the Church in the *Thirteen Articles*, Archbishop Cranmer notes that one of the two main meanings of the term 'Church' in Scripture is:

---

[534] Bray, *Tudor Church Reform*, pp.210-211.

...the congregation of all the saints and true believers, who really believe in Christ the Head and are sanctified by his Spirit. This is the living and truly holy mystical body of Christ, but known only to God, who alone understands the hearts of men.[535]

However, the issue which Article XIX was intended to address was not concerned with the invisible Church known to God alone, but with the nature of the Church as a visible human community. Hence the article talks about the latter, but says nothing about the former.

The visible Church of Christ is a congregation of faithful men

Article XIX begins its definition of the visible Church by describing it as a 'congregation'.

This wording is sometimes used as a justification for the idea that the fundamental unit of the Church is the congregation, in the sense of a group of people who gather together for worship in a particular place. On this reading of the article what it is saying is that the visible Church of Christ exists as a number of particular congregations.

This is not, however, what the article means. In the sixteenth century the word 'congregation,' like the word 'coetus' used in the Latin version of the article, meant a group of people of whatever size. We can see this, for instance, in the way that in the quotation from the *Thirteen Articles* given above Cranmer uses 'congregation' to refer to the whole of the invisible Church. In Article XIX the term is used to refer to the whole of the Church of Christ visible in this world. In the words of Tyrell Green: 'By 'congregation' (coetus) is here meant, not a body of people assembled in one place, but the whole number of God's people.'[536] Behind this usage lies the use of the term congregation to refer to the people of God in Old Testament passages such as Exodus 12:19, Joshua 22:18 and Psalm 74:2.

Article XIX goes on to say that the visible Church is made up of 'faithful men.' The term 'men' is used here generically to refer to human beings whether male or female. When it says that these people are 'faithful' what it means is that they are those that profess the Christian faith. As Gibson notes:

---

[535] *Thirteen Articles*, Article 5 'The Church', in Bray, *Documents of the English Reformation*, p.189.
[536] Tyrell Green. op. cit. p. 129.

It cannot be taken as implying anything as to the character of the faith in the members of the Church, or as if it indicated the presence of a true and lively faith in all who belong to the body; but it refers simply to those who 'profess and call themselves Christians' That this is so is shown by the fact that a later article (XXVI) expressly states...that 'in the visible Church the evil are ever mingled with the good.' Thus the Church consists of the bad as well as the good, and therefore the word 'faithful' must be understood in the sense explained above.[537]

That this is the correct meaning of 'faithful' in Article XIX is indicated by the fact that it corresponds to the distinction drawn by Cranmer in the article on the Church in the *Thirteen Articles* between those belonging to the invisible Church, who, as we have seen, are the 'the saints and true believers, who really believe in Christ the Head and are sanctified by his Spirit' and the members of the visible Church who are 'all who are baptized in Christ, who have not openly denied him nor been lawfully and by his Word excommunicated.'[538]

...in the which the pure word of God is preached and the sacraments be duly ministered according to Christ's ordinance in all those things that of necessity are requisite to the same.

Article XIX continues by setting out the two marks which it thinks characterise the visible Church. In the light of the parallel definition in the *Reformatio Legum Ecclesiasticarum* it is clear that the 'word of God' means Holy Scripture and the reason that the adjective 'pure' is used is probably to distinguish preaching that is based solely on Scripture and in that sense is pure from preaching that is tainted by an admixture of human traditions (such as legendary stories about the saints) which the English Reformers felt had been characteristic of the late Medieval Church. Article XXV will go on to explain that 'the sacraments,' properly so called, are the two dominical sacraments of Baptism and the Supper of the Lord. Articles XXVII, XXVIII and XXX and the services of Baptism and Holy Communion in the book of Common Prayer further explain what the English Church understood by ministering the sacraments 'according to

---

[537] Gibson, op. cit. p.502.
[538] Bray, *Documents of the English Reformation*, p.189.

Christ's ordinance in all those things that of necessity are requisite to the same.'

What the Articles do not do is to explain in either in Article XIX or elsewhere is why these are the two distinguishing characteristics of the visible Church. The same is also true when a similar definition of the characteristics of the visible Church is offered in the *Refomatio Legum Ecclesiasticarum.* However, given that we know the English Reformers were seeking to put forward a biblically based theology, the most likely explanation is that they believed that these were the two key characteristics of the visible Church to be found in Scripture. What seems plausible in the light of the biblical material is that they believed that in both the Old and the New Testaments the congregation of God's people was marked out by being a community in which God's word was preached , first by Moses and the prophets in the Old Testament and then by Christ and the Apostles in the New, and that they also believed that in the New Testament it was marked out as well by baptising people and celebrating the Lord's Supper in accordance with Christ's commands (see Matthew 28:19, 1 Corinthians 11:23-25, Acts 2:37-42).

As the setting of the definition of the visible Church in the *Reformatio Legum Ecclesiasticarum* makes clear, as well as setting out what the Reformers thought were the key characteristics of the visible Church, this definition also had the secondary function of excluding any necessity of accepting the authority of the Bishop of Rome. If the definition of the visible Church was that it was 'a congregation of faithful men, in the which the pure word of God is preached and the sacraments be duly ministered according to Christ's ordinance in all those things that of necessity are requisite to the same' then the Church of England could be said to belong to it even though it had rejected the authority of the Pope in under Henry VIII in 1534 and again under Elizabeth I in 1559.[539]

It should also be noted that in the homily 'Of the Coming Down of the Holy Ghost: for Whitsunday in the *Second Book of Homilies* these marks of the visible Church are used polemically to prove that 'the Bishops of Rome, and their adherents, are not the true Church of Christ'[540] According to the homily this is because

---

[539] See 'The abjuration of Papal Supremacy by the Clergy, 1534 ' and 'The Act of Uniformity, 1559' in Bray *Documents of the English Reformation* pp. 109-110 and 329-334.
[540] *The Homiles*, pp.337-338.

...neither are they *built upon the foundation of the Apostles and Prophets* (Ephesians 2:20) retaining the sound and pure doctrine of Christ Jesu; neither yet do they order the sacraments or else the ecclesiastical keys, in such sort as he did first institute and ordain them, but have so intermingled their own traditions and inventions by chopping and changing, by adding and plucking away, that now they may seem to be converted into a new guise. Christ commended to his Church a sacrament of his Body and Blood: they have changed it into a sacrifice for the quick and the dead. Christ did minister to his Apostles, and the Apostles to other men indifferently under both kinds: they have robbed the lay people of the cup, saying that for them one kind is sufficient. Christ ordained no other element to be used in Baptism, but only water, whereunto when the word is joined, it is made, as St. Augustin saith, a full and perfect sacrament: they being wiser in their own conceit than Christ, think it is not well nor orderly done unless they use conjuration, unless they hallow the water; unless there be oil, salt, spittle, tapers, and such other dumb ceremonies, serving to no use, contrary to the plain rule of St. Paul, who willeth *all things* to be done in the Church *unto edification* (1 Corinthians 14: 5).[541]

In order to understand Article XIX in its original historical context it is important to be aware that its definition of the visible Church was used, and was intended to be used, in this anti-Roman way. However, this use of the definition is not inherent in the definition itself. This means that it is perfectly possible for someone to assent to this definition, but to dissent from the conclusion drawn in the homily that the definition means that the Church of Rome should not be seen as belonging to the visible Church.

In this connection it is important to note the point made by Gibson that the consistent recognition of Roman orders by the Church of England has indicated that it has never regarded the Church of Rome as ceasing to belong the Church of Christ:

...the English Church accepts the Orders of the Church of Rome, and has never denied the priesthood of, or attempted to re-

---

[541] Ibid, p.337.

ordain, any Roman priests who have sought admission to her Communion. If the Church of Rome were regarded as apostate, her ordinations would never be accepted as conveying a valid commission. The fact, then, that they are so accepted in the English Church is conclusive on this point, and further argument is needless.[542]

What is said in the homily notwithstanding, the general approach taken by the Church of England has traditionally been to regret the errors that have been seen in the Church of Rome while still regarding her as belonging to the true Church of Christ.

This approach is classically expressed by Richard Hooker in the *Laws of Ecclesiastical Polity*. In the face of the Puritan call for a total rejection of Rome and all her works, Hooker declares:

> Notwithstanding, so far as lawfully we may, we have held and do hold fellowship with them. For even as the Apostle doth say of Israel that they are in one respect enemies, but in another beloved of God, in like sort with Rome we dare not communicate concerning sundry her gross and grievous abominations, yet touching those main parts of Christian truth wherein they constantly still persist, we gladly acknowledge them to be of the family of Jesus Christ; and our hearty prayer unto God almighty is, that being co-joined so far forth with them, they may at the length (if it be His will) so yield to frame and reform themselves, that no distraction remain in anything, but that we 'all may with one heart and mouth glorify God, the Father of our Lord and Saviour,' whose Church we are.[543]

In the quotation from the homily the use of the 'ecclesiastical keys', that is to say the use of the judicial authority given by Christ to St. Peter and the rest of the Apostles (Matthew 16:19, 18:18), is seen as one of the marks of the Church and this is also the case in Article 3 of the Eleven Articles of

---

[542] Gibson, op. cit. p.509.
[543] Hooker, *Laws of Ecclesiastical Polity*, Bk. III Ch. i.10. Since the 1960s the churches of the Anglican Communion and the Roman Catholic Church have begun to move towards the sort of rapprochement that Hooker hoped for. For this see the agreed statement of the International Anglican-Roman Catholic Commission for Unity and Mission, *Growing Together in Unity and Mission*, London: SPCK, 2007.

1559. The reason that the keys are not mentioned in Article XIX is probably to be explained by the distinction made by the Elizabethan Dean of St. Paul's, Alexander Nowell, in his *Catechism* of 1570 between preaching and the right administration of the sacraments as the 'chief and necessary marks of the church' and the use of ecclesiastical discipline as a mark of a 'well ordered' church.[544] Although the Articles as a whole stress the importance of ecclesiastical discipline – see Articles XXVI and XXXIII - Article XIX is concerned with the 'chief and necessary' marks of the Church and therefore does not mention the power of the keys.

As the Church of Jerusalem, Alexandria, and Antioch have erred: so also the Church of Rome hath erred, not only in their living and manner of ceremonies, but also in matters of faith.

Considered purely in the context of Article XIX itself the last section of the article does not seem to follow from what precedes it. Why does a statement that various churches have erred follow a definition of the marks of the visible Church?

However, when Article XIX is viewed in relation to what is said in the *Reformatio Legum Ecclesiasticarum* the connection becomes clear. The article is a whole is intended to provide a refutation of the claims being made on behalf of the Church of Rome. The last section of the article serves this purpose by explaining that the like other historic churches of Christendom the Church of Rome has been subject to error and as such it does not constitute an infallible guide to which other churches, such as the Church of England, should submit.

The reason that the Churches of Jerusalem, Alexandria and Antioch are mentioned is because they were the three historic patriarchates of the Eastern Church. As Gibson notes:

> No particular errors are specified in any case; but it is not difficult to point to periods during the great Arian controversy when each of the three Eastern Churches mentioned in the Article fell into serious errors. Thus the Church of Antioch went wrong at the Council of the Dedication in 341, when a defective creed acceptable to the Arians was accepted in lieu of the Nicene faith.

---

[544] G E Corrie (ed), *Nowell's Catechism*, Cambridge: CUP/Parker Society, 1853, p.175.

The Church of Alexandria certainly 'erred' when Athanasius was in banishment and Gregory or George of Cappadocia ruling the See. The Church of Jerusalem was also infected with Arianism for a considerable time. [545]

The errors of Rome are likewise not specified. Gibson suggests that what the article has in mind is errors committed by Rome during the Patristic period: 'she erred when her Bishop Liberius accepted an Arian creed; when Zosimus vindicated Pelagius; and when Honorius accepted the Monothelite heresy.[546] It is possible that these examples of historic error may have been part of what the article has in mind. However, what is said in the *Reformatio Legum Ecclesiasticarum* suggests that more recent examples of Roman error may also have been in mind. In addition, the language of the article ('not only in their living and manner of ceremonies, but also in matters of faith') indicates that that the errors with which it is concerned are not confined to the sort of doctrinal errors highlighted by Gibson.

As Griffith Thomas observes, we can see the sorts of errors of which the English Reformers thought that Rome was guilty from what is said in the Articles as a whole.

> Thus, in its 'living' can be proved by the celibacy of the clergy (Article XXXII); in its 'manner of Ceremonies,' the error speaking to the congregation in an unknown tongue (Article XXIV) and denial of the cup to the laity may be adduced (Article XXX); in regard to 'matters of Faith,' the errors are almost too numerous to mention, including the use of Tradition (Article VI), the works of supererogation (Article XIV), purgatory (Article XXII), the seven Sacraments (Article XXV), Transubstantiation (Article XXVIII) and several more.[547]

It is noteworthy that this section of the article talks about the 'Church of Rome' and this can be seen as an additional indication that in spite of its errors the Roman church is regarded as a belonging to the true Church just like the other three churches mentioned.

---

[545] Gibson, op. cit. p.507
[546] Ibid, p.507.
[547] Griffith Thomas, op. cit. p.173.

Note: Article XIX and the Church of England's approach to ecumenical relations:

Article VII of the Augsburg Confession declares that 'it is sufficient for the true unity of the Christian church that the Gospel be preached in conformity with a pure understanding of it and the sacraments be administered in accordance with the divine Word.' Article XIX has no equivalent to this declaration and Anglican thinking about what is required for the visible unity of the church has instead found expression in the declaration by the Lambeth Conference of 1920 ('The Appeal to All Christian People') that the visible unity of the Church will involve the 'whole-hearted acceptance' of:

> The Holy Scriptures, as the record of God's revelation of himself to man, and as being the rule and ultimate standard of faith; and the Creed commonly called Nicene, as the sufficient statement of the Christian faith, and either it or the Apostles' Creed as the baptismal confession of belief:
> The divinely instituted sacraments of Baptism and the Holy Communion, as expressing for all the corporate life of the whole fellowship in and with Christ:
> A ministry acknowledged by every part of the Church as possessing not only the inward call of the Spirit, but also the commission of Christ and the authority of the whole body.[548]

The Lambeth Conference also suggested that the Episcopate is 'the one means of providing such a ministry' and that 'it is now and will prove to in the future the best instrument for maintaining the unity and continuity of the Church.'[549]

The ecumenical policy followed by the Church of England in recent years has involved a hybrid approach based on both Article XIX and the Lambeth Appeal. Thus it has recognised other churches as belonging to the one true Church of Christ on the basis that they have the marks of the visible Church specified in Article XIX, but it has also insisted that such recognition is not sufficient for the visible unity of the Church. For this a reconciled pattern of ministry based on the episcopate,

---

[548] G Bell (ed), *Documents on Christian Unity 1920-1930*, Oxford: OUP, 1930, p.3
[549] Ibid, pp.3-4.

together with the establishment of agreed forms of collegial and conciliar oversight, is seen as necessary.[550]

---

[550] For this see *Called to Witness and Service*, London: CHP, 1999, p.23.

Article XX

∞

Of the Authority of the Church

The Church hath power to decree rites or ceremonies and authority in controversies of faith; and yet it is not lawful for the Church to ordain anything contrary to God's word written, neither may it so expound one place of Scripture, that it be repugnant to another. Wherefore, although the Church be a witness and a keeper of Holy Writ: yet, as it ought not to decree anything against the same, so besides the same ought it not to enforce anything to be believed for necessity of salvation.

De Ecclesiae Auctoritate

Habet Ecclesia ritus statuendi ius et in fidei controversiis auctoritatem; quamvis Ecclesiae non licet quicquam instituere quod verbo Dei scripto adversetur, neque unum Scripturae locum sic exponere potest, ut alteri contradicat. Quare licet Ecclesia sit divinorum librorum testis et conservatrix; attamen, ut adversus eos nihil decernere, ita praeter illos nihil credendum de necessitate salutis debet obtrudere.

Article XIX having defined the nature of the visible Church, Article XX goes on to consider the scope and limits of its authority in matters of faith and order.

The article as we have it today is a composite. The opening section (The Church...and yet), which seems to have been influenced by the article on the Church in the *Wurtemburg Confession,* has been added to the rest of the article, which was Article XXI of the *Forty Two Articles* and is almost identical to the statement on the limits of the authority of the Church in the *Reformatio Legum Ecclesiasticarum.*[551]

---

[551] Bray, *Tudor Church Reform*, p.181.

The authority of the opening section became a matter of dispute in the seventeenth century, with the argument being put forward by some on Puritan side that it had never been properly authorised by Convocation and even that it had been added to the text by Archbishop Laud.

The Puritan argument is supported by the fact that the section is not present in a number of early copies of the Articles. It is not present in:

• The Latin MS signed by Archbishop Parker and the other bishops on 29 January 1563.

• The English 'minute' of the Articles in the English State Papers dated 31 January 1563.

• The fair copy of this English minute, also among the state papers and entitled 'Articles of religion agreed on, 1562, in the Convocation house.'

• The English version of the Articles printed by Jugge and Cawood in 1563,

• The English MS of Archbishop Parker signed by the bishops in the Convocation of 1571.

• One Latin and one English edition, printed by Jugge and Cawood in 1571.

On the other hand, the additional section is present in:

• An early Latin draft of the Articles among the Elizabethan State Papers.

• The early Latin edition of Reynold Wolfe in 1563, explicitly authorised by the Queen.

• Two or more English edition of Jugge and Cawood in 1571.

• Six or more English editions from 1581-1628 and in all subsequent copies

- The transcript made by the public notary in 1637 from an original copy of the Articles deposited in the registry of the See of Canterbury.

The evidence of the manuscripts and the early printed editions of the Articles is thus divided. However, three considerations undermine the argument that the English and Latin manuscripts in the Parker collection present the final text of the Article XX as agreed by Convocation and authorised by the Crown: (1) these manuscripts are in what Hardwick calls a 'slovenly condition,' containing a variety of corrections, (2) they are in a private rather than an official archive and (3) they lack the normal indications that a text has royal authority.[552] In addition, the earliest printed edition that has the opening clause of Article XX (Wolfe's Latin text of 1563) has explicit royal authorisation, while the earliest edition that omits the clause (Jugge and Cawood's English text of 1563) lays no claim to any kind of royal or ecclesiastical sanction. Furthermore, the transcript made by the public notary in 1637, to which Archbishop Laud was able to appeal successfully in his trial in 1644, shows that Convocation had authorised a version of the Articles which included the opening words of Article XX.

All this evidence taken together indicates that there was a text of the Articles in circulation in 1563 in which Article XX lacked its current opening section. However, it also indicates that in the same year there was a text in circulation that did have this section and that it was this second, expanded, version of the text that was authorised the Crown and by Convocation and thus came to possess legal authority.

We do not know when the text was expanded or by whom. Hardwick suggests it may have been added in Convocation before the text of the Articles was submitted to the Queen for approval or that it may have been added while text was in the hands of the Royal Council.[553] However, in the absence of any definite evidence neither of these suggestions can be verified.

---

[552] Hardwick , op. cit. p.143.
[553] Ibid, p.144.

The Church hath power to decree rites or ceremonies and authority in controversies of faith

The purpose of the new opening section of the article is to respond to the arguments of those on the Protestant side of the Church who argued against the Elizabethan settlement of religion on the grounds that it involved the Church of England imposing rules that went beyond what could be derived directly from Scripture. As Burnet explains:

> As to the first part of the Article, concerning the power of the Church, either with relation to ceremonies or points of faith, the dispute lies only with those who deny all Church power, and think that Churches ought to be in all things limited by the rules set in Scripture; and that where the Scriptures are silent, there ought to be no rules made, but that all men should be left to their liberty; and in particular, that the appointing new ceremonies, looks like a reproach to the Apostles, as if their constitutions had been so defective, that those defects must be supplied by the inventions of men: which they oppose so much the more, because they think that all the corruptions of Popery began at some rites which seemed at first not only innocent, but pious; but were afterwards abused to superstition and idolatry, and swelled up to that bulk as to oppress and stifle true religion with their number and weight.[554]

In response to these arguments the opening section affirms that the Church does have authority in relation to both rites and ceremonies and controversies about faith.

The Church here means the Christian Church in general as opposed to 'particular or national' churches which are referred to in Article XXXIV. However, this does not mean that the English Reformers believed that only the Church as a whole could makes authoritative decisions about rites and ceremonies or matters of faith. At the Reformation the Church of England itself made decisions in both these areas and the English Reformers though that it was right to do so. For the English Reformers the Church existed at a variety of levels. It existed at the international level and on this level it could make decisions by means

---

[554] Burnet, op.cit., p.269.

of General Councils (something that is discussed in Article XXI), but it also existed at the national level and on this level it could make decisions through a properly constituted national council of the Church, which in the case of the Church of England meant the two Convocations meeting under the authority of the Crown.

It is not clear what the precise difference is between 'rites' and 'ceremonies.' One possibility is that 'rites' refers to particular events with religious significance and 'ceremonies' refers to the particular actions involved in these events. Thus an ordination would be a 'rite' and the questions and answers, the laying on of hands with prayer and giving of the Scriptures that take place during an ordination would be 'ceremonies.' Another possibility is that 'rites' refer to words and 'ceremonies' to accompanying actions.[555] A third possibility is that the two terms are simply synonymous. Whatever their precise meaning what is clear, however, is that 'rites and ceremonies' refer to outward activities performed corporately by Christians as part of their faith and the way that these outward activities take place.

'Controversies of faith' means disputes over the meaning of the Christian faith. Thus in terms of the Articles themselves, Articles XVI and XVII are concerned with 'controversies of faith' about post-baptismal sin and predestination respectively.

The claim that the Church has authority in these two areas follows on from what is said about the nature of the church in Article XIX. To quote Tyrell Green:

> The Church being a visible society of men, Divinely organised, it follows that there must be an inherent power of ordering whatever is necessary for the corporate life of her members; like other societies, she must have authority to enact and enforce the rules which her members are bound to observe.[556]

As Gibson notes in his commentary on this article, the fact that the Church has this authority in regard to rites and ceremonies is assumed throughout the Bible:

---

[555] Griffith Thomas, op.cit. p.283.
[556] Tyrell-Green, op.cit. p.135.

It obviously belonged to the Jewish Church. Although there was an elaborate ritual and ceremonial law with stated feasts ordained by God Himself, yet the Jewish Church claimed and exercised the power to add other feasts, such as Purim and Dedication, to those of Divine appointment. Our Lord's words, 'The scribes and Pharisees sit on Moses seat; all thing whatsoever they bid you, these do and observe' (Matthew 23:2-3), imply that power to make regulations still remained with the authorities; and we see from the Acts and the Epistles that when the Christian Church was established, such powers were exercised from the first in it as occasion required. Thus we find St. Paul incidentally laying down definite regulations in his Epistles on various details, e.g. that men are to worship with the head uncovered, women with the head covered (1 Corinthians 11); on the conduct of public worship by the prophets (1 Corinthians 14:27); that women are to keep silence in the churches (1 Corinthians 14:34; cf.1 Timothy 2:12). He lays down the general principle. 'Let all things be done decently and in order' (1 Corinthians 14:40) and appeals to the 'custom' of the Churches as if it were final and decisive and individuals ought to conform to it. 'If any man seemeth to be contentious, we have no other custom, neither the Churches of God.' (1 Corinthians 11:16).[557]

It could, of course, be argued that the Church's authority to make and enforce rules with regard to rites and ceremonies is now limited to those rules for Church order which are contained in the New Testament. This was precisely the argument developed by some of the Puritan theologians at the end of the 16th century, but as Richard Hooker argues at length in *The Laws of Ecclesiastical Polity* this argument is problematic because (a) there is nothing in Scripture itself to suggest that this is the case and (b) the New Testament simply does not provide us with a detailed and comprehensive blueprint covering all the possible future activities of the Church.[558]

Given the absence of a detailed blueprint, the Church has to decide what rites and ceremonies would, in a specific set of circumstances, best give expression to the overall biblical message and to

---

[557] Gibson, op.cit. p.517.
[558] Hooker, *Laws of Ecclesiastical Polity*, Bks II-III.

those specific statements relating to Church order that the Bible does contain. It is as it does this that it exercises its proper God given authority in this area.

As Browne notes in his commentary on this article, the Bible also implies that the Church has authority in matters of faith:

> The Church is a society founded by God, for the very purpose of preserving, maintaining, and propagating the truth. If she had no power to discern truth from error, how would this be possible? Her ministers are enjoined to teach and preach the truth of the Gospel; not simply to put the Bible into the hands of the people and leave them to read it. Their commission is. 'Go and teach all nations...teaching them to observe all things whatsoever I have commanded you' (Matthew 28:19-20). They are 'by sound doctrine to convince the gainsayers' (Titus 1:9). They are 'to feed the Church of God' (Acts 20:28): to give 'the household of God their portion of meat in due season' (Luke 12:42). The chief pastors of the Church are to 'commit to faithful men, who shall be able to teach others also' that truth which they have themselves received (2 Timothy 2:2). And they are enjoined to 'rebuke men sharply, that they may be sound in the faith.' (Titus 1:13).
>
> All this implies authority – authority to declare truth, to maintain truth, to discern truth from error, to judge when controversies arise, whether one party is heretical or not, and to reject from communion such as are in grievous falsehood and error. [559]

Just as in matters to do with rites and ceremonies the Church is not limited to what is explicitly laid down in the Bible, so also in matters to with faith the Church is not limited to simply repeating what is explicitly said in Scripture. In order to make the meaning of the Bible clear and to refute those who misinterpret it the Church has the freedom to summarise and paraphrase biblical teaching and to use technical terms such as the Trinity, the two natures of Christ and original sin which are not to be found in the Bible itself. We can see the Church doing this in the

---

[559] Browne, op.cit. p.477.

Catholic Creeds mentioned in Article VIII and this is what the Church of England is doing in the Articles.

...and yet it is not lawful for the Church to ordain anything contrary to God's word written, neither may it so expound one place of Scripture, that it be repugnant to another

However, although the Church does have the degree of freedom with regard to rites and ceremonies and matters of faith that has just been described there are two key limits to what the Church has the authority to do.

First, in terms of rites and ceremonies it cannot put in place anything that is directly contrary to Scripture. Scripture is 'God's word written.' As such it carries God's own authority and so for the Church to ordain anything against Scripture would be to for the Church to seek to place its own authority above the authority of God himself and that is something that the Church is not free to do. Thus for the English Reformers the form of the liturgy and the use of vestments were matters on which the Church was competent to decide, but the Church could not sanction the worship of images or the adoration of the host since this would be contrary to the second commandment (see Articles XXII and XXVIII)

Secondly, in expounding Scripture the Church is not free to emphasise one part of Scripture in such away that it contradicts another. Thus, in terms of issues highlighted in the articles, the Church is not free so to emphasise the biblical teaching about Christ's humanity as to contradict his divinity or so to emphasise his divinity as to contradict his humanity (Article II). Likewise the Church is not free so to emphasise the importance of good works as to obscure the fact that we are justified by faith or so to emphasise the importance of faith as to imply that good works do not matter (Articles XI and XII).

As O'Donovan explains, the logic behind the Reformers' inclusion of this second prohibition is that this prohibition is necessary in order to uphold the authority of Scripture:

> Unless we can think that Scripture is readable as whole, that it communicates a unified outlook and perspective, we cannot attribute doctrinal authority to it, but only to some part of it at the cost of some other part. The authority of Scripture, then,

presupposes the possibility of a harmonious reading; correspondingly, a church which presumes to offer an unharmonious or diversifying reading may be supposed to have in mind an indirect challenge to the authority of Scripture itself.[560]

Wherefore, although the Church be a witness and a keeper of Holy Writ: yet, as it ought not to decree anything against the same, so besides the same ought it not to enforce anything to be believed for necessity of salvation.

This last section of Article XX begins by affirming the positive role that Church has in relation to Scripture. It tells us that the Church is 'a witness and keeper of Holy Writ.' What this means is helpfully expounded by Browne:

> We, the children of the Church, must, in the first instance at least, receive the word of God from her. She, by our parents and her ministers, puts the Bible into our hands, even before we could seek it for ourselves. To her care the Lord has entrusted it. She keeps it, and testifies to us that it is the word of God, and teaches us the truths contained in it. Her ministers are enjoined 'to hold fast the form of sound words' (2 Timothy 1:13); 'to preach the word instant in season and out of season' (2 Timothy 4:2). And so she leads, by preaching and catechizing, and other modes of instruction, to take the Bible in our hands and read it for ourselves.
>
> In these and many similar modes, the Church is a witness, as well as a keeper of Holy Writ. We can hardly conceive of a state of things in which it could be otherwise. If the Church had not carefully guarded the Scriptures at first, they would have been scattered and lost, and spurious writings would have partially taken the place of the true. If she did not, by her teaching and her ministry, witness to us that the Scriptures were from above and so lead us to read and reverence them; we should be obliged to wait till the full maturity of reason and manhood, before we could learn what was the word of truth; and should then have patiently to go through for ourselves all the evidence, which might be

---

[560] O'Donovan, op.cit. p.57.

necessary to convince us, that the Bible, and not the Koran or the Veda was that which contained 'the lively oracles of God.'[561]

However ('yet') the fact that God has in this sense entrusted the Bible to the Church does not mean that the Church has authority over or alongside the Bible. Because the Bible is 'God's word written,' the Church does not has the right to nullify the authority of Scripture by decreeing on its own authority something contrary to what the Bible says. Because the Bible contains 'all things necessary to salvation' (Article VI) the Church does not have the right to decree that anything that is not in Scripture has to be believed or observed in order for people to be saved. The authority of the Church is always a derivative authority that is dependent on its fidelity to its role as a witness and keeper of Holy Scripture. In the words of O'Donovan:

> The church's authority never floats free of Scripture, and can never be posited independently of Scripture, as though it could dispense with its text and establish its own commentary irrespective of what the text contained.[562]

---

[561] Browne, op.cit. pp.474-475. It might be objected that Browne give insufficient weight to the testimony of the Holy Spirit in assuring us that these writings are God's word written. However, his basic point would still stand, as it is the normally the testimony of the Church that leads people to read the Bible and so receive the witness of the Spirit.

[562] O'Donovan, op.cit. p. 115.

Article XXI

∞

Of the Authority of General Councils

General Councils may not be gathered together without the commandment and will of princes. And when they be gathered together, forasmuch as they be an assembly of men, whereof all be not governed with the Spirit and word of God, they may err and sometime have erred, even in things pertaining to God. Wherefore things ordained by them as necessary to salvation have neither strength nor authority, unless it may be declared that they be taken out of Holy Scripture.

De auctoritate Conciliorum Generalium

Generalia Concilia sine iussu et voluntate principum congregari non possunt. Et ubi convenerint, quia ex hominibus constant, qui non omnes Spiritu et verbo Dei reguntur, et errare possunt, et interdum errarunt, etiam in his quae ad normam pietatis pertinent. Ideoque quae ab illis constituuntur, ut ad salutem necessaria, neque robur habent neque auctoritatem nisi ostendi possint e sacris literis esse desumpta.

This article was originally Article XXII of the *Forty Two Articles*. It has not been traced to any earlier source. There have been some slight changes in both the English and Latin versions. In the English version of 1553 the words 'not only in worldly things, but also' preceded the words 'in things pertaining to God.' There was no equivalent to these words in the Latin version and in 1563 they were dropped and 'even' was added. In the Latin versions of 1553 and 1563 the second sentence read 'verbis Dei' ('words of God') in 1571 this was brought into line with the English version by being altered to 'verbo Dei' ('word of God').

What is said in Article XXI closely parallels what is said about the councils of the Church in the *Reformatio Legum Ecclesiasticarum*:

> Although we freely grant great honour to the councils, and especially to the ecumenical ones, yet we judge that all of them must be placed far below the dignity of the canonical Scriptures, and even among the councils themselves we make a huge distinction. For some of them, such as the special four, Nicaea, the first of Constantinople, Ephesus and Chalcedon, we embrace and accept with great reverence. And we make the same judgement with regard to many others which were held later on, in which we see and confess that the most holy fathers determined many things, in a most serious and holy manner, concerning the blessed and highest Trinity, our Lord and Saviour Jesus Christ, and the redemption of mankind procured by him. But we do not regard them as binding on our faith except in so far as they can be proved out of the Holy Scriptures. For it is most obvious that some councils have occasionally erred, and defined things which are contrary to each other, partly in actions and partly even in faith. Therefore the councils are to be studied with honour and Christian reverence, but at the same time are to be tested against the godly, certain and right rule of the Scriptures.[563]

Article XXI follows on from the previous article because it, too, is concerned with the relation of the authority of the Church to the authority of Scripture. As Griffith Thomas explains:

> It is placed here because General councils were one important way of expressing Church Authority, and thus the Article is one application of the principles laid down in Article XX. Since the Church has authority, we ask how it has been sought and its decisions declared, and we naturally turn to those General Councils where it has been expressed and exercised.[564]

The question of the authority of General Councils was of particular importance to the English Reformers at the time when Article XXI was

---

[563] Bray, *Tudor Church Reform*, p.183.
[564] Griffith Thomas, op.cit. p.291.

drawn up. This was for three reasons. First, those who remained loyal to Rome appealed to the authority of the Councils of the Medieval Church in support of the Roman position on matters such as the number of the sacraments, the doctrine of transubstantiation, and the denial of the cup to the laity at Holy Communion. Secondly, it was suggested at the time of the Reformation that the holding of a General Council would be the proper way to end the divisions in the Church. Thirdly, Pope Paul III had summoned what he declared to be a General Council of the Church, the Council of Trent, in 1545 and this continued to meet and to define matters of faith and order raised by the Reformation until 1563.

In the face of all these three attempts to appeal to a General Council to settle the issues raised by the Reformation, it was necessary for the Church of England to declare what it thought of the authority of General Councils and so that is what Article XXI does.

General Councils may not be gathered together without the commandment and will of princes.

The term 'General Council' is used here to refer to an international gathering representing the Church as a whole as opposed to a more local national, provincial or diocesan council.

The statement that such a council 'may not be gathered together without the commandment and will of princes' can be understood in two ways.

First, it can be understood as being simply a statement of the political reality of the 16th century. Pope Paul III and his successors were only able to hold the Council of Trent because of the agreement of the Holy Roman Emperor and other Catholic monarchs and if a more general Council of the Church had been held in the 16th century it would also have required the approval of the European monarchs of the time. For example, no bishops of the Church of England would have been able to attend such a Council without the approval of Elizabeth I.

However, this opening statement is not simply a declaration of political reality. It also expresses the belief that the authority given to kings and princes by God in Scripture extends to the calling of General Councils of the Church. This point is made by Thomas Rogers, the earliest commentator on the Articles. He declares:

Great is the power and authority of kings and princes by the word of God. For, as the defence of religion is committed to them, so must they see that all men do their duties. That these things the better may be performed, they are, as just occasion is offered, not as men under the power of others, to summon, but as supreme governors within their own territories and dominions, to command all sorts of men to meet together: and that either to the implanting of truth where it is not, or to the suppressing of sin, errors, idolatry, and superstition, where or in whomsoever it doth arise or is rooted. Such councils were holden, both in the time of the Mosaical government by the commandment of the most godly kings, David, Solomon, Asa, Hezakiah and Josiah (1 Chronicles 28:1, 1 Kings 8:1, 2 Chronicles 15:9, 29:4 and 34:29) ; and since the gospel hath been received into kingdoms and commonweals, by Christian princes, kings and emperors, who gathered councils both general, as the Nicene was by Constantine the Great, the Council of Constantinople by Theodosius the elder, the council of Ephesus by Theodosius the younger, the council of Chalcedon by Marcian; and national and provincial; so the council at Franckfort, Rhemes, Turon, Arelate and Moguntia, by the will and council of Charles the Great; at Matison by Gunthranus, at Paris and Orleans, by the direction and appointment of Childebert, were kept and holden.

And never yet hath there been a council, either general or national, or whatsoever (I only except the councils held by the apostles and apostolical men in a troublesome state and time of the church, there being then no Christian princes and emperors to countenance the truth,) either begun or ended to the glory of God, but it hath been, I say not called only, but confirmed also by some godly emperor, king or queen.[565]

The use of the term 'supreme governors' in this quotation is significant. This is the term that was used by Elizabeth I in the Art of Uniformity of 1559 to describe her authority in relation to the Church of England.[566] Rogers is therefore making the point that there is a continuity between the role attributed to the English monarch in relation to the Church of

---

[565] Rogers, op.cit. p.205.
[566] See Bray, *Documents of the English Reformation*, p.319.

England by the settlement of religion in 1559 and the role attributed to kings and princes in general in relation to General Councils in Article XXI. This also means that there is continuity between what is said about the role of princes in Article XXI and what is said about the role of the English monarch in Article XXXVII. Both express the belief that the God given authority of kings and princes extends also to the oversight of the Church.

And when they be gathered together, forasmuch as they be an assembly of men, whereof all be not governed with the Spirit and word of God, they may err and sometime have erred, even in things pertaining to God.

What is said in this section of the article reflects what is said elsewhere in the Articles about the nature of the visible Church and the persistence of sin even in believers. As we have seen, Article XIX affirms the liability to error of particular churches. If we ask why they are liable to err the answer is given firstly in Article XXVI which declares that 'in the visible Church the evil be ever mingled with the good' and secondly in Articles IX, XV and XVI which affirms the continuing presence of sin even in those who have been reborn in Christ. Churches which are made up of people who are all affected to a greater or lesser extent by sin are bound to err because sin will inevitably lead people to turn away from God and what God wants either in their thinking or their actions or both. Councils of the Church, being made up of those who belong to the visible churches, also consist of sinners and therefore they too are liable to err.

The traditional response to the position taken in Article XXI is to say that in spite of the presence of sin in the Church in general the leaders of the Church are preserved from error when they gather together in Council. However, As Browne observes in his commentary on this article, there seems to be no biblical basis for this response:

> There is no distinct promise of infallibility to councils in Scripture. Nay! There is probably no distinct allusion to councils at all. To the bishops and rulers of the Church indeed there is a promise of guidance and presence, and Christians are enjoined to 'obey' and 'follow the faith' of those who have the rule over them (Hebrews 13:7 and 17 Compare Acts 20:28-31, Titus 1:13, 3:10 etc).Hence the judgement of our own spiritual guides is much to be attended to; and when our spiritual rulers meet together and agree on

matters either of doctrine or of discipline, there is no question, but that their decisions are worthy of all consideration and respect. Yet infallibility is certainly not promised to any one bishop or pastor, and though they are assured of Christ's presence and guidance, yet promises of this kind are all more or less conditional; and it is only to the universal Church that the assurance belongs 'the gates of hell shall not prevail against it.' Individual bishops, we know, may err. Hence assemblies of individual bishops may err; because, thought they have the grace of ordination, yet all may not be pious men, 'governed with the spirit and word of God.'[567]

Article XXI not only affirms the theoretical possibility that General Councils may err, but it also affirms that they have in fact erred 'even in things pertaining to God,' that is to say, in relation to matters that lie at the very heart of the faith. Neither the article nor the corresponding section of the *Reformatio Legum Ecclesiasticarum* specify which Councils have erred. However, it is not difficult to find examples of Councils which, from the perspective of the theology of the English Reformers, provide examples of error.

In the Patristic period:

- The Council of Ariminum in 350 secured a temporary triumph for Arianism, thus going against the doctrine of the Trinity as expounded in Article I.

- The Council of Ephesus in 449 declared in favour of the doctrine known as Eutychianism which held that Christ's humanity was swallowed up in his divinity, thus going against the permanence of Christ's humanity as upheld in Articles II and IV.

- The Second Council of Nicaea in 787 agreed that it was legitimate to give adoration to sacred images, something rejected in Article XXII.

In the Medieval period:

---

[567] Browne, op. cit, p.487.

- The Fourth Lateran Council of 1215 taught the doctrine of the transubstantiation of the elements at the Holy Communion, a belief rejected as unbiblical in Article XXVIII.

- The Council of Constance in 1414 taught that the cup should not be given to the laity at Holy Communion, something that is rejected as an error in Article XXX.

- The Council of Florence in 1439 taught belief in purgatory and in the existence of seven sacraments, teachings rejected in Articles XXII and XXV respectively.

Wherefore things ordained by them as necessary to salvation have neither strength nor authority, unless it may be declared that they be taken out of Holy Scripture.

Because Councils are liable to error and have erred their decisions cannot be regarded as being automatically correct ('wherefore'). It follows that there needs to be some criterion for deciding which of their decisions are correct and which are not. In line with what has already been said in Articles VI and XX, the article therefore declares that the touchstone for deciding whether or not matters decided by them have 'strength' or 'authority' is the teaching of Holy Scripture.

Like Articles VI and XX, Article XXI focuses on the issue of matters 'necessary for salvation.' In the case of what is said in this article this is because a key point of contention between those who supported the English Reformation and those who remained loyal to Rome was precisely the issue of whether it was necessary to accept the teaching of the those Councils that propagated beliefs and practices accepted by Rome but not by the Reformers, or else be a heretic and therefore liable to damnation. The response of the Church of England as set out in this article is that someone wishing to be saved is under no necessity to accept the teaching of these Councils unless it can be shown (as in fact it cannot be) that their teaching has a biblical basis.

In the words of Beveridge in his commentary on this article:

What is not contained in the scriptures, nor may be proved from them, though all the councils in the world should ordain it as necessary to salvation, their ordaining it as necessary to salvation cannot make it so.[568]

Note: The attitude of the Church of England to the First Four Councils

As we have seen, the *Reformatio Legum Ecclesiasticarum* declares that Church of England regards the first four General Councils as 'special' and views them with 'great reverence.' In line with this declaration Church of England theology from that time onwards has tended to focus on the importance of the first four Councils. That is why, for example, Anglican textbooks on Patristic theology have tended to concentrate on the first five centuries and the teaching of the first four councils.

However, this does not mean that at the Reformation the Church of England made an absolute distinction between the first four Councils and all subsequent ones. Thus the *Reformatio Legum Ecclesiasticarum*, having declared its reverence for the first four Councils, goes on to say that 'we make the same judgement with regard to many others which were held later on.'

The reason that the Tudor Church of England did not make an absolute distinction between the first four Councils and those that came later was because its criterion for judging a Council was whether or not the teaching of a Council was faithful to Scripture. The Church of England believed that the teaching of the first four Councils concerning the Trinity and the Person of Christ met this criterion, but so did the teaching of later Councils on these and other subjects. In so far as this was the case the teaching of these later Councils was also worthy of reverence. What mattered was not the number of a Council, but the biblical nature of its teaching. Thus an Act of Parliament in the first year of Elizabeth I's reign (1 Eliz. Cap.1.) states:

> ...nothing is to be adjudged heresy, but that which heretofore has been so adjudged by the authority of the Canonical Scriptures, or the first four General Councils, or some other General Council, wherein the same has been declared heresy by the express word of Holy Scripture.[569]

---

[568] Beveridge, op.cit. p. 397.
[569] Gibson, op.cit, p.536.

It is also worth noting that the homily 'Against Peril of Idolatry' in the *Second Book of Homilies* talks about 'six councils which were allowed and received of all men'[570] and that among sixteenth and seventeenth century Church of England theologians Richard Hooker and Lancelot Andrewes accorded special significance to the first four Councils, but Richard Field and Henry Hammond accorded special significance to the first six.[571] This indicates that although there was a general tendency to grant particular significance to the first four Councils there was a continuing diversity of opinion about the matter.

---

[570] *The Homilies*, p.144
[571]Gibson, op.cit, p.536

Errors to be avoided in the Church: Articles XXII-XXIV

This is the second set of articles concerning the Church. It deals with errors stemming from those loyal to Rome on the one hand and from some of the radical Protestant groups on the other.

Article XXII gives an example of the misuse of Church authority by rejecting the teaching upheld by those who had remained loyal to Rome concerning purgatory, pardons the use of images and the invocation of the saints. It contends that this teaching is not only unsupported by, but contrary to, the teaching of Scripture.

Article XXIII rejects the arguments of those Protestants who held that they had the right to minister in the Church solely on the basis of their own conviction that they have been called to do so. It declares that those who minister in the Church need to be 'lawfully called and sent.'

Article XXIV returns to the position taken by those who remained loyal to Rome, arguing against them that the traditional Medieval practice of using Latin rather than the vernacular as the language of the liturgy was illegitimate.

Article XXII

∞

Of Purgatory

The Romish doctrine concerning Purgatory, Pardons, worshipping and adoration as well of Images as of Reliques, and also Invocation of Saints, is a fond thing vainly invented, and grounded upon no warranty of Scripture; but rather repugnant to the word of God.

De Purgatorio

Doctrina Romanensium de Purgatorio, de Indulgentiis, de veneratione tum Imaginum tum Reliquiarum, nec non de Invocatione Sanctorum, res est futilis, inaniter conflicta, et nullis Scripturarum testimoniis innititur; imo verbo Dei contradicit.

This article was originally Article XXIII of the *Forty Two Articles*. There were two changes to the article in the 1563 revision of the Articles. Firstly the words 'Romish doctrine' (Doctrina Romanensium) was substituted for 'the doctrine of school-authors' (doctrina scholasticorum). The purpose of this substitution was to make it clear that the article was not condemning simply the erroneous teaching of certain theologians of the Middle Ages, but also the contemporary teaching of the Church of Rome and those who remained loyal to her. Secondly the word 'perniciose' (pernicious) which had no equivalent in the English version of the article was dropped before 'contradicit' at the end of the Latin text. It was presumably judged superfluous on the grounds that anything 'repugnant to the word of God' must necessarily be pernicious.

The purpose of the article is to reject a series of beliefs which were central to the piety of the Medieval English Church,[572] but which the

---

[572] See E Duffy, *The Stripping of the Altars*, New Haven and London: Yale University Press, 1992, Part I.

English Reformers believed were contrary to biblical teaching. As Griffith Thomas notes, this article follows on from the previous two because it:

> ....deals with certain doctrines set forth by Church and conciliar authority, which are here condemned as unscriptural. Thus they afford an example of the wrong use of that Church authority stated in Articles XX and XXI.[573]

The title of the article is not an accurate summary of its contents. It seems to have been chosen because purgatory is the first item on the list of beliefs rejected by the article. A modern equivalent to the title would be 'Of Purgatory etc.'

...a fond thing vainly invented, and grounded upon no warranty of Scripture; but rather repugnant to the word of God.

The word 'fond' is used here in its old sense of 'credulous' or 'foolish' and 'vainly' means 'pointlessly or 'without purpose'. The sense of the final clause of the article would thus be brought out by its being paraphrased as '(doctrines which) have no grounding in Scripture, but are rather repugnant to Scripture and which are therefore foolish and invented to no purpose.'

Purgatory

As Burnet explains, the doctrine of purgatory rejected by the article is the belief that:

> ...every man is liable to both temporal and eternal punishment for his sins; that God, upon the account of the death and the intercession of Christ, does indeed pardon sin as to its eternal punishment; but the sinner is still liable to temporal punishment, which he must expiate by acts of penance and sorrow in this world, together with such other sufferings as God shall think fit to lay upon him: but if he does not expiate these in this life, there is a state of misery and suffering in the next world, where the soul is

---

[573] Griffith Thomas, op.cit. p.298.

to bear the temporal punishment of its sins; which may continue longer or shorter, till the day of judgement.[574]

The reason why the English Reformers believed this belief to be unbiblical is explained in the homily 'Of Prayer' in the *Second Book of Homilies*. The third part of this homily addresses the question of whether it is right to pray for the dead. It argues that it is not right to do so, declaring that the dead are beyond the help of the living:

> ...let us not deceive ourselves, thinking that either we may help other, or other may help us by their good and charitable prayers in time to come. For, as the Preacher saith, *When the tree falleth, whether it be toward the south or toward the north, in what place soever the tree falleth, there it lieth* (Ecclesiastes 11.3); meaning thereby, that every mortal man dieth either in the state of salvation or damnation, according as the words of the Evangelist John do also plainly import, saying, *He that believeth on the Son of God hath eternal life, but he that believeth not on the Son shall never see life but the wrath of God abideth upon him* (John 3.36). Where is then the third place which they call purgatory? Or where shall our prayers help and profit the dead?[575]

The homily also declares that the only true purgatory is the death of Christ and no other purgation is either necessary or possible:

> The only purgatory wherein, we must trust to be saved, is the death and blood of Christ; which if we apprehend with a true and steadfast faith, it purgeth and cleanseth us from all our sins (1 John 1.7), even as well as if he were now hanging upon the cross. *The blood of Christ,* saith St. John, *hath cleansed us from all sin.* The blood of Christ, saith St. Paul, *hath purged our consciences from dead works to serve the living God* (Hebrews 9.14). Also in another place he saith, *We be sanctified* and made holy *by the offering up of the body of Jesus Christ done once for all* (Hebrews 10.10). Yea, he addeth more, saying, *With the one oblation of his blessed body and precious blood, he hath made perfect for ever and ever all them that*

---

[574] Burner, op.cit. pp.290-291.
[575] *The Homilies*, p. 242

are sanctified (Hebrews 10.14). This then is that purgatory, wherein all Christian men put their whole trust and confidence, nothing doubting, but if they truly repent them of their sins, and die in perfect faith, that then they shall forthwith pass from death to life.

If this kind of purgation will not serve them, let them never hope to be released by other men's prayers, though they should continue therein unto the world's end. He that cannot be saved by faith in Christ's blood, how shall he look to be delivered by man's intercessions? Hath God more respect to man on earth, than he hath to Christ in heaven? *If any man sin*, saith St. John *we have an Advocate with the Father, even Jesus Christ the righteous, and he is the propitiation for our sins"* (1 John 2.1). But we must take heed that we call upon this Advocate, while we have space given us in this life, lest when we are once dead, there be no hope of salvation left unto us. For as every man sleepeth with his own cause, so every man shall rise again with his own cause. And look in what state he dieth, in the same state he shall be also judged, whether it be to salvation, or damnation.[576]

In summary, for the English Reformers there were only two destinations for the dead, heaven or hell, the fate of the departed was fixed at the point of death and the blessed dead had no need of further purgation because they have been perfectly cleansed from their sin by the work of Christ and once they die they enter fully into this perfection. This belief is further reflected in the burial service in the *Book of Common Prayer* which declares that 'the souls of the faithful, after they are delivered from the burden of the flesh, are in joy and felicity.'

Pardons

'Pardons' refers to the doctrine of indulgences that we looked at in connection with Article XIV, the doctrine that the merits of the saints together with merits of the Mother of God and the superabundant merit of Christ constituted a 'a treasury of merit' which the Church could apply to the relief of the punishments being suffered by those in purgatory. The English Reformers rejected this belief for two reasons. Firstly, as we have

---

[576] *The Homilies*, p.243.

just seen they did not believe that there is such a place as purgatory. Secondly, as we saw when looking at Article XIV, they held that because the Saints were also sinners and their best deeds were simply acts of obedience owed to God they did not have an excess of merit that could be applied to meet the spiritual needs of others.

worshipping and adoration as well of Images as of Reliques

What is rejected here is the use in Christian worship of any images of God, Christ or the saints, whether two or three dimensional, and any adoration of the relics of the saints.

The reason for the rejection of the use of images and relics is set out in detail in the sixty nine pages of the homily 'Against Peril of Idolatry.' This homily makes four key points against the use of images, which, it says, are idols under another name.

Firstly, it argues that images are forbidden by God in the Old Testament:

> For when God had chosen to himself a peculiar and special people from amongst all other nations that knew not God, but worshipped idols and false gods, he gave unto them certain ordinances and laws to be kept and observed of his said people. But concerning none other matter did he give either more or more earnest and express laws to his said people, than those that concerned the true worshipping of him, and the avoiding and fleeing of idols and images, and idolatry for that, both the said idolatry is most repugnant to the right worshipping of him and his true glory, above all other vices, and that he knew the proneness and inclination of man's corrupt kind and nature, to that most odious and abominable vice.[577]

In support of this argument it cites a range of Old Testament texts such as Exodus 20:4-5, Deuteronomy 4:25-28, Psalm 97:7, Isaiah 40:18-21 and Ezekiel 6:3-7.

Secondly, it declares that the use of images is also rejected by the New Testament:

---

[577] Ibid, p.126.

...the scriptures of the New Testament do in sundry places make mention with rejoicing, as for a most excellent benefit and gift of God, that they which received the faith of Christ, were *turned from their dumb* and dead *images, unto the true and living God, who is* to be *blessed for ever* (Romans 1:25), namely in these places, the fourteenth and seventeenth of the Acts of the Apostles (Acts 14:15, 17:30) the eleventh to the Romans (Romans 11:30), the first Epistle to the Corinthians, the twelfth chapter (1 Corinthians 12:2-3), to the Galatians, the fourth (Galatians 4:8-9), and the first to the Thessalonians, the first chapter (1 Thessalonians 8-9).

And in likewise the said idols or images, and worshipping of them, are, in the scriptures of the New Testament, by the Spirit of God much abhorred and detested, and earnestly forbidden: as appeareth both in the forenamed places, and also many other besides, as in the seventh and fifteenth of the Acts of the Apostles (Acts 7:41-42, 15:20,29), the first to the Romans, where is set forth the horrible plague of idolaters, given over by God *into a reprobate sense* to work all wickedness and abominations not to be spoken, as usually spiritual and carnal fornication go together (Romans 1:23-32). In the first Epistle to the Corinthians, the fifth chapter, we are forbidden once to keep company, or to eat and drink with such as be called brethren or Christians that do worship images (1 Corinthians 5:11). In the fifth to the Galatians, the worshipping of images is numbered amongst the *works of the flesh* (Galatians 5:20), and in the first to the Corinthians it is called the service of devils, and that such as use it, shall be destroyed (1 Corinthians 10:20-22). And in the sixth chapter of the said Epistle, and the fifth to the Galatians, is denounced, *that such image worshippers shall never come into the inheritance of the kingdom of heaven* (1 Corinthians 6:9-10,Galatians 5:20-21) And in sundry other places is threatened, that the *wrath of God shall come upon all such*. And therefore St. John in his Epistle exhorteth us as his *dear children to beware of images* (1 John 5:21).[578]

Thirdly, it contends that the Early Church followed the position taken in the Old and New Testaments, stating that that the testimony of 'the old

---

[578] Ibid, pp.132-133.

learned and godly doctors of the Church' and of 'ancient histories ecclesiastical,' shows that in agreement with biblical teaching:

> ...images and image worshipping were in the primitive Church (which was most pure and uncorrupt) abhorred and detested, as abominable and contrary to true Christian religion. And that when images began to creep into the Church, they were not only spoken and written against by godly and learned bishops, doctors, and clerks but also condemned by whole councils of bishops and learned men assembled together, yea, the said images by many Christian emperors and bishops were defaced, broken, and destroyed, and that above seven hundred and eight hundred years ago, and that therefore it is not of late days (as some would bear you in hand) that images and image worshipping have been spoken and written against.[579]

Fourthly, it notes that experience shows that the worship[580] of images in the Church leads people to exactly the sort of pagan idolatry condemned in Scripture. Having outlined the similarities between the descriptions of the worship of pagan idols in Scripture and the Fathers and the practices of those who worship images within the Church, the homily states:

> Wherefore, when we see men and women on heaps to go on pilgrimage to images, kneel before them, hold up their hands before them, set up candles, burn incense before them, offer up gold and silver unto them, hang up ships, crouches, chains, men and women of wax before them, attributing health and safeguard, the gifts of God, to them, or the saints whom they represent, as they rather would have it: who I say, who can doubt, but that our image maintainers, agreeing in all idolatrous opinions, outward rites, and ceremonies with the Gentile idolaters, agree also with them in committing most abominable idolatry?[581]

---

[579] Ibid, p.152.
[580] The homily rejects any distinction between worship and adoration, arguing that they are simply two names for the same thing.
[581] Ibid, p.167.

With regard to the worship of the relics of the saints, the homily goes on to maintain that this is something that is even worse than the idolatry of the pagans:

> But in this they pass the folly and wickedness of the Gentiles: that they honour and worship the reliques and bones of our Saints, which prove that they be mortal men, and dead, and therefore no gods to be worshipped, which the gentiles would never confess of their gods for very shame. But the reliques we must kiss and offer unto, specially on Relique Sunday. And while we offer, that we should not be weary or repent us of our cost, the music and minstrelsy goeth merrily, all the offertory time, with praising and calling upon those saints, whose relics be then in presence. Yea, and the water also wherein those relics have been dipped, must with great reverence be reserved, as very holy and effectuous. Is this agreeable to St. Chrysostom, who writeth thus of reliques? (Chrysostom, *Homily of the Seven Macabees*): "Do not regard the ashes of the saints' bodies, nor the relics of their flesh and bones, consumed with time: but open the eyes of thy faith, and behold them clad with heavenly virtue, and the grace of the Holy Ghost, and shining with the brightness of the heavenly light." But our idolaters found too much vantage of relics and relic water, to follow St. Chrysostom's counsel.[582]

According the homily, what the cult of relics shows is that:

> ...our image-maintainers have not only made images, and set them up in temples, as did the gentiles' idolaters their idols, but also that they have had the same idolatrous opinions of the saints, to whom they have made images, which the Gentiles' idolaters had of their false gods, and have not only worshipped their images with the same rites, ceremonies, superstition, and all circumstances, as did the gentiles' idolaters their idols, but in many points also have far exceeded them in all wickedness, foolishness, and madness.[583]

---

[582] Ibid, p.168
[583] Ibid, p.169.

Invocation of Saints

The practice of the invocation of the Saints was based on the belief that being holy people, who had gone into the direct presence of God but who still cared for Christians undergoing the trials of life in this world, the saints would take the prayers of the faithful to God and that this would be more efficacious than if the faithful prayed to God directly.

In the homily 'Of Prayer' this argument is rejected completely. It argues that the Bible and the Fathers both teach us that God can and should be prayed to directly. Its conclusion is:

> Let us not therefore put our trust or confidence in the Saints, or Martyrs that be dead. Let us not call upon them nor desire help at their hands: but let us always lift up our hearts to God in the name of his dear Son Christ for whose sake as God hath promised to hear our prayers, so he will truly perform it. Invocation is a thing proper unto God: which if we attribute unto the Saints, it soundeth to their reproach, neither can they well bear it at our hands. When Paul had healed a certain lame man which was impotent in his feet, at Lystra, the people would have done sacrifice to him and Barnabas; who, rending their clothes, refused it, and exhorted them to worship the true God (Acts 14:8-18). Likewise in the Revelation, when St. John fell before the angel's feet to worship him, the angel would not permit him to do it, but commanded him that he should *worship God* (Revelation 19:10, 22:8-9). [584]

These examples, it says:

> ...declare unto us that the saints, and angels in heaven, will not have us to do any honour unto them that is due and proper unto God. He only is our Father; he only is omnipotent; he only knoweth and understandeth all things; he only can help us at all times and in all places; *he suffereth the sun to shine upon the good and the bad, he feedeth the young ravens that cry unto him, he saveth both man and beast, he will not that any one hair of our head shall perish* (Matthew 5:45, Ps 147:9, 36:6, Luke 12:7,

---

[584] Ibid, p.137

21:18), but is always ready to help and preserve all them that put their trust in him according as he hath promised, saying, *Before they call, I will answer, and whiles they speak, I will hear* (Isaiah 65.24). Let us not, therefore, anything mistrust his goodness; let us not fear to come before the throne of his mercy; let us not seek the aid and help of saints; but *let us come boldly ourselves* (Hebrews 4:16, 10:19-23), nothing doubting but God for Christ's sake, *in whom he is well pleased* (Matthew 17:5), will hear us without a spokesman and accomplish our desire in all such things as shall be agreeable to his most holy will.[585]

For all these reasons, therefore, the practices specified in Article XXII were seen by the English Reformers as repugnant to biblical teaching and were therefore abolished by the Church of England under Edward VI and Elizabeth I.[586]

Note 1: The development of the teaching of the Church of England after the breach with Rome

Even after the Church of England had rejected the authority of the Church of Rome it initially maintained traditional medieval practice in the areas covered by Article XXII while modifying the theology popularly attached to them.

Thus the *Ten Articles* of 1536 allowed the use of images and the honouring of the Saints providing it was made clear that the images and Saints were not be worshipped, but were to be used as teaching aids to provide people with good examples of what it meant to live the Christian life. They also allowed people to continue to pray to the Saints, providing it was made clear that they would not hear the faithful more quickly that Christ himself and that particular Saints should not be approached for particular needs, and for the dead, although admitting that the precise location or state of the dead was something that Scripture did not make clear.[587]

A similar line was also taken towards the veneration of the Saints and the use of Images in the three additional Articles composed by

---

[585] Ibid, p.137.
[586] See Duffy, op.cit. Pt II for details.
[587] Bray, *Documents of the English Reformation*, pp. 171-174.

Cranmer alongside the *Thirteen Articles* of 1538.[588] By the time of Edward VI, however, the thinking of Cranmer and others in the leadership of the Church of England had moved in a much more firmly Protestant direction on these matters and the position taken in Article XXIII of the *Forty Two Articles* and subsequently in Article XXII of the *Thirty Nine Articles* was the result. This fact is significant, because it indicates that those responsible for Article XXII were aware of a compromise position which would have allowed for the retention by the Church of England of the use of images, prayers to the Saints and prayers for the dead, but eventually decided that this compromise position was untenable.

Note 2: Newman's argument in *Tract Ninety*.

In Tract Ninety of the *Tracts for the Times* , *Remarks on Certain Passages in the Thirty-Nine Articles*, John Newman attempts to show that Article XXII need not be a stumbling block to Anglicans of a Catholic persuasion. He argues that what is said in the article and the homilies about purgatory, pardons, images, relics or the invocation of the Saints is concerned with certain specific errors on these subjects associated with the Church of Rome and does not rule out acceptance either of a 'primitive' doctrine on these matters held in the Early Church or the teaching of the Council of Trent, which had not ruled on these subjects when the article was drawn up.[589]

The problem with his argument is that if you read the article in the light of the homilies and in the light of the development of Church of England teaching highlighted in Note 1 above it is clear that by 1553 the English Reformers had no place in their theology for any doctrine of purgatory, pardons, images, relics or invocation of the Saints and that Article XXII was intended to reflect this position.

This clearly differentiates the teaching of the article from the teaching of the Council of Trent. Any discussion of Article XXII between the Protestant and Catholic traditions within Anglicanism or between Anglicans and Roman Catholics needs to take this fact into account.

Note 3: Prayer and the Departed and The Mystery of Salvation

---

[588] Ibid, pp. 213-221.
[589]See http://www.newmanreader.org/works/viamedia/volume2/tract90/tract90-1.html#section6

The 1971 report of the Archbishops Commission on Christian Doctrine of the Church of England, *Prayer and the Departed*, considered the question of 'prayer in relation to those who have died.'[590] The members of the commission were divided on the questions of whether it is right to pray in public for the dead and whether it is right to ask the faithful departed to pray for us.

They were, however, able to agree on the following statement about private prayer for the dead:

> The members of the Commission believe, with varying degrees of confidence, that the practice is at least not a clear contravention of Scripture; and they are unanimous in regarding it as an appropriate private practice for those who find it an expressive way of realizing the Communion of Saints and the manifest New Testament truth that death does not put an end to our fellowship with those in Christ. It is only appropriate, however, when the overall emphases of the New Testament are retained. Those who practice it must not lose sight of the fact, which prayer for the dead has sometimes in the past obscured in Christian minds, that 'blessed are the dead which die in the Lord from henceforth' (Revelation 14:13); and they will not forget either that this life is the God-given time for decision for or against Christ, so that what we do here will affect our destinies hereafter (see, for example, John 8:21, 24). Full weight must be given to the antitheses of saved and lost, wheat and tares, for him and against him, in Christ or without Christ, heirs or aliens, which run through all strands of the New Testament. At the same time, the hope of the restoration of all things, and of the summing up of all creation in Christ, when **God** shall be all and in all, is also present in the New Testament (Acts 3:21, Ephesians 1:10, Colossians 1:20, 1 Corinthians 15:28) giving a basis for the hope and prayer that in the end all God's purposes of love will be fulfilled. And a final caveat for those who wish to pray for the Christian dead is that such prayer must be

---

[590] The Archbishops Commission on Christian Doctrine, *Prayer and the Departed*, London: SPCK, 1971, p.13.

conceived broadly, in reverent recognition of the extent of our ignorance and without over-elaboration of doubtful detail.[591]

The commission also suggested three forms of prayer which Anglicans of all theological persuasions might be able to use in relation to the issue of praying for the dead and seeking their prayers for us.

The first was a prayer for the Christian departed. This ran:

> May God in his infinite love and mercy bring the whole church, living and departed in the Lord Jesus, to a joyful resurrection and the fulfilment of his eternal kingdom. [592]

The second was a prayer for the non-Christian dead. This ran:

> O God of infinite mercy and justice who has made man in thine own image, and hatest nothing that thou hast made, we rejoice in thy love for all creation and commend all men to thee, that it them thy will be done, in and through Jesus Christ our Lord.[593]

The third was a prayer concerning the communion of the saints living and departed which the commission hoped would help to bridge differences of opinion on the question of asking for the prayers of the saints. This ran:

> We thank you, O God, for your Grace revealed in all the Saints, and we pray for faith and courage, hope and love like theirs, through their example and in fellowship with them, through Jesus Christ our Lord.[594]

The 1995 Doctrine Commission report *The Mystery of Salvation* also commented on the issues of praying for the dead and asking for their prayers for us. On the first issue it declared that it was right to mention the Christian dead in prayer and to commend to God those who did not have an explicit faith in Christ:

---

[591] Ibid, pp.40-41.
[592] Ibid, p.51.
[593] Ibid, p. 55.
[594] Ibid, p.59.

We confess our belief in the Communion of Saints, and Christian prayer is one expression of that communion. It is therefore appropriate to mention the Christian dead in Christian prayer, in thanksgiving for their lives and as an affirmation that they are in the hands of God who works in them the good purpose of his perfect will. This kind of prayerful remembrance of the faithful departed is prayer in Christ and an expression of love for them. In the spirit, through Christ, we are made free to remember and love the faithful departed, in a trusting love which overcomes the barrier of death.

Furthermore, because Scripture makes it clear that God created, loves and sustains all humanity, and that Christ died for the sins of the whole world, to pray in the name of Christ for God's will to be done may appropriately include a prayer of commendation 'for those whose faith is known to God alone.'[595]

On the second issue it stated that the issue of the saints praying for us has to be seen in the context of the praise and prayer offered to God by all God's people living and departed within the Communion of Saints:

In the Communion of Saints, heaven and earth are united in a common worship, and it is in this context that the prayers of the Christian dead should be seen. Christians pray for one another on Earth; this of course does not take away from the centrality of Christ as the one High Priest who intercedes for us. We join our praises with those of the saints, and that praise is always the praise of God's holy, loving and righteous will; praise and prayer are united in the longing that God's will may be done. In the end it is Christ, the true once and future King, who is the Lord of both the old and the new creation, and it is in him that the mystery of the prayerful relations between the living and the departed must find its true expression.[596]

What these reports indicate is that opinion in the Church of England is divided on the question of the need and the possibility of praying for

---

[595] *The Mystery of Salvation*, p.197.
[596] Ibid p.198.

those who have died and the rightness of asking the faithful departed to pray for us.

However, there does seem to be a growing consensus that commending the departed, including those who have died without explicit Christian faith, to the mercy of God is not something that is ruled out by Scripture and may be an appropriate form of private Christian prayer and also that the question of asking the departed to pray for us has to be considered in the light of our belief in the Communion of Saints living and departed and their common participation in offering prayer and praise to God.

Note 4: Article XXII and work for the unity of the Church.

The Church of England is not only divided over the issues of praying for the dead and asking for them to pray for us, but also over the issues of purgatory and the adoration of images and relics. While there are many in the Church of England who would continue to uphold the line taken by Article XXXII on these issues there are also many other for whom prayer for the dead and to the saints, a belief in purgatory and the use of images and relics is a central part of their faith.

In its official doctrine and liturgy the Church of England still operates within the boundaries set by Article XXII, but if the Church is to be genuinely united in its faith and practice the divisions that exist in the Church of England over the issues covered in the article will need to be the subject of continuing internal theological debate.

The disparity between the teaching of Article XXII and the beliefs and practices of the Roman Catholic and Orthodox churches means that the issues covered in the article will need to be the subject of ecumenical debate as well. Thus far they are not issues that have been addressed in the Anglican-Roman Catholic and Anglican-Orthodox dialogues.

Article XXIII

∞

Of Ministering in the Congregation

It is not lawful for any man to take upon him the office of public preaching or ministering the sacraments in the congregation, before he be lawfully called and sent to execute the same. And those we ought to judge lawfully called and sent, which be chosen and called to this work by men who have public authority given unto them in the congregation to call and send ministers into the Lord's vineyard.

De vocatione Ministrorum

Non licet cuiquam sumere sibi munus publice praedicandi aut administrandi sacramenta in ecclesia, nisi prius fuerit ad haec obeunda legitime vocatus et missus. Atque illos legitime vocatos et missos existimare debemus, qui per homines, quibus potestas vocandi ministros atque mittendi in vineam Domini publice concessa est in ecclesia, co-optati fuerint et asciti in hoc opus.

This article is concerned with the issue of who may minister in the Church. Article XIX defined the visible Church as a body in which the word is preached and the sacraments are ministered. Article XXIII now goes on to say who may preach and who may minister the sacraments.

The article was originally Article XXIV of the *Forty Two Articles.* The substance of the article underwent no change between 1553 and 1571. However, in 1571 the present English and Latin titles were substituted for the original title, which had been retained in 1563, 'No man may minister in congregation except he be called' ('Nemo in ecclesia ministret nisi vocatus').

As the Latin version's use of the words licet ('permitted') and legitime ('legitimately') indicate, the words 'lawful' and 'lawfully' in the English version are used to refer to what is lawful in the sense of being right in the sight of God rather than in the sense of being laid down in the laws of England. The use of the word ecclesia in the Latin version also makes it clear that the word 'congregation' is used in the English version in the same way as in Article XIX, namely, to refer to the visible Church of Christ as a whole.

The ultimate source of the article seems to have been Article XIV of the *Augsburg Confession*: 'It is taught among us that nobody should publicly teach or preach or administer the sacraments in the church without a regular call.'[597] However, its immediate origin was Article 10 of the *Thirteen Articles* of 1538 ('The ministers of the Church') which clarified the teaching of Augsburg article by laying down that a regular call meant a call by those with appropriate authority in the Church:

> Concerning the ministers of the Church, we teach that no-one ought to teach publicly or administer the sacraments unless lawfully called by those in the Church who, according to the Word of God and the customs of each country, have the right and call to ordain.[598]

As Hardwick explains in his history of the Articles, the purpose of Article XXIII is to counter the error of those radical Protestants:

> ...who maintained that any one, believing himself to be called to the work of the ministry, was bound to exercise his functions as a preacher in defiance of all church authority. [599]

This error is highlighted in the account of contemporary heresies in the *Reformatio Legum Ecclesiasticarum* which talks about:

> ...the madness of those who divorce the institution of ministers from the church, denying that certain teachers, pastors, and ministers ought to be appointed to particular places, neither do they grant lawful callings nor the laying on of hands, but they grant the power of teaching publicly to everyone who has even a smattering of sacred learning, and claims the Spirit for himself,

---

[597] Leith, op.cit, p.72.
[598] Bray, *Documents of the English Reformation*, p.199.
[599] Hardwick, op.cit. p.102.

nor do they allow them only to teach, but also to govern the church and distribute the sacraments, which things are clearly repugnant to the writings of the apostles.[600]

It is not lawful for any man to take upon him the office of public preaching or ministering the sacraments in the congregation...

In response to this error the article begins by declaring (a) that there is a ministry of word and sacrament in the Church and (b) this ministry is not one that someone can take upon themselves. As Tyrell Green puts in his commentary on this article:

> That men may enjoy the blessings of the Gospel it must first be preached to them. Preachers, therefore, must be sent (Romans 10:15). Thus Christ sent forth his Apostles (John 20:21); and the Mission was handed on by them to others, so that the setting apart of certain members with authority to preach the Word publicly, and to be her ministers in sacred ordinances, dates from the very beginning of the Church's existence (Acts 13:1-3, 14:23, Ephesians 4:11-12; Philippians 1:1). Such ministers of the Church are spoken of in the New Testament as 'ambassadors of Christ' (2 Corinthians 5:20), 'ministers of Christ' (1 Corinthians 4:1), or 'of God' (2 Corinthians 6:4) and 'stewards of the mysteries of God' (1 Corinthians 4:1: cf. Colossians 1:25; Titus 1:7); they cannot of themselves assume authority as such, but must be called to the office by God Himself (Acts 20:28; Hebrews 5:4).[601]

...before he be lawfully called and sent to execute the same. And those we ought to judge lawfully called and sent, which be chosen and called to this work by men who have public authority given unto them in the congregation to call and send ministers into the Lord's vineyard.

Ministers, therefore, must be appointed to their ministries by God. The question that then arises is what form this appointment should take. The English Reformers were clear that there are instances in the New

---

[600] Bray, *Tudor Church Reform*, p.201
[601] Tyreall Green, op.cit. p.165.

Testament in which individuals are appointed to their ministries directly by God. As Rogers writes in his commentary on this article:

> Some are sent immediately from God himself. So sent was by God the Father, both Jesus Christ and John the Baptist (John 20:21, 1:6); by God the Son, in his state mortal, the twelve apostles, in his state immortal and glorious, St. Paul (Matthew 10:15, Acts 9:15).[602]

However, the Reformers regarded such direct appointment by God as exceptional rather than normal. As they saw it, the normal pattern, established in New Testament times and continued since, was for individuals to be appointed to exercise ministry by means of ordination by existing ministers of the church, who were themselves ordained by properly ordained ministers in a chain of ordination going back to the Apostles themselves.[603] To quote Rogers again:

> ...some...are by men sent: so in the primitive church by the apostles were pastors and elders ordained, who by the same authority ordained other pastors and teachers (Acts 14:22, 1 Timothy 4:14). Whence it is that the church as it hath been, so it shall till the end of the world be provided for.[604]

Tyrell Green explains the point in more detail:

> We find in the New Testament: -
>
> (a) That election by the people did not constitute a man a minister. See. e.g., Acts 6:5-6, where, after the Seven Deacons had been chosen by the whole body of the brethren, we read that they were admitted to their office by the imposition of the Apostles' hands.

---

[602] Rogers, op.cit. p.238
[603] Tyrell Green notes that 'in the Latin text the words 'co-optati and adsciti' correspond to the English 'chosen and called'; both Latin words imply that Ministers must be admitted to their office by those who are themselves ministers.' (p.167)
[604] Rogers, op.cit. p.238.

(b) Neither did the inward call of the Holy Spirit itself alone suffice. See Acts 13:2-3, where we have the account of the Ordination of SS. Barnabas and Paul by imposition of hands in obedience to a Divine command, although they had already received the call of the Holy Spirit.

(c) We gather, therefore, that from the very foundation of the Church, *Ordination*, has been considered *necessary*. See the passages above quoted, and notice especially how, when the Apostles were passing way from the earth, provision was made for the permanence of a duly ordained ministry (1 Timothy 3:4, 14, 5:22; 2 Timothy 1:6, 2:2; Titus 1:5).[605]

While Article XXIII is clear that there needs to be a lawfully appointed ministry of word and sacrament, nothing is said in Article XXIII either about the form that this ministry should take or about which ministers: 'have public authority given unto them in the congregation to call and send ministers into the Lord's vineyard.' As Burnet puts it in his commentary on the article:

That which is simply necessary as a means to preserve the order and union of Christians, and to maintain the reverence due to holy things is, that no man enter upon any part of the holy ministry, without he be chosen and called to it by such as have an authority so to do; that, I say, is fixed by the Article: but men are left more at liberty as to their thoughts concerning the subject of this lawful authority.[606]

Or, As O'Donovan puts it:

The formulation of Article 23 carefully avoids construing...ordained ministry in terms of the threefold order of bishops, priests, and deacons; neither does it allude to the succession of orders which maintains continuity with the earliest church. To neither of these things were Elizabethan churchmen, at least, indifferent; yet in stating what they thought essential to

---

[605] Tyrell Green, op.cit. p.166
[606] Burnet. op.cit. p.345.

the order of any church, they were content to stipulate nothing more than an ordained ministry of word and sacrament.[607]

As the Preface to the 1550 Ordinal makes clear, the English Reformers believed that:

> It is evident unto all men diligently reading Holy Scripture and ancient authors, that from the Apostles' time there hath been these orders of ministers in Christ's Church - bishops, priests and deacons.[608]

Furthermore, not only did they believe as a matter of historical fact that there had been these three orders of ministry in the Church since the time of the Apostles, but they also believed as a matter of theological principle that these orders of ministry should be continued in the Church. Thus the Preface to the 1550 Ordinal explains that is in order that 'these orders may be continued and reverently used and esteemed in this Church of England' that 'it is requisite that no man (not being at this present bishop, priest nor deacon) shall execute any of them except he be called, tried, examined and admitted according to the form hereafter following.'[609]

In addition, the English Reformers continued the Patristic and Medieval practice of allowing only bishops to ordain. Thus the only form of ordination permitted by the ordination rites contained in the 1550 Ordinal and the revised 1552 Ordinal which followed it is episcopal ordination. This meant that as far as the Church of England was concerned, those with 'public authority given unto them in the congregation to call and send ministers into the Lord's vineyard' were exclusively the bishops.

It is important to note, however, that at no point did the English Reformers make a negative judgement about the orders of those foreign Protestant churches that had not maintained the historic threefold order when they broke away from Rome and there is also evidence that during

---

[607] O'Donovan, op.cit. p.119.

[608] Text in Bray, *Documents of the English Reformation*, p. 277. For the historical evidence in support of this statement see J B Lightfoot's dissertation 'The Christian Ministry' in St. *Paul's Epistle to the Philippians*, 4ed, London & New York: Macmillan, 1891, pp.186-234

[609] Ibid, p.278.

the sixteenth and seventeenth centuries those who had received presbyteral ordination outside England were occasionally permitted to serve as ministers in the Church of England without being re-ordained.[610]

This practice only came to an end following the restoration of episcopal ministry in the Church of England after the Civil War. When an episcopally led Church of England was restored as the established church in England it was faced with the question of what view it should take of the orders of those who had received presbyteral ordination in England during the period of the Commonwealth. The decision it came to was that their orders should not be recognised and this decision was reflected in the alterations made to the Preface to the Ordinal in 1662. These alterations introduced the present wording that states that:

> No man shall be accounted or taken to be a lawful bishop, priest, or deacon in the Church of England, or suffered to execute any of the said functions, except he be called, tried, examined and admitted thereunto, according to the Form hereafter following, or hath had formerly Episcopal Consecration or Ordination.

This wording made episcopal ordination an absolute pre-requisite for the exercise of ordained ministry in the Church of England and although it was aimed at those who had received presbyteral ordination in England the effect was also to make a negative judgement about the orders of non-episcopal Protestant churches abroad, at least in so far as ministry in the Church of England was concerned. However, the Church of England never made a formal judgement that the orders of these churches were invalid and that there was no lawful ministry of word and sacrament within them.

Overall we can say that at the Reformation the Church of England maintained that the best form of the ministry of word and sacrament was the historic threefold order of ministry that had existed in the Church since the time of the Apostles. This in turn meant that the best way for people to receive lawful authority to exercise the ministry of word and sacrament was by means of episcopal ordination. What the Church of England did not maintain, however, and what is not stated in Article XXXIII, is that there can only ever be a lawful ministry of word and

---

[610] For this see N Sykes, *Old Priest and New Presbyter*, Cambridge: CUP, 2008 and Griffith Thomas, op.cit. pp. 330-332.

sacrament where the threefold order and episcopal ordination are present in a church.

Note: The contemporary view of the Church of England about ordination and non-episcopal orders.

In line with the Preface to the Ordinal the Church of England continues to maintain that episcopal ordination is a requirement in order for someone to serve as a minister of the Church of England. This is laid down in Canon C1 'Of Holy Orders in the Church of England' which declares:

> The Church of England holds and teaches that from the apostles' time there have been these orders in Christ's Church: bishops, priests, and deacons; and no man shall be accounted or taken to be a lawful bishop, priest, or deacon in the Church of England, or suffered to execute any of the said offices, except he be called, tried, examined, and admitted thereunto according to the Ordinal or any form of service alternative thereto approved by the General Synod under Canon B 2, authorized by the Archbishops of Canterbury and York under Canon C 4A or has had formerly episcopal consecration or ordination in some Church whose orders are recognized and accepted by the Church of England.

However, this does not mean that the Church of England does not acknowledge the existence of God given ministries of word and sacrament in churches in which historic threefold order of ministry has not been maintained and in which episcopal ordination is not practiced. As was noted in relation to Article XIX, the Lambeth Conference of 1920 declared that the visible unity of the Church needs to include:

> A ministry acknowledged by every part of the Church as possessing not only the inward call of the Spirit, but also the commission of Christ and the authority of the whole body.[611]

As was also noted, the Conference further declared that the Episcopate is 'the one means of providing such a ministry' and that 'it is now and will prove to in the future the best instrument for maintaining the unity and

---

[611] G Bell (ed), *Documents on Christian Unity 1920-1930*, Oxford: OUP, 1930, p.3

continuity of the Church.'[612] This did not mean, however, that the Conference saw no value in the ministries of non-episcopal churches. Rather, the Conference stated:

> It is not that we call in question for a moment the spiritual reality of the ministries of those Communions which do not possess the Episcopate. On the contrary, we thankfully acknowledge that these ministries have been manifestly blessed and owned by the Holy Spirit as effective means of grace.[613]

These statements by the Lambeth Conference of 1920 have set the framework for subsequent Anglican ecumenical theology and they are reflected in the ecumenical agreements with non-episcopal churches into which the Church of England has entered subsequently.

We can see this, for example in the *Reuilly Agreement* of 1999 between the Church of England and the other British and Irish Anglican churches and the French Lutheran and Reformed churches. In this agreement it is stated that:

> Anglicans believe that the historic episcopate is a sign of the apostolicity of the whole Church. The ordination of a bishop in historic succession (that is, in intended continuity with the apostles themselves) is a sign of God's promise to be with the Church, and also the way the Church communicates its care for continuity in the whole of its faith, life and mission, and renews its intention and determination to manifest the permanent characteristics of the Church of the apostles. Anglicans hold that the full visible unity of the Church includes the historic episcopal succession.[614]

However, the agreement also contains a series of mutual acknowledgements between the signatory churches, two of which declare:

---

[612] Ibid, pp.3-4.
[613] Ibid, pp.3-4.
[614] *Called to Witness and Service*, London: CHP, 1999, p.31.

We acknowledge that one another's ordained ministries are given by God as instruments of grace for the mission and unity of the Church and for the proclamation of the word and the celebration of the sacraments.

We acknowledge one another's orders as possessing not only the inward call of the Spirit but also Christ's commission through the church, and look forward to the time when the fuller visible unity of our churches makes possible the interchangeability of ministers.[615]

What we see here is a clear and unequivocal acknowledgement by the Church of England of the ministries of word and sacrament in the (non-episcopal) French Lutheran and Reformed churches. A similar acknowledgement is given by the Church of England to the ministries of two other non-episcopal churches in the 1988 *Meissen Agreement* with the Evangelical Church in Germany and the 2002 *Anglican-Methodist Covenant* with the Methodist Church in Great Britain.

Furthermore, under Canons B43 and B44 ordained ministers from non-episcopal churches can lawfully exercise a ministry of word and sacrament in Church of England churches without needing to receive episcopal ordination, although they do this as ministers of their own churches rather than as Church of England ministers and if they take a service of Holy Communion this counts as a service of their church rather than as a service of the Church of England.

---

[615] Ibid pp.36-37.

Article XXIV

∞

Of speaking in the Congregation in such a tongue as the people understandeth

It is a thing plainly repugnant to the word of God and the custom of the primitive Church, to have public prayer in the Church, or to minister the sacraments in a tongue not understanded of the people.

De precibus publicis dicendis in lingua vulgari

Lingua populo non intellecta publicas in Ecclesia preces peragere aut sacramenta administrare, verbo Dei et primitivae Ecclesiae consuetudine plane repugnat.

This Article originated as Article XXV of the Forty Two Articles. In its original form it read as follows:

Men must speak in the Congregation in such tongue as the people understandeth

It is most seemly, and most agreeable to the word of God, that in the congregation nothing be openly read, or spoken in a tongue unknown to the people, the which thing St. Paul did forbid, except some were present that should declare the same.

Agendum est in Ecclesia lingua quae sit populi nota

Decentissimum est et Verbo Dei maxime congruit, ut nihil in Ecclesia publice ligature aut recitetur lingua populd ignota, idque Paulus fieri vetuit, nisi adesset qui interpretatur.

In 1563 the original titles were retained, but the body of the article in English and Latin was changed to the present text apart from the fact that the words 'and the custom of the Primitive Church' were left out of the English version. In 1571 the titles were changed to their present form and words left out of the English version in 1563 were inserted into it in order to bring it in line with the Latin text.

The article is the second of two articles on the ministry. It follows on from Article XXIII, because that article says who may lead worship and this article goes on to say that they must lead not lead worship in a way that will prevent those in the congregation understanding what is said.

The background to the article was the practice of the Western Church of the Middle Ages of using Latin as the language of the liturgy even though this was not the language commonly used by most people in the countries of Western or central Europe. As W. G. Wilson and J.H. Templeton explain in their commentary on this article:

> The two greatest world-conquering powers of antiquity, Greece and Rome, spread their languages, Greek and Latin throughout their domains. In the West this meant that Latin became the official tongue; the standard version of the Scriptures, St. Jerome's Vulgate, and the Church's liturgy were in Latin. It was natural that this should be the case, for Latin was then the language used by educated people throughout the greater part of the Roman Empire, and it was very fitting that Latin should be used in the worship of the Church. But Latin gradually became added language, unintelligible to the majority of the people, for racial and cultural differences effected modifications of the general imperial language, and various dialects developed which eventually led to modern European languages, such as English, French, Spanish or Italian. Nevertheless, the Roman Church insisted on the use of Latin for her services, and tried to justify its retention on the grounds that it strengthened the unity of the Church, was conducive to reverence, and helped to preserve the Faith since it was less liable than modern languages to suffer corruption.[616]

---

[616] W G Wilson and J H Templeton, *Anglican Teaching*, Dublin: Association for Promoting Christian Knowledge, 1962, pp. 150-151.

As Eamon Duffy further explains, the result of this history was that in the English Church of the immediate pre-Reformation period:

> ...the available models of prayer – supremely in the day-to-day liturgy of the parish churches, but also in monastic piety and the great literary models of devotion – were all in Latin. The highest form of prayer was uttered by the priest at the sacring, the moment of consecration of the Mass. It was part of the power of the words of consecration that they were hidden, too sacred to be communicated to the 'lewed', and this very element of mystery gave legitimacy to the sacred character of Latin itself, as higher and holier than the vernacular. Moreover, since the words of scripture and the liturgy came from God, they were held to convey power even to those who did not fully comprehend them. One author, writing to help lay men and women participate properly in the Mass, compared the beneficial effect of such uncomprehending hearing at mass to that of a charm upon adders.[617]

The existing Roman practice was upheld by the Roman Catholic Church at the Council of Trent. Canon IX of Chapter IX of the Twenty Second session of the Council in September 1562 declared:

> If any one saith, that the rite of the Roman Church, according to which a part of the canon and the words of consecration are pronounced in a low tone, is to be condemned; or, that the mass ought to be celebrated in the vulgar tongue only...let him be anathema.[618]

In the Church of England, by contrast, the Reformation saw the introduction of a vernacular liturgy. Archbishop Cranmer introduced a litany (a sequence of prayers asking for God's help) in English in 1544 and in 1548 he also introduced an English Order for Communion which was inserted into the Latin Mass after the communion of the Priest. Finally, in 1549 and 1552 he produced two complete books of services,

---

[617] Duffy, op. cit. pp.217-218.
[618] J Waterworth (ed) *The canons and decrees of the sacred and oecumenical Council of Trent*, at http://history.hanover.edu/texts/trent/ct22.html.

the First and Second Prayer Books, in which Latin was entirely replaced by English.

During the reign of Queen Mary the Church of England reverted to the use of Latin, but with the accession of Elizabeth I English services were re-introduced. The primary purpose of Article XXIV is to justify this return to an English liturgy, but it may also have been intended as a response to what was said at Trent.

It is a thing plainly repugnant to the word of God and the custom of the primitive Church, to have public prayer in the Church, or to minister the sacraments in a tongue not understanded of the people.

In contrast to the 1553 prototype which made the positive point that having services in English was 'most seemly, and most agreeable to the word of God', Article XXIV in its final form takes a negative line, rejecting the traditional practice as 'plainly repugnant to the word of God and the custom of the primitive Church.'

The reasoning behind this rejection of the traditional practice is set out in the homily 'Of Common Prayer and Sacraments in a Tongue Understood' in the *Second Book of Homilies.*

The homily begins its consideration of this subject by declaring that the use of the vernacular in the liturgy is supported by reason:

> ...reason, if it might rule, would soon persuade us, to have our Common Prayer and administration of Sacraments in a known tongue, both for that to pray commonly is, for a multitude to ask one and the self thing with one voice, and one consent of mind, and to administer a Sacrament is, by the outward word and element, to preach to the receiver the inward and invisible grace of God; and also for that both these exercises were first instituted, and are still continued, to the end that the congregation of Christ might, from time to time, be put in remembrance of their unity in Christ, and that, as members all of one body, they ought both in prayers and otherwise to seek and desire one another's commodity, and not their own without others.[619]

---

[619] *The Homilies*, pp.256-257.

However, in line with what is said in Article XXIV it then goes onto argue that appeal to reason is superfluous because the use of a vernacular liturgy has the support of:

> 'both the plain and manifest words of the Scripture, and also the consent of the most learned and ancient writers.'[620]

In relation to the witness of Scripture, the homily puts forward three arguments.

First, the homily appeals to St. Paul's teaching in 1 Corinthians about the need for worship to be edifying to those taking part in it:

> Paul to the Corinthians saith, *Let all things be done to edifying* (1 Corinthians 14.26). Which cannot be, unless common prayers, and administration of Sacraments, be in a tongue known to the people. For where the prayers spoken by the minister and the words in the administration of the Sacraments be not understood of them that be present, they cannot thereby be edified. For as, when the trumpet that is blown in the field giveth an uncertain sound, no man is thereby stirred up to prepare himself to the fight (1 Corinthians 14:7-8); and as when an instrument of music maketh no distinct sound, no man can tell what is piped.; even so, when prayers or administration of Sacraments shall be in a tongue unknown to the hearers, which of them shall be thereby stirred up to lift up his mind to God, and to beg with the minister at God's hand, those things which in the words of his prayers the minister asketh? or who shall in the ministration of the Sacraments, understand what invisible grace is to be craved of the hearer to be wrought in the inward man? Truly no man at all. For, saith St. Paul, *he that speaketh in a tongue unknown shall be to the hearer an alien* (14.27), which in a Christian congregation is a great absurdity.
>
> For we are *not strangers* one to another, *but* we are *the citizens of the saints and of the household of God* (Ephesians 2.19); *yea, and members of one body* (1 Corinthians 10.17, 12.12). And therefore, whiles our minister is in rehearsing the prayer that is made in the name of us all, we must give diligent ears to the

---

[620] Ibid. p.257.

words spoken by him and in heart beg at God's hand those things that he beggeth in words. And to signify that we do so, we say, Amen, at the end of the prayer that he maketh in the name of us all. And this thing can we not do for edification unless we understand what is spoken. Therefore it is required of necessity that the common prayer be had in a tongue that the hearers do understand.[621]

Secondly, it argues that even in the Early Church, when the Apostles possessed the miraculous gift of speaking in other languages, the use of an unknown language was seen as being intolerable, and it must be even more intolerable now when this gift of speaking in other languages is no longer present:

If ever it had been tolerable to use strange tongues in the congregation, the same might have been in the time of Paul and the other Apostles, when they were miraculously endued with gifts of tongues. For it might then have persuaded some to embrace the Gospel when they had heard men that were Hebrews born and unlearned speak the Greek, the Latin, and other languages. But Paul thought it not tolerable then; and shall we use it now when no man cometh by that knowledge of tongues otherwise than by diligent and earnest study? God forbid. For we should by that means bring all our Church exercises to frivolous superstition, and make them altogether unfruitful[622].

Thirdly, the homily considers the account of the worship of the early Church given in Acts 4 and concludes that this shows that worship took place in a language that everyone present was able to understand:

Luke writeth that when Peter and John were discharged by the princes and high priests of Jerusalem, '*they came to their fellows and told them all that the princes of the priests and elders had spoken to them, Which when they heard, they lifted up their voice together to God with one assent and said, 'Lord, thou art he that hast made heaven and earth, the sea, and all things that are in*

---

[621] Ibid p. 257.
[622] Ibid. pp.257-258.

them,' &c. (Acts 4.23-24). Thus could they not have done, if they had prayed in a strange tongue that they had not understood. And no doubt of it, they did not all speak with several voices, but someone of them spake in the name of them all, and the rest giving diligent ear to his words consented thereunto: and therefore it is said that they lifted up their voice together. St. Luke saith not, *their voices* as many, but *their voice*, as one. That one voice therefore was in such language as they all understood, otherwise they could not have lifted it up with the consent of their hearts. For no man can give consent of the thing that he knoweth not.[623]

In relation to the witness of the Fathers about 'the custom of the primitive Church' the homily refers to the writings of St. Justin, St. Basil the Great, St. John Chrysostom, Dionysius, St. Cyprian, St. Ambrose, St. Jerome, St. Augustine and the Code of the Emperor Justinian. It contends that these writings all show that in the early centuries of the Church 'there was no strange or unknown tongue used in the congregations of Christians'[624] and that consequently the laity were able to take part in the liturgy with understanding and to say a meaningful 'Amen' in response to the prayers. For example, it notes that:

Basilius Magnus and Johannes Chrysostomus, did in their time prescribe public orders of public administration, which they call Liturgies; and in them they appointed the people to answer to the prayers of the minister, sometime, 'Amen,' sometime, 'Lord have mercy upon us,' sometime, 'And with thy spirit,' and 'We have our hearts lifted up to the Lord,' &c.; which answers, the people could not have made in due time, if the prayers had not been made in a language that they understood. [625]

For another example, it quotes St. Ambrose as saying:

...that nothing should be done in the Church in vain; and that this thing ought chiefly to be laboured for, that the unlearned also

---

[623] Ibid, p. 258.
[624] Ibid. P.258.
[625] Ibid. p.259.

might take profit, lest any part of the body should be dark, through ignorance.[626]

If we compare the understanding of the purpose of liturgical language reflected in the quotation from Duffy with the understanding of its purpose set out in the homily and presupposed in Article XXIV, what we find is that the Medieval viewpoint is that liturgical language has a spiritual power which exists regardless of whether it is understood or not, whereas the viewpoint of the English Reformers is that liturgical language only has spiritual power when people know what it means and are therefore able to make an informed response to what is said.

Because the key thing for the English Reformers was that the liturgy should be understood they objected not only to the liturgy being said in a unknown language, but also to the liturgy being said inaudibly, as when the words of consecration in the Mass were deliberately said in a 'low tone' that kept them from the ears of the laity.

Griffith Thomas suggests that the change in the language of the article between 1553 and 1563 was intended to rule out this kind of inaudible language as well:

> The change from 'unknown' (*ignota*) to 'not understanded' (*non intellecta*) shows that the prohibition is concerned with either a foreign tongue, or even the mother-tongue unintelligently rendered. A tongue 'not understanded' obviously includes a voice that is not audible. This gives point to the rubrical directions found in the Prayer Book ordering a 'loud voice' and 'turning him to the people.[627]

Since what the English Reformers was concerned about was thus intelligibility they were happy to permit Latin to go on being used in the liturgy in settings such as the college chapels in the universities where it was understood by those taking part in the services. The Church of England also continued to use Latin as the internationally understood theological and legal language. That is why, for instance, the Articles were produced in both Latin and English and why the *Reformatio Legum Ecclesisticarum* was written in Latin.

---

[626] Ibid. pp.259-260.
[627] Griffith Thomas, op. cit. 340.

In the twentieth and twenty first centuries the principle that the liturgy should be in a 'tongue understanded of the people' led the Church of England to produce a series of modern language services as alternatives to the services in the *Book of Common Prayer*, the services in *Common Worship* being the most recent of these.

In the twentieth century the Roman Catholic Church also accepted the notion of a vernacular liturgy with section 36 of the Second Vatican Council's *Constitution on the Sacred Liturgy* allowing the use of the 'mother tongue' in ways to be decided by the 'competent territorial ecclesiastical authority' and approved by the Apostolic See.[628] Today most Roman Catholic services are in the vernacular, although the Latin rite is still extensively used.

---

[628] W M Abbott S.J. (ed) *The Documents of Vatican II*, London: Geoffrey Chapman, 1967, p.150.

The Sacraments: Articles XXV–XXXI

The third sequence of articles concerning the Church looks at the Church's sacraments.

The opening articles in the sequence give general teaching about the sacraments. Article XXV sets out the Church of England's position on the nature and number of the sacraments and Article XXVI declares against objections from Protestant radicals that the celebration of the sacraments by a morally unworthy minister does not affect the spiritual efficacy of the sacraments concerned.

The next two articles, XXVII and XXVIII, explain the Church of England's view of Baptism and the Lord's Supper.

Article XXIX argues against both Roman and Lutheran teaching that those who receive the Lord's Supper unworthily do not partake of the body and blood of Christ

Finally, Articles XXX-XXXI argue against the Medieval and Roman practice of giving communion in only one kind and against any idea that at the Mass the priest re-offers Christ in order to obtain the remission of sins for those alive and those in purgatory.

Article XXV

∞

Of the Sacraments

Sacraments ordained of Christ be not only badges or tokens of Christian men's profession, but rather they be certain sure witnesses and effectual signs of grace and God's good will towards us, by the which He doth work invisibly in us, and doth not only quicken, but also strengthen and confirm, our faith in Him.

There are two Sacraments ordained of Christ our Lord in the Gospel, that is to say, Baptism and the Supper of the Lord.

Those five commonly called Sacraments, that is to say, Confirmation, Penance, Orders, Matrimony, and Extreme Unction, are not to be counted for Sacraments of the Gospel, being such as have grown partly of the corrupt following of the Apostles, partly are states of life allowed in the Scriptures; but yet have not the like nature of Sacraments with Baptism and the Lord's Supper, for that they have not any visible sign or ceremony ordained of God.

The Sacraments were not ordained of Christ to be gazed upon or to be carried about, but that we should duly use them. And in such only as worthily receive the same, have they a wholesome effect or operation: but they that receive them unworthily, purchase to themselves damnation, as Saint Paul saith.

De Sacramentis

Sacramenta a Christo instituta non tantum sunt notae professionis Christianorum, sed certa quaedam potius testimonia et efficacia signa gratiae atque bonae in nos voluntatis Dei, per quae invisibiliter ipse in nobis operatur, nostramque fidem in se, non solum excitat verum etiam confirmat.

Duo a Christo Domino nostro in Evangelio instituta sunt Sacramenta, scilicet, Baptismus et Coena Domini.

Quinque illa vulgo nominata Sacramenta, scilicet, Confirmatio, Poenitentia, Ordo, Matrimonium, et Extrema Unctio, pro Sacramentis Evangelicis habenda non sunt, ut quae partim a prava Apostolorum imitatione profluxerunt, partim vitae status sunt in Scripturis quidem probati, sed Sacramentorum eandem cum Baptismo et Coena Domini rationem non habentes, ut quae signum aliquod visibile seu ceremoniam a Deo institutam non habeant.

Sacramenta non in hoc instituta sunt a Christo ut spectarentur aut circumferrentur sed ut rite illis uteremur. Et in his duntaxat qui digne percipiunt, salutarem habent effectum: qui vero indigne perci piunt, damnationem, ut inquit Paulus, sibi ipsis acquirunt.

Article XXV is the first of series of six articles (Articles XXV-XXXI) which are concerned with the topic of the sacraments. Article XXV is an introductory article which sets out the Church of England's overall view of the nature and number of the sacraments.

The origins of the article go back to Article XIII of the *Augsburg Confession*, 'The Use of the Sacraments.' This states:

> It is taught among us that the sacraments were instituted not only to be signs by which people might be again identified outwardly as Christians, but that they are signs and testimonies of God's will towards us for the purpose of awakening and strengthening our faith. For this reason they require faith, and they are rightly used when they are received in faith and that the purpose of strengthening faith.[629]

This statement was used by Archbishop Cranmer as the basis for the opening section of Article 9 of the *Thirteen Articles*, again entitled 'The use of the Sacraments,' the opening section of which runs as follows:

---

[629] Leith, op.cit. p.72.

We teach that the sacraments which have been instituted by the Word of God are not only signs of profession among Christians, but even more, sure witnesses and effective signs of grace and of God's good will towards us. Through them, God works in us invisibly, and causes grace into us invisibly, if we receive them rightly, and faith is also awaken through them and confirmed in those who use them.[630]

This section of the *Thirteen Articles* was then re-used by Cranmer as the basis for the final paragraph of Article XXVI of the *Forty Two Articles*, 'Of the Sacraments' (De Sacramentis) This article declares:

> Our Lord Jesus Christ hath knit together a company of new people with Sacraments, most few in number, most easy to be kept, most excellent in signification, as is Baptism and the Lord's Supper.

> The Sacraments were not ordained of Christ to be gazed upon, or to be carried about, but that we should rightly use them. And in such only as a worthily receive the same, they have a wholesome effect and operation, [and yet not that of the work wrought, as some men speak, which word, as it is strange, and an unknown to Holy Scripture; so it engendereth no godly, but a very superstitious sense.]

> But they that receive the Sacraments unworthily purchase to themselves damnation, as St. Paul saith.

> Sacraments ordained by the Word of God be not only badges, and tokens of Christian men's profession, but rather they be certain sure witnesses, and effectual signs of grace, and God's good will towards us, by the which he doth work invisibly in us, and doth not only quicken but also strengthen and confirm our faith in him.

> *Dominus noster Jesus Christus Sacramentis numero paucissimis, observatu facillimis, significatione praestantissimis, societatem novi populi colligavit, sicuti est Baptismus et Coena Domini.*

---

[630] Bray, *Documents of the English Reformation*, p. 198.

Sacramenta non institute sunt a Christo ut spectarentur aut circumferrentur, sed ut rite illis uteremur: Et in his duntaxat qui digne percipient, salutarem habent effectum, [idque non ex opera, ut quidem loquuntur, operato; quae vox, ut peregrina est et Sacris literis ignota, sic parit sensum minime pium sed admodum superstitiosum.]

Qui vero indigne percipient, damnationem (ut inquit Paulus) sibi ipsis acquirunt.

Sacramenta per Verbum Dei institute, non tantum sunt notae professionis Christianorum, sed certa quaedam potius testimonia et efficacia signa gratiae atque bonae in nos voluntatis Dei, per quae invisibiliter ipse in nobis operator, nostramque fidem in se non solum excitat, verum etiam confirmat.

In 1563 this article was extensively recast.

(1) The first paragraph was dropped entirely.

(2) The first section of the second paragraph was combined with the third paragraph and moved down to become the final paragraph of Article XXV with the second section of the second paragraph (in square brackets) being omitted.

(3) The fourth paragraph was revised with 'ordained of Christ' replacing 'ordained of the Word of God' and moved up to become the opening paragraph of Article XXV.

(4) Two new paragraphs were added (paragraphs two and three of Article XXV) explaining the number of the sacraments and the difference between the two sacraments ordained by Christ and the five other rites reckoned to be Sacraments by the Medieval Church.

In its final form Article XXV consists of four paragraphs which consider three subjects, the nature of the sacraments, the number of the sacraments and the use of the sacraments. As Gibson explains in his commentary on the article, its purpose is:

(1) to condemn the inadequate views of sacraments held by the Anabaptists, and to state their true position; (2) to distinguish between the two 'Sacraments of the Gospel' and the other five 'commonly called Sacraments'; and (3) to insist upon the necessity of a right disposition on the part of the recipient of them.[631]

Sacraments ordained of Christ be not only badges or tokens of Christian men's profession, but rather they be certain sure witnesses and effectual signs of grace and God's good will towards us, by the which He doth work invisibly in us, and doth not only quicken, but also strengthen and confirm, our faith in Him.

This first paragraph of the article begins by stating what sacraments are not. Sacraments are not simply an outward sign that someone is a Christian. The reason this mistaken view of the sacraments is mentioned is because it was taught by some of the more radical Protestants at the time of the Reformation. Evidence that they taught this is provided by the *Simplex ac pia deliberatio* of the reforming Archbishop of Cologne, Hermann of Wied, which was translated into English in 1547. This mentions that the radicals:

> ...withdraw from the sacraments, which they will to be nothing else than outward signs of our profession and fellowship, as the badges of captains be in war.[632]

Further evidence is provided by the *Reformatio Legum Ecclesiasticarum* which describes the heresy of those:

> ...who so dilute the sacraments that they want them to be understood as mere bare signs and mere external symbols, by which signs, however, the religion of Christian people may be recognized by others.[633]

---

[631] Gibson, op. cit. p.588
[632] Ibid. p.589.
[633] Bray, *Tudor Church Reform*, p.203.

In the place of this diluted view of the sacraments Article XXV offers a threefold positive account of the nature of the sacrament.

Firstly, the sacraments are 'sure witnesses and effectual signs of grace and God's good will towards us.' That is to say, the sacraments are reliable witnesses that enable us to understand God's grace and good will towards us through testifying to what God has done for us in Jesus Christ.

This point is explained by Alexander Nowell in his catechism. He notes that the outward and visible witness provided by sacraments is needed because of our spiritual limitations as human beings:

> S. [A sacrament] is an outward testifying of God's good-will and bountifulness toward us, through Christ by a visible sign representing an invisible and spiritual grace, by which the promises of God touching forgiveness of sins and eternal salvation given through Christ, are, as it were sealed, and the truth of them is more certainly confirmed in our hearts.
>
> M. Of how many parts consisteth a sacrament?
>
> S. Of two parts: the outward element, or visible sign, and the invisible grace.
>
> M. Why would God so have us to use outward signs?
>
> S. Surely we are not endued with mind and understanding so heavenly and divine, that the graces of God do appear clearly of themselves to us, as it were to angels. By this mean therefore God hath provided for our weakness, that we which are earthly and blind should in outward elements and figures, as it were in certain glasses, behold the heavenly graces which otherwise we were not able to see. And greatly for our behoof [benefit] it is that God's promises should be also presented to our senses, that they may be confirmed to our minds without doubting.[634]

Secondly, the sacraments are not only outward and visible witnesses. On the basis of New Testament passages such as John 3:5, 6:56, Romans 6:3-4 and 1 Corinthians 10:16, the English Reformers held that the

---

[634] Nowell, op. cit. p. 205.

sacraments are also instruments by which God's grace works invisibly but effectively in our lives. That is what the article means when it says that the sacraments are 'effectual signs...by the which He doth work invisibly in us.' In the words of Richard Hooker, the sacraments are to be viewed not simply as:

> ...naked signs and testimonies assuring us of grace receive before, (but as they are indeed and in verity) for means effectual whereby God when we take the sacraments delivereth onto our hands that grace available unto eternal life, which grace the sacraments represent or signify.[635]

Thirdly, as witnesses to God's grace and effectual instruments of that grace the sacraments are means by which God both 'quickens', that is to say, creates, and also strengthens our faith in him. As the homily 'Of Common Prayer and Sacraments in a Tongue Understood' puts it, through the sacraments God 'embraceth us, and offereth himself to be embraced by us.'[636]

Gibson suggests that 'quicken' refers to the effect of baptism while 'strengthen' refers to the effect of the Lord's Supper.[637] However, the text itself does not divide the effects of the two sacraments in this way. As far as the article itself is concerned both sacraments can be used by God to quicken faith and both sacraments can be used by God to strengthen it.

There are two Sacraments ordained of Christ our Lord in the Gospel, that is to say, Baptism and the Supper of the Lord.

Those five commonly called Sacraments, that is to say, Confirmation, Penance, Orders, Matrimony, and Extreme Unction, are not to be counted for Sacraments of the Gospel, being such as have grown partly of the corrupt following of the Apostles, partly are states of life allowed in the Scriptures; but yet have not the like nature of Sacraments with Baptism and the Lord's Supper, for that they have not any visible sign or ceremony ordained of God.

---

[635] Hooker, *Laws of Ecclesiastical Polity*, Bk V. LVIII.5.
[636] *The Homilies*, p.253.
[637] Gibson, op.cit. p. 592.

The background to this section of the article is the dispute which took place between the Roman Catholic and Protestant sides at the Reformation as to the number of the sacraments. Prior to the Middle Ages there was no agreement about the number of the sacraments. During the Middle Ages, however, the twelfth century theologian Peter Lombard had laid down in the fourth book of his *Four Books of Sentences* that there are seven sacraments, Baptism, Confirmation, the Eucharist, Penance, Extreme Unction, Orders and Matrimony. His list was not immediately accepted, but his view eventually prevailed, being defined as the orthodox view of the matter at the Council of Florence in 1439.

At the time of the Reformation this traditional medieval list continued to be upheld by the Church of Rome. Thus the first canon of the seventh session of the Council of Trent, declared:

> If anyone says that that the sacraments of the New Law were not all instituted by our Lord Jesus Christ, or that there are more or less that seven, namely baptism, confirmation, Eucharist, penance, extreme unction, order and matrimony, or that any of these seven is not truly and intrinsically a sacrament, let him be anathema.[638]

On the Protestant side at the Reformation, however, the issue of how many sacraments there were was re-opened both on the Continent and in England. Initially, the English Reformers followed the Lutheran position and held that there were three sacraments, Baptism, the Lord's Supper and Penance/Absolution. This was the position taken, for example, in the *Ten Articles* of 1536.

In the *King's Book* of 1543 the Church of England reverted to the medieval seven sacraments and in Article XXVI of the *Forty Two Articles* the number of the sacraments is left undefined.

However the *Reformatio Legum Ecclesiasticarum* of 1553 is quite clear that there are only two sacraments. In its section 'Of Sacraments' it states that the Church of England accepts only Baptism and the Eucharist as 'true and proper sacraments of the New Testament.'[639] Article XXV takes the same line as does the homily 'Of Common Prayer and Sacraments' *in the Second Book of Homilies* which declares:

---

[638] Leith, op.cit. p.425
[639] Bray, *Tudor Church Reform* p.227.

...as for the number of them, if they should be considered according to the exact signification of a Sacrament, namely for visible signs expressly commanded in the New Testament, whereunto is annexed the promise of free forgiveness of our sin, and of our holiness, there be but two; namely, Baptism and the Supper of the Lord.[640]

Article XXV itself does not say why there are only two sacraments properly so called. In the homily, however, it is explained that the reason is because only Baptism and the Supper of the Lord fit the definition of a sacrament which it lays down. In similar fashion, the words quoted above from the *Reformatio Legum Ecclesiasticarum* follow on from a definition of what a sacrament is:

Three things must come together for a sacrament to be perfect. First, there must be an obvious and appropriate sign, which can be clearly discerned. Second, there is the promise of God which is represented to us and fully confirmed by the external sign. Third there is the command of God, by which the necessity is placed on us, both to do these things and to commemorate them. Since these three things occur with the authority of the Scriptures only in baptism and the eucharist , we accept only these two as true and proper sacrament of the New Testament.[641]

Given what is said in the homily and in the *Reformatio Legum Ecclesiasticarum,* and in the absence of any other explanation, is it reasonable to conclude that the reason that that Article XXV sees only Baptism and the Eucharist as being true sacraments is because only they fit the threefold criteria of a promise from God, a visible sign and a biblical mandate.

The requirement for a biblical mandate explains why Article XXV declares that 'There are two sacraments ordained of Christ our Lord in the Gospel, that is to say, Baptism and the Supper of the Lord.' This is not meant to suggest that there are other sacraments that are not ordained by Christ in the Gospel. What it is meant to say is that because only Baptism and the Supper of the Lord are ordained by Christ in the Gospel

---

[640] *The Homilies* p.255.
[641] Bray, *Tudor Church Reform* p.227.

475

only they have the necessary biblical mandate to be considered true sacraments. 'In the Gospel' here means 'in the Gospels' and what the article is referring to are the accounts of the institution of the Eucharist in Matthew 26:26-29, Mark 14:22-25 and Luke 22:19-24 (as well as St. Paul's parallel account in 1 Corinthians 11:23-26), the command to baptise given by the risen Christ in Matthew 28:19 and the accounts of the significance of baptism and the Eucharist in John 3:3-6 and 6:25-59.

Conversely, when the article goes on to say in the next paragraph that the five 'commonly called Sacraments' are 'not to be counted for Sacraments of the Gospel' what this means is that they were not ordained by Christ in the Gospels. They therefore have no biblical mandate and so are not truly sacraments at all. The same point is made at the end of the paragraph where we are told that they 'have not any visible sign or ceremony ordained of God.'

If these five rites are not sacraments the question that then arises is what they are instead. The article answers this question by stating that they are 'such as have grown partly of the corrupt following of the Apostles, partly are states of life allowed in the Scriptures.'

As Gibson explains, 'corrupt following of the Apostles' means 'a bad imitation of them.'[642] This applies to Confirmation, Penance and Extreme Unction. In Acts we see the Apostles laying on hands so that people receive the gift of the Holy Spirit (Acts 8:15-17, 19:6), declaring to penitent people the forgiveness of their sins (Acts 2:37-39) and praying for sick people that they might be made well (Acts 3:1-10, 9:32-41, 14:8-10). We also find Jesus giving authority to the Apostles to forgive sins in John 20:21-23 and an injunction to the elders of the Church to pray for the sick that they may be forgiven and healed in James 5:13-16. These aspects of the New Testament record underlie the rites of Confirmation, Penance and Extreme Unction, but they do not in themselves constitute the specific God given mandate to perform certain acts that would be necessary in order for these rites to qualify as sacraments under the article's definition of the term.

Furthermore, there is a mismatch between what is described in the New Testament and the rites that developed in the later Church. In the case of Confirmation the mismatch is because in Acts 8 and 19 the Apostles lay on hands to bestow the Spirit for the first time rather than to strengthen those who have already received the Spirit at baptism. In the

---

[642] Gibson, op. cit. p.603.

case of Penance it is because in the New Testament the forgiveness of sins is linked to repentance, faith, baptism and mutual confession rather than being tied to auricular confession to a priest and the performance of specific acts of penance. In the case of Extreme Unction it is because in the New Testament hands are laid on the sick to heal them rather than to prepare them for death.

That leaves Orders and Matrimony. These are described by the article as 'states of life allowed in the Scriptures.' As the Latin equivalent 'probati' indicates, the word 'allowed' used here means 'approved'. In the view of the article, therefore, ordination and marriage are states of life approved by God, but according to the article they are still not sacraments because they do not have a sign ordained by Christ himself.

Orders can be seen as being instituted by Christ himself in the commission given to the Apostles as the first ministers of the Church in John 20:21-23. It also has the outward and visible sign of the laying on of hands and the inward grace of the Holy Spirit given to those ordained. However, the outward sign was not mandated by Christ himself. Matrimony was instituted by God at creation (Genesis 2:18-24), is a sign of divine grace (Ephesians 5:21-33) and involves an outward ceremony. However, once again, the outward rite was not mandated by Christ himself.

The Sacraments were not ordained of Christ to be gazed upon or to be carried about, but that we should duly use them. And in such only as worthily receive the same, have they a wholesome effect or operation: but they that receive them unworthily, purchase to themselves damnation, as Saint Paul saith.

The final section of the article turns to the question of the right use of the sacraments. This section begins by rejecting the medieval practices of making the consecrated elements of the Eucharist a focus for adoration or carrying them in procession. This subject is referred to again in Article XXVIII and both there and in this article the point is made that Christ ordained that the elements at the Eucharist should be eaten and drunk rather than that they should be worshipped or carried about.

Since there is no evidence that the water of baptism was ever the subject of adoration or carried in procession this opening statement appears to refer only to the Eucharist. Why then is the plural 'sacraments' used? One possibility is that this is simply a mistake, but it is difficult to see why such an obvious error was never spotted before the article was finally issued. A second and more likely explanation noted by Gibson[643] and Tyrell Green[644] is that this wording reflects a Tudor practice of referring to the two elements of the Eucharist as sacraments. Thus the second exhortation in the Communion Service in the 1559 Prayer Book refers to 'the holy sacraments of his blessed body and blood' and Queen Elizabeth's injunctions of 1559 likewise refer to 'the Sacraments of the Body and Blood of our Saviour Jesus Christ.'

If this second explanation is correct it means that the opening sentence of this section should be seen as meaning 'the Sacraments of his body and blood were not ordained of Christ to be gazed upon or to be carried about, but that we should duly use them.' This would then lead naturally into the discussion of the worthy reception of the body and blood in the final sentence of the article. That this sentence is concerned with the Eucharist is shown by its reference to the teaching of St. Paul in 1 Corinthians 11:27-32 about how the Corinthians have brought judgement upon themselves by their unworthy eating and drinking of the Lord's Supper.

The first clause of the final sentence stresses that the elements at the Eucharist only have a 'wholesome effect or operation' as effectual signs of grace if we receive them worthily. What worthy reception means is explained in the homily 'Of the worthy receiving and reverent esteeming of the body and blood of Christ' in the *Second Book of Homilies*. After looking at the subject in detail, the homily summarises its argument in its concluding paragraph. This runs as follows:

> Thus have ye heard, how ye should come reverently and decently to the Table of the Lord, having the knowledge of his word, of the thing itself and the fruits thereof, bringing a true and constant faith, the root and wellspring of all newness of life, as well in praising God and loving our neighbour as purging our conscience from filthiness. So that neither the ignorance of the thing shall cause us to contemn it, nor unfaithfulness make us void of fruit, nor sin and iniquity procure us God's plagues, but shall by faith in knowledge and amendment of life in faith be here so united to Christ our Head in his mysteries to our comfort, that after we

---

[643] Ibid, p.610
[644] Tyrell Green, op.cit, p.199.

shall have full fruition of him indeed to our everlasting joy and eternal life to the which he bring us that died for us and redeemed us, Jesus Christ the righteous...[645]

What we see here are the three elements which the English Reformers believed to be necessary for the right reception of the sacrament.

- First, there needs to be knowledge of the meaning of the sacrament based on Scripture.

- Secondly, there needs to be faith that in the sacrament Christ offers us the benefits of what he did for us on the cross when his body was broken for us and his blood shed for us.

- Thirdly, there needs to be freedom from un-repented sin. Only when these three elements are present do we receive the sacrament 'rightly, worthily and with faith' and so partake of Christ's body and blood.

A similar point is made in the exhortation prior to communion in the Communion service in the Book of Common Prayer:

> Judge therefore yourselves brethren, that ye be not judged of the Lord; repent you truly for your sins past; have a lively and steadfast faith in Christ our Saviour, amend your lives and be in perfect charity with all men; so shall ye be meet partakers of these holy mysteries.

The second clause of the sentence warns that those who receive unworthily 'purchase for themselves damnation.' These words are a reference to the teaching of St. Paul in 1 Corinthians 11:29 'For any one who eats and drinks without discerning the body eats and drinks judgement upon himself.' As Gibson notes in his commentary on this article:

> ...the 'damnation' spoken of here and in the Authorised Version of 1 Cor 11:29 (the passage alluded to, is not necessarily final

---

[645] *The Homilies* p.328.

condemnation. It is rather that 'judgement' with which 'we are chastened of the Lord, *that we may not be condemned with the world*' (ver.32); i.e. the Apostle is speaking of a temporal chastisement, the object of which was to wean the unworthy communicant from his sin, and lead him to repentance, so that he might escape what is commonly called 'damnation.'[646]

According to the biblical witness God's chastisements can be very severe. When the Communion service in the Book of Common Prayer talks about our unworthy reception of the sacrament leading God to 'plague us with divers diseases and sundry kinds of death' it is only echoing St. Paul's words in 1 Corinthians 11:30 'that is why many of you are weak and ill and some of you have died.' However, God's chastisements are never arbitrary and, however severe they are, they are always merciful in that their purpose us to break the grip of sin on our lives so that we can enter into the fullness of life that God longs to give us rather than be cut off from him for ever.

---

[646] Gibson, op.cit. p.611

Article XXVI

∞

Of the Unworthiness of the Ministers, which hinders not the effect of the Sacraments

Although in the visible Church the evil be ever mingled with the good, and sometime the evil have chief authority in the ministration of the word and sacraments; yet forasmuch as they do not the same in their own name, but in Christ's, and do minister by His commission and authority, we may use their ministry both in hearing the word of God and in the receiving of the sacraments. Neither is the effect of Christ's ordinance taken away by their wickedness, nor the grace of God's gifts diminished from such as by faith and rightly do receive the sacraments ministered unto them, which be effectual because of Christ's institution and promise, although they be ministered by evil men.

Nevertheless it appertaineth to the discipline of the Church that inquiry be made of evil ministers, and that they be accused by those that have knowledge of their offences; and finally, being found guilty by just judgement, be deposed.

De vi institutionum divinarum, quod eam non tollat malitia Ministrorum

Quamvis in Ecclesia visibili bonis mali semper sunt admixti, atque interdum ministerio verbi et sacramentorum administrationi praesint ; tamen cum non suo sed Christi nomine agant, eiusque mandato et auctoritate ministrent, illorum ministerio uti licet cum in verbo Dei audiendo tum in sacramentis percipiendis. Neque per illorum malitiam effectus institutorum Christi tollitur aut gratia donorum Dei minuitur quoad eos qui fide et rite sibi oblata percipiunt, quae propter institutionem Christi et promissionem efficacia sunt, licet per malos administrentur.

> *Ad Ecclesiae tamen disciplinam pertinet, ut in malos ministros inquiratur, accusenturque ab his qui eorum flagitia noverint; atque tandem, iusto convicti iudicio, deponantur.*

Article XXV having addressed the nature, number and use of the sacraments, Article XXVI goes on to consider how the sacraments relate to the personal worthiness (or unworthiness) of the person who ministers them.

The ultimate origins of this article can be traced back to Article VIII of the *Augsburg Confession*. This declares:

> Again, although the Christian church, properly speaking, is nothing else than the assembly of all believers and saints, yet because in this life many false Christians, hypocrites, and even open sinners remain among the godly, the sacraments are efficacious even if the priests who administer them are wicked men, for as Christ himself indicated, 'The Pharisees sit on Moses' seat' (Matt 23:2).
>
> Accordingly the Donatists and all others who hold contrary views are condemned.[647]

The teaching of this Article was then reflected in Article V of the *Thirteen Articles* which states:

> And although the evil are mixed together with the good in the church, as understood in the second sense,[648] and even sometimes preside over the ministry of the Word and sacraments, yet when they minister not in their own but in Christ's name, we may use their ministry both in hearing the Word and in receiving the sacraments, as it is written: 'Whoever hears you, hears me.' Nor is the effect or the grace of the gifts of Christ, properly received,

---

[647] Leith, op.cit. p.70. The Donatists were a group within the North African Church from the 4-8 centuries. They held that only the sacraments administered by their clergy were efficacious, the sacraments of the Catholic Church not being efficacious because they were ministered by clergy who had compromised with the Imperial authorities. Their theology was critiqued by St. Augustine and came to be seen by the wider Church as heretical.

[648] That is, the Church as a visible human institution rather than as the invisible company of those who belong to Christ.

diminished by their wickedness; for they are efficacious on account of the promise and ordination of Christ, even if they are manifested by evil men.[649]

This statement in the *Thirteen Articles* was then expanded and re-worked by Cranmer to form Article XXVII of the *Forty Two Articles* and a slightly amended version of this article forms Article XXVI of the *Thirty Nine Articles*.

Article XVVII was amended in three ways. In 1563 the Latin version was amended so as to replace 'eos' (such) with 'malos ministros' (evil ministers) in the final paragraph. In 1571 the English text of the final paragraph was amended to make it conform to the Latin. Finally, in 1571 the present English and Latin titles were introduced to replace the original title 'The wickedness of the ministers doth not take away the effectual operation of God's ordinances' (Ministrorum militia non tollit efficaciam institutionum divinarum).

The purpose of Article XXVI is to counter the teaching and practice of radical Protestant groups who boycotted the ministry of ministers they considered to be evil. This teaching and practice is referred to in the account of heresies in the *Reformatio Legum Ecclesiasticarum* which notes that the Anabaptists:

...separate themselves from the body of the church and refuse to come to the most holy table of the Lord with everyone else, saying that they are held back by the unworthiness of the ministers or of the other brethren...[650]

It is also referred to by Rogers in his commentary on the *Articles*. He notes that:

The Anabaptists will not have the people to use the ministry of evil ministers; and think the service of wicked ministers unprofitable and not effectual; affirming, that no man who is himself faulty, can preach the truth to others. [651]

---

[649] Bray, *Documents of the English Reformation*, p. 190.
[650] Bray, *Tudor Church Reform*, p.201.
[651] Rogers, op.cit. p.271.

Although in the visible Church the evil be ever mingled with the good, and sometime the evil have chief authority in the ministration of the word and sacraments; yet forasmuch as they do not the same in their own name, but in Christ's, and do minister by His commission and authority, we may use their ministry both in hearing the word of God and in the receiving of the sacraments. Neither is the effect of Christ's ordinance taken away by their wickedness, nor the grace of God's gifts diminished from such as by faith and rightly do receive the sacraments ministered unto them, which be effectual because of Christ's institution and promise, although they be ministered by evil men.

In response to the teaching and practice of the radical Protestant groups, Article XXVI insists that there are inevitably wicked ministers in the visible Church, but that their personal wickedness should not deter us from receiving their ministry since they minister on behalf of Christ and the activity of God through them is not blocked by their shortcomings.

The theology underlying what is said here is well expressed by Bishop Beveridge in his commentary on this Article. He begins by explaining that:

> The visible Church, as we have seen before, is a congregation of faithful men; yet all are not truly faithful that are of this congregation: but the church whilst floating in the world is like Noah's ark, wherein there are both clean and unclean beasts; and like the floor our Saviour speaks of, wherein there is both wheat and chaff. So that though in the triumphant church above all are good and none hath bad as well as good; yet the militant church below hath bad as well as good, sinners as well as saints in it. Neither are the people only, but the priests also, oftentimes tainted with sin, and rebels against God whose ambassadors they are: not only such as the sacraments are administered to, but also such as administer the sacraments, are often defiled with sin, though consecrated unto Christ. Their office indeed is holy, but their persons are often sinful: their work is always a good and

godly work; but their hearts are frequently evil and wicked hearts.[652]

Beveridge then argues that in spite of their personal wickedness such ministers should not be boycotted because:

> ...if they be rightly called to the work, if it be their office to preach the word and administer the sacraments, we may hear the one and receive the other effectually at their hands, notwithstanding any personal infirmities they may lie under, or be guilty of. [653]

He gives three biblical examples in support of this argument.

The first is Jesus' words in Matthew 23:2-3 'The scribes and the Pharisees sit on Moses' seat; so practice and observe whatever they tell you, but not what they do; for they preach, but do not practice.' Beveridge comments:

> That the Scribes and Pharisees were unworthy ministers of God's word is clear, in that they said and did not; yet for all that they said and did not, the Jews were bound to do as they said: yea, our Saviour commands them to be attentive in hearing the word, though they were unworthy that delivered it. He doth not immediately command that they should be deposed from preaching the word to the people, but that the people should be diligent in hearing them: which is a plain demonstration that the word was not hindered by their ministry, but that for all the unworthiness of those that it was administered by, yet it might be effectual those it was administered to.[654]

The second is the appointment of the members of the tribe of Levi to act as priests in the Old Testament (Leviticus 28:1-29:46). Here Beveridge notes:

> God did not pick out only holy persons to administer his sacraments and offer the sacrifices, but he appointed a certain

---

[652] Beveridge, op.cit. pp.445-446.
[653] Ibid p.447.
[654] Ibid, p.447.

tribe, the tribe of Levi to do it. Though otherwise they might be unworthy for so holy and great a work, yet if they were of the

tribe of Levi, if it was their office to do it, the work itself was not made ineffectual by their personal infirmities.[655]

The third is the role of Judas Iscariot in baptising along with the other disciples in John 4:2. In the words of Beveridge:

...it is observable, that our Saviour also had one among his disciples that administered the sacrament of baptism, John 4:2; I say even amongst them he had one that was unworthy to do it, even a very Judas; yet, for all that, he suffered his sacrament to be administered by him, as well as any of the rest, though he knew him to be what he was.[656]

According to Beveridge, what lies behind these three examples is the truth expressed in Article XXVI that ministers do not act in their own name, but in the name of Christ:

It is not their own word they preach, but Christ's; not their own sacraments they administer, but Christ's; and therefore, be their own sins what they will, the ordinance is still Christ's ordinance; the institution of it is from Christ; the promises annexed to it are made by Christ; and we cannot think that Christ's grace should be hindered by man's sin; or that because ministers are not faithful to Christ, Christ should not therefore be faithful to his people in performing the promises made to them; which promises were not made to the administration of the promises by faithful persons, but to the ordinances in general, as duly administered even by such as are truly and rightly called to it. So that the ordinance is never the better for being administered by worthy, nor is it the worse for being administered by unworthy persons. Whether the

---

[655] Ibid pp.447-448.
[656] Ibid p.448.

ministers be worthy or unworthy, it is still by the grace of Christ his ordinances are made effectual.[657]

In terms of those coming to receive the sacraments or hear the preaching of the Word what this means is that:

> ...he that receives grace from an ordinance cannot thank the minister for his worthiness, but Christ for his goodness: and he that receives no grace must not blame the unworthiness of the minister, but the faithlessness of his own heart. For be the minister worthy or unworthy, if I come with faith to an ordinance I am sure to go with grace from it.[658]

Nevertheless it appertaineth to the discipline of the Church that inquiry be made of evil ministers, and that they be accused by those that have knowledge of their offences; and finally, being found guilty by just judgement, be deposed.

The fact that the worthiness of the minister is not required in order for the faithful to benefit from the celebration of the sacraments or the preaching of the word might seem to point to the conclusion that the worthiness of ministers was an issue of no importance. However, the article rejects this conclusion. It argues instead that proper discipline needs to be exercised against unworthy ministers. As Bray puts in his commentary:

> ...there is no excuse for tolerating either moral laxity or doctrinal deviance in the Christian ministry. It may be true that God's grace is able to overcome the defects caused by such things, but we also have a responsibility to make sure that both the preaching of the Gospel and its preachers are as pure as they can reasonably be expected to be. We are all sinners and make mistakes but that is not a pretext for deliberately denying the truth or for consciously living in a way that the Bible condemns. There is all the difference in the world between a man like Apollos, who was insufficiently instructed in the meaning of baptism but otherwise perfectly sound in the faith (Acts 18:24-28) and someone like Simon

[657]Ibid, p.448.
[658] Ibid, p..448-449.

Magus, who thought he could buy the power of the Holy Spirit (Acts 8:18-24). The former was a believer with more to learn – like us all!- but the latter had no idea what the Gospel was about and responded to in a way that contradicted its very nature. When we meet that kind of thing, as we do whenever we come across ministers who openly reject the Christian faith by their

teaching and lifestyle, we have a duty to protest and do what we can to remove them from the position that they have abused. [659]

In the contemporary Church of England the means by which the discipline called for in Article XXVI is exercised is through the *Ecclesiastical Jurisdiction Measure* 1963[660] for matters involving doctrine, ritual and ceremonial and the *Clergy Discipline Measure* 2003 for other matters.[661] These provide for precisely the inquiry and just judgement called for by the article.

---

[659] Bray, *The Faith We Confess*, pp.148-149.
[660] This can be found at
http://www.opsi.gov.uk/RevisedStatutes/Acts/ukcm/1963/cukcm_19630001_en_1
[661] This can be found at
http://www.cofe.anglican.org/about/churchlawlegis/clergydiscipline/

Article XXVII

∞

Of Baptism

Baptism is not only a sign of profession and mark of difference whereby Christian men are discerned from other that be not christened, but is also a sign of regeneration or new birth, whereby, as by an instrument, they that receive baptism rightly are grafted into the Church; the promises of the forgiveness of sin, and of our adoption to be the sons of God, by the Holy Ghost are visibly signed and sealed; faith is confirmed, and grace increased by virtue of prayer unto God. The baptism of young children is in any wise to be retained in the Church as most agreeable with the institution of Christ.

De Baptismo

Baptismus non est tantum professionis signum ac discriminis nota qua Christiani a non Christianis discernantur, sed etiam est signum regenerationis, per quod, tanquam per instrumentum, recte baptismum suscipientes Ecclesiae inseruntur; promissiones de remissione peccatorum atque adoptione nostra in filios Dei per Spiritum Sanctum visibiliter obsignantur; fides confirmatur, et vi divinae invocationis gratia augetur. Baptismus parvulorum omnino in Ecclesia retinendus est, ut qui cum Christi institutione optime congruat.

Article XXVII has its origins in Article XXVIII of the *Forty Two Articles*. This article was changed in two ways to become the present Article XXVII.

In 1563 the current last sentence replaced the weaker statement in the original article that:

The custom of the Church to christen young children is to be recommended and in any wise to be retained in the Church (Mos Ecclesisiae baptizandi parvulos et laudandus et omnino in Ecclesia retinendus).

In 1571 the English version of the Latin words 'signum regenerationis' in the second clause of the first sentence, which had read 'sign and seal of regeneration' in the 1553 and 1563 texts, was altered to read simply 'sign of regeneration' thus giving a straight equivalent to the Latin text.

The purpose of Article XXVII is to counter the ideas of those radical Protestant groups who maintained that baptism was simply an outward sign of Christian commitment and who denied that it should be administered to infants and young children. We have already noted in connection with Article XXV that the *Reformatio Legum Ecclesiasticarum* rejects the first of these ideas as heretical and it goes on to reject the second idea as well, criticising the 'cruel ungodliness' of those who 'do not want [baptism] to be administered to infants, though for no reason whatsoever.'[662]

Baptism is not only a sign of profession and mark of difference whereby Christian men are discerned from other that be not christened.

Although the English Reformers did not see it as sufficient to say that baptism was only an external sign of Christian faith, nevertheless, as the opening words of Article XXVII indicate, this was part of what they thought baptism was about. There are two points made in these words.

The first point is that baptism is 'a sign of profession.' What this means is that baptism is an outward indication of what it means to live as a Christian. We can see this from the words of the closing exhortation in the service for the baptism of infants in the *Book of Common Prayer*, in which, drawing on St. Paul's teaching in Romans 6:1-11, the minister declares:

Baptism doth represent unto us our profession; which is to follow the example of our saviour Christ, and to be made like unto him; that as he died and rose again for us, so should we, who are

---

[662] Bray, *Tudor Church Reform*, p.205.

baptized, die from sin and rise again unto righteousness, continually mortifying all our evil and corrupt affections, and daily proceeding in all virtue and godliness of living.

The second point is that baptism is an outward mark distinguishing Christian from non Christians, just as under the old covenant circumcision was an outward mark distinguishing Jews from non Jews. For the English Reformers a non-baptised Christian would have been a contradiction in terms. Baptism was an indispensable sign of identity.

This is a view of things that has become largely obscured in our society because of the high number of people who have been baptised, but give no other indication of Christian belief or practice. It is, however, a view of things that is still very clear in situations in which people convert to Christianity from another religion. In his book *Christian Faith Today* Stephen Neill notes, for example, that:

> In India the high-caste Hindu attaches such significance to baptism as would satisfy the most high-flying Christian orthodoxy. A Hindu, if he wishes, may accept in his heart all the tenets of the Christian faith; he may be regular at Christian worship and may contribute largely from his means in support of the Christian Church. He may even openly profess himself to be a friend and follower of Jesus. If he stops short of baptism, and is careful not to offend against the rules of his caste, his position in the Hindu community is unendangered and unimpaired. But let him take the fatal step, and all is altered. He is at once cut off from home and family, from all social ties, and from all his ancient roots in the life of his community. To his own people he is as one dead. It is baptism alone that makes the separation irrevocable.[663]

...but is also a sign of regeneration or new birth, whereby, as by an instrument, they that receive baptism rightly are grafted into the Church; the promises of the forgiveness of sin, and of our adoption to be the sons of God, by the Holy Ghost are visibly signed and sealed; faith is confirmed, and grace increased by virtue of prayer unto God

---

[663] S Neill., *Christian Faith Today*, London: Penguin, 1958, p.179.

Although the Reformers thus see baptism as an outward mark of Christian profession and identity for them it is more than this. It is also 'a sign of regeneration and new birth'. In this clause the word sign is being used in a different sense from the way in which it us used in the first clause of the article. In that clause 'sign' means simply an outward and visible mark, whereas in this clause it means what Article XXV has called an 'effectual sign' – a sign that effects what it signifies. In the case of the current article this means that baptism not only signifies 'regeneration or new birth' but actually effects it. In the language of Article XVII, baptism is the 'instrument' God uses to bring new birth about.

It is because baptism brings about new birth that in the service of baptism in the *Book of Common Prayer* the person who has been baptised is described as 'regenerate.' The use of this language goes back to two New Testament passages, John 3:5 and Titus 3:5, where the effects of baptism are described in terms of regeneration or new birth.[664]

In the history of the Church of England since the Reformation, and particularly in the nineteenth and twentieth centuries, the use of the term 'baptismal regeneration' became a cause of controversy between High Church Anglicans on the one hand and Evangelicals on the other. The former insisted that the language of the Bible and Prayer Book meant that those who were baptised were born again in Christ, while the latter were unwilling to say that someone who had been baptised, but showed no sign of Christian faith could be truly said to be born again.[665] If we look at the teaching of the English Reformers, however, it would appear that they took a third position.

We can see this, for example, in Nowell's *Catechism*. In this Alexander Nowell describes the effects of baptism in terms of regeneration through the death and resurrection of Christ and then gives the following exchange between the Master and the Scholar:

M. Do all generally, and without difference, receive this grace?

---

[664] For the interpretation of these two passages see E Ferguson, *Baptism in the Early Church*, Grand Rapids and Cambridge: Eerdmans, 2009, pp. 142-5 and 162-4.
[665] This dispute was the context for the 'Gorham Case' a Victorian cause celebre in which the High Church Bishop of Exeter, Henry Phillpotts, refused to institute an Evangelical clergyman, the Revd G C Gorham, to a living in his diocese because he found him unsound on the doctrine of baptismal regeneration.

S. The only faithful receive this fruit: but the unbelieving, in refusing the promises offered them by God, shut up the entry against themselves, and go away empty. Yet they do not thereby make that the sacraments lose their force and nature.[666]

What Nowell is saying here is that baptism really delivers God's gift of a new birth, but that this gift has to be received and where it is not received then the gift is unfruitful. Someone who is baptised is truly born again, but this fact is of no spiritual benefit to them unless they live out the new life that God has given them.

It is this understanding baptism that is in the background when Article XXVII declares that the effects of baptism are imported by God to those 'that receive baptism rightly.' 'Rightly' here does not mean that the right acts have been performed in the sense of the candidate being baptised with water in the name of the Trinity. What it means is that those who have been baptised must receive rightly what God has given to them and what this involves is explained in the Prayer Book catechism in which the question 'What is required of persons to be baptized?' is given the answer 'Repentance, whereby they forsake sin: and faith, whereby they steadfastly believe the promises of God, made to them in the Sacrament.'

For the English Reformers, then, baptism gives the person baptised God's gift of new life, but in order to be fruitful this gift has to be received and the way it is received is through repentance and faith.

Article XXVI next goes on to describe the consequences of baptism rightly received. It lists four of these, being grafted into the Church, being given the sign and seal of forgiveness and adoption, faith being confirmed and grace being increased.

The idea that those who receive baptism rightly are grafted into the Church is also found in the baptism service in the *Book of Common Prayer* where those baptised are said to be 'regenerate and grafted into the body of Christ's Church.' There are two ideas from St. Paul in the background here. The first is the image used by St. Paul in Romans 11:17-24 of Gentile Christians being grafted into God's people in the way that a wild olive shoot is grafted into a cultivated olive tree. The second is St. Paul's teaching in 1 Corinthians 12:13 that all Christians, whether Jews or Greeks, slaves or free people, where all baptised into the one body of

---

[666] Nowell, op.cit. p.208.

Christ which is the Church. What these two passages have in common is the idea that those who formerly did not belong to the people of God now belong to it and what the article and the Prayer Book are saying is that baptism is the means by which this takes place.

The idea that forgiveness and sins and adoption are given to us in baptism is also rooted in the teaching of the New Testament. In Acts 2:38 St. Peter declares 'Repent and be baptized every one of you for the forgiveness of your sins' and in Galatians 3:26-27 St. Paul teaches that those who have been baptized into Christ are 'sons of God, through faith.' The idea of sealing is likewise biblical, being fund in passages such as Ephesians 1:13 'in him you also, who have heard the word of truth, the gospel of your salvation, and have believed in him, were sealed with the promised Holy Spirit.' The connection between this last passage and baptism is that is by means of the Holy Spirit given in baptism that Christians are sealed.

As Gibson explains:

> With regard to the expression employed in the Article 'signed and sealed' (obsignantur), its force will be clearly seen when it is remembered that 'a seal is appended to a deed of gift or any other grant, when the donor, who has promised it, *actually makes the thing promised over to the receiver* and thereby assures the possession of it to him.'[667]

What this means is that baptism is the point at which the forgiveness of sins and adoption as God's children are actually bestowed on those who are baptised. It is this belief that underlies the prayer before the baptism in the *Book of Common Prayer* 'sanctify this Water to the mystical washing way of sin; and grant that the persons now to be baptized therein may receive the fullness of they grace, and ever remain in the number of thy faithful and elect children; through Jesus Christ our Lord.'

We have just noted that in the New Testament it is by means of the Holy Spirit that we are sealed and this is reflected in the grammatical construction of Article XXVII. Both in the English and the Latin versions of the article 'by the Holy Ghost' (per Spiritum Sanctum) refers to 'signed and sealed/obsignantur' rather than to 'our adoption to be sons of

---

[667] Gibson, op.cit. p.625. Italics in the original.

God.'[668] The Holy Spirit is the effective agent who bestows the benefits of baptism upon us.

The precise meaning of the final words in this section of the article 'faith is confirmed, and grace increased by virtue of prayer unto God' is not easy to ascertain. To quote Gibson again:

> No Scriptural authority can be urged, as in the case of the statements already made, for connecting these blessings with the administration of Baptism. Moreover, the Article contemplates the Baptism of infants, in whose case faith cannot be looked for; and yet the expression before us is 'faith is confirmed and grace increased' – words which of necessity presuppose an already existent 'faith' and 'grace' which can be 'confirmed' and increased.'[669]

The most likely explanation seems to be that these words are a description of what takes place in those baptised subsequent to baptism. In the baptism service in the *Book of Common Prayer* there is a prayer by the congregation in response to the exhortation after the reading of the Gospel, the first part of which runs as follows:

> Almighty and everlasting God, heavenly Father, we give thee humble thanks, for that thou hast vouchsafed to call us to the knowledge of this grace and faith in thee: Increase this knowledge and confirm this faith in us evermore.

What is asked for in these words correspond quite closely to the blessings referred to in Article XXVII and it is asked for on the basis of a recollection of the significance of baptism. What would make sense of the notion that 'faith is confirmed, and grace increased by virtue of prayer unto God' would be if those responsible for the wording of the article held that as a general rule faith was confirmed and grace increased subsequent to baptism because the recollection of baptism led to a prayer for further divine blessing which in turn led to God granting an increase in faith and a growth in grace in the life of the believer.

---

[668] For the details see Ibid pp, 629-30.
[669] Ibid, p.632.

This is not provable, but it makes sense of the wording of the article. It also corresponds to the way in which the Christian life actually unfolds. As Bray comments:

> Baptism confirms faith because once the promise has been received it serves as a reassurance that it will be fulfilled. People who embark on married life seldom realise what they are letting themselves in for, and they discover the implications of their commitment as they go along. So it is with Christian faith. We begin with little idea of what it really means, but find out by experience. As we analyze that, we can turn to our baptism to see what it is that we have committed ourselves to and what we can expect in the future. As things start to work out in that way, our trust in the promises of God is strengthened and confirmed, because we know what is coming and see it unfolding in front of our eyes. Finally, the grace of God works more fully and deeply in our lives as we open ourselves up to him in prayer. Infants grow in it as their parents and godparents pray for them, and those who are truly saved will start praying for themselves as soon as they understand what it means. The prayers of a little child may be simple and naïve, but they are not to be despised, because, Jesus said, it is the faith of a child which makes up the kingdom of heaven (Matthew 19:14).[670]

The baptism of young children is in any wise to be retained in the Church as most agreeable with the institution of Christ.

As has already been explained, the final section of Article XXVII is designed to combat the teaching of some of the radical Protestant groups that infants and children should not be baptised. The justification offered for the baptism of young children in this section of the article is rather general. It is simply said to be 'most agreeable with the institution of Christ.'

However, more light is shed on why the English Reformers believed that the baptism of young children ought to be maintained in the words of the *Reformatio Legum Ecclesiasticarum*. In response to the teaching of those who rejected infant baptism this declares:

---

[670] Bray, *The Faith We Confess*, p. 155.

...the children of Christians do not belong any less to God and the church than the children of the Hebrews once did, and since circumcision was given to them in infancy so also baptism ought to be imparted to our children, since they are participants in the same divine promise and covenant, and have been accepted by Christ with the greatest human kindness.[671]

There are two arguments in this quotation.

The first argument is that infant baptism is justified because of the continuity between circumcision and baptism.

This argument is developed by Nowell in his *Catechism*. Nowell argues that given that the grace of God is more plentifully revealed in the New Testament than in the Old it would be wrong if the sign of that grace was denied to the children of Christians when it was available to the children of Old Testament times:

> S...the Jews' children, being not yet by age capable of faith and repentance, were nevertheless circumcised; by which visible sign God shewed himself in the Old Testament to be the Father of young children and of the seed of his people. Now sith it is certain that the grace of God is both more plentifully poured and more clearly declared in the Gospel by Christ, than at that time it was in the Old Testament by Moses, it were a great indignity if the same grace should now be thought to be either obscurer or in any part abated.

> M. Go on forward.

> S. Sith it is certain that our infants have the force, and as it were the substance of baptism common with us, they should have wrong done them if the sign, which is inferior to the truth itself, should be denied them; and the same, which greatly availeth to testifying of the mercy of God and confirming his promises, being taken away, Christians should be defrauded of a singular comfort which they that were in old time enjoyed, and so should our infants be more hardly dealt with in the New Testament under Christ, than was dealt with the Jews' infants in the Old Testament

---

[671] Bray, *Tudor Church Reform* p.205.

under Moses. Therefore most great reason it is that by baptism, as by the print of a seal, it be assured to our infants that they be heirs of God's grace, and of the salvation promised to the seed of the faithful.[672]

The second argument is that children were accepted by Christ himself. The biblical basis for this argument is the story of Christ welcoming children in Matthew 19:13-15, Mark 10:13-16 and Luke 18:15-17. In the service for the baptism of infants in the Book of Common Prayer the Gospel reading is Mark 10:13-15 and this then forms the basis for the following exhortation justifying the practice of infant baptism:

> Beloved, ye hear in this Gospel the words of our Saviour Christ, that he commanded the children to be brought unto him; how he blamed those that would have kept them from him; how he exhorteth all men to follow their innocency. Ye perceive how by his outward gesture and deed he declared his good will toward them; for he embraced them in his arms, he laid his hands upon them, and blessed them. Doubt ye not therefore, but earnestly believe, that he will likewise favourably receive this present Infant; that he will embrace him with the arms of his mercy; that he will give unto him the blessing of eternal life, and make him partaker of his everlasting kingdom. Wherefore we being thus persuaded of the good will of our heavenly Father towards this Infant, declared by his Son Jesus Christ; and nothing doubting but that he favourably alloweth this charitable work of ours in bringing this Infant to his holy Baptism

It was for these reasons that the Tudor Church of England thought that infant baptism should be retained. They were aware of the obvious objection that to receive baptism rightly means to exercise repentance and faith and infants are capable of neither. Their answer was that there are two parts to baptism, the promise of God and the human response. In the case of the baptism of adults the two go together, but in the case of infants the promise of God is given when the baptism takes place and the response then follows later when the infant is old enough to respond for his or herself. To quote Nowell again:

---

[672] Nowell, op.cit. pp.209-210.

M. Sith infants cannot by age perform those things that thou speakest of, why are they baptized?

S. That faith and repentance go before baptism, is required only in persons so grown in years, that by age they are capable of both. But to infants the promise made to the Church by Christ, in whose faith are baptized, shall for the present time be sufficient; and then afterward, when they are grown to years, they must needs themselves acknowledge the truth of their baptism, and have the force thereof to be lively in their souls, and to be represented in their life and behaviours.[673]

For the Reformers confirmation fitted into the picture because it was the occasion when those baptised in infancy could publicly 'ratify and confirm' their personal acceptance of the promises made on their behalf by their Godparents at baptism and receive strengthening through the Holy Spirit to live the Christian life.

Thus in the Prayer Book confirmation service the bishop asks the candidates:

Do ye here, in the presence of God, and of this Congregation, renew the solemn promise and vow that was made in your name at your Baptism; ratifying and confirming the same in your own persons, and acknowledging yourselves bound to believe and to do all those things, which your Godfathers and Godmothers then undertook for you?

He also prays for them making clear the connection between their baptism and their confirmation:

Almighty and everliving God, who hast vouchsafed to regenerate these thy servants by Water and the Holy Ghost, and hast given unto them forgiveness of all their sins: Strengthen them, we beseech thee, O Lord, with the Holy Ghost the Comforter, and daily increase in them thy manifold gifts of grace; the spirit of wisdom and understanding; the spirit of counsel and ghostly

---

[673] Ibid p.209.

strength; the spirit of knowledge and true godliness; and fill them, O Lord, with the spirit of thy holy fear, now and for ever. Amen.

and

Defend, O Lord, this thy Child [or this thy Servant] with thy heavenly grace, that he may continue thine for ever; and daily increase in thy Holy Spirit, more and more, until he come unto thy everlasting kingdom. Amen.

The final point to note is that although Article XXVII affirms the propriety of infant baptism this does not mean that the Church of England rejects the baptism of adult candidates who have not previously been baptised in infancy. Provision was made for this in the 1662 revision of the *Book of Common Prayer* and with the decline in the number of infants being brought for baptism the proportion of adult baptism in the Church of England is steadily increasing.

Note: Infant baptism and ecumenical relations between Anglicans and Baptists.

Historically, the belief in, and practice of, infant baptism by the Church of England in line with Article XXVII has been a central difficulty in the way of the development of closer ecumenical relations between the Church of England and the Baptists.

However, the 2005 report of conversations between the Church of England and the Baptist Union of Great Britain, *Pushing at the Boundaries of Unity*, suggests a way forward on this issue. In his chapter in the report entitled 'One baptism: a Baptist perspective,' the Baptist theologian Paul Fiddes argues that the traditional polarisation between the advocates of infant and adult baptism can be overcome if we think in terms of the existence of two 'equivalent stories' of the journey of Christian initiation. He states:

If baptism is truly to be a means a means of binding Christians together ('one baptism'), we must then compare not simple moments – but journeys, and this means listening to others' stories of their journey. One journey, a Baptist experience, may be from infant blessing through Christian nurture in childhood to believers' baptism, laying on of hands for gifts of the Spirit, and then increasing use of those gifts in ministry in the world. An Anglican or Reformed journey might be from infant baptism, through Christian nurture in childhood, to public profession of faith, and laying on of hands in confirmation for gifts of the Spirit, to be used in ministry in the world.[674]

For Fiddes, recognising these as two equivalent journeys open up the possibility of the mutual recognition by the supporters of infant and adult baptism of each other's patterns of Christian initiation:

> We are in a broken situation where churches have different beliefs about baptism, owing to different interpretations of Scripture and the different paths they have taken in history. Without abandoning their convictions, Baptists might be able to value and affirm someone's whole journey of experience, and not just the moment of public profession of faith on which attention is usually fixed; they might be able gladly to recognize how God has used every stage of the journey for saving purposes. Correspondingly, those who baptize infants as well as believers (since all churches practise believers' baptism in the case of older converts) might feel more free to offer some parents the option of delaying the baptism of their child until a later age, with the alternative of a service of infant blessing.[675]

In support of this position he points to the commentary on paragraph 12 of the World Council of Churches' report *Baptism, Eucharist and Ministry*. This notes that:

> In some churches which unite both infant-baptist and believer-baptist traditions, it has been possible to regard as equivalent alternatives for entry into the church both a pattern whereby baptism in infancy is followed by later profession of faith and a pattern whereby believers' baptism follows upon a presentation and blessing in infancy. This example invites other churches to

---

[674] P Fiddes 'One baptism: a Baptist contribution' in *Pushing at the Boundaries of Unity*, London: CHP, 2005, pp.41-42
[675] Ibid p 42

decide whether they, too, could not recognize equivalent alternatives in their reciprocal relationships and in church union negotiations.[676]

Fiddes approach might not be accepted by all his fellow Baptists, but it does indicate a possible way forward for ecumenical relations between Anglicans and Baptists which would allow both sides to maintain their traditional positions while at the same time recognising the integrity of the other sides' approach.

---

[676] *Baptism, Eucharist and Ministry*, Geneva: WCC, 1982), p.5.

Article XXVIII

∞

Of the Lord's Supper

The Supper of the Lord is not only a sign of the love that Christians ought to have among themselves, one to another, but rather it is a sacrament of our redemption by Christ's death: insomuch that to such as rightly, worthily, and with faith receive the same, the bread which we break is a partaking of the body of Christ, and likewise the cup of blessing is a partaking of the blood of Christ.

Transubstantiation (or the change of the substance of bread and wine) in the Supper of the Lord, cannot be proved by Holy Writ, but is repugnant to the plain words of Scripture, overthroweth the nature of a Sacrament, and hath given occasion to many superstitions.

The body of Christ is given, taken, and eaten in the Supper, only after an heavenly and spiritual manner. And the mean whereby the body of Christ is received and eaten in the Supper is Faith.

The Sacrament of the Lord's Supper was not by Christ's ordinance reserved, carried about, lifted up, or worshipped.

De Coena Domini

Coena Domini non est tantum signum mutae benevolentiae Christianorum inter sese, verum potius est sacramentum nostrae per mortem Christi redemptionis. Atque ideo rite digne et cum fide sumentibus, panis quem frangimus est communicatio corporis Christi: similiter poculum benedictionis est communicatio sanguinis Christi.

Panis et vini transubstantiatio in Eucharistia ex sacris literis probari non potest, sed apertis Scripturae verbis adversatur, sacramenti naturam evertit, et multarum superstitionum dedit occasionem.

Corpus Christi datur, acciptur, et manducatur in Coena, tantum coelestis et spirituali ratione. Medium autem quo corpus Christi accipitur et manducatur in Coena, fides est.

Sacramentum Eucharistiae ex institutione Christi non servabatur, circumferebatur, elevabatur, nec adorabatur.

Article XXVVIII is the first of a series of four articles dealing with the Lord's Supper. It begins the series by giving a general overview of how the Lord's Supper is to be understood. The origins of the present article go back to Article XXIX of the *Forty Two Articles* and cannot be traced back to any earlier source.

When Article XXIX was revised to create the present article in 1563 the first, third and fourth paragraphs remained the same with the exception of the addition of the words 'overthroweth the nature of a Sacrament' in the second paragraph. The third paragraph, however, was completely changed.

The third paragraph of the 1553 article followed up the denial of the doctrine of transubstantiation in the previous paragraph by arguing that the ascension of Christ into heaven, together with the inability of human bodies to be in more than one place at the same time, means that is impossible to believe in the bodily presence of Christ's flesh and blood in the sacramental elements at the Lord's Supper. The article states:

> Forasmuch as the truth of Man's nature requireth, that the body of one, and the self same man cannot be at one time in diverse places, but must needs be in some one certain place: Therefore the body of Christ cannot be present at one time in many, and diverse places. And because (as Holy Scripture doth teach) Christ was taken up into heaven, and there shall continue unto the end of the world, a faithful man ought not, either to believe, or openly to confess the real, and bodily presence (as they term it) of Christ's flesh and blood, in the Sacrament of the Lord's Supper.

*Quum naturae humanae veritas requirat, ut unius eiusdemque
hominis corpus in multis locis simul esse non posset, sed in uno
aliquo et definito loco esse oporteat, idcicrco Christi corpus, in
multis et diversis locis, eodem tempore, praesens non potest. Et
quoniam ut tradunt Sacrae literae, Christus in Coelum fuit sublatus,
et ibi usque ad finem sculi est permansurus, non debet quisquam
fidelium carnis eius et sanguinis Realem et Corporem (ut
loquuntur) praesentiam in Eucharistia vel credere vel profiteri.*

When the present article was created this paragraph was totally deleted
and replaced by the present third paragraph which describes how the
body of Christ is given and received at the Lord's Supper.

With this revision the present article falls into four paragraphs
covering four subjects.

The first paragraph declares is not just a sign of the love
Christians have for one another but a means of partaking Christ's body
and blood. The second paragraph rejects the doctrine of
Transubstantiation. The third paragraph describes how the body of
Christ is received and the fourth paragraph rejects a number of Medieval
practices as contrary to Christ's ordinance.

**The Supper of the Lord is not only a sign of the love that Christians
ought to have among themselves, one to another, but rather it is a
sacrament of our redemption by Christ's death: insomuch that to
such as rightly, worthily, and with faith receive the same, the bread
which we break is a partaking of the body of Christ, and likewise the
cup of blessing is a partaking of the blood of Christ.**

The first three clauses of this paragraph are a response to the teaching of
certain radical Protestant groups that saw the Lord's Supper purely as a
sign of the love that Christians ought to have for one another. Their
position, building on St. Paul's teaching in 1 Corinthians 10:17, was that
the partaking of the Lord's Supper was a manifestation of the oneness of
the Church as the body of Christ and therefore a sign of the love that
Christians should have for one another as members of the body. The
article does not reject this idea but says that it does not go far enough as a
description of the significance of the Lord's Supper.

According to the article this is because the Lord's Supper is in fact 'a sacrament of our redemption by Christ's death.' Article XXV has already defined a sacrament as an effectual signs of grace through which God works invisibly in us and in the case of the sacrament of the Lord's Supper what we have is effectual sign 'of our redemption by Christ's death.' That is to say, it is the outward sign of Christ's death on the cross for us by means of which the spiritual benefits of that death become effective in us, what the Prayer Book Catechism calls 'the strengthening and refreshing of our souls by the Body and Blood of Christ.'

The final part of the paragraph explains why the Lord's Supper is 'a sacrament of our redemption by Christ's death.' Like the teaching of the radical Protestant groups the article draws on St. Paul's words in 1 Corinthians 10:16-17, but the article focuses of his declaration that when Christians partake of the bread and wine they partake of the body and blood of Christ. According to the article this declaration means that when the Lord's Supper is celebrated 'the bread which we break is a partaking of the body of Christ, and likewise the cup of blessing is a partaking of the blood of Christ.'

This paragraph does not explain what partaking means. A discussion of this subject is postponed until the second and third paragraphs of the article. What it does affirm is that partaking only takes place in the case of those who receive the article 'rightly, worthily, and with faith.' No explanation of these words is provided by the article itself, but an explanation is provided in the homily 'Of the worthy receiving and reverend esteeming of the body and blood of Christ' in the *Second Book of Homilies* to which we have already referred in looking at Article XXV. As we have seen when look at that article what the homily lays down is that worthy reception involves, knowledge, faith and freedom from un-repented sin. Only when these three elements are present do we receive the sacrament 'rightly, worthily and with faith' and so partake of Christ's body and blood.

This last point raises the question of what happens when someone in whom these elements are missing receives the sacrament. If they do not partake of the body and blood of Christ then what does happen? This is not an issue that is addressed in this article, but it is addressed in Article XXIX 'Of the wicked which eat not the body of Christ in the use of the Lord's Supper' and we shall look at it there.

Transubstantiation (or the change of the substance of bread and wine) in the Supper of the Lord, cannot be proved by Holy Writ, but is repugnant to the plain words of Scripture, overthroweth the nature of a Sacrament, and hath given occasion to many superstitions.

The second paragraph of the article begins to address the issue of what it means to partake of the body and blood of Christ, by rejecting the Medieval doctrine of transubstantiation, the doctrine that at the Lord's Supper the faithful receive the body and blood of Christ because at the moment of consecration the substance of the bread and the substance of the wine have ceased to exist and have been replaced by the body and blood of Christ.

This view of what happens at the Lord's Supper makes use of the philosophical distinction between the substance of a something and its accidents. The substance of something is what is in itself whereas its accidents are those qualities that it has that appear to the senses, its colour, its feel, its smell, its taste and so forth. In normal circumstances the substance and accidents of something go together. Thus a football is a football in terms of its substance and has the accidents appropriate to this fact (which is why we can perceive that it is a football). However, in the case of the elements at the Lord's Supper, it is argued, since Jesus said 'this is my body' and 'this is my blood' (Matthew 26:26-27, Mark 14:22-24, Luke 22:19-20, 1 Corinthians 11:24-25) the accidents of the bread and wine remain (so that they look, taste and smell like bread and wine) but the substance of them changes into the body and blood of Christ. This what the article is referring to when it talks about 'the change of the substance of bread and wine.'

The use of the term 'transubstantiation' to describe the change in the elements first occurs in the eleventh century and the use of the term was upheld at the Fourth Lateran Council of 1215, Canon 1 of which declared that the body and blood of Christ 'are truly contained in the sacrament of the altar under the forms of bread and wine; the bread being changed *(transsubstantiatio)* by divine power into the body, and the wine into the blood.'[677] It was also upheld at the thirteenth session of the Council of Trent in 1551 which stated that:

> ...since Christ our Redeemer declared that to be truly His own body which He offered under the form of bread, it has, therefore, always been a firm belief in the Church of God, and this holy council declares it anew, that by the consecration of the bread and wine a change is brought about of the whole substance of the bread into the substance of the body of Christ our Lord, and of the whole substance of the wine into the substance of his blood. This change the holy Catholic Church properly and appropriately calls transubstantiation. [678]

Article XXVIII rejects the doctrine of transubstantiation for four reasons. These are helpfully explained by Gibson as follows:

> (1) **Cannot be proved by Holy Writ.**[679] It is hard to see how a philosophical theory such as Transubstantiation confessedly is, can ever be 'proved by Holy Writ.' Romanists point to the words of institution, Τουτό ἐστιν τό σωμά μου [this is my body]. But though they can certainly be claimed in favour of the real Presence, yet to bring into them a theory of 'accidents' remaining while the substance is changed, is to read into this text that which is certainly not contained in it, and what we deny can reasonably be inferred from it.

> (2) It **is repugnant to the plain words of Scripture**. According to the theory now under consideration, what remains after consecration is no longer 'bread' and has no claim to be so called. But Scripture freely speaks of what is received as 'bread,' e.g. 'As often as ye eat this bread and drink of this cup, ye proclaim the Lord's death until he come...Let a man prove himself, and so let him eat of the bread and drink of the cup' (1 Corinthians 11:26, 28).

---

[677] Fourth Lateran Council, Canon I, text at http://www.fordham.edu/halsall/basis/lateran4.html
[678] Council of Trent, Session 13 Ch IV, text in Leith, op. cit., p. 432.
[679] 'Writ' means Scripture.

(3) It **overthroweth the nature of a Sacrament**. It is of the essence of a sacrament that there should be in it two parts – the 'outward visible sign' and the 'inward spiritual grace' But if 'bread,' the outward visible sign in the Eucharist, no longer remains after consecration, one of the two essential parts has been destroyed, and the 'nature of a sacrament' is overthrown.

(4) It **hath given occasion to many superstitions**. These words are only too painfully true, and in support of them reference can be made to the medieval stories of alleged miracles, such as those freely instanced by Paschasius Radbert,[680] in which the Host has disappeared and the Infant Christ Himself been seen, or where drops of blood have been seen to flow from the consecrated wafer.[681]

The body of Christ is given, taken, and eaten in the Supper, only after an heavenly and spiritual manner. And the mean whereby the body of Christ is received and eaten in the Supper is Faith.

The second paragraph of the article having declared that partaking of the body and blood of Christ at the Lord' Supper ought to not to be understood in terms of the doctrine of Transubstantiation, the third paragraph goes on to explain how it should be understood. For reasons that are not clear, it only talks about the 'body of Christ,' but presumably what it says Christ's body would also apply to his blood.

It says that the body of Christ is 'given, taken and eaten' after a 'heavenly and spiritual manner.' What this means is that it is given, taken eaten in a way that corresponds to the fact that Christ's body is in heaven and not through a material eating, but through the work of the Holy Spirit. Furthermore the medium through which the body of Christ is received and eaten is faith.

These points are explained in more detail by Alexander Nowell in his *Catechism*.

Like Article XXVIII, Nowell rejects the idea that there is any change in the substance of the elements at the Lord's Supper anymore

---

[680] Paschasius Radbertus (c 790-865) was a theologian who included such stories in his treatise *Of the Body and Blood of Christ*.
[681] Gibson, op.cit. p.657-658.

than there is a change in the substance of the water at baptism. Nevertheless, he says, at the Lord's Supper, by the Holy Spirit and through faith, we are fed and sustained by God to eternal life:

> S. In both the sacraments the substances of the outward things are not changed; but the word of God and heavenly grace coming to them (Ephesians 5;26, Galatians 3:27, Titus 3:5), there is such efficacy, that as by baptism we are once regenerate in Christ, and are first, as it were, joined and grafted into his body (John 3;5, Titus 3:5); so, when we rightly receive the Lord's Supper, with the very divine nourishment of his body and blood (John 6:35, 51, 54, 55, 1 Corinthians 11:28-29) most full of health and immortality, given to us by the work of the Holy Ghost, and received of us by faith, as the mouth of our soul, we are continually fed and sustained to eternal life, growing together in them both into one body with Christ (John 6:51, 54 etc).[682]

According to Nowell we truly received what is promised to us in word and sign at the Lord's Supper and, as Article XXVIII declares, it is through faith that we are able to do this:

> M. Is there then not an only figure, but the truth itself of the benefits that thou hast rehearsed, delivered in the supper?

> S. What else? For sith [since] Christ is the truth itself (John 1:17, 14:6), it is no doubt but that the thing which he testifieth in words, and representeth in signs, he performeth also in deed, and delivereth it unto us; and that he as surely maketh them that believe in him partakers of his body and blood (John 6:54, 56, 64), as they surely know that they have received the bread and wine with their mouth and stomach.

> M. Sith we be in the earth, and Christ's body in heaven, how can that be that thou sayest?

---

[682] Nowell, op.cit. p. 214.

S. We must lift our souls and hearts from earth, and raise them up by faith to heaven, where Christ is (John 6:62, 64, Colossians 3:1, Hebrews 4:14, 16).

M. Sayest thou then the mean to receive the body and blood of Christ standeth upon faith?

S. Yea. For when we believe that Christ died to deliver us from death, and that he rose again to procure us life (John 6:35, Acts 4:10,12, Romans 4:24-25, 5:8, 14:9) we are partakers of the redemption purchased by his death, and of his life, and all other his good things; and with the same conjoining wherewith the head and the members are knit together (1 Corinthians 6:15, 12:27, Ephesians 4;15, 16, 5:29-30), he coupleth us to himself by secret and marvelous virtue of his Spirit, even so that we be members of his body, and be of his flesh and bones, and do grow into one body with him. [683]

The Sacrament of the Lord's Supper was not by Christ's ordinance reserved, carried about, lifted up, or worshipped.

Because the Medieval Church believed that the consecrated bread and wine were permanently changed into the body and blood of Christ it believed that the consecrated bread represented the localised presence of God in the midst of his people. This being the case, consecrated hosts were reserved, not only for the purpose of giving communion to the sick who were unable to attend Mass, but as objects of worship and they were also elevated and carried in procession at the Feast of Corpus Christi and at other times, once again for the purposes of worship.

The thirteenth session of the Council of Trent upheld this theology and practice. It declared that there is:

...no room for doubt that all the faithful of Christ may, in accordance with a custom always received in the Catholic Church, give to this holy sacrament in veneration the worship of *latria*, which is due to the true God. Neither is it to be less adored for the reason that it was instituted by Christ the Lord in order to be

---

[683] Ibid, p.215.

received. For we believe in it the same God is present of who the eternal Father, when introducing him into the world, says: *And let all the angels of God adore him*; whom the Magi falling down, adores; who finally, as the Scriptures testify, was adored by the Apostles in Galilee.

On this basis it also upheld the reservation and veneration of the sacrament and the practice of carrying it in procession.[684]

Article XXVIII rejects the Medieval practices endorsed by Trent. Both here and in Article XXV the point is made that these practices lack dominical authority. For the English Reformers the key thing was that at the Last Supper Jesus told his disciples to take and eat and take and drink in thankful remembrance of his death on their behalf. In their view this command meant that that the consecrated bread should be eaten and that it would be wrong to use it for any other purpose.

The fundamental theological point here is helpfully explained by Bicknell in his commentary on this article:

> We hold that the Christian religion has a two-fold foundation, Christian experience and historic fact. Both are necessary. Each reinforces the other. In order that experience may be kept Christian, it needs constantly to be tested by the New Testament. In support of the doctrine of the Eucharist, we can appeal not only to Christian experience throughout the ages and to the intrinsic moral and spiritual value of its symbolism, but also to the mind and promise of Christ as revealed in the historic fact of its institution. The sense of His presence and of the new life that he imparts is no mere product of collective imagination. It is guaranteed by his actual word and act. But there is nothing in His institution or in the outward signs to suggest in any way that He gave us the Eucharist in order that through the consecrated elements He might dwell among us to-day by an abiding external presence comparable to His presence during His life on earth. 'The presence is given under a form which indicates that it is to be received.' Any other use is not only unauthorized and goes beyond the declared purpose of Christ, but is in danger of

---

[684] Council of Trent, Session 13, Chs V-VI, in Leith, op. cit., pp.432-433.

obscuring that purpose by suggesting that 'the value of the Sacrament is intended to reside in itself.'[685]

It is important to realise that the primary concern of Article XXXVIII at this point is to reject the reservation of the elements at the Lord's Supper for the purposes of subsequent adoration. It does not address the issue of whether it may be proper to reserve the sacrament in order to give it to the sick or to form the basis of a service extended communion when a priest is not available.

Note: the ARCIC I agreed statement on the Eucharist

Given the disagreement between Church of England and Roman Catholic theology on the doctrine of the Eucharist in the 16th century highlighted by Article XXVIII, it is important to note the agreement on the Eucharist between Anglican and Roman Catholic theologians expressed in the ARCIC I agreed statement on Eucharistic Doctrine in 1971.

In the section of this statement on 'The Presence of Christ' it declares:

> Communion with Christ in the eucharist presupposes his true presence, effectually signified by the bread and wine which, in this mystery, become his body and blood. The real presence of his body and blood can, however, only be understood within the context of the redemptive activity whereby he gives himself, and in himself reconciliation, peace and life, to his own. On the one hand, the eucharistic gift springs out of the paschal mystery of Christ's death and resurrection, in which God's saving purpose has already been definitively realised. On the other hand, its purpose is to transmit the life of the crucified and risen Christ to his body, the church, so that its members may be more fully united with Christ and with one another.
>
> Christ is present and active, in various ways, in the entire eucharistic celebration. It is the same Lord who through the proclaimed word invites his people to his table, who through his minister presides at that table, and who gives himself sacramentally in the body and blood of his paschal sacrifice. It is

---

[685] Bicknell, op.cit., pp. 507-508, citing W Temple *Christus Veritas* p.241,

the Lord present at the right hand of the Father, and therefore transcending the sacramental order, who thus offers to his church, in the eucharistic signs, the special gift of himself.

The sacramental body and blood of the Saviour are present as an offering to the believer awaiting his welcome. When this offering is met by faith, a life giving encounter results. Through faith Christ's presence which does not depend on the individual's faith in order to be the Lord's real gift of himself to his church becomes no longer just a presence for the believer, but also a presence with him.

Thus, in considering the mystery of the eucharistic presence, we must recognize both the sacramental sign of Christ's presence and the personal relationship between Christ and the faithful which arises from that presence.

The Lord's words at the last supper, "Take and eat; this is my body", do not allow us to dissociate the gift of the presence and the act of sacramental eating. The elements are not mere signs; Christ's body and blood become really present and are really given. But they are really present and given in order that, receiving them, believers may be united in communion with Christ the Lord.[686]

This statement is in line with the teaching of Article XXVIII in that it declares that at the Eucharist Christ gives the gifts of his body and blood to be received by faith in order that the believer may be united in communion with him. The ARCIC I statement on the Eucharist as a whole was agreed to be 'consonant in substance' with the faith of the Church of England by General Synod in 1986.

It should also be noted, however, that in the ARCIC I 'Elucidation' on Eucharistic Doctrine published in 1979 recorded continuing disagreement on the issue of the adoration of Christ in the reserved sacrament. It stated that there are those who still find 'any kind of adoration of Christ in the reserved sacrament unacceptable' and who believe that:

---

[686] Text in C Hill and E J Yarnold (eds), *Anglicans and Roman Catholics: The search for unity*, London: SPCK, 1994, pp.20-21.

...this devotion can hardly fail to produce such an emphasis upon the association of Christ's sacramental presence with the consecrated bread and wine as to suggest too static and localized a presence that disrupts the movement as well as the balance of the whole eucharistic action (cf. Article 28 of the Articles of Religion).[687]

---

[687] Ibid p.28.

Article XXIX

∞

Of the wicked which do not eat the body of Christ, in the use of the Lord's Supper

The wicked and such as be void of a lively faith, although they do carnally and visibly press with their teeth (as S. Augustine saith) the sacrament of the body and blood of Christ, yet in no wise are they partakers of Christ, but rather to their condemnation do eat and drink the sign or sacrament of so great a thing.

De manducatione corporis Christi, et impios illud non manducare

Impii et viva fide destituti, licer carnaliter et visibilitur (ut Augustinus loquitur) corporis et sanguinis Christi sacramentum dentibus premant, nullo tamen modo Christi participes efficiuntur; sed potius tantae rei sacramentum seu symbolum ad iudicium sibi manducant et bibunt.

This article has its origins in the revision of the Articles during the reign of Elizabeth I. It first appears in Archbishop Parker's MS which was signed by the bishops of the Convocation of Canterbury on January 29 1563. It is also found in two English MSS of about the same date in the Public Record Office, in one of which there is a marginal note which states 'This is the original but not passed.'

However, in a Latin MS of the same date which is also in the Record Office the article is missing. The article is also missing in the edition of the Articles published a few months later by direct authority of Queen Elizabeth by Wolfe, the royal printer. It is also missing in all the printed copies of the Articles up to 1571.

The article appears again in May 1571. The bishops of the Upper House of the Convocation of Canterbury had looked again at the articles and a copy including Article XXIX was subscribed to by Archbishop Parker and ten other bishops. In spite of objections from Bishop Guest of

Rochester the article was also included in the copy of the Articles which was subsequently ratified by Elizabeth I and it is found thereafter in all printed copies of the Articles, both Latin and English.

What this evidence suggests is that after having been agreed by the bishops the article was subsequently omitted, either during the passage of the Articles through the Lower House of the Convocation of Canterbury or at an even later stage due the direct intervention of the Queen. The most plausible explanation for its omission was it was felt likely to create difficulties for those loyal to Rome who remained within the Church of England or to cause an impediment to a political or matrimonial alliance with the Lutheran states in Germany. By 1571 the breach with Rome was complete following the Pope's excommunication of Queen Elizabeth and an alliance with the Lutherans was no longer in prospect. The reasons for its omitting the article therefore no longer applied.

The purpose of the article is to answer a question raised by what has been said in the previous article. If those who receive the elements 'rightly, worthily, and with faith' partake of the body and blood of Christ what is consumed by those receive the sacrament in an unworthy fashion?

The answer given to this question in Medieval theology was that those who receive the sacraments unworthily receive the body and blood of Christ, but receive no spiritual benefit thereby, but rather incur divine judgement. Article XXIX rejects this Medieval approach, which was maintained by those who remained loyal to Rome and supplies an alternative answer.

The wicked and such as be void of a lively faith, although they do carnally and visibly press with their teeth (as S. Augustine saith) the sacrament of the body and blood of Christ, yet in no wise are they partakers of Christ

The article begins by describing those who receive the sacrament unworthily as 'the wicked and such as be void of a lively faith.' This could either refer to two sets of people, those who are morally wicked and those who lack faith, or to a single set of people, those who are both morally wicked and lacking in faith. Either way it is clear that it is referring to those who do not meet the requirements for worth reception of the sacrament set out in the previous article.

517

The article then refers to a saying of St. Augustine in the twenty sixth of his lectures on St. John's Gospel. This lecture is on John 6:41-59 and the passage cited in the article runs as follows

> In a word, he now explains how that which he speaks of comes to pass, and what it is to eat His body and drink His blood. 'He that eateth my flesh, and drinketh my blood, dwelleth in me, and I in him.' This it is, therefore, for a man to eat that meat and drink that drink, to dwell in Christ, and to have Christ dwell in him. Consequently, he that dwelleth not in Christ, and in who Christ dwelleth not, doubtless eateth not His flesh [spiritually] not drinketh his blood [although he may press the sacrament of the body and blood of Christ carnally and visibly with his teeth], but rather doth he eat and drink the sacrament of so great a thing to his own judgement, because he, being unclean, has presumed to come to the sacraments of Christ, which no man taketh worthily except that he is pure: of such it is said, 'Blessed are the pure in heart, for they shall see God.'[688]

It has been suggested that the words in square bracket have been interpolated and are due not to St. Augustine, but to Bede in whose commentary on John they are also found. Be that as it may, the full quotation is what the author of Article XXIX had in mind and it makes clear the theological logic of what is said in a compressed fashion in the article.

The logic is that according to John 6:54 eating Christ's flesh and drinking his blood means a mutual indwelling between an individual and Christ. In John's Gospel this indwelling involves faith (John 6:35) and obedience to Christ's commands (John 14:23-24, 15:10) and consequently those who do not believe and are not obedient in the way they behave do not dwell in Christ and therefore do not eat his flesh or drink his blood. That is why they are not 'partakers of Christ.'

..but rather to their condemnation do eat and drink the sign or sacrament of so great a thing.

---

[688] St. Augustine, *Lectures or Tractates on the Gospel According to St.John,* XXVI:18, in P Schaff (ed), *Nicene and Post Nicene Fathers,* Vol VII, Edinburgh: T&T Clark, 1991, p.173.

The Article then goes on to say that those who receive the sacrament, but do not feed on Christ, eat the outward and visible signs of Christ's body and blood but do not receive the reality which those signs signify. No only that, but they eat these outward signs 'to their condemnation.'

The article takes this latter idea from 1 Corinthians 11:27-30 where St. Paul declares:

> Whoever, therefore, eats the bread or drinks the cup of the Lord in an unworthy manner will be guilty of profaning the body and blood of the Lord. Let a man examine himself, and so eat of the bread and drink of the cup. For any one who eats and drinks without discerning the body eats and drinks judgement upon himself. That is why many of you are weak and ill, and some have died. But if we judged ourselves truly, we should not be judged. But when we are judged by the Lord, we are chastened so that we may not be condemned along with the world.

This passage is referred to in Article XXV and, as we noted when looking at that article, the condemnation referred to in it is not eternal damnation, but rather a temporal, though potentially very severe, judgement designed to bring us back to God and therefore avoid eternal damnation at the last judgement.

This passage is also quoted in the exhortation before communion in the *Book of Common Prayer*. This exhortation provides a pastoral application of the teaching in Articles XXV and XXIX in that in it the minister warns the congregation of the danger of an unworthy reception of the sacrament and exhorts them to amend their lives accordingly:

> Dearly beloved in the Lord, ye that mind to come to the holy Communion of the Body and Blood of our Saviour Christ, must consider how Saint Paul exhorteth all persons diligently to try and examine themselves, before they presume to eat of that Bread, and drink of that Cup. For as the benefit is great, if with a true penitent heart and lively faith we receive that holy Sacrament; (for then we spiritually eat the flesh of Christ, and drink his blood; then we dwell in Christ, and Christ in us; we are one with Christ, and Christ with us;) so is the danger great, if we receive the same unworthily. For then we are guilty of the Body

and Blood of Christ our Saviour; we eat and drink our own damnation, not considering the Lord's Body; we kindle God's wrath against us; we provoke him to plague us with divers diseases, and sundry kinds of death. Judge therefore yourselves, brethren, that ye be not judged of the Lord; repent you truly for your sins past; have a lively and steadfast faith in Christ our Saviour; amend your lives, and be in perfect charity with all men; so shall ye be meet partakers of those holy mysteries.

An additional pastoral application of the teaching about the unworthy reception of the sacrament in these articles can be found in the warning about a forthcoming celebration of Holy Communion which is also contained in the communion service in the *Book of Common Prayer.* In this warning the minister first of all informs the congregation that he intends to celebrate the sacrament, warns them of the need to make spiritual preparation:

Dearly beloved, on _ day next I purpose, through God's assistance, to administer to all such as shall be religiously and devoutly disposed the most comfortable Sacrament of the Body and Blood of Christ; to be by them received in remembrance of his meritorious Cross and Passion, whereby alone we obtain remission of our sins, and are made partakers of the kingdom of heaven. Wherefore it is our duty to render most humble and hearty thanks to Almighty God our heavenly Father, for that he hath given his Son our Saviour Jesus Christ, not only to die for us, but also to be our spiritual food and sustenance in that holy Sacrament. Which being so divine and comfortable a thing to them who receive it worthily, and so dangerous to them that will presume to receive it unworthily; my duty is to exhort you in the mean season to consider the dignity of that holy mystery, and the great peril of the unworthy receiving thereof; and so to search and examine your own consciences, and that not lightly, and after the manner of dissemblers with God: but so that ye may come holy and clean to such a heavenly Feast, in the marriage-garment required by God in holy Scripture, and be received as worthy partakers of that holy Table.

He then explains that the way to make adequate preparation is through self examination leading to repentance and appropriate action:

> The way and means thereto is; First, to examine your lives and conversations by the rule of God's commandments; and whereinsoever ye shall perceive yourselves to have offended, either by will, word, or deed, there to bewail your own sinfulness, and to confess yourselves to Almighty God, with full purpose of amendment of life. And if ye shall perceive your offences to be such as are not only against God, but also against your neighbours; then ye shall reconcile yourselves unto them; being ready to make restitution and satisfaction, according to the uttermost of your powers, for all injuries and wrongs done by you to any other; and being likewise ready to forgive others that have offended you, as you would have forgiveness of your offences at God's hand; for otherwise the receiving of the holy Communion doth nothing else but increase your damnation. Therefore if any of you be a blasphemer of God, an hinderer or slanderer of his Word, an adulterer, or be in malice, or envy, or in any other grievous crime, repent you of your sins, or else come not to that holy Table; lest, after the taking of that holy Sacrament, the devil enter into you, as he entered into Judas, and fill you full of all iniquities, and bring you to destruction both of body and soul.

Finally, he offers the possibility of private confession and absolution to any whose consciences are still troubled:

> And because it is requisite, that no man should come to the holy Communion, but with a full trust in God's mercy, and with a quiet conscience; therefore if there be any of you, who by this means cannot quiet his own conscience herein, but requireth further comfort or counsel, let him come to me, or to some other discreet and learned Minister of God's Word, and open his grief; that by the ministry of God's holy Word he may receive the benefit of absolution, together with ghostly counsel and advice, to the quieting of his conscience, and avoiding of all scruple and doubtfulness.

Note: the teaching of the *Formula of Concord*

The Lutheran *Formula of Concord* of 1577 takes the opposite view of the eating of the sacrament by the wicked than that taken in Article XXIX. As can seen in the extract from the *Formula of Concord* below, it holds that 'unworthy, unbelieving, false, and wicked Christians' eat the body of Christ at the Lord's Supper, albeit in a manner that is 'injurious and damning.'

This extract also shows the reason that the *Formula of Concord* takes a different position from Article XXIX is due to a different understanding on what it means to feed on the flesh of Christ. The English Reformers held that there is only one means of feeding on the body and blood of Christ, the feeding by faith which takes place when a worthy recipient receives the elements at the Lord's Supper. The Lutheran Reformers, on the other hand held that there was a twofold feeding, a spiritual feeding by faith and an 'oral' or 'sacramental' feeding that takes place when the bread and wine are consumed whether by the faithful or by the wicked. In the words of the *Formula of Concord*:

> There is, therefore, a two-fold eating of the flesh of Christ, one spiritual, of which Christ treats especially John 6:54, which occurs in no other way than with the Spirit and faith, in the preaching and meditation of the Gospel, as well as in the Lord's Supper, and by itself is useful and salutary, and necessary at all times for salvation to all Christians; without which spiritual participation also the sacramental or oral eating in the Supper is not only not salutary, but even injurious and damning [a cause of condemnation].
>
> But this spiritual eating is nothing else than faith, namely, to hear God's Word (wherein Christ, true God and man, is presented to us, together with all benefits which He has purchased for us by His flesh given into death for us, and by His blood shed for us, namely, God's grace, the forgiveness of sins, righteousness, and eternal life), to receive it with faith and appropriate it to ourselves, and in all troubles and temptations firmly to rely, with sure confidence and trust, and to abide in the consolation that we have a gracious God, and eternal salvation on account of the Lord Jesus Christ. [He who hears these things related from the Word of God, and in faith receives and applies;

them to himself, and relies entirely upon this consolation (that we have God reconciled and life eternal on account of the Mediator, Jesus Christ),-he, I say, who with true confidence rests in the Word of the Gospel in all troubles and temptations, spiritually eats the body of Christ and drinks His blood.]

The other eating of the body of Christ is oral or sacramental, when the true, essential body and blood of Christ are also orally received and partaken of in the Holy Supper, by all who eat and drink the consecrated bread and wine in the Supper-by the believing as a certain pledge and assurance that their sins are surely forgiven them, and Christ dwells and is efficacious in them, but by the unbelieving for their judgement and condemnation, as the words of the institution by Christ expressly declare, when at the table and during the Supper He offers His disciples natural bread and natural wine, which He calls His true body and true blood, at the same time saying: Eat and drink. For in view of the circumstances this command evidently cannot be understood otherwise than of oral eating and drinking, however, not in a gross, carnal, Capernaitic,[689] but in a supernatural, incomprehensible way; to which afterwards the other command adds still another and spiritual eating, when the Lord Christ says further: This do in remembrance of Me, where He requires faith [which is the spiritual partaking of Christ's body].

Therefore all the ancient Christian teachers expressly, and in full accord with the entire holy Christian Church, teach, according to these words of the institution of Christ and the explanation of St. Paul, that the body of Christ is not only received spiritually by faith, which occurs also outside of [the use of] the sacrament, but also orally, not only by believing and godly, but also by unworthy, unbelieving, false, and wicked Christians.[690]

The fundamental hermeneutical issue at stake here is whether John 6 and the accounts of the words of institution at the Last Supper in the Synoptic Gospels and 1 Corinthians testify to two types of feeding on Christ as the

---

[689] 'Capernaitic' means 'cannibalistic. '

[690] *Formula of Concord* Ch 7:61-66. Text at http://www.bookofconcord.org/sd-supper.php

Lutherans held or whether, as the English Reformers thought, John 6 explains the true meaning of the eating and drinking of Christ's body and blood referred to in the words of institution.

The theological differences between Anglican and Lutheran theology highlighted in this note have not been addressed in the Anglican-Lutheran theological dialogues that have taken place in recent years and they remain an unresolved issue between the Anglican and Lutheran traditions.

Article XXX

∞

Of Both Kinds

The Cup of the Lord is not to be denied to the lay people; for both parts of the Lord's sacrament, by Christ's ordinance and commandment, ought to be ministered to all Christian men alike.

De Utraque Specie

Calix Domini laicis non est denegandus, utraque enim pars Dominici sacramenti, ex Christi institutione et praecepto, omnibus Christianis ex aequo administrari debet.

This article was introduced when the Articles were revised in 1563 and it has remained unchanged since then. It does not appear to go back to any previous source.

The purpose of the article is to reject the medieval practice of giving the laity the bread only and not also the wine at communion, a practice which was endorsed by the Roman Catholic Church at the twenty first session of the Council of Trent in 1562.

The words of St. Paul in 1 Corinthians 11:28 'Let a man examine himself and so eat of the bread and drink of the cup' indicate that at Corinth both the elements were received at the Lord's Supper and there is no evidence to suggest that this was not also the case in the other churches during the New Testament period.

There is also clear evidence that during the Patristic period it continued to be the practice to receive both the bread and the wine.

For example, in the second century St. Justin Martyr declares in his *First Apology*, in the earliest account of the celebration of the Eucharist we possess:

> And when the president has given thanks, and all the people have expressed their assent, those who are called by us deacons give to

each of those present to partake of the bread and wine mixed with water over which the thanksgiving was pronounced, and to those who are absent they carry away a portion. [691]

Likewise, in the fourth century we find St. Cyril of Jerusalem declaring in his twenty second *Catechetical Lecture*:

> Wherefore with full assurance let us partake as of the body and Blood of Christ: for in the figure of bread is given to thee His Body, and in the figure of wine His Blood; that thou by partaking of the Body and Blood of Christ, mayest be made of the same body and the same blood with him. For thus we come to bear Christ in us, because His Body and Blood are distributed through our members; thus it is that, according to the blessed Peter, we become partakes of the divine nature [2 Peter 1:4]. [692]

There is also clear evidence that there were groups in the Early Church who abstained from receiving the cup, but that this was strongly condemned by the leaders of the Catholic Church. Thus Pope Leo the Great writes in the fifth century of certain followers of the Manichaean heresy who 'entirely refuse to drink the Blood of our redemption' and declares that 'men of this sort, whose sacrilegious deceit has been detected, are to be expelled by priestly authority from the fellowship of the saints.'[693] Later on in the same century Pope Gelasius I notes that there are certain people who 'abstain from partaking of the chalice of the sacred Blood' and states that they should:

> ...either receive the sacrament in its entirety, or be repelled from the entire sacrament, because the division of one and the same mystery cannot take place without great sacrilege.[694]

---

[691] Justin Martyr, *First Apology,* Ch LXV, in A Roberts, and J Donaldson (eds), *The Ante Nicene Fathers,* Vol I, Edinburgh & Grand Rapids: T&T Clark/ Eerdmans, 1996, p.185.

[692] Cyril of Jerusalem, *Catechetical Lectures,* XXII:3, in P Schaff and H Wace (eds), *The Nicene and Post Nicene Fathers* (second series), Vol. VII, Edinburgh and Grand Rapids: T&T Clark/Eerdmans, 1996, p.151.

[693] Leo the Great, *Homily XLI* in Gibson, op.cit., p.678.

[694] Gelasius I, *Corpus Juris Canon.* Decret.III.ii.12 in Ibid, p.678.

The practice of receiving the Eucharist in one kind also continued to be condemned in the early Middle Ages. It was condemned by the eighth Canon of the Council of Clermont in 1185 and in 1118 Pope Pascal II writes that the bread and wine should be given separately in the Eucharist following Christ's example, except in the case of infants and the very infirm who could not swallow bread.[695]

However, during the Middle Ages the practice of giving the bread only to the laity became widespread, probably out of reverence and a desire to avoid scandal should the wine be accidentally spilt while it was being administered. Reforming elements within the Church hoped that this practice would be condemned at the Council of Constance (1414-1417), but instead the Council affirmed that notwithstanding the fact that Christ ministered 'to his apostles under the forms of both bread and wine' and that it was the custom in the Early Church for everyone to receive the sacrament in both kinds, nevertheless the later Church had the authority to order that it should be given to the laity under one kind only. The Council also declared that priests who communicate the laity under the forms of both bread and wine should be excommunicated. [696]

At the Reformation the Protestant reformers reinstituted the practice of giving communion in both kinds. Thus Article XXII of the *Augsburg Confession* states:

> Among us both kinds are given to laymen in the sacrament. The reason is that there is a clear command and order of Christ, 'Drink of it all of you' (Matthew 26:27).Concerning the chalice Christ here commands with clear words that all should drink of it.[697]

In response the twenty first session of the Council of Trent in 1562 reasserted the later Medieval practice, stating:

> ...this holy Synod, instructed by the Holy Spirit, who is the spirit of wisdom and of understanding, the spirit of counsel and of godliness, and following the judgement and usage of the Church itself, declares and teaches, that laymen, and clerics when not consecrating, are not obliged, by any divine precept, to receive the

---

[695] Ibid, pp.678-679.
[696] Council of Constance, Session 13, at http://www.papalencyclicals.net/Councils/ecum16.htm
[697] Leith, op.cit.,p.79.

sacrament of the Eucharist under both species ; and that neither can it by any means be doubted, without injury to faith, that communion under either species is sufficient for them unto salvation.[698]

It went on to state that the authority given to the Church in regard to the dispensing of the sacraments meant that it had the power to do this:

...this power has ever been in the Church, that, in the dispensation of the sacraments, their substance being untouched, it may ordain, or change, what things soever it may judge most expedient, for the profit of those who receive, or for the veneration of the said sacraments, according to the difference of circumstances, times, and places. And this the Apostle seems not obscurely to have intimated, when he says; Let a man so account of us, as of the ministers of Christ, and the dispensers of the mysteries of God [1 Corinthians 4:1]. And indeed it is sufficiently manifest that he himself exercised this power,- as in many other things, so in regard of this very sacrament; when, after having ordained certain things touching the use thereof, he says; The rest I will set in order when I come [1 Corinthians 11:34]. Wherefore, holy Mother Church, knowing this her authority in the administration of the sacraments, although the use of both species has,--from the beginning of the Christian religion, not been unfrequent, yet, in progress of time, that custom having been already very widely changed, she,- induced by weighty and just reasons,- has approved of this custom of communicating under one species, and decreed that it was to be held as a law; which it is not lawful to reprobate, or to change at pleasure, without the authority of the Church itself.[699]

In the English Reformation the Church of England at first continued later medieval practice with the *Act of the Six Articles* of 1539 declaring 'that communion in both kinds is not necessary *ad salutem*, by the law of God,

---

[698] Council of Trent, Session XXI, Ch 1, text at http://history.hanover.edu/texts/trent/ct21.html
[699] Council of Trent, Session XXI, Ch 2

to all persons.'[700] However, by agreement with Convocation communion in both kinds was legalised in the reign of Edward VI and was provided for by the Prayer Books of 1549 and 1552.

In the reign of Mary the Church of England returned to the medieval practice, only to revert to communion in both kinds after the accession of Elizabeth I. In 1559 the tenth of the Eleven Articles declared:

> I am of that mind also, that the holy communion or sacrament of the body and blood of Christ, for the due obedience of Christ's institution, for the due obedience of Christ's institution, and to express the virtue of the same, ought to be ministered unto the people under both kinds; and that it is avouched by certain fathers of the Church to be a plain sacrilege, to rob them of the mystical cup, for whom Christ hath shed his most precious blood, seeing he himself hath said: Drink ye all of this; (1 Corinthians 11:25) considering also that in the time of the ancient doctors of the Church, as Cyprian, Jerome, Augustine, Gelasius and others, six hundred years after Christ and more, both the parts of the sacrament were ministered to the people.[701]

As we have seen, the present article was then introduced in 1563. Its defensive tone may well indicate that it was intended as a response to the decree of the Council of Trent of the previous year.

The Cup of the Lord is not to be denied to the lay people; for both parts of the Lord's sacrament, by Christ's ordinance and commandment, ought to be ministered to all Christian men alike.

Although the initial reason for introducing communion in one kind may have been, as I have indicated, a pragmatic decision based on reverence and a desire to avoid scandal, this practice was defended on two theological grounds.

As can be seen in the decrees of the Councils of Constance and Trent, the first ground was the belief that the Church had the authority to decide in what form the sacrament should be administered.

---

[700] Bray, *Documents of the English Reformation*, p.224.
[701] Ibid, p.351.

The second ground was what is known as the doctrine of 'concomitance.' This was the doctrine that because Christ is a single whole person he is fully present in both the bread and the wine. As the thirteenth session of the Council of Trent put it:

> Christ is whole and entire under the form of the bread and under any part of that form: likewise the whole Christ is present under the form of the wine and under all its parts.[702]

It followed that a lay person who received only the bread nevertheless fed on the whole Christ and so his or her communion with Christ was unimpaired.

The English Reformers countered these arguments with two of their own.

The first, which can be seen in the *Eleven Articles,* was an appeal to tradition. Certain of the Fathers taught that denying the cup to the laity was sacrilege and the tradition of the Church for the first six hundred years or more was that both bread and wine were given to the people. The implicit argument here is that if communion in both kinds was good enough for the Early Church why was a later change of practice justified?

The second, which is found in the *Augsburg Confession,* the *Eleven Articles* and Article XXX is the fact that according to the accounts of the institution of the sacrament in the Synoptic Gospels and I Corinthians Christ gave the wine as well as the bread to his disciples {Matthew 26:27, Mark 14:23, Luke 22:20, 1 Corinthians 11:25) and gave a direct command that they should all drink it (Matthew 26:27). The implicit argument here is that whatever the authority the Church may legitimately have in liturgical matters does not extend to disregarding what Christ did and what Christ commanded. As Bicknell puts it:

> The Church has, indeed, authority to decree rites and ceremonies, but not in contradiction to Scripture and to Our Lord's own words. It cannot be denied that the practice [of communion in one kind] has a certain practical convenience. But we cannot set that against the plain direction of Christ. The danger of irreverence can be reduced to a minimum. The Church of England in company

---

[702] Council of Trent, Session XXII, Ch III, text in Leith, op.cit, p.431.

with the Churches of the East is content to hold fast to the primitive and Scriptural practice.[703]

Note: Contemporary Roman Catholic theology and practice

In the Roman Catholic Church today it is normal, but not universal, for the laity as well as the clergy to receive the wine as well as the bread at the Mass. However, the Church continues to use the doctrine of concomitance to defend the legitimacy of administering the sacrament in one kind.

The *Catechism of the Catholic Church* declares:

> Since Christ is sacramentally present under each of the species, communion under the species of bread alone makes it possible to receive all the fruits of Eucharistic grace. For pastoral reasons this manner of receiving communion has been legitimately established as the most common form of the Latin rite. But 'the sign of communion is more complete when given under both kinds, since in that form the sign of the Eucharistic meal appears more clearly.' This is the usual form of receiving communion in the Eastern rites.[704]

---

[703] Bicknell, op.cit. pp. 514-515.

[704] *Catechism of the Catholic Church*, p.314. The 'Eastern rites' are the rites of those churches that use Orthodox liturgical tradition but are in communion with Rome.

Article XXXI

∞

Of the one oblation[705] of Christ finished upon the Cross

The offering of Christ once made is the perfect redemption, propitiation, and satisfaction for all the sins of the whole world, both original and actual, and there is none other satisfaction for sin but that alone. Wherefore the sacrifices of Masses, in the which it was commonly said that the priests did offer Christ for the quick and the dead to have remission of pain or guilt, were blasphemous fables and dangerous deceits.

De unica Christi oblatione in Cruce perfecta

Oblatio Christi, semel facta, perfecta est redemptio, propitiatio, et satisfactio pro omnibus peccatis totius mundi, tam originalibus quam actualibus; neque praeter illam unicam est ulla alia prop peccatis expiatio. Unde missarum sacrificia, quibus vulgo dicebatur sacerdotem offerre Christum in remissionem poenae aut culpae pro vivis et defunctis, blasphema figmenta sunt et pernitiosae imposturae.

This article first appears as Article XXX of the *Forty Two Articles* in 1553. The wording of the article as a whole does not appear to go back to any earlier source, but some of the expressions in the second paragraph echo a draft article produced by Archbishop Cranmer for the discussions with the Lutherans in 1538.[706]

A number of changes were made to the article in 1563 and 1571 First, the English title, which in the 1553 text read 'Of the perfect oblation of Christ made upon the cross,' was changed to the present version in order to bring it into line with the Latin title. Secondly, 'propitiation'

---

[705] An oblation is the act of offering something to God. In this case it refers to Christ's offering of himself to the Father.

[706] Gibson, op.cit., p.688

replaced 'the pacifying of God's displeasure' in the English text of the first sentence to make it correspond mode directly to the Latin 'propitiatio.' Thirdly, in the second sentence 'guilt' was substituted for 'sin' in the English text in order to bring it into line with the Latin 'culpae.' Fourthly, 'blasphema' was introduced into the Latin text to qualify 'figmenta.' Fifthly, 'blasphemous' then replaced 'forged' in the English text in 1571 to make it correspond with the Latin.

The article has two purposes. The first is to emphasise the sufficiency of the sacrifice made by Christ on the cross. The second is to condemn in consequence the 'sacrifices of Masses.' What precisely is means by the term 'sacrifices of Masses' is disputed and we shall we be looking at this issue in due course.

The offering of Christ once made is the perfect redemption, propitiation, and satisfaction for all the sins of the whole world, both original and actual, and there is none other satisfaction for sin but that alone.

In its first sentence Article XXXI piles up a whole series of statements about the offering of Christ. The purpose of including all these statements is to leave no room for doubt or evasion about the scope of what Christ achieved on the cross.

The sentence begins by talking about the offering of Christ deliberately uses the language of priesthood, drawing on the use of this language in the Epistle to the Hebrews in passages such as Hebrews 10:11-14:

> And every priest stands daily at his service, offering repeatedly the same sacrifices, which can never take away sins. But when Christ had offered for all time a single sacrifice for sins, he sat down at the right hand of God, then to wait until his enemies should be made a stool for his feet. For by a single offering he has perfected for all time those who are sanctified.

Following the teaching of Hebrews the use of the word 'of' in the first clause of Article XXXI is meant to operate in two ways. First, what took place on the cross was the offering of Christ in the sense that he was the priest, the person making the offering. Secondly what took place on the cross was the offering of Christ in the sense that he was not only the priest, but also the victim. He was not only the person making the sacrifice but the person being sacrificed.

The article goes on to say, following verses such as Hebrews 7:27, 9:12 and 10:12, that the offering of Christ was 'once made.' This is not only a historical observation noting the fact that Christ did only die once, but a theological assertion. The point that it is making, in line with Hebrews, is not only that Christ's offering was not repeated, but also that it did not need to be. This is because, as Article XXXI will go on to explain, Christ's offering of himself was sufficient to deal with all sin for all time.

In order to start to explain the all sufficient character of Christ's offering the article next goes on to use three terms to describe it, 'redemption,' 'propitiation' and 'satisfaction.'

The term redemption is taken from New Testament passages such as Matthew 20:28, Romans 3:24 and Ephesians 1:7. It expresses the fact that the death of Christ set us free from our captivity to sin.

The term propitiation is taken from New Testament passages such as Romans 3:25, Hebrews 2:17 and 1 John 3:2. [707] It expresses the fact that the death of Christ assuages God's righteous anger ('wrath') against our sinfulness.

The term satisfaction reflects the thought of the medieval theologian St. Anselm. It expresses the fact 'that the claims of Divine justice were met and satisfied in the Death of Christ.'[708]

Taken together these three terms indicate the comprehensive scope of what Christ achieved on the cross. It set us free from our bondage to sin *and* assuaged God's wrath against us *and* satisfied the demands of God's justice.[709]

The article then continues by saying that that Christ's death dealt not just with some sin but 'all the sins of the whole world.' All the sins that there ever have been or ever will be have been dealt with by Christ's death on the cross. This does not mean everyone will be saved, but it does mean that if anyone is lost it is not because Christ's work was insufficient to save them, but because they have decided, knowingly or unknowingly, to reject what he has done for them.

---

[707] Many modern translations prefer to use the word 'expiation' in these passages.
[708] Griffith Thomas, op.cit. , p.415
[709] A similar point about the all embracing character of what Christ has done for us is made in the communion service in the *Book of Common Prayer* when it describes Christ's death as 'a full, perfect and sufficient, sacrifice, oblation and satisfaction for the sins of the whole world.

Just in the case there was any doubt left, the article further specifies that Christ's death dealt with both 'original' and 'actual' sin, a point previously made in Article II. As Article IX explains, original sin is the 'fault and corruption of nature' that exists in every human being as a result of the Fall Actual sins are the sins that flow from this corruption of our natures. The death of Christ dealt with both.

Finally, because of the comprehensive nature of what Christ's death achieved it follows that 'there is not satisfaction for sin but that alone.' Because Christ has done what the article has just said he has done, no other way of dealing with sin is either necessary or possible. 'Satisfaction' here seems to be used in a wider sense than earlier in the article. 'No other satisfaction for sin' means 'no other way of dealing with sin' and is meant to include the concepts of redemption and propitiation.

Wherefore the sacrifices of Masses, in the which it was commonly said that the priests did offer Christ for the quick and the dead to have remission of pain or guilt, were blasphemous fables and dangerous deceits.

The key linking word in Article XXXI is the word 'wherefore' at the start of the second sentence. What it means is that because all that is said in the first sentence is true what is said in the second sentence follows.

As we have already noted, the precise meaning of 'sacrifices of Masses' is disputed. The best way to attain clarity about the meaning of the second sentence as whole is to postpone consideration of the precise meaning of the term and to begin by noting that whatever 'sacrifices of Masses' are they are regarded by the article as 'blasphemous fables and dangerous deceits' because it is said that in them 'the priests did offer Christ for the quick and the dead to have remission of pain or guilt.'

This statement parallels the rejection of the idea of the offering of Christ in the Mass in the *Augsburg Confession* and the *Eleven Articles*.

As we saw when looking at Article II, Article XXIV of the *Augsburg Confession* notes that the Lutheran reformation condemns:

> ...the abominable error...according to which it was taught that our Lord Christ had by his death made satisfaction for original sin, and had instituted the Mass as a sacrifice for other sins. This transformed the Mass into a sacrifice for the living and the dead, a

sacrifice by means for which sin was taken away and God was reconciled.[710]

In like manner Article IX of the Eleven Articles states that:

> ...the doctrine that maintaineth the mass to be propitiatory sacrifice for the quick and the dead, and a mean to deliver souls out of purgatory, is neither agreeable to Christ's ordinance nor grounded upon doctrine apostolic, but contrariwise most ungodly and most injurious to the precious redemption of our Saviour Christ, and his only sufficient sacrifice offered once and for ever on the altar of the cross. [711]

If we compare these statements with what is said in Article XXXI what we learn is that the statement in Article XXXI reflects a concern that was shared by Protestant reformers in both Germany and England about a form of teaching current in their day which held that the Mass was a sacrifice in which Christ was offered to make propitiation both for the living and for the dead in purgatory

The point that is made explicitly in the Eleven Articles and implicitly in Article XXXI through its use of 'wherefore' is that this teaching denies the sufficiency of what Christ did for us on the cross. If Christ really did die on the cross to deal with all sin, original and actual, for all time then why does the Mass need to be offered to make propitiation for the sins of the living and the dead? Or, to put the same thing the other way round, if the Mass needs to offered to make propitiation for the living and the dead does this not show that what Christ did on the cross was not sufficient to save them from their sins?

Article XXXI dismisses any such ideas as 'blasphemous fables and dangerous deceits.' They are 'blasphemous fables' because they are fictions that deny the truth of what God has done for us in Christ. They are 'dangerous deceits' because they are falsehoods that lead people to trust in false hopes by looking to the offering of the Mass to save them from sin rather than putting their whole trust in what Christ did for them on the cross.

---

[710] Leith, op.cit. p.84.
[711] Bray, *Documents of the English Reformation*, p.350.

All this is clear and undisputed. This is the point that Article XXXI is seeking to make. What is disputed, however, is whether what is condemned by Article XXXI is simply popular late medieval theology unsupported by the official teaching of the Roman Catholic Church or is the official teaching of the Roman Catholic Church as codified at the Council of Trent.

Gibson puts forward the former view. He makes two points.

The first is that the Article is not concerned to deny the general idea that the Eucharist should be viewed in sacrificial terms:

> Had it been the intention of its compilers to deny this doctrine, nothing would have been easier than for them to use words which would have conveyed their meaning without any ambiguity. As a matter of fact, however, it is not even 'the sacrifice of the Mass' which is condemned, but the sacrifices of Masses (missarum sacrificia), and in connection with them a current theory (in which it was commonly said,' quibus vulgo dicebatur) rather than a formal statement of doctrine.[712]

The second is that the decrees of the twenty second session of the Council of Trent about the sacrifice of the Mass being 'truly propitiatory for the living and the dead' were not:

> ....present to the minds of those who formulated the Article, for they were not in existence, as the subject was only considered at Trent in the autumn of 1562, nearly ten years later...It was the popular teaching alone which the Reformers had before them...[713]

On the other hand, Griffith Thomas argues that the use of the term 'Masses' rather than 'Mass' is not significant because:

> ...the Church of Rome frequently uses the plural of the Mass, and the Council of Trent does the same thing without any idea of

---

[712] Gibson, op.cit., p.692.
[713] Ibid.p.694.

making a doctrinal distinction. Masses (in the plural) are merely several instances of the same thing, Mass. [714]

He also argues that nothing much, if anything, can be 'argued from the phrase 'commonly said' which can be found several times in the Prayer Book to denote ordinary popular practices and usages; e.g. 'Commonly called Christmas Day.' [715]

However, the most important point that he makes is that even though the Council of Trent formulated its teaching after Articles XXXI was originally compiled, nevertheless what it says about the Mass is precisely what is rejected in the article.

Thus chapter II of session twenty two of the Council of Trent declares:

> ...inasmuch as in this divine sacrifice which is celebrated in the mass is contained and immolated in an un-bloody manner the same Christ who once offered Himself in a bloody manner on the altar of the cross, the holy council teaches that this is truly propitiatory and has this effect, that if we, with a sincere heart and upright faith, with fear and reverence draw near to God, we obtain mercy and find grace in seasonable aid. For, appeased by this sacrifice, the Lord grants the grace and gift of penitence and pardons even the gravest of crimes and sins.[716]

It goes on to say:

> Wherefore. according to the tradition of the Apostles, it is rightly offered not only for the sins, punishments, satisfactions and other necessities of the faithful who are still living, but also for those departed in Christ but not yet fully purified.[717]

In the light of the points that he makes, supported by the evidence from Trent, Griffith Thomas' conclusion seems justified:

---

[714] Griffith Thomas op.cit. p.417.
[715] Ibid, p.418.
[716] Leith, op.cit., p.439
[717] Ibid., p.439.

The Article, following Scripture, says Christ was offered on the Cross 'once for all'; the Council of Trent teaches that there are as many offerings of Christ as there are Masses celebrated. Scripture and our Article say that Christ's death is the one and all- sufficient propitiation for sin; Trent says that every Mass is a propitiatory sacrifice for sin. Surely nothing can be clearer than the condemnation of the sacrifice of the Mass by our Article, and its use of the plural is evidently intended to cover all the instances of celebration which are continually occurring, and to put them in contrast with and opposition to the uniqueness of Calvary. [718]

Note: Eucharistic sacrifice

It is important to note that what is condemned in Article XXXI is a specific error, the offering of Christ at the Mass as a propitiatory sacrifice for the living and the dead. What the article does not condemn is every use of the language of sacrifice to describe what happens at the Eucharist.

Since at least the second century Christians have described the Eucharist in sacrificial terms and have seen in the Eucharist the 'pure offering' prophesied in Malachi 1:11

For from the rising of the sun to its setting my name is great among the nations, and in every place incense is offered to my name, and a pure offering; for my name is great among the nations, says the Lord of hosts.[719]

As many theologians have argued there are two ways in which such sacrificial language has been, and can be, used which do not involve seeing the Eucharist as a propitiatory sacrifice in a way that contradicts Article XXXI.

Firstly, like the Passover, the Eucharist can be seen as a commemorative sacrifice in the sense that at the Eucharist, as we eat the bread and drink the wine, we recall the sacrifice of Christ offered for us and the benefits of that sacrifice become real and effective in our midst as we receive Christ's body that was broken for us and his blood which was shed for us.

---

[718] Griffith Thomas, op.cit. p.418.
[719] For a convenient summary of the evidence see Browne, op.cit. , p.p. 437-447.

Secondly, the Eucharist is a sacrifice in the sense that it is a key occasion at which we can offer ourselves to God as a 'living sacrifice' (Romans 12:2). As we receive Christ's body and blood at the Eucharist we are united to Christ our great High Priest as the members of his body (1 Corinthians 10:17). As Eric Mascall and Michael Green put it, this means that at the Eucharist we offer to God 'ourselves as re-appropriated in Christ.' [720] and on this basis we come to God, bringing him our praise and thanksgiving and our prayers for our own needs and those of others.

This dual understanding of Eucharistic sacrifice can be found in *Saepius Officio,* the response by the Archbishops of Canterbury and York on behalf of the Church of England to the condemnation of Anglican orders by Pope Leo XIII in his1896 Encyclical *Apostolicae Curae.* One of the grounds for the condemnation of Anglican orders by Pope Leo was that Anglicans lacked a sacrificial view of the Eucharist. In *Saepius Officio* the Archbishops refute this accusation, declaring that in the Eucharist the Church of England continues:

> ...a perpetual memory of the precious death of Christ, who is our Advocate with the Father and the propitiation for our sins, according to His precept, until His coming again. For first we offer the sacrifice of praise and thanksgiving; then next we plead and represent before the Father the sacrifice of the cross, and by it we confidently entreat remission of sins and all other benefits of the Lord's Passion for all the whole Church; and lastly we offer the sacrifice of ourselves to the Creator of all things which we have already signified by the oblations of His creatures. This whole action, in which the people have necessarily to take its part with the priest, we are accustomed to call the Eucharistic sacrifice.[721]

In this statement pleading and representing the sacrifice of the cross is a form of active remembering. As Anglicans recall the death of Christ once offered so they ask God for the remission of sins and all other benefits which the cross made possible.

---

[720] E.Mascall and M.Green 'Eucharistic Sacrifice' in C. Buchanan, E. Mascall, J. I. Packer and G Leonard, *Growing into Union,* London: SPCK, 1970. p.191.
[721] *Saepius Officio*, London, Longman Green and Co, 1897, p.15.

The same understanding of Eucharistic sacrifice can also be found in ARCIC I. In its agreed statement on Eucharistic doctrine, which, as we have seen, the General Synod declared to be 'consonant in substance' with the Church of England's teaching ARCIC I declares first of all that what Christ achieved on the cross was once for all and therefore unrepeatable:

> Christ's redeeming death and resurrection took place once and for all in history. Christ's death on the cross, the culmination of his whole life of obedience, was the one, perfect and sufficient sacrifice for the sins of the world. There can be no repetition of or addition to what was then accomplished once for all by Christ. Any attempt to express a nexus between the sacrifice of Christ and the Eucharist must not obscure this fundamental fact of the Christian faith.[722]

However, it then goes on to say,

> ...God has given the Eucharist to his Church as a means through which the atoning work of Christ on the cross is proclaimed and made effective in the life of the church. The notion of memorial as understood in the Passover celebration at the time of Christ i.e. the making effective in the present of an event in the past has opened the way to a clearer understanding of the relationship between Christ's sacrifice and the Eucharist. The Eucharistic memorial is no mere calling to mind of a past event or of its significance, but the church's effectual proclamation of God's mighty acts. Christ instituted the Eucharist as a memorial (anamnesis) of the totality of God's reconciling action in him. In the Eucharistic prayer the church continues to make a perpetual memorial of Christ's death, and his members, united with God and one another, give thanks for all his mercies, entreat the benefits of his passion on behalf of the whole Church, participate in these benefits and enter into the movement of his self-offering.[723]

---

[722] Text in Hill and Yarnold (eds), op.cit., p. 20
[723]. Ibid, p.20

The Discipline of the Church:
Articles XXXII-XXXVI

The final sequence of articles concerning the Church has to do with various aspects of the Church's discipline

Article XXXII defends the marriage of Priests against those who wanted to retain the Medieval discipline of compulsory clerical celibacy.

Article XXXIII defends the Church's discipline of excommunication.

Article XXXIV argues that the traditions and ceremonies of the Church can legitimately vary in different times and places, that individuals should not unilaterally break traditions and ceremonies instituted by proper authority and not contrary to Scripture and that national churches (such as the Church of England) have the authority to change or abolish those rites and ceremonies of the Church instituted by human authority.

Article XXXV contends that the model sermons contained in the Church of England's *First and Second Book of Homilies* contain godly, wholesome and necessary material and should be read in an intelligible fashion.

Finally Article XXXVI defends the Church of England's ordination rites as contained in the 1549 and1552 Ordinals on the grounds that they contain all the necessary elements for the ordination and consecration of bishops, priests and deacons and contain nothing that is 'superstitious and ungodly.'

Article XXXII

∞

Of the Marriage of Priests

Bishops, Priests, and Deacons are not commanded by God's laws either to vow the estate of single life or to abstain from marriage. Therefore it is lawful also for them, as for all other Christian men, to marry at their own discretion, as they shall judge the same to serve better to godliness.

De Conjugio Sacerdotum

Episcopis, Prebyteris et Diaconis nullo mandato divino praeceptum est, ut aut coelibatum voveant aut a matrimonio absteneant. Licet igitur etiam illis, ut caeteris omnibus Christianis, ubi hoc ad pietatem magis facere iudicaverint, pro suo arbitratu matrimonium contrahere.

Article XXXII is the first of four articles covering various aspects of the discipline of the Church of England.

This article has its origins in Article XXXI of the *Forty Two Articles*. The original form of this article, as found in the MS of the *Forty Two Articles* signed by the Royal Chaplains ran as follows:

Coelibatus ex verbo Dei praecipitur nemini

Episcopis, Presbyteris, et Diaconis non est mandatum ut coelibatum voveant, neque jure divino coguntur matrimonio abstinere, *si donum not habeant, tametsi voverint, quandoquidem hoc voti genus verbo Dei repugnant.*

The words in italics 'if they do not have the gift, whatever they have vowed, seeing that this kind of vow is repugnant to the word of God,' which encouraged priests to break their vows of celibacy, were omitted from the final form of the article, which in its English form stated:

> The state of single life is commanded to no Man by the Word of God

> Bishops, priests, and deacons are not commanded to vow the state of single life without marriage, neither by God's law are they compelled to abstain from matrimony.

In 1563 Archbishop Parker added the second clause of the present article, giving a positive assertion of the lawfulness of clerical marriage to supplement the purely negative argument of the 1553 article that such marriage is not forbidden by Scripture.

In the earliest centuries of the Church there is ample evidence that there were married clergy. For instance St. Clement of Alexandria who lived in the second half of the second and the beginning of the third centuries mentions married priests and deacons (*Stromateis* III:12) and the fifth century historian Socrates refers to a married episcopate in the Eastern churches (*Ecclesiastical History* V:22). The Council of Gangra in 324 anathematised those who separated themselves from a married priest and the Council of Nicaea in 325 rejected a proposal to impose a rule of celibacy on the clergy.[724]

From the beginning of the fourth century onwards, however, there was a growing feeling, beginning in the Church in Spain, that clergy ought to be celibate and by the end of the century compulsory clerical celibacy had been agreed at a council held in Carthage, with councils at Toledo and Arles taking the same line early in the fifth century.

This move towards a celibate clergy received the support of the Popes. Nevertheless, as late as the eleventh century married clergy were still common in the Western Church. In 1074, however, Pope Gregory VII issues a decree forbidding the laity to receive ministry from married priests and in the English church, under the influence of St. Anselm, an absolute rule of clerical celibacy was imposed from 1102 onwards.

In the Eastern Church, by contrast, it remained normal for priests and deacons to be married and this position was formally endorsed by

---

[724] However, there also seems to have been an unwritten custom that clergy should not marry after ordination, see Bicknell, op.cit. pp. 390-391.

the Council of Trullo in 692. From the sixth century onwards, however, bishops came to be chosen from the ranks of the monks or from those parochial clergy who were unmarried.

At the time of the Reformation the Protestant side rejected compulsory clerical celibacy on the grounds that this practice lacked support from the Bible or the Early Church and had led to a situation in which it had been common for the clergy to have concubines and to engage in other forms of sexual immorality.[725] Rome, on the other hand resisted calls to resist the abandonment of clerical celibacy and this position was maintained by the twenty fourth session of the Council of Trent in November 1563.[726]

In the Church of England clerical celibacy remained the law even after the breach with Rome, but in 1547 a large majority in Convocation agreed:

> That all such canons, laws, statutes, decrees, usages and customs, heretofore made, had, or used that forbid any person to contract matrimony, or condemn matrimony already contracted by any person, for any vow or promise of priesthood, chastity or widowhood, shall henceforth cease, be utterly void, and of none effect. [727]

Then in 1549 an Act of Parliament repealed all the laws and canons forbidding clerical marriage and declared that all were free to marry provided that they did so according to the rite in the new Prayer Book.

As Burnet explains, the issue of whether clerical celibacy should be retained or abandoned was a matter of great controversy:

> There was not any one point that was more severely examined at the time of the Reformation than this: for, as the irregular practices and dissolute lives of both seculars and regulars[728] had very much prejudiced the world against the celibate of the Roman

---

[725] See, for example *Augsburg Confession* XXIII.

[726] Clerical celibacy remains the norm for those churches in the Western tradition within the Roman Catholic Church (see *Catechism of the Catholic Church*, p.354). In the Eastern rite churches in union with Rome, however, the Eastern custom of permitting married deacons and priests has been retained.

[727] J Strype, *Cranmer*, Bk II:C:IV, cited in Gibson, op.cit., p.703

[728] That is, both the ordinary parochial clergy and those in monastic orders.

Clergy, which was considered as the occasion of all these disorders; so, on the other hand, the marriage of the Clergy, and also of those of both sexes who had taken vows, gave great offence. They were represented as persons that could not master their appetites, but that indulged themselves in carnal pleasures and interests. Thus, as the scandals of the unmarried Clergy had alienated the world much from them; so the marriage of most of the Reformers was urged as an ill character both of them and of the Reformation; as a doctrine of libertinism, that made the Clergy look to like the rest of the world, and involved by them in the common pleasures, concerns and passions of human life.[729]

This issue was also a personal one for both Archbishop Cranmer and Archbishop Parker, both of whom had married.

The purpose of Article XXXII is to defend the legitimacy of clerical marriage in the face of the criticism of it noted by Burnet.

The title of the article is somewhat misleading as it covers the marriage of bishops and deacons as well as priests. The best explanation is that deacons were generally regarded as priests in preparation and all bishops were necessarily also priests so the marriage of priests was the key issue.

Bishops, Priests, and Deacons are not commanded by God's laws either to vow the estate of single life or to abstain from marriage.

The article starts its defence of the legitimacy of clerical marriage by declaring that there is nothing in Scripture that commands the clergy to be celibate. As Gibson notes in his commentary on this article ' There is certainly no single passage of Holy Scripture which can be cited as containing any command to the clergy either to 'vow the estate of single life,' or to 'abstain from marriage.'[730] On the contrary, he says, 'the injunctions of St. Paul distinctly contemplate the ordination of married men, and contain no hint that they are expected to abstain from the use of marriage.'[731]

---

[729] Burnet, op.cit. p.485
[730] Gibson, op.cit. p.696
[731] Ibid. p.697

The evidence for the latter claim can be found in the following passages:

> Do we not have the right to be accompanied by a wife, as the other apostles and the brothers of the Lord and Cephas? (1 Corinthians 9:5)

> Now a bishop must be above reproach, the husband of one wife, temperate, sensible, dignified, hospitable, an apt teacher... (1Timothy 3:2)

> Let deacons be the husband of one wife, and let them manage their children and their households well. (1Timothy 3:12)

> This is why I left you in Crete, that you might amend what was defective, and appoint elders in every town as I directed you, if any man is blameless, the husband of one wife, and his children are believers and not open to the charge of being profligate or insubordinate. (Titus 1:5-6)

> It is also worth noting that Philip the deacon was married (Acts 21:9) and that Aquila and Priscilla seemed to have exercised a joint ministry as St. Paul's 'co-workers' as a married couple (Acts 18:2, Romans 16:3, 1 Corinthians 16:19).

To quote Gibson again, 'These texts are conclusive. There is plainly nothing unscriptural in the existence of a married clergy.' [732]

For the English Reformers this Scriptural argument was decisive. Because they believed that 'it is not lawful for the Church to ordain anything that is contrary to God's word written,' (Article XX) they held that the biblical evidence meant that the Church did not have the authority to declare that the clergy had to be celibate. In the words of Burnet: 'The adding a law upon this head to the law of Christ, seems to assume an authority that he has not given the Church.' [733]

---

[732] Ibid., p.697.
[733] Ibid,. p.487.

Therefore it is lawful also for them, as for all other Christian men, to marry at their own discretion, as they shall judge the same to serve better to godliness.

While the English Reformers were therefore clear that compulsory clerical celibacy should not be imposed by the Church this did not mean that they therefore felt that the clergy had to be married.

They held that in principle it was as 'lawful' according to the law of God, for a member of the clergy to marry as for anyone else. However, they were aware that both Christ and St. Paul had affirmed the rightness of celibacy as a vocation to which some people may be called by God (Matthew 19:1-12, 1 Corinthians 7:1-9) and that, even for those without a specific celibate vocation, personal circumstances, or the inability to find the right person to marry, might rule out the possibility of marriage at any particular time. They therefore also held that the decision about whether or not to marry was one that could only be made by each individual member of the clergy 'at their own discretion'

However, the article also adds an important qualification to its declaration that it is lawful for the clergy to marry at their own discretion, namely that each individual needs to judge what will 'serve better to godliness.' That is to say, the decision whether or not to marry must not be simply made on the grounds of personal needs or desires, but on a judgement by an individual about what will help them to live a more godly life in the specific circumstances in which God has called them to serve him.

Griffith Thomas[734] suggests that this qualification may be a response to the *Injunctions* issued by Queen Elizabeth I in 1559 which note:

> ...there hath grown offence and some slander to the Church by a lack of discreet and sober behaviour in many ministers of the Church, both in choosing of their wives and in indiscreet living with them.[735]

In the face of what was said in the Injunctions and the particular examples of clerical behaviour that lay behind it, Archbishop Parker may

---

[734] Griffith Thomas, op.cit, p.429.
[735] Bray, *Documents of the English Reformation*, p.342.

have felt in necessary to emphasise that clerical marriage should be an aid to godliness and that both the choice of clergy wives and the behaviour of married clergy needed to reflect this fact. In other words, he is issuing a warning not to enter too lightly into marriage or to undertake marriage in a manner unbefitting the clerical calling.

Article XXXIII

∞

Of Excommunicated Persons, how they are to be avoided

That person which by open denunciation of the Church is rightly cut off from the unity of the Church and excommunicated, ought to be taken of the whole multitude of the faithful as an heathen and publican, until he be openly reconciled by penance and received into the Church by a judge that hath authority thereto.

De Excommunicatis Vitandis

Qui per publicam Ecclesiae denunciationem rite ab unitate Ecclesiae praecisus est et excommunicatus, is ab universa fidelium multitudine, donec per poenitentiam publice reconciliatus fuerit arbitrio iudicis competentis, habendus est tanquam ethnicus et publicanus.

This article is taken from Article XXXII of the *Forty Two Articles*. The only change in 1563 was the substitution of the present titles for the original titles 'Excommunicate persons are to be avoided' and 'Excommunicati vitandi sunt.' The article cannot be traced back to any earlier source.

As Tyrell Green notes:

> The object both of this Article and Article XXXIV is the regulation of the internal discipline and usages of the Church, upon which subject there was much warm discussion in England in the reign of Edward VI.[736]

---

[736] Tyrell Green, op cit. p.271.

In this particular article the focus is on the Church's exercise of the discipline of excommunication.

In Old Testament passages such as Genesis 17:14, Exodus 12:19, Leviticus 7:20 and Ezra 10:8 we find references to the exclusion of someone from participation in the life of the people of Israel. The person so excluded would be cut off from both the social and religious life of God's people. It is this Jewish practice of excommunication (which could be either temporary or permanent depending on the severity of the offence) that is referred to in Luke 6:22, John 9:22, 12:42 and 16:2.

In Matthew 18:15-18, the New Testament passage referred to in Article XXXIII, we find that Christ gives the Church as the renewed Israel the right to exercise the discipline of excommunication given to Israel in the Old Testament:

> If your brother sins against you, go and tell him his fault, between you and him alone. If he listens to you, you have gained your brother. But if he does not listen, take one or two others along with you, that every word may be confirmed by the evidence of two or three witnesses. If he refuses to listen to them, tell it to the church; and if he refuses to listen even to the church, let him be to you as a Gentile and a tax collector. Truly, I say to you, whatever you bind on earth shall be bound in heaven, and whatever you loose on earth shall be loosed in heaven.

As Browne comments:

> Our Lord Himself gave power to His Church to excommunicate and absolve. In Matthew 18:15-18, He enjoins that, if one brother or fellow Christian sin against another, and refuse to listen to a private rebuke, or to the admonition of others to whom the offence be told, then the grievance is to be communicated to the Church. But if, when it is told to the Church, the erring brother still neglects to hear and show penitence; then he is to be looked on no longer as a Christian and a brother, but it is said 'Let him be unto thee as an heathen man and a publican' (ver. 17). The meaning of this would be intelligible enough to the first disciples of Christ. They had been bred Jews, and knew that Jews had no communion with heathen men and publicans, not merely in religious ordinances, but not even to eat. This direction then

Christ gives to His Church, that those, who having sinned openly against their brethren would not listen to her godly admonitions, should be separated from the fellowship of the faithful and treated as heathen or publicans. Then, to confirm the Church in her authority, to assure her that her censures and her remission of censure both had a warrant from God, He adds: 'Verily I say unto you, Whatsoever ye shall bind on earth shall be bound in heaven: and whatever ye loose on earth shall be loosed in heaven (ver.18). In this context there can be no reasonable question, that the binding means to place in a state of bondage or excommunication from Church privilege, that the loosing signifies to restore again to the freedom of Christian communion.[737]

In Matthew 16:19 and John 20:23 this same power of binding and loosing is given by Christ to St. Peter and to the Apostles as a whole to exercise on behalf of the Church as its leaders. In 1 Corinthians and 1Timothy we then find this power being exercised by St. Paul.

In 1 Corinthians 5:1-5 we find him instructing the Christians at Corinth to expel from their midst someone who has been living with his father's wife:

It is actually reported that there is immorality among you, and of a kind that is not found even among pagans; for a man is living with his father's wife. And you are arrogant! Ought you not rather to mourn? Let him who has done this be removed from among you. For though absent in body I am present in spirit, and as if present, I have already pronounced judgement in the name of the Lord Jesus on the man who has done such a thing. When you are assembled, and my spirit is present, with the power of our Lord Jesus, you are to deliver this man to Satan for the destruction of the flesh, that his spirit may be saved in the day of the Lord Jesus.

There has long been a debate amongst commentators on this passage about what delivering a person 'to Satan for the destruction of the flesh' means, but the most satisfactory explanation is that is a way of describing the consequences of someone being excluded from the Church. As J T South puts it, it means 'putting him outside the sphere of God's protection

---

[737] Browne, op.cit. pp.767-768.

within the church, and leaving him exposed to the satanic forces of evil in hope that the experience would cause him to repent and return to the fellowship of the church.' [738]

In 1 Timothy 1:19-20 St. Paul tells Timothy that:

> By rejecting conscience, certain persons have made shipwreck of their faith, among them Hymenaeus and Alexander, whom I have delivered to Satan that they may learn not to blaspheme.

Given the meaning of delivery to Satan in 1 Corinthians 5, the most plausible explanation of this passage is that here too we are talking about people being excommunicated, in this case for some unspecified form of blasphemy.

As Browne argues, in addition to the passages already mentioned we also need to take note of:

> ...many passages, in which the Apostles enjoin upon Christians to withdraw from the company of brethren, who do not live according to their Christian profession, but who are either impure in their lives, or heretical in their belief. (See Romans 16:17, 1 Corinthians 5:9, 15:33, 2 Corinthians 6:14, 17, 2 Thessalonians 3:6, 14, 2 John 10-11). These, though not all directly bearing on the subject, show, that Christians ought to keep themselves from all communion with ungodly men; and therefore make it probable, that they should be enjoined to exclude them from Church-fellowship.[739]

In the Early Church a formal system of excommunication developed which involved three stages or degrees of discipline.

First there was the formal admonition of the offender, which was solemnly repeated once or twice in accordance with St. Paul's teaching in Titus 3:10-11.

---

[738] J T South, *Disciplinary Practices in Pauline Texts*, Lewiston: Mellen Biblical Press, 1992, p.43. For a discussion of the passage as a whole see A C Thiselton, *The First Epistle to the Corinthians*, Grand Rapids & Carlisle: Eerdmans/Paternoster Press, 2000, pp. 384-400.
[739] Browne, op.cit. p.769.

Secondly. if this admonition was disregarded the 'lesser excommunication' involving suspension from the Eucharist would follow. Those under this discipline would still be allowed to attend the service of the catechumens prior to the Eucharist, but they would not be allowed to be present at the Eucharist itself.

Thirdly, there was the 'greater excommunication' which was imposed for more heinous offences or for those who remained obstinately impenitent in regard to lesser offences.

As R W Jelf explains, as a result of this greater excommunication people:

> ...were not only shut out from all public services of the Church, of whatsoever kind, but from all civil and social intercourse with the Christian community: and notice was customarily given of the sentence, at least to the neighbouring Churches, sometimes to all the Churches in the world, that they too might refuse to admit the offenders to their communion. [740]

This greater excommunication could last for months, years, or even the rest of someone's life, depending on the severity of their offence and whether or not they exhibited appropriate penitence.

Within this pattern of discipline it was ordinarily the bishop who pronounced the judgement of excommunication and also granted reconciliation to the penitent. However, in cases of extreme necessity, such as the danger of imminent death, presbyters, or even deacons, acting under the bishop's authority, might reconcile the sinner to communion and grant him or her the absolution of their sins.

This threefold disciplinary pattern became the basis for the subsequent disciplinary practice of the Church and it formed the basis for the disciplinary approach taken by the Church of England at the Reformation.

The theological rationale for the exercise of discipline by the Church in New Testament times and subsequently is helpfully explained by Dietrich Bonhoeffer in his book *The Cost of Discipleship*. In his chapter on the Church as the community on the saints Bonhoeffer writes that the Church:

---

[740] R W Jelf, *The Thirty Nine Articles of the Church of England*, London, Oxford and Cambridge: Rivingtons, 1873, p.374.

...is a community of men and women who have genuinely encountered the grace of God, and who walk worthily of the gospel by not casting that grace recklessly away.[741]

This means, he argues, that:

> ...the preaching of forgiveness must always go hand-in-hand with the preaching of repentance, the preaching of the gospel with the preaching of the law. Nor can the forgiveness of sin be unconditional – sometimes sin must be retained. It is the will of the Lord himself that the gospel should not be given to dogs. He too held that the only way to safeguard the gospel was by preaching repentance. If the Church refuses to face the stern reality of sin, it will gain no credence when it talks of forgiveness. Such a Church sins against its sacred trust and walks unworthily of the gospel. It is an unholy Church, squandering the precious treasure of the Lord's forgiveness. Nor is it enough simply to deplore in general terms that the sinfulness of man infects even his good works. It is necessary to point out concrete sins, and to punish and condemn them. This is the proper use of the power of the keys (Matthew 16:19, 18:18, John 20:23), which the Lord bequeathed to his Church. Even the Reformers laid great emphasis on this power. It is essential for the Church to exercise it, for the sake of holiness, for the sake of the sinner and for its own sake. If the Church is to walk worthily of the gospel, part of its duty will be to maintain ecclesiastical discipline. Sanctification means driving out the world from the Church as well as separating the Church from the world. [742]

The purpose of the exercise of discipline, he says:

> ...is not to establish a community of the perfect, but a community of men who really live under the forgiving mercy of God. Discipline in a congregation is a servant of the precious grace of God. If a member of the Church falls into sin, he must be

---

[741] D Bonhoeffer, *The Cost of Discipleship*. London: SCM, 1959, p. 259.
[742] Ibid., pp. 359-60

admonished and punished, lest he forfeit his own salvation and the gospel be discredited.[743]

It is important to emphasise Bonhoeffer's point that discipline is for the benefit of the sinner as well as for the sake of the Church as a whole. As Stanley Hauerwas observes in his commentary on Matthew, paradoxical though it may seem at first sight:

> ...excommunication is a form of love. Excommunication is not to throw someone out of the church, but rather to help them to see that they have become stumbling block and are, therefore, already out of the church. Excommunication is a call to come home by undergoing the appropriate penance.[744]

Because excommunication is a call to the sinner to come home the proper end of the process of excommunication is only achieved when the person who has undergone discipline is restored to full participation in the life of the Church. As P E Hughes comments on St. Paul's plea for the restoration of a penitent offender in 2 Corinthians 2:5-11, the primary end of all discipline within the Christian community is 'the reformation and therefore the restoration of the guilty person.' In consequence:

> Discipline which is so inflexible as to leave no place for repentance and reconciliation has ceased to be truly Christian; for it is no less a scandal to cut off the penitent sinner from all hope of re-entry into the fellowship of the redeemed community than it is to permit flagrant wickedness to continue unpunished in the Body of Christ. [745]

In the words of Article XVI, we cannot 'deny the place of forgiveness to such as truly repent.' This means that there not only needs to be a process for excommunicating people, but also a process, known to the sinner, by which he or she may be restored.

---

[743] Ibid., p.360.
[744] S Hauerwas , *Matthew*, London: SCM, 2006, p.165.
[745] P E Hughes, *The Second Epistle to the Corinthians*, Grand Rapids: Eerdmans, 1992, pp.66-67.

That person which by open denunciation of the Church is rightly cut off from the unity of the Church and excommunicated, ought to be taken of the whole multitude of the faithful as an heathen and publican, until he be openly reconciled by penance and received into the Church by a judge that hath authority thereto.

For the process of discipline and restoration outlined above to be effective two things need to be in place.

First, there needs to be a public process by which the Christian community, or those acting on its behalf, can impose a sentence of excommunication when this is appropriate and can then subsequently restore the penitent offender when the time for this is right. The process needs to be public so that the both the offender and the community from which they are being excluded, or to which they are being restored, know where they stand.

It is this public process that is referred to in Article XXXIII when it talks about someone being 'rightly cut off from the unity of the church and excommunicated' by means of 'open denunciation' and about them then being 'openly reconciled by penance and received into the Church by a judge that hath authority thereto.' Because the article is dealing with the matter at the level of general principle the article does not specify who the judge should be, but it needs to be someone who has the authority to administer the law of the Church in this matter.

Secondly, in order to be effective the discipline of excommunication needs to be observed by the community from which the offender has been excluded. The person who has been excommunicated will never be brought to appreciate the magnitude of their offence and their need for repentance and restoration if everyone treats them as if nothing has changed. Hence the article declares that the person who is still excommunicate 'ought to be taken by the whole multitude of the faithful as an heathen and publican.' What precisely this involves is not spelt out, but it seems to be a reference to the 'greater excommunication' that would involve the suspension of both religious and social relations with the person concerned. As the title of Article XXXIII suggests, it would mean avoiding having any dealings with them and would thus be the equivalent of the practice of shunning that is still found among some of the stricter Mennonite churches today.

Note: Excommunication in the post-Reformation Church of England

In the *Book of Common Prayer* there are a number of references to excommunication.

- The rubric at the beginning of the Communion service provides for someone being refused admission to the sacrament 'by reason of malicious and open contention with his neighbours, or other open sin without repentance.'

- Also in the communion service provision is made for the announcement of excommunications after the recitation of the Nicene Creed.

- The rubric at the beginning of the burial service states that it should not be used in the case of someone who has died excommunicate.

- At the beginning of the service of commination it is stated that the service is intended as a stop gap until the restoration of the 'godly discipline' of the Early Church that:

...at the beginning of Lent, such persons as stood convicted or notorious sin were put to open penance, and punished in this world, that their souls might be saved in the day of the Lord; and that others, admonished by their example, might be the more afraid to offend.

There are also numerous references to excommunication in the Canons of 1604

- Canons II-VIII declare that excommunication is due to those who impugn the laws of the Church.

- Canons IX-XII declare that it is due to schismatics.

- Canon CIX declares that it is due to offenders against religion, morality and good order in church. This Canon also makes provision for 'notorious crimes and scandals' to be referred to the ecclesiastical courts.

- Canon LXV requires ministers 'solemnly to denounce recusants and excommunicants'

- Canon LXVIII prohibits clergy from refusing to use the burial service 'except the party deceased were denounced excommunicated, *majori excommunicatione*, for some grievous and notorious crime, and no man able to testify of his repentance.'

As Gibson notes, this last canon explicitly recognises the distinction coming down from the days of the Early Church between the 'lesser excommunication' involving suspension from Holy Communion and the 'greater excommunication' for more serious offences which would totally exclude someone from the society of the faithful and involve their being denied a Christian funeral.[746]

Because of the establishment of the Church of England, excommunication also carried with it a range of civil pains and penalties. Until 1813 excommunication was routinely used as a penalty for those who were in contempt of the ecclesiastical courts, which until 1858 covered matters such as matrimonial disputes and inheritance, and under an Act of George III excommunication was also used for a time as a penalty for those who were in contempt of the civil courts as well.

The civil consequences of excommunication were gradually abolished, as was its use as a penalty for being in contempt of court, and the revision of the canons and the development of modern language services in the Church of England that took place during the twentieth and twenty first centuries have left the Church of England with virtually no provision for excommunication.

The references to excommunication in the *Book of Common Prayer* have no parallels in *Common Worship* and the Canons that are now in force also have no reference to excommunication except in the case of Canon B16 'Of notorious offenders not to be admitted to Holy Communion' which is for the most part simply a repetition of what is said in the opening rubric of the Prayer Book Communion service.

---

[746] Gibson, op.cit. p.713-714.

There is thus some provision for lesser excommunication (although in practice it is rarely used), but no provision for at all for greater excommunication as envisaged in Article XXXIII. The question this raises is whether this is a healthy state of affairs for the Church of England to be in, given that excommunication is a practice which has firm roots in Scripture and tradition and which has important theological arguments in its favour.

As Bicknell puts it in his commentary on this article:

> We need a new recognition of the practical holiness demanded from all members of the Body of Christ. This is not to fall into the Puritan error of limiting the church to those who are actually holy. So long as a man is making an effort after holiness, even with many lapses, there is room for him in the Church. But there should be no place for those who do not even desire to live up to the standard of Christ and who actively set at naught Christian principles. The power of excommunication has been abused in the past, but there is no reason why it should be neglected. What is needed to-day is an awakening to the sense that churchmanship carries with it definite obligations.[747]

---

[747] Bicknell, op.cit., p.400.

Article XXXIV

∞

Of the Traditions of the Church

It is not necessary that traditions and ceremonies be in all places one or utterly alike; for at all times they have been diverse, and may be changed according to the diversity of countries, times, and men's manners, so that nothing be ordained against God's word.

Whosoever through his private judgement willingly and purposely doth openly break the traditions and ceremonies of the Church which be not repugnant to the word of God, and be ordained and approved by common authority, ought to be rebuked openly that other may fear to do the like, as he that offendeth against the common order of the Church, and hurteth the authority of the magistrate, and woundeth the conscience of the weak brethren.

Every particular or national Church hath authority to ordain, change, and abolish ceremonies or rites of the Church ordained only by man's authority, so that all things be done to edifying.

De Traditionibus Ecclesiasticis

Traditiones atque caeremonias easdem non omnino necessarium est esse ubique, aut prorsus consimiles; nam et variae semper fuerunt et mutari possunt, pro regionum temporum et morum diversitate, modo nihil contra verbum Dei instituatur.

Traditiones et caeremonias ecclesiasticas quae cum verbo Dei non pugnant et sunt autoritate publica institutae atque probatae, quisquis privato consilio volens et data opera publice violaverat, is ut qui peccat in publicum ordinem Ecclesiae, quique laedit autoritatem magistratus, et qui infirmorum fratrum conscientias vulnerat, publice, ut caeteri timeant, arguendus est.

Quaelibet Ecclesia particularis sive nationalis autoritatem habet instituendi mutandi aut abrogandi caeremonias aut ritus ecclesiasticos, humana tantum autoritate institutos, modo omnia ad aedificationem fiant.

Article XXXIV developed in three stages.

First Cranmer included a statement about the legitimacy of diversity within the Church in the fifth of the *Thirteen Articles* of 1538. This ran as follows (the words that became the basis of Article XXXIV are in italics):

> *Traditiones* vero, et ritus, *atque caeremoniae*, quae vel ad decorum vel ordinem vel disciplinam ecclesiae ab hominibus sunt institutae, *non omnino necesse est ut eaedem sint ubique aut prorsus similes. Hae enim et variae fuere, et variati possunt pro regionum et morum diversitate*, ubi decus decensque ordo principibus rectoribus regionum videbuntur postulare; ita tamen ut *nihil* varietur aut *instituatur contra verbum Dei manifestum.*

> *Traditions* and rites and *ceremonies*, which have been instituted by men either for decency, or order, or church discipline, *need not be identical everywhere, or even very similar. They have always been diverse, and may vary according to the differences of region and custom*, when decency and good order are seen to be advocated by the princes and rules of these regions, provided that *nothing* differ from, or *be instituted which is contrary to, the plain Word of God.*[748]

Secondly, when Article XXXIII of the *Forty Two Articles* was drawn up the material from the *Thirteen Articles* was used as the basis for the current first paragraph (with the exception of the word 'times' in the English text and 'temporum' in the Latin one) with entirely new material being added to form the present second paragraph.

---

[748] Bray, *Documents of the English Reformation*, p.190 (adapted).

Thirdly, in 1563 the words 'times' and 'temporum' were added to the English and Latin texts of the first paragraph and the present third paragraph was added, utilising material from the twenty three doctrinal Articles drawn up by the bishops in 1560/61 (see p.50 footnote 51).

Article XXXIV in its final form has two purposes.

The first is to justify, against the objections of Rome, the right of the Church of England to make those changes in her 'traditions and ceremonies' which she had carried out.

The second is to challenge the behaviour of those Protestants who felt that the Church of England had not changed enough and were unwilling to conform to 'traditions and ceremonies' that they though were still too redolent of Rome.

It is not necessary that traditions and ceremonies be in all places one or utterly alike; for at all times they have been diverse, and may be changed according to the diversity of countries, times, and men's manners, so that nothing be ordained against God's word.

The first paragraph of the article beings with the summary claim that 'it is not necessary that traditions and ceremonies be in all places one of utterly alike.' The phrase 'Traditions and ceremonies' is used here to refer to the practices of the Church and does not include doctrinal traditions. This is clear both from the contents of the paragraph in the *Thirteen Articles* on which the first paragraph of Article XXXIII is based and on the fact that in the final paragraph of Article XXXIII the equivalent phase that is used is 'ceremonies or rites.'

Having made this summary claim the paragraph goes on to give two justifications for it. The first justification is historical 'at all times they have been diverse.' The article itself does not go into details, but the sort of historic diversity that is referred to here is helpfully summarised by Wilson and Templeton in their commentary on this article. They write:

> The basis of the right to change customs is the historical fact that customs have varied in the past. Local branches of the Catholic Church in various places developed, often unconsciously, customary ways of worship, and formulated rules for the guidance of their members. Such customs and rules varied from place to place, and were recognized and approved by many of the highest authorities in the Church. For instance, a ceremonial feet-

washing (the 'Pedilavium') accompanied Baptism in the Gallican Church and in Milan, but was not practised in Spain or in Rome. Many non –Roman customs and usages were practiced in the early Celtic Church. The Eucharist was celebrated on Wednesdays and Fridays in Africa and Jerusalem but not in Rome. Saturday was observed as a day of fasting in Rome and North Africa but not in Milan. St. Ambrose, Bishop of Milan (375-397 A.D.) advised St. Augustine to conform to local customs: 'When I am here (in Milan) I do not fast on Saturday; but when I am in Rome I do: whatever Church you may come to, conform to its custom, if you would avoid either giving or receiving offence.

It is evident, therefore, that in the Primitive Church absolute uniformity in rites and ceremonies was not considered desirable or essential. [749]

In addition to such examples, the English Reformers would also have been aware that Pope Gregory the Great had endorsed the principle of local diversity when he told St. Augustine of Canterbury to make his own selection from the varying customs of the churches as the basis for the practice of the English church.

St. Augustine had written to Pope Gregory asking:

> Since we hold the same Faith, why do customs vary in different Churches? Why, for instance, does the method of saying Mass differ in the holy Roman Church and the Churches of Gaul?

The Pope's reply was:

> My brother, you are familiar with the usage of the Roman Church, in which you were brought up. But if you have found customs, whether in the Church of Rome or of Gaul or any other that may be more acceptable before God, I wish you to make a careful selection of them, and teach the Church of the English, which is still young in the Faith, whatever you have been able to learn with profit from the various Churches. For things should not be loved for the sake of places, but places for the sake of good things.

---

[749] Wilson and Templeton, op.cit. p.158.

Therefore, select from each of the Churches whatever things are devout and honest and right; and when you have bound them, as it were, into a sheaf, let the minds of the English grow accustomed to it. [750]

The implicit argument that the article is making by appealing to such historical examples is that if such diversity of practice was accepted in the past then there is no reason why it should not still be acceptable in the present.

The second justification for the claim that there can be a legitimate diversity of 'traditions and ceremonies' is implicit in the words 'so that nothing be ordained against God's word.' For the English Reformers the one absolutely binding authority for the practice of the Church is the word of God contained in the Bible. This is a point that is made in Articles VI, XX and XXI. Because that which is taught in the Bible has binding authority any tradition or ceremony that is contrary to Scripture must not be practiced in the Church. On the other hand this also means that anything that is not contrary to Scripture cannot be automatically ruled out as wrong even if it contradicts the established practice of the Church. Where God has not seen fit to give any binding teaching through Scripture the Church is free to develop new forms of practice that are in accordance with 'the diversity of countries, times, and men's manners.'

A good example of this last point is provided by baptism. Because of what is said in Scripture it is clear that the Church is under an obligation to baptise people, using water, in the name of the Father, the Son and the Holy Spirit. However, because the precise form of the baptismal rite is not otherwise specified in Scripture, particular local churches are free to develop their own forms of baptismal service by, for example, administering baptism indoors and by pouring, rather than outdoors and by full immersion, in places where the weather is cold or there is not a large supply of water, or by adding additional ceremonies such as anointing or foot washing or clothing people with new garments in order to bring out the full meaning of what is taking place at baptism.

---

[750] Bede, *A History of the English Church and People*, Bk I.27, Harmondsworh; Penguin , 1997, p.73.

Whosoever through his private judgement willingly and purposely doth openly break the traditions and ceremonies of the Church which be not repugnant to the word of God, and be ordained and approved by common authority, ought to be rebuked openly that other may fear to do the like, as he that offendeth against the common order of the Church, and hurteth the authority of the magistrate, and woundeth the conscience of the weak brethren.

Having said that the traditions and ceremonies of the Church are in principle open to change the article goes on to say that they cannot, however, simply be rejected on the basis of the 'private judgement' of individuals. This point is aimed at those of a Protestant persuasion who were refusing to conform to the practices of the Church of England on the grounds that they had been insufficiently reformed.

The article makes it clear that what is being discussed here is the rejection by an individual of traditions and ceremonies that have (a) been put in place by those with appropriate institutional authority within the Church to do so ('ordained and approved by common authority') and (b) are not 'repugnant to the word of God.' Where a tradition or ceremony is contrary to the teaching of Scripture then an individual would be justified in opposing it as Luther did, for instance, when he rejected the practice of the selling of indulgences. This was obviously a vital point for the English Reformers to make because otherwise they would have been forced, for example, to condemn the actions of the English martyrs of Queen Mary's reign who refused to conform to the traditions and ceremonies of Mary's restored Catholicism. However, when something is not contrary to the teaching of Scripture then an individual is not justified in opposing it if the proper authorities have sanctioned it.

According to the article anyone who does this needs to be 'rebuked openly' for three reasons.

Firstly, they are someone who 'offendeth against the common order of the Church'. This, for the English Reformers, was a serious matter. As the statement 'Of Ceremonies' in the *Book of Common Prayer* puts it:

> And although the keeping or omitting of a Ceremony, in itself considered, is but a small thing; yet the wilful and contemptuous transgression and breaking of a common order and discipline is no small offence before God, Let all things be done among you,

saith Saint Paul, in a seemly and due order: The appointment of the which order pertaineth not to private men; therefore no man ought to take in hand, nor presume to appoint or alter any publick or common Order in Christ's Church, except he be lawfully called and authorized thereunto.

Secondly, they are someone who 'hurteth the authority of the magistrate.' In a church like the sixteenth century Church of England the order of the church was sanctioned by the authority of the state. This meant that to rebel against the order of the church also involved rejecting the authority of the rulers appointed by God in opposition to the teaching of Romans 13:1-7 and 1 Peter 2:13-14.[751]

Thirdly, they are someone who 'woundeth the conscience of the weak brethren.' This is a reference to St. Paul's teaching in 1 Corinthians 8:1-13 and Romans 14:13-23 about the necessity of considering the impact on our fellow Christians of the way we exercise our Christian freedom. The point that is being made by the article through this reference is that if someone decides to unilaterally break the law of the Church this could cause unnecessary offence or difficulties of conscience to other Christians who believe that the law needs to be upheld. Individuals should therefore refrain from breaking the law in order to avoid this happening even if they think what the law says is not actually required by God's word.

Every particular or national Church hath authority to ordain, change, and abolish ceremonies or rites of the Church ordained only by man's authority, so that all things be done to edifying.

The final section of the article addresses the issue of at what level of Church life decisions about 'ceremonies and rites' should be made. In opposition to the claim made by Rome that such decisions should only be made by the Church worldwide and with the agreement of the Pope, the article argues that such decisions should be made at the level of the national church.

---

[751] It is perhaps worth noting, because it often forgotten, that it is still the case that the laws of the Church of England form part of English law and that therefore breaking these laws by, for example, failing to observe the Canons, is as much a breach of the law as say, driving through a red light or falsifying one's tax return. Breaking church law is simply breaking the law.

This was for two reasons.

Firstly, the English Reformers believed that one of the things that distinguished the Christian from the Jewish dispensation was that under Christianity God's people consisted not of one nation but of several and each of these had the right to determine their own rites and ceremonies where there was nothing laid down in Scripture. In the words of Burnet:

> It is certain, that all the parts of the Catholic Church ought to hold a communion one with another, and mutual commerce and correspondence together; but this difference is to be observed between the Christian and the Jewish religion, that the one was tied to one nation, and to one place, whereas the Christian religion is universal, to be spread to all nations, among people of different climates and languages, and of different customs and tempers; and therefore, since the power in indifferent matters is given to the Church only in order to edification, every nation must be the judge of that within itself. [752]

Secondly, the reason why the English Reformers believed that decisions should be taken at the national rather than the diocesan or congregational level was that they believed that as in the case of Old Testament Israel the national church and the national state formed a single national community. Thus, in the words of Richard Hooker 'there is not any man of the Church of England but the same man is also a member of the commonwealth; nor any man a member of the commonwealth, which is not also of the Church of England.'[753] In line with this belief they held that just as civil law was decided at the national level and applied to the whole nation so also church law should be decided at the national level and apply to the whole of the national church.

In the final section the article also reiterates that point that only those rites and ceremonies can be changed which have been introduced by human beings ('ordained only by man's authority'). Those aspects of the Church's life in which there are rules laid down by Scripture cannot be altered (except, of course, to bring them back into line with Scripture where they have departed from it).

---

[752] Burnet, op.cit. p.508.

[753] Hooker, *Laws of Ecclesiastical Polity* VIII.1.2 . 'Commonwealth' here means the English nation.

The words 'that all things be done to edifying' is a reference back to St. Paul's teaching, in this case 1 Corinthians 14:26 in which, in the context of a discussion of Christian worship, the Apostle states the principle 'Let all things be done for edification.' Edification means that which builds up people in their relationship with God. Applying this principle the article insists that in deciding whether or not to ordain, change, or abolish rites or ceremonies what the national church has to decide is whether doing this will build up the members of that church in their relationship with God.

Note 1; Diversity in recent ecumenical statements

In line with Article XXXIV recent ecumenical agreements entered into by the Church of England have continued to affirm the importance of appropriate diversity in the life of the Church.

Thus the Porvoo agreement of 1992 declares that:

> Visible unity, however, should not be confused with uniformity. 'Unity in Christ does not exist despite and in opposition to diversity, but is given with and in diversity.' Because this diversity corresponds with the many gifts of the Holy Spirit to the church, it is a concept of fundamental ecclesial importance, with relevance to all aspects of the life of the Church, and is not a mere concession to theological pluralism. [754]

Thus also the Anglican-Methodist Covenant of 2001 states that the catholicity of the Church means that:

> ...it aims to hold together the rich diversity of gifts and insights generated by the breadth of Christian response through many cultures. Diverse expressions of the gospel answer to the diversity of human needs and situations.[755]

Note 2: *The Windsor Report* on the limits to the autonomy of national churches.

---

[754] *The Porvoo Common Statement*, p.14.
[755] *An Anglican-Methodist Covenant*, p.31.

The principle laid down in Article XXXIV that, subject to the authority of Scripture, each national church is free to develop its own traditions and ceremonies has been a cornerstone of Anglican ecclesiology. However, in the light of recent disputes in the Anglican Communion on the issue of same-sex relationships it has increasingly come to be recognised that the autonomy of each national church also has to be qualified by the requirements of being in communion with other churches.

This point is made, for instance, in the *Windsor Report* of 2004. This report affirms that each autonomous church:

> ...has the unfettered right to order and regulate its own local affairs, through its own system of government and law. Each such church is free from direct control by any decision of any ecclesiastical body external to itself in relation to its exclusively internal affairs (unless that external decision is authorised under, or incorporated in, its own law).[756]

However, it then goes on to argue that some matters treated by and within a church may have what it calls a 'dual character.' This means that they may be of both 'internal (domestic) and external (common) concern.' In its view autonomy includes: the right of a church to make decisions about the latter:

> ...provided those internal decisions are fully compatible with the interests, standards, unity and good order of the wider community of which the autonomous body forms part. If they are not so compatible, whilst there may be no question about their legal validity, they will impose strains not only upon that church's wider relationship with other churches, but on that church's inner self-understanding as part of "the One, Holy, Catholic and Apostolic Church" in relation to some of its own members.[757]

As a result, says the report, autonomy should not be seen as denoting 'unlimited freedom' but rather 'freedom-in-relation,' that is to say freedom that is 'subject to limits generated by the commitments of communion.' In consequence: 'the very nature of autonomy itself obliges

---

[756] *The Windsor Report*, London: Anglican Communion Office, 2004, p.48
[757] Ibid p.48.

each church to have regard to the common good of the global Anglican community and the Church universal.' [758]

Summing up its argument the report declares:

> Since autonomy is closely related to interdependence and freedom-in-relation, there are legitimate limits (both substantive and procedural) on the exercise of this autonomy, demanded by the relationships and commitments of communion and the acknowledgement of common identity. Communion is, in fact, the fundamental limit to autonomy. In essential matters of common concern to the worldwide fellowship of churches (affairs, that is, which touch both the particular church and the wider community of which it forms part), we believe that each church in the exercise of its autonomy should:

> • consider, promote and respect the common good of the Anglican Communion and its constituent churches (as discerned in communion through the Instruments of Unity)

> • maintain its communion with fellow churches, and avoid jeopardising it, by bringing potentially contentious initiatives, prior to implementation, to the rest of the communion in dialogue, consultation, discernment and agreement in communion with the fellowship of churches (through the Instruments of Unity), and

> • be able to depart, where appropriate and acceptable, on the basis of its own corporate conscience and with the blessing of the communion, from the standards of the community of which is an autonomous part, provided such departure is neither critical to the maintenance of communion nor likely to harm the common good of the Anglican Communion and of the Church universal (again, as determined by the Instruments of Unity).[759]

---

[758] Ibid, pp.48-49.

[759] Ibid, p.49. The Instruments of Communion are the key institutions that link together churches of the Anglican Communion. They are the Archbishop of Canterbury, the Lambeth Conference, the Primates Meeting and the Anglican Consultative Council.

Article XXXV

∞

Of Homilies

The second Book of Homilies, the several titles whereof we have joined under this Article, doth contain a godly and wholesome doctrine and necessary for these times, as doth the former Book of Homilies which were set forth in the time of Edward the Sixth: and therefore we judge them to be read in Churches by the ministers diligently and distinctly, that they may be understood of the people.

Of the Names of the Homilies

1 Of the right Use of the Church
2 Against peril of Idolatry
3 Of the repairing and keeping clean of Churches
4 Of good Works: first of Fasting
5 Against Gluttony and Drunkenness
6 Against Excess of Apparel
7 Of Prayer
8 Of the Place and Time of Prayer
9 That Common Prayers and Sacraments ought to be ministered in a known tongue
10 Of the reverend estimation of God's Word
11 Of Alms-doing
12 Of the Nativity of Christ
13 Of the Passion of Christ
14 Of the Resurrection of Christ
15 Of the worthy receiving of the Sacrament of the Body and Blood of Christ
16 Of the Gifts of the Holy Ghost
17 For the Rogation-days
18 Of the state of Matrimony

19 Of Repentance
20 Against Idleness
21 Against Rebellion

De Homiliis

Tomus secundus Homiliarum, quarum singulos titulos huic Articulo subiunximus, continet piam et salutarem doctrinam et his temporibus necessarium, non minus quam prior tomus Homiliarum, quae editae sunt tempore Edwardi Sexti: itaque eas in Ecclesiis per ministros diligenter et clare, ut a populo intelligi possint, recitandas esse iudicamus.

Catalogus Homiliarum

   1 *De recto Ecclesiae*
   2 *Adversus idolatariae pericula*
   3 *De reparandis ac purgandis Ecclesii*
   4 *De bonis operibus*
   5 *De ieiunio*
   6 *In gulae atque ebrietatis vitia*
   7 *In nimis sumptuosos vestium apparatus*
   8 *De oratione sive precatione*
   9 *De loco et tempore orationi destinatis*
  10 *De publicis precibus ac sacramentis, idiomate vulgari omnibusque noto, habendis*
  11 *De sacrosancta verbi divini auctoritate*
  12 *De eleemosyna*
  13 *De Christi nativitate*
  14 *De Dominica passione*
  15 *De resurrectione Domini*
  16 *De digna corporis et sanguinis Dominici in coena Domini participatione*
  17 *De donis Spiritus Sancti*
  18 *In diebus, qui vulgo Rogationum dicti sunt, concio*
  19 *De matrimonii statu*
  20 *De otio seu socordia*
  21 *De poenitantia*

Article XXXV developed in three stages.

The first stage was Article XXXIV of the *Forty Two Articles*. Referring to the First Book of Homilies issued in Edward VI's reign, this states:

> The homilies of late given and set out by the king's authority, be godly and wholesome, containing doctrines to be received of all Men and therefore are to be read to the people diligently, distinctly and plainly.

The second stage was in 1563. In the revised Articles published in that year the opening paragraph of the present Article formed the concluding paragraph of the article on the Traditions of the Church. The list of homilies in the *Second Book of Homilies* was then included as a separate article. The English and Latin versions of this list were in their present forms except that the English version lacked a reference to the homily 'Against Rebellion' which was not added to the Homilies until 1571.

The third stage was in 1571 when the article achieved its present form with the opening paragraph and the list of homilies being brought together into one article and the reference to the homily 'Against Rebellion' being added to the English version of the list of homilies. It is unclear why the Latin version of the article was not revised to refer to this additional homily and it is also unclear why in English list has the homilies 'Of Repentance' and 'Against Idleness' in the wrong order (the Latin list is correct on this point).

A further difference between the English and Latin lists of the homilies is that while the English version lists the fourth homily under the one heading 'Of good works: first of fasting' the Latin version lists the two parts of the homily under two headings 'De bonis operibus' (Of good works) and 'De ieiunio' (Of fasting). It is because the two parts of this homily are listed separately in the Latin version that the Latin version lists the same number of homilies as the English version in spite of lacking the homily 'Against Rebellion.'

As Griffith Thomas notes, the word English word 'homily' is derived from the Greek word ὁμιλία meaning 'conversation' or 'intercourse' (see Luke 24:14, Acts 20:11, 1 Corinthians 15:33) It was used from the fifth century onwards 'to signify a simple discourse for people when there was no sermon.'[760] At least as early as the time of St. Jerome homilies taken from the writings of the Fathers were used for this purpose and this practice was formally sanctioned by the Council of Vasens in 529 and the Council of Rheims in 813.[761] The practice of using homilies continued through the Middle Ages and was picked up by the Continental Reformers. Luther, for example, prepared a collection of sermons for reading in parish churches.

Possibly influenced by his knowledge of Luther's example, Archbishop Cranmer seems to have conceived the idea of a book of homilies for the Church of England as early as 1539. As Jelf explains, the reason such a book was needed was that:

> Not only were the bulk of the clergy generally very ignorant, but many of them were only half acquainted with the first principles of the Reformation, and many others mistook their new-found liberty for utter license so that the greatest uncertainty and confusion prevailed in the teaching that issues from the pulpits, and it was found needful repeatedly to prohibit preaching, except under special sanction. Consequently we hear of as many as 8000 parishes at one time as being destitute of preaching ministers; and some means of supplying such a want was peremptorily required.[762]

In 1540 a collection of discourses called the *Postils* was published by Richard Taverner with Cranmer's sanction and encouragement and in 1542 the bishops, meeting in the southern Convocation, agreed 'to make certain homilies for stay of such errors as were then by ignorant people sparkled among the people.'[763] In 1543 a number of homilies written by members of the Lower House of Convocation were produced by the Prolocutor of that House, but at that point the project seems to have lapsed due to opposition from King Henry VIII.

Following the accession of Edward VI, however, the *First Book of Homilies*, which seems to have made use of the material produced in 1542-3 plus some more recent material, was published in 1547 by royal

---

[760] Griffith Thomas op.cit. p.448

[761] Jelf, op.cit. p. 383.

[762] Ibid, p.383.

[763] Bishop Stephen Gardiner, letter to Lord Protector Somerset, June 10, 1547 quoted in J Griffith (ed) *The Two Books of Homilies*, Oxford: OUP, 1859, p.vii.

authority with the title 'Certain Sermons, or Homilies, appointed by the King's Majesty to be declared and read by all Parsons, Vicars, or Curates every Sunday in their churches where they have cure.'

The homilies were published with a preface by Edward VI and, in the words of Peter Toon, his royal injunctions of 1547:

> ...required every parish church in England to have a copy of the whole Bible in English, the Paraphrases on the Gospels and Acts by Erasmus (translated by Nicholas Udall) and the Homilies, and to use these as the basis for reading, studying and preaching from the Bible. Thus the Homilies were part of a larger plan to bring the message of the word of God to the people of England.[764]

In addition the Prayer Books of 1549 and 1552 made provision for one of the Homilies to be read in the place of a sermon in the service of Holy Communion.

The homilies in the *First Book of Homilies* are anonymous and some of the authors are unknown, but it seems that Archbishop Cranmer was the author of 'A fruitful exhortation to the Reading of Holy Scripture,' 'Of the Salvation of all Mankind by only Christ,' 'Of the true lively and Christian faith' and 'Of Good works annexed unto Faith,' Archdeacon John Harpesfield was the author of 'Of the Misery of all Mankind,' the Bishop of London, John Bonner, was the author 'Of Christian Love and Charity' and Edward VI's chaplain Thomas Becon was the author of 'Against Whoredom and Uncleanness.'

The Homilies were widely used during Edward's reign and in 1549, in recognition that they were rather lengthy for reading in church, they were divided into smaller parts which could then be read separately.

During the reign of Queen Mary the Homilies had no official sanction, although the homilies 'Of the Misery of all Mankind,' and "Of Christian Love and Charity' were re-used in an alternative set of Homilies produced during her reign.

After the accession of Elizabeth I the Act of Uniformity of 1559 re-authorised the 1552 Prayer Book and in consequence once again sanctioned the use of the Edwardine Homilies. They were therefore re-issued in 1559 and 1562 with a new preface from Elizabeth I. During the

---

[764] P. Toon, 'The Articles and Homilies' in S. Sykes and J. Booty (eds), *The Study of Anglicanism.* London and Minneapolis: SPCK/Fortress Press, 1988, p.138.

reign of Edward VI it had been planned to produce additional homilies covering additional topics and this plan came to fruition when after careful scrutiny and a number of alterations by the Queen and her advisers the *Second Book of Homilies* was published in the summer of 1563 under the title 'The Second Tome of Homilies of such matters as were promised and intituled in the former part of Homilies: sent out by the authority of the Queen's Majesty, and to be read in every Parish Church agreeably.'

The Bishop of Salisbury, John Jewel, seems to have been the editor of this second collection. As in the case of the First Book of Homilies, not all the authors of the homilies in this collection are known, but the evidence suggests that Jewel was the author of 'Of the right Use of the Church,' 'Against peril of Idolatry' (drawing on the work of Heinrich Bullinger), 'Of the repairing and keeping clean of Churches,' 'Of Prayer ' 'Of the Place and Time of Prayer,' 'That Common Prayers and Sacraments ought to be ministered in a known tongue,' 'Of the worthy receiving of the Sacrament of the Body and Blood of Christ,' 'Of the Gifts of the Holy Ghost' and 'Against Idleness,' that the Bishop of Durham, James Pilkington, was the author 'Against Gluttony and Drunkenness' and 'Against Excess of Apparel' and that the Archbishop of Canterbury, Matthew Parker, and the Bishop of London, Edmund Grindal, wrote 'Of Good Works: first of Fasting.' The homilies 'Of the Passion of Christ' and 'Of the Resurrection of Christ 'were taken from Taverner's *Postils* and 'Of the state of Matrimony' was a combination of material from the Nuremburg Reformer Veit Dietrich and from St. John Chrysostom.

As previously noted, the homily 'Against Rebellion', which was written by Archbishop Parker, was added in 1571.

The second Book of Homilies, the several titles whereof we have joined under this Article, doth contain a godly and wholesome doctrine and necessary for these times, as doth the former Book of Homilies which were set forth in the time of Edward the Sixth.

The purpose of the *First Book of Homilies* is set out in Edward VI's Preface. This declares that 'the king's most excellent majesty' in order that:

>...all Curates, of what learning soever they may be, may have some godly and fruitful lessons in a readiness to read and declare unto

their parishioners for their edifying, instruction and comfort; hath caused a Book of Homilies to be made and set forth, wherein is contained certain wholesome and godly exhortations, to move the people to honour and worship Almighty God, and diligently to serve him, every one according to their degree, state and vocation.[765]

A similar explanation of the purpose of the Homilies is contained in the Preface by Elizabeth I. This notes that:

...they which are appointed ministers have not the gift of preaching sufficiently to instruct the people which is committed unto them, whereof great inconveniences might rise, and ignorance still be maintained, if some honest remedy be not speedily found and provided...

This being the case, Queen Elizabeth:

...hath by the advice of her most honourable counsellors, for her discharge on this behalf, caused a Book of Homilies, which heretofore was set forth by her most loving brother, a Prince of most worthy memory, Edward the Sixth, to be printed anew, wherein are contained certain wholesome and godly exhortations, to move the people to honour and worship Almighty God, and diligently to serve him, every one according to their degree, state and vocation.[766]

If we look at the contents of the *First Book of Homilies* we find that it fulfils the purpose set out in these Prefaces in a number of ways.

First, the opening homily 'A Fruitful Exhortation to the Reading of Holy Scripture' sets the tone for the whole collection by emphasising that it is through knowledge of, and obedience to, Scripture that we can live in the way that God requires and so attain eternal life.

Secondly, the homilies 'Of the misery of all mankind', 'Of the salvation of mankind by only Christ', 'Of the true, lively and Christian Faith' and 'Of good works annexed unto Faith' explain the doctrine of

---

[765] *The Homilies*, p.3. 'Curates' in this context means all those having a cure of souls.
[766] Ibid, p.1.

justification by faith and the importance of good works as an expression of saving faith.

Thirdly, the homilies 'Of Christian Love and Charity', 'How dangerous a thing it is to fall from God' and 'Against the Fear of Death' warn of the nature and importance of Christian love and against apostasy and the fear of death.

Fourthly, the homily 'Concerning Good Order and Obedience' explains that Christians need to obey the civil authorities appointed by God.

Fifthly, the homilies 'Against Swearing and Perjury,' 'Against Whoredom and Uncleanness' and 'Against Contention and Brawling' warn against three forms of personal immorality.

Taken together these homilies give an overall introduction to what it means to live a godly life, rightly responding to what God has done for us in Christ and then highlight certain aspects of Christian conduct which were seen as needing particular emphasis.

The *Second Book of Homilies* was not given a Preface and we lack any direct explanation of its purpose. However, we can infer the purposes it was meant to achieve by looking at its contents.

First, the *Second Book of Homilies* was intended to supply appropriate teaching for the each of the major festivals in the Christian year so that congregations would understand what it was that was being celebrated. We can see this from the inclusion of the homilies 'Of the Nativity of Christ,' 'Of the Passion of Christ,' 'Of the Resurrection of Christ,' 'Of the Gifts of the Holy Ghost' and 'For the Rogation-days' which provide homilies for Christmas, Easter and Pentecost and for the key agricultural festival of Rogationtide.

Secondly, it was intended to reinforce the teaching given in the *First Book of Homilies*. The homily 'Of the reverend estimation of God's Word' reinforces the teaching of the homily 'A Fruitful Exhortation to the Reading of Holy Scripture' in the earlier collection by responding to some common objections to the biblical material such as the ungodly life style of the Old Testament Patriarchs or the curses against the wicked contained in the Psalms. The homily 'Of Repentance' underlines the teaching of the earlier homilies 'Of the salvation of mankind by only Christ', 'Of the true, lively and Christian Faith' and 'Of Good works annexed unto faith' by explaining that reconciliation to God involves repentance, faith in the promises of salvation God concerning salvation through Christ and amendment of life resulting in the performance of good works. Finally, the homily 'Against Rebellion' underlines the teaching of the earlier homily 'Concerning Good Order and Obedience' by stressing the importance of obeying the rulers appointed by God and the unlawfulness of rebellion against them.

Thirdly, it was intended to give guidance about the kind of behaviour that Christians should engage in and the sort of behaviour that they should avoid. These topics are covered by the homilies 'Of Good Works: first of Fasting,' 'Against Gluttony and Drunkenness,' 'Against Excess of Apparel,' 'Of Alms-doing,' 'Of the state of Matrimony,' and 'Against Idleness.'

Fourthly, it was intended to give guidance about the nature and importance of Christian worship and, related to this, the need to keep churches clean and in good repair. We can see this purpose reflected in the homilies 'Of the right Use of the Church,' 'Against peril of Idolatry,' 'Of the repairing and keeping clean of Churches,' 'Of Prayer,' 'Of the Place and Time of Prayer,' 'That Common Prayers and Sacraments ought to be ministered in a known tongue,' and 'Of the worthy receiving of the Sacrament of the Body and Blood of Christ.'

Peter Toon suggests that the right worship of God is the key message that the *Second Book of Homilies* is meant to convey:

> Even as Cranmer believed that justification by faith was the primary message that must be heard in 1547, Jewel held that in 1563 the primary message was the purity and right ordering of Christian worship – free from a medieval images cult.[767]

The great length of the homily 'Against peril of Idolatry,' which is by far the longest homily in either of the Books of Homilies, indicates that Bishop Jewel did see avoiding idolatry in worship as a matter of great importance. However, if the *Second Book of Homilies* is considered as a whole there is nothing to indicate that 'the purity and right ordering of Christian worship' is its primary message. As has just been noted, the homilies contained in it are there for a variety of purposes and there is no reason to see one purpose as more primary than the others.

---

[767] Toon, op.cit. p.140.

Article XXXV states that both of the Books of Homilies contain 'doctrine,' that is to say teaching, which is (a) 'godly', (b) 'wholesome' and (c) 'necessary for these times.'

When it says that the teaching of the Books of Homilies is 'godly' what the article means is that this teaching is in accordance with what God is like, what he has done for the salvation of the world and how he wants human beings to behave in response. The article does not explain the basis of its judgement that the teaching of the Books of Homilies is godly, but from what we know of the overall theological approach of the English Reformers we can infer that the reason for this judgement lies in the fact that this teaching is rooted in the teaching of Scripture which, being God's word, is the touchstone for godliness.

An example of the way that the teaching of the Books of Homilies is rooted in Scripture can be seen in the homily 'Of good works annexed unto Faith' in the *First Book of Homilies* which supports its opening argument that good works 'acceptable and pleasant unto God' cannot be performed without faith by quoting John 15:4-5, Hebrews 11:5-6 and Romans 14:23:

> Now by God's grace, shall be declared the second thing that before was noted of faith, that without it, can no good work be done, accepted and pleasant unto God. For *as a branch can not bear fruit of it self, saith our Saviour Christ, except it abide in the vine: so cannot you, except you abide in me. I am the vine, and you be the branches. He that abideth in me, and I in him, he bringeth forth much fruit: for without me, you can do nothing* (John 15.4-5). And St. Paul proveth that the Enoch had faith, *because he pleased God: for without faith* (saith he) *it is not possible to please God* (Hebrews 11.6). And again to the Romans he saith, *Whatsoever work is done without faith, it is sin.* (Romans 14.23).[768]

A further example can be seen in the homily 'Of Repentance and true Reconciliation unto God' in the *Second Book of Homilies* which basis its emphasis on the importance on the importance of repentance on the teaching of Matthew, Luke, Acts and Joel.

---

[768] *The Homilies* p.35.

...no doctrine is so necessary in the Church of God, as is the doctrine of repentance and amendment of life. And verily the true preachers of the Gospel of the kingdom of heaven, and of the glad and joyful tidings of salvation, have always in their godly Sermons and Preachings unto the people, joined these two together, I mean repentance and forgiveness of sins, even as our Saviour Jesus Christ did appoint himself, saying, *So it behoved Christ to suffer, and to rise again the third day, and that repentance and forgiveness of sins should be preached in his Name among all Nations* (Luke 24:46-47). And therefore the holy Apostle doeth in the Acts speak after this manner: *I have witnessed both to the Jews and to the Gentiles, the repentance towards God, and faith towards our Lord Jesus Christ* (Acts 20:21). Did not John Baptist, Zacharias' son, begin his ministry with the doctrine of repentance, saying, *Repent, for the kingdom of God is at hand*? The like doctrine did our Saviour Jesus Christ preach himself, and commanded his Apostles to preach the same (Matthew 3:2, 4:17).

I might here allege very many places out of the Prophets, in the which this most wholesome doctrine of repentance is very earnestly urged, as most needful for all degrees and orders of men, but one shall be sufficient at this present time. These are the words of Joel the Prophet. *Therefore also now the Lord saith, Return unto me with all your heart, with fasting, weeping, and mourning, rent your hearts and not your clothes, and return unto the Lord your God, for he is gracious and merciful, slow to anger, and of great compassion, and ready to pardon wickedness* (Joel 2.12-13).Whereby it is given us to understand, that we have here a perpetual rule appointed unto us, which ought to be observed and kept at all times, and that there is none other way whereby the wrath of God may be pacified, and his anger assuaged, that the fierceness of his fury, and the plagues of destruction, which by his righteous judgement he had determined to bring upon us, may depart, be removed and taken away.[769]

The claim that the teaching of the Books of Homilies is 'wholesome' follows on from the claim that it is godly. 'Wholesome' in this context means spiritually health giving (in the same way that wholesome food is

---

[769] *The Homilies*, pp.381-382.

physically health giving) and the teaching of the Book of Homilies is spiritually health giving because it gives truthful teaching about God and how he wants people to behave and thus enables them to respond in faith and obedience.

The teaching is said to be 'necessary for the times' because it addresses those issues which in the opinion of the English Reformers were pressing for the English church in the 16th century. Thus the homilies teach about justification by faith in order to counter a prevalent tendency to rely on good works for salvation, they teach about the importance of Scripture in order to encourage people who were not used to doing so to study the Bible for themselves and trust what it says and they teach about the need to avoid gluttony and drunkenness because these were prevalent forms of ungodliness in Tudor England.

and therefore we judge them to be read in Churches by the ministers diligently and distinctly, that they may be understanded of the people.

If the teaching of the Books of Homilies was godly, wholesome and necessary for the times it was important that people had the opportunity to hear this teaching for themselves. The last clause of Article XXXV was intended to ensure that this happened in the face of opposition to the Homilies from some of the clergy. As Bishop Forbes notes:

> The last clause in the Article, 'we judge them to be read in the Church diligently and distinctly' was to meet the case of the lower clergy who disliked the changed tone of thought in the Articles, or many of their statements, some of whom neglected to read the Homilies at all, while others read them in such a way that they were utterly unintelligible to the people.[770]

Note: The place of the Homilies in the Church of England today

The Books of Homilies are little known and very rarely used in the contemporary Church of England. Unlike the *Book of Common Prayer*, *Common Worship* makes no provision for them to be read in church.

---

[770] A P Forbes, *An Explanation of The Thirty Nine Articles,* London: Parker and Co, 1890, p. 699.

However, the Homilies cannot be disregarded by anyone who accepts that the *Thirty Nine Articles* provide authoritative guidance for the contemporary Church. This is for three reasons.

Firstly, Article XI explicitly refers to the homily 'Of the salvation of mankind by only Christ' ('the Homily of Justification') as giving further explanation about why the teaching 'that we are justified by faith only' is 'a most wholesome doctrine and full of comfort.' The homily acts as the authoritative commentary on the article.

Secondly, as we have just seen, Article XXXV declares that the teaching contained in the Books of Homilies is 'godly' and 'wholesome.' There is a general consensus among commentators that this statement commits people to a general rather than specific assent to the teaching of the Homilies. As Browne puts it:

> We are not expected to express full concurrence with every statement, or every exposition of Holy Scripture contained in them, but merely, in the general, to approve of them, as a body of sound and orthodox discourses, and well adapted for the times, for which they were composed.[771]

Even with this caveat what is said in Article XXXV obliges us to take the Homilies seriously. If overall they are 'a body of sound and orthodox discourses' then we should be willing to give our attention to them and to see what we can learn from them.

Thirdly, as we have seen on numerous occasions in the course of this commentary, on the subjects on which they overlap the Homilies and the Articles contain the same basic teaching, with the Homilies giving this teaching in more detail. It is therefore not possible to play off the teaching of the Articles against the teaching of the Homilies. If you accept the one you are obliged to accept the other.

The need to give due attention to the Homilies for these three reasons does not mean that the Homilies should still be used today for their original purpose. Even when they were first published they were often found to be too lengthy for general congregational use and today there is the additional issue of the linguistic changes that have taken

---

[771] Browne, op.cit, p.777, see also Gibson, op.cit, pp.726-727 and Griffith Thomas, op.cit. p.449.

place since the sixteenth century which have made the English of the Homilies difficult for the ordinary reader or listener to follow.

What these difficulties mean is that that rather than the Homilies being read out in churches in the place of sermons they should be used as a resource for study and reflection on the topics that they cover with the results of this study and reflection being communicated in a more contemporary and 'user friendly' fashion.

A particular issue that is raised by the Homilies for the Church of England today is the very strong criticism of the Roman Catholic Church contained in the homilies 'Against peril of Idolatry' and 'Of the Gifts of the Holy Ghost.' For example, the latter homily declares:

> ...look what our Saviour Christ pronounced of the Scribes and Pharisees, in the Gospel, the same may be boldly and with safe conscience pronounced of the Bishops of Rome, namely that they have forsaken, and daily do forsake, the commandments of God, to erect and set up their own constitutions. Which thing being true, as all they which have any light of God's word must needs confess, we may well conclude according to the rule of Augustine, that the Bishops of Rome and their adherents, are not the true Church of Christ, much less then, to be taken as chief heads and rulers of the same.[772]

How do we handle this sort of material in terms of relations between Anglicans and Roman Catholics today? This question is part of the general problem of how we handle the condemnations of each other's theology and practice that were issued by both sides at the Reformation. The answer which was developed in the course of Protestant-Catholic ecumenical dialogue during the twentieth century is to acknowledge what was said in the sixteenth century, but then seek to understand the theological issues lying behind what was said and see whether it is possible for us today to reach theological agreement about them.

In the case of the quotation from the *Second Book of Homilies* just given, for instance, this means acknowledging that among the English Reformers the view was held for serious theological reasons that the Church of Rome no longer possessed the marks of the visible Church because it had forsaken the commandments of God by ceasing to preach

---

[772] *The Homilies,*p.336.

the pure word of God, ceasing to administer the sacraments rightly, and abandoning the proper exercise of ecclesiastical discipline.[773] It also means acknowledging, however, that theological developments since the Reformation, and especially during last century, mean that most Anglicans, and the Church of England as a corporate body, no longer hold to this negative judgement about the Roman Catholic Church. This is because agreement has been reached between Roman Catholics and Anglicans about the nature of the Christian message, about the sacraments and about the exercise of authority within the Church in a way that did not seem possible at the time of the Reformation.[774]

---

[773] Ibid, p.336.

[774] See, for example, the agreed statement of the International Anglican-Roman Catholic Commission for Unity and Mission, *Growing Together in Mission and Unity*, London: SPCK, 2007.

Article XXXVI

∞

Of Consecration of Bishops and Ministers

The Book of Consecration of Archbishops and Bishops and ordering of Priests and Deacons, lately set forth in the time of Edward the Sixth and confirmed at the same time by authority of Parliament, doth contain all things necessary to such consecration and ordering; neither hath it anything that of itself is superstitious or ungodly. And therefore whosoever are consecrated or ordered according to the rites of that book, since the second year of King Edward unto this time, or hereafter shall be consecrated or ordered according to the same rites, we decree all such to be rightly, orderly, and lawfully consecrated or ordered.

De Episcoporum et Ministrorum Consecratione

Libellus de Consecratione Archiepiscoporum et Episcoporum et de ordinatione Presbyterorum et Diaconorum, editus nuper temporibus Edwardi Sexti et auctoritate Parliamenti illis ipsis temporibus confirmatus, omnia ad eiusmodi consecrationem et ordinationem necessaria continet; et nihil habet quod ex se sit aut supersitiosum aut impium. Itaque quicunque iuxta ritus illius libri consecrati aut ordinati sunt, ab anno secundo praedicti Regis Edwardi usque ad hoc tempus aut in posterum iuxta eosdem ritus consecrabuntur aut ordinabuntur, rite, atque ordine, atque legitime statuimus esse et fore consecratos et ordinatos.

Article XXXVI dates from 1563 and was a replacement for Article XXXV of the *Forty Two Articles*. As Gibson notes, this original article 'was of a much more general character, referring to the Book of Common Prayer as a whole, and not only to the Ordinal.' [775] The article ran as follows:

---

[775] Gibson, op.cit. p.729

Of the Book of Prayers and Ceremonies of the Church of England

The Book which of very later time was given to the Church of England by the King's authority and the Parliament, containing the manner and form of praying, and ministering the sacraments in the Church of England, likewise also the book of Ordering Ministers of the Church, set forth by the foresaid authority, are godly, and in no point repugnant to the wholesome doctrine of the Gospel, but agreeable thereunto, furthering and beautifying the same not a little; and therefore all faithful members of the Church of England, and chiefly of the ministers of the word, they ought to be received, and allowed with all readiness of mind, and thanksgiving, and to be commended to the people of God.

De Libro Precationum et caeremoniarum Ecclesiae Anglicanae

Liber qui nuperrime authoritate Regis et Parliamenti Ecclesiae Anglicanae traditus est, continens modum et formam orandi, et Sacramenta administrandi in Ecclesia Anglicana: similiter et libellus eadem authoritate editus de ordinatione ministrorum Ecclesiae, quoad doctrine veritatem, pii sunt, et salutatri doctrinae Evangelii in nullo repugnant sed congruunt, et eadem non parum promovent et illustrant, atque ideo ab omnibus Ecclesiae Anglicanae fidelibus membris, et maxime a ministris verbi eum omni promptitutidne animorum et gratiarum actione, recipendi, appropandi, et populo Dei commendandi sunt.

A comparison of this article with Article XXXVI shows that the latter article is completely new with nothing of the previous article remaining and that it has a much more specific focus.

The focus of Article XXXVI is on two issues. Does the Church of England have valid ordination rites and therefore are those ordained in the Church of England validly ordained? It answers both questions in the affirmative, arguing that its ordination rites are valid and therefore that all those ordained according to them should be regarded as validly ordained.

The Book of Consecration of Archbishops and Bishops and ordering of Priests and Deacons, lately set forth in the time of Edward the

Sixth and confirmed at the same time by authority of Parliament, doth contain all things necessary to such consecration and ordering; neither hath it anything that of itself is superstitious or ungodly.

During the reign of Edward VI two Ordinals were produced. The first Ordinal was produced in 1550 and a second, revised, Ordinal was produced in 1552. The 1552 Ordinal was given legal authority by the Act of Uniformity of 1552 which referred both to the 1552 Prayer Book and the 1552 Ordinal.[776] This legal authority was lost when the Act of Uniformity was repealed by Mary Tudor and when the 1559 Act of Uniformity of Elizabeth I in turn rescinded Mary Tudor's action it mentioned only the *Book of Common Prayer* and failed to mention the Ordinal. This may have been simply an oversight or, more likely, because the 1552 Ordinal was bound together with the 1552 Prayer Book mention of the Prayer Book may have been intended to cover both.

As Griffith Thomas notes:

> The authorities evidently considered the Ordinal of 1552 restored, because it was used at [Archbishop] Parker's Consecration, and there is no record of any Consecration or Ordination being performed with any other form than that of 1552. But criticism was raised in regard to this point, that Elizabeth's Act did not expressly mention the Ordinal, and as a result those who were favourable to the Church of Rome maintained that the Ordinations and Consecrations were invalid, because they held that the Ordinal of 1552 was still repealed by the Statute of Mary. [777]

Doubt about the authority of the 1552 Ordinal was eventually settled legally by an Act of Parliament passed in 1566 which declared the validity of Consecrations performed according to the 1552 rite and determined that 1552 ordination rites should be used in future. Three years earlier, however, the same issue was addressed theologically by Article XXXVI.

It was the specific need in 1563 to affirm the validity of the Ordinal that explains the difference between this article and Article XXXV

---

[776] See Bray, *Documents of the English Reformation*, pp.282-283.
[777] Griffith Thomas, op.cit., pp.453-454.

of the *Forty Two Articles*. In 1563 was clearly felt unnecessary to defend the 1552 Prayer Book since its authority had already been guaranteed by the 1559 Act of Uniformity. It was, however, still necessary to defend the Ordinal and so this is the focus of Article XXXVI.

The first two clauses specify the subject of the article. The reference to 'the Book of Consecration of Archbishops and Bishops and ordering of Priests and Deacons' is clearly intended as a catch all reference covering both the 1550 and 1552 Ordinals since the article later goes on to talk about all those consecrated or ordained according to 'the rites of that Book' since 'the second year of the forenamed King Edward unto this time.' The second year of King Edward VI was 1549[778] and therefore the article refers to the 1552 Ordinal in terms of its being a second revised edition of the Ordinal that was first issued in 1550. There is one book, but it is the authority of its second edition that is being defended.

The reference to the Book being 'confirmed at the same time by authority of Parliament,' which is unnecessary for dating purposes, is intended to emphasise the legal authority of the 1552 Ordinal. It was an Ordinal authorised by Parliament and therefore legally valid.

Having specified the 1552 Ordinal as the subject of the article and noted its legal authority, the article goes on to state that this ordinal 'doth contain all things necessary to such Consecration and Ordering.' What it does not tell us is what these necessary things are. However, we can work this out from what is said in the Preface to the 1550 Ordinal which the Elizabethan Church of England adopted un-amended.

This Preface makes it clear that the Church of England ordination rites are intended to continue the practice of the Early Church with regard to ministry and ordination and it notes that in the Early Church no one might presume to exercise ordained ministry:

> ...except he were first called, tried, examined, and known to have such equalities as were requisite for the same; and also by public

---

[778] As previously noted in the 16th century the calendar year started on 25 March. In our terms the first Edwardine Ordinal, which was published before 25 March, was published in 1550, but in Elizabethan terms it was published in 1549 and hence in the second year of Edward VI's reign.

prayer, with imposition of hands, were approved and admitted thereunto.[779]

The two elements mentioned in this quotation are what the Elizabethan Church of England saw as the necessary qualifications for the exercise of ordained ministry and both of them are present in the 1552 Ordinal.

All those ordained as bishops, priests and deacons have been 'called, tried and examined' by the Church prior to the Ordination service. This is indicated in the rites for deacons and priests when the Archdeacon declares that he has enquired of the candidates for ordination and thinks they are 'apt and meet, for their learning and godly conversation, to exercise their ministry duly, to the honour of God, and the edifying of his church.' It is also indicated in the rite for the consecration of a bishop when the candidate is presented by two other bishops as 'this godly and well-learned man.' In addition, in all three rites the candidates are examined orally concerning their fitness for ministry in front of the congregation by the ordaining or consecrating bishop or archbishop.

All those ordained or consecrated according to the 1552 Ordinal are also 'approved and admitted' by means of 'public prayer, with imposition of hands.' In all three rites prayer is offered for the candidates and the bishop or archbishop then lays hands on them to ordain them.[780] In the Medieval Church there was a diversity of opinion about what actions and words were necessary for a valid ordination. The English Reformers took the view that all that was specified in the New Testament was prayer and the laying on of hands (see Acts 6:6 and 13:3) and both of these were present in the 1552 rites.

It is because the two elements needed to qualify someone to exercise ordained ministry are thus present that the article draws the conclusion that the rites contain 'all things necessary to such consecrating and ordering.'

Article XXXVI goes on to say that the 1552 rite does not contain anything that 'that of itself is superstitious or ungodly.' Commentators on the Articles see these words as a response to Puritan objections to the 1552 Ordinal. Jelf, for example, declares that these words are 'directed

---

[779] Bray, *Documents of the English Reformation*, p.277. 'Equalities' means what we would now call 'qualities.'
[780] For details see P Bradshaw 'Ordinals' in S Sykes and J Booty (eds), *The Study of Anglicanism*, pp.146-157.

against an opposite class of objections, proceeding mainly from the Puritans, who object that we are guilty of blasphemy in pretending that our bishops can confer the gift of the Holy Ghost; and in declaring that the priest, in virtue of his ordination, has power to forgive sins.' [781]

It is clear that such objections to the 1552 Ordinal did exist. Archbishop John Whitgift and Richard Hooker, for example, defend the use of the formula 'Receive the Holy Ghost' and the giving of the power to remit and retain sins against Puritan objections in Whitgift's *Defence of the Answer the Admonition*, Tract II, Chapter ii, Division 4 and in Hooker's *Laws of Ecclesiastical Polity*, LXVII: 5-8.

However, the writings of Whitgift and Hooker date from well after Article XXXVI was drawn up and those commentators who suggest that this part of the Article was a response to the Puritans do not provide any specific evidence to indicate that who were later to be known as Puritans objected to the 1552 Ordinal as 'superstitious and ungodly' prior to the drawing up of Article XXXVI in 1563. Furthermore, no such evidence has been put forward by other scholars.

In the absence of any such evidence we cannot therefore say that the words in question were a response to Puritan objections to the Ordinal. There is simply no evidence that this was the case. The truth is that we simply do not know for certain why these words were included in the Article. It may be that they were a response to a specific objection to the Ordinal that we no longer know about. Alternatively, it may be that they were intended simply to supplement the declaration that the Ordinal contains everything necessary for valid ordinations with a defence in advance against any possible hypothetical objection to the Ordinal as superstitious and ungodly.

However, for the purpose of giving assent to the Article with a good conscience it is not necessary to know why precisely these words were included in the Article. What matters is whether we can agree with their assessment that the Ordinal does not contain anything that is 'superstitious and ungodly.'

It is at this point that the Puritan objection to the Ordinal properly comes into the picture. The Article may not have been a response to the Puritan objection to the Ordinal, but if the Puritan objection to the

---

[781] Jelf, op.cit., p.388. See also, Browne, op.cit, p.783, Gibson, op.cit., p.731, Griffith Thomas, op.cit., p.456 and Tyrell Green, op.cit, p.292,.

Ordinal is correct then we cannot say with the Article that the Ordinal does not contain anything 'superstitious and ungodly.'

As Jelf notes, there are two parts to the Puritan objection. The first is the claim that it is blasphemous to suggest that a bishop can convey the Holy Spirit to people at ordination. In the ordination service for a priest and the consecration service for a bishop the laying on of hands is accompanied by the formula 'receive the Holy Ghost' and this is said to be blasphemous because Christ alone can give the Spirit and not human beings.

As Bishop Burnet notes in his commentary on this article the response that can be made to this criticism of the Ordinal is that according to Scripture the Holy Spirit was not given solely to the Apostles, but is also given to all those who are called by God to the ordained ministry.

> And since the several functions and administrations that are in the Church are by the Apostle said to flow *from one and the same Spirit* [I Corinthians 12:11], all of them from the *Apostles* down to the *Pastors and Teachers* [Ephesians 4:11-12], we may then reckon that the Holy Ghost, though in a much lower degree, is given by those who are inwardly moved by God to undertake that holy office. So that though that extraordinary effusion that was poured out on the Apostles, was in them in a much higher degree, and was accompanied with most amazing characters; yet still such as do sincerely offer themselves up, on a divine motion, to this service receive a lower portion of this Spirit.[782]

Seen in this light, says Burnet:

> ...these words, *Receive the Holy Ghost,* may be understood to be of the manner of a wish and a prayer; as if it were said *May thou receive the Holy Ghost;* and so it will better agree with what follows. *And be thou a faithful dispenser of the word and sacraments.* Or, it may be observed, that in those sacred missions the Church and Churchmen consider themselves as acting in the *name* and *person* of Christ. In baptism it is expressly said, *I baptize in the name of the Father, &c.* In the Eucharist we repeat the

---

[782] Burnet, op.cit. p.515-516.

words of Christ, and apply them to the elements, as said by him. So we consider such as deserve to be admitted to those holy functions, as persons called and sent of God; and therefore the Church, in the name of Christ sends them; and because he gives a portion of his Spirit to those whom he sends, therefore the Church, in his name says *Receive the Holy Ghost*. And in this sense, and with this respect, the use of these words may be well justified.[783]

The second part of the Puritan objection is that it is wrong to suggest that the priest can forgive sins by virtue of his ordination as is suggested by the inclusion of the words 'Whose sins thou dost forgive they are forgiven; and whose sins thou dost retain, they are retained' as part of the rite for the ordination of priests in the 1552 Ordinal.

The point that needs to be made in relation to this argument is that while it is true that is only God who can forgive sins (Mark 2:7-10), because the Church is the body of Christ it is the channel through which God acts to bestow forgiveness and hence we find in the Gospels that the Church is given the authority to forgive and retain sins (Matthew 16:19, 18:18, John 20:23). The priest then fits into the picture as the person who bestows the forgiveness of sins on behalf of Christ acting through the Church in the same way that, as we have already noted, a priest baptizes on behalf of Christ and consecrates the elements at Holy Communion on behalf of Christ. The priest forgives sins, that is to say, not because of any virtue inherent in him or her as a private individual, but as part of his her activity on behalf of Christ acting in and through his Church. As Griffith Thomas puts it, the words in the ordination service 'Whose sins thou dost forgive they are forgiven; and whose sins thou dost retain, they are retained' are 'a definite personal application to the one individual of the general authority given by our Lord to the whole Church.'[784]

The Puritan objection to this aspect of the Ordinal would thus only have force if the Church as a whole were unable to exercise the 'power of the keys' by forgiving or retaining sins and this would be something that would be impossible to square with the witness of the Gospels.

---

[783] Ibid, p.516.
[784] Griffith Thomas, op.cit., p.456.

Because the rites in the1552 Ordinal contain nothing that is superstitious or ungodly, but do contain all that is necessary for the consecrating and ordering of bishops priests and deacons the conclusion set out in the final sentence of Article XXXVI 'therefore' follows:

...whosoever are consecrated or ordered according to the rites of that book, since the second year of King Edward unto this time, or hereafter shall be consecrated or ordered according to the same rites, we decree all such to be rightly, orderly, and lawfully consecrated or ordered.

In the final clause of this sentence 'rightly, orderly and lawfully' like their Latin counterparts 'rite, atque ordine, atque legitime' are synonyms, with three words being used instead of one for rhetorical effect. They all mean that anyone who is consecrated or ordained or according to the Edwardine Ordinal is properly consecrated or ordained.

Note: Article XXXVI and the 1662 and *Common Worship* Ordinals.

As we have seen, Article XXXVI refers to the 1552 Ordinal since this was the Ordinal which was in use when it was drawn up. This Ordinal has since been superseded by the Ordinal attached to the 1662 Prayer Book and, recently, by the contemporary language rites in the *Common Worship Ordination Services*. This fact raises the question of how what is said in Article XXXVI relates to these later Ordinals.

The line that the Church of England has taken on this matter is that these later Ordinals contain the same necessary elements as the 1552 rites. They too involve the ordination or consecration of those who have been 'called, tried and examined' and who posses the requisite qualities needed for ordination. They too involve 'public prayer, with imposition of hands.' They are also like the 1552 rites in that they contain nothing in them that is superstitious or ungodly. It follows that the same judgement made in Article XXXVI about those ordained or consecrated according the 1552 Ordinal has been made by the Church of England about those ordained or consecrated according to the 1662 or *Common Worship* rites. They too are 'rightly, orderly and lawfully consecrated or ordered.'

In the case of the 1662 rites this point is made explicitly in Canon A 8. This states:

> The Form and Manner of Making, Ordaining, and Consecrating of Bishops, Priests, and Deacons, annexed to The Book of Common Prayer and commonly known as the Ordinal, is not repugnant to the Word of God; and those who are so made, ordained, or consecrated bishops, priests, or deacons, according to the said Ordinal, are lawfully made, ordained, or consecrated, and ought to be accounted, both by themselves and others, to be truly bishops, priests, or deacons.

The *Common Worship Ordinal* does not have its own Canonical endorsement, but because it is seen as being in fundamental conformity with the 1662 Ordinal what is said in Canon A8 about those ordained according to the 1662 rites is taken to refer to those ordained according to this Ordinal as well.

Christians and Civil Society:
Articles XXXVII-XXXIX

The *Articles* conclude with three articles that discuss different aspect of the relationship between Christians and the society in which they live.

Article XXXVII re-affirms and explains the role of the monarch as the supreme governor of the Church of England and in that context denies the jurisdiction in England of the Bishop of Rome. It also defends against the objections of some radical Protestants the right of the state to take life and legitimacy of Christians serving in the military.

Article XXXVIII argues against the claims of some radical Protestants that the goods of Christians should not be held in common, but also stresses the importance of alms-giving to the poor and needy.

Article XXXIX rejects 'vain and rash swearing' but against the objections of some radical Protestants argues that it is legitimate for Christians to take oaths when asked to by a magistrate for a legitimate reason.

Article XXXVII

∞

Of the Civil Magistrates

The Queen's Majesty hath the chief power in this realm of England and other her dominions, unto whom the chief government of all estates of this realm, whether they be ecclesiastical or civil, in all causes doth appertain, and is not nor ought to be subject to any foreign jurisdiction.

Where we attribute to the Queen's Majesty the chief government, by which titles we understand the minds of some slanderous folks to be offended, we give not to our princes the ministering either of God's word or of sacraments, the which thing the Injunctions also lately set forth by Elizabeth our Queen doth most plainly testify: but that only prerogative which we see to have been given always to all godly princes in Holy Scriptures by God himself, that is, that they should rule all estates and degrees committed to their charge by God, whether they be ecclesiastical or temporal, and restrain with the civil sword the stubborn and evil-doers.

The Bishop of Rome hath no jurisdiction in this realm of England.

The Laws of the Realm may punish Christian men with death for heinous and grievous offences.

It is lawful for Christian men at the commandment of the Magistrate to wear weapons and serve in the wars.

De Civilibus Magistratibus

Regia Maiestas in hoc Angliae regno ac caeteris eius dominiis summam habet potestatem, ad quam omnium statuum huius regni, sive illi ecclesiastici sive civiles, in omnibus causis suprema gubernatio pertinet, et nulli externae iurisdictioni est subiecta, necesse debet.

Cum Regiae Maiestati summam gubernationem tribuimus, quibus titulis intelligimus animos quorundam calumniatorum offendi, non damus regibus nostris aut verbi Dei aut sacramentorum administrationem, quod etiam Iniunctiones ab Elizabetha Regina nostra nuper editae apertissime testantur: sed eam tantum prerogativam quam in Sacris Scripturis a Deo ipso omnibus piis principibus videmus semper fuisse attributam, hoc est, ut omnes status atque ordines fidei suae a Deo commissos, sive illi ecclesiastici sint sive civiles, in officio contineant, et contumaces ac delinquentes gladio civili coerceant.

Romanus Pontifex nullam habet iurisdictionem in hoc regno Angliae.

Leges regni possunt Christianos propter capitalia et gravia crimina morte punire.

Christianis licet ex mandato Magistratus arma portare et iusta bella administrare.

Article XXXVII is a reworking dating from 1563 of Article XXXVI of the *Forty Two Articles* which ran as follows:

Of Civil Magistrates

The King of England is supreme head in earth, next under Christ, of the Church of England and Ireland.

The Bishop of Rome hath no jurisdiction in this realm of England

The civil Magistrate is ordained, and allowed of God: wherefore we must obey him, not only for fear of punishment, but also for conscience sake.

The civil laws may punish Christian men with death, for heinous, and grievous offences.

It is lawful for Christians, at the commandment of the Magistrate, to wear weapons, and to take part in lawful wars.

De civilibus Magistratibus

Rex Angliae est supremum caput in terries, post Christum, Ecclesiae Anglicanae & Hibernicae.

Romanus Pontifex nullum habet jurisdictionem in hoc Regno Angliae.

Magistratus civilis est a Deo ordinatus atque probatus, quamobrem illi, non solum propter iram, sed etiam, propter conscientam, obedientum est.

Leges civiles possunt Christanos propter capitalia & gravia crimina morte punire.

Christianis licet ex mandato magistratus arma portare & iusta bella administrare.

The changes that took place in 1563 were as follows

• The first and third paragraphs of the original article were dropped and were replaced by two new paragraphs discussing in some detail the royal supremacy over the Church exercised by Elizabeth I.

• The paragraph about the Bishop of Rome was moved down to become the third paragraph of the new article.

• In the penultimate paragraph of the English version of the new article the term 'the civil laws' became the 'the laws of the Realm' although the Latin 'leges civiles' remained the same.

• In the final paragraph of the English version of the new article the adjective 'lawful' qualifying the word 'wars' was omitted even though the phrase 'iusta bella' was retained in the Latin version.

The article in its revised form has three objects. The first is to assert and explain the tenet of royal supremacy. The second is to reject the jurisdiction in England of the Pope. The third is to defend the right of the government to defend the imposition of the death penalty and Christian involvement in war over against the pacifist position taken by some radical Protestant groups.

The Queen's Majesty hath the chief power in this realm of England and other her dominions, unto whom the chief government of all estates of this realm, whether they be ecclesiastical or civil, in all causes doth appertain, and is not nor ought to be subject to any foreign jurisdiction.

Article XXXVII begins with a political claim about the authority belonging to Elizabeth I as the Queen of England. What is said here reflects the declaration made in the preamble to the Act in Restraint of Appeals in 1533 that 'this realm of England is an empire'[785] This declaration meant two things. First, because an empire was a state that was legally wholly independent, it meant that no appeal could be made from a decision by the monarch or the courts administering royal justice to any foreign authority, whether that was to another monarch such as the Holy Roman Emperor, or in ecclesiastical matters to the Pope in Rome. Secondly, following the precedent set by the law code of Justinian in the Christian Empire of the sixth century the claim that England was an empire meant that its monarch, as one who possessed imperial authority, had authority over both the state and the Church.

As Stephen Neill notes, what people saw when they looked at the law code of Justinian was a ruler:

> ...who was *fons utrisque juris*, the source of the law of the Church as well as of the law of the State. It was the business of the patriarchs and bishops to put the law into effect, but the law they administered was the law of the Christian emperor, and it was under his authority that they administered it.[786]

---

[785] Bray, *Documents of the English Reformation*, p. 78.
[786] S C Neill, *Anglicanism*, 4ed, London: Mowbray, 1977, p.38.

It is this imperial authority that was claimed by Henry VIII in the Act of Supremacy of 1534 and by Elizabeth I in the Act of Supremacy of 1559, both of which refer to the 'imperial crown of this realm'[787] and it is this imperial authority that is also asserted in the opening paragraph of Article XXXVII.

Where we attribute to the Queen's Majesty the chief government, by which titles we understand the minds of some slanderous folks to be offended, we give not to our princes the ministering either of God's word or of sacraments, the which thing the Injunctions also lately set forth by Elizabeth our Queen doth most plainly testify: but that only prerogative which we see to have been given always to all godly princes in Holy Scriptures by God himself, that is, that they should rule all estates and degrees committed to their charge by God, whether they be ecclesiastical or temporal, and restrain with the civil sword the stubborn and evil-doers.

The point that is being made in the second paragraph of Article XXXVII is that the government over the Church asserted in the first paragraph has a very specific meaning. It is clear from the Injunctions issued by Elizabeth I in 1559 and from the present paragraph that some disaffected conservative clergy were arguing that people should not take the oath contained in the Act of Supremacy, because this oath gave Queen Elizabeth the right to minister within the Church as if she was ordained.

The Article makes it clear that this is not what the Queen's role as 'supreme governor' of the Church involves. Negatively it states that this role does not involve 'the ministering of either God's word or of sacraments.' Positively, it states that what it does means is the exercise of the prerogative:

> ...which we see to have been given always to all godly princes in Holy Scriptures by God himself, that is, that they should rule all estates and degrees committed to their charge by God, whether they be ecclesiastical or temporal, and restrain with the civil sword the stubborn and evil-doers.

---

[787] For the Acts of Supremacy see Bray, *Documents of the English Reformation*, pp.113-114 and 318-328.

The theology underlying this claim is set out in the homily 'Concerning good order and obedience to rulers and magistrates' in the *First Book of Homilies* which was updated during Queen Elizabeth's reign to make it absolutely clear that it applied to her.

This homily states, first of all, that royal authority comes directly from God. The homily starts by declaring that:

> Almighty God hath created and appointed all things, in heaven, earth, and waters, in a most excellent, and perfect order. In heaven, he hath appointed distinct and several orders and states of archangels and angels. In earth he hath assigned and appointed kings and princes, with other governors under them, in all good and necessary order.[788]

The homily then goes on to argue on the basis of quotations from Proverbs and Wisdom that monarchs, and the royal officers who act on their behalf, have their authority immediately from God. It also notes that this rules out the idea put forward by Papal advocates in the Middle Ages that as Vicar of Christ the Pope had the authority over monarchs and the right to appoint or depose them. Monarchs have their authority from God and the Pope has no standing in the matter.

> For Almighty God is the only author and provider for this forenamed state and order, as it is written of God, in the book of the Proverbs: *Through me kings do reign, through me counsellors make just laws, through me do princes bear rule, and all judges of the earth execute judgement, I am loving to them that love me* (Proverbs 8.15, 17).Here let us mark well, and remember that the high power and authority of kings, with their making of laws, judgements and offices, are the ordinances not of man, but of God: and therefore is this word (through me) so many times repeated. Here is also well to be considered and remembered, that this good order is appointed by God's wisdom, favour, and love, especially for them that love God, and therefore he saith, I love them that love me.

---

[788] *The Homilies.*, p.78.

Also in the Book of Wisdom we may evidently learn, that a king's power, authority, and strength, is a great benefit of God, given of his great mercy, to the comfort of our great misery. For thus we read there spoken to kings, *Hear, O ye kings, and understand: learn, ye that be judges of the ends of the earth; give ear, ye that rule the multitudes: for the power is given you of the Lord, and the strength, from the Highest* (Wisdom 6.1-3). Let us learn also here by the infallible word of God, that kings and other their officers, are ordained of God, who is Most Highest: and therefore they are here diligently taught to apply and give themselves, to knowledge and wisdom, necessary for the ordering of God's people, to their governance committed.. And they be here also taught by Almighty God, that they should acknowledge themselves, to have all their power and strength not from Rome, but immediately of God Most Highest.[789]

This, then, is what Article XXXVII has in mind when it states that monarchs should rule all those 'committed to their charge by God.' The article also specifies that by the authority given to them by God monarchs should rule 'all estates and degrees...whether they be ecclesiastical or temporal.' This part of the article is designed to rule out the idea that the Church might constitute a separate sphere of authority not subject to rule by the monarch.

As the homily on 'Good order and obedience' further explains, the English Reformers held that this idea was ruled out by the teaching of St. Paul in Romans 13 which indicated that everyone without exception was subject to the rulers appointed by God:

Thus Saint Paul writeth to the Romans: *Let every soul submit himself unto the authority of the higher powers, for there is no power but of God. The powers that be, be ordained of God. Whosoever therefore withstandeth the power, withstandeth the ordinance of God: but they that resist, or are against it, shall receive to themselves damnation. For rulers are not fearful to them that do good, but to them that do evil. Wilt thou bee without fear of that power? Do well then, and so shalt thou be praised of the same, for he is the minister of God, for thy wealth. But and if thou do that*

---

[789]Ibid., p.79.

which is evil, then fear, for he beareth not the sword for nought, for he is the minister of God, to take vengeance on him that doeth evil. Wherefore ye must needs obey, not only for fear of vengeance, but also, because of conscience, and even for this cause pay ye tribute, for they are God's ministers serving for the same purpose (Romans 13.1-6).

Here let us learn of Saint Paul the chosen vessel (Acts 9:15) of God, that all persons having souls (he excepteth none, nor exempteth none, neither Priest, Apostle, nor Prophet, saith St. Chrysostom) do owe of bounden duty, and even in conscience, obedience, submission, and subjection to the high powers, which be set in authority by God, for as much as they be God's Lieutenants, God's Presidents, God's Officers, God's Commissioners, God's Judges, ordained of God himself, of whom only they have all their power, and all their authority. And the same Saint Paul threateneth no less pain, then everlasting damnation to all disobedient persons, to all resisters against this general, and common authority, for as much as they resist not man, but God.[790]

The reference in the article to rulers restraining 'with the civil sword the stubborn and evil-doers' makes it clear that it is indeed Romans 13 that the article has in mind and it also forms a link with what is said about the death penalty and Christian participation in war at the end of the article.

The Bishop of Rome hath no jurisdiction in this realm of England.

The term 'jurisdiction' means 'legal authority' and during the Middle Ages there was repeated tension between the English monarchy and the Papacy about the relationship between the authority of the Pope as the head of the Church and that of the king as the ruler of the English state. This tension focussed on issues such as who had the right to make church appointments and the right of appeal to the courts in Rome about legal issues relating to England. Various Acts of Parliament were passed to limit the exercise of Papal power in England, but the fact that the Pope had some proper rights of jurisdiction in England was accepted.

[790] Ibid., p.80.

What happened at the English Reformation can be seen in one sense as being a continuation of previous medieval attempts to determine the right relationship between royal and papal authority. In another sense it was something radically new because at the Reformation the English state and the English church formally rejected any Papal jurisdiction in England. In the 1530s a series of Acts of Parliament abolished all legal appeals from England to Rome, any role for the Papacy in making church appointments in England and any payments to the Papacy relating to such appointments.[791] Then in March and May 1534 the Convocations of Canterbury and York passed resolutions denying that 'the Roman pontiff has any greater jurisdiction bestowed on him by God in the Holy Scriptures than any other foreign bishop.' This meant in effect that the Pope had no jurisdiction in England. This conclusion was accepted by the Universities of Oxford and Cambridge and the abolition of Papal supremacy in England was approved by Parliament and passed into statute in November of that year.[792]

This Henrician legislation was rescinded during the reign of Mary Tudor, but was restored by Elizabeth I's Act of Supremacy of 1559.[793] In the light of this historical background the statement in Article XXXVII 'the Bishop of Rome hath no jurisdiction in this realm of England' is one sense simply a statement of legal reality. Under the 1559 Act of Supremacy Papal jurisdiction in England had been abolished.

However, the statement in Article XXXVII is also a statement of theological conviction. It is intended to mean not only that the Pope has no jurisdiction in England, but that he ought not to have any jurisdiction in England.

The reasons why the English Reformers believed that the Pope ought not to have any jurisdiction in England are explained in the homily on 'Good order and obedience' to which we have already referred.

This homily notes that all that has been said about obedience to God given authority should not be understood 'in any condition, of the pretensed power of the Bishop of Rome'. It then goes on to state that there are two reasons for not accepting 'the usurped power of the Bishop

---

[791] For these Acts of Parliament see Bray, *Documents of the English Reformation,* pp. 72-110.
[792] Ibid, pp.109-110.
[793] Ibid, pp.319-20.

of Rome, which he most wrongfully challengeth, as the successor of Christ and Peter.'[794]

The first reason is that the claim that the Pope has jurisdiction as the successor of St. Peter 'hath no sufficient ground in holy Scripture.'[795] As far as the English Reformers were concerned, Christ's words to St. Peter in Matthew 16:18 'You are Peter and on this rock I will build my Church,' the traditional cornerstone of Papal claims did not constitute a grant of universal jurisdiction to Peter as Bishop of Rome or to subsequent Bishops of Rome as his successors.

The second reason is what the homily calls 'the fruits and doctrine' of the Papal claim. As the homily sees it, the claim to jurisdiction made by the Papacy involves an encroachment on the rightful authority belonging to the rulers appointed by God and thus a repudiation of the teaching about due obedience to rulers given by Christ and by St. Peter;

> For our Saviour Christ, and S. Peter, teacheth most earnestly and agreeably obedience to Kings, as to the chief and supreme rulers in this world, next under God: but the Bishop of Rome teacheth, that they that are under him, are free from all burdens and charges of the common wealth, and obedience toward their Prince, most clearly against Christ's doctrine and S. Peter's.[796]

The homily declares that 'Christ and St. Peter 'not only taught obedience to kings, but also practised obedience in their conversation and living. For we read that they both paid tribute to the King (Matthew 17:24-27).'[797]

The homily also cites 1 Peter 2:13-15:

> Be subject for the Lord's sake to every human institution, whether it be to the emperor as supreme, or to governors as sent by him to punish those who do wrong and to praise those who do right. For it is God's will that by doing right you should put to silence the ignorance of foolish men.

and notes:

---

[794] *The Homilies*, p.85.
[795] Ibid. p.85.
[796] Ibid, p.85.
[797] Ibid. p.85.

St Peter doth not say, Submit yourselves unto me, as supreme head of the Church: neither saith he, Submit your selves from time to time to my successors in Rome: but he saith, *Submit your selves unto your king, your supreme head*, and unto those that he appointeth in authority under him, for that you shall so show your obedience, *it is the will of God,* God's will that you be in subjection to your head and king. This is God's ordinance, God's commandment, and God's holy will, that the whole body of every realm, and all the members and parts of the same, shall be subject to their head, their king, and that, as St. Peter writeth, *for the Lords sake* (1 Peter 2.13), and, as St. Paul writeth, *for conscience sake*, and not for fear only (Romans 13.5).[798]

From these quotations from the homily we can thus see that the repudiation of the authority of the Bishop of Rome in Article XXXVII was based on the belief that (a) this authority had no scriptural basis and (b) the claims made for it undermined the proper obedience that was due to the rulers appointed by God.

The Laws of the Realm may punish Christian men with death for heinous and grievous offences.

It is lawful for Christian men at the commandment of the magistrate to wear weapons and serve in the wars.

As has already been indicated, the purpose of the final two sentences of Article XXXVII is to counter the pacifist teaching of the some radical Protestant groups. Like the Quakers subsequently they held that it was not legitimate for Christians ever to kill other people.

A good example of this position can be found in the Swiss Anabaptist Confession of Faith dating from 1527, the *Schleitheim Confession*. As can be seen below, section VI of this confession argues that the right to use 'the sword', that is the right to put people to death or to engage in warfare, is one that is given to secular magistrates, but cannot be used by Christians, amongst whom excommunication is the supreme penalty, and that for that reason Christians cannot be magistrates.

---

[798] Ibid, p.86.

We are agreed as follows concerning the sword: The sword is ordained of God outside the perfection of Christ. It punishes and puts to death the wicked, and guards and protects the good. In the Law the sword was ordained for the punishment of the wicked and for their death, and the same (sword) is (now) ordained to be used by the worldly magistrates.

In the perfection of Christ, however, only the ban is used for a warning and for the excommunication of the one who has sinned, without putting the flesh to death - simply the warning and the command to sin no more.

Now it will be asked by many who do not recognize (this as) the will of Christ for us, whether a Christian may or should employ the sword against the wicked for the defence and protection of the good, or for the sake of love.

Our reply is unanimously as follows: Christ teaches and commands us to learn of Him, for He is meek and lowly in heart and so shall we find rest to our souls. Also Christ says to the heathenish woman who was taken in adultery, not that one should stone her according to the Law of His Father (and yet He says, As the Father has commanded me, thus I do), but in mercy and forgiveness and warning, to sin no more. Such (an attitude) we also ought to take completely according to the rule of the ban.

Secondly, it will be asked concerning the sword, whether a Christian shall pass sentence in worldly disputes and strife such as unbelievers have with one another. This is our united answer. Christ did not wish to decide or pass judgement between brother and brother in the case of the inheritance, but refused to do so. Therefore we should do likewise.

Thirdly, it will be asked concerning the sword, Shall one be a magistrate if one should be chosen as such? The answer is as follows: They wished to make Christ king, but He fled and did not view it as the arrangement of His Father. Thus shall we do as He did, and follow Him, and so shall we not walk in darkness. For He Himself says, He who wishes to come after Me, let him deny himself and take up his cross and follow Me. Also, He Himself forbids the (employment of) the force of the sword saying, The worldly princes lord it over them, etc., but not so shall it be with you. Further, Paul says, Whom God did foreknow He also did predestinate to be conformed to the image of His Son, etc. Also

Peter says, Christ has suffered (not ruled) and left us an example, that ye should follow His steps.

Finally it will be observed that it is not appropriate for a Christian to serve as a magistrate because of these points: The government magistracy is according to the flesh, but the Christian's is according to the Spirit; their houses and dwelling remain in this world, but the Christian's are in heaven; their citizenship is in this world, but the Christian's citizenship is in heaven; the weapons of their conflict and war are carnal and against the flesh only, but the Christian's weapons are spiritual, against the fortification of the devil. The worldlings are armed with steel and iron, but the Christians are armed with the armour of God, with truth, righteousness, peace, faith, salvation and the Word of God. In brief, as in the mind of God toward us, so shall the mind of the members of the body of Christ be through Him in all things, that there may be no schism in the body through which it would be destroyed. For every kingdom divided against itself will be destroyed. Now since Christ is as it is written of Him, His members must also be the same, that His body may remain complete and united to its own advancement and upbuilding.[799]

Article XXXVII takes a different view of the matter, arguing that even in a Christian society the laws of the land may rightly punish people with death for 'heinous and grievous offences' and that at the command of the magistrates (that is to say, the ruling authorities of the state) Christians may bear arms and take part in war.

The theological thinking behind the position taken in the article is, once again, set out in the homily on 'Good order and obedience.' This declares:

We read in the Book of Deuteronomy, that all punishment pertaineth to God, by this sentence, *Vengeance is mine, and I will reward* (Deuteronomy 32.35). But this sentence we must understand to pertain also unto the magistrates which do exercise God's room, in judgement and punishing, by good and godly laws, here in earth. And the places of Scripture, which seem to remove from among all Christian men, judgement, punishment,

---

[799] J H Leith, *Creeds of the Churches*, pp.287-289.

or killing ought to be understood, that no man of his own private authority may be judge over other, may punish, or may kill, but we must refer all judgement to God, to kings, and rulers, and judges under them, which be God's officers to execute justice, and by plain words of Scripture, have their authority and use of the sword granted from God (Romans 13:4), as we are taught by St. Paul, the dear and chosen Apostle, of our Saviour Christ, whom we ought diligently to obey, even as we would obey our Saviour Christ, if he were present.[800]

Unlike the *Schleitheim Confession,* which draws a distinction between the behaviour permitted to non- Christians and how Christians are called to behave, this statement in the homily draws a distinction between the private activity of individuals and the public acts performed by those exercising governing authority on behalf of God. Following the approach taken by St. Paul in Romans 12:9-13:6 the homily holds that in relation to the private activity of individuals the teaching of Deuteronomy that vengeance belongs only to God means that they are not allowed to judge, punish, or kill, but instead must practice an ethic of love and non-retaliation towards those who do them harm (Romans 12:9-25). Those who exercise public authority on behalf of God, however, are allowed to judge and punish, and even inflict the punishment of death, precisely because they are acting not on their own behalf, but are acting as agents of the judgement of God (Romans 13:1-6).

Seen in this context it is legitimate for a Christian state to inflict the death penalty and for Christians to take part in war under the authority of their rulers because in both cases the power of the sword given to rulers by God is being duly exercised. It should be noted here that in this view of the matter war is regarded as being, in the words of Oliver O'Donovan, 'an extraordinary extension of ordinary acts of judgement.' That is to say, just as governing authorities normally take action by means of the policing and judicial systems of their countries to enact the justice of God in response to various forms of injustice, so also, on occasion, they have to resort to war for the same reason.[801] In this view war is permissible as a means of seeking to achieve justice in response to some form of injustice that would otherwise continue.

---

[800] *The Homilies*, p.80.
[801] O O'Donovan, *The Just War Revisited*, Cambridge: CUP, 2003 Ch 1.

When the Latin version of the article talks about Christians taking part in a just war, a 'iusta bella,' it is this sort of permissible warfare that is meant. This means, of course, that not all war is legitimate. If Christians may take up arms in a just war, equally they should not take up arms in a war that is unjust, a war that has as its object for example, not the pursuit of justice, but the pursuit of military glory or territorial aggrandisement for their own sake.

Note 1: Canon A7

The view of royal authority set out in Article XXXVII continues to be upheld by the Church of England. It is specifically affirmed in Canon A7, 'Of the Royal Supremacy' which states:

> We acknowledge that the Queen's excellent Majesty, according to the laws of the realm, is the highest power under God in this kingdom, and has supreme authority over all persons, in all causes, as well ecclesiastical as civil.

Note 2: Ecumenical discussion of Papal authority

The issue of Papal primacy and the jurisdiction relating to it is a topic that has been addressed in the context of the work of ARCIC.[802] The current state of ecumenical discussion between Anglicans and Roman Catholics on this matter is well summarised in paragraph 75 of the 2007 IARCCUM report *Growing Together in Mission and Unity*. This states that:

> While some Anglicans are coming to value the ministry of the Bishop of Rome as a sign and focus of unity, there continue to be questions about whether the Petrine ministry as exercised by the Bishop of Rome exists within the Church by divine right; about the nature of papal infallibility; and about the jurisdiction ascribed to the Bishop of Rome as universal primate.[803]

Note 3: Anglican attitudes to capital punishment

---

[802] See 'Authority in the Church II' in C Hill and E Yarnold (eds), *Anglicans and Roman Catholics: The Search for Unity*, London: SPCK/CTS, 1994, pp. 62-75,
[803] *Growing Together in Mission and Unity*, p.38.

From the sixteenth to the mid twentieth century Anglicans continued to maintain the position about the legitimacy of the death penalty taken by Article XXXVII, although there was continuing discussion about what constituted the 'heinous and grievous offences' for which the death penalty might rightly be applied.

In the second half of the twentieth century, however, Anglican opinion moved against the imposition of capital punishment.

Thus in England the Upper and Lower Houses of the Convocations of Canterbury and York agreed in 1961 and 1962 passed motions supporting the abolition of capital punishment:

> ...this House would welcome the introduction, and adoption by Parliament, of a Bill providing for:

> (1) The abolition of capital punishment, or at least its complete suspension for a period of five years;

> (2) Such punishment and treatment for the convicted person as (*Canterbury Lower House*, 2, Treatment for the convicted person which) would assist in his own reclamation and ensure the safety of society;

> (3) Suitable compensation for the relatives or dependents of the victims of homicide.[804]

In 1983 a debate on capital punishment in the General Synod opposed the re-introduction of the death penalty by a large majority.

Internationally, Resolution 33; 3 b of the Lambeth Conference of 1988 urged the Church to speak out against:

> ...all governments who practice capital punishment, and encourages them to find alternative ways of sentencing offenders so that the divine dignity of every human being is respected and yet justice is pursued.[805]

---

[804] *Acts of the Convocations of Canterbury and York 1921-1970*, London: SPCK 1971 p.153

[805] R Coleman (ed) , *Resolutions of the Lambeth Conferences 1867-1988*, Toronto: Anglican Book Centre, 1992 p.214.

These statements make clear the current Anglican opposition to imposition of capital punishment as part of the normal system of punishment. It is important to distinguish, however, between the judgement that capital punishment should not normally be imposed by a state as part of its penal code and a belief that it would never be right under any circumstances for the ruling authorities to exercise 'the power of the sword' by taking someone's life.

It is only the latter position that is in conflict with what is said in Article XXXVII and this position is impossible to maintain without abandoning the idea that the state has any right to impose punishment at all (a position that Anglicans have never taken). This is because the possibility of death forms the horizon for all lesser penalties that the state may impose.

As Oliver O'Donovan explains:

There are basic conditions for any penal system, and they can be derived from the words of Genesis 9:6 promulgating the Noachic covenant: 'Whoever sheds the blood of man, by man shall his blood be shed.' This is not the formulation of the *lex talionis* as a determination of penalty; it is, rather, an expression of the basis of retributive practice itself. We are all mortal, and our life has a limited expectancy. That fact gives all crime and all punishment its meaning. Two years in prison are 'two good years of my life'; if we were immortal, they would count for nothing. A heavy fine is a drain on resources needed for food, clothing, and shelter. Corporal punishment weakens the bodily constitution. Every serious injury is an assault, directly or indirectly, on the victim's life; so every punishment, too, is an assault on the victim's life.

What we are looking for in a system of punishment is a flexible range of intermediate punishments that hedge that infringement of life around with alternatives, so that we are not driven too quickly back upon the ultimate resort of taking life directly. The art of penal development is the multiplication of a carefully differentiated range of intermediate assaults. Yet its horizon is the ultimate penalty of death itself. Even if a society formally abolishes the death penalty from its criminal sanctions, it does not abolish death as its ultimate recourse, for when crime become uncontrollable by normal means, resorts to making war upon it. The armed patrol takes the place of the hangman.[806]

O'Donovan's argument is illustrated in the British context by the fact that although Britain has formally abolished the death penalty, British law nevertheless makes provision for members of the armed forces or the police to take life on behalf of the state in situations where this is judged to be necessary. When this happens the state is exercising the 'power of the sword' and this is something to which the Church of England has not objected, thus indicating that it still holds that in extreme circumstances the ruling authorities 'may punish Christian men with death'

Note 4: Anglican attitudes to war

Resolution 25 of the Lambeth Conference of 1930 declared that: 'The Conference affirms that war as a method of settling international disputes is incompatible with the teaching and example of our Lord Jesus Christ.'[807] This resolution was re-affirmed by subsequent Lambeth Conferences and it has sometimes been appealed to by bodies such as the Anglican Pacifist Fellowship as endorsing a pacifist position that warfare as such is incompatible with obedience to Christ.

This pacifist position would be incompatible with the teaching of Article XXXVII, but it is not what was intended by the 1930 resolution. This is clear from the report of the committee on 'The life and witness of the Christian community' that lay behind the resolution. The report of this committee states:

> War, as a method of settling international disputes, is incompatible with the teaching and example of Our Lord Jesus Christ. We believe that as the Christian conscience has condemned infanticide and slavery and torture, it is now called to condemn war as an outrage on the Fatherhood of God and the brotherhood of all mankind. We do not deny the right of a nation to defend itself if attacked, or to resort to force in fulfilment of international obligations, but it is the duty of the Christian Church

---

[806] O O'Donovan, *The Ways of Judgement*, Grand Rapids: Eerdmans, 2005 pp.122-123.
[807] Coleman, op.cit, p.75.

to create a world-wide public opinion which will condemn a nation that resorts to war from a motive of self-interest or a mistaken conception of honour as guilty of a crime against humanity.[808]

Seen in the light of this quotation it is clear that the words that became Resolution 25 were not meant to rule out any resort to war by a nation and thus any Christian participation in war. What they were meant to rule out was a nation resorting to war to settle an international dispute out of self-interest or a mistaken conception of honour.

The fact that Resolution 25 was not understood as completely ruling out Christian participation in war is shown by the fact that there was no opposition from the churches of the Anglican Communion to Anglicans participating in the conflict against the Axis powers during World War II. This is because this conflict was seen as an example of self-defence and the fulfilment of international obligations.

---

[808] *The Report of the Lambeth Conference 1930*: London: SPCK, 1930 p.98.

Article XXXVIII

∞

Of Christian men's goods which are not common

The riches and goods of Christians are not common, as touching the right, title, and possession of the same, as certain Anabaptists do falsely boast. Notwithstanding every man ought of such things as he possesseth liberally to give alms to the poor, according to his ability.

De illicita bonorum communicatione

Facultates et bona Christianorum non sunt communia quoad ius et possessionem, ut quidam Anabaptistae falso iactant; debet tamen quisque de his quae possidet, pro facultatum ratione, pauperibus eleemosynas benigne distribuere.

This article was originally Article XXXVII of the *Forty Two Articles*. The substance of the article has remained unchanged since 1553, but the original English and Latin titles ('Christian men's goods are not common' and 'Christianorum bona non sunt communia') were changed to the present titles in 1571.

Griffith Thomas notes that the current Latin title of the article is rather difficult to interpret, but that it has been suggested that it should be rendered 'Of the unlawfulness of Acting as if all Goods were common.'[809]

The purpose of the article is to respond to the teaching of a number of radical Protestant groups which held that Christians ought to practice a pattern of life in which all possessions were held in common. The *Reformatio Legum Ecclesiasticarum* notes in its list of heresies that:

---

[809] Griffith Thomas, op.cit.p 480.

It is also proclaimed by the same Anabaptists that there shall be a forced sharing of goods and possessions, which they insist on even physically so strongly, that they leave nobody with anything of his own.[810]

The riches and goods of Christians are not common, as touching the right, title, and possession of the same, as certain Anabaptists do falsely boast.

The evidence that we have indicates that the 'Anabaptist' insistence on possessions being held in common was based on the example of the earliest church in Jerusalem as recorded in Acts 2:44-45 and 4:32. We read in these texts that: 'all who believed were together and had all things in common; and they sold their possessions and goods and distributed them to all, as any had need' and that 'the company of those who believed were of one heart and soul, and no one said that any of the things which he possessed was his own, but they had everything in common.' Those Protestant groups who advocated community of possessions held that these examples provided a pattern that should be followed by the Christians of the sixteenth century.

We can see this, for example, in Article 5 of the *Congregational Order* produced by Swiss Anabaptists in 1527:

> Of all the brothers and sisters of this congregation none shall have anything of his own, but rather, as the Christians in the time of the apostles held all in common, and especially stored up a common fund, from which aid can be given to the poor, according as each will have need, and as in the apostles' time permit no brother to be in need.[811]

Article XXXVIII rejects the idea that 'none shall have anything of his own,' declaring that it is wrong to suggest that 'right, title and possession' of 'riches and goods' should be held by Christians in common. What the article does not do is give any explanation of why this idea is wrong. However, we can infer why those who drew up the article thought this idea was wrong from what is said in the *Reformatio Legum*

---

[810] Bray, *Tudor Church Reform*, p.199.
[811] http://dir.groups.yahoo.com/group/AnabaptistPioneers/message/684

Ecclesiasticarum. This text follows its description of Anabaptist teaching about the forced sharing of goods and possessions with the statement:

> In this they speak strangely, since they can discover that theft is prohibited by the law of God by divine scripture, and they can see that almsgiving, which we offer out of our own resources, is praised in both Testaments, neither of which would be possible unless the ownership of their goods and possessions were left to Christians.[812]

What the *Reformatio Legum* is doing here is drawing on the principle laid down in Article XX that it is not legitimate to 'so expound one place of Scripture, that it be repugnant to another.' As it sees the matter, an interpretation of Acts 2 and 4 that sees these passages as teaching that people should not hold private possessions has to be wrong because this would then make these texts repugnant to other parts of Scripture which assume that people will have private possessions that are capable of being stolen and that can be given away as alms to assist the poor and needy.

This approach of appealing to the wider teaching of Scripture is the one followed by Thomas Rogers in the earliest commentary on Article XXXVIII. He declares:

> Against community of goods and riches be all those places (which are infinite) of holy scripture, that either condemn the unlawful getting, keeping, or desiring of riches, which, by covetousness [1 Corinthians 5:11, Ephesians 5:3], thievery [1 Peter 4:15], extortion [1 Corinthians 5:11, 6:10], and the like wicked means, many do attain; or do commend liberality [Acts 20:35, 1 Thessalonians 4:10, James 2:15-16], frugality [1 Timothy 5:8], free and friendly lending [Matthew 5:42, Luke 6:35], honest labour [Ephesians 4:28, 2 Thessalonians 3:8], and lawful vocations to live and thrive by [Acts 20:34, 1 Thessalonians 2:9, 2 Thessalonians 3:8]. All of which do show that Christians are to have goods of their own, and that riches ought not to be common.[813]

---

[812] Bray, *Tudor Church Reform*, p.199.
[813] Rogers, op.cit., pp.352-353.

Later commentators have taken a similar approach. Beveridge, for example, declares that 'community of goods' is an idea that subverts 'the whole scope of the holy scriptures' since:

> ...what signify the commands of God, *Thou shalt not steal,* Exod XX.15, and *Thou shalt not covet thy neighbour's house,* ver.17? If I have as much right to my neighbour's goods as himself, how can I be said to steal anything from him, when it is no more but to receive what is my own of him? Or why should I be forbidden to covet his house, when it is my own as well as his? And what means that place of scripture also, *It is a more blessed thing to give than to receive?* Acts XX.35. For if one man hath no more right to what he enjoys than another, how can one man be said to give to another, or the other to receive anything as a gift from him? Certainly by this rule I cannot steal anything from another, though I take all that he hath from him; neither can he be said to give any thing to me, though he bestoweth all he hath upon me. For if I take anything from him, I take no more than what is my own as well as his; and if he bestows any thing upon me, he gives me that which is no more than mine own, and so according to this fancy (for an opinion I cannot call it) there could not be any stealing, neither need there be any giving. I could not steal though I would, and I need not give though I could. And further, admit this dream to be a truth, why should we be commanded to provide for our families, 1 Tim.v.8? to give to him that asketh of us, and to lend to him that would borrow lf us, Matt.v.42? Why should St. Paul's hands minister to his necessities, Acts xx.34, and labour night and day that he might not be chargeable to any, 1 Thess. ii.9? And many like places we find in scripture, which would signify nothing, if one man had no more title to or propriety in what he enjoys than another.[814]

This appeal to the teaching of Scripture as a whole still leaves unresolved, however, the question of how to interpret Acts 2:44-45 and 4:32. How should we understand these verses?

---

[814] Beveridge, op.cit. pp.606-607.

The approach taken by commentators on Article XXXVIII has been to argue that a careful reading of Acts shows that while the first Christians generously shared what they had with each other out of gratitude to God and love for their neighbour their possessions nevertheless remained their own.

Browne, for instance, comments:

> The self–devotion of the primitive Christians affords a most instructive example for all succeeding generations. It sprang from and intense feeling of love and gratitude to the Saviour; and while it was fervent and enthusiastic, it was reasonable and necessary. Had there not been self-sacrifice among the rich; what would become of the poor of the flock, whose name was, for Christ's sake cast out as evil?[815]

However, he says:

> ...even at this very time we find the right of the owners to their property fully recognised in the Scriptures and by the Apostles, so as abundantly to show, that no absolute community of goods had been exacted. The very fact that it written, 'No man said that ought of the things that he possessed was his own,' shews that the possessions were acknowledged to be theirs by others, though voluntarily renounced by themselves; and that therefore it was a voluntary renunciation, and not made according to an obligation imposed on them by the Church. Also, St. Peter said to Ananias: 'Whilst it remained, was it not thine own? and after it was sold, was it not in thine power?' (Acts v.4). So that, before the property was sold, there was no necessity upon him to give it up to the Apostles. His sin was not in the retaining of his goods, but in pretending to give all, and yet keeping back a part.[816]

In similar fashion, Gibson writes:

---

[815] Browne, op.it., pp.831-832.
[816] Ibid, p.832.

...a careful consideration of the whole account given by S. Luke of the early Church in Jerusalem, shows conclusively that what he is here describing is not so much an institution as a temper and spirit. Most certainly the rights of private property were not superseded. Mary the mother of John Mark still retained her own home (Acts xii.12); while the words of s. peter to Ananias prove that no necessity was laid upon him to sell his property 'Whilst it remained, did it not remain thine own? and after it was sold was it not in thy power?'[817]

Notwithstanding every man ought of such things as he possesseth liberally to give alms to the poor, according to his ability.

If the first part of the article defends the existence of private possessions, the second part of the article declares that those who have possessions should be willing to share them generously with the poor and needy. The article does not explain why they should be willing to share their possessions in this way, but it seems probable that just like the first part of the article is offering an interpretation of Acts 2:44-45 and Acts 4:32. The first part of the article tells us what we should not deduce from these verses, namely that we should not deduce from them that private property should be abolished. The second part of the article tells us what we should deduce from them, namely that we should be generous in our giving to the poor and needy in the same way that the first Christians were.

The English Reformers did not base their belief in the importance of charity to the poor and needy solely on the early chapter of Acts. This is made clear in the homily 'Of Almsdeeds and Mercifulness' in the *Second Book of Homilies* which reinforces what is said in Article XXXVIII about the importance of almsgiving and which draws on the teaching of Scripture as a whole and on the teaching of the Fathers.

This homily declares that:

Amongst the manifold duties that Almighty God requireth of his faithful servants, the true Christians, by the which he would that both his Name should be glorified, and the certainty of their vocation declared, there is none that is more acceptable unto him,

---

[817] Gibson, op.cit., p.785.

or more profitable for them, than are works of mercy and pity, showed unto the poor which be afflicted with any kind of misery.[818]

In support of this contention the homily then refers to Deuteronomy 15:11, Proverbs 19:17, Isaiah 58:7, Matthew 10:42, 25:35-40, Mark 9:41, 1 Thessalonians 5:14, Hebrews 13:16, James 2:5 as well as Tobit 4:7 and 16 and Ecclesiasticus 35:2 and 6-7 from the Apocrypha[819] and to the biblical and apocryphal examples of Abraham, Lot, Job and Tobit. It also refers to the teaching of St. John Chrysostom and St. Augustine and it summarises this material by stating:

> Ye have heard before, dearly beloved, that to give alms unto the poor, and to help them in time of necessity, is so acceptable unto our Saviour Christ, that he counteth that to be done to himself, that we do for his sake unto them. Ye have heard also how earnestly both the Apostles, Prophets, holy Fathers, and Doctors, do exhort us unto the same. And ye see how well beloved and dear unto God they were, whom the Scriptures report unto us to have been good alms men. Wherefore if either their good examples, or the wholesome counsel of godly Fathers, or the love of Christ, whose especial favour we may be assured by this means to obtain may move us, or do any thing at all with us: let us provide us that from henceforth we shew unto Godward this thankful service, to be mindful and ready to help them that be poor and in misery.[820]

The homily also goes on to argue that almsgiving is not only acceptable to God, but also beneficial to the giver because it 'is profitable, to purge the soul from the infection and filthy spots of sin'[821] Aware that this idea might seem to be a variance with a belief in justification by faith, the homily explains that this is not case because:

---

[818] *The Homilies* p.275.
[819] For the purposes of the homily these texts from the Apocrypha are described as Scripture.
[820] Ibid p.279.
[821] Ibid p. 280.

The meaning...of these sayings in the Scriptures and other holy writings: *Almsdeeds do wash away our sins*, and, *mercy to the poor doth blot out our offences* (Tobit 12:9, Proverbs 16:6, Daniel 4:27) , is, that we doing these things according to God's will and our duty, have our sins indeed washed away, and our offences blotted out: not for the worthiness of them, but by the grace of God *which worketh all in all* (1 Corinthians 12:6), and that for the promise that God hath made to them that are obedient unto his commandment, that he which is the truth, might be justified in performing the truth, due to his true promise. Alms deeds do wash away our sins, because God doth vouchsafe then to repute us as clean and pure, when we do them for his sake, and not because they deserve or merit our purging, or for that they have any such strength and virtue in themselves.[822]

The final section of the homily addresses the fear that giving to poor will simply end up impoverishing the giver. It contends that the teaching of Scripture makes it clear that this fear is unjustified:

Hearken then, whosoever thou art, that fearest lest by giving to the poor, thou shouldest bring thyself to beggary. That which thou takest from thyself, to bestow upon Christ, can never be consumed and wasted away. Wherein thou shalt not believe me; but if thou have faith, and be a true Christian, believe the Holy Ghost, give credit to the authority of God's word, that thus teacheth. For thus saith the Holy Ghost by Salomon: *He that giveth unto the poor, shall never want* (Proverbs 28:27). Men suppose that by hoarding and laying up still, they shall at length be rich, and that by distributing and laying out, although it be for most necessary and godly uses, they shall be brought to poverty. But the Holy Ghost, which knoweth all truth, teacheth us another lesson, contrary to this. He teacheth us that there is a kind of dispending,[823] that shall never diminish the stock, and a kind of saving that shall bring a man to extreme poverty. For where he saith, that the good almsman shall never have scarcity, he addeth: *But he that turneth away his eyes from such as be in necessity, shall*

---

[822] Ibid p.282.
[823] Giving away

suffer great poverty himself (Proverbs 28:27). How far different then is the judgement of man, from the judgement of the Holy Ghost?

The holy Apostle Paul, a man full of the Holy Ghost, and made privy even of the secret will of God teacheth: that the liberal almsgiver shall not thereby be impoverished. *He that ministreth (saith he) seed unto the sower, will minister also bread unto you for food, yea, he will multiply your seed, and increase the fruits of your righteousness* (2 Corinthians 9.10). He is not content here to advertise them that they shall not lack, but he showeth them also, after what sort God will provide for them. Even as he provided seed for the sower, in multiplying it and giving great increase, so he will multiply their goods, and increase them, that there shall be great abundance.[824]

It may be assumed that the teaching contained in the homily is the kind of theology that lies behind the exhortation to give generously towards the poor and needy contained in the second part of Article XXXVIII. The homily acts as a kind of extended commentary on the teaching of the article.

Note: Subsequent Church of England teaching about wealth and poverty.

Until the nineteenth century Church of England writers tended to argue that the fact that society contained both those who were rich and those who were poor was a result of the providence of God and that therefore both the rich and the poor ought to accept the station in life in which God had placed them and strive to live virtuously within them.

In his commentary on Article XXXVIII Burnet declares, for instance:

Both the rich and the poor have rules given them, and there are virtues suitable to each state of life. The rich ought to be sober and thankful, modest and humble, bountiful and charitable, out of the abundance that God has given them, and not to set their hearts upon uncertain riches, but to trust in the living God, and to

---

[824] Ibid, p.284.

make the best use of them that they can. The poor ought to be patient and industrious, to submit to the providence of God, and to study to make sure of a better portion in another state, than God has thought fit to give them in this world. [825]

In the nineteenth century, however, this view of the matter was challenged by Church of England writers such as F D Maurice, Charles Kingsley and J M Ludlow who argued that the social inequality of Victorian Britain ought to be ascribed not to the providence of God, but rather to the exploitation of the poor by the rich in a way that was contrary to God's will. They advocated the development of a 'Christian socialism' that would result in a society in which wealth was more equitably distributed and in which everyone would have the opportunity to flourish in the way that God intended. The Christian Socialist tradition stemming from such writers has been an important of the subsequent history of the Church of England and can be seen to be the tradition underlying significant Church of England statements about the state of society such as Archbishop William Temple's 1942 manifesto *Christianity and Social Order*[826] and the 1985 report on Urban Priority Areas, *Faith in the City.*[827]

The Church of England as a whole, however, whilst accepting that the existence of disparities of wealth in society cannot simply be ascribed to the providence of God and that the exploitation of the poor by the rich is contrary to God's will, has not accepted that Christian socialism is the only legitimate Christian response to issues of wealth and poverty. It has instead refused to commit itself to any one economic theory and has insisted that economic and social changes by themselves cannot bring about the changes that are needed in society because the problems of society are ultimately rooted in human sinfulness and cannot be resolved without the change of heart leading to love for God and neighbour brought about by acceptance of the Gospel.

We can see this kind of approach in the commentary on Article XXXVIII by Bicknell. He writes:

---

[825] Burnet, op.cit, p.586.
[826] W Temple, *Christianity and Social Order*, Harmondsworth: Penguin Books, 1942.
[827] The Archbishop of Canterbury's Commission on Urban Priority Areas, *Faith in the City*, London: CHP, 1985.

The Church is not tied down to any one economic theory, but it is bound to assert Christian principles. That is where the church has failed. It has made little or no protest against the exploitation of the poor and weak. Men have been allowed to suppose that Christian morality applies only to private life and not to business relationships. Prominent members of the church have been known to be getting money by means that involved the suffering and loss of their fellow men and women and the Church has not rebuked them. Men have salved their consciences by gifts to the Church taken from money gained at the cost of the lives of their employees. The Christian conscience has acquiesced in the existence of slums and the employment of sweated labour. In all attempts at reform the Church has too often taken the side of wealth rather than righteousness. These ugly facts underlie the demand that the Church should adopt socialism. The Church is bound to face the evils for which socialism attempts to supply a remedy, in the light of the Gospel. But she is not bound to accept the remedy offered by socialism without investigation. She must always insist that external conditions by themselves cannot secure righteousness, though they may do much to hinder it. The real root of all social problems lies in the perverted will and heart of man, in other words, in human sin. No economic reconstruction apart from love can bring true and lasting satisfaction. [828]

---

[828] Bicknell, op.cit.pp.557-558.

Article XXXIX

∞

Of a Christian man's Oath

As we confess that vain and rash swearing is forbidden Christian men by our Lord Jesus Christ, and James his Apostle, so we judge that Christian religion doth not prohibit but that a man may swear when the magistrate requireth in a cause of faith and charity, so it be done according to the Prophet's teaching in justice, judgement, and truth.

De Iureiurando

Quemadmodum iuramentum vanum et temerarium a Domino nostro Iesu Christo et Apostolo eius Iacobo Christianis hominibus interdictum esse fatemur, ita Christianorum religionem minime prohibere censemus quin, iubente magistratu in causa fidei et caritatis iurare liceat, modo id fiat iuxta Prophetae doctrinam in iustitia, in iudicio, et veritate.

Article XXXIX was originally Article XXXVIII of the *Forty Two Articles*. As in the case of Article XXXVIII the substance of this article was retained unchanged when it became part of the *Thirty Nine Articles*, but the original English and Latin titles, 'Christian men may take an oath' and 'Licet Christianis jurare,' were changed to their present form.

Article XXXIX is also like Article XXXVIII in that its purpose is to counter what the English Reformers saw as a misinterpretation of Scripture by some radical Protestant groups. In the case of Article XXXIX what is being countered is the argument that Scripture prohibits Christians from making oaths of any kinds, even when asked to do so in a court of law.

We can find this teaching, for example, in the Swiss Anabaptist Confession of faith, the *Schleitheim Confession* of 1527 which declares:

We are agreed as follows concerning the oath: The oath is a confirmation among those who are quarrelling or making promises. In the Law it is commanded to be performed in God's Name, but only in truth, not falsely. Christ, who teaches the perfection of the Law, prohibits all swearing to His [followers], whether true or false - neither by heaven, nor by the earth, nor by Jerusalem, nor by our head - and that for the reason He shortly thereafter gives, For you are not able to make one hair white or black. So you see it is for this reason that all swearing is forbidden: we cannot fulfil that which we promise when we swear, for we cannot change [even] the very least thing on us.[829]

The *Reformatio Legum Ecclesiasticarum* lists as a heresy the fact that 'the Anabaptists even give up the lawful use of oaths,'[830] and it is this heresy which Article XXXIX is designed to counteract.

As we confess that vain and rash swearing is forbidden Christian men by our Lord Jesus Christ, and James his Apostle

The article begins by accepting that certain forms of swearing are forbidden to Christians. It describes these as 'vain and rash swearing' and it states that such swearing is prohibited both by Christ himself and by St. James.

The biblical passages which the article is referring to here are Matthew 5:33-37 and James 5:12.

In the former passage, which is the passage referred to in the *Schleitheim Confession*, Christ declares:

Again you have heard that it was said to the men of old, 'You shall not swear falsely, but shall perform to the Lord what you have sworn.' But I say to you, Do not swear at all, either by heaven, for it is the throne of God, or by the earth, for it is his footstool, or by Jerusalem, for it is the city of the great King. And do not swear by your head, for you cannot make one hair white or black. Let what you say be simply 'Yes' or 'No'; anything more than this comes from the evil one.

---

[829] J Leith, *Creeds of the Churches*, p.289.
[830] Bray, *Tudor Church Reform*, p. 201.

In the second passage, which seems to be an echo of the first, St. James writes:

> But above all, my brethren, do not swear, either by heaven or by earth or with any other oath, but let your yes be yes and your no be no, that you may not fall under condemnation.

so we judge that Christian religion doth not prohibit but that a man may swear when the magistrate requireth in a cause of faith and charity, so it be done according to the Prophet's teaching in justice, judgement, and truth.

At first sight these two passages do appear to give biblical backing to the argument that all oaths of whatever kind are forbidden to Christians. However, the English Reformers held that Scripture as a whole does not support this idea. We can see this in the same section of the *Reformatio Legum Ecclesiasticarum* which rejects this idea as heretical. This section goes on to states that in this matter the Anabaptists go against:

> ...the teaching of the Scriptures and the examples of the Fathers of the Old Testament, as well as the Apostle Paul, and even of Christ, even of God the Father whose oaths are often recorded in Holy Writ.[831]

This appeal to the wider teaching of Scripture is not developed in the *Reformatio Legum,* but it is developed in the homily 'Against Swearing and Perjury' in the *First Book of Homilies.* This homily gives a series of biblical examples to demonstrate that 'lawful swearing is not forbidden, but commanded by Almighty God.' It declares:

> ...we have examples of Christ, and godly men, in Holy Scripture, that did swear themselves, and required oaths of others likewise. And God's Commandment is, *Thou shalt dread thy Lord GOD, and shalt swear by his Name* (Deuteronomy 6.13). And Almighty God by his Prophet David saith, *All men shall be praised that swear by him* (Psalms 63.11).

---

[831] Ibid p.201.

Thus did our Saviour Christ swear divers times, saying, *Verily, verily* (John 3.3,5,11). And S. Paul sweareth thus, *I call God to witness* (2 Corinthians 1.23). And Abraham (waxing old) required an oath of his servant, that he should procure a wife for his son Isaac, which should come of his own kindred (Genesis 24.3): and the servant did swear that he would perform his masters will. Abraham also being required, did swear unto Abimelech the king of Geraris, that he should not hurt him, nor his posterity (Genesis 21.23), and likewise did Abimelech swear unto Abraham. And David did swear to be and continue a faithful friend to Jonathan, and Jonathan did swear to become a faithful friend unto David (1 Samuel 18:3, 20:12-17, 42).

Also God once commanded, that if a thing were laid to pledge to any man, or left with him to keep, if the same thing were stolen, or lost, that the keeper thereof should be sworn before judges, that he did not convey it away, nor used any deceit in causing the same to be conveyed away, by his consent or knowledge (Exodus 22:10-11). And Saint Paul saith, that in all matters of controversy between two persons, whereas one saith, Yea, and the other, Nay, so as no due proof can be had of the truth, the end of every such controversy must be an oath ministered by a judge (Hebrews 6.16).[832]

In view of this wider teaching of Scripture and their conviction that Scripture is consistent in its teaching, the English Reformers held that the words of Christ and St. James appealed to by the Protestant radicals could not be seen as an absolute ban on all oaths. As the homily goes on to say, with reference to the teaching of Christ in Matthew:

...when Christ so earnestly forbad swearing, it may not be understood, as though he did forbid all manner of oaths: but he forbiddeth all vain swearing and forswearing both by God, and by his creatures, as the common use of swearing in buying, selling, and in our daily communication, to the intent every Christian mans word should be as well regarded in such matters, as if he should confirm his communication with an oath. For 'every Christian man's word' (saith S. Jerome) 'should be so true, that it

---

[832] *The Homilies*, pp.52-53.

should be regarded as an oath.' And Chrysostom witnessing the same, saith, 'It is not convenient to swear: for what needeth us to swear, when it is not lawful for one of us to make a lie unto another?'[833]

Against the background of this conviction that oaths as such are not forbidden by Scripture, Article XXXIX addresses the specific issue of whether Christians may swear an oath when required to do so by a magistrate. The radical Protestant groups, like the Quakers subsequently, saw this as something that Christians could not do, but Article XXXIX says that they may do it, but under two conditions.

The first condition is that the cause for which the oath is required is 'a cause of faith and charity.' This is a compressed phrase which seems to be shorthand for 'a cause in which faith in God is expressed by the protection of the innocent and the conviction of the guilty.' This interpretation of the phrase makes sense in the context of the article. It is also consistent with the way in which faith is used throughout the *Thirty Nine Articles* to refer to faith in God and the way in which the meaning of charity is understood in the homily 'Of Christian love and charity' in the *First Book of Homilies.*

In this homily the question is raised 'If charity require to think, speak, and do well unto every man, both good and evil, how can magistrates execute justice upon malefactors, with charity?'[834] The answer that is then given to this question is that charity as exercised by magistrates has two forms or 'offices'.

The first office is:

> ...to cherish good and harmless men; not to oppress them with false accusations, but to encourage them with rewards, to do well and to continue in well doing, defending them with the sword from their adversaries.[835]

---

[833] Ibid, p.54.
[834] Ibid p.49.
[835] Ibid, p.50.

The second office is 'to rebuke, correct, and punish vice, without regard of person; and this is to be used only against those that be evil men and malefactors.'

When charity is understood in this way then the taking of an oath in a court case can be seen as an act of charity in so far as the taking of an oath, by helping to establish the truth about a particular matter, serves to protect 'good and harmless men' against oppression and false accusation and to ensure that the vices of evil men and malefactors are exposed so that they can be rebuked, corrected and punished.

The second condition is that not only should an oath be made for a right cause, but it should also be made in a right way. In this connection the article refers to Jeremiah 4:2 and notes that in this verse the prophet says that God's people should swear 'in justice, judgement and truth.' What swearing in this way means is explained in the homily 'Against Swearing and Perjury' referred to above. This declares:

> God by the Prophet Jeremy saith, Thou shalt swear, The Lord liveth, in truth, in judgement, in righteousness (Jeremiah 4.2). So that whosoever sweareth when he is required of a judge, let him be sure in his conscience that his oath have three conditions, and he shall never need to be afraid of perjury. First, he that sweareth, may swear truly, that is, he must (setting apart all favour and affection to the parties) have the truth only before his eyes, and for love thereof, say and speak that which he knoweth to be truth, and no further. The second is, he that taketh an oath, must do it with judgement, not rashly and unadvisedly, but soberly, considering what an oath is. The third is, he that sweareth, must swear in righteousness: that is, for the very zeal and love which he beareth to the defence of innocency, to the maintenance of the truth, and of the righteousness of the matter or cause: all profit, disprofit, all love and favour unto the person for friendship or kindred laid apart.[836]

Note: The oaths of allegiance and obedience

Although the Church of England continues to believe that Scripture does not forbid the use of oaths in appropriate ways, for appropriate causes,

---

[836] Ibid, p.53.

on appropriate occasions. However, it also recognises that there are people who have conscientious scruples about making oaths and it makes provision for their scruples in Canons C13 and 14. These canons set out the oaths of allegiance to the monarch and obedience to an archbishop or bishop made by all members of the clergy and alongside the normal formula 'I, AB do swear' an alternative formula, taken from the 1978 Oaths Act, is set down which says 'I, AB, do solemnly, sincerely and truly declare and affirm.'

Subject Index

Act in Restraint of Appeals (1533) 601

Act of the Six Articles (1539) 24–25, 528–29

Act of Uniformity (1559) 44, 425, 576, 589–90

Acts of Supremacy (1534 and 1559) 44, 602, 606

Admonition to Parliament, second 371

adoption, as sons of God 489, 491, 493–95

Adoptionism 214

Albertus Magnus 351

Alexander of Hales 351

Alexandria, Council (326) 229

Alley, William (Bishop of Exeter) 162–64, 271

almsgiving 572, 580, 617, 619, 622–25

ambiguity, avoidance 16–17

Ambrose of Milan, St. 314, 327, 346, 350, 463–64, 564

Anabaptists 12 n.4, 37, 39–41
  and goods held in common 617–19
  and oath-taking 628–30
  and pacifism 608–10
  and sacraments 471, 483, 484
  and salvation 393–94
  and sin 39–40, 304, 305, 359–60
  and the Trinity 104–5
 see also Protestantism, radical

Anastasius (chronicler) 224

Andrewes, Lancelot 430

angels, belief in 116–17, 136

Anglican Communion 82–90
  current situation 88–89
  and diversity 570–71
  Instruments of Unity 571
  Ireland 82–84, 88–89
  and Lambeth Conferences 86–87
  New Zealand 85–86
  Scotland 85
  United States of America 84–85

Anglican Covenant 89–90

Anglican Pacifist Fellowship 615

Anglican-Methodist Covenant 337–38, 456, 569

Anglican-Orthodox Joint Doctrinal Commission (1976) 225

Anglicanism, and confessionalism 17–19

Anglican–Lutheran Dialogue 337

Anglican–Roman Catholic International Commission (ARCIC) 338–39, 363, 407 n.543, 513–15, 541, 612

Anselm of Canterbury, St. 327 n.421, 534, 544

anthropapathism 112

anthropomorphisms, in Old Testament 109

Antinomianism 387, 390

Apocrypha 54, 57, 60, 69, 237–38, 240–41, 242–43, 246–47, 263–65, 267–68

Apollinarianism 143

Apostles' Creed 19, 46, 87, 102, 286–91
  authority 238, 410
  and descent into Hell 160, 162–63, 168
  and English Reformation 299
  and God as Trinity 115
  and Jesus Christ 133, 150
  name 289
  and resurrection of Christ 174
  and Scripture 291
  structure 291
  text 298–99

Aquinas, St. Thomas 344 n.455, 351

Archbishops' Commission on Christian Doctrine 70–72, 116–17, see also Doctrine Commission

Arianism 105, 127, 128–30, 132, 143, 221–22, 408–9, 427

Ariminum, Council (350) 427

Arius 128–29

Arminianism 67–68, 90, 380–81
  Remonstrance (1610) 381

Arminius, Jacobus 68, 380

Article I, 'Of Faith in the Holy Trinity' 103–25
  on unity and attributes of God 28, 105–20, 123

Article II, 'Of the Word, or Son of God' 126–59
and Parker 102, 128
Article III, 'Of the going down of Christ into Hell' 160–73
Article IV, 'Of the Resurrection of Christ' 174–213
Article V, 'Of the Holy Ghost' 214–36
Article VI, 'Of the Sufficiency of the Holy Scriptures for Salvation' 237–39, 240–68
Article VII, 'Of the Old Testament' 238, 269–85
Article VIII, 'Of the Three Creeds' 19, 238, 260, 286–300
Article IX, 'Of Original or Birth Sin' 154, 302, 303–10
Article X, 'Of Free Will' 301, 311–19
Article XI, 'Of the Justification of Man' 302, 320–29
Article XII, 'Of Good Works' 301, 330–41
Article XIII, 'Of Works before Justification' 301, 342–48
Article XIV, 'of Works of Supererogation' 301, 349–56, 358–59
Article XV, 'Of Christ alone without Sin' 328, 357–64, 366
Article XVI, 'of Sin after Baptism' 301, 365–73
and indefectibility of grace 67
Article XVII, 'Of Predestination and Election' 20–21, 301, 374–91
and Reformed theology 20–21, 65
Article XVIII, 'Of obtaining eternal salvation only by the name of Christ' 302, 392–99
Article XIX, 'Of the Church' 401–11
Article XX, 'Of the Authority of the Church' 260, 412–21
authorisation of Article 413–14
and controversies of faith 416, 418–19
and rites and ceremonies 415–18
Article XXI, 'Of the Authority of General Councils' 260, 422–30
in New Zealand 85–86
Article XXII, 'Of Purgatory' 432–46, 542

Article XXIII, 'Of Ministering in the Congregation' 369, 447–56, 542
and ministry of lay people 67
Article XXIV, 'Of speaking in the Congregation in such a tongue as the people understandeth' 457–65
Article XXV, 'Of the Sacraments' 467–80
and Confirmation 67
Article XXVI, 'Of the Unworthiness of the Ministers' 481–88
Article XXVII, 'Of Baptism' 489–502
and infant baptism 75, 489–90, 495, 496–502
Article XXVIII, 'Of the Lord's Supper' 503–15
Article XXIX, 'Of the wicked which do not eat the body of Christ' 21, 507, 516–24
and Reformed theology 20, 21
Article XXX, 'Of Both Kinds' 525–31
Article XXXI, 'Of the one oblation of Christ finished upon the Cross' 154, 532–42
Article XXXII, 'Of the Marriage of Priests' 543–49
Article XXXIII, 'Of Excommunicated Persons' 550–60
Article XXXIV, 'Of the Traditions of the Church' 542, 561–71
Article XXXV, 'Of Homilies' 542, 572–86
Article XXXVI, 'Of Consecration of Bishops and Ministers' 542, 587–96
Article XXXVII, 'Of the Civil Magistrates' 597, 598–616
in New Zealand 85–86
and papal jurisdiction 67
Article XXXVIII, 'Of Christian men's goods which are not common' 597, 617–27
and almsgiving 617, 619, 622–25
and common property 617–21
Article XXXIX, 'Of a Christian man's Oath' 597, 628–34
Articles of 1660/61 50 n.51, 563
ascension of Christ 144, 167, 174–75, 182–89, 191, 193, 274, 504
assurance 64, 65–66

Athanasian Creed 19, 84, 238, 286–90
  damnatory clauses 294–95, 300
  and English Reformation 299
  name 289
  structure 292
  text 296–98
Athanasius, St. 123, 161, 252, 264, 287, 409
Athenagoras, On the Resurrection of the Dead 198–99, 209
atonement, as universal 155, 159
Augsburg Confession (1530) 12, 21, 154, 342
  and call to ministry 448
  and communion in both kinds 527, 530
  and good works 330
  and justification by faith 331
  and marks of the Church 401
  and Mass as sacrifice 535–36
  and sacraments 28, 468, 482
  and sin 154
  and Ten Articles 22
  and Thirteen Articles 26–29
  and unity of the Church 410
Augustine of Canterbury, St. 564
Augustine of Hippo, St. 463
  and almsgiving 623
  and Eucharist 516, 518, 529
  and free will 311–12, 314
  and God as Trinity 121, 122, 287
  and good works 330–31, 346
  and grace 314
  and Holy Spirit 220–21, 229, 234
  and justification 327 n.421
  and predestination 21, 40, 64, 377–78
  and reconciliation through death of Christ 153–54, 159
  and Scripture 252, 273–74
authority
  of Christ 189, 191, 193, 407–8
  of the Church 400, 412–21, 423, 433, 528, 529–30, 547
  civil 26, 40, 43, 54–55, 82, 84, 85–86, 561, 566–67, 579, 580, 597–616
  of Creeds 238, 260, 290
  and Eleven Articles 46, 49

  and Forty Two Articles 43, 51
  of General Councils 260–61, 400, 422–30
  imperial 601–2
  for ministry 447–56
  of Old Testament 238, 277–78, 283–85
  of papacy 39, 46–47, 50, 405, 597, 598, 603, 605–8, 612
  and radical Protestantism 40
  of rulers 424–26, 601–5, 606–7, 611–12
  of Scripture 238, 244–45, 254–57, 264–68, 400, 419–21, 423, 547, 565
  and Thirty Eight Articles 54

Bancroft, Richard (Archbishop of Canterbury) 29, 67, 387
Bandstra, A 276
baptism
  and adoption as sons of God 489, 491, 493–95
  of adults 500
  and Apostles' Creed 299, 300, 410
  and Church of Rome 406
  and diversity of practices 565
  and ecclesiastical election 381–82
  and faith 489, 491, 493, 495–96
  and forgiveness 292
  and Holy Spirit 494–95
  of infants 40, 43, 75, 489–90, 495, 496–502
  and original sin 304, 308–10
  as outward mark 491
  post-baptismal sin 360, 362–63, 365–73, 416
  and regeneration 69, 304, 308–9, 362, 491–93, 510
  as sign of profession 490–91
  see also confirmation
Baptism, Eucharist and Ministry (World Council of Churches report) 501–2
Baptists, and Church of England 500–502
Barrett, William 64–66
Barth, Karl, Church Dogmatics 110–11, 138–41, 155–59, 194, 217–18, 386

Basil of Caesarea, St. 232–33, 327, 463

Bauckham, R J 191–92, 201, 246, 253–55

Becon, Thomas 576

Bede, the Venerable 223, 518

Bellarmine, Cardinal Robert 246

Benedict VIII, Pope 224

Bernard of Clairvaux, St. 64

Beveridge, W 90
  and General Councils 428–29
  and goods held in common 620
  and Holy Spirit 230–31
  and humanity and divinity of Christ 143–44, 150
  and nature of God 112
  and resurrection of Christ 175–76
  and sacraments 484–87

Bible
  authority 238, 244–45, 254–57, 264–68, 400, 419–21, 423, 547, 565
  Canon 54, 69, 237–38, 240–43, 246–47, 263–67
  diversity and coherence 253–59
  inspiration 69, 247–48, 283
  Latin 23
  and Thirty Nine Articles 93–94
  translations 86
  vernacular 25
  see also Scripture

Bicknell, E J 90–91, 112–14, 512–13, 530–31, 560, 626–27

Biel, Gabriel 344 n.455

bishops 410
  appointment 11
  consecration 587–89, 591
  and episcopal ordination 452–55
  and excommunication of offenders 554
  marriage 544–45, 546

The Bishops Book (1537) 23–24, 25, 50
  blasphemy against the Spirit 232, 234, 373

Body of Christ
  Church as 211
  and Eucharist 51–55

Bonhoeffer, Dietrich 554–56

Bonner, John (Bishop of London) 576

Book of Common Prayer (1552) 44, 47, 49, 72, 576
  assent to 73–74, 76, 78–80, 81
  and baptism 490–91, 492, 494, 495, 498
  Catechism 281–82, 299, 319, 336, 493, 506
  and confirmation 499–500
  and Creeds 299
  and death of Christ 534 n.709
  and descent into Hell 168–73
  and excommunication 558
  funeral service 435
  general confession 306–7
  and grace 314
  and Ordinal 14, 43, 73–74, 79–80, 90, 261, 589
  and post-baptismal sin 372
  and reception of Eucharist 479–80, 519–21
  revision of 1662 70
  and Royal Declaration of 1628 67–68, 72
  and sacraments 404–5
  and traditions and ceremonies 566–67

Bradford, John 105

Bray, Gerald 22–23, 65–66, 287, 362–63, 487–88, 496

Browne, E H
  and Books of Homilies 584
  and the Church 418, 420–21
  and Creeds 295
  and excommunication 551–52, 553
  and free will 318
  and General Councils 426–27
  and goods held in common 621
  and grace 315
  and Jesus Christ 131
  and predestination 381–82
  and salvation 396
  and sufficiency of Scripture 252
  and works 331–32

Bruce, F F 167–68, 275

Bucer, Martin 12

Bullinger, Heinrich 30–31, 36, 359, 577

Burges, Cornelius 15

Burn, A E 222

Burnet, Gilbert, Exposition of the XXXIX
   Articles 90–91
   and the Church 415
   and clerical celibacy 545–46, 547
   and comprehension 16–17
   and Creeds 289, 294–95
   and English and Latin versions 62
   and good works 336–37, 348
   and ministry in the Church 451
   and national churches 568
   and nature of God 109
   and Ordinal 593–94
   and purgatory 433–34
   and salvation 395–96
   and sin 366–67
   and sufficiency of Scripture 261
   and supererogation 358–59
   and wealth and poverty 625–26

Caesarius of Arles, St. 287
Caird, G B 190, 354–55
Calvin, John 12, 20, 30, 168 n.226
   and Eucharistic theology 21
   and predestination 379, 380
Calvinism
   and Arminianism 67–68, 90
   and Church of England 64–66, 67–70,
   90–91, 371–72
   and Eucharist 20
   and indefectible grace 64, 66–67, 371
   and predestination 8, 20–21, 64–67,
   155, 372, 378, 390
Cambridge University, and assent to
   Articles 81–82
canon law, Reformation reforms 15
Canons of 1604
   and excommunication 558–59
   II-VIII 558
   V 80–81
   IX-XII 558
   XXXVI 74–76, 81, 93
   LXV 559
   LXVIII 559
   CIX 558–59
Canons
   A2 80
   A5 80, 93, 168

A7 612
A8 596
B2 454
B16 559
B43 456
B44 456
C1 454
C4A 454
C13 634
C14 634
C15 77–79, 300
E5 78
E8 78
capital punishment 597, 598, 599, 601,
   608–11, 612–15
Cardwell, Edward 66–67
Carthage, Council (387/390) 544
Catechism
   Book of Common Prayer 281–82, 299,
   319, 336, 493, 506
   of the Catholic Church 355–56, 531
   see also Nowell, Alexander
Cecil, Sir William 31–32
celibacy
   clerical 24, 25, 39, 409, 542, 543–44
   lay 24–25
Chalcedon, Council (451) 11, 142, 220,
   226, 286, 423, 425
Chalcedonian definition 142–43, 172
changelessness of God 109–11
Charlemagne, Emperor 223–24, 287,
   425
Charles I, and Calvinism 67–68, 70
Cheke, Sir John 31, 34
Chesterton, G K 255
Childs, B. S. 121–22
Christian socialism 626–27
Church
   and authority of Scripture 419–21,
   423
   diversity of traditions and ceremonies
   561–71
   as God's elect 381–82, 385–86
   invisible 402–3, 404
   marks of 42, 401, 404–5, 407–8, 410,
   585

visible 400, 401–11, 447–48, 481–82, 484

visible unity 410–11, 454–56, 569

Church of England
attitudes to war 615–16
and Books of Homilies 583–86
and Calvinism 64–66, 67–70, 90–91, 371–72
and General Council 429–30
as national church 568–69
Supreme Governor 425–26, 597, 599, 600, 601–2

Church of England Empowering Act (New Zealand; 1928) 86

Church of Ireland 82–84, 88–89, 379

Church of New Zealand 85–86

Church and state
and civil authority 26, 37, 40, 43, 54–55, 82–83, 84–86, 561, 566–67, 579, 580
and diversity of opinion 13
and national church 568–69
see also supremacy, royal

churches, national 568–69, 570–71

Clement of Alexandria, St. 544

clergy
celibacy 24, 25, 39, 409, 542, 543–44
subscription to Articles 63, 70–72, 73–82, 87

Clergy Discipline Measure (2003) 488

Clerical Subscription Act (1865) 76–78

Clermont, Council (1185) 527

Collinson, Patrick 59

Common Worship 465
and Books of Homilies 583
and Creeds 299–300
and excommunication 559–60
Ordinal 596

communion of saints 291, 443, 444–46

comprehension, and statements of faith 16–17

Comprehension Bill (1689) 75

concomitance, doctrine of 530, 531

concupiscence, and sin 37, 69, 181, 303, 308–10

confession and absolution, private 25, 521

Confession of Faith (Scotland; 1560) 85

confirmation 476, 499–500

congregation, and Church 403, 448

Congregational Order (Anabaptist) 618

Constance, Council (1414-17) 428, 527, 529

Constantine the Great 425

Constantinople
First Council (381) 220, 226, 286, 423, 425
Second Council (553) 145

Councils, General 11, 260–61, 400, 416, 422–30
liability to error 426–28
and Scripture 428–29
and secular rulers 424–26

Cox, Richard (Bishop of Ely) 51

Cranfield, C E B 169–71, 172

Cranmer, Thomas (Archbishop of Canterbury) 17, 23, 104, 128
and the Church 402–3, 404
and clerical marriage 546
and descent into Hell 171
and diversity in the Church 562
and English liturgy 459–60
and good works 343
and Holy Spirit 215
and homilies 575–76
and incarnation 133
and predestination 376–78, 388
and resurrection of Christ 175
and sacraments 468–69, 483, 532
Of the Salvation of Mankind 155
and Scripture 246, 248–53, 255, 259, 262
and Six Articles 24
and Thirteen Articles 26, 29, 162, 175, 402–3, 442, 468–69, 562
and Thirty Nine Articles 61
see also Forty Two Articles

creation
renewal 118–19, 211–13
and role of the Spirit 232
see also God, as creator

creeds 286–300
authority 238, 260, 290
ecumenical 11, 21, 39, 46

and Scripture 260, 288–89, 290–95,
299, 419
  texts 296–99
  Thirty Nine Articles as 17–19, 94
Cromwell, Thomas 23
Crossan, J D 208
Cyprian of Carthage, St. 327 n.421, 463,
529
Cyril of Jerusalem, St. 526

damnation 201–7, 301, 307–8
  and unworthy reception of sacraments
  467, 469, 477–80, 516, 519–20, 522
death of Christ
  as reconciling 151–53, 155, 159
  as sacrifice 150–59, 187–88, 532–36,
  539–41
death penalty 597, 598, 599, 601, 608–
  11, 612–15
Declaration of Assent 76–80, 300
departed, prayer for 434–35, 441, 443–
  46
devils, belief in 116–17
dialogue, interfaith 396–99
Dietrich, Veit 577
Dionysius 463
discipline, ecclesiastical 408, 487–88,
  542, 550–60
Dissenters, and subscription to Articles
  75–76
diversity in traditions and ceremonies
  561, 563–65, 569
Docetism 143
doctrine, non-scriptural 260–61
Doctrine in the Church of England
  (1938) 116–17, 133–34
Doctrine Commission, The Mystery of
  Salvation 123–24, 155, 200, 201–2,
  212–13, 396–99, 444–45
  see also Archbishops' Commission on
Christian Doctrine
Donatists 482
Dort, Synod (1619) 68
Duffy, E 459, 464

Eastern Church 408–9
  and clerical marriage 544–45

and communion in both kinds 531
and procession of the Spirit 220–21,
  225–30
Ecclesiastical Jurisdiction Measure
  (1963) 488
ecumenism
  and Article XXII 446
  and baptism 500–502
  and Books of Homilies 585
  and diversity 569
  and justification 337–39
  and papal primacy 612
  and treasury of merit 355–56
  and visible Church 410–11
Edward VI
  and church discipline 550
  and communion in both kinds 529
  and Forty Two Articles 29–30, 43
  and Ordinal 587–90
  see also First Book of Homilies
election 374–91
  conditional 380–81
  ecclesiastical 381–82
  identity of the elect 382–83, 386
Eleven Articles (1561) 43–50, 82, 407–
  8, 529, 530, 536
Elizabeth I 13–14, 44, 424
  authority in the Church 46–47, 49, 52,
  54–55
  and Eucharist 516–17, 529
  Injunctions 548, 602
  and Lambeth Articles 66, 378–79
  and liturgy in English 460
  and Second Book of Homilies 576–77,
  578
  as Supreme Governor 425–26, 600,
  602
  and toleration 58
  see also Eleven Articles; Thirty Eight
Articles
emotions, of God 109–10
empty tomb 177–78, 210
enhypostatic union 145
Ephesus
  Council of 431 423, 425
  Council of 449 427

Episcopal Church of the United States of America 84–85
Epistle to Diognetus 279
Erasmus, Desiderius 576
eschatology
   and Forty Two Articles 41
   and Thirty Eight Articles 56
   see also judgement; punishment, eternal
eternity
   eternal life 198, 200, 204–5
   eternal punishment 164, 202–5
Eucharist 503–15
   ARCIC agreed statement 513–15, 541
   and body and blood of Christ 506
   communion in both kinds 24, 25, 47–48, 406, 409, 428, 466, 525–30
   and concomitance doctrine 530, 531
   and Cranmer 31
   and Forty Two Articles 43
   and Real Presence 57, 508, 513–14
   reception 479–80, 505–6, 516–24
   and Reformed theology 20, 21
   reservation of elements for the sick 513
   and reservation and veneration of elements 477–78, 503, 511–13, 514–15
   and role of faith 505, 506, 509–11, 514, 522–23
   as sacrifice 539–41
   as sign of unity 505
   suspension from 554, 558–60
   and transubstantiation 24, 39, 52, 409, 428, 503–4, 507–9
Eutychianism 143, 175, 427
Evangelical Church in Germany 314
excommunication 542, 550–60, 608–9
   in New Testament 551–54
   in Old Testament 551
   in post-Reformation Church 558–60
Extreme Unction 476–77

faith, and Eucharist 505, 506, 509–11, 514, 522–23
   see also baptism; justification; statements of faith

Faith in the City 626
faith and practice
   and diversity of opinion 12–14
   in early Christianity 10–11
   and ecumenical councils 11, 17, 422–30
   and good works 330–36, 337–39, 348, 581
   in Judaism 10
   Reformation statements 12–14
Feathers Tavern Petition 76 n.99
Fee, G D 178
Fiddes, Paul 500–502
Field, Richard 430
filioque clause 220–30
First Book of Homilies (1547) 14, 29, 43, 84, 265, 574, 575–76, 577–79, 581–82
   'Against the Fear of Death' 579
   'Against Swearing and Perjury' 579, 630–32, 633
   'Against Whoredom and Uncleanness' 576, 579
   'Against Contention and Brawling' 579
   'Concerning Good Order and Obedience' 579, 580, 603–5, 606–8, 610–11
   'A fruitful exhortation to the Reading of Holy Scripture' 576, 578
   'How Dangerous a Thing it is to Fall from God' 370–71, 579
   'Of Christian Love and Charity' 576, 579, 632–33
   'Of Good Works annexed unto Faith' 280–81, 314, 334–36, 345–47, 576, 578, 579, 581
   'Of the Misery of All Mankind' 306, 313, 576, 578
   'Of the Salvation of Mankind' 321–27, 576, 578, 579, 584
   'Of the true, lively and Christian Faith' 578, 579
   'A short declaration of the true, lively and Christian faith' 272–74, 332–34, 576
Florence, Council (1439) 428, 474
Forbes, A P 90, 583

forgiveness
  by ordained minister 594
  for post-baptismal sin 366–72
Formula of Concord (1577) 522–24
Forsyth, P T 148
Forty Two Articles (1553) 13 n.6, 29–
    43, 44, 50, 330
  and baptism 489–90
  and the Church 412
  and civil magistrates 599–600
  contents 35–36
  and Cranmer 29–31, 33–34, 36, 41–42,
    57, 61, 100–101, 104, 215
  and descent of Christ into Hell 162,
    164, 171
  development 29–34
  and diversity in the Church 562
  and Eucharist 504–5, 532
  and excommunication 550
  and free will 311
  and General Councils 422
  and goods held in common 617
  and grace 316–17, 342–43
  and Holy Spirit 215, 373
  and Holy Trinity 100, 103
  and Homilies 574
  and images 442
  and Jesus Christ 126, 128
  and justification by faith 320
  and Lutheranism 27
  and marriage of priests 543–44
  and Medieval Catholicism 37, 38–39,
    432–33
  and ministering in the Church 447
  nature 36–43
  and oath-taking 628
  and Old Testament 41, 269–71
  and Ordinal 587–88, 590
  and original sin 304
  and post-baptismal sin 365
  and predestination 375
  and purgatory 432
  and radical Protestantism 36–37, 271
  and sacraments 28, 469–70, 474
  and salvation through Christ 392
  and Scripture and Creeds 237, 243–
    44, 286

sources 36
  and sufficiency of Scripture 242
  and Thirty Eight Articles 51, 52–57
  and use of Latin 457–58
  and visible Church 401
  and works 342–43
free will 311–19
  and Calvinism 69
  and radical Protestantism 39–40
Funk, R W 208

Gallican Confession 310
Gangra, Council (324) 544
Gelasius I, Pope 526, 529
genealogies, New Testament 136, 137
generation of Son from Father 57, 218–
    19
Gentilly, Council (767) 223
Germany, Evangelical Church 337
Gibson, E. C. S. 90
  and Apocrypha 265
  and baptism 494, 495
  and the Church 403–4, 406–7, 416–17
  and clerical celibacy 546–47
  and Creeds 288
  and descent into Hell 160, 167, 173
  and Eastern Churches 408–9
  and excommunication 559
  and Forty Two Articles 36, 41, 51–52
  and free will 312
  and goods held in common 621–22
  and Holy Spirit 215, 233, 234
  and Institution of a Christian Man 23–
    24
  and Jesus Christ 149, 152, 154, 160,
    167, 173
  and Mass as sacrifice 537
  and Ordinal 587
  and post-baptismal sin 369, 373, 390
  and predestination 387
  and reconciliation 152
  and sacraments 470–71, 473, 476,
    478, 479–80
  and sin 309–10
  and subscription 75–76, 81
  and Thirteen Articles 26
  and transubstantiation 508–9

and the Trinity 104–5, 215, 229–30
and Virgin Mary 358
and works 342–44
and Württemburg Confession 56
Global Anglican Futures Conference
  (GAFCON) 89
Gnosticism
  and God as creator 114
  and humanity of Jesus Christ 133
God
  as creator 114–20, 134, 291
  as free of limitations 108–12
  as love 200
  as one, living and true 105–7
  perfections 112–14, 123
  as Trinity 45–46, 100–102, 103–5,
  120–25, 193, 214, 292–93
  unity 45–46, 100, 105–7, 122–23
  wrath 152–53, 155, 159, 301, 307–8,
  534
goodness of God 113–14
goods, held in common 41, 43, 597,
  617–27
Gorham case 492 n.665
grace
  co-operating 314, 315–16
  congruous 342–44
  and free will 311–18
  indefectibility 64, 66–67, 371
  prevenient 69, 311, 313–15, 319, 337–
  38, 343
  and sacraments 26, 28, 38, 467–69,
  471–72, 477, 506, 509
  and works 313, 319, 343–48
Gregory I 'the Great', Pope 564–65
Gregory VII, Pope 544
Gregory Nazianzen, St. 264
Gregory of Nyssa, St. 228–29, 230
Grenz, Stanley 385–86
Griffith Thomas, W. H. 90
  and authority of the Church 433
  and clerical marriage 548
  and Creeds 19, 289–90
  and Eucharist 52
  and General Councils 423
  and God as Trinity 120–21
  and goods held in common 618

and Homilies 574–75
and liturgy and language 464
and Mass as sacrifice 537–39
and Ordinal 589, 594
and original sin 306, 307–8, 310
and predestination 380
and Roman Catholicism 408
and salvation 394–95
and Scripture 242, 264
and subscription to Articles 58
and works of supererogation 350–51
Grindal, Edmund (Bishop of London)
  73, 577
Growing Together in Mission and Unity
  612
Guest, Edmund (Bishop of Rochester)
  51, 516–17

Hadrian I, Pope 223–24
Hammond, Henry 430
Hampton Court Conference (1604) 66–
  67, 371, 387
Hanson, A T 276
Hanson, A T and Hanson, R P C 146–7
Hardwick, Charles
  and Forty Two Articles 32, 44, 51, 61
  and Irish Articles 82–83
  and Thirteen Articles 27
  and Thirty Nine Articles 61, 62 n.71,
  63, 67, 92–93, 317, 357–58, 393, 414,
  448
  and Westminster Assembly 69–70
Harmony of the Confessions of Faith of
the Orthodox and Reformed Churches
  20
Harpesfield, John 576
Hatfield, Synod (680) 223
Hauerwas, Stanley 556
Hell
  Christ's descent into 160–73
  and eternal punishment 205–6
  New Testament imagery 201–2
Henry II (Holy Roman Emperor) 224
Henry VIII 22, 24–25, 575, 602
  and Ten Articles 22
Henson, Herbert Hensley (Bishop of
  Durham) 70

heresies
  Christological 127–30, 143, 175, 182
  Trinitarian 104–5, 214–15
Heron, A I C 132
Hilary of Poitiers, St. 221, 264, 327
Hippolytus of Rome, St. 252
Holy Ghost see Holy Spirit
Holy Spirit 101–2, 214–36, 292
  and baptism 494–95
  blasphemy against 232, 234, 373
  as breath of God 219
  and direct revelation 243–44
  divinity 230–36
  and Eucharist 509–11
  and filioque clause 220–30
  and free will 318–19
  and incarnation of Christ 138–41, 232
  and Old Testament 277
  and ordination 593
  as paraclete 227, 233
  procession from Father and Son 216–30
  sin against 40, 360, 365–73
  as witness to Scripture 421 n.561
Homilies see First Book of Homilies;
  Second Book of Homilies
Homily of Repentance (1571) 152–53
Hooker, Richard
  and authority of the Church 417
  and General Councils 430
  and justification by faith 328
  and national church 568
  and nature of God 113
  and nature of Jesus Christ 145, 185
  and Ordinal 592
  and righteousness 339 n.446
  and Roman Catholicism 407
  and sacraments 473
Hooper, John (Bishop of Worcester) 30–31, 36–37, 163–64
Hughes, P E 556
human nature, and original sin 303–10, 323

Ignatius of Antioch, St. 161
images 22, 48, 419, 427, 431, 436–42, 446

immortality 212
  and damnation 202–7
impassibility of God 111–12
incarnation 127–28, 132–41, 150
  and Holy Spirit 138–41, 232
indulgences 352, 355–56, 435–36, 442, 566
infant baptism 40, 43, 75, 489–90, 495, 496–502
The Institution of a Christian Man/Bishops' Book (1537) 23–24, 25, 50
interfaith dialogue 396–99
Irenaeus of Lyons, St. 114, 120, 123
Irish Articles (1615) 82–84, 100, 379

James I and VI
  and Calvinism 67, 387
  and Cambridge University 81
Jelf, R W 280, 554, 575, 591–93
Jerome (Hierome), St. 240, 243, 263, 264, 265, 463, 529, 575, 631–32
Jerusalem Declaration 89
Jesus Christ 126–59
  ascension 144, 167, 174–75, 182–89, 191, 193, 274, 504
  Christological heresies 127–30, 143, 175, 182
  death 149–59
  descent into Hell 160–73
  divine nature 105, 127–32, 143, 146–47, 158–59, 185, 291–92, 293, 419
  enhypostatic union 145
  human nature 127–28, 132–41, 143–47, 158–59, 171–72, 175–82, 184–85, 361, 419, 427
  as judge 187, 193–208
  as king 185, 189–93, 197–98
  as priest 185, 187–89
  as prophet 185, 186–87
  resurrection 167, 174–213
  salvation only in his name 392–99
  as second Adam 159, 212
  as second person of the Trinity 142–49
  self-limitation 148–49
  as sinless 328, 357–64

as Son of Man 144 n.187
suffering 149–59
as Word of God 129–31, 161, 186, 193, 214
Jesus Seminar 208
Jewel, John (Bishop of Salisbury) 60, 247–48, 577
Apology for the Church of England 14
John Chrystostom 249, 251, 327 n.421, 463, 577, 605
and almsgiving 623
and good works 314, 346–47
Liturgy of 145–46
and oath-taking 632
and relics 439
John of Damascus, St. 161–62, 218–19, 252
judgement, final 187, 193–208
justice, divine 196–97, 308, 324–25, 534, 611
justification
definition 321–22
in ecumenical agreements 337–39
by faith 38, 301, 320–29, 579, 583–84
and new perspective on Paul 339–41
and predestination 374, 377, 378, 383–84, 386–87
and works 25, 38, 301, 329, 330–41, 342–48, 354, 419
Justin Martyr, St. 463, 525–26
Justinian, lawcode 601

Kelly, J N D 221–2, 224
keys, ecclesiastical 407–8, 555
king, Christ as 185, 189–93, 197–98
King's Book (1543) 25, 474
Kingsley, Charles 626
Knox, D B 117–18
Knox, John, and Confession of Faith 85

laity
denial of chalice to 406, 409, 428, 466, 525–30
and subscription to Articles 59–60, 80
Lambeth Articles (1595) 64–66, 67, 83, 371, 378–79, 388
Lambeth Conferences

1888 86
1920 410, 454–55
1930 86–87, 615–16
1968 87
1978 225
1988 225, 613
Lampe, G. W. H. 17
Lateran Council, Fourth (1215) 11–12, 428, 507–8
Latimer, Hugh (Bishop of Worcester) 29
Latin
Bible in 23
liturgy in 409, 431, 457–65
Thirty Nine Articles in 62–63, 464
latitudinarianism 90, 91, 396
Laud, William (Archbishop of Canterbury) 68, 414
Laurence, Richard 390
laws of nature 117–18, 119–20, 395
Leo I 'the Great', Pope 526
Leo III, Pope 224
Leo X, Pope 352
Leo XIII, Pope, Apostolicae Curae 540
Lewis, C S 134–35, 184, 200–201, 206–7
Liberal Protestantism 151
Licensed Lay Workers, and declaration of assent 78
life, eternal 198, 200, 204–5
liturgy, vernacular 38, 409, 431, 457–65
Liturgy of St. John Chrysostom 145–46
Lombard, Peter 344 n.455, 474
Lord's Supper see Eucharist
Ludlow, J M 626
Luther, Martin 12
and homilies 575
and indulgences 352, 566
and predestination 376, 391–92
and sacraments 22
Lutheranism
and Eucharistic theology 21, 52, 522–24, 532
and sacraments 474
see also Augsburg Confession; Formula of Concord; Württemburg Confession

MacCulloch, Diarmaid 34, 377
magistrates, civil

and the Church 26, 37, 40, 43, 54–55, 82–83, 84–86, 561, 566–67, 579, 597–616
and death penalty 608–11
and oath-taking 597, 628, 630, 632
and radical Protestants 6–8–10
Manichaeism 526
marks of the Church 42, 401, 404–5, 407–8, 410, 585
marriage
as non-sacramental 477
of priests 542, 543–49
Mary: Grace and Hope in Christ (ARCIC II report) 363
Mary, Blessed Virgin
immaculate conception 357–59, 363
and sinlessness 363–64
virginity 140–41
Mary Tudor 33, 43–44, 50, 529, 566, 576, 589
Mascall, E and Green, M 540
Mass
private 25, 47–48
seen as sacrifice 154, 532–33, 535–39
Maurice, F D 626
Meissen Agreement 456
Melancthon, Philip 376, 390
Mennonites, and shunning 557
mercy, divine 197, 324–25, 370, 372
merit
of Christ 273, 320, 323–25, 328, 337, 351–52, 355–56, 435
congruous 38
human 198, 199, 347–48, 350–51, 355, 435–36
Micronius, Martin (Marten de Cleyne) 162
military service 597, 600, 601, 608–12
Millenarii 41
Miller, P. D. 10, 106–7
Miller, Victoria 66
ministry
authority for 447–56
consecration for 587–96
and ecclesiastical discipline 487–88
lawful 447–56
qualifications for 591

threefold order 451–52, 453–54
and use of vernacular language 457–65
mission 398–99
monotheism, Old Testament 105–7
Monothelitism 409
Montague, Richard, Apello Caesarem 68
Moravian Church 337
Moscow Agreed Statement 225–26
Motyer, J A 203, 204
Muhlen, Heribert 234
The Mystery of Salvation 123–24, 155, 200, 201–2, 212–13, 396–99, 444–45

The Necessary Doctrine and Erudition for any Christian Man (1543) 25, 29, 31
Neill, S C 12, 491, 601
Nestorianism 143
New Testament
authority 257, 266–67
Douai-Reims translation 351
genealogies 136, 137
and idols 436–37
and Old Testament 272–77
New Zealand, and Thirty Nine Articles 85–86
Newdigate, Sir Roger 76
Newman, John Henry, Tracts for the Times 442
Nicaea
Council of 325 11, 103, 286–87, 289, 423, 425, 544
Council of 787 427
Nicene Creed 11, 18–19, 46, 85, 87, 102, 286–88, 290
authority 238, 410
and descent into Hell 160
and English Reformation 299
filioque clause 220–30
and God as Trinity 115
and Jesus Christ 129, 131, 150
name 289
structure 291–92
text 296
Novatians 366
Nowell, Alexander, Catechism

and angels and devils 116
and baptism 492–93, 497–99
and Creeds 150–51
and Eucharist 509–11
and final judgement 194–95, 207
and marks of the Church 408
and nature of God 115, 117
and sacraments 472
and virgin birth of Christ 137–38, 140

Oath of Allegiance 634
Oath of Obedience 634
Oath of Supremacy 81
oath-taking 41, 43, 597, 628–34
O'Donovan, Oliver 61–62, 91–92, 100–101
and ascension 182
and authority of Scripture 419–21
and death penalty 614–15
and descent into Hell 171
and free will 316
and justification 328–29
and ministry in the Church 451–52
and Old Testament 284–85
and predestination 383–85
and war 611
Oecumenicus 327 n.421
Old Roman Creed 287
Old Testament
authority 238, 277–78, 283–85
and excommunication 551
and Holy Spirit 277
and idols 436
and moral commandments 277–83
and New Testament 272–77
and salvation 274, 276–77
as Scripture 266
omnipotence of God 112–13, 123
omnipresence of God 232
omniscience of God 113, 148–49, 232
orders
non-episcopal 453, 454–56
as non-sacramental 477
recognition 540, 588
Ordinal 14, 73–74, 76, 78–80, 261, 452–54
1662 595–96

and Article XXXVI 542, 587–96
Common Worship 596
and Forty Two Articles 587–88, 590
objections to 591–94
Preface 452, 453, 454, 590–91
validity 589–90
ordination for ministry 450–55, 587–96
Origen of Caesarea 327 n.421, 366
original sin 39, 69, 154, 301, 303–10, 313, 535
Oxford University, and assent to Articles 81–82
Oxford University Act (1854) 81

pacifism 601, 608, 615
Packer, J I
and final judgement 196, 199–200, 205
and impassibility of God 111–12
and Thirty Nine Articles 16, 17–18, 19, 21, 94
Pannenberg, Wolfhart 133
papacy
primacy 612
and procession of the Spirit 223–24
rejection of jurisdiction 39, 46–47, 50, 67, 405, 597, 598, 599, 601, 605–8, 612
paraclete (counsellor) 227, 233
paradise 166–67
pardons see indulgences
Parker, Matthew (Archbishop of Canterbury) 13–14, 104, 413, 589
and blasphemy against the Holy Spirit 373
and clerical marriage 544, 546, 548–49
and Eleven Articles 44, 50, 82
and free will 312, 317
and good works 330
and Holy Spirit 101–2, 214–15
and justification by faith 321
and reception of Eucharist 516
and Scripture and creeds 237, 243, 244, 246–47
and Second Book of Homilies 577
and Thirty Eight Articles 51, 52–55,

56, 60–61, 100–102, 104, 128, 164
and Württemburg Confession 56, 128, 214, 243
Parker, T M 306
Pascal II, Pope 527
Paschasius Radbertus 509
Paul III, Pope 424
Paul, St., new perspective on 339–41
Pearson, John 15, 16, 183–84
Pelagianism 39, 303, 304–8
Pelagius 304, 409
penance 369, 476–77, 550, 556
and absolution 25
perfection, counsels of 350–51
perfections of God 112–14, 123, 196
perseverance, and predestination 65, 381, 387–88
Persons of Holy Trinity 45–46, 120–24, 193, 214–18, 292–93
Peter Martyr 376–77
Phillpotts, Henry (Bishop of Exeter) 492 n.665
Philpot, John (Bishop of Winchester) 33–34
Photius of Constantinople 327 n.421
Pilkington, James (Bishop of Durham) 577
Pius V, Pope 58
Porvoo agreement (1992) 569
Postils 575, 577
poverty, and wealth 625–27
Prayer Book of 1552 see Book of Common Prayer (1552)
prayer for the dead 434–35, 441, 443–46
Prayer and the Departed 443–46
preaching
  authority for 447–56
  in vernacular language 457–65
predestination 301, 374–91, 416
  and Augustine 21, 40, 64
  Calvinistic view 8, 20–21, 64–67, 155, 372, 378, 390
  as in Christ 383–84
  consequences 388–90
  double 20, 64, 372, 379–81
  and justification 374, 377, 378, 383–

84, 386–87
  and missio dei 384–85
  and perseverance 65, 381, 387–88
  and radical Protestantism 317
priest, Christ as 185, 187–89
procession of Spirit from Father 216–30
  double 220–29
  single 220, 223–24, 226–27, 229
property, common 41, 43, 597, 617–27
prophet, Christ as 185, 186–87
propitiation
  death of Christ as 532–33, 534, 539
  Mass as 536, 539
Prosper of Aquitaine, St. 327 n.421, 377–78
Protestantism, and canon of Scripture 237–38, 240–43, 246–47, 263–66
Protestantism, Liberal 151
Protestantism, radical 36–37
  and authority 40, 497
  and authority to preach and teach 448–49
  and baptism 490, 496
  and the creeds 288, 290
  and eschatology 41, 56
  and Eucharist 50, 5065
  and free will 39–40, 312, 317
  and goods held in common 597, 617–18
  and Holy Spirit 40, 100, 101
  and justification 321
  and oath-taking 597, 628–32
  and pacifism 601, 608
  and predestination 317
  and sacraments 466, 471, 483, 484
  and salvation 302, 393–94
  and Scripture 237, 243–44
  and sin 39–40, 301, 304–8, 359–60, 366
  and traditions and ceremonies 563, 566
  and two natures of Christ 127, 175
punishment
  capital 597, 598, 599, 601, 608–11, 612–15
  eternal 164, 202–5

purgatory 38, 409, 428, 431, 432–35, 442, 446
  and indulgences 352
  and propitiation the Mass 536
Puritans
  and authority of the Church 413, 417
  and Elizabethan Church 59–60, 371
  and Jacobean Church 66–67, 80–81, 379, 387
  objections to Ordinal 591–94
  and Roman Catholic Church 407
Pushing at the Boundaries of Unity 500–501

Quakers (Religious Society of Friends) 608, 632
Quicunque vult see Athanasian Creed

radical Reformers see Protestantism, radical
Ramsey, Michael (Archbishop of Canterbury) 211
Ramsey, I T (Bishop of Durham) 87
Readers, and declaration of assent 78
Reccared (Visigothic king) 221–22
reconciliation, through death of Christ 151–53, 155, 159, 397, 513, 579
reconciliation of sinners 369, 550, 554–56
redemption
  particular 390
  through death of Christ 534
Reformatio Legum Ecclesiasticarum 15, 104
  and authority of the Church 412
  and baptism 496–97
  and Church of Rome 408–9
  and Creeds 289–90, 299
  and free will 312
  and General Councils 427, 429
  and goods held in common 617–19
  and Holy Trinity 104, 123, 215
  and infant baptism 490
  and Jesus Christ 127–28, 151, 175, 182
  and justification and sin 360
  and Latin 464

  and ministry in the Church 448–49
  and oath-taking 629, 630
  and original sin 305
  and predestination 388–90, 391 n.519
  and sacraments 471, 474–75, 483
  and salvation 393–94
  and Scripture 242–44, 260 n.348, 266, 271, 404
  and visible Church 402, 404–5
  and works of supererogation 349–50, 351
Reformation
  and Old Testament 271
  statements of faith 12–14, 18–19
Reformed theology, and theology of Articles 19–22, 90–91
regeneration, and baptism 69, 304, 308–9, 362, 491–93, 510
relics of saints 436, 439, 442, 446
religion, true 13–14
Relton, H M 147–8
repentance, and forgiveness 366–72, 555–56, 579, 581–82
resurrection
  of Christ 167, 174–213
  corporate and cosmic significance 211–13
  general 165–66, 195–96, 198
  of saints 179
Reuilly Agreement 455
revelation
  direct 243–44
  in Scripture 255, 301
Rheims, Council (813) 575
Ridley, Nicholas 29, 32, 105
righteousness
  original 303, 304, 306
  and sanctification 329, 338
  see also justification
rites and ceremonies, and authority of the Church 415–18
Rogers, John 29–30
Rogers, Thomas 14, 19, 90, 262, 278–79, 310, 353–54, 363, 424–26, 450, 483, 619
Roman Catholicism
  and Books of Homilies 585–86

and canon of Scripture 237, 243, 246–47

and communion in both kinds 525–31

errors 408–9

and number of sacraments 409, 473–74

and Scripture and tradition 245–46, 251 n.337, 409

and theology of Thirty Nine Articles 91

and vernacular liturgy 465

and visible Church 400, 401–2, 406–9

see also papacy; scholasticism; Trent, Council

Routley, Eric 20

Royal Declaration of 1628 67–68, 72

Rufinus, St. 264

Sabellianism 104

sacraments 466, 467–80

and biblical mandate 474–77

ex opere operato 38, 53, 466

number 54, 404, 409, 428, 466, 473–74

right use 467, 469, 477–80

as signs of grace 26, 28, 38, 467–69, 471–73, 477, 506, 509

and unworthiness of minister 40, 67, 481–88

and visible Church 404–5, 481–82, 484

see also Baptism; Eucharist

sacrifice

Christ's death as 150–59, 187–88, 532–34

Eucharistic 539–41

Mass seen as 154, 532–33, 535–39

in Old Testament 156, 158

Saepius Officio 540

saints

communion of saints 291, 443, 444–46

invocation 431, 440, 442, 444

merits 435–36

relics 436, 439, 442, 446

veneration 441–42

salvation

and death of Christ 149–59, 532–33

and justification by faith 301, 347–48

and nature of Christ 128, 129, 138, 140

and Old Testament 274, 276–77

only by the name of Christ 392–99

and other faiths 396–97

and sufficiency of Scripture 237, 240–68, 421

and teaching of General Councils 428

and the Trinity 123–25

see also predestination

sanctification, and righteousness 329, 338

satisfaction, death of Christ as 534–35

Schleitheim Confession 608–10, 611, 628–29

Schmalkaldic league 56

scholasticism 38, 301

and grace 342–48

and works of supererogation 351

Scottish Episcopal Church 85

Scottish Episcopal Relief Act (1792) 85

Scripture

and Councils 423

and creeds 260, 288–89, 290–95, 299

and early fathers 251–52

and General Councils 428–29

and sacraments 474–76

and self-revelation of God 255, 301

as story 253–59

as sufficient for salvation 237, 240–68, 421

and tradition 245–46, 262–63, 409

and transubstantiation 508

Second Book of Homilies 265, 572–74, 577, 579–82

'Against Disobedience and Wilful Rebellion' 363–64, 573, 574, 577, 580–81

'Against Excess of Apparel' 572, 577, 580

'Against Gluttony and Drunkenness' 572, 577, 580

'Against Idleness' 573, 574, 577, 580

'Against Peril of Idolatry' 430, 436–39, 572, 577, 580, 585

'For the Rogation-days' 572, 579

'Of Alms-doing' 572, 580, 622–25
'Of the Coming Down of the Holy Ghost and his Manifold Gifts' 318, 405–6, 572, 577, 579, 585
'Of Common Prayer and Sacraments in a Tongue Understood' 460–64, 473, 474–75, 572, 577, 580
'Of Good Works: first of fasting' 572, 574, 577, 580
'Of the Nativity of Christ' 572, 579
'Of the Passion of Christ' 572, 577, 579
'Of the Place and Time of Prayer' 572, 577, 580
'Of Prayer' 434–36, 440–41, 572, 577, 580
'Of the repairing and keeping clean of Churches' 572, 577, 580
'Of Repentance and True Reconciliation unto God' 363, 367–68, 373, 573, 579, 581
'Of the Resurrection of Our Saviour Jesus Christ' 179–82, 572, 577, 579
'Of the reverend estimation of God's Word' 572, 579
'Of the right Use of the Church' 577, 580
'Of the state of Matrimony' 572, 577, 580
'Of the worthy receiving and reverent esteeming of the body and blood of Christ' 478–79, 506, 572, 577, 580
Sermon on the Mount 336
Sheehan, T 208
Shema, as statement of faith 10, 106–7, 122
sheol 165–67, 171–72
sin
  against Holy Spirit 40, 360, 365–73
  and concupiscence 37, 69, 181, 303, 308–10
  deadly 366–67, 369
  and death of Christ 534–35
  post-baptismal 360, 362–63, 365–73
  and radical Protestantism 39–40, 301, 304–8, 359–60, 366
  and reconciliation with God 151–53, 155, 159
  see also original sin
sinlessness of Christ 328, 357–64
Six Articles (1539) 24–25, 528–29

Smail, T 196–97, 217, 219–20, 226–28, 234–36
socialism, Christian 626–27
Socrates (church historian) 544
Son of God see Jesus Christ
South, J T 552–53
state see Church and state
statements of faith
  Articles as 10–12, 13–14
  and comprehension 16–17
  and ecumenical councils 11, 17
  and Fourth Lateran Council 11–12
  Reformation 12–14, 18–19, 20
Strickland, William 59
Subscription and Assent (1968) 77–79, 84, 87
substance, and accidents 507–8
substance, divine 123, 132, 143, 230–31, 292, 293
suffering
  of God 111–12, 146
  of Jesus Christ 149–59
  and providential care 118–20
supererogation 38, 301, 349–56, 358–60, 409
supremacy, royal 73–74, 425–26, 597, 599, 600, 601, 606, 612
Supreme Governor, monarch as 425–26, 597, 599, 600, 601–2
swearing see oath-taking
Swete, Henry 233
Swiss Confessions, First and Second (1536, 1566) 100

Tarasius (Patriarch of Constantinople) 223–24
Taverner, Richard 575, 577
Temple, William (Archbishop of Canterbury) 129–30, 636
Ten Articles (1536) 13 n.6, 22–23, 24, 33
  and Creeds 288, 290
  and images 441

and justification 23, 322–23
and purgatory 23
and sacraments 474
Ten Commandments 281–83, 336
Tertullian 369 n.493
Theodore of Tarsus (Archbishop of
Canterbury) 223
Thirteen Articles (1538) 26–29, 36
  and the Church 402–3, 404
  and descent into Hell 162
  and diversity in the Church 562
  and Holy Trinity 103, 122, 214
  and justification 322–23
  and ministry in the Church 448
  and resurrection of Christ 174–75
  and sacraments 468–69, 482–83
  and Son of God 126–27, 128
  and traditions and ceremonies 563
  and use of images 442
Thirty Eight Articles (1563) 50–63, 73,
  242
  and Forty Two Articles 51, 52–57, 378
  revision of 1571 57–63
Thirty Nine Articles
  assent to 72, 76–80
  attempts to supplement or revise 64–
  72
  as comprehensive 16–17
  contemporary context 93
  as creed 17–19, 94
  development 22–63
  eclecticism 21
  in English and Latin 62–63, 464
  and Forty Two Articles 40–41, 57–63
  historical context 12–13, 90, 92–93
  interpretation 90–94
  and Lutheranism 27
  need for commentary on 8–9
  public reading 77, 78
  purpose 12–15
  as Reformed theology 19–22, 90–91
  and Roman Catholic theology 91
  and Scripture 93–94
  shape 95–96
  as statement of faith 8, 10–12
  subscription to 63, 70–72, 73–82, 92–
  93

Toledo, Council (589) 221–23
Toleration Act (1689) 75
Toon, Peter 88, 91, 576, 580
Torrance, T F 186, 188–89
Towards a Theology for Inter-Faith
  Dialogue 396–97
tradition, and Scripture 245–46, 262–
  63, 409
transubstantiation 24, 39, 52, 409, 428,
  503–4, 507–9
Travis, S H 202
Trent, Council (1545-63) 38, 56, 338,
  424
  Canons and Decrees 12, 309, 442,
  459–60
  and clerical celibacy 545
  and communion in one kind 525, 527–
  28, 529, 530
  and Mass as sacrifice 537–39
  reservation and veneration of elements
  511–12
  and sacraments 474
  and Scripture 237, 245–47
  and transubstantiation 508
Tri-theism 122
Trinity
  and attributes of God 108–20, 123
  faith in 103–24
  and salvation 123–25
  and three Persons 45–46, 120–24,
  193, 214–15, 292–93
  Trinitarian heresies 104–5, 214–15
  and unity of God 45–46, 100, 105–8,
  122–23
Trullo, Council (692) 545
Tyacke, Nicholas 64
Tyrell Green, E
  and adoration of the Eucharist 478
  and authority of the Church 416
  and excommunication 550
  and ministry in the Church 449, 450–
  51
  and nature of Christ 131, 132
  and sin 309–10
  and visible Church 403

Udall, Nicholas 576

unity, visible 410–11, 454–56, 569
Universities Test Act (1871) 81–82
Vasens, Council (529) 575
Vatican Council, Second 251 n.337, 465
Vermigli, Peter Martyr 376–78
virgin birth 132–41

war
  Christian service in 597, 600, 601,
    608–11
  and Church of England 615–16
  just war 612
Waterland, Daniel 62–63
wealth and poverty 625–27
Webster, John 147, 251, 255
Wentworth, Peter 59
Westcott, B F 172, 187–88
Western Church
  and Apostles' Creed 287
  and Athanasian Creed 287
  and procession of the Spirit 220–21,
    224–30
Westminster Assembly (1643) 68–70
Westminster Confession (1648) 70, 85,
    100, 379, 388
Whitaker, William 64–65, 378
Whitgift, John (Archbishop of
    Canterbury) 65–66, 73, 592
Whitgift's Articles 73–74, 78
Wied, Hermann (Archbishop of
    Cologne) 321, 471
will of God 390–91
Williams, D J 204
Wilson, W G and Templeton, J H 108,
    458, 563–64
Windsor Report (2004) 569–71
Witherington, Ben 137
Wolfe, Reynold (royal printer) 413, 414,
    516
Word see Jesus Christ
works
  and final judgement 199
  and grace of God 313, 319, 343–47
  and justification 25, 38, 301, 329, 330–
    41, 342–48, 419, 581
  of supererogation 38, 301, 349–56,
    358–60, 409

World Council of Churches, Baptism,
    Eucharist and Ministry 501–2
wrath of God 152–53, 155, 159, 301,
    307–8, 534
Wright, N. T.
  and general resurrection 165–66,
    176–77, 178–79, 212
  and judgement 207–8
  and new perspective on Paul 340–41
  and resurrection of Christ 210
  and Scripture 255–58, 266–67
  and suffering 118–19
Württemburg Confession (1552) 21, 56
  and the Church 412
  and free will 312
  and good works 330–31
  and Holy Spirit 214
  and Jesus Christ 126, 128
  and justification 321
  and Scripture 243

Zwingli, Huldrych 12, 101

Index of Biblical Citations

OLD TESTAMENT

Genesis
1-3 119
1 114
1:1 131
1:2 232
2:7 212, 219
2:18-24 477
6:12 169
8:21 305
9:6 614
12:3 385
17:14 551
18:9-15 140
19:24 201
21:1-7 140
21:23 631
24:3 631

Exodus
12:19 403, 551
20:2-17 281–82
20:4-5 436
20:15 620
20:17 620
22:10-11 631

Leviticus
7:20 551
19:18 281
25 280
28:1-29:46 485

Numbers
23:19 108

Deuteronomy
4:2 262
4:25-28 436
4:35 106
5:6-21 281–82
6:4-5 10, 106–107
6:4 105, 281

6:6-9 10
6:10-15 10
6:13 630
6:16-19 10
6:20–25 10
7:6-8 385
7:6-7 382
7:6 384
12:32 262
15:11 623
18:15 186
29:29 382
30:3 111
32:16 110
32:35 610

Joshua
1:7 353
22:18 403

Judges
13:1-20 140

1 Samuel
1:1-2:11 141
10:1 280
14:4-23 250
15:29 108
16:13 280
18:3 631
20:12-17 631
20:42 631

1 Kings
1:38-40 280
8:1 425
17:17-24 179

1 Chronicles
28:1 425

2 Chronicles
15:3 105
15:9 425

20:7 250
20:17 250
20:29 250
29:4 425
34:29 425

Ezra
10:8 551

Job
19:25-26 165
40:9 109

Psalms
2:7 383
14:1-3 305
16 177
16:9-11 165
16:10 165, 167
33:6 219, 232
34:15 109
36:6 440
40:6 156
42:2 105
49:15 165
51:1-10 313
59:10 314
63:11 630
66:13-15 151
73:24 165
74:2 403
78:40 109
86:13 165
90:2 108
97:7 436
102:25 109
102:26-7 110
104 114
105:6 382
110:1 183, 189–90
116:10 274
135:4 382
139 108
139:7-12 232

143:2 313
147:9 440

Proverbs
8:15 603
8:17 603
15:3 108
16:6 624
19:17 623
28:27 624–25
30:5-6 262

Ecclesiastes
7:20 305, 368
11:3 434

Isaiah
1:10-11 156
1:21 196
2:3 385
6:9-10 231
14:9-10 165
25:8 165
26:19 165
34:9 201
35:4 197
40:18-21 436
40:28 108
42:1 385
42:5 114
45:21 197
49:14-16 111
53:6 305
55:7 368
58:7 623
60 277
61:1 232
63:16 273
64:6 347
65:24 441
66:24 201, 203

Jeremiah
4:1 378
4:2 633
7:21-23 156
10:10 105, 106

18:8 110

Ezekiel
6:3-7 436
20:1 353
36:26-27 317
37:1-14 219
47-48 277

Daniel
4:27 624
7:14 144 n.187
12:2 165

Hosea
6:1 368
6:2 178–79
11:1 109
11:8-9 111
13:14 180
14:2 371

Joel
2:12-13 582

Amos
5:21-24 156

Malachi
1:2-3 384
1:11 539
3:6 108

APOCRYPHA

Tobit
4:7 623
4:10-11 265
4:16 623
12:9 624

Judith
16:17 203

Wisdom
6:1-3 604

Ecclesiasticus
5:7 371
23:11 265
35:2 623
35:6-7 62

**OTHER JEWISH
WRITINGS**

4 Maccabees
9:9 204 n.269

NEW TESTAMENT

Matthew
1:16 136
1:18-25 135
1:18 138, 140
1:20 138, 140
3:2 582
3:16 121, 216
3:17 121
4:1-11 361
4:2 144
4:17 582
5:17-21 283
5:19 353–54
5:33-37 629
5:42 619, 620
5:45 182, 440
6:25-30 114
7:13-14 200
7:23 201
7:24 250
10:5-6 256
10:15 450
10:20 216
10:29-30 113
10:42 623
11:23 165
11:25 121
11:27 101, 204
12:28 231
12:31-37 366
12:31 377
12:33ff. 199
12:33 332, 333

12:36-37 199
16:18 291, 607
16:19 407, 552, 555,
  594
17:5 441
17:24-27 607
18:8 203
18:15-18 551
18:18 407, 555, 594
19:1-12 548
19:13-15 498
19:14 496
19:16-30 283
19:16-17 280–81,
  334
19:18-19 281, 334
19:26 112
20:28 534
22:34-40 281, 283
23:2-3 417, 485
23:2 482
25:31-46 195
25:34ff. 200
25:35-40 623
25:41 201, 205
25:46 202, 204
26:2 144
26:26-29 476
26:26-27 507
26:27 527, 530
26:38 144
27:51-53 179
28:1-8 177
28:9 177
28:16-20 386
28:18 189
28:19-20 418
28:19 121, 232, 405,
  476
28:20 108, 184, 353

Mark
2:7-10 594
3:28-30 366
3:29 232, 234, 377
6:3 136
6:5-6 148

7:7 353–54
7:14-23 278
9:7 353
9:41 623
9:47 205
9:48 201, 203
10:13-6 498
10:17-31 283
10:22 350
11:18-27 165
12:28-34 281, 283
12:32 105
13:32 148, 149
14:22-25 476
14:22-24 507
14:23 530
14:33 144
16:1-8 177
16:16 295, 394
16:19 183

Luke
1:26-2:20 135
1:35 138, 140, 232
2:49 235
2:52 144, 235
3:23 136
3:52 148, 149
4:1-13 361
6:22 551
6:35 619
9:34-35 184
11:13 216
11:20 231
12:7 440
12:10 366
12:42 418
15-17 498
15:11-32 291
15:35 350
17:7-10 354
17:10 354
18:18-30 283
21:18 441
22:19-24 476
22:19-20 507
22:20 530

23:43 167
24:1-11 177
24:14 574
24:25-27 273
24:30 177
24:31 177
24:36-43 177
24:39 144
24:44-47 273
24:46-47 582
24:50-51 188

John
1:1-18 129
1:1 121, 130, 131,
  186
1:6 450
1:13 136, 140
1:14 144
1:17 510
1:18 121, 129 n.168
1:29 155, 361–62
2:1-11 134
3:1-15 140
3:1-13 378
3:3-6 476
3:3 631
3:5-7 232
3:5 472, 492, 510,
  631
3:6 318
3:11 631
3:16 291
3:18 295
3:26 394
3:36 109, 295, 381,
  434
4:1 486
4:6 144
4:8 149
4:24 108
4:34 193
5:19 101, 193
5:20 219
5:25-9 195
5:26 131
5:28-29 200

5:39 275
6:1-14 134
6:29 346
6:35 510–11, 518
6:38 193
6:41-42 136
6:44 315
6:51 510
6:54 510, 518, 522
6:55 510
6:56 472, 510
6:57 131
6:62 183, 511
6:64 510–11
6:68 249
7:16-18 193
8:21 443
8:24 443
8:28 193
8:46 361
8:56 275
9:22 551
10:5 353
10:7 273
10:25 193
10:27 353
10:30 130 n.171, 227
11:1-44 179
11:25 212
12:41 275
12:42 551
12:48 250
12:49 193
14-17 233
14:6 510
14:16 216, 233
14:23-24 518
14:23 250, 449
14:26 216, 233
14:28 227
15:4-5 315, 345, 581
15:10 518
15:26-27 186
15:26 121, 216, 217, 227, 233
16:2 551
16:7 217, 227, 233

16:8-14 233
16:13-14 121
17:1 121
17:3 105, 106
17:4 193
17:8 121
17:18 121
17:23 121
19:30 144
20:1-18 177
20:19 177
20:21-23 476, 477
20:21 449, 450
20:22 217, 219, 227–28
20:23 552, 555, 594
20:26-28 177
20:26 177
20:28 121
21:9-14 177

Acts
1:1-11 189
1:1 187
1:6-11 182–83
1:8 186
1:9-11 183
1:9 184
2:22-36 275
2:22-34 177
2:24-31 167
2:33-34 183
2:33 216, 217
2:34-35 189
2:37-42 405
2:37-39 476
2:37 342
2:38 292, 494
2:44-45 618, 620–21, 622
3:1-10 476
3:14 361
3:21 183, 443
3:22-23 186
3:28 275
4:10 511
4:12 394, 511

4:23-24 462–63
4:32 618, 620–21, 622
5:3-4 231
5:3 121
5:4 234, 621
6:5-6 450
6:6 591
7:41-42 437
8:13-27 275
8:15-17 476
8:18-24 487
8:30-35 275
9:11 343
9:15 450, 605
9:32-41 476
10 344
10:2-5 394
10:9-16 278
12:12 622
12:15 166
13:1-3 449
13:2-3 451
13:3 591
14:8-18 440
14:8-10 476
14:15 437
14:22 450
15 279
15:1-29 278
15:1-2 394
15:20 278, 283
15:28-29 278
15:29 437
16:14 315
16:17 217
16:37 279
17:26-28 114
17:27 108
17:32 208
18:2 547
18:24-28 487
19:6 476
20:11 574
20:17 183
20:21 582
20:28-31 426

20:28 121, 418, 449
20:34 619, 620
20:35 619, 620
21:9 547
22:25 279
23:6-10 165
24:30 177
25:11-12 279
28:25-28 231

Romans
1-3 154
1:3 136
1:6-7 382
1:18-3:26 153
1:20 108, 119
1:21-23 119
1:22 283
1:23-32 437
1:25 437
2:4 114
3:21-23 283
3:21-5:9 325
3:21-4:8 291
3:23-25 324
3:23 305
3:24 534
3:25 155, 326, 534
4 275
4:24-25 511
5 153
5:1 153
5:3 219
5:5 236
5:8 154, 511
5:10-11 152
5:12-21 154, 159, 305
6:1-11 212, 292, 490–91
6:3-4 472
6:11 207
6:12 309
6:23 180, 204
7:7-25 307
7:7-12 283
7:7 309
8 256

8:1-17 378
8:1-2 208
8:1 309
8:3-5 325
8:6-7 308–309
8:9 216–17
8:10 207
8:11 216
8:15 236
8:18-25 118–19
8:18-22 211
8:26-27 234
8:28-30 377
8:29 140, 383
8:30 378
9:5 121
9:13 384
9:22-23 380
9:23-24 377
9:30-10:13 325
10:4 324
10:15 449
10:20 315
11:17-24 493
11:30 437
12:1 151
12:2 540
12:9-13:6 611
12:9-25 611
13:1-7 567
13:1-6 605, 611
13:1 278
13:4 611
13:5 608
13:8-10 283
14:9 511
14:13-23 567
14:14 278
14:23 345
15:6 121
15:20 437
16:3 547
16:17 553
16:26 108
16:27 113
17:30 437

1 Corinthians
1:2 382
2:10-11 232
2:10 121
2:11 121
3:11 394
3:16 216, 231
4:1 449, 528
5:1-5 552
5:7 155
5:9 553
5:11 437, 619
6:9-10 437
6:10 619
6:11 338
6:15 511
6:19 231
7:1-9 548
7:25 350
8:1-13 567
8:4 106, 121
9:5 547
10:1-4 275–76
10:14-22 283
10:16-17 506
10:16 472
10:17 461, 505, 540
10:20-22 437
11 417
11:16 417
11:23-26 476
11:23-25 405
11:24-25 507
11:25 530
11:26 508
11:27-32 478
11:27-30 519
11:28-29 510
11:28 508, 525
11:29 479–80
11:30 480
11:34 528
12:2-3 437
12:4-11 234
12:4-6 232
12:6 624
12:11 593

12:12 461
12:13 493–94
12:27 511
14:5 406
14:7-8 461
14:26 461, 569
14:27 417, 461
14:34 417
14:40 417
15 256
15:1-58 291
15:3-5 178
15:5 179
15:6-8 179
15:6 210
15:10 315
15:21-22 305
15:21 144
15:24-25 189
15:24 192
15:28 192, 443
15:33 553, 574
15:44 212
15:45-50 159
15:45 212
15:50 212
15:51-52 195
15:52-53 212
15:55 180
15:57 180, 250
16:19 547

2 Corinthians
1:23 631
2:5-11 556
3:3 105
3:5 313
3:14 232
3:17 140
3:18 231
4:13 273–74
5:2-4 166
5:8 166
5:9-10 195
5:17 159, 207
5:18-20 152
5:21 138, 159, 328,

361
6:4 449
6:14 553
6:17 553
8:9 144
9:10 625
11:4 295
11:13-15 295
13:14 121
20:11 199

Galatians
1:8-9 394
1:8 295, 353
1:9 42, 222 n.298
2:1-21 278
2:16 326–27
2:20-3:29 325
2:20 315–16
3:6-9 275
3:26-27 494
3:26 510
4:4 136
4:6 217, 236
4:8-9 437
5:1-12 278
5:6 333
5:14 283
5:17 307, 309
5:18 234
5:20-21 437
5:20 437

Ephesians
1:3-3:21 291
1:4-5 377–78
1:4 383
1:5-9 380
1:7 534
1:10 308, 443
1:11-12 378
1:13-14 378
1:13 493
2:1-3 153
2:3 305, 313
2:6 181, 212
2:8-9 325

2:10 315
2:12 204
2:16 152
2:19 461
2:20 406
2:22 121
4:4-6 232
4:6 121
4:9-10 144
4:8-10 183
4:9 167
4:11-12 449, 593
4:15 511
4:16 511
4:28 619
4:30 234
5:2 155
5:3 619
5:21-33 477
5:26 510
5:29-30 511

Philippians
1:1 449
1:19 217
1:23 166
2:6 121
2:7 136, 144
2:12-13 316
2:12 337
2:13 380
3:2-11 325
3:20 182

Colossians
1:15 131
1:16-17 114
1:19-20 152
1:20 213, 443
1:25 449
2:8-15 292
2:9 121
2:12 212
2:13-15 291
2:16-23 278
2:20 353
2:23 353

3:1-2 181
3:1 511
3:5-9 181
3:5 309
3:7 337
3:12-13 182
3:17 332

1 Thessalonians
1:8-9 437
1:9 105, 109
1:10 183
2:9 619, 620
4:10 382
4:13-18 291
5:14 623

2 Thessalonians
1:7-10 195
1:8-9 200
1:9 201, 202, 204
1:11 380
3:6 553
3:8 619
3:14 553

1 Timothy
1:17 354
1:19-20 553
2:4 386
2:5 105, 144
2:12 417
3:2 547
3:3–12 10
3:4 451
3:12 547
3:14 451
3:16 10–11, 183
4:1 353
4:14 450
5:8 619, 620
5:22 451

2 Timothy
1:6 451
1:13 420
2:2 418, 451

2:13 108, 113
3:16-17 354
3:16 247, 266, 283
4:2 420

Titus
1:5-6 547
1:5 451
1:7 449
1:9 418
1:13 418, 426
3:4 114
3:5 232, 492, 510
3:10-11 553
3:10 426

Hebrews
1:2 186
1:3 131, 144
1:5-12 131
1:8 121
2:7 144
2:14-18 144
2:14 144
2:17 361, 534
4:12 250
4:13 113
4:14 183, 511
4:15 144, 361
4:16 441, 511
5:4 449
6:2 202
6:4-8 367
6:16 631
6:18 108
7:11-10:18 278
7:26-28 138
7:27 362, 534
9:1-10:18 158
9:12 362, 534
9:14 232, 361, 434
9:24-26 187
9:24 183
9:26 155
10:5 144
10:10 144, 362, 434
10:11-14 533

10:12 534
10:14 435
10:19-23 441
11 272, 275
11:5-6 581
11:6 345
11:10 276
11:13-16 276–77
11:26 275
12:22 277
13:7 426
13:15 131, 188
13:16 623
13:17 426

James
1:17 108, 182
2:5 623
2:8-13 283
2:15-16 619
2:17-19 333
2:18 333
2:19 121
3:2 362
5:12 629–30
5:13-16 476

1 Peter
1:1 382
1:2 232
1:3-5 181
1:10-12 276
1:11 217, 277
1:19 138, 155, 157, 361
2:4-10 291
2:4-5 332
2:13-15 607–608
2:13-14 278, 567
2:13 608
2:22 138, 361
2:25 313
3:17-22 168–73
3:18-20 162–3, 168–71
3:18 169
3:19-20a 170, 172

3:19 170–71
3:20 169
3:22-4:1 169
3:22 183
4:6 168–71
4:15 619

2 Peter
1:1 121
1:4 526
1:5-7 333
1:10 333
1:21 232, 266
2:4 169
2:20-22 367
3:16 267 n.356

1 John
1:7 434
1:8-9 291
1:8 362, 368
2:1 435
2:22-23 293
3:2 534
3:5 362
3:9 232
5:4 250
5:21 283, 437

2 John
7-9 295
10-11 553

Jude
6 169
7 201
20-21 232

Revelation
1:7 193
1:8 108
1:18 165
5:1-10 189–91
5:5 191
5:6 183
5:9 191
7:4-17 291

12:10-11 191–92
14:10-11 201
14:13 443
19:3 201
19:10 440
20:7-14 197
20:11-15 195
20:11 199
21-22 256, 277
21:1-22:5 291
21:10 277
21:11-15 200
22:8-9 440
22:16 191
22:18-19 262

CPSIA information can be obtained
at www.ICGtesting.com
Printed in the USA
LVHW080111191219
641031LV00011B/1229/P

9 780956 856074